W9-ABI-137

Introduction to Information Systems

Essentials for the e-Business Enterprise

InformationTechnology

At **McGraw-Hill Higher Education**, we publish instructional materials targeted at the higher education market. In an effort to expand the tools of higher learning, we publish texts, lab manuals, study guides, testing materials, software, and multimedia products.

At **McGraw-Hill/Irwin** (a division of McGraw-Hill Higher Education), we realize technology will continue to create new mediums for professors and students to manage resources and communicate information with one another. We strive to provide the most flexible and complete teaching and learning tools available and offer solutions to the changing world of teaching and learning.

McGraw-Hill/Irwin is dedicated to providing the tools necessary for today's instructors and students to navigate the world of Information Technology successfully.

Seminar Series – McGraw-Hill/Irwin's Technology Connection seminar series, offered across the country every year, demonstrates the latest technology products and encourages collaboration among teaching professionals.

Osborne/McGraw-Hill – A division of the McGraw-Hill Companies known for its best-selling Internet titles, *Harley Hahn's Internet & Web Yellow Pages* and the *Internet Complete Reference*, offers an additional resource for certification and has strategic publishing relationships with corporations such as Oracle Corporation, Corel Corporation, and America Online. For more information, visit Osborne at www.osborne.com.

Digital Solutions – McGraw-Hill/Irwin is committed to publishing Digital Solutions. Taking your course online doesn't have to be a solitary venture. Nor does it have to be a difficult one. We offer several solutions, which will let you enjoy all the benefits of having course material online. For more information, visit www.mhhe.com/ digital_solutions.

Packaging Options – For more about our discount options, contact your local McGraw-Hill/Irwin sales representative at 1-800-338-3987, or visit our website at www.mhhe.com/it.

Introduction to Information Systems

Essentials for the e-Business Enterprise

Eleventh Edition

James A. O'Brien

College of Business Administration
Northern Arizona University

Boston   Burr Ridge, IL   Dubuque, IA   Madison, WI   New York   San Francisco   St. Louis
Bangkok   Bogotá   Caracas   Kuala Lumpur   Lisbon   London   Madrid   Mexico City
Milan   Montreal   New Delhi   Santiago   Seoul   Singapore   Sydney   Taipei   Toronto

McGraw-Hill Higher Education

A Division of The **McGraw-Hill** Companies

INTRODUCTION TO INFORMATION SYSTEMS
ESSENTIALS FOR THE E-BUSINESS ENTERPRISE

Published by McGraw-Hill/Irwin, an imprint of The McGraw-Hill Companies, Inc. 1221 Avenue of the Americas, New York, NY, 10020. Copyright © 2003, 2001, 2000, 1997, 1994, 1991, 1988, 1985, 1982, 1978, 1975, by The McGraw-Hill Companies, Inc. All rights reserved. No part of this publication may be reproduced or distributed in any form or by any means, or stored in a database or retrieval system, without the prior written consent of The McGraw-Hill Companies, Inc., including, but not limited to, in any network or other electronic storage or transmission, or broadcast for distance learning.

Some ancillaries, including electronic and print components, may not be available to customers outside the United States.

This book is printed on acid-free paper.

domestic   2 3 4 5 6 7 8 9 0 DOW/DOW 0 9 8 7 6 5 4 3 2
international   2 3 4 5 6 7 8 9 0 DOW/DOW 0 9 8 7 6 5 4 3 2

ISBN 0-07-247264-2

Vice president/Editor-in-chief: *Robin J. Zwettler*
Publisher: *George Werthman*
Senior sponsoring editor: *Rick Williamson*
Developmental editor: *Kelly L. Delso*
Senior marketing manager: *Paul Murphy*
Project manager: *Scott Scheidt*
Production supervisor: *Michael McCormick*
Freelance design coordinator: *Jennifer McQueen*
Senior supplement coordinator: *Mark Mattson*
Media technology producer: *Greg Bates*
Cover illustrator: *Kevin Ghiglione*
Photo researcher: *Jeremy Cheshareck*
Compositor: *The GTS Companies*
Typeface: 10/12 Janson Text
Printer: *Von Hoffman Press*

Library of Congress Cataloging-in-Publication Data

O'Brien, James A., 1936–
    Introduction to information systems : essentials for the E-business
enterprise / James A. O'Brien.—11th ed.
        p.   cm.
    Includes bibliographical references and index.
    ISBN 0-07-247264-2 (alk. paper)
    1. Business—Data processing. 2. Management—Data processing. 3. Management
information systems.   I. Title.
HF5548.2 .O23   2003
658.4'038—dc21   2001054663

INTERNATIONAL EDITION ISBN 0-07-115109-5
Copyright © 2003. Exclusive rights by The McGraw-Hill Companies, Inc. for manufacture and export. This book cannot be re-exported from the country to which it is sold by McGraw-Hill. The International Edition is not available in North America.

http://www.mhhe.com

To your love, happiness, and success

James A. O'Brien is an adjunct professor of Computer Information Systems in the College of Business Administration at Northern Arizona University. He completed his undergraduate studies at the University of Hawaii and Gonzaga University and earned an M.S. and Ph.D. in Business Administration from the University of Oregon. He has been professor and coordinator of the CIS area at Northern Arizona University, professor of Finance and Management Information Systems and chairman of the Department of Management at Eastern Washington University, and a visiting professor at the University of Alberta, the University of Hawaii, and Central Washington University.

Dr. O'Brien's business experience includes working in the Marketing Management Program of the IBM Corporation, as well as serving as a financial analyst for the General Electric Company. He is a graduate of General Electric's Financial Management Program. He has also served as an information systems consultant to several banks and computer services firms.

Jim's research interests lie in developing and testing basic conceptual frameworks used in information systems development and management. He has written eight books, including several that have been published in multiple editions, as well as in Chinese, Dutch, French, Japanese, or Spanish translations. He has also contributed to the field of information systems through the publication of many articles in business and academic journals, as well as through his participation in academic and industry associations in the field of information systems.

Preface

Essentials for the e-Business Enterprise

The Eleventh Edition is an introduction to information systems and information technology for business students who are or will be managers, entrepreneurs, and business professionals in today's e-business enterprises. The goal of this text is to help business students learn how to use and manage information technologies to revitalize business processes, conduct electronic commerce, improve business decision making, and gain competitive advantage. Thus, it places a major emphasis on the role of Internet technologies in providing a technology platform for electronic business, commerce, and collaboration within and among internetworked enterprises and global markets.

These are the essential aspects of the e-business enterprise that this text brings to the study of information systems. Of course, as in all my texts, this edition:

- Loads the text with **real world cases,** examples, and exercises about real people and companies in the business world.
- Organizes the text around a simple **five-area framework** that emphasizes the IS knowledge a business end user needs to know.
- Distributes and integrates IS foundation theory throughout the text instead of concentrating it in several early chapters.
- Places a major emphasis on the strategic role of information technology in gaining competitive advantage, supporting electronic business operations and decision making, and enabling electronic commerce and enterprise collaboration.

Audience

This text is designed for use in undergraduate courses in Management Information Systems that are required in many Business Administration or Management programs as part of the common body of knowledge for all business majors. Thus, this edition treats the subject area known as Information Systems (IS), Management Information Systems (MIS), or Computer Information Systems (CIS) as a major functional area of business that is as important to management education as are the areas of accounting, finance, operations management, marketing, and human resource management.

Key Features

The new Eleventh Edition is filled with new e-business and e-commerce topics and real world examples that provide students with a solid e-business foundation for their studies and work in business.

All New Real World Cases and Examples

This text provides all new up-to-date real world case studies. These are not fictional stories, but actual situations faced by business firms and other organizations as reported in current business and IS periodicals. This includes four real world case studies in each chapter that apply specifically to that chapter's contents.

In addition, each chapter contains several application exercises, including two hands-on spreadsheet or database software assignments and new Internet-based real world assignments in most chapters. Also, many new highlighted in-text real world examples have been added to illustrate concepts in every chapter. The purpose of this variety of learning and assignment options is to give instructors and students many opportunities to apply each chapter's material to real world situations.

Cisco Systems: e-Business and e-Commerce Leader	Top telecom manufacturer Cisco Systems uses 36 manufacturing plants, of which it owns but two. One of them is downstairs from the San Jose office of Randy Pond, Senior Vice President for Operations. The rest belong to top contract manufacturers like Jabil Circuit and Solectron. It's "virtual manufacturing," Pond says, made possible by a "suite of Internet-based tools and processes that lets me manage an extended enterprise I don't own as if I do own it."

The key, says Pond, is "real-time data on a real-time basis so my partners know what goes on in my business every single day." As much as possible, Cisco and a partner work with the same stream of e-business information, doubling its value. Every day Cisco compiles its inventory, forecast for each model, order backlog, and thirteen weeks of daily data about parts and subassemblies; every day its partner compiles data on in-process inventory, cycle time by process step, optimal lot size, and yield; every night computers combine the Internet data streams into a river of information; every morning everyone knows what to build that day.

Cisco works the other end of the process—e-commerce—the same way. Eighty seven percent of Cisco's sales are entered directly from the Net and available instantaneously. Except for commodity parts, Cisco's e-business supply chain is as visible and as live as a televised football game. Validation and testing are also Internet-based. Autotest, a homemade tool, tests machines as they are built and won't print a packing label for a machine unless every test has been done and passed. Another tool checks a customer's order as he enters it, to make sure that he hasn't asked for incompatible gear.

The benefits of real-time e-business add up to about $400 million a year, by Pond's reckoning, plus up to a $1 billion saving in capital costs—from equipment Cisco doesn't carry on its books, improved utilization by suppliers, and minimal inventory [18].

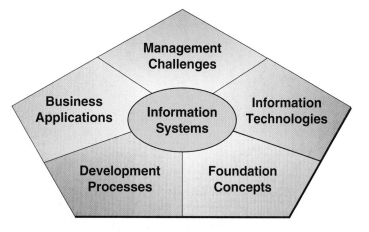

Figure 1

The five-area information systems framework.

New Chapters on Electronic Business and Commerce

This edition expands its coverage of e-business and e-commerce with two new chapters that emphasize how Internet and Web technologies provide the technological infrastructure and business tools that enable internetworked enterprises to engage in electronic business and commerce. This is demonstrated, not only in the text materials in Chapters 7 and 8, but in other chapters and Real World Cases and examples in the text. Examples include General Electric, Duke Energy, Netro Corp., Lightwave Systems, Charles Schwab, Harrah's, DuPont, Otis, Orvis, Boeing, Citigroup, Deere & Co., Covisint, Johnson Controls, and Dana Corp., to name a few.

An Information Systems Framework

This text reduces the complexity of an introductory course in information systems by using a conceptual framework that organizes the knowledge needed by business students into five major areas (see Figure 1):

- **Foundation Concepts.** Fundamental business information systems concepts including trends, components, and roles of information systems (Chapter 1) and competitive advantage concepts and applications (Chapter 2). Other behavioral, managerial, and technical concepts are presented where appropriate in selected chapters.

- **Information Technologies.** Major concepts, developments, and managerial issues involved in computer hardware, software, telecommunications networks, and data resource management technologies (Chapters 3, 4, 5, and 6). Other technologies used in e-business systems are discussed where appropriate in selected chapters.

- **Business Applications.** How the Internet, intranets, extranets, and other information technologies are used in e-business enterprises to support electronic business and commerce and business decision making (Chapters 7, 8, and 9).

- **Development Processes.** Developing and implementing e-business strategies and systems using several strategic planning and application development approaches (Chapter 10).

- **Management Challenges.** The challenges of e-business technologies and strategies, including security and ethical challenges and global IT management (discussed in many chapters, but emphasized in Chapters 11 and 12).

Strategic, International, and Ethical Dimensions

This text also contains substantial text material and cases reflecting the strategic, international, and ethical dimensions of information systems. This can be found not only in Chapters 2, 11, and 12, but also in all other chapters of the text. This is especially evident in many real world cases and examples, such as Capital One Financial, Moen Inc., GM, Fidelity Investments, Staples, Dell Computer, Litton, Exodus

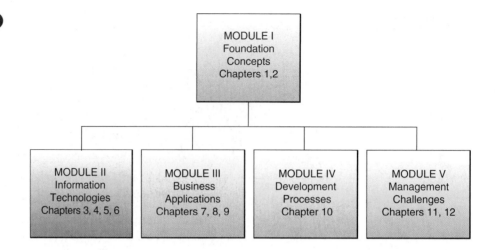

Figure 2

The modular organization or the text.

Communications, Visa International, AGM Container, DoubleClick, Microsoft, DHL Worldwide Express, IBM, The Timken Company, and many, many others. These examples repeatedly demonstrate the strategic and ethical challenges of managing e-business technologies for competitive advantage in global business markets and in the global information society in which we all live and work.

Modular Structure of the Text

The text is organized into five modules that reflect the five major areas of the framework for information systems knowledge mentioned earlier. See Figure 2. Also, each chapter is organized into two distinct sections. This is done to avoid proliferation of chapters, as well as to provide better conceptual organization of the text and each chapter. This organization increases instructor flexibility in assigning course material since it structures the text into modular levels (i.e., modules, chapters, and sections) while reducing the number of chapters that need to be covered.

Each chapter starts with Chapter Highlights and Learning Objectives and ends with a Summary, Key Terms and Concepts, a Review Quiz tied directly to the Key Terms and Concepts, Discussion Questions, and Application Exercises. Real World Cases are placed at the beginning of the two sections of each chapter (with a brief analysis), and at the end of each chapter, to help students understand the chapter material in the context of examples from the real world of business.

Changes to This Edition

Besides providing all new Real World Cases, the Eleventh Edition expands the e-business orientation and content that was the hallmark of the Tenth Edition by providing two full chapters of e-business and e-commerce coverage (Chapters 7 and 8). However, at the urging of reviewers, coverage of other topics has been condensed or eliminated to reduce the overall length of the text. For example, coverage of intranets and extranets (formerly in Section I of Chapter 7) was condensed and moved to Chapter 6, Telecommunications and Networks. Detailed coverage of enterprise collaboration systems (formerly in Section II of Chapter 7) has also been condensed and moved to the new edition's section on cross-functional e-business systems in Chapter 7.

Highlights of these and other changes are as follows:

● Chapter 7, *Electronic Business Systems*, now provides students with two solid sections on e-business. Section I on e-business systems features new content on cross-functional enterprise applications, including enterprise application integration (EAI), enterprise resource planning (ERP), customer relationship management (CRM), supply chain management (SCM), online transaction processing (OLTP), and enterprise collaboration systems (ECS). Section II contains updated coverage of more traditional e-business applications that support activities in each of the functional areas of business.

- Chapter 8, *Electronic Commerce Systems*, is a major revision and expansion of the former edition's section on electronic commerce. Section I emphasizes the fundamental components and processes of e-commerce systems, while Section II explores key applications and issues in e-commerce, including B2C and B2B marketplaces, requirements for success, and clicks and bricks strategies. Coverage of supply chain management and online transaction processing has been moved to Chapter 7.

Introductory coverage of managerial challenges in Chapter 1 and competitive advantage issues in Chapter 2 has been simplified at the urging of reviewers in order to reduce the number of topics covered in these two early foundation chapters. Chapter 6, Telecommunications and Networks, was restructured to better organize coverage of the Internet, intranets, and extranets moved over from the Tenth Edition's chapter on The Internetworked Enterprise, as well as new coverage of network management and P2P networks. New material on enterprise information and knowledge portals is included in the coverage of e-business decision support systems in Chapter 9, while coverage of e-business technology management and global data access issues was revised and expanded in Chapter 12. In addition, many real world examples used to illustrate major topics throughout the text have been replaced with more current in-text examples of actual companies engaged in e-business and e-commerce.

Teaching and Learning Resources

A **presentation manager Instructor CD-ROM** is available to adopters and offers the following resources for course presentation and management:

- An Instructor's Resource Manual, authored by Margaret Trenholm-Edmunds of Mount Allison University, contains suggestions for using the book in courses of varying lengths, detailed chapter outlines with teaching suggestions for use in lectures, and answers to all end-of-chapter questions, application exercises, and problems and case study questions. Teaching tips for incorporating the video clips are included for many chapters.

- A Test Bank, authored by Margaret Trenholm-Edmunds of Mount Allison University, contains true-false, multiple choice, fill-in-the-blank, and short essay questions.

- Computerized/Network Testing with Brownstone Diploma software is fully networkable for LAN test administration; tests also can be printed for standard paper delivery or posted to a website for student access.

- Slide shows in Microsoft PowerPoint, authored by Margaret Trenholm-Edmunds of Mount Allison University, are available for each chapter to support classroom discussion of chapter concepts and real world cases.

- Data/solutions files, authored by James N. Morgan of Northern Arizona University, for the database and spreadsheet application exercises in the text are included.

- Video clips are available that highlight how specific companies apply and use information technology.

The McGraw-Hill/Irwin Information Systems Video Library contains 14 10- to 12-minute videos on numerous companies demonstrating use of a variety of IT areas like intranets, multimedia, or computer-based training systems, and concepts like client/server computing and business process reengineering. This library is available free to adopters. For further information, visit www.mhhe.com/business/mis/videos or contact your local McGraw-Hill/Irwin sales representative. A video lecture guide for all 14 videos is included in the Instructor's Resource Manual.

Digital Solutions

- Website/OLC—The book's website at http://www.mhhe.com/obrien provides resources for instructors and students using the text. The Online Learning Center (OLC) builds on the book's pedagogy and features with self-assessment quizzes, extra material not found in the text, Web links, and other resources for students and instructors.

- Pageout—our Course Website Development Center. Pageout offers a syllabus page, website address, Online Learning Center content, online quizzing, gradebook, discussion forum, and student Web page creation.

Packaging Options

The McGraw-Hill/Irwin *Advantage*, O'Leary, and Laudon Interactive computing series are collections of software application manuals and interactive computer-based training products for Microsoft Office. In addition, we offer several paperback Internet literacy books or CDs, perfect for introducing the World Wide Web, e-mail, and Web page design to students. These texts and CDs are available for discounted packaging options with any McGraw-Hill/Irwin title. For more about our discount options, contact your local McGraw-Hill/Irwin sales representative or visit our website at www.mhhe.com/it.

In addition, a software casebook—*Application Cases in MIS: Using Spreadsheet and Database Software and the Internet*, fourth edition, by James N. Morgan of Northern Arizona University—is available to supplement the hands-on exercises in this edition. This optional casebook contains an extensive number of hands-on cases, many of which include a suggested approach for solving each case with the Internet, spreadsheet, or database management software packages to develop solutions for realistic business problems.

Acknowledgments

The author wishes to acknowledge the assistance of the following reviewers whose constructive criticism and suggestions helped invaluably in shaping the form and content of this text.

Noushin Ashrafi, *University of Massachusetts–Boston*

Harry C. Benham, *Montana State University*

Karen E. Bland-Collins, *Morgan State University*

Warren Boe, *University of Iowa*

Ranjit Bose, *University of New Mexico–Albuquerque*

Gurpreet Dhillon, *University of Nevada–Las Vegas*

Doris Duncan, *California State University–Hayward*

Sean B. Eom, *Southeast Missouri State University*

Dale Foster, *Memorial University of Newfoundland*

Robert Fulkerth, *Golden Gate University*

Yvonne A. Greenwood, *Penn. State University–Berks-Lehigh Valley*

Babita Gupta, *California State University–Monterey*

Phillip Johnson, *College of William and Mary*

Michelle L. Kaarst-Brown, *University of Richmond*

Ronald J. Kizior, *Loyola University–Chicago*

Douglas M. Kline, *Sam Houston State University*

Andrew G. Kotulic, *York College of Pennsylvania*

Martha Leva, *Penn. State University–Abington*

Elizabeth E. Little, *The University of Central Oklahoma*

Stephen L. Loy, *Eastern Kentucky University*

Joan B. Lumpkin, *Wright State University*

Randy Maule, *California State University–Monterey*

Pam Milstead, *Louisiana Tech University*

Murli Nagasundaram, *Boise State University*

Margaret H. Neumann, *Governors State University*

Rene F. Reitsma, *St. Francis Xavier University*

Erik Rolland, *University of California–Riverside*

Dolly Samson, *Weber State University*

Tod Sedbrook, *University of Northern Colorado*

Richard S. Segall, *Arkansas State University*

Gerhard Steinke, *Seattle Pacific University*

Dana V. Tesone, *University of Hawaii and Nova Southeastern University*

E. Lamar Traylor, *Our Lady of Lake in Houston*

Craig VanLengen, *Northern Arizona University*

H. Joseph Wen, *New Jersey Institute of Technology*

Jennifer J. Williams, *University of Southern Indiana*

Karen L. Williams, *University of Texas–San Antonio*

My thanks also go to James N. Morgan of Northern Arizona University, who is the author of the software casebook that can be used with this text and who developed most of the hands-on Application Exercises in the text, as well as the data/solutions files on the Instructor CD-ROM. I am also grateful to Margaret Trenholm-Edmunds of Mount Allison University, the author of the Instructor's Resource Manual, for her revision of this valuable teaching resource.

Much credit should go to several individuals who played significant roles in this project. Thus, special thanks go to the editorial and production team at Irwin/McGraw-Hill, especially Rick Williamson, senior sponsoring editor; Kelly Delso, developmental editor; Paul Murphy, senior marketing manager; Scott Scheidt, project manager; and Jennifer McQueen, designer. Their ideas and hard work were invaluable contributions to the successful completion of the project. Thanks also to Kay Pinto, whose word processing skills helped me meet my manuscript deadlines. The contributions of many authors, publishers, and firms in the computer industry that contributed case material, ideas, illustrations, and photographs used in this text are also thankfully acknowledged.

A Special Acknowledgment

A special acknowledgment goes to Omar El Sawy, Arvind Malhotra, Sanjay Gosain, and Kerry Young for their award-winning *MIS Quarterly* article, "IT-Intensive Value Innovation in the Electronic Economy: Insights from Marshall Industries"; to Ravi Kalakota and Marcia Robinson for the latest version of their groundbreaking book, *E-Business 2.0: Roadmap for Success*; and to Patricia Seybold for her best-selling book on e-commerce: *Customers.com: How to Create a Profitable Business Strategy for the Internet and Beyond*. Their pioneering works were invaluable sources for my coverage of e-business and e-commerce topics in this new edition.

Acknowledging the Real World of Business

The unique contribution of the hundreds of business firms and other computer-using organizations that are the subject of the real world cases, exercises, and examples in this text is gratefully acknowledged. The real-life situations faced by these firms and organizations provide the readers of this text with a valuable demonstration of the benefits and limitations of using the Internet and other information technologies to enable electronic business and commerce, and enterprise communications and collaboration in support of the business processes, managerial decision making, and strategic advantage of the e-business enterprise.

James A. O'Brien

Brief Contents

Contents

Module I   Foundation Concepts

Module II   Information Technologies

Module III   Business Applications

Chapter 8

Electronic Commerce Systems   253

Chapter 9

Decision Support Systems   291

Module IV   Development Processes

Module V   Management Challenges

Introduction to Information Systems

Essentials for the e-Business Enterprise

Management
Challenges

Business
Applications · Module
I

Information
Technologies

Development
Processes

Foundation
Concepts

Module I

Foundation Concepts

Why study information systems? Why do businesses need information technology? What do you need to know about the use and management of information technologies in business? The introductory chapters of Module I are designed to answer these fundamental questions about the role of information systems in e-business enterprises.

- **Chapter 1: Foundations of Information Systems in Business** presents an overview of the five basic areas of information systems knowledge needed by business professionals, including the conceptual system components and major types of information systems.

- **Chapter 2: Competing with Information Technology** introduces fundamental concepts of competitive advantage through information technology, and illustrates strategic applications of information systems that can gain competitive advantages for today's global e-business enterprise.

After completing these chapters, you can move on to study chapters on information technologies (Module II), business applications (Module III), development processes (Module IV), and the management challenges of information systems (Module V).

Management
Challenges

Business
Applications Module
I
Information
Technologies

Development
Processes Foundation
Concepts

Chapter 1

Foundations of Information

Systems in Business

Chapter Highlights

Learning Objectives

After reading and studying this chapter, you should be able to:

1. Explain why knowledge of information systems is important for business professionals and identify five areas of information systems knowledge they need.

2. Give examples to illustrate how electronic business, electronic commerce, or enterprise collaboration systems could support a firm's business processes, managerial decision making, and strategies for competitive advantage.

3. Provide examples of the components of real world information systems. Illustrate that in an information system, people use hardware, software, data, and networks as resources to perform input, processing, output, storage, and control activities that transform data resources into information products.

4. Provide examples of several major types of information systems from your experiences with business organizations in the real world.

5. Identify several challenges that a business manager might face in managing the successful and ethical development and use of information technology in a business.

Foundation Concepts: Information Systems and Technologies

Why Information Systems Are Important

The blending of Internet technologies and traditional business concerns is impacting all industries and is really the latest phase in the ongoing evolution of business. All companies need to update their business infrastructures and change the way they work to respond more immediately to customer needs [12].

Why study information systems and information technology? That's the same as asking why anyone should study accounting, finance, operations management, marketing, human resource management, or any other major business function. Information systems and technologies (including e-business and e-commerce technologies and applications) have become a vital component of successful businesses and organizations. They thus constitute an essential field of study in business administration and management. That's why most business majors must take a course in information systems. Since you probably intend to be a manager, entrepreneur, or business professional, it is just as important to have a basic understanding of information systems as it is to understand any other functional area in business.

The Real World of Information Systems

Let's take a moment to bring the real world into our discussion of the importance of information systems (IS) and information technology (IT). Read the Real World Case on General Electric on the next page. Then let's analyze it together. See Figure 1.1.

Figure 1.1

Stuart Scott, CIO of GE Industrial Systems, directs the continued development of GE's Support Central knowledge management system.

Source: Derek Dudek

General Electric Company:
Implementing e-Business and e-Commerce Initiatives

No company has made as vocal a commitment to radically transforming business by shifting to e-business and e-commerce as General Electric. What motivated GE has been a fear that new competition would cut into its extraordinary profits. That's what former CEO Jack Welch tried to hammer into his managers in January 1999, ordering them "to destroy their businesses and rebuild them for the Internet . . . before start-up dotcoms get the chance to destroy you." From that moment, the shift to e-business became a policy imperative, with every GE business unit jumping to integrate its suppliers and customers with its internal processes.

Welch had four major business strategies: globalization, business services, e-business, and the total quality program known as Six Sigma. Instead of unveiling a fifth, new CEO Jeff Immelt says, "The best thing I can do is drive GE's four initiatives broader and deeper." Under the banner of "No back office," for instance, he's telling managers to digitize or outsource the parts of their businesses that don't touch the customer. Immelt also supports the development of "digital cockpits" or corporate information portals that let managers track the vitals of their businesses moment by moment. All told, e-business is supposed to save GE $1.6 billion in 2001.

Leading GE's technology charge is CIO Gary Reiner. And Reiner isn't afraid to pose provocative questions and technology-based solutions concerning the business potential of information technology and its impact on the company's performance. Thus, Reiner has been spearheading nothing less than a cultural revolution at GE. The goal is to take full advantage of the Internet to sell products and services, streamline internal operations, and purchase materials and supplies. As a consequence, GE is far ahead of the 50 largest corporations in the United States in squeezing benefits out of the Web.

GE's drive to apply Internet power everywhere—an initiative once dubbed "destroyyourbusiness.com" and now more soberly called digitization—has been three-sided. On the sell side, online sales across GE's divisions grew from nearly nothing in 1998 to more than $7 billion in 2000, about 5 percent of company revenue. That fell short of an eventual goal of 30 percent—but was still more than double Amazon.com's sales, as GE sold everything from mutual funds to jet engine repair services on the Web.

On the buy side, by the end of 2000, GE had purchased more than $6 billion in goods and services through online auctions, and this year it plans to spend $14 to $30 billion online. Engineers in its locomotive business, for example, developed a Web tool that lets GE hold up to 100 auctions a day for companies to bid on contracts to supply GE with materials and services. Online auctions are expected to cut purchasing costs at GE through reductions in prices and transaction costs by over $600 million in 2001.

The rest of the $1.6 billion in costs GE plans to vaporize in 2001 will come from the make side—the internal processes the company is juicing up with Internet technologies. For example, one of the keys to the planned cost reductions is an invasion of Net-based collaboration tools. The company has made a huge commitment to the Lotus Development tools QuickPlace (which lets employees set up web-based work spaces) and Sametime (for realtime online meetings), which permit ad hoc collaboration without help from the IT department.

These tools streamline the company's communication in myriad ways. Thus, GE's recruiting teams can set up QuickPlaces to trade information about prospective hires. And GE engineers share drawings, design requirements, and production schedules with foremen on manufacturing floors. In all, GE has created almost 18,000 QuickPlaces for 250,000 users, says CTO Larry Biagini. "And if we have an engineering project with someone outside the company, we'll set up a QuickPlace or Sametime session and invite outside people."

There's also Support Central, a companywide knowledge management system developed using software from GE's Fanuc division. Employees sign on and complete a survey about their areas of expertise. The responses are added to a knowledge base so people with questions anywhere in GE can find people with answers. "Someone may have a question about, say, titanium metallurgy, and they'll be able to find documents about it, or send e-mail or initiate an online chat with someone who can help," says Stuart Scott, CIO of GE Industrial Systems. The result of all this collaboration? Faster workflow and quicker, smarter decisions, GE executives say.

Case Study Questions

1. Are the buy, sell, and make e-business and e-commerce initiatives of GE applicable to other companies—both large and small? Give examples to support your answer.

2. Could the business value of GE's Web-based collaboration tools be as great as their executives claim? Why or why not?

3. Evaluate the business value of Jeff Immelt's e-business directives for GE. Do you agree with their strategic importance for GE at this time? Explain your answer.

Source: Adapted from Kathy Robello, "The e-Biz 25," *Business Week e-biz*, May 14, 2001, p. EB54; Paul Strassman, "GE's B2B Retreat," *Computerworld*, July 2, 2001, p. 27; Desiree DeMeyer and Don Steinberg, "The Smart Business 50—General Electric," *Smart Business*, September 2001, p. 72; and Jerry Useem, "It's All Yours Jeff, Now What?" *Fortune*, September 17, 2001, p.19. 2001 Time Inc. All rights reserved. Reprinted from Ziff Davis *Smart Business*, September 2001, with permission. Copyright 2001 Ziff Davis Media Inc. All rights reserved.

Analyzing General Electric Company

We can learn a lot about the importance of information technology and information systems from the Real World Case of General Electric Company.

This case dramatizes just one of the countless examples of the business challenges and opportunities created by the growth of the Internet and the World Wide Web. Former CEO Jack Welch drove General Electric into major e-business initiatives in 1999 to counter an expected dot-com invasion into GE's many businesses. Every GE business unit developed e-commerce and e-business systems to use the Web to connect with their suppliers and customers. New CEO Jeff Immelt is continuing the digitization process by encouraging e-business projects that transform internal processes and provide managers with online information for decision making. GE business units are focused on digitizing their buy, sell, and make processes in a variety of ways. Online auctions for suppliers, online sales to customers, and Web-based collaboration tools for employees are just a few examples as GE moves to save $1.6 billion in operating costs in 2001 and transform itself into a premier e-business enterprise.

Thus, information technologies, including Internet-based information systems, are playing a vital and expanding role in business. Information technology can help all kinds of businesses improve the efficiency and effectiveness of their business processes, managerial decision making, and workgroup collaboration and thus strengthen their competitive positions in a rapidly changing marketplace. This is true whether information technology is used to support product development teams, customer support processes, interactive electronic commerce transactions, or any other business activity. Internet-based information technologies and systems are fast becoming a necessary ingredient for business success in today's dynamic global environment.

What You Need to Know

There is no longer any distinction between an IT project and a business initiative. IT at Marriott is a key component of the products and services that we provide to our customers and guests at our properties. As such, there's very little that goes on within the company that either I personally or one of my top executives is not involved in [13].

Those are the words of Carl Wilson, executive vice-president and CIO of Marriott International. So even top executives and managers must learn how to apply information systems and technologies to their unique business situations. In fact, business firms depend on all of their managers and employees to help them manage their use of information technologies. So the important question for any business professional or manager is: What do you need to know in order to help manage the hardware, software, data, and network resources of your business, so they are used for the strategic success of your company?

An IS Framework for Business Professionals

The field of information systems encompasses many complex technologies, abstract behavioral concepts, and specialized applications in countless business and nonbusiness areas. As a manager or business professional you do not have to absorb all of this knowledge. Figure 1.2 illustrates a useful conceptual framework that organizes the knowledge presented in this text and outlines what you need to know about information systems. It emphasizes that you should concentrate your efforts in five areas of knowledge:

- **Foundation Concepts.** Fundamental behavioral, technical, business, and managerial concepts about the components and roles of information systems. Examples include basic information system concepts derived from general systems theory, or competitive strategy concepts used to develop e-business applications of information technology for competitive advantage. Chapters 1 and 2 and other chapters of the text support this area of knowledge.

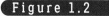

Figure 1.2

This framework outlines the major areas of information systems knowledge needed by business professionals.

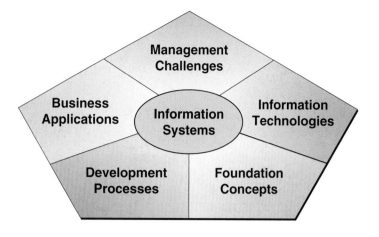

- **Information Technologies.** Major concepts, developments, and management issues in information technology—that is, hardware, software, networks, data resource management, and many Internet-based technologies. Chapters 3 through 6 provide you with coverage of such topics that supports this area of information systems knowledge.

- **Business Applications.** The major uses of information systems for the operations, management, and competitive advantage of an e-business enterprise, including electronic business, commerce, collaboration and decision making using the Internet, intranets, and extranets are covered in Chapters 7 through 9.

- **Development Processes.** How business professionals and information specialists plan, develop, and implement information systems to meet e-business opportunities using several application development approaches. Chapter 10 helps you gain such knowledge as well as an appreciation of the e-business issues involved.

- **Management Challenges.** The challenges of effectively and ethically managing e-business technologies, strategies, and security at the end user, enterprise, and global levels of a business. Chapters 11 and 12 specifically cover these topics, but all of the chapters in the text emphasize the managerial challenges of information technology in today's global e-business environment.

In this chapter, we will discuss some of the foundation concepts of information systems and introduce other topics that give you an overview of the five areas of IS knowledge covered in this text.

What Is an Information System?

Let's begin with a simple definition of an information system, which we will expand in the next few pages. An **information system** can be any organized combination of people, hardware, software, communications networks, and data resources that collects, transforms, and disseminates information in an organization. See Figure 1.3. People have relied on information systems to communicate with each other using a variety of physical devices *(hardware)*, information processing instructions and procedures *(software)*, communications channels *(networks)*, and stored data *(data resources)* since the dawn of civilization.

Information Technologies

Business professionals rely on many types of information systems. Some information systems use simple manual (paper-and-pencil) hardware devices and informal (word-of-mouth) communications channels. However, in this text, we will

Figure 1.3

Information systems rely on people, and a variety of hardware, software, data, and communications network technologies as resources to collect, transform, and disseminate information in an organization.

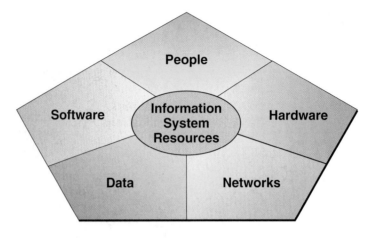

concentrate on *computer-based information systems* that use computer hardware and software, the Internet and other telecommunications networks, computer-based data resource management techniques, and many other **information technologies** to transform data resources into an endless variety of information products for consumers and business professionals. Now let's look at some of the basic foundation concepts of information systems and technologies.

System Concepts: A Foundation

System concepts underlie the field of information systems. That's why we need to discuss how generic system concepts apply to business firms and the components and activities of information systems. Understanding system concepts will help you understand many other concepts in the technology, applications, development, and management of information systems that we will cover in this text. For example, system concepts help you understand:

- **Technology.** That computer networks are systems of information processing components that use a variety of hardware, software, data management, and telecommunications network technologies.
- **Applications.** That electronic business and commerce applications involve interconnected business information systems.
- **Development.** That developing ways to use information technology in business includes designing the basic components of information systems.
- **Management.** That managing information technology emphasizes the quality, strategic business value, and security of an organization's information systems.

What Is a System?

What is a *system*? A system can be most simply defined as a group of interrelated or interacting elements forming a unified whole. Many examples of systems can be found in the physical and biological sciences, in modern technology, and in human society. Thus, we can talk of the physical system of the sun and its planets, the biological system of the human body, the technological system of an oil refinery, and the socioeconomic system of a business organization.

However, the following generic system concept provides a more appropriate foundation concept for the field of information systems: a **system** is a group of interrelated components working together toward a common goal by accepting inputs and producing outputs in an organized transformation process.

Such a system (sometimes called a *dynamic* system) has three basic interacting components or functions:

- **Input** involves capturing and assembling elements that enter the system to be processed. For example, raw materials, energy, data, and human effort must be secured and organized for processing.

- **Processing** involves transformation processes that convert input into output. Examples are a manufacturing process, the human breathing process, or mathematical calculations.
- **Output** involves transferring elements that have been produced by a transformation process to their ultimate destination. For example, finished products, human services, and management information must be transmitted to their human users.

Example

A manufacturing system accepts raw materials as input and produces finished goods as output. An information system is a system that accepts resources (data) as input and processes them into products (information) as output. A business organization is a system where economic resources are transformed by various business processes into goods and services. ●

Feedback and Control

The system concept becomes even more useful by including two additional components: feedback and control. A system with feedback and control components is sometimes called a *cybernetic* system, that is, a self-monitoring, self-regulating system.

- **Feedback** is data about the performance of a system. For example, data about sales performance is feedback to a sales manager.
- **Control** involves monitoring and evaluating feedback to determine whether a system is moving toward the achievement of its goal. The control function then makes necessary adjustments to a system's input and processing components to ensure that it produces proper output. For example, a sales manager exercises control when reassigning salespersons to new sales territories after evaluating feedback about their sales performance.

Example

A familiar example of a self-monitoring, self-regulating system is the thermostat-controlled heating system found in many homes; it automatically monitors and regulates itself to maintain a desired temperature. Another example is the human body, which can be regarded as a cybernetic system that automatically monitors and adjusts many of its functions, such as temperature, heartbeat, and breathing. A business also has many control activities. For example, computers may monitor and control manufacturing processes, accounting procedures help control financial systems, data entry displays provide control of data entry activities, and sales quotas and sales bonuses attempt to control sales performance. ●

Other System Characteristics

Figure 1.4 uses a business organization to illustrate the fundamental components of a system, as well as several other system characteristics. Note that a system does not exist in a vacuum, rather, it exists and functions in an *environment* containing other systems. If a system is one of the components of a larger system, it is a *subsystem*, and the larger system is its environment.

Several systems may share the same environment. Some of these systems may be connected to one another by means of a shared boundary, or *interface*. Figure 1.4 also illustrates the concept of an *open system*; that is, a system that interacts with other systems in its environment. In this diagram, the system exchanges inputs and outputs with its environment. Thus, we could say that it is connected to its environment by input and output interfaces. Finally, a system that has the ability to change itself or its environment in order to survive is an *adaptive system*.

Example

Organizations such as businesses and government agencies are good examples of the systems in society, which is their environment. Society contains a multitude of such systems, including individuals and their social, political, and economic institutions. Organizations themselves consist of many subsystems, such as departments, divisions, process teams, and other workgroups. Organizations are examples of open systems because they interface and interact with other systems in their environment. Finally, organizations are examples of adaptive systems, since they can modify themselves to meet the demands of a changing environment. ●

Components of an Information System

We are now ready to apply the system concepts we have learned to help us better understand how an information system works. For example, we have said that an information system is a system that accepts data resources as input and processes them into information products as output. How does an information system accomplish this? What system components and activities are involved?

Figure 1.5 illustrates an **information system model** that expresses a fundamental conceptual framework for the major components and activities of information systems. An information system depends on the resources of people (end users and IS specialists), hardware (machines and media), software (programs and procedures), data (data and knowledge bases), and networks (communications media and network support) to perform input, processing, output, storage, and control activities that convert data resources into information products.

This information system model highlights the relationships among the components and activities of information systems. It provides a framework that emphasizes four major concepts that can be applied to all types of information systems:

Figure 1.4

A business is an example of an organizational system where economic resources (input) are transformed by various business processes (processing) into goods and services (output). Information systems provide information (feedback) on the operations of the system to management for the direction and maintenance of the system (control) as it exchanges inputs and outputs with its environment.

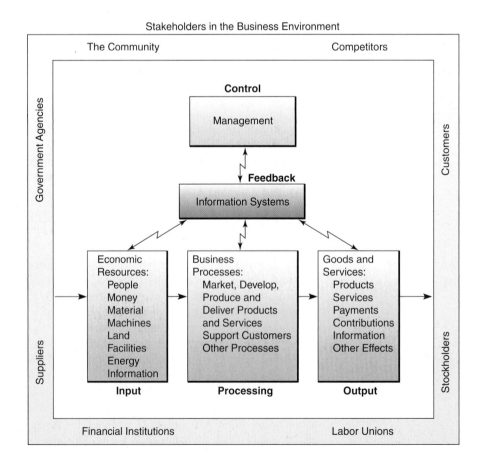

Stakeholders in the Business Environment

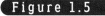

Figure 1.5

The components of an information system. All information systems use people, hardware, software, data, and network resources to perform input, processing, output, storage, and control activities that transform data resources into information products.

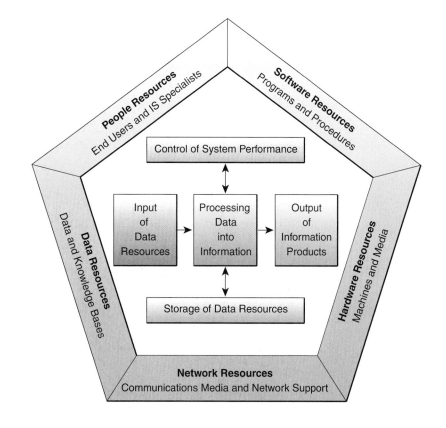

- People, hardware, software, data, and networks are the five basic resources of information systems.
- People resources include end users and IS specialists, hardware resources consist of machines and media, software resources include both programs and procedures, data resources can include data and knowledge bases, and network resources include communications media and networks.
- Data resources are transformed by information processing activities into a variety of information products for end users.
- Information processing consists of input, processing, output, storage, and control activities.

Information System Resources

Our basic IS model shows that an information system consists of five major resources: people, hardware, software, data, and networks. Let's briefly discuss several basic concepts and examples of the roles these resources play as the fundamental components of information systems. You should be able to recognize these five components at work in any type of information system you encounter in the real world. Figure 1.6 outlines several examples of typical information system resources and products.

People Resources

People are required for the operation of all information systems. These people resources include end users and IS specialists.

- **End users** (also called users or clients) are people who use an information system or the information it produces. They can be accountants, salespersons, engineers, clerks, customers, or managers. Most of us are information system end users. And most end users in business are **knowledge workers,** that is, people who spend most of their time communicating and collaborating in teams and workgroups and creating, using, and distributing information.

Figure 1.6

Examples of information system resources and products.

Information Systems Resources and Products
People Resources Specialists—systems analysts, software developers, system operators. End Users—anyone else who uses information systems.
Hardware Resources Machines—computers, video monitors, magnetic disk drives, printers, optical scanners. Media—floppy disks, magnetic tape, optical disks, plastic cards, paper forms.
Software Resources Programs—operating system programs, spreadsheet programs, word processing programs, payroll programs. Procedures—data entry procedures, error correction procedures, paycheck distribution procedures.
Data Resources Product descriptions, customer records, employee files, inventory databases.
Network Resources Communications media, communications processors, network access and control software.
Information Products Management reports and business documents using text and graphics displays, audio responses, and paper forms.

- **IS specialists** are people who develop and operate information systems. They include systems analysts, software developers, system operators, and other managerial, technical, and clerical IS personnel. Briefly, systems analysts design information systems based on the information requirements of end users, software developers create computer programs based on the specifications of systems analysts, and system operators help to monitor and operate large computer systems and networks.

Hardware Resources

The concept of **hardware resources** includes all physical devices and materials used in information processing. Specifically, it includes not only **machines,** such as computers and other equipment, but also all data **media,** that is, tangible objects on which data are recorded, from sheets of paper to magnetic or optical disks. Examples of hardware in computer-based information systems are:

- **Computer systems,** which consist of central processing units containing microprocessors, and a variety of interconnected peripheral devices. Examples are hand-held, laptop, or desktop microcomputer systems, midrange computer systems, and large mainframe computer systems.

- **Computer peripherals,** which are devices such as a keyboard or electronic mouse for input of data and commands, a video screen or printer for output of information, and magnetic or optical disks for storage of data resources.

Software Resources

The concept of **software resources** includes all sets of information processing instructions. This generic concept of software includes not only the sets of operating instructions called **programs,** which direct and control computer hardware, but also the sets of information processing instructions called **procedures** that people need.

It is important to understand that even information systems that don't use computers have a software resource component. This is true even for the information systems of ancient times, or the manual and machine-supported information systems still used in the world today. They all require software resources in the form of information processing instructions and procedures in order to properly capture, process, and disseminate information to their users.

The following are examples of software resources:

- **System software,** such as an operating system program, which controls and supports the operations of a computer system.
- **Application software,** which are programs that direct processing for a particular use of computers by end users. Examples are a sales analysis program, a payroll program, and a word processing program.
- **Procedures,** which are operating instructions for the people who will use an information system. Examples are instructions for filling out a paper form or using a software package.

Data Resources

Data are more than the raw material of information systems. The concept of data resources has been broadened by managers and information systems professionals. They realize that data constitute valuable organizational resources. Thus, you should view data as **data resources** that must be managed effectively to benefit all end users in an organization.

Data can take many forms, including traditional alphanumeric data, composed of numbers and alphabetical and other characters that describe business transactions and other events and entities. Text data, consisting of sentences and paragraphs used in written communications; image data, such as graphic shapes and figures; and audio data, the human voice and other sounds, are also important forms of data.

The data resources of information systems are typically organized, stored, and accessed by a variety of data resource management technologies into:

- Databases that hold processed and organized data.
- Knowledge bases that hold knowledge in a variety of forms such as facts, rules, and case examples about successful business practices.

For example, data about sales transactions may be accumulated, processed, and stored in a web-enabled sales database that can be accessed for sales analysis reports by managers and marketing professionals. Knowledge bases are used by knowledge management systems and expert systems to share knowledge or give expert advice on specific subjects. We will explore these concepts further in later chapters.

Data versus Information. The word **data** is the plural of *datum*, though data commonly represents both singular and plural forms. Data are raw facts or observations, typically about physical phenomena or business transactions. For example, a spacecraft launch or the sale of an automobile would generate a lot of data describing those events. More specifically, data are objective measurements of the *attributes* (the characteristics) of *entities* (such as people, places, things, and events).

Example

Business transactions such as buying a car or an airline ticket can produce a lot of data. Just think of the hundreds of facts needed to describe the characteristics of the car you want and its financing, or the details for even the simplest airline reservation. ●

People often use the terms *data* and *information* interchangeably. However, it is better to view data as raw material resources that are processed into finished information products. Then we can define **information** as data that have been converted into a meaningful and useful context for specific end users. Thus, data are usually subjected to a value-added process (we call *data processing* or *information processing*) where (1) its form is aggregated, manipulated, and organized; (2) its content is analyzed and evaluated; and (3) it is placed in a proper context for a human user. So you should view information as processed data placed in a context that gives it value for specific end users.

Example

Names, quantities, and dollar amounts recorded on sales forms represent data about sales transactions. However, a sales manager may not regard these as information. Only after such facts are properly organized and manipulated can meaningful sales information be furnished, specifying, for example, the amount of sales by product type, sales territory, or salesperson. ●

Network Resources

Telecommunications technologies and networks like the Internet, intranets, and extranets have become essential to the successful electronic business and commerce operations of all types of organizations and their computer-based information systems. Telecommunications networks consist of computers, communications processors, and other devices interconnected by communications media and controlled by communications software. The concept of **network resources** emphasizes that communications technologies and networks are a fundamental resource component of all information systems. Network resources include:

- **Communications media.** Examples include twisted-pair wire, coaxial cable, and fiber-optic cable; and microwave, cellular, and satellite wireless technologies.
- **Network support.** This generic category emphasizes that many hardware, software, and data technologies are needed to support the operation and use of a communications network. Examples include communications processors such as modems and internetwork processors, and communications control software such as network operating systems and Internet browser packages.

Information System Activities

Let's take a closer look now at each of the basic **information processing** (or **data processing**) activities that occur in information systems. You should be able to recognize input, processing, output, storage, and control activities taking place in any information system you are studying. Figure 1.7 lists business examples that illustrate each of these information system activities.

Input of Data Resources

Data about business transactions and other events must be captured and prepared for processing by the **input** activity. Input typically takes the form of *data entry* activities such as recording and editing. End users typically enter data directly into a computer system, or record data about transactions on some type of physical medium such as a paper form. This usually includes a variety of editing activities to ensure that they have recorded data correctly. Once entered, data may be transferred onto a machine-readable medium such as a magnetic disk until needed for processing.

For example, data about sales transactions can be recorded on source documents such as paper sales order forms. (A **source document** is the original formal record of a transaction.) Alternately, salespersons can capture sales data using computer keyboards or optical scanning devices; they are visually prompted to enter data correctly by video displays. This provides them with a more convenient and efficient **user interface,** that is, methods of end user input and output with a computer system. Methods such as optical scanning and displays of menus, prompts, and fill-in-the-

Figure 1.7

Business examples of the basic activities of information systems.

Information System Activities
● **Input.** Optical scanning of bar-coded tags on merchandise.
● **Processing.** Calculating employee pay, taxes, and other payroll deductions.
● **Output.** Producing reports and displays about sales performance.
● **Storage.** Maintaining records on customers, employees, and products.
● **Control.** Generating audible signals to indicate proper entry of sales data.

blanks formats make it easier for end users to enter data correctly into an information system.

Processing of Data into Information

Data are typically subjected to **processing** activities such as calculating, comparing, sorting, classifying, and summarizing. These activities organize, analyze, and manipulate data, thus converting them into information for end users. The quality of any data stored in an information system must also be maintained by a continual process of correcting and updating activities.

Example

Data received about a purchase can be (1) *added* to a running total of sales results, (2) *compared* to a standard to determine eligibility for a sales discount, (3) *sorted* in numerical order based on product identification numbers, (4) *classified* into product categories (such as food and nonfood items), (5) *summarized* to provide a sales manager with information about various product categories, and, finally, (6) used to *update* sales records. ●

Output of Information Products

Information in various forms is transmitted to end users and made available to them in the **output** activity. The goal of information systems is the production of appropriate **information products** for end users. Common information products include messages, reports, forms, and graphic images, which may be provided by video displays, audio responses, paper products, and multimedia. We routinely use the information provided by these products as we work in organizations and live in society. For example, a sales manager may view a video display to check on the performance of a salesperson, accept a computer-produced voice message by telephone, and receive a printout of monthly sales results.

Information Quality

What characteristics would make information products valuable and useful to you? One way to answer this important question is to examine the characteristics or attributes of **information quality.** Information that is outdated, inaccurate, or hard to understand would not be very meaningful, useful, or valuable to you or other end users. People want information of high quality, that is, information products whose characteristics, attributes, or qualities make the information more valuable to them. It is useful to think of information as having the three dimensions of time, content, and form. Figure 1.8 summarizes the important attributes of information quality and groups them into these three dimensions.

Storage of Data Resources

Storage is a basic system component of information systems. Storage is the information system activity in which data and information are retained in an organized manner for later use. For example, just as written text material is organized into words, sentences, paragraphs, and documents, stored data are commonly organized into fields, records, files, and databases. This facilitates its later use in processing or its retrieval as output when needed by users of a system. These logical data elements are shown in Figure 1.9 and are discussed further in Chapter 5.

Control of System Performance

An important information system activity is the **control** of its performance. An information system should produce feedback about its input, processing, output, and storage activities. This feedback must be monitored and evaluated to determine if the system is meeting established performance standards. Then appropriate system activities must be adjusted so that proper information products are produced for end users.

For example, a manager may discover that subtotals of sales amounts in a sales report do not add up to total sales. This might mean that data entry or processing procedures need to be corrected. Then changes would have to be made to ensure that all sales transactions would be properly captured and processed by a sales information system.

A summary of the attributes of information quality. This outlines the attributes that should be present in high-quality information products.

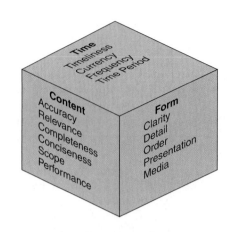

Time Dimension

Timeliness	Information should be provided when it is needed.
Currency	Information should be up-to-date when it is provided.
Frequency	Information should be provided as often as needed.
Time Period	Information can be provided about past, present, and future time periods.

Content Dimension

Accuracy	Information should be free from errors.
Relevance	Information should be related to the information needs of a specific recipient for a specific situation.
Completeness	All the information that is needed should be provided.
Conciseness	Only the information that is needed should be provided.
Scope	Information can have a broad or narrow scope, or an internal or external focus.
Performance	Information can reveal performance by measuring activities accomplished, progress made, or resources accumulated.

Form Dimension

Clarity	Information should be provided in a form that is easy to understand.
Detail	Information can be provided in detail or summary form.
Order	Information can be arranged in a predetermined sequence.
Presentation	Information can be presented in narrative, numeric, graphic, or other forms.
Media	Information can be provided in the form of printed paper documents, video displays, or other media.

Recognizing Information Systems

As a business professional, you should be able to recognize the fundamental components of information systems you encounter in the real world. This means that you should be able to identify:

- The people, hardware, software, data, and network resources they use.
- The types of information products they produce.
- The way they perform input, processing, output, storage, and control activities.

This kind of understanding will help you be a better user, developer, and manager of information systems. And that, as we have pointed out in this chapter, is important to your future success as a manager, entrepreneur, or professional in business.

Analyzing GE's Information Systems

Refer back to the Real World Case on General Electric on page 5. Now let's try to recognize or visualize the resources used, activities performed, and information products produced by some of their information systems.

IS Resources. People resources include end users like GE's online customers, suppliers, and employees, and IS specialists like software engineers, CIOs Gary Reiner and Stuart Scott, and CTO Larry Biagini. Hardware resources include the thousands

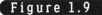

Figure 1.9

Logical data elements. This is a common method of organizing stored data in information systems.

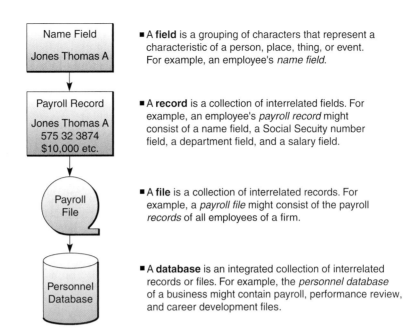

- A **field** is a grouping of characters that represent a characteristic of a person, place, thing, or event. For example, an employee's *name field*.

- A **record** is a collection of interrelated fields. For example, an employee's *payroll record* might consist of a name field, a Social Security number field, a department field, and a salary field.

- A **file** is a collection of interrelated records. For example, a *payroll file* might consist of the payroll *records* of all employees of a firm.

- A **database** is an integrated collection of interrelated records or files. For example, the *personnel database* of a business might contain payroll, performance review, and career development files.

of PCs and servers and other computers that GE must be using. Software resources include everything from Web browsers to e-business software that runs e-commerce websites, holds online auctions, and supports online collaboration. You can just visualize all of the communications media and network support components that would be part of the network resources that GE would need to support the e-business and e-commerce process of such a large global enterprise. Finally, GE undoubtedly has vast data resources of files and databases of data about their customers, suppliers, employees, products, and other necessary business information, including the knowledge bases that are part of their Support Central knowledge management system.

Information Products. The information products we can most easily visualize are the displays on customer, supplier, and employee networked PCs that provide information about GE's online products and services from e-commerce catalog and auction websites, support the online collaboration of company workgroups and teams, and provide managers with online information from "digital cockpit" information portals.

IS Activities. Some of the input activities we can visualize are the input of website navigation clicks, e-commerce and e-business data entries and selections, and online collaboration queries and responses made by customers, suppliers, and employees. Processing activities are accomplished whenever any of GE's computers executes the programs that are part of their e-business and e-commerce software resources. Output activities primarily involve the display or printing of the information products we identified earlier. Storage activities take place whenever business data is stored and managed in the files and databases on the disk drives and other storage media of GE's computer systems. Finally, we can visualize several control activities, including the use of passwords and other security codes by customers, suppliers, and employees for entry into GE's e-business and e-commerce websites, and access of their databases and knowledge bases.

So you see, analyzing an information system to identify its basic components is not a difficult task. Just identify the resources that the information system uses, the information processing activities it performs, and the information products it produces. Then you will be better able to identify ways to improve these components, and thus the performance of the information system itself. That's a goal that every business professional should strive to attain.

Foundation Concepts: Business Applications, Development, and Management

The Fundamental Roles of IS Applications in Business

There are three fundamental reasons for all business applications of information technology. They are found in the three vital roles that information systems can perform for a business enterprise.

- Support of its business processes and operations.
- Support of decision making by its employees and managers.
- Support of its strategies for competitive advantage.

We will introduce these roles and applications in this chapter, and cover them in more detail later. The strategic applications of information systems for competitive advantage will be covered in Chapter 2. Business applications of information technology for electronic business operations, electronic commerce, enterprise collaboration, and decision making will be discussed in Chapters 7, 8, and 9.

Analyzing Duke Energy

Read the Real World Case on Duke Energy on the next page. We can learn a lot about the challenges of introducing e-business into a company from this example. See Figure 1.10.

Duke Energy chose a guerilla approach to introducing e-business into their company. They created an e-team of professionals from a variety of business functions whose two-year mission was to encourage Duke's business units to develop and implement a variety of strategic e-business initiatives. The e-team would provide seed money, systems consulting, and project liaison and management services to help a business unit develop and implement a variety of e-business applications. The team was especially supportive of projects that would add significant value to Duke's customer relationships. Examples of successful e-business projects at Duke were a customer Web portal and an online auction system. Within eighteen months, the

Figure 1.10

Led by A. R. Mullinax, chief e-business officer (second from right), Duke Energy's e-team worked to sell e-business approaches to the company's business units.

Source: Marc Berlow

Duke Energy: Introducing e-Business throughout the Business Enterprise

On the first business day of the new millennium, Duke Energy initiated a guerrilla approach to e-business. A small band of advocates began to roam the utility, living in the business units, seeding pilot projects, assisting with implantations, coordinating resources, and spreading success stories. Eighteen months later, having launched more than a dozen successful Internet initiatives that saved the company $52 million last year alone, the "e-team" is now handing off the projects to the businesses. "Then," says senior vice president and chief e-business officer A.R. Mullinax, "we will declare victory." Here's how they did it.

In late 1999, Duke's corporate policy committee, at the urging of CIO Cecil Smith, authorized Mullinax to begin to harness the Internet. The goal was to weave e-business into the Duke fabric. "We didn't want to turn Duke into a dot-com," Mullinax recalls. "We wanted to find uses of the Internet that would advance our existing business."

Mullinax, then senior vice president for procurement, was given free reign to recruit a team and carry out the mission. He chose Ted Schultz from strategic planning; Steve Bush, finance and administration; Dave Davies, IT project management; Amy Baxter and Dennis Wood, procurement; Elizabeth Henry, customer focus; and Anne Narang, Web design. "Everybody brought strengths to the table," Mullinax says, "and the other ingredient was chemistry. We worked well as a team."

From the start, the team planned to disband in 24 months. "You should get to the point where you don't need an e-business officer any more than you need a chief telephone officer," Mullinax says.

The team spent the first month getting a good perspective on the Charlotte, N.C.–based company, which ranks 17th among the Fortune 100. Then, team members literally moved into the businesses. If a unit had already launched an Internet initiative, a team member would advise on strategy and implementation. If a unit was new to the Web, a team member would spearhead an initiative.

The e-team had a budget, but its mantra was "Invest little, save big." It looked for business units that could use Internet tools in the most effective way, particularly those units where customers were dependent on information, and easy access to that information would add value to the relationship. "We could have taken on hundreds of initiatives, but we looked for the ones that would give us the most return compared with the level of effort it was going to take," Mullinex explains.

Henry worked at Duke Solutions, which advises very large industrial, commercial, and institutional customers, such as Northfield, Illinois–based Kraft Foods, Inc., on energy management. "I was attached at the hip to Duke Solutions' e-business strategist Jeffrey Custer," she recalls. "It worked so well to be with them, hearing what their issues were every day." Custer, director of corporate development at Duke Solutions, agrees. "You have a fear when you hear that corporate is going to create a new group, but they were different," he says. "I was the lead; they were here to provide support and seed money. They kept the focus and kept me moving."

Meanwhile, Schultz worked with Duke Energy Trade and Marketing in Houston, which provides energy to very large customers, such as city power companies. Henry and Schultz correctly suspected that the needs of the two customer sets would be similar. The e-team members funded and helped the businesses stage comprehensive focus groups to gather information on what customers wanted. That turned out to be a customizable Web portal where clients could obtain services like online billing and account status as well as energy industry information.

Custer says the focus groups made a big difference. "I had some fantastic things I wanted to put on the site, but the customers said, 'That's great, but this is what I need today,'" he says. The e-team funded the prototype, and the businesses provided coding and content-generation services. Within 90 days, version 1.0 of the my.duke-energy.com customer portal was up and running.

The iterative, 90-day cycle was a hallmark of the e-team, and it kept them in touch with customers. "When you go off and work on something for six months, even if it's bad, you've invested too much, so you try to put the round peg into the square hole," Custer says. "But their strategy was ask the customer, prototype it, show it to them, make changes and do it again, keep it moving. You get a lot more feedback and buy-in that way."

While Henry and Schultz worked on the customer portal, Wood brought online auctions to Global Sourcing, Duke Energy's procurement unit. Working with FreeMarkets Inc., a Pittsburgh-based online auction company, Wood also explained the process and benefits to supply chain folks throughout the businesses. More important, he invited them all to the first live auction in May of last year. Says Wood, "You can explain things all day long, but when they see it, it clicks."

Top management is proud of the e-team's results. "E-business has helped accelerate cost savings, and we are also seeing performance enhancements," said executive vice president and chief administrative officer, Ruth Shaw.

Case Study Questions

1. Should Duke Energy's guerilla approach to introducing e-business be adopted by other companies? Why or why not?

2. Select and evaluate one of Duke Energy's e-business projects. What are its business benefits and limitations?

3. Are any of Duke Energy's e-business initiatives applicable to other companies? Explain your answer.

Source: Adapted from Kathleen Melymuka, "Energizing the Company," *Computerworld*, August 13, 2001, pp. 48, 49. Reprinted by permission.

Figure 1.11

The three major roles of the business applications of information systems. Information systems provide an organization with support for business processes, operations, decision making, and competitive advantage.

Information Systems

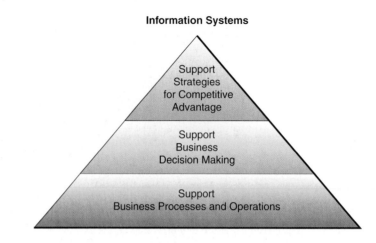

Support Strategies for Competitive Advantage

Support Business Decision Making

Support Business Processes and Operations

e-team had helped launch over a dozen e-business initiatives that saved the company $52 million in one year.

Figure 1.11 illustrates the three major roles of the business applications of information systems. Let's look at a retail store as a good example of how these three fundamental roles can be implemented by a business.

Example

As a consumer, you have to deal regularly with the information systems that support business operations at the many retail stores where you shop. For example, most retail stores now use computer-based information systems to help them record customer purchases, keep track of inventory, pay employees, buy new merchandise, and evaluate sales trends. Store operations would grind to a halt without the support of such information systems.

Information systems also help store managers and other business professionals make better decisions and attempt to gain a competitive advantage. For example, decisions on what lines of merchandise need to be added or discontinued, or on what kind of investment they require, are typically made after an analysis provided by computer-based information systems. This not only supports the decision making of store managers, buyers, and others, but also helps them look for ways to gain an advantage over other retailers in the competition for customers. For example, Figure 1.12 illustrates a financial forecast report produced by a management information system.

Gaining a strategic advantage over competitors requires innovative use of information technology. For example, store management might make a decision to install touch-screen kiosks in all of their stores, with links to their e-commerce website for online shopping. This might attract new customers and build customer loyalty because of the ease of shopping and buying merchandise provided by such information systems. Thus, strategic information systems can help provide products and services that give a business a comparative advantage over its competitors. ●

Trends in Information Systems

The business applications of information systems have expanded significantly over the years. Figure 1.13 summarizes these changes.

Until the 1960s, the role of most information systems was simple: transaction processing, record-keeping, accounting, and other *electronic data processing* (EDP) applications. Then another role was added, as the concept of *management information systems* (MIS) was conceived. This new role focused on developing business applications that provided managerial end users with predefined management reports that would give managers the information they needed for decision-making purposes.

Figure 1.12

A financial forecast report produced by a management information system.

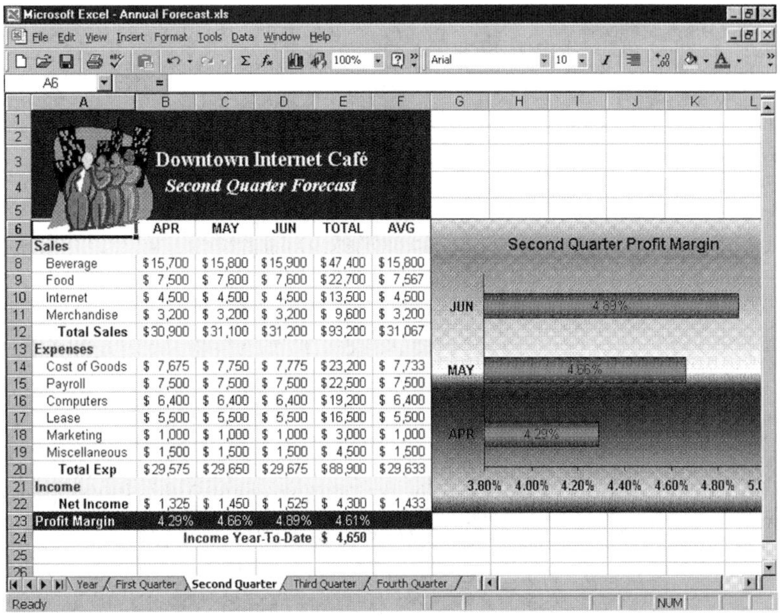

	APR	MAY	JUN	TOTAL	AVG
Sales					
Beverage	$15,700	$15,800	$15,900	$47,400	$15,800
Food	$ 7,500	$ 7,600	$ 7,600	$22,700	$ 7,567
Internet	$ 4,500	$ 4,500	$ 4,500	$13,500	$ 4,500
Merchandise	$ 3,200	$ 3,200	$ 3,200	$ 9,600	$ 3,200
Total Sales	$30,900	$31,100	$31,200	$93,200	$31,067
Expenses					
Cost of Goods	$ 7,675	$ 7,750	$ 7,775	$23,200	$ 7,733
Payroll	$ 7,500	$ 7,500	$ 7,500	$22,500	$ 7,500
Computers	$ 6,400	$ 6,400	$ 6,400	$19,200	$ 6,400
Lease	$ 5,500	$ 5,500	$ 5,500	$16,500	$ 5,500
Marketing	$ 1,000	$ 1,000	$ 1,000	$ 3,000	$ 1,000
Miscellaneous	$ 1,500	$ 1,500	$ 1,500	$ 4,500	$ 1,500
Total Exp	$29,575	$29,650	$29,675	$88,900	$29,633
Income					
Net Income	$ 1,325	$ 1,450	$ 1,525	$ 4,300	$ 1,433
Profit Margin	4.29%	4.66%	4.89%	4.61%	
		Income Year-To-Date	$ 4,650		

Source: Courtesy of Microsoft.

By the 1970s, it was evident that the prespecified information products produced by such management information systems were not adequately meeting many of the decision-making needs of management. So the concept of *decision support systems* (DSS) was born. The new role for information systems was to provide managerial end users with ad hoc and interactive support of their decision-making processes. This support would be tailored to the unique decision-making styles of managers as they confronted specific types of problems in the real world.

In the 1980s, several new roles for information systems appeared. First, the rapid development of microcomputer processing power, application software packages, and telecommunications networks gave birth to the phenomenon of *end user computing*. Now, end users could use their own computing resources to support their job requirements instead of waiting for the indirect support of corporate information services departments.

Second, it became evident that most top corporate executives did not directly use either the reports of management information systems or the analytical modeling capabilities of decision support systems, so the concept of *executive information systems* (EIS) was developed. These information systems were created to give top executives an easy way to get the critical information they want, when they want it, tailored to the formats they prefer.

Third, breakthroughs occurred in the development and application of artificial intelligence (AI) techniques to business information systems. *Expert systems* (ES) and other *knowledge-based systems* forged a new role for information systems. Today, expert systems can serve as consultants to users by providing expert advice in limited subject areas.

An important new role for information systems appeared in the 1980s and continued through the 1990s. This is the concept of a strategic role for information systems, sometimes called *strategic information systems* (SIS). In this concept, information technology becomes an integral component of business processes, products, and services that help a company gain a competitive advantage in the global marketplace.

Finally, the rapid growth of the Internet, intranets, extranets, and other interconnected global networks of the 1990s has dramatically changed the capabilities of information systems in business at the beginning of the twenty-first century. Internetworked enterprise and global **electronic business and commerce** systems are revolutionizing the operations and management of today's business enterprises. Let's take a closer look at this development.

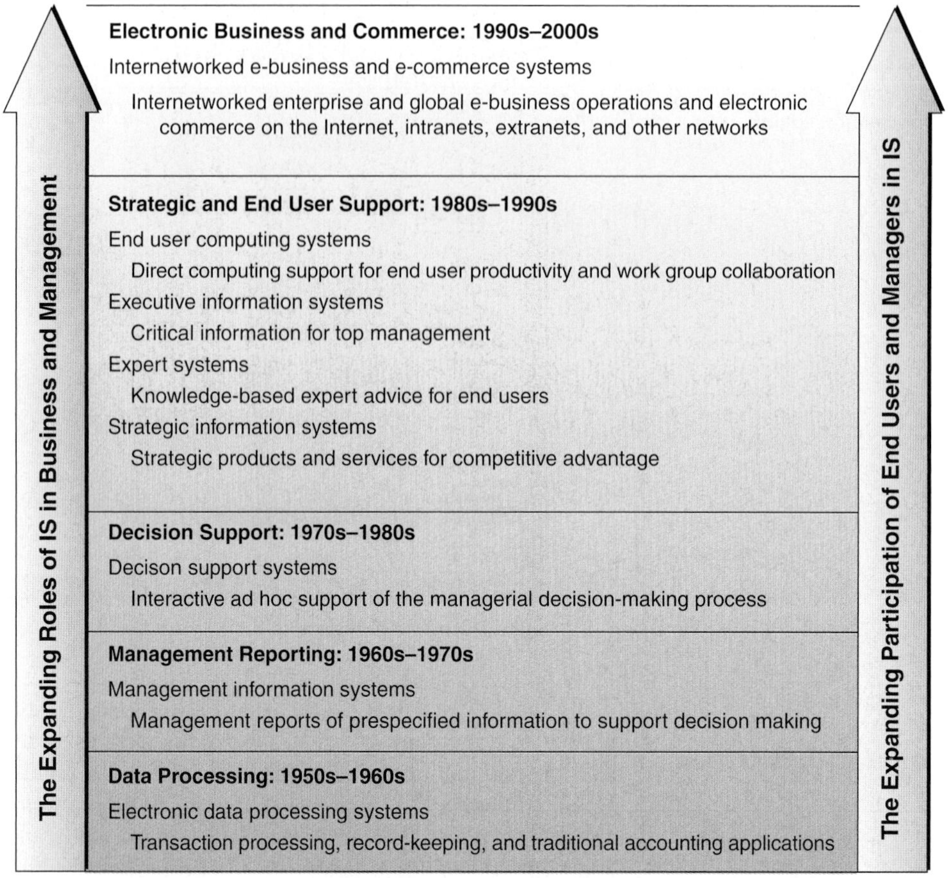

Figure 1.13

The expanding roles of the business applications of information systems. Note how the roles of computer-based information systems have expanded over time. Also, note the impact of these changes on the end users and managers of an organization.

The Expanding Roles of IS in Business and Management →

The Expanding Participation of End Users and Managers in IS →

Electronic Business and Commerce: 1990s–2000s
Internetworked e-business and e-commerce systems
Internetworked enterprise and global e-business operations and electronic commerce on the Internet, intranets, extranets, and other networks

Strategic and End User Support: 1980s–1990s
End user computing systems
Direct computing support for end user productivity and work group collaboration
Executive information systems
Critical information for top management
Expert systems
Knowledge-based expert advice for end users
Strategic information systems
Strategic products and services for competitive advantage

Decision Support: 1970s–1980s
Decison support systems
Interactive ad hoc support of the managerial decision-making process

Management Reporting: 1960s–1970s
Management information systems
Management reports of prespecified information to support decision making

Data Processing: 1950s–1960s
Electronic data processing systems
Transaction processing, record-keeping, and traditional accounting applications

The e-Business Enterprise

There is an overriding change in information technology on whose importance business executives, academicians, and technologists all agree. The explosive growth of the Internet and related technologies and applications is revolutionizing the way businesses are operated and people work, and how information technology supports business operations and end user work activities.

Businesses are becoming **e-business enterprises.** The Internet and Internet-like networks—inside the enterprise **(intranets),** and between an enterprise and its trading partners **(extranets)**—have become the primary information technology infrastructure that supports the business operations of many companies. E-business enterprises rely on such technologies to (1) reengineer and revitalize internal business processes, (2) implement electronic commerce systems among businesses and their customers and suppliers, and (3) promote enterprise collaboration among business teams and workgroups. Figure 1.14 illustrates how an e-business enterprise depends on the Internet, intranets, extranets, and other information technologies to implement and manage e-business operations and electronic commerce and collaboration. Thus in this text, we can define **e-business** as the use of Internet technologies to internetwork and empower business processes, electronic commerce, and enterprise communication and collaboration within a company and with its customers, suppliers, and other business stakeholders.

Enterprise collaboration systems involve the use of groupware tools to support communication, coordination, and collaboration among the members of networked teams and workgroups. An e-business enterprise depends on intranets, the Internet, extranets, and other networks to implement such systems. For example, employees and external consultants may form a *virtual team* that uses a corporate intranet and an extranet for electronic mail, videoconferencing, electronic discussion groups, and Web pages of work-in-progress information to collaborate on business projects.

Figure 1.14

An e-business enterprise depends on the Internet, intranets, and extranets to implement and manage electronic business operations, enterprise collaboration, and electronic commerce.

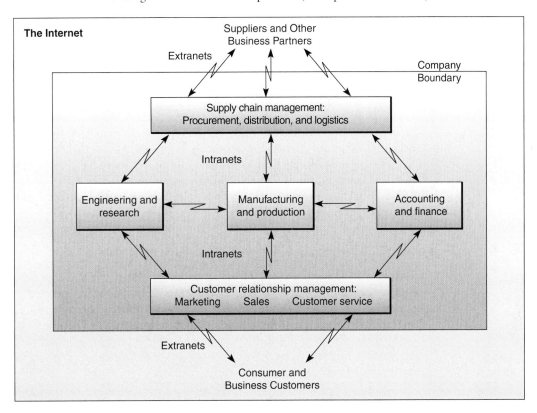

Electronic commerce is the buying and selling, and marketing and servicing of products, services, and information over a variety of computer networks. An e-business enterprise uses the Internet, intranets, extranets, and other networks to support every step of the commercial process. This might include everything from advertising, sales, and customer support on the World Wide Web, to Internet security and payment mechanisms that ensure completion of delivery and payment processes. For example, electronic commerce systems include Internet websites for online sales, extranet access of inventory databases by large customers, and the use of corporate intranets by sales reps to access customer records for customer relationship management. Now let's look in more detail at how one company is using the Internet for electronic business and commerce.

Cisco Systems: e-Business and e-Commerce Leader	Top telecom manufacturer Cisco Systems uses 36 manufacturing plants, of which it owns but two. One of them is downstairs from the San Jose office of Randy Pond, Senior Vice President for Operations. The rest belong to top contract manufacturers like Jabil Circuit and Solectron. It's "virtual manufacturing," Pond says, made possible by a "suite of Internet-based tools and processes that lets me manage an extended enterprise I don't own as if I do own it." The key, says Pond, is "real-time data on a real-time basis so my partners know what goes on in my business every single day." As much as possible, Cisco and a partner work with the same stream of e-business information, doubling its value. Every day Cisco compiles its inventory, forecast for each model, order backlog, and thirteen weeks of daily data about parts and subassemblies; every day its partner compiles data on in-process inventory, cycle time by process step,

optimal lot size, and yield; every night computers combine the Internet data streams into a river of information; every morning everyone knows what to build that day.

Cisco works the other end of the process—e-commerce—the same way. Eighty seven percent of Cisco's sales are entered directly from the Net and available instantaneously. Except for commodity parts, Cisco's e-business supply chain is as visible and as live as a televised football game. Validation and testing are also Internet-based. Autotest, a homemade tool, tests machines as they are built and won't print a packing label for a machine unless every test has been done and passed. Another tool checks a customer's order as he enters it, to make sure that he hasn't asked for incompatible gear.

The benefits of real-time e-business add up to about $400 million a year, by Pond's reckoning, plus up to a $1 billion saving in capital costs—from equipment Cisco doesn't carry on its books, improved utilization by suppliers, and minimal inventory [18].

Types of Information Systems

Conceptually, the applications of information systems in the real world can be classified in several different ways. For example, several types of information systems can be classified as either operations or management information systems. Figure 1.15 illustrates this conceptual classification of information systems applications. Information systems are categorized this way to spotlight the major roles each plays in the operations and management of a business. Let's look briefly at some examples of how information systems exist in the business world.

Operations Support Systems

Information systems have always been needed to process data generated by, and used in, business operations. Such **operations support systems** produce a variety of information products for internal and external use. However, they do not emphasize producing the specific information products that can best be used by managers. Further processing by management information systems is usually required. The role

---

Figure 1.15   Operations and management classifications of information systems. Note how this conceptual overview emphasizes the main purposes of information systems that support business operations and managerial decision making.

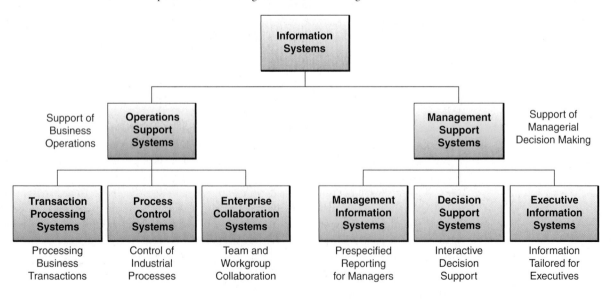

Figure 1.16   A summary of operations support systems with examples.

Operations Support Systems
● **Transaction processing systems.** Process data resulting from business transactions, update operational databases, and produce business documents. Examples: sales and inventory processing and accounting systems.   ● **Process control systems.** Monitor and control industrial processes. Examples: petroleum refining, power generation, and steel production systems.   ● **Enterprise collaboration systems.** Support team, workgroup, and enterprise communications and collaboration. Examples: e-mail, chat, and videoconferencing groupware systems.

of a business firm's operations support systems is to efficiently process business transactions, control industrial processes, support enterprise communications and collaboration, and update corporate databases. See Figure 1.16.

Transaction processing systems are an important example of operations support systems that record and process data resulting from business transactions. They process transactions in two basic ways. In *batch processing*, transactions data are accumulated over a period of time and processed periodically. In *real-time* (or online) processing, data are processed immediately after a transaction occurs. For example, point-of-sale (POS) systems at many retail stores use electronic cash register terminals to electronically capture and transmit sales data over telecommunications links to regional computer centers for immediate (real-time) or nightly (batch) processing. See Figure 1.17.

Process control systems monitor and control physical processes. For example, a petroleum refinery uses electronic sensors linked to computers to continually monitor chemical processes and make instant (real-time) adjustments that control the refinery process. **Enterprise collaboration systems** enhance team and workgroup communications and productivity, and are sometimes called *office automation systems*.

Figure 1.17

QuickBooks is a popular accounting package that automates small business accounting transaction processing while providing business owners with management reports.

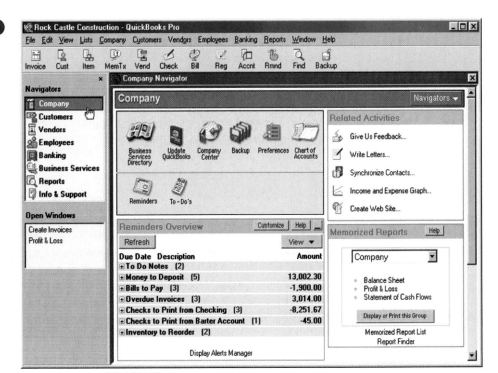

Source: Courtesy of QuickBooks.

For example, knowledge workers in a project team may use electronic mail to send and receive electronic messages, and videoconferencing to hold electronic meetings to coordinate their activities.

Management Support Systems

When information system applications focus on providing information and support for effective decision making by managers, they are called **management support systems.** Providing information and support for decision making by all types of managers and business professionals is a complex task. Conceptually, several major types of information systems support a variety of decision-making responsibilities: (1) management information systems, (2) decision support systems, and (3) executive information systems. See Figure 1.18.

Management information systems provide information in the form of reports and displays to managers and many business professionals. For example, sales managers may use their networked computers and Web browsers to get instantaneous displays about the sales results of their products and to access their corporate intranet for daily sales analysis reports that evaluate sales made by each salesperson. **Decision support systems** give direct computer support to managers during the decision-making process. For example, advertising managers may use an electronic spreadsheet program to do what-if analysis as they test the impact of alternative advertising budgets on the forecasted sales of new products. **Executive information systems** provide critical information from a wide variety of internal and external sources in easy-to-use displays to executives and managers. For example, top executives may use touchscreen terminals to instantly view text and graphics displays that highlight key areas of organizational and competitive performance. See Figure 1.19.

Other Classifications of Information Systems

Several other categories of information systems can support either operations or management applications. For example, **expert systems** can provide expert advice for operational chores like equipment diagnostics, or managerial decisions such as loan portfolio management. **Knowledge management systems** are knowledge-based information systems that support the creation, organization, and dissemination of business knowledge to employees and managers throughout a company. Information systems that focus on operational and managerial applications in support of basic business functions such as accounting or marketing are known as **functional business systems.** Finally, **strategic information systems** apply information technology to a firm's products, services, or business processes to help it gain a strategic advantage over its competitors.

It is also important to realize that business applications of information systems in the real world are typically integrated combinations of the several types of information systems we have just mentioned. That's because conceptual

Figure 1.18   A summary of management support systems with examples.

Management Support Systems
• **Management information systems.** Provide information in the form of prespecified reports and displays to support business decision making. Examples: sales analysis, production performance, and cost trend reporting systems.
• **Decision support systems.** Provide interactive ad hoc support for the decision-making processes of managers and other business professionals. Examples: product pricing, profitability forecasting, and risk analysis systems.
• **Executive information systems.** Provide critical information from many sources tailored to the information needs of executives. Examples: systems for easy access to analyses of business performance, actions of competitors, and economic developments to support strategic planning.

Figure 1.19

Executive information systems provide information to executives in a variety of easy-to-use formats.

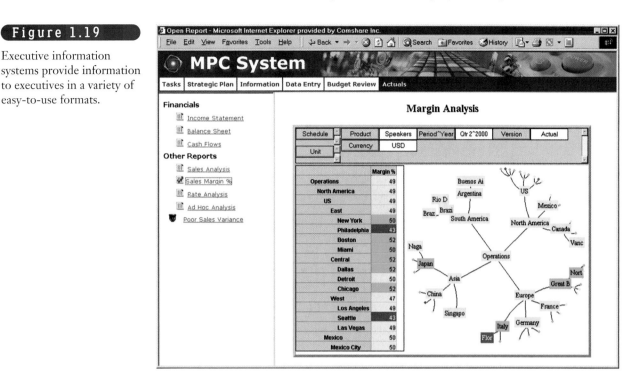

classifications of information systems are designed to emphasize the many different roles of information systems. In practice, these roles are combined into integrated or **cross-functional informational systems** that provide a variety of functions. Thus, most information systems are designed to produce information and support decision making for various levels of management and business functions, as well as do record-keeping and transaction processing chores. So whenever you analyze an information system, you will probably see that it provides information for a variety of managerial levels and business functions.

Figure 1.20 summarizes these categories of information system applications. We will explore many examples of the use of information systems in business in Chapters 7, 8, and 9.

Figure 1.20

A summary of other categories of information systems with examples.

Other Categories of Information Systems

- **Expert systems.** Knowledge-based systems that provide expert advice and act as expert consultants to users. Examples: credit application advisor, process monitor, and diagnostic maintenance systems.
- **Knowledge management systems.** Knowledge-based systems that support the creation, organization, and dissemination of business knowledge within the enterprise. Examples: intranet access to best business practices, sales proposal strategies, and customer problem resolution systems.
- **Strategic information systems.** Support operations or management processes that provide a firm with strategic products, services, and capabilities for competitive advantage. Examples: online stock trading, shipment tracking, and e-commerce Web systems.
- **Functional business systems.** Support a variety of operational and managerial applications of the basic business functions of a company. Examples: information systems that support applications in accouting, finance, marketing, operations management, and human resource management.

Figure 1.21

Internetworked information systems and technologies must be managed to support e-business strategies, processes, and organizational structures and culture to increase the customer and business value of an e-business enterprise.

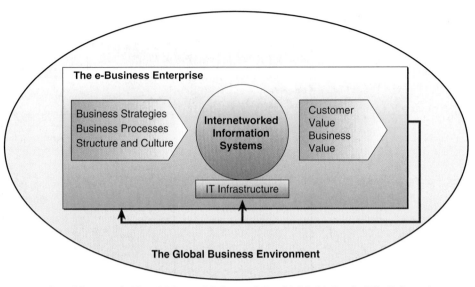

Source: Adapted from Mark Silver, M. Lynne Markus, and Cynthia Mathis Beath, "The Information Technology Interaction Model: A Foundation for the MBA Core Course," *MIS Quarterly*, September 1995, p. 366, and Allen Lee, "Inaugural Editor's Comments," *MIS Quarterly*, March 1999, pp. v–vi. Reprinted with permission from the *MIS Quarterly*.

Managerial Challenges of Information Technology

Prospective managers and business professionals like you should become aware of the problems and opportunities presented by the use of information technology and learn how to effectively confront such managerial challenges. Today's internetworked e-business information systems play a vital role in the business success of an enterprise. For example, the Internet, intranets, and extranets can provide much of the IT infrastructure a business needs for e-business operations, effective management, and competitive advantage. However, Figure 1.21 emphasizes that information systems and their technologies must be managed to support the business strategies, business processes, and organizational structures and culture of an enterprise to increase its customer and business value in a global business environment.

Success and Failure with IT

That's because computer-based information systems, though heavily dependent on information technologies, are designed, operated, and used by people in a variety of organizational settings and business environments. Thus, the success of an information system should not be measured only by its *efficiency* in terms of minimizing

Figure 1.22

Turning business failure into business success with information technology.

From Failure to Success with IT	
The Boeing Company	**Thomson Consumer Electronics**
Business Failure Costly delays ($1.6 billion in 1997) in obtaining 6 million parts to build each aircraft with unintegrated IT systems.	**Business Failure** Retailers not getting quick replenishment of core products with old inventory systems.
New IT Solution Integrate entire supply chain into internal production systems.	**New IT Solution** Demand collaboration system with top retailers that link directly into internal production and logistics systems.
Business Success Output capacity up 100% in 4 years. Aircraft lead times reduced by 60%.	**Business Success** Out-of-stock scenarios reduced to 1% with forecast accuracy now above 95%.

Source: Adapted from Peter Fingar, Harsha Kumar, and Tarun Sharma, *Enterprise e-Commerce* (Tampa, FL: Meghan-Kiffer Press, 2000), p. 176.

Developing information systems solutions to business problems can be viewed as a multistep process or cycle.

costs, time, and the use of information resources. Success should also be measured by the *effectiveness* of information technology in supporting an organization's business strategies, enabling its business processes, enhancing its organizational structures and culture, and increasing the customer and business value of the enterprise.

However, it is important that you realize that information technology and information systems can be mismanaged and misapplied so that IS performance problems create both technological and business failure. For example, Figure 1.22 outlines two dramatic examples of how information technology contributed to business failure and success at two major corporations.

Developing e-Business Solutions

Developing information system solutions to business problems is a major challenge for many business professionals today. As a business professional, you will be responsible for proposing or developing new or improved uses of information technologies for your company. As a business manager, you will also frequently manage the development efforts of information systems specialists and other business end users.

Most computer-based information systems are conceived, designed, and implemented using some form of systematic development process. Figure 1.23 shows that several major activities are involved in a complete IS development cycle. In this development process, end users and information specialists *design* information system applications based on an *analysis* of the business requirements of an organization. Examples of other activities include *investigating* the economic or technical feasibility of a proposed application, acquiring and learning how to use the software required to *implement* the new system, and making improvements to *maintain* the business value of a system.

We will discuss the information systems development process further in Chapter 10. Many of the business and managerial challenges that arise in developing and implementing new uses of information technology will be explored in Chapters 11 and 12. Now let's look at an example of the challenges faced and overcome by a company that developed and installed a major new information system application. This example emphasizes how important good systems development practices are to a business.

A-DEC Inc.: Challenges in Systems Development

After turning on Baan Co.'s enterprise resource planning (ERP) suite of business software, A-DEC expected it to automate much of their manufacturing, distribution, and financial information processing. But they soon fell behind on processing orders, building products, and then shipping the goods to dealers. "We lost a lot of business," said CIO Keith Bearden, who was brought in to manage A-DEC's information systems three months into the rollout. To get by, the Newberg, Oregon, dental equipment maker even had to fill some orders outside the system "because workers didn't understand it, and the performance was so bad," he said. At A-DEC, business changes initially were fought, Bearden said. End-user training also fell short at first, he said, and the IT department underestimated the processing power that Baan's software required.

After Bearden was hired, he pulled together a stabilization team from all parts of the company. It took about six months of systems development work to fix the performance issues by changing databases and upgrading A-DEC's servers and network. Another six months were spent redesigning business processes and training users. All that work basically doubled the cost of the project, Bearden said. "We spent a lot of money just cleaning up problems," he said. Even now, 50-plus key users spend 20 percent of their work time looking for ways to improve A-DEC's use of the software.

But the company now is getting some of the benefits it expected, Bearden said. For example, inventory levels have been cut by about 30 percent since the new system was put into use. And one of A-DEC's four product lines has been switched to a fast turnaround modular manufacturing approach that wasn't feasible before [17].

Ethics and IT

As a prospective manager, business professional, and knowledge worker, you should consider the **ethical responsibilities** generated by the use of information technology. For example, what uses of information technology might be considered improper, irresponsible, or harmful to other individuals or to society? What is the proper business use of the Internet and an organization's IT resources? What does it take to be a **responsible end user** of information technology? How can you protect yourself from computer crime and other risks of information technology? These are some of the questions that outline the ethical dimensions of information systems that we will discuss and illustrate with Real World Cases in Chapter 11 and other chapters of this text. Figure 1.24 outlines some of the ethical risks that may arise in the use of information technology. The following example illustrates some of the ethical challenges in the use of business resources to access the Internet.

3M Corp. and Others: Internet Ethics

Faced with international controversies over pornography and hate speech on the Internet, employers are setting policies to limit Internet usage to business purposes. They also are penalizing employees who send out abusive electronic mail, "flame" people on newsgroups, or visit inappropriate sites on the World Wide Web.

For most companies, an Internet usage policy is straightforward. It generally informs employees that their Internet access is a company resource that should be used only for their jobs. "3M's policy is simply put: that the Web must be used for business purposes. If people get on and abuse it, then you've got a problem with that individual and need to handle it," said Luke Crofoot, a marketing services supervisor at 3M in St. Paul, Minnesota.

Firms that want more control over their employees develop detailed Internet usage policies. Companies that have detailed usage policies include the Chase Manhattan Bank NA; Johnson Controls, Inc.; Pioneer Hi-Bred International Inc.; and Monsanto Co. But some attorneys take a tougher stance. Says Neal J. Friedman, a Washington attorney who specializes in online law, "Employees need to know they have no right of privacy and no right of free speech using company resources" [19].

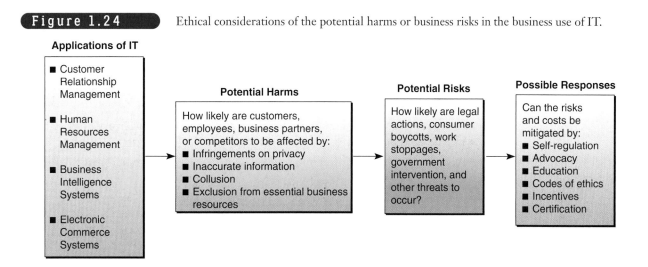

Figure 1.24 Ethical considerations of the potential harms or business risks in the business use of IT.

Challenges of IT Careers

Information technology and its uses in information systems have created interesting, highly paid, and challenging career opportunities for millions of men and women. So learning more about information technology may help you decide if you want to pursue an IT-related career. Employment opportunities in the field of information systems are excellent, as organizations continue to expand their use of information technology. However, this poses a resource management challenge to many companies, since employment surveys continually forecast shortages of qualified information systems personnel in a variety of job categories. Also, job requirements in information systems are continually changing due to dynamic developments in business and information technology.

One major recruiter is the IT industry itself. Thousands of companies develop, manufacture, market, and service computer hardware, software, data and network products and services, or provide e-business and commerce applications and services, end user training, or business systems consulting. However, the biggest need for qualified people comes from the millions of businesses, government agencies, and other organizations that use information technology. They need many types of IS professionals to help them support the work activities and supply the information needs of their employees, managers, customers, suppliers, and other business partners. Let's take a look at IT career challenges at a leading e-commerce company.

Amazon.com: IT Career Challenges

John Vlastelca is the technical recruiting manager of Amazon.com Inc. in Seattle. He says: "We have a huge demand for people who have experience building relationships with customers online—people who bring together a retailing background and some IT background. We hire smart folks, and they are working their butts off. There is a heavy dose of informality. People aren't title-centric; the best idea wins and the career path is often a vertical crossover to management or content areas.

"The one thing that drives us is an obsession with the customer. What helps us make our selection decision is the question, 'Is this a technical person who views technology as a means to an end, where the end is the customer? Or does this person define him or herself as just a Java programmer?'

"But the bar is incredibly high here. It is really hard for my team to find the combination of skills—the software engineer who really understands the customer and the business. So half don't make it because they are not strong enough technically. Other reasons have to do with soft skills—being open to ideas, just raw smarts and not being passionate enough. The problem space we operate in is unexplored territory" [10].

The IS Function

In summary, successful management of information systems and technologies presents major challenges to business managers and professionals. Thus, the information systems function represents:

- A major functional area of business that is as important to business success as the functions of accounting, finance, operations management, marketing, and human resources management.

- An important contributor to operational efficiency, employee productivity and morale, and customer service and satisfaction.

- A major source of information and support needed to promote effective decision making by managers and business professionals.

- A vital ingredient in developing competitive products and services that give an organization a strategic advantage in the global marketplace.

- A dynamic, rewarding, and challenging career opportunity for millions of men and women.

- A key component of the resources, infrastructure, and capabilities of today's e-business enterprises.

Summary

- **Why Information Systems Are Important.** An understanding of the effective and responsible use and management of information systems and technologies is important for managers, business professionals, and other knowledge workers in today's internetworked enterprises. Information systems play a vital role in the e-business and e-commerce operations, enterprise collaboration and management, and strategic success of businesses that must operate in an internetworked global environment. Thus, the field of information systems has become a major functional area of business administration.

- **An IS Framework for Business Professionals.** The IS knowledge that a business manager or professional needs to know is illustrated in Figure 1.2 and covered in this chapter and text. This includes (1) *foundation concepts:* fundamental behavioral, technical, business, and managerial concepts like system components and functions, or competitive strategies; (2) *information technologies:* concepts, developments, or management issues regarding hardware, software, data management, networks, and other technologies; (3) *business applications:* major uses of IT for business processes, operations, decision making, and strategic/competitive advantage; (4) *development processes:* how end users and IS specialists develop and implement business/IT solutions to problems and opportunities arising in business; and (5) *management challenges:* how to effectively and ethically manage the IS function and IT resources to achieve top performance and business value in support of the business strategies of the enterprise.

- **System Concepts.** A system is a group of interrelated components working toward the attainment of a common goal by accepting inputs and producing outputs in an organized transformation process. Feedback is data about the performance of a system. Control is the component that monitors and evaluates feedback and makes any necessary adjustments to the input and processing components to ensure that proper output is produced.

- **An Information System Model.** An information system uses the resources of people, hardware, software, data, and networks to perform input, processing, output, storage, and control activities that convert data resources into information products. Data are first collected and converted to a form that is suitable for processing (input). Then the data are manipulated and converted into information (processing), stored for future use (storage), or communicated to their ultimate user (output) according to correct processing procedures (control).

- **IS Resources and Products.** Hardware resources include machines and media used in information processing. Software resources include computerized instructions (programs) and instructions for people (procedures). People resources include information systems specialists and users. Data resources include alphanumeric, text, image, video, audio, and other forms of data. Network resources include communications media and network support. Information products produced by an information system can take a variety of forms, including paper reports, visual displays, multimedia documents, electronic messages, graphics images, and audio responses.

- **Business Applications of Information Systems.** Information systems perform three vital roles in business firms. Business applications of IS support an organization's business processes and operations, business decision making, and strategic competitive advantage. Major application categories of information systems include operations support systems, such as transaction processing systems, process control systems, and enterprise collaboration systems, and management support systems, such as management information systems, decision support systems, and executive information systems. Other major categories are expert systems, knowledge management systems, strategic information systems, and functional business systems. However, in the real world most application categories are combined into cross-functional information systems that provide information and support for decision making and also perform operational information processing activities. Refer to Figures 1.16, 1.18, and 1.20 for summaries of the major application categories of information systems.

Key Terms and Concepts

These are the key terms and concepts of this chapter. The page number of their first explanation is in parentheses.

1. Computer-based information system (8)
2. Control (9)
3. Data (13)
4. Data or information processing (15)
5. Data resources (13)
6. Developing business/IT solutions (29)
7. E-business enterprise (22)
8. Electronic business (21)
9. Electronic commerce (23)
10. End user (11)
11. Enterprise collaboration systems (22)
12. Extranet (22)
13. Feedback (9)
14. Hardware resources (12)
    a. Machines
    b. Media

15. Information (13)
    a. Products (15)
    b. Quality (15)
16. Information system (7)
17. Information system activities (11)
    a. Input
    b. Processing
    c. Output
    d. Storage
    e. Control
18. Information system model (10)
19. Information technology (IT) (8)
20. Intranet (22)
21. IS knowledge needed by business professionals (4)
22. Knowledge workers (11)
23. Management challenges of IS (30)
    a. Ethics and IT (30)
    b. IT career challenges (31)
    c. IT success and failure (28)
24. Network resources (14)

25. People resources (11)
    a. IS specialists
    b. End users
26. Roles of IS applications in business (20)
    a. Support of business processes and operations
    b. Support of business decision making
    c. Support of strategies for competitive advantage
27. Software resources (12)
    a. Programs
    b. Procedures
28. System (8)
29. Trends in information systems (20)
30. Types of information systems (24)
    a. Cross-functional systems (27)
    b. Management support systems (26)
    c. Operations support systems (24)

Review Quiz

Match one of the previous key terms and concepts with one of the following brief examples or definitions. Look for the best fit for answers that seem to fit more than one key term or concept. Defend your choices.

_____ 1. You should know some fundamental concepts about information systems and their technologies, development processes, business applications, and management challenges.

_____ 2. People who spend most of their workday creating, using, and distributing information.

_____ 3. Computer hardware and software, networks, data management, and other technologies.

_____ 4. Information systems support an organization's business processes, operations, decision making, and strategies for competitive advantage.

_____ 5. Using IT to reengineer business processes to support e-business operations.

_____ 6. Using Web-based decision support systems to support sales managers.

_____ 7. Using information technology for electronic commerce to gain a strategic advantage over competitors.

_____ 8. A system that uses people, hardware, software, and network resources to collect, transform, and disseminate information within an organization.

_____ 9. An information system that uses computers and their hardware and software.

_____ 10. Anyone who uses an information system or the information it produces.

_____ 11. A company that uses the Internet, corporate intranets, and interorganizational extranets for electronic business operations, e-commerce, and enterprise collaboration.

_____ 12. The buying, selling, marketing, and servicing of products over the Internet and other networks.

_____ 13. The use of groupware tools to support collaboration among networked teams.

_____ 14. A group of interrelated components working together toward the attainment of a common goal.

_____ 15. Data about a system's performance.

_____ 16. Making adjustments to a system's components so that it operates properly.

_____ 17. Facts or observations.

_____ 18. Data that have been placed into a meaningful context for an end user.

_____ 19. The act of converting data into information.

_____ 20. An information system uses people, hardware, software, network, and data resources to perform input, processing, output, storage, and control activities that transform data resources into information products.

_____ 21. Machines and media.

_____ 22. Computers, disk drives, video monitors, and printers are examples.

_____ 23. Magnetic disks, optical disks, and paper forms are examples.

_____ 24. Programs and procedures.

_____ 25. A set of instructions for a computer.

_____ 26. A set of instructions for people.

_____ 27. End users and information systems professionals.

_____ 28. Using the keyboard of a computer to enter data.

_____ 29. Computing loan payments.

_____ 30. Printing a letter you wrote using a computer.

_____ 31. Saving a copy of the letter on a magnetic disk.

_____ 32. Having a sales receipt as proof of a purchase.

_____ 33. Information systems can be classified into operations, management, and other categories.

_____ 34. Includes transaction processing, process control, and end user collaboration systems.

_____ 35. Includes management information, decision support, and executive information systems.

_____ 36. Information systems that perform transaction processing and provide information to managers across the boundaries of functional business areas.

_____ 37. Information systems have evolved from a data processing orientation to the support of strategic decision making, end user collaboration, and electronic business and commerce.

_____ 38. Internet-like networks and websites inside a company.

_____ 39. Interorganizational Internet-like networks among trading partners.

_____ 40. You need to be a responsible end user of IT resources in your company.

_____ 41. Managing the IT resources of a company effectively and ethically to improve its business performance and value.

_____ 42. Using the Internet, intranets, and extranets as the IT platform for internal business operations, electronic commerce, and enterprise collaboration.

Discussion Questions

1. How can information technology support a company's business processes and decision making, and give it a competitive advantage? Give examples to illustrate your answer.

2. How does the use of the Internet, intranets, and extranets by an e-business enterprise support their e-commerce activities?

3. Refer to the Real World Case on General Electric in the chapter. If you were the new CEO of GE, what other e-business moves would you recommend for the company? Defend your proposals.

4. Why do big companies still fail in their use of information technology? What should they be doing differently?

5. How can a manager demonstrate that he or she is a responsible end user of information systems? Give several examples.

6. Refer to the Real World Case on Duke Energy in the chapter. What are some other methods for introducing e-business into a company? Which do you prefer? Why?

7. What are some of the toughest management challenges in developing IT solutions to solve business problems and meet new e-business opportunities?

8. Why are there so many conceptual classifications of information systems? Why are they typically integrated in the information systems found in the real world?

9. In what major ways have the roles of information systems applications in business expanded during the last 40 years? What is one major change you think will happen in the next 10 years?

10. Can the business use of Internet technologies help a company gain a competitive advantage? Give an example to illustrate your answer.

Application Exercises

Complete the following exercises as individual or group projects that apply chapter concepts to real world business situations.

1. Using the Internet for Business Research

Search the Internet for additional information and business examples about some of the topics or companies in this chapter. For example, use search engines like Google or Fast Search to research the latest developments in e-business, e-commerce, IT ethics and security, or IT careers. Or find and visit the websites of companies in the Real World Cases in this chapter. Look for examples of the business use of information technology in your search.

  a. Prepare a one- or two-page summary of some of your findings and the sources you used.

  b. End your paper with a few sentences describing one thing you have learned from your research that might help you in your future career in business.

2. Visiting the Smart Business Supersite

The Smart Business Supersite (www.smartbiz.com) is dubbed the "how-to resource for business" site.

Nearly every colorful icon on the tool bar across the top of the home page leads to useful, relevant material such as columns on electronic privacy, violence in the workplace, and internal marketing. (See Figure 1.25.)

You can also click on the browse button to call up a Windows-like menu of subjects. Then choose *Computing in Business* to get a precise index of all relevant material at the site. The Jobs/Careers section includes relevant articles and a message board. People Finder is a unique section that offers users a venue for locating speakers and consultants.

  a. Prepare a one- or two-page summary describing the *Computing in Business* material you found most interesting and relevant as a business end user.

  b. End your paper with a few sentences describing one thing you have learned from your research that might help you in your future career in business.

Figure 1.25

The Smart Business Supersite.

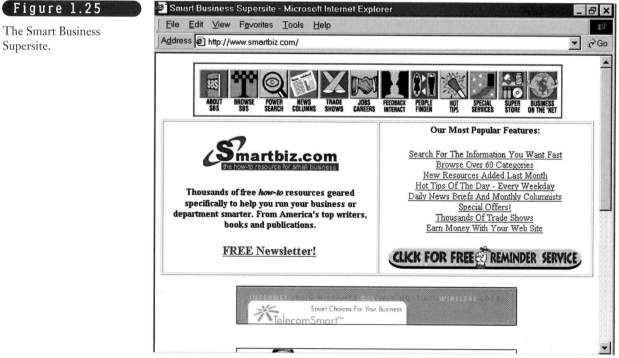

Source: Courtesy of Smart Business Supersite, © 2000.

3. **Jefferson State University: Recognizing IS Components**

Students in the College of Business Administration of Jefferson State University use their desktop and laptop microcomputers for a variety of assignments. For example, a student may use a word processing program stored on the microcomputer system's hard disk drive and proceed to type a case study analysis. When the analysis is typed, edited, and properly formatted to an instructor's specifications, the student may save it on a floppy disk, e-mail a copy to the instructor via the Internet, and print out a copy on the system's printer. If the student tries to save the case study analysis using a file name he or she has already used for saving another document, the program will display a warning message and wait until it receives an additional command.

Make an outline to identify the information system components in the preceding example.

a. Identify the people, hardware, software, network, and data resources and the information products of this information system.

b. Identify the input, processing, output, storage, and control activities that occurred.

4. **Office Products Corporation: Recognizing IS Components**

Office Products Corporation receives more than 10,000 customer orders a month, drawing on a combined inventory of over 1,000 office products stocked at the company's warehouse. About 60 PCs are installed at the Office Products headquarters and connected in a local area network to several IBM Netfinity servers. Orders are received by phone or mail and entered into the system by customer representatives at network computers, or they are entered directly by customers who have shopped at the electronic commerce website developed by Office Products. Entry of orders is assisted by formatted screens that help users follow data entry procedures to enter required information into the system, where it is stored on the magnetic disks of the Netfinity servers.

As the order is entered, a server checks the availability of the parts, allocates the stock, and updates customer and part databases stored on its magnetic disks. It then sends the order pick list to the warehouse printer, where it is used by warehouse personnel to fill the order. The company president has a networked PC workstation in her office, as do the controller, sales manager, inventory manager, and other executives. They use simple database management inquiry commands to get responses and reports concerning sales orders, customers, and inventory, and to review product demand and service trends.

Make an outline that identifies the information system components in Office Products' order processing system.

a. Identify the people, hardware, software, data, and network resources and the information products of this information system.

b. Identify the input, processing, output, storage, and control activities that occurred.

5. **Western Chemical Corporation: Recognizing the Types and Roles of Information Systems**

Western Chemical uses the Internet and an electronic commerce website to connect to its customers and suppliers, and to capture data and share information about sales orders and purchases. Sales and order data are processed immediately, and inventory and other databases are updated. Videoconferencing and electronic mail services are also provided. Data generated by a chemical refinery process are captured by sensors and processed by a computer that also suggests answers to a complex refinery problem posed by an engineer. Managers and business professionals access reports on a periodic, exception, and demand basis, and use computers to interactively assess the possible results of alternative decisions. Finally, top management can access text summaries and graphics displays that identify key elements of organizational performance and compare them to industry and competitor performance.

Western Chemical Corporation has started forming business alliances and using intranets, extranets, and the Internet to build a global electronic commerce website to offer their customers worldwide products and services. Western Chemical is in the midst of making fundamental changes to their computer-based systems to increase the efficiency of their e-business operations and their managers' ability to react quickly to changing business conditions.

Make an outline that identifies:

a. How information systems support (1) business operations, (2) business decision making, (3) strategic advantage, (4) an e-business enterprise, and (5) electronic commerce at Western Chemical.

b. There are many different types of information systems at Western Chemical. Identify as many as you can in the preceding scenario. Refer to Figure 1.16, 1.18, and 1.20 to help you. Explain the reasons for your choices.

Ford and UPS Logistics:
The Business Value of Information Technology

Ford Motor Company and UPS Logistics Group are seeing productivity gains six months sooner than expected from an information system designed to make new car and truck delivery faster and more predictable. Ford has adopted proprietary logistics application software from UPS Logistics, a division of United Parcel Service, Inc., the world's largest package delivery company. It replaces a group of homegrown systems and manual processes that weren't able to give Ford managers a complete status report on its cars and trucks as they are en route to local Ford dealerships across the United States and Canada.

In February 2000, Ford began work with UPS Logistics in an effort that has already knocked four days out of the typical 14- or 15-day cycle for moving a vehicle from a manufacturing plant to a dealership. By doing so, Ford also has seen the value of its vehicle inventory shrink by $1 billion, which, in turn, is expected to cut annual inventory carrying costs by $125 million, according to officials at the automaker.

The ultimate goal for the two companies is to decrease delivery time by two more days—for a total of six—and they're almost there. "We're optimistic in achieving 4 percent or 5 percent additional improvement by the end of the year," says Frank Taylor, Ford's vice president of material, planning, and logistics. That could translate into eliminating as much as another day from the process by the beginning of 2002.

Historically, Ford gave their local dealerships estimated delivery dates that weren't accurate. Those dates were then passed along to waiting customers. In addition, railroad or trucking delays would further alter the schedule. Ultimately, Ford didn't have a good handle on the status of its vehicles in transit. "Once you shipped it, you couldn't give a reliable date, even plus or minus a few days, when anyone could see it or where it was," Taylor says. "And now we can."

For example, Pete Greiner, owner of the Greiner Ford dealership in Casper, Wyoming, says he began to see better delivery forecasts last summer, about six months into the process. In the past, Greiner would tell waiting customers that their cars and trucks would arrive within a range of several days. Sometimes that wasn't good enough. "We've had consumers get so frustrated because they had vacations or hunting trips coming up, they'd say, 'If you can't get the truck in time, I'm going elsewhere,'" Greiner says. "Now we can say to customers, 'We firmly believe your truck will be here August 25,' and by golly, it shows up."

Most of Ford's legacy systems for tracking vehicles' delivery were homegrown point solutions that didn't give the company a unified view of events. In fact, a lot of the information used for tracking vehicles was scribbled down on paper. The new Ford online system tracks cars and trucks by vehicle identification number (VIN). Workers from UPS Logistics and Ford, as well as people at the railroads and trucking companies that haul Ford vehicles, use hand-held computers to scan the bar codes from each VIN as the vehicle proceeds from a plant via rail or truck to a dealership.

Executives from both Atlanta-based UPS Logistics and Ford declined to comment on how much the project has cost. One hundred and twenty people are involved: 93 from UPS Logistics and 27 from Ford.

Aside from technology changes, rearranging the people processes of companies along the distribution chain has also helped improve delivery performance. For example, Ford has persuaded some of its 6,000 dealerships to extend the hours during which they will receive and unload new vehicles. Previously, dealers typically accepted vehicles Mondays through Fridays from 9 A.M. to 5 P.M., when most of their office and maintenance staff were at work. Now, many local dealers have made work assignment changes so they can take delivery in the evenings and on weekends.

UPS Logistics helped Ford figure out that having a wider window for delivery meant less of a backlog on Ford's railroad and highway carrier routes. UPS Logistics monitors the traffic at railroad offices and out in the field, says Andy Gonta, vice president of automotive shipping at Canadian National Railway Co. in Montreal, Canada. Before, a shipment of cars and trucks "would hit a facility on a Friday and would sit until Monday, and so would the vehicles that hit on Saturday or Sunday," Gonta explains. "It would take you until Wednesday to get it sorted out."

Next on Ford's agenda: an extranet application designed to let local dealerships track specific vehicles in transit in real time. The system will allow dealers to extract data from Ford's many different back-end manufacturing systems, combine it with information from rail and truck carriers and funnel it all into a middleware system that will collate the information and make it Web-enabled and accessible online. Ford said it expects to roll out the application in 2002. Right now, 21 Ford dealers are testing it. Ultimately, Taylor says the system will be "very close" to UPS's own Web-based package-tracking application.

Case Study Questions

1. What are the business benefits to Ford of its partnership with UPS Logistics?

2. How do Internet technologies help make e-business applications more feasible for local car dealers?

3. What other e-business applications could Ford develop to help its local car dealers? Give an example.

Source: Adapted from Kim Nash, "Ford's Vehicle Delivery Project Ahead of Plan," *Computerworld*, October 1, 2001, p. 30. Reprinted by permission.

Hewlett-Packard and Staff-Leasing: Success and Failure with Customer Relationship Management

True story. One of the Big Three Detroit automakers put together a customer relationship management (CRM) system that helped it decide which cars to manufacture based on what was going out of dealers' lots. It worked great.

Well, except for one catch. According to Eric Almquist, VP at Mercer Management Consulting, the company's marketing team had just created sales incentives to get rid of a lot of lime-green cars, which no one wanted. As consumers snapped up the special deals on the cars, the CRM software noticed the surge of sales in lime-green cars and instructed the factory to produce more. The automaker lost millions of dollars before it caught the error.

No one doubts that CRM software is powerful stuff. It can slash call center costs, make a sales force dramatically more productive, and glue together offline and online sales efforts. Everyone knows stories like the one Stephen Pratt, global practice leader for Deloitte Consulting's CRM efforts, likes to tell about the telecommunications equipment manufacturer that used CRM software to coordinate its Web and offline technical-support teams. Tech support began running so smoothly that within six months, happy customers signed up for an additional $15 million in contracts.

But CRM can also go terribly wrong, causing interdepartmental chaos or never taking hold among key employees. The nightmare scenarios are all too common. Based on interviews with thousands of clients, Gartner Inc. projects that in the next five years, 55 percent of all CRM projects will fail to meet objectives. That failure rate represents a big financial risk, considering that CRM systems cost an average of $35,000 per call-center agent to deploy, and that setup and maintenance of CRM sales software typically cost $28,000 to $40,000 per salesperson (over three years). How can you avoid ending up on the CRM casualty list? Head off the most common mistakes before they happen.

CRM projects usually involve different departments, which means skilled diplomacy is in order. "Traditionally sales, marketing, and service have been enemies," Pratt says. "Marketing would blame sales for not closing leads, sales would blame marketing for not generating enough leads, and service would blame them both for too-high expectations. Asking them to work together goes against their DNA." The trick is to find leadership that can cajole or force various fiefdoms to do the right thing.

Rob Schauble, director of technology for Hewlett-Packard's customer support division, gathered managers from marketing, production, sales, and customer service in order to get the cooperation he needed to install CRM software from Motive Communications on all the computers HP sells. The package would let HP technical support more quickly diagnose and fix a customer's problem. Rather than going over anyone's head, Schauble invited everyone with a stake in the project to help map out a strategy from the start.

His initiative paid off; more than a year after the project's completion, he estimates that the software saves HP millions of dollars by reducing the time it takes to identify problems.

No amount of high-level cooperation will protect a CRM project from rank-and-file employees who hate it. Lisa Harris, CIO at HR-services firm Staff-Leasing based in Bradenton, Florida, faced rebellion from the staff when she installed Oracle CRM software that helped solve some customers' problems online—without the help of a live operator. Call-center employees felt that the software threatened their jobs, so they quietly discouraged customers from using it. "Our operators would say, 'Wouldn't you rather call up? I'll take care of everything you need,'" Harris says. She stuck with the online CRM, but also began talking to employees about the software. She changed their work routines to include more customer hand-holding and less data entry, which was increasingly done online.

CRM software is complex to install because it often touches many different legacy systems. Four years ago, Staff-Leasing's Harris says she spent millions of dollars integrating a CRM application for a previous employer. But when she was finished, it took operators too long to get data on screen. The company had bogged down the performance of the new CRM implementation by trying to integrate too many complicated systems. The project ended up a total failure, she says.

But Harris says that new software products that link related e-business applications into suites, like the one she is using from Oracle, typically work better together. However, analysts say that such suites are a relatively new and immature technology. CRM systems are further complicated by the move of their underlying networking technology from private networks of servers and PCs (client/server networks), to Web-enabled systems. For example, early versions of Oracle's Web-enabled CRM suite, released early in 2000, tried to do too much too soon, which resulted in problems for their users, according to Wendy Close, CRM research director for Gartner, Inc. Close also adds that Web-based systems, including PeopleSoft's latest offering, have fewer features than client/server versions.

Case Study Questions

1. What are some of the potential benefits of CRM systems to a business?

2. What are several reasons why many CRM systems fail to meet the expectations of their business users?

3. What are some possible solutions to such problems? Give an example to illustrate your answer.

Source: Adapted from Brian Caulfield, "Facing up to CRM," *Business 2.0*, August/September 2001, pp. 149–150. 2001 Time Inc. All rights reserved

Management
Challenges

Business
Applications

Module I

Information
Technologies

Development
Processes

Foundation
Concepts

Chapter 2

Competing with Information

Technology

Chapter Highlights

Learning Objectives

After reading and studying this chapter, you should be able to:

1. Identify several basic competitive strategies and explain how they can use information technologies to confront the competitive forces faced by a business.

2. Identify several strategic uses of information technologies for electronic business and commerce, and give examples of how they give competitive advantages to a business.

3. Give examples of how business process reengineering frequently involves the strategic use of e-business technologies.

4. Identify the business value of using e-business technologies for total quality management, to become an agile competitor, or to form a virtual company.

5. Explain how knowledge management systems can help a business gain strategic advantages.

Fundamentals of Strategic Advantage

Strategic IT

Technology is no longer an afterthought in forming business strategy, but the actual cause and driver [23].

This chapter will show you that it is important that you view information systems as more than a set of technologies that support efficient business operations, work-group and enterprise collaboration, or effective business decision making. Information technology can change the way businesses compete. So you should also view information systems strategically, that is, as vital competitive networks, as a means of organizational renewal, and as a necessary investment in technologies that help a company adopt strategies and business processes that enable it to reengineer or reinvent itself in order to survive and succeed in today's dynamic e-business environment.

Analyzing Capital One

Read the Real World Case on Capital One on the next page. We can learn a lot about the strategic business uses of information technologies from this case. See Figure 2.1.

Capital One Financial uses information technology as a strategic foundation for their business strategies and business practices and has thus gained a preeminent profit position among credit card companies. For example, Capital One's Information Based Strategy (IBS), relies heavily on information technology to perform a host of sophisticated market research, customer relationship management, and marketing processes that enable them to discover and create over a 100,000 unique customer and credit card product combinations. Another example is their Global Service Logistics call-routing system that gives call center representatives detailed information on customers and prospects and the products to sell them. To make this all

Figure 2.1

Marge Connelly (right), executive vice president of operations and IT infra-structure, and Laura Olle, senior vice president of IT systems development, lead over 1,000 IT professionals at Capital One.

Source: Walter P. Calahan

Capital One Financial Corporation: Using Information Technology for Competitive Advantage

Capital One Financial Corporation is the most profitable credit card company in the United States. The secret to the success of the Falls Church, Virginia-based credit card issuer is a test-and-learn philosophy that the company has dubbed its Information Based Strategy (IBS). Calling IBS "customer relationship management" (CRM) is an understatement, as the strategy goes above and beyond what most CRM packages do. IBS is a 6-year-old process that pervades all of the technology and business activities at Capital One.

IBS is a three-step approach: Step 1 is to create an idea for a new product offering, find a target population and a business case and then change the environment for members of this group to see how they react. Step 2 involves gathering data on the test and analyzing the results. Step 3 is aimed at using the test results to do micro segmentation, or to identify which people are most receptive to specific product types and conduct additional marketing campaigns based on those results.

"We identify people who will be positively attracted to the product, so the response rates are high, the cost of acquisition isn't outrageous, and at the same time people are an appropriate price to charge off [write off losses from accounts that default," says Wylie Schwieder, vice president of customer relations at Capital One. Capital One then analyzes the results of the test to determine what the appropriate prices or interest rates should be, says Schwieder. Company leaders look for relevant characteristics among the test group "and see whether we can go elsewhere in the United States to find more people who share those characteristics. Then we do a direct-mail campaign based on that," he adds.

For example, Capital One has used IBS to track visitors' activities and offer customized promotions on its website. It has studied which online visitors it has successfully converted into customers and has used that information to buy banner ads on other websites whose visitor demographics match those of its ideal customers. Using these tactics, the company has doubled its goal of opening 1 million new accounts online. Capital One's customer base has burgeoned from 6 million in 1995 to 33 million today. Capital One currently nets about 25,000 new customers each day.

Capital One conducted 45,000 tests last year, averaging 120 per day. The company has created 100,000 combinations. People in every part of the company are perpetually testing and segmenting—matching credit card offers to potential customers who might be interested, matching customers to sales representatives who can best help them, matching sales reps to the appropriate product campaigns, and so on. For instance, IBS significantly enhances risk-based pricing for Capital One—the process of setting different interest rates and fees based on a person's creditworthiness. Most banks make these decisions using credit scores or algorithms that are calculated based on a person's income and credit history.

Through testing and learning about how cardholders perform, Capital One is able to use more information about prospective customers to determine what to offer them to allow it to come up with a much wider variety of prices and terms. For example, when a call comes in, the customer is identified and his record is run through a database to determine what he might possibly want to discuss. The call is then routed to the representative who's the most qualified to address the customer's concerns.

This match is based on 12 different customer characteristics—including the products he already has, account status, and responsiveness to previous campaigns—and five different employee characteristics, such as training, skills, and availability. When an incoming call reaches the appropriate representative, his PC displays the caller's account and personal information, with scripts suggesting good products to cross-sell. For instance, a customer who regularly pays off all of his balances might be routed to a representative who will be able to target-market a platinum card with a bigger credit line.

The call-routing software, one of the few shrink-wrapped applications that Capital One uses, is Cisco Systems' Global Service Logistics (GSL) system. "Everyone will say they use GSL the same way we do, but I think we use it more intelligently than they do," says Schwieder. "We use many more attributes in judging where the call goes. And we gather more data about that call than anyone else does. I say this with a high degree of confidence. And we use that data as a basis for creating decision rules that get embedded in our applications."

The amount of technology required to support IBS is immense. Capital One has spent hundreds of millions of dollars building and refining systems based on IBS. More than 1,000 IT professionals continue to enhance and maintain IBS-driven systems, which encompass every piece of technology used by the company's 3,000 call center representatives and 16,000 other employees. As Marge Connelly, Capital One's executive vice president of operations and IT infrastructure says: "Our IT organization is the central nervous system of Capital One."

Case Study Questions

1. How does Capital One use information technology to give them a competitive advantage among credit card companies? Use the strategies outlined in Figures 2.3, 2.5, and 2.8 to help you answer.

2. Can other companies apply the concepts and methods used by Capital One without spending the hundreds of millions of dollars they have? Give examples to illustrate your answer.

3. Visit the Capital One website (www.capitalone.com) and evaluate the business and customer value of its content. How do you rate its effectiveness as an e-commerce website? Explain your rating.

Source: Adapted from Jackie Cohen, "Growth Formula," *Computerworld*, July 2, 2001, pp. 36, 38. Reprinted by permission.

possible, Capital One has spent hundreds of millions of dollars on hardware, software, network, and data management technologies, and the IT professionals who help develop and maintain their IBS-driven systems.

Competitive Strategy Concepts

The strategic role of information systems involves using information technology to develop products, services, and capabilities that give a company major advantages over the competitive forces it faces in the global marketplace. This creates **strategic information systems,** information systems that support or shape the competitive position and strategies of an e-business enterprise. So a strategic information system can be any kind of information system (TPS, MIS, DSS, etc.) that helps an organization gain a competitive advantage, reduce a competitive disadvantage, or meet other strategic enterprise objectives [31]. Let's look at several basic concepts that define the role of such strategic information systems.

How should a business professional think about competitive strategies? How can competitive strategies be applied to the use of information systems by an e-business enterprise? Figure 2.2 illustrates an important conceptual framework for understanding and applying competitive strategies. A firm can survive and succeed in the long run if it successfully develops strategies to confront five **competitive forces** that shape the structure of competition in its industry. These are: (1) rivalry of competitors within its industry, (2) threat of new entrants, (3) threat of substitutes, (4) the bargaining power of customers, and (5) the bargaining power of suppliers [34].

Figure 2.2 also illustrates that businesses can counter the threats of competitive forces that they face by implementing five basic **competitive strategies** [31].

- **Cost Leadership Strategy.** Becoming a low-cost producer of products and services in the industry. Also, a firm can find ways to help its suppliers or customers reduce their costs or to increase the costs of their competitors.

Figure 2.2

Businesses can develop competitive strategies to counter the actions of the competitive forces they confront in the marketplace.

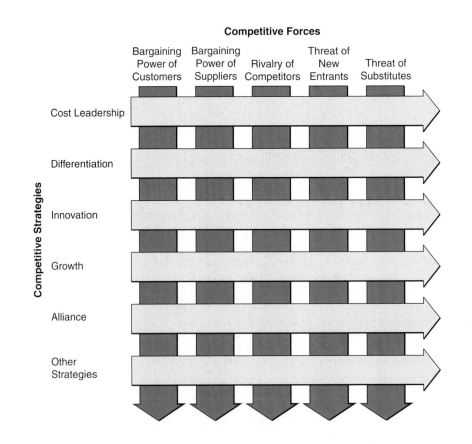

- **Differentiation Strategy.** Developing ways to differentiate a firm's products and services from its competitors' or reduce the differentiation advantages of competitors. This may allow a firm to focus its products or services to give it an advantage in particular segments or niches of a market.

- **Innovation Strategy.** Finding new ways of doing business. This may involve the development of unique products and services, or entry into unique markets or market niches. It may also involve making radical changes to the business processes for producing or distributing products and services that are so different from the way a business has been conducted that they alter the fundamental structure of an industry.

- **Growth Strategies.** Significantly expanding a company's capacity to produce goods and services, expanding into global markets, diversifying into new products and services, or integrating into related products and services.

- **Alliance Strategies.** Establishing new business linkages and alliances with customers, suppliers, competitors, consultants, and other companies. These linkages may include mergers, acquisitions, joint ventures, forming of "virtual companies," or other marketing, manufacturing, or distribution agreements between a business and its trading partners.

Strategic Uses of Information Technology

How can business managers use investments in information technology to directly support a firm's competitive strategies? Figure 2.3 answers that question with a summary of the many ways that information technology can help a business implement the five basic competitive strategies. Figure 2.4 provides examples of how specific companies have used strategic information systems to implement each of these five basic strategies for competitive advantage. Note the major use of Internet technologies for electronic business and commerce applications. In the rest of this chapter, we will discuss and provide examples of many strategic uses of information technology.

Figure 2.3

A summary of how information technology can be used to implement the five basic competitive strategies. Many companies are using Internet technologies as the foundation for such strategies.

Basic Strategies in the Business Use of Information Technology
Lower Costs • Use IT to substantially reduce the cost of business processes. • Use IT to lower the costs of customers or suppliers.
Differentiate • Develop new IT features to differentiate products and services. • Use IT features to reduce the differentiation advantages of competitors. • Use IT features to focus products and services at selected market niches.
Innovate • Create new products and services that include IT components. • Develop unique new markets or market niches with the help of IT. • Make radical changes to business processes with IT that dramatically cut costs, improve quality, efficiency, or customer service, or shorten time to market.
Promote Growth • Use IT to manage regional and global business expansion. • Use IT to diversify and integrate into other products and services.
Develop Alliances • Use IT to create virtual organizations of business partners. • Develop interenterprise information systems linked by the Internet and extranets that support strategic business relationships with customers, suppliers, subcontractors, and others.

Figure 2.4

Examples of how companies used information technology to implement five competitive strategies for strategic advantage. Note the use of Internet technologies for electronic business and commerce applications.

Strategy	Company	Strategic Information System	Business Benefit
Cost Leadership	Buy.com	Online price adjustment	Lowest price guarantee
	Priceline.com	Online seller bidding	Buyer-set pricing
	EBay.com	Online auctions	Auction-set prices
Differentiation	AVNET Marshall	Customer/supplier e-commerce	Increase in market share
	Ross Operating Valves	Online customer design	Increase in market share
	Consolidated Freightways	Customer online shipment tracking	Increase in market share
Innovation	Charles Schwab & Co.	Online discount stock trading	Market leadership
	Federal Express	Online package tracking and flight management	Market leadership
	Amazon.com	Online full service customer systems	Market leadership
Growth	Citicorp	Global intranet	Increase in global market
	Wal-Mart	Merchandise ordering by global satellite network	Market leadership
	Toys 'Я' Us Inc.	POS inventory tracking	Market leadership
Alliance	Wal-Mart/Procter & Gamble	Automatic inventory replenishment by supplier	Reduced inventory cost/increased sales
	Cisco Systems	Virtual manufacturing alliances	Agile market leadership
	Airborne Express/ Rentrak Corp.	Online inventory management/ shipment tracking	Increase in market share

Other Competitive Strategies

There are many other competitive strategies in addition to the five basic strategies of cost leadership, differentiation, innovation, growth, and alliance. Let's look at several key strategies that are also implemented with information technology. They are: locking in customers or suppliers, building switching costs, raising barriers to entry, and leveraging investment in information technology.

Investments in information technology can allow a business to **lock in customers and suppliers** (and lock out competitors) by building valuable new relationships with them. This can deter both customers and suppliers from abandoning a firm for its competitors or intimidating a firm into accepting less-profitable relationships. Early attempts to use information systems technology in these relationships focused on significantly improving the quality of service to customers and suppliers in a firm's distribution, marketing, sales, and service activities. Then businesses moved to more innovative uses of information technology.

Wal-Mart and Others

For example, Wal-Mart built an elaborate satellite network linking the point-of-sale terminals in all of its stores. The network was designed to provide managers, buyers, and sales associates with up-to-date sales and inventory status information to improve product buying, inventories, and store management. Then Wal-Mart began to use the operational efficiency of such information systems to offer lower cost, better-quality products and services, and differentiate itself from its competitors.

Companies like Wal-Mart began to extend their networks to their customers and suppliers in order to build innovative continuous inventory replenishment systems that would lock in their business. This creates **interenterprise information systems** in which the Internet, extranets, and other networks electronically link the computers of businesses with their customers and suppliers, resulting in new business alliances and partnerships. Extranets between businesses and their suppliers are prime examples of such strategic linkages. An even stronger e-business link is formed by *stockless* inventory replenishment systems such as those between Wal-Mart and Procter & Gamble. In that system, Procter & Gamble automatically replenishes Wal-Mart's stock of Procter & Gamble products [6, 27].

A major emphasis in strategic information systems has been to find ways to build **switching costs** into the relationships between a firm and its customers or suppliers. That is, investments in information systems technology, such as those mentioned in the Wal-Mart example, can make customers or suppliers dependent on the continued use of innovative, mutually beneficial interenterprise information systems. Then, they become reluctant to pay the costs in time, money, effort, and inconvenience that it would take to change to a company's competitors.

By making investments in information technology to improve its operations or promote innovation, a firm could also erect **barriers to entry** that would discourage or delay other companies from entering a market. Typically, this happens by increasing the amount of investment or the complexity of the technology required to compete in an industry or a market segment. Such actions would tend to discourage firms already in the industry and deter external firms from entering the industry.

Investing in information technology enables a firm to build strategic IT capabilities that allow it to take advantage of strategic opportunities when they arise. In many cases, this results when a company invests in advanced computer-based information systems to improve the efficiency of its own business processes. Then, armed with this strategic technology platform, the firm can **leverage investment in information technology** by developing new products and services that would not be possible without a strong IT capability. An important current example is the development of corporate intranets and extranets by many companies, which enables them to leverage their previous investments in Internet browsers, PCs, servers, and client/server networks. Figure 2.5 summarizes the additional strategic uses of IT we have just discussed.

Merrill Lynch and Charles Schwab	Merrill Lynch is a classic example of the use of several competitive strategies. By making large investments in information technology, along with a groundbreaking alliance with BancOne, they became the first securities brokers to offer a credit line, checking account, Visa credit card, and automatic investment in a money market fund, all in one account. This gave them a major competitive advantage for several years before their rivals could develop the IT capability to offer similar services on their own [31].

However, Merrill is now playing catch-up in online discount securities trading with Charles Schwab, e-Trade, and others. Schwab is now the leading online securities company with over 7.4 million customers in early 2001, far surpassing Merrill's online statistics. Thus, large investments in IT can make the stakes too high for some present or prospective players in an industry, but can evaporate over time as new technologies are employed by competitors [28].

Figure 2.5   Additional ways that information technology can be used to implement competitive strategies.

Other Strategic Uses of Information Technology

- Develop interenterprise information systems whose convenience and efficiency create switching costs that lock in customers or suppliers.
- Make major investments in advanced IT applications that build barriers to entry against industry competitors or outsiders.
- Include IT components in products and services to make substitution of competing products or services more difficult.
- Leverage investment in IS people, hardware, software, databases, and networks from operational uses into strategic applications.

The Value Chain and Strategic IS

Let's look at another important concept that can help you identify opportunities for strategic information systems. The value chain concept was developed by Michael Porter [34] and is illustrated in Figure 2.6. It views a firm as a series, chain, or network of basic activities that add value to its products and services, and thus add a margin of value to the firm. In the value chain conceptual framework, some business activities are primary processes; others are support processes. This framework can highlight where competitive strategies can best be applied in a business. That is, managers and business professionals should try to develop a variety of strategic uses of Internet and other technologies for those basic processes that add the most value to a company's products or services, and thus to the overall business value of the company. Figure 2.6 provides examples of how and where information technologies can be applied to basic business processes using the value chain framework.

Value Chain Examples

Figure 2.6 emphasizes that collaborative workflow intranet-based systems can increase the communications and collaboration needed to dramatically improve administrative coordination and support services. A career development intranet can help the human resources management function provide employees with professional development training programs. Computer-aided engineering and design extranets

---

Figure 2.6   The value chain of a firm. Note the examples of the variety of strategic information systems that can be applied to a firm's basic business processes for competitive advantage.

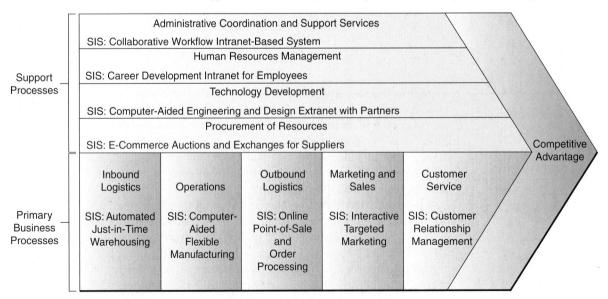

enable a company and its business partners to jointly design products and processes. Finally, e-commerce auctions and exchanges can dramatically improve procurement of resources by providing an online marketplace for a firm's suppliers.

Other examples of strategic applications of information systems technology to primary business processes are identified in Figure 2.6. These include automated just-in-time warehousing systems to support inbound logistic processes involving storage of inventory, computer-aided flexible manufacturing (CAM) systems for manufacturing operations, and online point-of-sale and order processing systems to improve out-bound logistics processes that process customer orders. Information systems can also support marketing and sales processes by developing an interactive targeted marketing capability on the Internet and its World Wide Web. Finally, customer service can be dramatically improved by a coordinated and integrated customer relationship management system.

Internet-Based Value Chains

Value chains can also be used to strategically position a company's Internet-based applications to gain competitive advantage. Figure 2.7 is a value chain model that outlines several ways that a company's Internet connections with its customers could provide business benefits and opportunities for competitive advantage. For example, company-managed Internet newsgroups, chat rooms, and electronic commerce websites are powerful tools for market research and product development, direct sales, and customer feedback and support.

A company's Internet connections with its suppliers could also be used for competitive advantage. Examples are online auctions and exchanges at suppliers' e-commerce websites, and online shipping, scheduling, and status information at an e-commerce portal that gives employees immediate access to up-to-date information from a variety of vendors. This can substantially lower costs, reduce lead times, and improve the quality of products and services [8].

Thus, the value chain concept can help you decide where and how to apply the strategic capabilities of information technology. It shows how various types of information technologies might be applied to specific business processes to help a firm gain competitive advantages in the marketplace.

Figure 2.7

This Internet value chain demonstrates the strategic business value of Internet-based applications that focus on a company's relationships with its customers.

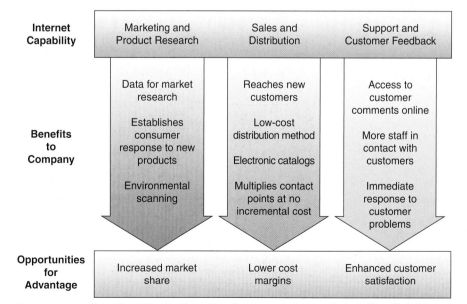

Source: Adapted from Mary Cronin, *Doing More Business on the Internet*, 2nd ed. (New York: Van Nostrand Reinhold, 1995), p. 61. Used by permission.

Identifying e-Business and e-Commerce Strategies

Companies need a strategic framework that can bridge the gap between simply connecting to the Internet and harnessing its power for competitive advantage. The most valuable Internet applications allow companies to transcend communication barriers and establish connections that will enhance productivity, stimulate innovative development, and improve customer relations [9].

E-business and e-commerce applications and Internet technologies can be used strategically for competitive advantage, as this text will repeatedly demonstrate. However, in order to optimize this strategic impact, a company must continually assess the strategic value of such applications. Figure 2.8 is a strategic positioning matrix that can help a company identify where to concentrate its use of Internet technologies to gain a competitive advantage with e-business and e-commerce. Let's take a look at the strategies that each quadrant of this matrix represents [9].

- **Cost and Efficiency Improvements.** This quadrant represents a low amount of internal company, customer, and competitor connectivity and use of IT via the Internet and other networks. So one recommended strategy would be to focus on improving efficiency and lowering costs by using the Internet and the World Wide Web as a fast, low-cost way to communicate and interact with customers, suppliers, and business partners. The use of e-mail, chat systems, discussion groups, and a company website are typical examples.

- **Performance Improvement in Business Effectiveness.** Here a company has a high degree of internal connectivity and pressures to substantially improve its business processes, but external connectivity by customers and competitors is still low. A strategy of making major improvements in business

Figure 2.8

A strategic positioning matrix helps a company optimize the strategic impact of Internet technologies for electronic business and commerce applications.

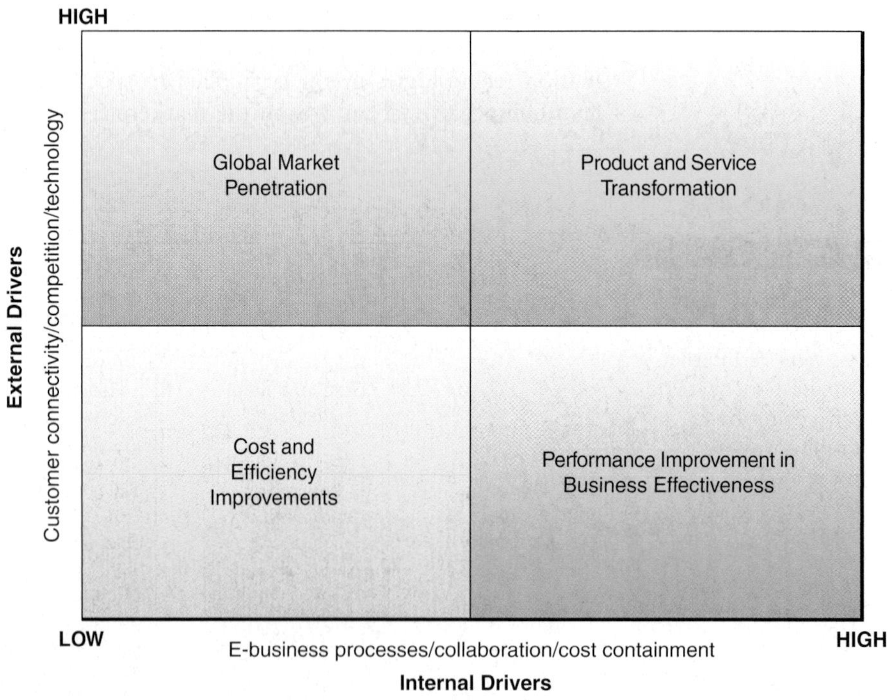

Source: Adapted and reprinted by permission of The Harvard Business School Press from Mary Cronin, *The Internet Strategy Handbook* (Boston: 1996), p. 20, and Don Tapscott, David Ticoll, and Alex Lowy, *Digital Capital: Harnessing the Power of Business Webs* (Boston: 2000), p. 220. Copyright © 1996, 2000 by the President and Fellows of Harvard College, all rights reserved.

effectiveness is recommended. For example, widespread internal use of Internet-based technologies like intranets and extranets can substantially improve information sharing and collaboration within the business and with its trading partners.

- **Global Market Penetration.** A company that enters this quadrant of the matrix must capitalize on a high degree of customer and competitor connectivity and use of IT. Developing e-business and e-commerce applications to optimize interaction with customers and build market share is recommended. For example, e-commerce websites with value-added information services and extensive online customer support would be one way to implement such a strategy.

- **Product and Service Transformation.** Here a company and its customers, suppliers, and competitors are extensively networked. Internet-based technologies, including e-commerce websites and e-business intranets and extranets, must now be implemented throughout the company's operations and business relationships. This enables a company to develop and deploy new Internet-based products and services that strategically reposition it in the marketplace. Using the Internet for electronic commerce transaction processing with customers at company websites, and e-commerce auctions and exchanges for suppliers are typical examples of such strategic e-business applications. Let's look at more specific examples.

e-Business Strategy Examples	
	Market creator. Use the Internet to define a new market by identifying a unique customer need. This model requires you to be among the first to market and to remain ahead of competition by continuously innovating. Examples: Amazon.com and E*TRADE.
	Channel reconfiguration. Use the Internet as a new channel to directly access customers, make sales, and fulfill orders. This model supplements, rather than replaces, physical distribution and marketing channels. Example: Cisco and Dell.
	Transaction intermediary. Use the Internet to process purchases. This transactional model includes the end-to-end process of searching, comparing, selecting, and paying online. Examples: Microsoft Expedia and eBay.
	Infomediary. Use the Internet to reduce the search cost. Offer the customer a unified process for collecting information necessary to make a large purchase. Examples: HomeAdvisor and Auto-By-Tel.
	Self-service innovator. Use the Internet to provide a comprehensive suite of services that the customer's employees can use directly. Self-service affords employees a direct, personalized relationship. Examples: Employease and Healtheon.
	Supply chain innovator. Use the Internet to streamline the interactions among all parties in the supply chain to improve operating efficiency. Examples: McKesson and Ingram Micro.
	Channel mastery. Use the Internet as a sales and service channel. This model supplements, rather than replaces, the existing physical business offices and call centers. Example: Charles Schwab [23].

| Section II | # Using Information Technology for Strategic Advantage |

Strategic Uses of IT

There are many ways that organizations may view and use information technology. For example, companies may choose to use information systems strategically, or they may be content to use IT to support efficient everyday operations. But if a company emphasized strategic business uses of information technology, its management would view IT as a major competitive differentiator. It would then devise business strategies that would use IT to develop products, services, and capabilities that would give the company major advantages in the markets in which it competes. In this section, we will provide many examples of such strategic business applications of information technology.

Analyzing Moen Inc.

Read the Real World Case on Moen Inc. on the next page. We can learn a lot about electronic business and commerce strategies from this example. See Figure 2.9.

Moen Inc. is a leader in the construction/home improvement and plumbing industries in innovative product designs and the use of Internet technologies for e-business and e-commerce applications. For example, they use their ProjectNet extranet to collaborate in product design with their suppliers, and thus have significantly reduced the time to design, manufacture, and bring new products to market, which has contributed to increases in their market share. Moen also developed a SupplyNet extranet which allows parts suppliers to report and check the status of their orders online. This application alone has generated millions in cost savings in reduced order processing costs. Their latest e-commerce project is to create a CustomerNet extranet to encourage their business customers to use the Web to place their orders, thus significantly reducing Moen's order processing costs and building closer relationships with their customers.

| Figure 2.9 |

Tim Baker is chief technology officer at Moen Inc., and leader of their Internet Program Office.

Source: Daniel Levin

Moen, Incorporated:
Implementing e-Business and e-Commerce Strategies

It used to be that if you were in the market for a new faucet, you could have any color as long as it was chrome. Plumbing fixtures were meant to be practical, not pretty. Then, in the mid-1990s, goosenecks, gold, and built-in water filters became popular. That's when faucet maker Moen Inc. decided it was really in the fashion business selling jewelry for the bathroom and began churning out new faucet designs in fresh finishes like silver, platinum, and copper as often as Donna Karan introduces a new ready-to-wear line.

Moen president Jeffrey A. Svoboda calls it the "9-to-5" strategy. If consumers had a choice of new styles and were able to mix parts, they might buy a new faucet once every five years instead of every nine years. "We would double the size of the market and enjoy a gain in market share," says Svoboda, who spent 20 years at General Electric Company and another three at Black & Decker Corp. before joining Moen in 1996. The only problem: Moen was selling many faucets designed in the '60s and '70s. The sleepy Midwestern company was lucky to introduce one new line a year.

So Svoboda decided to use the Internet to design jazzy products—fast. Sure, everyone believed that the Web could help speed communications, but few thought it could turbocharge product design and, in turn, manufacturing. Yet by collaborating on designs with suppliers over the Web, a new Moen faucet goes from drawing board to store shelf in 16 months, instead of the former 24 months. The time savings make it possible for Moen's 50 engineers to work on three times as many projects, and introduce from 5 to 15 fashion (or faucet) lines a year.

The change is paying off handsomely. More products reaching the market faster has helped boost sales by 17 percent since 1998—higher than the industry average of 9 percent over the same period. Moen has jumped from No. 3 in market share to a tie for No. 1 with archrival Delta Faucet Co. Both claim about 30 percent of the $2.5 billion North American faucet market. "Better communication means more rapid deployment of ideas," says Svoboda.

That doesn't mean big budgets and fuel-injected scheduling. Since 1996, technology chief Tim Baker and his now 20-member Internet Program Office have been setting priorities and laying out what can be accomplished with the resources they have. So far, Moen's Web initiatives have cost only $1.5 million, with money spent to hire software developers for in-house work and on outsourced features like an online design room that allows customers to mix and match shower fixtures. This is the new model for an effective Net strategy, say consultants: methodical, with a focus on the bottom line. "Companies are starting to ask what's the return on investment and how strategic is the Web to their core business," says Tim Byrne, a vice-president at Mercer Management Consulting Inc.

Moen has known the answer for years. That's why, in late 1998, Moen started sending electronic files of new product designs by e-mail. A few months later, it launched ProjectNet, an online extranet site where Moen can share digital designs simultaneously with suppliers worldwide. Every supplier can make changes immediately. Moen consolidates all the design changes on a master Web file. That way, design problems are discovered instantly and adjustments can be made just as fast, cutting the time it takes to lock in a final design to three days.

Next, the company attacked the cumbersome process of ordering parts from suppliers and updating them by fax or phone. In October 2000, the company launched its SupplyNet extranet site that allows parts suppliers to check the status of Moen's orders online. Every time Moen changes an order, the supplier receives an e-mail. If a supplier can't fill an order in time, it can alert Moen right away so the faucet maker can search elsewhere for the part. Today, the 40 key suppliers who make 80 percent of the parts that Moen buys use SupplyNet. The result: The company has shaved $3 million, or about 6 percent, off its raw-materials and work-in-progress inventories since October.

Moen's approach is like light-speed compared with competitors. Many still rely on fax machines to do most of their business. The percentage of companies using the Net to speed the supply chain in the construction/home improvement field, which includes plumbing, is expected to rise to just 7.7 percent in 2004, up from 3.2 percent in 2000, according to Forrester Research. "Moen is a step ahead of its peers in embracing Internet technologies," says analyst Navi Radjou of Forrester Research.

Moen may be ahead of its peers, but there's plenty of work to do. Technology chief Baker's most sensitive task is CustomerNet, the company's attempt to wire wholesalers, which account for 50 percent of the company's business. Unlike suppliers, who depend on Moen for most of their business, the company has little sway with wholesalers that buy plumbing, heating, and other products—not just faucets—from many manufacturers. Most still order by fax, even though that process causes errors up to 40 percent of the time.

Moen execs are undaunted. They're courting wholesalers with the same methodical determination that has made Moen a Web-smart company. By the end of the year, they expect the trickle of online orders to turn into a steady stream.

Case Study Questions

1. How is Moen using e-business and e-commerce technologies for competitive advantage? Include the appropriate strategies outlined in Figures 2.3, 2.5, and 2.8 in your analysis.

2. How effectively is Moen implementing "the new model for an effective Net strategy" mentioned in the case? Explain your answer.

3. How could other companies apply the e-business and e-commerce strategies that Moen is using to their businesses? Use an example from both a large and small business perspective to illustrate your answer.

Source: Adapted from Faith Keenan, "Opening the Spigot," *Business Week e.Biz*, June 4, 2001, pp. 17, 20. ©2001 McGraw-Hill Companies. Reprinted by permission.

Building a Customer-Focused e-Business

The driving force behind world economic growth has changed from manufacturing volume to improving customer value. As a result, the key success factor for many firms is maximizing customer value [9].

For many companies, the chief business value of becoming a **customer-focused e-business** lies in its ability to help them keep customers loyal, anticipate their future needs, respond to customer concerns, and provide top-quality customer service. This strategic focus on **customer value** recognizes that quality, rather than prices, has become the primary determinant in a customer's perception of value. From a customer's point of view, companies that consistently offer the best value are able to keep track of their customers' individual preferences, keep up with market trends, supply products, services, and information anytime, anywhere, and provide customer services tailored to individual needs [9]. And so electronic commerce has become a strategic opportunity for companies, large and small, to offer fast, responsive, high-quality products and services tailored to individual customer preferences.

Internet technologies can make customers the focal point of all e-business and e-commerce applications. Internet, intranet, and extranet websites create new chan-

---

Figure 2.10   How a customer-focused e-business builds customer value and loyalty in electronic commerce.

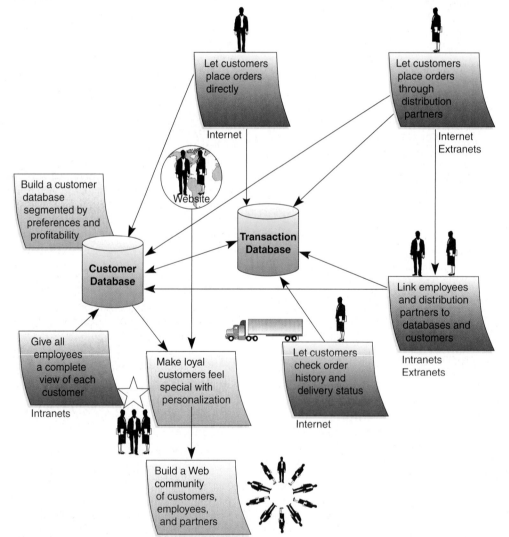

Source: Adapted from Patricia Seybold with Ronnie Marshak, *Customers.com: How to Create a Profitable Business Strategy for the Internet and Beyond* (New York: Times Books, 1998), p. 32.

nels for interactive communications within a company, with customers, and with the suppliers, business partners, and others in the external environment. This enables continual interaction with customers by most business functions and encourages cross-functional collaboration with customers in product development, marketing, delivery, service, and technical support [9].

Typically, e-commerce customers use the Internet to ask questions, air complaints, evaluate products, request support, and make and report their purchases. Using the Internet and corporate intranets, specialists in business functions throughout the enterprise can contribute to an effective response. This encourages the creation of cross-functional discussion groups and problem-solving teams dedicated to customer involvement, service, and support. Even the Internet and extranet links to suppliers and business partners can be used to enlist them in a way of doing business that ensures prompt delivery of quality components and services to meet a company's commitments to its customers [20]. This is how an e-business enterprise demonstrates its focus on customer value.

Figure 2.10 illustrates the interrelationships in a customer-focused e-business. Intranets, extranets, e-commerce websites, and web-enabled internal business processes form the invisible IT platform that supports this e-business model. This enables the e-business to focus on targeting the kinds of customers it really wants, and "owning" the customer's total business experience with the company. A successful e-business streamlines all business processes that impact their customers, and provides its employees with a complete view of each customer, so they can offer their customers top-quality personalized service. A customer-focused e-business helps their e-commerce customers to help themselves, while also helping them do their jobs. Finally, a successful e-business nurtures an online community of customers, employees, and business partners that builds great customer loyalty, while fostering cooperation to provide an outstanding customer experience [37]. Let's review a real world example.

Hilton Hotels: Customer-Focused e-Business	Hilton Hotels, via Hilton.com, has one of the fastest reservation services in the world: The average time to complete a reservation is less than two minutes. Frequent guests have services automatically tailored to their last visit, and meeting planners access the website for group reservations and floor plans of venues. Bruce Rosenberg, Hilton's vice president of market distribution, says, "The Web opened up people's eyes about how we can and should do business. We looked at all the business models—every customer segment from the business traveller, the tourist, the meeting planner, the travel agent—and identified an e-business way of doing business with them."

Hilton's e-business initiative required information from multiple business units, interactivity among the customer, Hilton.com, and Hilton's existing back-end reservation systems, and a high level of personalization. "We want profiles on the customers, their history with us and what they like and don't like, accessible no matter where they touch us in the world," Rosenberg says. Hilton has very good profiles of members of HHonors (the Hilton frequent-customer loyalty program), but not so good profiles, Rosenberg notes, for the tens of millions of customers that only occasionally stay with Hilton. "The new systems we are building will allow us to have a larger number of profiles and a finer segmentation of our customer base. The Web will enable us to reach them cost effectively and develop a deeper personal relationship. We just couldn't do this before by mailing material to them. The budgets weren't there to support it."

Hilton is implementing a direct-to-customer business model via the Web channel, targeting the frequent-traveller segment and providing a single point of contact. All customer segments can use the Web channel, including both individuals and travel agents—with some travel agents bypassed when individuals contact Hilton directly. To implement this e-business initiative, Hilton integrates workflows, reservation systems, call centers, and business processes with the common goal of obtaining more finely segmented customer data. The initiative required a strong vision to evolve to an e-business, many negotiations across business units within Hilton, alliances with other firms, investment in IT infrastructure, and integration of Internet-based application with a large database of segmented customer profiles and various existing reservation systems [40].

Reengineering Business Processes

One of the most important implementations of competitive strategies today is **business process reengineering** (BPR), most often simply called reengineering. Reengineering is a fundamental rethinking and radical redesign of business processes to achieve dramatic improvements in cost, quality, speed, and service. So BPR combines a strategy of promoting business innovation with a strategy of making major improvements to business processes so that a company can become a much stronger and more successful competitor in the marketplace.

However, Figure 2.11 points out that while the potential payback of reengineering is high, so is its risk of failure and level of disruption to the organizational environment [16]. Making radical changes to business processes to dramatically improve efficiency and effectiveness is not an easy task. For example, many companies have used cross-functional enterprise resource planning (ERP) software to reengineer, automate, and integrate their manufacturing, distribution, finance, and human resource business processes. While many companies have reported impressive gains with such ERP reengineering projects, many others have failed to achieve the improvements they sought (as we saw in the real world example of A-DEC in Chapter 1).

That's why *organizational redesign* approaches are an important enabler of reengineering, along with the use of information technology. For example, one common approach is the use of self-directed cross-functional or multidisciplinary *process teams*. Employees from several departments or specialties including engineering, marketing, customer service, and manufacturing may work as a team on the product development process. Another example is the use of *case managers*, who handle almost all tasks in a business process, instead of splitting tasks among many different specialists.

Figure 2.11 How business process reengineering differs from business improvement.		**Business Improvement**	**Business Reengineering**
	Definition	Incrementally improving existing processes	Radically redesigning business processes
	Target	Any process	Strategic business processes
	Primary Enablers	IT and work simplification	IT and organizational redesign
	Potential Payback	10%–50% improvements	10-fold improvements
	What Changes?	Same jobs, just more efficient	Big job cuts; new jobs; major job redesign
	Risk of Failure and Level of Disruption	Low	High

The Role of Information Technology

Information technology plays a major role in reengineering most business processes. The speed, information processing capabilities, and connectivity of computers and Internet technologies can substantially increase the efficiency of business processes, as well as communications and collaboration among the people responsible for their operation and management. For example, the order management process illustrated in Figure 2.12 is vital to the success of most companies [10]. Many of them are reengineering this process with enterprise resource planning software and Web-enabled electronic business and commerce systems. See Figure 2.13. Now, let's take a look at an example from Ford Motor Company.

Ford Motor Company: Driving e-Engineering

Ford believes the Internet is ushering in an even bigger wave of business transformation than reengineering. Call it e-engineering. Ford realizes it's not enough to put up simple websites for customers, employees, and partners. To take full advantage of the Net, they've got to reinvent the way they do business—changing how they design, manufacture, and distribute goods, collaborate inside and outside the company, and deal with suppliers.

Ford is using Web technologies to reengineer its internal business processes as well as those between the company and its dealers, suppliers, and customers. For example, Ford's global intranet connects thousands of designers in the United States and Europe so they can collaborate on design projects. Also, extranet links enable suppliers from all over the world to collaborate on the design, manufacture, and assembly of automotive components. All of these e-engineering initiatives are designed to slash costs, reduce time to market, and lower inventory and workforce levels, while improving the sales, quality, and consistency of Ford's products. Ford's global intranet brings 4,500 engineers from labs in the United States, Germany, and England together in cyberspace to collaborate on automobile design projects. The idea is to break down the barriers between regional operations so basic auto components are designed once and used everywhere. When design plans conflict, the software automatically sends out e-mail alerts to members of design teams. When all of the pieces are in place, the company hopes to transform the way it designs and produces cars, so it can quickly build them to order [21, 40].

Improving Business Quality

Information technology can be used strategically to improve business performance in many ways other than in supporting reengineering initiatives. One important strategic thrust is continuous quality improvement, popularly called **total quality management** (TQM). Previous to TQM, quality was defined as meeting established standards or specifications for a product or service. Statistical *quality control* programs were used to measure and correct any deviations from standards [10].

Figure 2.12

The order management process consists of several business processes and crosses the boundaries of traditional business functions.

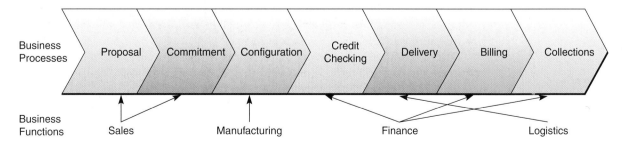

Figure 2.13

Examples of information technologies that support reengineering the sales and order management processes.

Reengineering Order Management
● Customer relationship management systems using corporate intranets and the Internet.
● Supplier managed inventory systems using the Internet and extranets.
● Cross-functional ERP software for integrating manufacturing, distribution, finance, and human resource processes.
● Customer-accessible e-commerce websites for order entry, status checking, payment, and service.
● Customer, product, and order status databases accessed via intranets and extranets by employees and suppliers.

Total Quality Management

Total quality management is a much more strategic approach to business improvement. Quality is emphasized from the customer's viewpoint, rather than the producer's. Thus, quality is defined as meeting or exceeding the requirements and expectations of customers for a product or service. This may involve many features and attributes, such as performance, reliability, durability, responsiveness, and aesthetics, to name a few [33].

TQM may use a variety of tools and methods to seek continuous improvement of quality, productivity, flexibility, timeliness, and customer responsiveness. According to quality expert Richard Schonberger, companies that use TQM are committed to:

1. Even better, more appealing, less-variable quality of the product or service.
2. Even quicker, less-variable response—from design and development through supplier and sales channels, offices, and plants all the way to the final user.
3. Even greater flexibility in adjusting to customers' shifting volume and mix requirement.
4. Even lower cost through quality improvement, rework reduction, and non-value-adding waste elimination [33].

GE's Six Sigma Quality Initiative

Six Sigma is the most fundamental, far-reaching and potentially significant initiative ever undertaken by General Electric (GE) to optimize its competitiveness.

Six Sigma is the mother of all quality efforts. To achieve it, GE will have to eliminate 9,999.5 of every 10,000 defects in its processes or only 3.4 defects per million opportunities. That's a tall order, but it's one that would add $8 billion to $12 billion to the bottom line.

GE's Superabrasives business, which produces industrial diamonds, has virtually completed the implementation of Six Sigma, giving a glimpse of what might be expected companywide in a few years. Figure 2.14 outlines the improvements that occurred.

The Six Sigma mantra for approaching any process is "define, measure, analyze, improve, control," and information technology enables many of those activities. GE uses IT to collect baseline quality data, model defect-free Six Sigma processes, automate those processes to lock in improvements, and monitor them to assure they remain defect-free.

For example, a foundation of Six Sigma is that customers define a defect. GE developed an extranet website called the "customer dashboard" that invites more than 1,000 key customers to identify the most critical-to-quality (CTQ) aspects of GE products and services that define a good performance and a defect. For example, if a customer chose speedy product delivery as a CTQ aspect, it would then define a good performance—say, five days. Anything slower is a defect.

Having defined the CTQ aspects, customers use the dashboard to provide regular, precise, quantitative feedback on how GE's processes measure up, giving a snapshot of its performance at a given moment and a trend line over time.

GE also developed an intranet website that helps all employees focus on the Six Sigma process. It provides information and status reports on every project and shares best practices among 6,000 "black belt" Six Sigma experts, who work full-time on the effort, and 30,000 "green belts," who integrate Six Sigma projects into their regular workloads [29].

Becoming an Agile Company

We are changing from a competitive environment in which mass-market products and services were standardized, long-lived, information-poor, and exchanged in one-time transactions, to an environment in which companies compete globally with niche market products and services that are individualized, short-lived, information-rich, and exchanged on an ongoing basis with customers [19].

Agility in business performance is the ability of a company to prosper in rapidly changing, continually fragmenting global markets for high-quality, high-performance, customer-configured products and services. An **agile company** can make a profit in markets with broad product ranges and short model lifetimes, and can produce orders in arbitrary lot sizes. It supports *mass customization* by offering individualized products while maintaining high volumes of production. Agile companies depend heavily on Internet technologies to integrate and manage business processes, while providing the information processing power to treat masses of customers as individuals.

To be an agile company, a business must implement four basic strategies. First, customers of an agile company perceive products or services as solutions to their individual problems. Thus, products can be priced based on their value as solutions, not on their cost to produce. Second, an agile company cooperates with customers, suppliers, and other companies, even *competition* with competitors. This allows a business to bring products to market as rapidly and cost-effectively as possible, no matter where resources are located and who owns them. Third, an agile company organizes so that it thrives on change and uncertainty. It uses flexible organizational structures keyed to the requirements of different and constantly changing customer opportunities. Finally, an agile company leverages the impact of its people and the knowledge they possess. By nurturing an entrepreneurial spirit, an agile company provides powerful incentives for employee responsibility, adaptability, and innovation [19]. Now let's take another look at AVNET Marshall, which is a great example of an agile company.

Figure 2.14

The results of GE's Six Sigma total quality management program in its Superabrasives division.

GE Superabrasives Business Process Results

- Operating margins rose from 9.8% to 25.5%.
- Variable manufacturing costs fell 50%.
- The number of carats per manufacturing run rose 500%.
- On-time deliveries improved 85%.
- Product quality improved 87%.
- Late deliveries to customers declined 85%.
- Billing mistakes fell 87%.
- Capital expenditures decreased 40%.

Source: Adapted from Kathleen Melymuka, "GE's Quality Gamble," *Computerworld*, June 8, 1998, p. 64. Copyright 1998 by Computerworld, Inc., Framingham, MA 01701. Reprinted from *Computerworld*.

**AVNET Marshall:
Agile for the
Customer**

*Marshall realized that customers, if given a choice, wanted everything: products
and services at the lowest possible cost, highest possible quality, greatest possible
customization, and fastest possible delivery time. At the limit, this translates to
the impossible goals of "Free.Perfect.Now"* [13].

Figure 2.15 reveals the components of the Free.Perfect.Now business model
that inspired the company then known as Marshall Industries to be an agile,
customer-focused company. AVNET Marshall developed the model as a clear,
simple, and powerful tool to focus its employees and its information technology
platform on serving its customers in the most agile and responsive ways.

The Free dimension emphasizes that most customers want the lowest cost for
value received, but are willing to pay more for a value-added services such as
inventory management. The Perfect dimension stresses that AVNET Marshall's
products and services should not only be defect-free, but that their quality can
be enhanced by added features, customization, and anticipation of the future
needs of the customer. Finally, the Now dimension of this business model emphasizes that customers want 24/7 accessibility to products and services, short delivery times, and consideration of the time-to-market for their own products [13].

AVNET Marshall's extensive use of Internet technologies for innovative Internet, intranet, and extranet e-commerce websites and services for its customers, suppliers, and employees is a cornerstone of their IT and e-business strategies. Such
technologies are essential to the agility and customer responsiveness that have made
them a successful e-business enterprise.

Creating a Virtual Company

*These days, thousands of companies, large and small, are setting up virtual corpora-
tions that enable executives, engineers, scientists, writers, researchers, and other professionals from around the world to collaborate on new products and services without ever
meeting face to face. Once the exclusive domain of Fortune 500 companies with banks
of powerful computers and dedicated wide area networks, remote networking is now
available to any company with a phone, a fax, and e-mail access to the Internet* [36].

Figure 2.15   The Free.Perfect.Now business model developed by AVNET Marshall to guide its
transformation into an agile, customer-focused company.

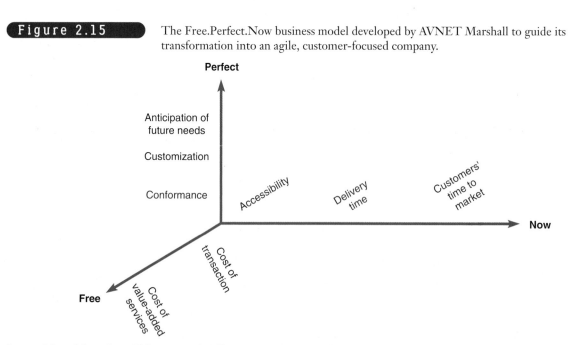

Source: Adapted from Omar El Sawy, Arvind Malhotra, Sanjay Gosain, and Kerry Young, "IT Intensive Value Innovation in the Electronic
Economy: Insights from Marshall Industries," *MIS Quarterly*, September 1999, p. 311. Reprinted with permission from the *MIS Quarterly*.

Figure 2.16

A network structure facilitates the creation of virtual companies.

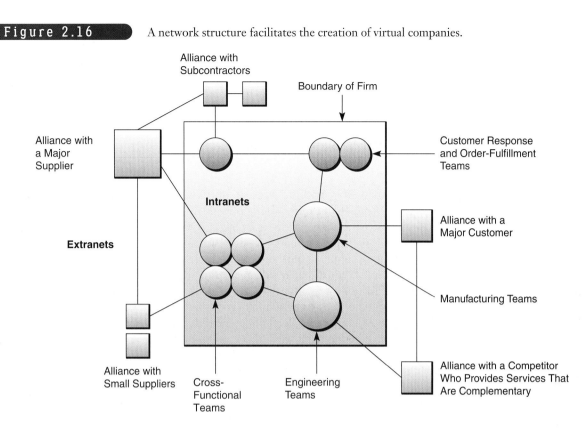

In today's dynamic global business environment, forming a **virtual company** can be one of the most important strategic uses of information technology. A virtual company (also called a *virtual corporation* or *virtual organization*) is an organization that uses information technology to link people, assets, and ideas.

Figure 2.16 illustrates that virtual companies typically use an organizational structure called a **network structure,** since most virtual companies are interlinked by the Internet, intranets, and extranets. Notice that this company has organized internally into clusters of process and cross-functional teams linked by intranets. It has also developed alliances and extranet links that form **interorganizational information systems** with suppliers, customers, subcontractors, and competitors. Thus, network structures create flexible and adaptable virtual companies keyed to exploit fast-changing business opportunities [4].

Virtual Company Strategies

Why are people forming virtual companies? Several major reasons stand out and are summarized in Figure 2.17. People and corporations are forming virtual companies as the best way to implement key business strategies that promise to ensure success in today's turbulent business climate.

Figure 2.17

The basic business strategies of virtual companies.

Strategies of Virtual Companies
● Share infrastructure and risk.
● Link complementary core competencies.
● Reduce concept-to-cash time through sharing.
● Increase facilities and market coverage.
● Gain access to new markets and share market or customer loyalty.
● Migrate from selling products to selling solutions.

For example, in order to exploit a diverse and fast-changing market opportunity, a business may not have the time or resources to develop the manufacturing and distribution infrastructure, people competencies, and information technologies needed. Only by quickly forming a virtual company of all-star partners can it assemble the components it needs to provide a world-class solution for customers and capture the market opportunity. Of course, today, the Internet, intranets, extranets, and a variety of other Internet technologies are vital components in creating a successful solution.

| Cisco Systems: Virtual Manufacturing | Cisco Systems is the world's largest manufacturer of telecommunications products. Jabil Circuit is the fourth largest company in the electronics contract manufacturing industry, with annual sales approaching $1 billion. Cisco has a *virtual manufacturing company* arrangement with Jabil and Hamilton Corporation, a major electronics parts supplier. Let's look at an example of how these three companies are involved in a typical business transaction.

An order placed for a Cisco 1600 series router (an internetwork processor used to connect small offices to networks) arrives simultaneously at Cisco in San Jose, California, and Jabil in St. Petersburg, Florida. Jabil immediately starts to build the router by drawing parts from three on-site inventories: Jabil's, one belonging to Cisco, and one owned and controlled by Hamilton. When completed, the router is tested and checked against the order in St. Petersburg by computers in San Jose, then shipped directly to the customer by Jabil. That triggers a Cisco invoice to the customer and electronic billings from Jabil and Hamilton to Cisco in San Jose. Thus, Cisco's virtual manufacturing company alliance with Jabil and Hamilton gives them an agile, build-to-order capability in the fiercely competitive telecommunications equipment industry [39]. |

Building a Knowledge-Creating Company

In an economy where the only certainty is uncertainty, the one sure source of lasting competitive advantage is knowledge. When markets shift, technologies proliferate, competitors multiply, and products become obsolete almost overnight, successful companies are those that consistently create new knowledge, disseminate it widely throughout the organization, and quickly embody it in new technologies and products. These activities define the "knowledge-creating" company, whose sole business is continuous innovation [32].

To many companies today, lasting competitive advantage can only be theirs if they become **knowledge-creating companies** or *learning organizations*. That means consistently creating new business knowledge, disseminating it widely throughout the company, and quickly building the new knowledge into their products and services.

Knowledge-creating companies exploit two kinds of knowledge. One is *explicit knowledge*—data, documents, things written down or stored on computers. The other kind is tacit knowledge—the "how-tos" of knowledge, which reside in workers. Successful **knowledge management** creates techniques, technologies, and rewards for getting employees to share what they know and to make better use of accumulated workplace knowledge. In that way, employees of a company are leveraging knowledge as they do their jobs [32].

Knowledge Management Systems

Making personal knowledge available to others is the central activity of the knowledge-creating company. It takes place continuously and at all levels of the organization [32]

Knowledge management has thus become one of the major strategic uses of information technology. Many companies are building **knowledge management**

systems (KMS) to manage organizational learning and business know-how. The goal of such systems is to help knowledge workers create, organize, and make available important business knowledge, wherever and whenever it's needed in an organization. This includes processes, procedures, patents, reference works, formulas, "best practices," forecasts, and fixes. As you will see in Chapter 9, Internet and intranet websites, groupware, data mining, knowledge bases, and online discussion groups are some of the key technologies that may be used by a KMS.

Knowledge management systems facilitate organizational learning and knowledge creation. They are designed to provide rapid feedback to knowledge workers, encourage behavior changes by employees, and significantly improve business performance. As the organizational learning process continues and its knowledge base expands, the knowledge-creating company works to integrate its knowledge into its business processes, products, and services. This helps the company become a more innovative and agile provider of high-quality products and customer services, and a formidable competitor in the marketplace [35]. Now let's close this chapter with an example of knowledge management strategies from the real world.

Siemens AG: Global Knowledge Management System	Joachim Doring is a Siemens vice president in charge of creating a high-tech solution to the age-old problem of getting employees to stop hoarding their know-how. His grand plan: Use the Internet to spread the knowledge of 461,000 co-workers around the globe so that people could build off one another's expertise. At the heart of his vision is a website called ShareNet. The site combines elements of a chat room, a database, and a search engine. An online entry form lets employees store information they think might be useful to colleagues—anything from a description of a successful project to a PowerPoint presentation. Other Siemens workers can search or browse by topic, then contact the authors via e-mail for more information.

So far, the payoff has been a dandy: Since its inception in April 1999, ShareNet has been put to the test by nearly 12,000 salespeople in Siemens' $10.5 billion Information & Communications Networks Groups, which provides telecom equipment and services. The tool, which cost only $7.8 million, has added $122 million in sales. For example, it was crucial to landing a $3 million contract to build a pilot broadband network for Telecom Malaysia. The local salespeople did not have enough expertise to put together a proposal, but through ShareNet they discovered a team in Denmark that had done a nearly identical project. Using the Denmark group's expertise, the Malaysia team won the job.

Better yet, the system lets staffers post an alert when they need help fast. In Switzerland, Siemens won a $460,000 contract to build a telecommunications network for two hospitals even though its bid was 30 percent higher than a competitor's. The clincher: Via ShareNet, colleagues in the Netherlands provided technical data to help the sales rep prove that Siemens' system would be substantially more reliable [15]. |

Summary

- **Strategic Uses of Information Technology.** Information technologies can support many competitive strategies. They can help a business cut costs, differentiate and innovate in its products and services, promote growth, develop alliances, lock in customers and suppliers, create switching costs, raise barriers to entry, and leverage its investment in IT resources. Thus, information technology can help a business gain a competitive advantage in its relationships with customers, suppliers, competitors, new entrants, and producers of substitute products. Refer to Figures 2.3 and 2.5 for summaries of the uses of information technology for strategic advantage.

- **Identifying e-Business and e-Commerce Strategies.** The Internet, intranets, extranets, and other Internet-based technologies can be used strategically for e-business and e-commerce capabilities that provide competitive advantage. This may result in major improvements in business efficiency and effectiveness, global market penetration, transforming products and services, and developing strategic applications and relationships with customers and business partners.

- **Building a Customer-Focused e-Business.** A key strategic use of Internet technologies is to build an e-business that develops its business value by making customer value its strategic focus. E-business enterprises use Internet, intranet, and extranet e-commerce websites and services to keep track of their customers' preferences; supply products, services, and information anytime, anywhere; and provide services tailored to the individual needs of their customers.

- **Reengineering Business Processes.** Information technology is a key ingredient in reengineering business operations by enabling radical changes to business processes that dramatically improve their efficiency and effectiveness. Internet technologies can play a major role in supporting innovative changes in the design of work flows, job requirements, and organizational structures in a company.

- **Improving Business Quality.** Information technology can be used to strategically improve the quality of business performance. In a total quality management approach, IT can support programs of continual improvement in meeting or exceeding customer requirements and expectations about the quality of products, services, customer responsiveness, and other features.

- **Becoming an Agile Company.** A business can use information technology to help it become an agile company. Then it can prosper in rapidly changing markets with broad product ranges and short model lifetimes in which it must process orders in arbitrary lot sizes, and can offer its customers customized products while maintaining high volumes of production. An agile company depends heavily on Internet technologies to help it be responsive to its customers with customized solutions to their needs and cooperate with its customers, suppliers, and other businesses to bring products to market as rapidly and cost-effectively as possible.

- **Creating a Virtual Company.** Forming virtual companies has become an important competitive strategy in today's dynamic global markets. Internet and other information technologies play an important role in providing computing and telecommunications resources to support the communications, coordination, and information flows needed. Managers of a virtual company depend on IT to help them manage a network of people, knowledge, financial, and physical resources provided by many business partners to quickly take advantage of rapidly changing market opportunities.

- **Building a Knowledge-Creating Company.** Lasting competitive advantage today can only come from innovative use and management of organizational knowledge by knowledge-creating companies and learning organizations. Internet technologies are widely used in knowledge management systems to support the creation and dissemination of business knowledge and its integration into new products, services, and business processes.

Key Terms and Concepts

These are the key terms and concepts of this chapter. The page number of their first explanation is in parentheses.

1. Agile company (57)
2. Business process reengineering (54)
3. Competitive forces (42)
4. Competitive strategies (42)
5. Creating switching costs (45)
6. Customer-focused e-business (52)
7. Identifying e-business and e-commerce strategies (48)
8. Knowledge-creating company (60)
9. Knowledge management system (60)
10. Leveraging investment in IT (45)
11. Locking in customers and suppliers (44)
12. Raising barriers to entry (45)
13. Strategic information systems (42)
14. Strategic uses of information technology (43)
15. Strategic uses of Internet technologies (47)
16. Total quality management (55)
17. Value chain (46)
18. Virtual company (59)

Review Quiz

Match one of the key terms and concepts listed previously with one of the brief examples or definitions that follow. Try to find the best fit for answers that seem to fit more than one term or concept. Defend your choices.

_____ 1. A business must deal with customers, suppliers, competitors, new entrants, and substitutes.

_____ 2. Cost leadership, differentiation of products, and new product innovation are examples.

_____ 3. Using investment in technology to keep firms out of an industry.

_____ 4. Making it unattractive for a firm's customers or suppliers to switch to its competitors.

_____ 5. Time, money, and effort needed for customers or suppliers to change to a firm's competitors.

_____ 6. Information systems that reengineer business processes or promote business innovation are examples.

_____ 7. Internet technologies enable a company to emphasize customer value as its strategic focus.

_____ 8. Highlights how strategic information systems can be applied to a firm's business processes and support activities for competitive advantage.

_____ 9. A business can find strategic uses for the computing and telecommunications capabilities it has developed to run its operations.

_____ 10. A business can use information systems to build barriers to entry, promote innovation, create switching costs, and so on.

_____ 11. Information technology can help a business make radical improvements in business processes.

_____ 12. Programs of continual improvement in meeting or exceeding customer requirements or expectations.

_____ 13. A business can prosper in rapidly changing markets while offering its customers individualized solutions to their needs.

_____ 14. A network of business partners formed to take advantage of rapidly changing market opportunities.

_____ 15. Many companies use the Internet, intranets, and extranets to achieve strategic gains in their competitive position.

_____ 16. Learning organizations that focus on creating, disseminating, and managing business knowledge.

_____ 17. Information systems that manage the creation and dissemination of organizational knowledge.

_____ 18. Analyzing the strategic business value of e-business and e-commerce applications.

Discussion Questions

1. Suppose you are a manager being asked to develop e-business and e-commerce applications to gain a competitive advantage in an important market for your company. What reservations might you have about doing so? Why?

2. How could a business use information technology to increase switching costs and lock in its customers and suppliers? Use business examples to support your answers.

3. How could a business leverage its investment in information technology to build strategic IT capabilities that serve as a barrier to entry by new entrants into its markets?

4. Refer to the Real World Case on Capital One in the chapter. Is Capital One's competitive position a temporary technology-based advantage, or a more enduring strategic business advantage? Defend your position.

5. What strategic role can information play in business process reengineering and total quality management?

6. How can Internet technologies help a business form strategic alliances with its customers, suppliers, and others?

7. How could a business use Internet technologies to form a virtual company or become an agile competitor?

8. Refer to the Real World Case on Moen Inc. in the chapter. What steps can Moen or other companies take to convince reluctant business customers to use their Web-based ordering systems? Give several examples.

9. Information technology can't really give a company a strategic advantage, because most competitive advantages don't last more than a few years and soon become strategic necessities that just raise the stakes of the game. Discuss.

10. MIS author and consultant Peter Keen says: "We have learned that it is not technology that creates a competitive edge, but the management process that exploits technology." What does he mean? Do you agree or disagree? Why?

Application Exercises

Complete the following exercises as individual or group projects that apply chapter concepts to real world business situations.

1. AVNET Marshall and Hilton Hotels: Customer-Focused e-Business

Visit the top-rated websites of AVNET Marshall (www.avnetmarshall.com) and Hilton Hotels (www.hilton.com), which are highlighted in the chapter as examples of customer-focused e-business companies. Check out many of their website features and e-commerce services.

a. Which site provided you with the best quality of service as a prospective customer? Explain.

b. How could these companies improve their website design and marketing to offer even better services to their customers and prospective customers?

2. Sabre's Travelocity and American Airlines: Competing for e-Travel Services

Visit the top-rated websites of Travelocity (www. travelocity.com), which is 70 percent owned by Sabre, and American Airlines (www.aa.com), the former corporate owner of Sabre. Check out their website features and e-commerce services.

a. How do their e-commerce websites and business models seem to differ?

b. Refer to the summaries of strategic uses of IT in Figures 2.3 and 2.5. Which strategies can you see each company using? Explain.

c. How could each company improve their competitive position in travel services e-commerce?

3. Assessing Strategy and Business Performance

The latest annual figures for eBay.com's net revenue, stock price, and earnings per share at the time of publication of this book are shown in Table 2.1. eBay™ is one of the firms identified in Figure 2.4 as following a cost leadership strategy. Update the data for eBay™ if more recent annual figures are available and get comparable data for at least one other firm from the set of firms listed in Figure 2.4. (You can get financial data about most companies by looking on their website for a link called investor relations or about the company. If necessary search the index or site map.)

a. Create a spreadsheet based on these data. Your spreadsheet should include measures of percentage change in revenues, earnings per share and stock price. You should also compute the price earnings (PE) ratio, that is stock price divided by earnings per share. (Note that some companies may have no earning for a particular year so that the PE ratio cannot be computed for that year.)

b. Create appropriate graphs highlighting trends in the performance of each company.

c. Write a brief (one page) report addressing how successful each company appears to be in maintaining strategic advantage? How important were general market conditions in affecting the financial performance of your companies?

Table 2.1	Year	Net Revenue (in millions)	Earnings per Share	Stock Price (at Year End)
eBay's financial performance.	1998	$186.129	$0.05	$40.21
	1999	224.724	0.08	62.59
	2000	431.424	0.17	33.00

4. Just-in-Time Inventory Systems for Pinnacle Manufacturing

Pinnacle Manufacturing is evaluating a proposal for the development of a new inventory management system that will allow it to use just-in-time techniques to manage the inventories of key raw materials. It is estimated that the new system will allow Pinnacle to operate with inventory levels for gadgets, widgets, and sprockets equaling 10 days of production and with inventories equaling only 5 days of production for cams and gizmos. In order to estimate the inventory cost savings from this system, you have been asked to gather information about current inventory levels at all of Pinnacle's production facilities. You have received estimates of the current inventory level of each raw material, the amount of each raw material used in a typical production day, and the average dollar value of a unit of each raw material. These estimates are shown in Table 2.2.

a. Create a spreadsheet based on estimates below. Your spreadsheet should include a column showing the number of days of inventory of each raw material currently held (inventory value divided by inventory used per production day). It should also include columns showing the inventory needed under the new system (inventory used per day times 10 or 5) and the reduction in inventory under the new system for each raw material. Finally you should include columns showing the dollar value of existing inventories, the dollar value of inventories under the new system, and the reduction in dollar value of the inventories held.

b. Assume that the annual cost of holding inventory is 10 percent times the level of inventory held. Add a summary showing the overall annual savings from the new system.

Table 2.2	Item	Inventory (units)	Units Used per Day	Cost per Unit
Pinnacle's inventory estimates.	Gadget	2,437,250	97,645	$2.25
	Widget	3,687,450	105,530	0.85
	Sprocket	1,287,230	29,632	3.25
	Cam	2,850,963	92,732	1.28
	Gizmo	6,490,325	242,318	2.60

GM, Fidelity Investments, and Staples: Expanding Strategic Web-Based Alliances

GM and Fidelity

One day in the middle of 2000, General Motors chairman John Smith was chatting with Edward C. Johnson, chairman and CEO of Fidelity Investments, which administers GM's employee savings program. Smith mentioned Virtual Advisor, a voice-enabled information-delivery system from GM subsidiary OnStar Corp. Johnson said Fidelity was looking at wireless systems to keep clients informed anytime, anywhere. Nine months later, Fidelity and GM announced an alliance that lets GM's 800,000 OnStar subscribers monitor their investments (and will eventually let them buy and sell stocks) from behind the wheel. But how much the pact will contribute to either firm's bottom line remains to be seen.

Business alliances among not-so-obvious allies are skyrocketing. According to Booz, Allen & Hamilton, the 1,000 largest U.S. companies earned less than 2 percent of their total revenue from alliances in 1980. By 1996, that percentage had hit 19 percent, and by 2002, it's slated to reach 35 percent. If you rely on the press releases that announce such partnerships, the reasons for them are many and convincing: cost reduction in the supply chain, access to new markets, and the opportunity to share in another respected company's reputation.

For example, GM gets free content for its in-car information service; and Fidelity wins access to more than 800,000 commuters who spend an average of 90 minutes per day in their cars. Under the GM–Fidelity agreement, subscribers to OnStar—GM's in-vehicle information-delivery system, which offers such services as stolen-vehicle tracking, emergency assistance, and directions—can manage their Fidelity accounts through Virtual Advisor, OnStar's hands-free interface. Initially launched in the Northeast, the program is expected to be available nationwide this summer.

"We're adding a new service to Virtual Advisor that we didn't have to build," says Mike Peterson, GM's director of the program. "We offered a distribution channel; they offered a service that's attractive to customers." Joseph Ferra, a senior vice president at Fidelity, says the investment firm wanted to establish a leadership position in a place where lots of people spend lots of time: their cars. "When you peel all the technology away, it's about improved customer service," he says, "We're expanding the ways customers can remain informed—anytime, in any mode."

Staples and Partners

When Staples decided to expand its website, Staples.com, one major goal for the Framingham, Massachusetts-based office supply retailer was to increase its product offerings without taking its eye off its core business: its 1,100 retail stores. Establishing partnerships was the way to accomplish that goal, according to Staples.com chief technology officer Mike Ragunas. "In our catalog, we've got 8,000 items," he says. "At Staples.com, we've integrated with wholesalers and manufacturers to offer 45,000."

Staples.com is seeking to limit its IT investment by acting as a portal to partners' websites, rather than linking to their order entry systems or creating a shared data center. This is especially notable at the company's business services center. Through this portal, Staples customers can do everything from insuring company cars to hiring debt-collection agencies.

Staples.com's partners bear the burden of making sure their websites can handle the traffic Staples sends their way. "We do not ask them to share our cost to create supporting content," Ragunas says. "The partners provide their own infrastructure . . . They have got to do their own build out." Staples.com and its partners don't share IT staff other than for network monitoring.

Here's where the monitoring comes in: When Staples.com executives were building the Web-based business services portal, one major worry was that poor service from any of the 35 partners, which tend to be young, small companies, could reflect badly on Staples. "With all those third parties, we needed to make sure they met our standards," Ragunas says.

Staples.com's solution is wide-ranging. For starters, the company "mystery shops" its own partners and grades them on timely response, politeness, and general customer service. Naturally, the partners know of this practice; they just don't know which calls are from Staples. Staples.com also performs network monitoring and usability testing of its partners' websites, each of which receives a weekly report card and any applicable customer comments. "Its almost like free consulting for these companies," Ragunas says. And, when a partner's score falls below a certain level, Staples.com representatives visit the laggard and help coach its customer service team.

Staples.com wouldn't say how much it spends on controlling the quality of these partnerships, but J. B. Lyon, vice president of business services, says the payoff is indisputable. In 1999, Staples.com's revenue was $94 million. Last year, following the launch of the business services portal, revenue grew to $512 million and repeat traffic increased by 287 percent. Lyon says the company's in-house studies show that the online services center was a major reason for the growth in repeat customers.

Case Study Questions

1. Why are Web-based technologies and e-business and e-commerce applications encouraging the growth of strategic alliances?

2. Do you see significant business and customer value in the Virtual Advisor application of GM and Fidelity? Explain your answer.

3. What are the benefits and challenges of using other companies as partners in an e-commerce website as Staples is doing? Visit www.staples.com to help you answer.

Source: Adapted from Steve Ulfelder, "Partners in Profit," *Computerworld ROI*, July/August 2001, pp. 25–28. Reprinted by permission.

Dell Computer and Litton:
Benefits and Challenges of B2B e-Commerce Strategies

More than once, Michael Dell has joked that the only thing more direct than the Internet is mental telepathy. He started moving Dell's business online in 1994. Three years later, Dell introduced its Premier Pages, an electronic catalog that allows corporate customers to purchase Dell machines over the Web. Those early efforts have enabled Dell to build its Internet sales to about $16 billion a year, accounting for half of its revenues.

But until the middle of last year, many of Dell's incoming corporate orders were still handled mainly by employees numbering in the hundreds. To cut that fat, Dell first had to make itself technologically capable of implanting itself more deeply into its business customers' electronic business systems. "It was obvious," Michael Dell says. "I don't want to overstate this as a brilliant blast."

Last year, Dell installed software from WebMethods, a maker of industrial-strength business-to-business integration software, based in Fairfax, Virginia. WebMethods' enterprise application integration (EAI) technology acts as a software translator and creates a kind of hub that, using the Web, allows instantaneous communication among networked companies' internal business systems.

For Dell, the first fruit of installing the WebMethods software is what Dell calls e-procurement, and it goes like this: A business customer pulls product information directly from Dell's server into the customer's purchasing system, which creates an electronic requisition. After the requisition is approved online by the customer, a computer-generated purchase order shoots over the Internet back to Dell.

The entire process can take 60 seconds. Dell says the system, which went live in the spring of 2000, has automatically cut errors in its procurement processes from about 200 per million transactions to 10 per million. And Dell has been able to shave $40 to $50 off the cost of processing each order. That adds up to $5 million a year in cost savings, since thousands of orders flow to Dell through its WebMethods system daily.

That system also looks good to business customers like David Capizzi, who joined Litton PRC three years ago as vice president for procurement. Litton makes big information technology systems that run things like the U.S. Treasury Department's human resources operation. Capizzi, a former contract manager with the U.S. Navy, was shocked by what he saw after he came onboard at Litton: It took an average of 16 days just to get a requisition to the purchasing honchos; getting a Dell PC took as long as a month.

Capizzi set about bringing Litton's procurement into the modern age, and Dell became one of its first partners in the effort. Litton hooked into Dell's new e-procurement system, and since July 2000, Litton employees have been able to log on to a Dell Premier Page and choose what they need from an online catalog that contains approved product configurations, options, and negotiated prices specific to Litton's account with Dell.

An order triggers a purchase requisition within Litton's internal system. If a manager does not act to approve or reject a requisition within 24 hours, it is routed to that person's manager for immediate response. After two approvals, the order goes to Dell, which starts building the machines. On average, delivery is two days after the order is placed.

For every early adopter like Litton, however, Dell faces many other partners who are skeptical—even though Dell is offering customers a sweet deal to sign on to its program. Often, a company that creates a WebMethods hub charges its customers to hook into it; the fees can run into the tens of thousands of dollars. Dell isn't charging its partners a penny to tie into its system.

Nonetheless, only about a dozen or so of Dell's thousands of corporate customers have signed up. Customers remain uncertain of the payoff, and there are costs involved, even with the free initial hookup. Tom Fountain, Dell's B2B chief, says that there are literally scores of different internal computer systems among Dell's customers. The WebMethods software that Dell uses can communicate with these disparate systems, but often not without some significant—and often expensive—customization that prospective B2B customers would have to incur.

But the PC industry and Dell's current major business challenges have only made Dell's push for efficiencies more urgent—the only way, really, for its last-man-standing strategy to succeed. So besides building automated factories, Dell is determined to weave customers and suppliers into its production network. In addition, Dell is experimenting with more exotic IT concepts such as data warehousing, event tracking, and demand shaping.

Ultimately, if Michael Dell is right, all these systems will merge to produce what he and several manufacturing gurus have come to call "frictionless trade." That's when a Web-enabled business enterprise automatically reacts to stimuli from hundreds of sources, makes thousands of adjustments in real time, and gets products to customers with whirlwind speed. Nowadays, no one in the industry is betting against Mr. Dell.

Case Study Questions

1. What are the strategic benefits and challenges of using the WebMethods technology for Dell and its business customers?

2. Does Litton's use of the Dell e-procurement system result in strategic or operational business benefits for the company? Explain your answer.

3. How realistic is a frictionless trade goal for Dell Computer? For other companies? Defend your position.

Management
Challenges

Business
Applications   M o d u l e   Information
II   Technologies

Development   Foundation
Processes   Concepts

Module II

Information Technologies

What challenges do information system technologies pose for business professionals? What basic knowledge should you possess about information technology? The four chapters of this module give you an overview of some of the major technologies used in e-business systems and their implications for business managers and professionals.

- **Chapter 3: Computer Hardware,** reviews trends and developments in microcomputer, midrange, and mainframe computer systems; basic computer system concepts; and the major types of technologies used in peripheral devices for computer input, output, and storage.

- **Chapter 4: Computer Software,** reviews the basic features and trends in the major types of application software and system software used to support enterprise and end user computing.

- **Chapter 5: Data Resource Management,** emphasizes management of the data resources of computer-using organizations. This chapter reviews key database management concepts and applications in business information systems.

- **Chapter 6: Telecommunications and Networks,** presents an overview of telecommunications networks, applications, and trends, and reviews technical telecommunications alternatives.

Management
Challenges

Business
Applications

Module
II

Information
Technologies

Development
Processes

Foundation
Concepts

Chapter 3

Computer Hardware

Chapter Outline

Learning Objectives

After reading and studying this chapter, you should be able to:

1. Identify the major types, trends, and uses of microcomputer, midrange, and mainframe computer systems.

2. Outline the major technologies and uses of computer peripherals for input, output, and storage.

3. Identify and give examples of the components and functions of a computer system.

4. Identify the computer systems and peripherals you would acquire or recommend for a business of your choice, and explain the reasons for your selections.

Section I

Computer Systems: End User and Enterprise Computing

All computers are systems of input, processing, output, storage, and control components. In this section, we will discuss the trends, applications, and some basic concepts of the many types of computer systems in use today. In Section II, we will cover the changing technologies for input, output, and storage that are provided by the peripheral devices that are part of modern computer systems.

Analyzing Boeing, Monster.com, and Others

Read the Real World Case of Boeing, Monster.com, and Others on the next page. We can learn a lot about the criteria and concerns of corporate PC buyers from this case. See Figure 3.1.

This case emphasizes that companies like Boeing, Monster.com, and others, focus on criteria that lower their total cost of ownership (TCO). Corporate buyers relegate low purchase price and the latest PC technology to secondary status in their purchasing decisions. Instead, they emphasize criteria like good performance at a reasonable price, readiness for future operating system versions, and connectivity. Corporate buyers also focus on less tangible criteria like the ease of purchase and deployment, a stable product line, and vendor service and support. Unless these criteria are met, the total cost of ownership for purchase, software updates, networking, training, user support, maintenance, and administration of PC systems for most companies will far outweigh any benefits provided by a low purchase price or advanced technical features.

Trends in Computer Systems

Today's computer systems come in a variety of sizes, shapes, and computing capabilities. Rapid hardware and software developments and changing end user needs continue to drive the emergence of new models of computers, from the smallest hand-held *personal digital assistant* for end users, to the largest multiple-CPU mainframe for the enterprise.

Figure 3.1

Joe Puglisi, CIO at EMCOR Group, rates uniform and consistent product lines, online order tracking, and quick delivery as key criteria when making PC purchase decisions.

Source: Seth Resnick

Boeing, Monster.com, and Others:
Corporate Criteria for Buying PC Systems

What do you look for in a new PC system? A big, bright screen? Zippy new processor? Capacious hard drive? Acres of RAM? Sorry, none of these is a real concern for corporate PC buyers. Numerous studies have shown that the price of a new computer is only a small part of the total cost of ownership (TCO). Support, maintenance, and other intangibles contribute far more heavily to the sum. Let's take a look.

Solid performance at a reasonable price. Corporate buyers know that their users probably aren't mapping the human genome or plotting trajectories to Saturn. They're doing word processing, order entry, sales contact management, and other essential business tasks. They need a solid, competent machine at a reasonable price, not the latest whiz-bang. "Mainstream machines from respected vendors are going to do the job fine," says Bob Jorgenson, a spokesman for The Boeing Co. in Seattle.

Operating system ready. "A change in an operating system is the most disruptive upgrade an enterprise has to face," says Paul Neilson, vice president of technical support at Monster.com, an online job-placement service in Maynard, Massachusetts. That's why many corporate buyers want their machines to be able to handle current operating systems and anticipated new ones. While many enterprises use Windows 9x or NT, they must be able to make a possible transition to Windows 2000 or XP, or even OS versions expected three to five years out. Primarily, that means deciding what hard disk space and RAM will be sufficient.

Connectivity. Networked machines are a given in corporate life, and Internet-worked machines are becoming a given. Buyers need machines equipped with reliable network interface cards or even wireless LAN capabilities. "With fewer cables to worry about, wireless LANs, especially when combined with laptop PCs, contribute to the flexibility of the workplace and the simplicity of PC deployment," says Matt Heller, vice president of operations at GoTo.com Inc. in Pasadena, California, which provides online search services to tens of thousands of affiliate companies. Many organizations are planning for Internet-based applications and need machines ready to make fast, reliable and secure connections. "Connection performance and ports are prime factors for us," says Chris Carrara, IT manager at Sartorious AG, a global lab technology manufacturer in Goettingen, Germany.

Ease of purchase and deployment. Buyers want purchasing to be an easy process, and you'd think vendors would feel the same way. However, while some vendors have made great efforts in smoothing the potholes in their ordering processes, others haven't. Vendors that offer online ordering and extranet support for customers are more appealing to buyers. "The ability to track orders online from inception to delivery is a plus," says Joe Puglisi, CIO at EMCOR Group, Inc., a global construction conglomerate in Norwalk, Connecticut. Dell Computer Corp. is one supplier that offers such tracking. Speed of delivery aids in rapid deployment to employees, and international delivery boosts global rollouts.

Besides getting it fast, corporate buyers want to get it right, too. Vendors that offer buyer-specific hardware configurations, such as Compaq Computer Corp. and Dell, earn the gold stars here. "It's important that we are able to supply standard configurations to remote sales partners with nationwide support," says Rick Beardsley, IT director at Indoff Inc., a drop-ship distributor in St. Louis. Software preconfiguration also saves time and ensures uniformity. "Dell allows us to create an image of all required software—operating system, office applications, even our own customized and proprietary apps—which they then load onto machines before they ship," says Neilson of Monster.com. This saves the systems folks from loading and testing the software themselves before handing it off to the employees.

Stable platform. All this preconfigured software isn't worth a whistle if a product line changes or, even worse, ceases production. Corporate buyers like product lines that don't change, which seems counter to the vendor tendency to constantly tweak and fiddle with machines in the never-ending race to be, momentarily, the best. "We prefer product lines that are uniform and consistent," says Puglisi of EMCOR.

Beardsley of Indoff concurs, adding, "Ideally, we favor machines we can keep buying for at least 18 months." You can't blame them. Every component change means another driver to keep track of, another wrinkle in service and support, another potential glitch to bog down IT staffers and rev up the cost meter.

Service and support. Corporate buyers aren't interested in 90-minute waits when they call a vendor's tech support hotline. If they don't get fast and accurate resolutions of all difficulties, they'll take their business elsewhere. And vendor support should be ubiquitous. If a corporate buyer sees a vendor with only a handful of service locations, he's going to look for another vendor. Organizations want to make sure that their users can get service wherever they may be, especially on the road. Some vendors arrange for extranet support so remote users can obtain access to software and other files from the Web. That can save a lot of time and difficulties on both ends.

Case Study Questions

1. Rank the corporate criteria for buying PC systems in their order of importance to a business. What are some of the business reasons behind your rankings?

2. Do the corporate criteria for buying PCs apply to small businesses in the same way? Why or why not?

3. Do the corporate criteria for buying PCs differ from those for buying a PC for your own use? Why or why not?

Source: Adapted from Edmund DeJesus, "Building PCs for the Enterprise," *Computerworld*, May 7, 2001, pp. 62–64. Reprinted by permission.

Figure 3.2   Examples of computer system categories.

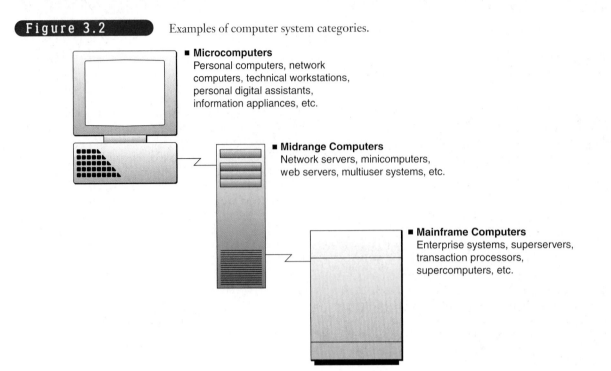

■ **Microcomputers**
Personal computers, network
computers, technical workstations,
personal digital assistants,
information appliances, etc.

■ **Midrange Computers**
Network servers, minicomputers,
web servers, multiuser systems, etc.

■ **Mainframe Computers**
Enterprise systems, superservers,
transaction processors,
supercomputers, etc.

Categories such as *mainframe, midrange computers,* and *microcomputers* are still used to help us express the relative processing power and number of end users that can be supported by different types of computers. But as Figure 3.2 illustrates, these are not precise classifications, and they do overlap each other. Thus, other names are commonly given to highlight the major uses of particular types of computers. Examples include personal computers, network servers, network computers, and technical workstations.

In addition, experts continue to predict the merging or disappearance of several computer categories. They feel, for example, that many midrange and mainframe systems have been made obsolete by the power and versatility of *client/server* networks of end user microcomputers and servers. Most recently, some industry experts have predicted that the emergence of network computers and *information appliances* for applications on the Internet and corporate intranets will replace many personal computers, especially in large organizations and in the home computer market. Only time will tell whether such predictions will equal the expectations of industry forecasters.

Computer Generations

It is important to realize that major changes and trends in computer systems have occurred during the major stages—or **generations**—of computing, and will continue into the future. The first generation of computers developed in the early 1950s, the second generation blossomed during the late 1960s, the third generation took computing into the 1970s, and the fourth generation has been the computer technology of the 1980s and 1990s. A fifth generation of computing systems and devices that accelerates the trends of the previous generations is expected to evolve in the early 21st century. Figure 3.3 highlights trends in the characteristics and capabilities of computers. Notice that computers continue to become smaller, faster, more reliable, less costly to purchase and maintain, and more interconnected within computer networks.

Whether we are moving into a *fifth generation* of computing is a subject of debate since the concept of generations may no longer fit the continual, rapid changes occurring in computer hardware, software, data, and networking technologies. But

Figure 3.3   Major trends in computer system capabilities.

	First Generation	Second Generation	Third Generation	Fourth Generation	Fifth Generation?
SIZE (Typical computers)	Room Size Mainframe	Closet Size Mainframe	Desk-Size Minicomputer	Desktop and Laptop Microcomputers	Networked Computers of all sizes
NETWORKING	None	Mainframe-Based Networks of Video Terminals	Mainframe and Minicomputer–Based Networks	Local Area and Client/Server Networks	The Internet, Intranets, and Extranets
CIRCUITRY	Vacuum Tubes	Transistors	Integrated Semi-conductor Circuits	Large-Scale Inte-grated (LSI) Semi-conductor Circuits	Very-Large-Scale Integrated (VLSI) Semiconductor Circuits
DENSITY (Circuits per component)	One	Hundreds	Thousands	Hundreds of Thousands	Millions
SPEED (Instructions/second)	Hundreds	Thousands	Millions	Tens of Millions	Billions
RELIABILITY (Failure of circuits)	Hours	Days	Weeks	Months	Years
MEMORY (Capacity in characters)	Thousands	Tens of Thousands	Hundreds of Thousands	Millions	Billions
COST (Per million instructions)	$10	$1.00	$.10	$.001	$.0001

in any case, we can be sure that progress in computing will continue to accelerate, and that the development of Internet-based technologies and applications will be one of the major forces driving computing in the 21st century.

Microcomputer Systems

The entire center of gravity in computing has shifted. For millions of consumers and business users, the main function of desktop PCs is as a window to the Internet. Computers are now communications devices, and consumers want them to be as cheap as possible [5].

Microcomputers are the most important category of computer systems for businesspeople and consumers. Though usually called a *personal computer*, or PC, a microcomputer is much more than a small computer for use by an individual. The computing power of microcomputers now exceeds that of the mainframes of previous computer generations at a fraction of their cost. Thus, they have become powerful networked *professional workstations* for business professionals.

Microcomputers come in a variety of sizes and shapes for a variety of purposes, as Figure 3.4 illustrates. For example, PCs are available as hand-held, notebook, laptop, portable, desktop, and floor-standing models. Or, based on their use, they include home, personal, professional, workstation, and multiuser systems. Most microcomputers are *desktops* designed to fit on an office desk, or *laptops* for those

Figure 3.4

Examples of microcomputer systems.

a. A notebook microcomputer.
Source: Stone.

b. The microcomputer as a professional workstation.
Source: Mug Shots-The Stock Market.

c. The microcomputer as a technical workstation.
Source: Andy Sacks/Stone.

who want a small, portable PC for their work activities. Figure 3.5 offers advice on some of the key features you should consider in acquiring a high-end workstation, multimedia PC, or beginner's system. This should give you some idea of the range of features available in today's microcomputers.

Some microcomputers are powerful **workstation computers** (technical workstations) that support applications with heavy mathematical computing and graphics display demands such as computer-aided design (CAD) in engineering, or investment and portfolio analysis in the securities industry. Other microcomputers are used as **network servers.** They are usually more powerful microcomputers that coordinate telecommunications and resource sharing in small local area networks (LANs), and Internet and intranet websites.

Network Computers

Network computers (NCs) are emerging as a serious business computing platform. NCs are known as *thin clients,* as compared to traditional *fat client* full-featured PCs. Somewhere in between are stripped-down PCs known as **NetPCs** or *legacy-free PCs,* designed for the Internet and a limited range of applications within a company. Examples are Compaq's iPaq, HP's e-PC, and eMachine's eOne. See Figure 3.6.

Figure 3.5   Recommended features for the three types of PC users.

Financial Pro	Multimedia Heavy	Newcomer
To track the market's every tremor, you'll need more than just a fast machine:	Media pros and dedicated amateurs will want at least a Mac G4 or a 750 MHz Intel chip, and:	Save money with a Celeron processor in the 500 MHz range. Also look for:
• 1 to 2 Gigahertz processor	• 30 GB hard drive or more	• 64MB RAM
• 128MB or 256MB RAM	• 18-inch or larger flat-screen CRT or flat-panel LCD	• 10 GB hard drive
• Cable-modem or DSL Internet connection	• High-end color printer	• Internal 56K modem
• 18-inch flat-panel display	• DVD-RAM or CD-RW drive	• 24X CD-ROM drive
• CD-RW drive for backup	• Deluxe speaker system	• Basic inkjet printer

Source: Adapted from "Rev Up for the Web," Technology Buyers Guide, *Fortune*, Summer 2000, p. 106.

Network computers are a microcomputer category designed primarily for use with the Internet and corporate intranets by clerical workers, operational employees, and knowledge workers with specialized or limited computing applications. NCs are low-cost, sealed, networked microcomputers with no or minimal disk storage. Users of NCs depend primarily on Internet and intranet servers for their operating system and Web browser, Java-enabled application software, and data access and storage. Examples include the Sun Ray 1, IBM Network Station, and the NCD Explora network computers. See Figure 3.7.

One of the main attractions of network computers is their lower cost of purchase, upgrades, maintenance, and support compared to full-featured PCs. Other benefits to business include ease of software distribution and licensing, computing platform standardization, reduced end user support requirements, and improved manageability through centralized management and enterprisewide control of computer network resources [4].

Figure 3.6

Comparing the network computer to the NetPC and the network terminal.

Network Computer

- Operating system, application software, and data storage are provided by Internet, intranet, or extranet servers
- Uses a web browser and can process Java-enabled software applications called *applets*
- Managed remotely and centrally by network servers
- Generally has no hard disk drive

NetPC (Legacy-free PC)

- Works like a PC, with its own software
- Has a hard drive, but may have no floppy drive or CD-ROM
- Box may have no expansion slots or serial or parallel ports
- Operating system and applications are managed centrally by network servers

Network Terminal

- An inexpensive terminal-like device without its own disk storage
- Depends on the servers in a network for most of its processing power
- Multiuser version of Windows 2000, Linux, or Unix as the server operating system
- Microsoft Office or Sun StarOffice-like multiuser software on the Internet or intranet Web server

Figure 3.7
information

Examples of a network computer: the Sun Ray 1 enterprise appliance (left), and an appliance, the Netpliance i-opener.

Source: Sun Microsystems.

Source: Netpliance.

Information Appliances

PCs aren't the only option: A host of smart gadgets and information appliances—from cellular phones and pagers to hand-held PCs and Web-based game machines—promise Internet access and the ability to perform basic computational chores [5].

Hand-held microcomputer devices known as **personal digital assistants** (PDAs) are some of the most popular devices in the **information appliance category.** PDAs use touch screens, pen-based handwriting recognition, or keypads so mobile workers can send and receive e-mail, access the Web, and exchange information such as appointments, to-do lists, and sales contacts with their desktop PCs or Web servers.

Information appliances may also take the form of *set-top boxes* and video-game consoles that connect to your home TV set. These devices enable you to surf the World Wide Web or send and receive e-mail and watch TV programs or play video games at the same time. An example is the Sony or Philips WebTV Plus Receiver, which uses Microsoft's WebTV network service. Other information appliances include wireless PDAs and cellular and PCS phones and wired telephone-based home appliances that can send and receive e-mail and access the Web.

Computer Terminals

Computer terminals are undergoing a major conversion to networked computer devices. *Dumb terminals*, which are keyboard/video monitor devices with limited processing capabilities, are being replaced by *intelligent terminals*, which are modified networked PCs, network computers, or other thin clients. Also included are **network terminals,** which may be *Windows terminals*, that are dependent on network servers for Windows software, processing power, and storage, or *Internet terminals*, which depend on Internet or intranet website servers for their operating systems and application software.

Intelligent terminals take many forms and can perform data entry and some information processing tasks independently. This includes the widespread use of **transaction terminals** in banks, retail stores, factories, and other work sites. Examples are automated teller machines (ATMs), factory production recorders, and retail point-of-sale (POS) terminals. These intelligent terminals use keypads, touch screens, and other input methods to capture data and interact with end users during a transaction, while relying on servers or other computers in the network for further transaction processing.

Figure 3.8

Hundreds of rack-mounted servers help power a Sun Microsystems iForce Center Internet hosting facility.

Source: Sun Microsystems.

Midrange Computer Systems

Midrange computers, including high-end network servers and minicomputers, are multiuser systems that can manage networks of PCs and terminals. Though not as powerful as mainframe computers, they are less costly to buy, operate, and maintain than mainframe systems, and thus meet the computing needs of many organizations. See Figure 3.8.

> *Burgeoning data warehouses and related applications such as data mining and online analytical processing are forcing IT shops into higher and higher levels of server configurations. Similarly, Internet-based applications, such as Web servers and electronic commerce, are forcing IT managers to push the envelope of processing speed and storage capacity and other [business] applications, fueling the growth of high-end servers* [17].

Midrange computers have become popular as powerful **network servers** to help manage large Internet websites, corporate intranets and extranets, and client/server networks. Electronic commerce and other business uses of the Internet are popular high-end server applications, as are integrated enterprisewide manufacturing, distribution, and financial applications. Other applications, like data warehouse management, data mining, and online analytical processing (which we discuss in Chapters 6 and 13), are contributing to the growth of high-end servers and other midrange systems [17].

Midrange computers first became popular as **minicomputers** for scientific research, instrumentation systems, engineering analysis, and industrial process monitoring and control. Minicomputers could easily handle such uses because these applications are narrow in scope and do not demand the processing versatility of mainframe systems. Thus, midrange computers serve as industrial process-control and manufacturing plant computers, and they still play a major role in computer-aided manufacturing (CAM). They can also take the form of powerful technical workstations for computer-aided design (CAD) and other computation and graphics-intensive applications. Midrange computers are also used as *front-end computers* to assist mainframe computers in telecommunications processing and network management.

Mainframe Computer Systems

Several years after dire pronouncements that the mainframe was dead, quite the opposite is true: Mainframe usage is actually on the rise. And it's not just a short-term blip. One factor that's been driving mainframe sales is cost reductions [of 35 percent or more]. Price reductions aren't the only factor fueling mainframe acquisitions. IS organizations are teaching the old dog new tricks by putting mainframes at the center stage of emerging applications such as data mining and warehousing, decision support, and a variety of Internet-based applications, most notably electronic commerce [17].

Mainframe computers are large, fast, and powerful computer systems. For example, mainframes can process hundreds of million instructions per second (MIPS). Mainframes also have large primary storage capacities. Their main memory capacity can range from hundreds of megabytes to many gigabytes of primary storage. And mainframes have slimmed down drastically in the last few years, dramatically reducing their air-conditioning needs, electrical power consumption, and floor space requirements, and thus their acquisition and operating costs. Most of these improvements are the result of a move from water-cooled mainframes to a newer air-cooled technology for mainframe systems [15]. See Figure 3.9.

Thus, mainframe computers continue to handle the information processing needs of major corporations and government agencies with high transaction processing volumes or complex computational problems. For example, major international banks, airlines, oil companies, and other large corporations process millions of sales transactions and customer inquiries each day with the help of large mainframe systems. Mainframes are still used for computation-intensive applications such as analyzing seismic data from oil field explorations or simulating flight conditions in designing aircraft. Mainframes are also widely used as *superservers* for the large client/server networks and high-volume Internet websites of large companies. And as previously mentioned, mainframes are becoming a popular business

Figure 3.9

This new IBM eServer z900 mainframe computer processes up to 2.5 billion instructions per second.

Source: IBM Corporation.

computing platform for data mining and warehousing, and electronic commerce applications [15].

Supercomputer Systems

Supercomputers have now become "scalable servers" at the top end of the product lines that start with desktop workstations. Market-driven companies, like Silicon Graphics, Hewlett-Packard, and IBM, have a much broader focus than just building the world's fastest computer, and the software of the desktop computer has a much greater overlap with that of the supercomputer than it used to, because both are built from the same cache-based microprocessors [12].

The term **supercomputer** describes a category of extremely powerful computer systems specifically designed for scientific, engineering, and business applications requiring extremely high speeds for massive numeric computations. The market for supercomputers includes government research agencies, large universities, and major corporations. They use supercomputers for applications such as global weather forecasting, military defense systems, computational cosmology and astronomy, microprocessor research and design, large-scale data mining, and so on.

Supercomputers use *parallel processing* architectures of interconnected microprocessors (which can execute many instructions at the same time in parallel). They can perform arithmetic calculations at speeds of billions of floating-point operations per second (*gigaflops*). Teraflop (1 trillion floating-point operations per second) supercomputers, which use advanced massively parallel processing (MPP) designs of thousands of interconnected microprocessors, are becoming available. Purchase prices for large supercomputers are in the $5 million to $50 million range.

However, the use of symmetric multiprocessing (SMP) and distributed shared memory (DSM) designs of smaller numbers of interconnected microprocessors has spawned a breed of *minisupercomputers* with prices that start in the hundreds of thousands of dollars. For example IBM's RS/6000 SP starts at $150,000 for a one-processing-node SMP computer. However, it can be expanded to hundreds of processing nodes, which drives its price into the tens of millions of dollars. For example, Blue Horizon, an IBM RS/6000 SP with 156 processing nodes and a total of 1,152 Power 3+ microprocessors, was installed at the San Diego Supercomputer Center during 2000. The system cost $50 million (less a substantial education discount), and has a peak processing capacity of 1.7 teraflops [18]. Thus, supercomputers continue to advance the state of the art for the entire computer industry. See Figure 3.10.

Technical Note: The Computer System Concept

As a business professional, you do not need a detailed technical knowledge of computers. However, you do need to understand some basic concepts about computer systems. This should help you be an informed and productive user of computer system resources.

A computer is more than a high-powered collection of electronic devices performing a variety of information processing chores. A computer is a *system*, an interrelated combination of components that performs the basic system functions of input, processing, output, storage, and control, thus providing end users with a powerful information processing tool. Understanding the computer as a **computer system** is vital to the effective use and management of computers. You should be able to visualize any computer this way, from the smallest microcomputer device, to a large computer network whose components are interconnected by telecommunications network links throughout a building complex or geographic area.

Figure 3.11 illustrates that a computer is a system of hardware devices organized according to the following system functions:

- **Input.** The input devices of a computer system include keyboards, touch screens, pens, electronic mouses, optical scanners, and so on. They convert

Figure 3.10

This Blue Horizon IBM RS/6000 SP at the University of California at San Diego Supercomputer Center, is one of the most powerful supercomputers in the world.

Source: UCSDSC.

data into electronic form for direct entry or through a telecommunications network into a computer system.

● **Processing.** The **central processing unit** (CPU) is the main processing component of a computer system. (In microcomputers, it is the **main microprocessor.** See Figure 3.12.) Conceptually, the circuitry of a CPU can be subdivided into two major subunits: the arithmetic-logic unit and the control

Figure 3.11   The computer system concept. A computer is a system of hardware components and functions.

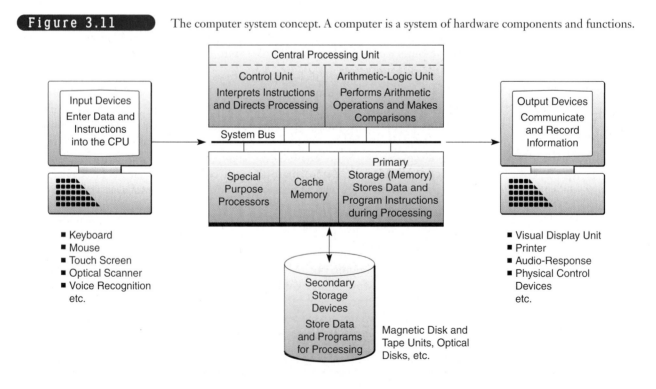

Figure 3.12

This Intel Pentium 4 microprocessor operates at 1.5 GHz clock speeds, and features 256K of cache memory and a Rapid Execution Engine with dual arithmetic-logic units that execute basic instructions at twice the clock speed of the core processor.

Source: Intel Corporation.

unit. It is the electronic circuits of the **arithmetic-logic** unit that perform the arithmetic and logic functions required to execute software instructions. The CPU also includes circuitry for devices such as *registers* and *cache memory* for high-speed, temporary storage of instruction and data elements, and may include various subsidiary processors.

- **Output.** The output devices of a computer system include video display units, printers, audio response units, and so on. They convert electronic information produced by the computer system into human-intelligible form for presentation to end users.

- **Storage.** The storage function of a computer system takes place in the storage circuits of the computer's **primary storage unit,** or *memory,* supported by **secondary storage** devices such as magnetic disk and optical disk drives. These devices store data and software instructions needed for processing.

- **Control.** The control unit of a CPU is the control component of a computer system. Its circuits interpret software instructions and transmit directions to the other components of the computer system.

Computer Processing Speeds

How fast are computer systems? Early computer operating speeds were measured in **milliseconds** (thousandths of a second) and **microseconds** (millionths of a second). Now computers operate in the **nanosecond** (billionth of a second) range, with **picosecond** (trillionth of a second) speed being attained by some computers. Such speeds seem almost incomprehensible. For example, an average person taking one step each nansecond would circle the earth about 20 times in one second!

We have already mentioned the *teraflop* speeds of some supercomputers. However, most computers can now process program instructions at *million instructions per second* (MIPS) speeds. Another measure of processing speed is *megahertz* (MHz), or millions of cycles per second, and *gigahertz* (GHz), or billions of cycles per second. This rating is commonly called the *clock speed* of a microprocessor, since it is used to rate microprocessors by the speed of their timing circuits or internal clock.

However, such ratings can be misleading indicators of the effective processing speed of microprocessors. That's because processing speed depends on a variety of factors including the size of circuitry paths, or *buses* that interconnect microprocessor components; the capacity of instruction processing *registers;* the use of high-speed *memory caches;* and the use of specialized microprocessors such as a math co-processor to do arithmetic calculations faster.

| Section II | # Computer Peripherals: Input, Output, and Storage Technologies |

The right peripherals can make all the difference in your computing experience. A top-quality monitor will be easier on your eyes—and may change the way you work. A scanner can edge you closer to that ever-elusive goal—the paperless office. Backup-storage systems can offer bank-vault security against losing your work. CD-ROM drives can be essential for education and entertainment. Memory cards, 3-D graphics, and other devices will help you configure your computer to meet your needs. Some may be the digital equivalent of chrome bumpers and tailfins, but the right choice of peripherals can make a big difference [10].

Analyzing Dresdner Bank and Wyndham International

Read the Real World Case Dresdner Bank and Wyndham International on the next page. We can learn a lot about the trade-offs between big centralized servers and small local servers from this case. See Figure 3.13.

The practice of placing small server computer systems throughout an organization's computer network is being reversed in many companies. Instead, they are reducing the number of local servers and consolidating many server functions into a smaller number of large networked servers that can be managed centrally. Companies expect big savings in hardware and reduced training and travel costs for server administrative and maintenance personnel. However, this must be balanced by the increased risk of system failure affecting more users and vital business processes, so increased server security and redundancy must be designed into these more-centralized systems. That's why most companies doing server consolidation continue to use a mix of large central servers and smaller servers in each branch office and other local sites.

Peripherals

A computer is just a high-powered "processing box" without peripherals. **Peripherals** is the generic name given to all input, output, and secondary storage devices that are part of a computer system. Peripherals depend on direct connections or

| Figure 3.13 |

Anthony Wilbert, systems manager at Dresdner Bank, is leading the bank's move to consolidate the thousands of servers in its worldwide network.

Source: Herman Bredehorst/Liaison Agency

Dresdner Bank and Wyndham International:
The Business Case for Server Consolidation

Think big. Or think small. Which is the best approach when it comes to managing IT resources? Well, one big idea currently percolating at Dresdner Bank AG focuses on thinking small. The Frankfurt-based bank is in the process of paring down the approximately 5,000 servers it maintains throughout Europe.

Depending on what's running at an individual branch, network administrators must manage a wide variety of server platforms, including IBM, Hewlett-Packard, and Sun Microsystems hardware running each vendor's flavor of Unix or Windows 2000. This IT potpourri evolved as the headquarters and branches added bits and pieces during the past decade, according to Anthony Wilbert, systems manager at Dresdner's IT services arm. "It's cheaper to have one big machine than hundreds of small machines," he says. However, Wilbert cautions that a big issue in consolidation decision making is factoring in the impact a server crash would have on the business and other system resources.

The bank's consolidation project began a year ago and will continue indefinitely. So far, the main result has been the installation of a Sun Enterprise 10000 server at headquarters. The bank's goal is to reduce its total number of servers, but Wilbert acknowledges that some branches will continue to run local applications on local servers.

Another "think small" advocate is Wyndham International Inc. in Dallas. The global hotel chain is putting the application that controls guest arrivals, departures, and billing onto two IBM eServer p680 computers running Unix. The same guest-management tasks used to require 165 servers scattered across 100 locations.

The Web helped push Wyndham to reevaluate the role that today's mega boxes play in a wide-ranging enterprise. A few years ago, the hotel chain picked Opera, a networked PC application from Columbia, Maryland–based Micros Systems Inc., as its guest-management system because the program allowed IT managers to upgrade and tune the program at all of its front desks from a central administrative center in Dallas. "We then wondered, 'If that's good at the workstation level, wouldn't it be good at the server level, too,'" recalls Gary Owen, vice president of IT operations.

Although companies expect to save costs through server consolidation—Wyndham estimates it will lower its hardware bills by as much as 40 percent in the coming year—learning to live with less comes with stumbling blocks. Managing fewer servers may be easier, but when things go wrong, everyone suffers, not just the workers at a single network node. Likewise, network scalability, security, and availability become so critical to a firm's health that there's almost no room for error.

Wyndham and Dresdner Bank aren't the only large companies pruning the tentacles of their client/server networks. Ten years ago, the placement of servers everywhere and anywhere was considered the best way to achieve high performance and computing availability. Nowadays, corporations are taking advantage of better networking gear, lower costs for high-end components like switches, and administrative tools that manage a small number of servers in central locations.

Companies start down the consolidation trail to reduce costs. Besides lower hardware costs, Wyndham expects to save "several hundred percent" over five years in reduced travel and training costs, according to a Wyndham spokesman.

Consolidation can also make networks more manageable. System performance monitor software like HP's OpenView, Computer Associates' Unicenter TNG, or Tivoli Systems' TM give administrators centralized control panels to keep servers and networks running at optimal speeds by monitoring performance and, in some cases, reallocating resources to break through bottlenecks.

Also, rather than buying high-end computing power packed into towers, many large companies are putting together racks of servers that fill a central data center much like the telecommunications gear that hums in communication closets. "By consolidating 50 one-processor servers into new-generation server racks, companies save not just on equipment costs but on the costs of power management and maintenance contracts," says Jonathan Eunice, principal server technology analyst at Illuminata, a technology research firm.

But companies with a large number of affiliated branches, such as Dresdner Bank, are often better served in a mixed environment. "Even today, a central data center is probably not good enough for, say, 800 offices," says Eunice. "You may really need a server in each branch. Here, distributed makes all the sense in the world. On the other hand, if you're dealing with a large office, as in an insurance company, where the network within a single building or campus is so reliable, so close to 100 percent available, then you don't really need servers on every floor, and you can have a single data center."

The crucial consideration, no matter how widely a company embraces consolidations, is system reliability. If all the computing resources are put in one basket, managers must watch that basket closely. "Really understand what service levels you want to provide," Eunice says. "Ask yourself what scalability will you need, how much headroom should you build into the system? Have you built in enough redundancy? Downtime is a huge no-no. If that server goes down, it's not just a local issue when your system is centralized."

Case Study Questions

1. What are the business and technical reasons why server consolidation is occurring in many large companies?

2. What are the potential problems that must be considered in a server consolidation strategy? How might they be solved?

3. Should a smaller business with several servers consider such a strategy? Why or why not?

Source: Adapted from Alan Joch, "Fewer Servers, Better Service," *Computerworld*, June 4, 2001, pp. 66, 67. Reprinted by permission.

Figure 3.14

Some advice about peripherals for a business PC.

Peripherals Checklist

- **Monitors.** Bigger is better for computer screens. Consider a 19-inch or 21-inch CRT monitor, or a 15-inch LCD flat panel display. That gives you much more room to display spreadsheets, Web pages, lines of text, open windows, etc. The clarity of a monitor's image is important, too. Look for models with at least an XGA resolution of 1024×768 pixels.

- **Printers.** Your choice is between laser printers or color inkjet printers. Lasers are better suited for high-volume business use. Moderately priced color inkjets provide high-quality images and are well-suited for reproducing photographs. Per-page costs are higher than for laser printers.

- **Scanners.** You'll have to decide between a compact, sheet-fed scanner or a flatbed model. Sheet-fed scanners will save desktop space, while bulkier flat-bed models provide higher speed and resolution. Resolution is a key measure of quality; you'll want at least 300 dpi.

- **Hard Disk Drives.** Bigger is better; as with closet space, you can always use the extra capacity. So go 5 to 10 gigabytes at the minimum, 30 gigabytes at the max.

- **CD-ROM and DVD Drives.** CD-ROM and DVD drives are becoming a necessity for software installation and multimedia applications. Consider a high-speed variable-speed model (20X to 32X) for faster, smoother presentations.

- **Backup Systems.** Essential. Don't compute without them. Removable mag disk cartridges (like the Iomega Zip and Jazz drives) are convenient and versatile, and fast too.

telecommunications links to the central processing unit of a computer system. Thus, all peripherals are **online** devices; that is, they are separate from, but can be electronically connected to and controlled by a CPU. (This is the opposite of **offline** devices that are separate from and not under the control of the CPU.) The major types of peripherals and media that can be part of a computer system are discussed in this section. See Figure 3.14.

Input Technology Trends

Figure 3.15 emphasizes that there has been a major trend toward the increased use of input technologies that provide a more **natural user interface** for computer users. You can now enter data and commands directly and easily into a computer system through pointing devices like electronic mice and touch pads, and technologies like optical scanning, handwriting recognition, and voice recognition. These developments have made it unnecessary to always record data on paper *source documents* (such as sales order forms, for example) and then keyboard the data into a computer in an additional data entry step. Further improvements in voice recognition and other technologies should enable an even more natural user interface in the future.

Figure 3.15

Input technology trends. Note the trend toward input methods that provide a more natural user interface.

	First Generation	Second Generation	Third Generation	Fourth Generation	Fifth Generation?
INPUT MEDIA/ METHOD	Punched Cards Paper Tape	Punched Cards	Key to Tape/Disk	Keyboard Data Entry Pointing Devices Optical Scanning	Voice Recognition Touch Devices Handwriting Recognition

TREND: Toward Direct Input Devices That Are More Natural and Easy to Use.

Pointing Devices

Keyboards are still the most widely used devices for entering data and text into computer systems. However, **pointing devices** are a better alternative for issuing commands, making choices, and responding to prompts displayed on your video screen. They work with your operating system's **graphical user interface** (GUI), which presents you with icons, menus, windows, buttons, bars, and so on, for your selection. For example, pointing devices such as electronic mouses and touchpads allow you to easily choose from menu selections and icon displays using point-and-click or point-and-drag methods. See Figure 3.16.

The **electronic mouse** is the most popular pointing device used to move the cursor on the screen, as well as to issue commands and make icon and menu selections. By moving the mouse on a desktop or pad, you can move the cursor onto an icon displayed on the screen. Pressing buttons on the mouse activates various activities represented by the icon selected.

The trackball, pointing stick, and touchpad are other pointing devices most often used in place of the mouse. A **trackball** is a stationary device related to the mouse. You turn a roller ball with only its top exposed outside its case to move the cursor on the screen. A **pointing stick** (also called a *trackpoint*) is a small button-like device, sometimes likened to the eraserhead of a pencil. It is usually centered one row above the space bar of a keyboard. The cursor moves in the direction of the pressure you place on the stick. The **touchpad** is a small rectangular touch-sensitive surface usually placed below the keyboard. The cursor moves in the direction your finger moves on the pad. Trackballs, pointing sticks, and touchpads are easier to use than a mouse for portable computer users and are thus built into most notebook computer keyboards.

Touch screens are devices that allow you to use a computer by touching the surface of its video display screen. Some touch screens emit a grid of infrared beams, sound waves, or a slight electric current that is broken when the screen is touched. The computer senses the point in the grid where the break occurs and responds with an appropriate action. For example, you can indicate your selection on a menu display by just touching the screen next to that menu item.

Figure 3.16

This IBM ThinkPad laptop microcomputer features a large LCD screen, built-in CD-ROM, floppy disk drives, stereo speakers, and a trackpoint pointing device.

Source: IBM Corporation.

Pen-Based Computing

Handwriting-recognition systems convert script into text quickly and are friendly to shaky hands as well as those of block-printing draftsmen. The pen is more powerful than the keyboard in many vertical markets, as evidenced by the popularity of pen-based devices in the utilities, service, and medical trades [10].

Pen-based computing technologies are being used in many hand-held computers and personal digital assistants. These small PCs and PDAs contain fast processors and software that recognizes and digitizes handwriting, handprinting, and hand drawing. They have a pressure-sensitive layer like a graphics pad under their slate-like liquid crystal display (LCD) screen. So instead of writing on a paper form fastened to a clipboard or using a keyboard device, you can use a pen to make selections, send e-mail, and enter handwritten data directly into a computer. See Figure 3.17.

A variety of other penlike devices are available. One example is the *digitizer pen* and *graphics tablet*. You can use the digitizer pen as a pointing device, or use it to draw or write on the pressure-sensitive surface of the graphics tablet. Your handwriting or drawing is digitized by the computer, accepted as input, displayed on its video screen, and entered into your application.

Speech Recognition Systems

Speech recognition is gaining popularity in the corporate world among nontypists, people with disabilities, and business travelers, and is most frequently used for dictation, screen navigation, and Web browsing [3].

Speech recognition promises to be the easiest method for data entry, word processing, and conversational computing, since speech is the easiest, most natural means of human communication. Speech input has now become technologically and economically feasible for a variety of applications. Early speech recognition products

Figure 3.17

Using a personal digital assistant (PDA) that accepts pen-based input for sales transaction processing.

Source: Jeff Sciortino.

Figure 3.18

Peter Corrales, owner of Barocco To Go in Greenwich Village, New York, ignores his PC keyboard and mouse to check inventory with voice recognition technology.

Source: IBM Corporation.

used *discrete speech recognition*, where you had to pause between each spoken word. New *continuous speech recognition* (CSR) software recognizes continuous, conversationally paced speech. See Figure 3.18.

Speech recognition systems digitize, analyze, and classify your speech and its sound patterns. The software compares your speech patterns to a database of sound patterns in its vocabulary and passes recognized words to your application software. Typically, speech recognition systems require training the computer to recognize your voice and its unique sound patterns in order to achieve a high degree of accuracy. Training such systems involves repeating a variety of words and phrases in a training session, as well as using the system extensively.

Examples of continuous speech recognition software are NaturallySpeaking by Dragon Systems, ViaVoice by IBM, VoiceXpress by Lernout & Hauspie, and FreeSpeech by Phillips. Most products have 30,000-word vocabularies expandable to 60,000 words, and sell for less than $200. Training to 95 percent accuracy may take several hours. Longer use, faster processors, and more memory make 99 percent accuracy possible [3].

Speech recognition devices in work situations allow operators to perform data entry without using their hands to key in data or instructions and to provide faster and more accurate input. For example, manufacturers use speech recognition systems for the inspection, inventory, and quality control of a variety of products; and airlines and parcel delivery companies use them for voice-directed sorting of baggage and parcels. Speech recognition can also help you operate your computer's operating systems and software packages through voice input of data and commands. For example, such software can be voice-enabled so you can send e-mail and surf the World Wide Web.

Speaker-independent voice recognition systems, which allow a computer to understand a few words from a voice it has never heard before, are being built into products and used in a growing number of applications. Examples include *voice-messaging computers*, which use speech recognition and voice response software to verbally guide an end user through the steps of a task in many kinds of activities. Typically, they enable computers to respond to verbal and Touch-Tone input over the telephone. Examples of applications include computerized telephone call switching, telemarketing surveys, bank pay-by-phone bill-paying services, stock quotations services, university registration systems, and customer credit and account balance inquiries.

Optical Scanning

Few people understand how much scanners can improve a computer system and make your work easier. Their function is to get documents into your computer with a minimum of time and hassle, transforming just about anything on paper—a letter, a logo, or a photograph—into the digital format that your PC can make sense of. Scanners can be a big help in getting loads of paper off your desk and into your PC [10].

Optical scanning devices read text or graphics and convert them into digital input for your computer. Thus, optical scanning enables the direct entry of data from source documents into a computer system. For example, you can use a compact desktop scanner to scan pages of text and graphics into your computer for desktop publishing and Web publishing applications. Or you can scan documents of all kinds into your system and organize them into folders as part of a *document management* library system for easy reference or retrieval.

There are many types of optical scanners, but they all employ photoelectric devices to scan the characters being read. Reflected light patterns of the data are converted into electronic impulses that are then accepted as input into the computer system. Compact desktop scanners have become very popular due to their low cost and ease of use with personal computer systems. However, larger, more expensive *flatbed scanners* are faster and provide higher resolution color scanning. See Figure 3.19.

Another optical scanning technology is called **optical character recognition** (OCR). OCR scanners can read the OCR characters and codes on merchandise tags, product labels, credit card receipts, utility bills, insurance premiums, airline tickets, and other documents. OCR scanners are also used to automatically sort mail, score tests, and process a wide variety of forms in business and government.

Figure 3.19

Using a flatbed scanner for desktop publishing.

Source: Melissa Farlow.

Figure 3.20

Using an optical scanning wand to read bar coding of inventory data.

Source: Image Bank.

Devices such as hand-held optical scanning **wands** are frequently used to read OCR coding on merchandise tags, product labels, and other media. Many business applications involve reading *bar coding*, a code that utilizes bars to represent characters. One common example is the Universal Product Code (UPC) bar coding that you see on product labels, product packaging, and merchandise tags. For example, the automated checkout scanners found in supermarkets read UPC bar coding. Supermarket scanners emit laser beams that are reflected off a UPC bar code. The reflected image is converted to electronic impulses that are sent to the in-store computer, where they are matched with pricing information. Pricing information is returned to the terminal, visually displayed, and printed on a receipt for the customer. See Figure 3.20.

Other Input Technologies

Magnetic stripe technology is a familiar form of data entry that helps computers read credit cards. The iron oxide coating of the magnetic stripe on the back of such cards can hold about 200 bytes of information. Customer account numbers can be recorded on the mag stripe so it can be read by bank ATMs, credit card authorization terminals, and many other types of magnetic stripe readers.

Smart cards that embed a microprocessor chip and several kilobytes of memory into debit, credit, and other cards are popular in Europe, and becoming available in the United States. One example is Holland, where over 8 million smart debit cards have been issued by Dutch banks. Smart debit cards enable you to store a cash balance on the card and electronically transfer some of it to others to pay for small items and services. The balance on the card can be replenished in ATMs or other terminals.

The smart debit cards used in Holland feature a microprocessor and either 8 or 16 kilobytes of memory, plus the usual magnetic stripe. The smart cards are widely used to make payments in parking meters, vending machines, newsstands, pay telephones, and retail stores [9].

Digital cameras represent another fast-growing set of input technologies. Digital still cameras and digital video cameras (digital camcorders) enable you to shoot, store, and download still photos or full motion video with audio into your PC. Then you can use image-editing software to edit and enhance the digitized images and include them in newsletters, reports, multimedia presentations, and Web pages [8].

Figure 3.21

Output technology trends. Note the trend from paper documents to more natural forms of video, audio, and multimedia output.

	First Generation	Second Generation	Third Generation	Fourth Generation	Fifth Generation?
OUTPUT MEDIA/ METHOD	Punched Cards Printed Reports and Documents	Punched Cards Printed Reports and Documents	Printed Reports and Documents Video Displays	Video Displays Audio Responses Printed Reports and Documents	Video Displays Voice Responses Hyperlinked Multimedia Documents

TREND: Toward Direct Output Methods That Communicate Naturally, Quickly, and Clearly.

The computer systems of the banking industry can magnetically read checks and deposit slips using **magnetic ink character recognition** (MICR) technology. Computers can thus sort and post checks to the proper checking accounts. Such processing is possible because the identification numbers of the bank and the customer's account are preprinted on the bottom of the checks with an iron oxide-based ink. The first bank receiving a check after it has been written must encode the amount of the check in magnetic ink on the check's lower right-hand corner. The MICR system uses 14 characters (the 10 decimal digits and 4 special symbols) of a standardized design. Equipment known as *reader-sorters* read a check by first magnetizing the magnetic ink characters and then sensing the signal induced by each character as it passes a reading head. In this way, data are electronically captured by the bank's computer systems.

Output Technologies and Trends

Computers provide information to you in a variety of forms. Figure 3.21 shows you the trends in output media and methods that have developed over the generations of computing. As you can see, video displays and printed documents have been, and still are, the most common forms of output from computer systems. But other natural and attractive output technologies such as **voice response** systems and multimedia output are increasingly found along with video displays in business applications.

For example, you have probably experienced the voice and audio output generated by speech and audio microprocessors in a variety of consumer products. Voice messaging software enables PCs and servers in voice mail and messaging systems to interact with you through voice responses. And of course, multimedia output is common on the websites of the Internet and corporate intranets.

Video Output

Of all the peripherals you can purchase for your system, a [video] monitor is the one addition that can make the biggest difference. Forget about faster processors, bigger hard drives, and the like. The fact is, the monitor is the part of your system you spend the most time interacting with . . . Invest in a quality monitor, and you'll be thankful every time you turn on your computer [10].

Video displays are the most common type of computer output. Most desktop computers rely on **video monitors** that use a *cathode ray tube* (CRT) technology similar to the picture tubes used in home TV sets. Usually, the clarity of the video display depends on the type of video monitor you use and the graphics circuit board installed in your computer. These can provide a variety of graphics modes of increasing capability. A high-resolution, flicker-free monitor is especially important if you spend a lot of time viewing multimedia on CDs or the Web, or the complex graphical displays of many software packages.

The biggest use of **liquid crystal displays** (LCDs) is to provide a visual display capability for portable microcomputers and PDAs, though the use of "flat panel" LCD video monitors for desktop PC systems is growing. LCD displays need significantly

Figure 3.22

Using a flat panel LCD video monitor for a desktop PC system.

Source: Index Stock/Picture Quest

less electric current and provide a thin, flat display. Advances in technology such as *active matrix* and *dual scan* capabilities have improved the color and clarity of LCD displays. See Figure 3.22.

Printed Output

Printing information on paper is still the most common form of output after video displays. Thus, most personal computer systems rely on an inkjet or laser printer to produce permanent (hard copy) output in high-quality printed form. Printed output is still a common form of business communications, and is frequently required for legal documentation. Thus, computers can produce printed reports and correspondence, documents such as sales invoices, payroll checks, bank statements, and printed versions of graphic displays.

Inkjet printers, which spray ink onto a page one line at a time, have become the most popular, low-cost printers for microcomputer systems. They are quiet, produce several pages per minute of high-quality output, and can print both black-and-white and high-quality color graphics. **Laser printers** use an electrostatic process similar to a photocopying machine to produce many pages per minute of high-quality black-and-white output. More expensive color laser printers and multifunction inkjet and laser models that print, fax, scan, and copy are other popular choices for business offices. See Figure 3.23.

Storage Trends and Trade-Offs

Data and information must be stored until needed using a variety of storage methods. For example, many people and organizations still rely on paper documents stored in filing cabinets as a major form of storage media. However, you and other computer users are more likely to depend on the memory circuits and secondary storage devices of computer systems to meet your storage requirements. Figure 3.24 illustrates major trends in primary and secondary storage methods. Progress in very-large-scale integration (VLSI), which packs millions of memory circuit elements on tiny semiconductor memory chips, is responsible for continuing increases in the main-memory capacity of computers. Secondary storage capacities are also escalating into the billions and trillions of characters, due to advances in magnetic and optical media.

Figure 3.23

An inkjet printer produces high-quality color output.

Source: Corbis.

There are many types of storage media and devices. Figure 3.25 illustrates the speed, capacity, and cost relationships of several alternative primary and secondary storage media. Note the cost/speed/capacity trade-offs as one moves from semiconductor memories to magnetic disks, to optical disks, and to magnetic tape. High-speed storage media cost more per byte and provide lower capacities. Large-capacity storage media cost less per byte but are slower. This is why we have different kinds of storage media.

However, all storage media, especially memory chips and magnetic disks, continue to increase in speed and capacity and decrease in cost. Developments like automated high-speed cartridge assemblies have given faster access times to magnetic tape, and the speed of optical disk drives continues to increase.

Note in Figure 3.25 that semiconductor memories are used mainly for primary storage, though they are sometimes used as high-speed secondary storage devices. Magnetic disk and tape and optical disk devices, on the other hand, are used as secondary storage devices to greatly enlarge the storage capacity of computer systems. Also, since most primary storage circuits use RAM (random access memory) chips,

Figure 3.24 Major trends in primary and secondary storage media.

	First Generation	Second Generation	Third Generation	Fourth Generation	Fifth Generation?
PRIMARY STORAGE	Magnetic Drum	Magnetic Core	Magnetic Core	LSI Semiconductor Memory Chips	VLSI Semiconductor Memory Chips
TREND: Toward Large Capacities Using Smaller Microelectronic Circuits.					
SECONDARY STORAGE	Magnetic Tape Magnetic Drum	Magnetic Tape Magnetic Disk	Magnetic Disk Magnetic Tape	Magnetic Disk Optical Disk Magnetic Tape	Optical Disk Magnetic Disk
TREND: Toward Massive Capacities Using Magnetic and Optical Media.					

Figure 3.25

Storage media cost, speed, and capacity trade-offs. Note how cost increases with faster access speeds, but decreases with the increased capacity of storage media.

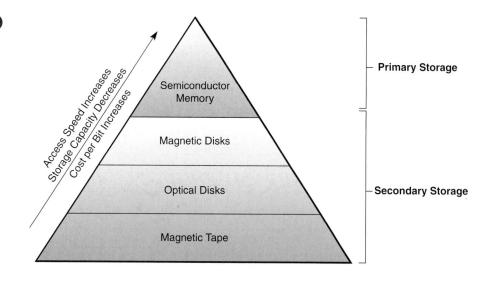

Computer Storage Fundamentals

which lose their contents when electrical power is interrupted, secondary storage devices provide a more permanent type of storage media.

Data are processed and stored in a computer system through the presence or absence of electronic or magnetic signals in the computer's circuitry or in the media it uses. This is called a "two-state" or **binary representation** of data, since the computer and the media can exhibit only two possible states or conditions. For example, transistors and other semiconductor circuits are either in a conducting or nonconducting state. Media such as magnetic disks and tapes indicate these two states by having magnetized spots whose magnetic fields have one of two different directions, or polarities. This binary characteristic of computer circuitry and media is what makes the binary number system the basis for representing data in computers. Thus, for electronic circuits, the conducting (ON) state represents the number one, while the nonconducting (OFF) state represents the number zero. For magnetic media, the magnetic field of a magnetized spot in one direction represents a one, while magnetism in the other direction represents a zero.

The smallest element of data is called a **bit,** or binary digit, which can have a value of either zero or one. The capacity of memory chips is usually expressed in terms of bits. A **byte** is a basic grouping of bits that the computer operates as a single unit. Typically, it consists of eight bits and represents one character of data in most computer coding schemes. Thus, the capacity of a computer's memory and secondary storage devices is usually expressed in terms of bytes. Computer codes such as ASCII (American Standard Code for Information Interchange) use various arrangements of bits to form bytes that represent the numbers zero through nine, the letters of the alphabet, and many other characters. See Figure 3.26.

Storage capacities are frequently measured in **kilobytes** (KB), **megabytes** (MB), **gigabytes** (GB), or **terabytes** (TB). Although kilo means 1,000 in the metric system, the computer industry uses K to represent 1,024 (or 2^{10}) storage positions. Therefore, a capacity of 10 megabytes, for example, is really 10,485,760 storage positions, rather than 10 million positions. However, such differences are frequently disregarded in order to simplify descriptions of storage capacity. Thus, a megabyte is roughly 1 million bytes of storage, a gigabyte is roughly 1 billion bytes and a terabyte represents about 1 trillion bytes, while a **petabyte** is over 1 quadrillion bytes!

Direct and Sequential Access

Primary storage media such as semiconductor memory chips are called **direct access** or random access memories (RAM). Magnetic disk devices are frequently called

Figure 3.26

Examples of ASCII computer code.

Character	ASCII Code	Character	ASCII Code	Character	ASCII Code
0	00110000	A	01000001	N	01001110
1	00110001	B	01000010	O	01001111
2	00110010	C	01000011	P	01010000
3	00110011	D	01000100	Q	01010001
4	00110100	E	01000101	R	01010010
5	00110101	F	01000110	S	01010011
6	00110110	G	01000111	T	01010100
7	00110111	H	01001000	U	01010101
8	00111000	I	01001001	V	01010110
9	00111001	J	01001010	W	01010111
		K	01001011	X	01011000
		L	01001100	Y	01011001
		M	01001101	Z	01011010

direct access storage devices (DASDs). On the other hand, media such as magnetic tape cartridges are known as **sequential access** devices.

The terms *direct access* and *random access* describe the same concept. They mean that an element of data or instructions (such as a byte or word) can be directly stored and retrieved by selecting and using any of the locations on the storage media. They also mean that each storage position (1) has a unique address and (2) can be individually accessed in approximately the same length of time without having to search through other storage positions. For example, each memory cell on a microelectronic semiconductor RAM chip can be individually sensed or changed in the same length of time. Also any data record stored on a magnetic or optical disk can be accessed directly in approximately the same time period. See Figure 3.27.

Sequential access storage media such as magnetic tape do not have unique storage addresses that can be directly addressed. Instead, data must be stored and retrieved using a sequential or serial process. Data are recorded one after another in a predetermined sequence (such as in numeric order) on a storage medium. Locating an individual item of data requires searching the recorded data on the tape until the desired item is located.

Figure 3.27

Sequential versus direct access storage. Magnetic tape is a typical sequential access medium. Magnetic disks are typical direct access storage devices.

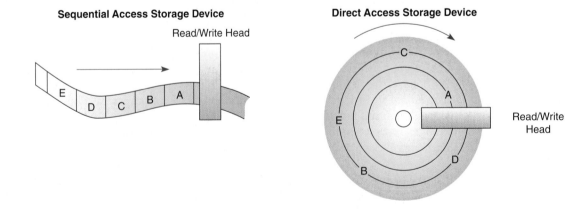

Semiconductor Memory

Memory is the coalman to the CPU's locomotive: For maximum PC performance, it must keep the processor constantly stoked with instructions. Faster CPUs call for larger and faster memories, both in the cache where data and instructions are stored temporarily, and in the main memory [10].

The primary storage (main memory) of your computer consists of microelectronic **semiconductor memory** chips. It provides you with the working storage your computer needs to process your applications. Plug-in memory circuit boards containing 32 megabytes or more of memory chips can be added to your PC to increase its memory capacity. Specialized memory can help improve your computer's performance. Examples include external cache memory of 512 kilobytes to help your microprocessor work faster, or a video graphics accelerator card with 16 megabytes of RAM for faster and clearer video performance. Removable credit-card-size and smaller "flash memory" RAM cards can also provide several megabytes of erasable direct access storage for PDAs or hand-held PCs.

Some of the major attractions of semiconductor memory are its small size, great speed, and shock and temperature resistance. One major disadvantage of most semiconductor memory is its **volatility.** Uninterrupted electric power must be supplied or the contents of memory will be lost. Therefore, emergency transfer to other devices or standby electrical power (through battery packs or emergency generators) is required if data are to be saved. Another alternative is to permanently "burn in" the contents of semiconductor devices so that they cannot be erased by a loss of power.

Thus, there are two basic types of semiconductor memory: random access memory (RAM) and read only memory (ROM).

- **RAM: random access memory.** These memory chips are the most widely used primary storage medium. Each memory position can be both sensed (read) and changed (written), so it is also called read/write memory. This is a volatile memory.

- **ROM: read only memory.** Nonvolatile random access memory chips are used for permanent storage. ROM can be read but not erased or overwritten. Frequently used control instructions in the control unit and programs in primary storage (such as parts of the operating system) can be permanently burned in to the storage cells during manufacture. This is sometimes called *firmware*. Variations include PROM (programmable read only memory) and EPROM (erasable programmable read only memory), which can be permanently or temporarily programmed after manufacture.

Magnetic Disk Storage

Multigigabyte magnetic disk drives aren't extravagant, considering that full-motion video files, sound tracks, and photo-quality images can consume colossal amounts of disk space in a blink [10].

Magnetic disks are the most common form of secondary storage for your computer system. That's because they provide fast access and high storage capacities at a reasonable cost. Magnetic disk drives contain metal disks that are coated on both sides with an iron oxide recording material. Several disks are mounted together on a vertical shaft, which typically rotates the disks at speeds of 3,600 to 7,600 revolutions per minute (rpm). Electromagnetic read/write heads are positioned by access arms between the slightly separated disks to read and write data on concentric, circular tracks. Data are recorded on tracks in the form of tiny magnetized spots to form the binary digits of common computer codes. Thousands of bytes can be recorded on each track, and there are several hundred data tracks on each disk surface, thus providing you with billions of storage positions for your software and data. See Figure 3.28.

Figure 3.28   Magnetic disk media: A hard magnetic disk drive and a 3 1/2-inch floppy disk.

Source: Quantum.

Source: Eric Kamp/Index Stock Photography.

Types of Magnetic Disks

There are several types of magnetic disk arrangements, including removable disk cartridges as well as fixed disk units. Removable disk devices are popular because they are transportable and can be used to store backup copies of your data offline for convenience and security.

- **Floppy disks,** or magnetic diskettes, consist of polyester film disks covered with an iron oxide compound. A single disk is mounted and rotates freely inside a protective flexible or hard plastic jacket, which has access openings to accommodate the read/write head of a disk drive unit. The 3 1/2-inch floppy disk, with capacities of 1.44 megabytes, is the most widely used version, with a newer Superdisk technology offering 120 megabytes of storage.

- **Hard disk drives** combine magnetic disks, access arms, and read/write heads into a sealed module. This allows higher speeds, greater data recording densities, and closer tolerances within a sealed, more stable environment. Fixed or removable disk cartridge versions are available. Capacities of hard drives range from several hundred megabytes to many gigabytes of storage.

RAID Storage

RAID computer storage equipment—big, refrigerator-size boxes full of dozens of interlinked magnetic disk drives that can store the equivalent of 100 million tax returns—hardly gets the blood rushing. But it should. Just as speedy and reliable networking opened the floodgates to cyberspace and e-commerce, ever-more-turbocharged data storage is a key building block of the Internet [11].

Disk arrays of interconnected microcomputer hard disk drives have replaced large-capacity mainframe disk drives to provide many gigabytes of online storage. Known as **RAID** (redundant arrays of independent disks), they combine from 6 to more than 100 small hard disk drives and their control microprocessors into a single unit. RAID units provide large capacities with high access speeds since data are accessed in parallel over multiple paths from many disks. RAID units also provide a *fault tolerant* capacity, since their redundant design offers multiple copies of data on several disks. If one disk fails, data can be recovered from backup copies automatically stored on other disks. *Storage area networks* (SANs) are high-speed *fiber channel* local area networks that can interconnect many RAID units and thus share their combined capacity through network servers with many users.

Magnetic Tape Storage

Tape storage is moving beyond backup. Disk subsystems provide the fastest response time for mission-critical data. But the sheer amount of data users need to access these days as part of huge enterprise applications, such as data warehouses, requires afford-able [magnetic tape] storage [16].

Magnetic tape is still being used as a secondary storage medium in business applications. The read/write heads of magnetic tape drives record data in the form of magnetized spots on the iron oxide coating of the plastic tape. Magnetic tape devices include tape reels and cartridges in mainframes and midrange systems, and small cassettes or cartridges for PCs. Magnetic tape cartridges have replaced tape reels in many applications and can hold over 200 megabytes.

One growing business application of magnetic tape involves the use of high-speed 36-track magnetic tape cartridges in robotic automated drive assemblies that can directly access hundreds of cartridges. These devices provide lower-cost storage to supplement magnetic disks to meet massive data warehouse and other online business storage requirements. Other major applications for magnetic tape include long-term *archival* storage and backup storage for PCs and other systems [16].

Optical Disk Storage

CD-ROM technology has become a necessity. Most software companies have stopped distributing their elephantine programs on floppies altogether. Many corporations are now rolling their own CDs to distribute product and corporate information that once filled bookshelves [10].

Optical disks are a fast-growing storage medium. One version for use with microcomputers is called **CD-ROM** (compact disk–read only memory). CD-ROM technology uses 12-centimeter (4.7 inch) compact disks (CDs) similar to those used in stereo music systems. Each disk can store more than 600 megabytes. That's the equivalent of over 400 1.44 megabyte floppy disks or more than 300,000 double-spaced pages of text. A laser records data by burning permanent microscopic pits in a spiral track on a master disk from which compact disks can be mass-produced. Then CD-ROM disk drives use a laser device to read the binary codes formed by those pits.

CD-R (compact disk–recordable) is a popular optical disk technology. CD-R drives or *CD burners* are commonly used to permanently record digital music tracks or digital photo images on CDs. The major limitation of CD-ROM and CD-R disks is that recorded data cannot be erased. However, **CD-RW** (CD-rewritable) drives have now become available that record and erase data by using a laser to heat a microscopic point on the disk's surface. In CD-RW versions using magneto-optical technology, a magnetic coil changes the spot's reflective properties from one direction to another, thus recording a binary one or zero. A laser device can then read the binary codes on the disk by sensing the direction of reflected light.

Optical disk capacities and capabilities have increased dramatically with the emergence of an optical disk technology called **DVD** (digital video disk or digital versatile disk). DVDs can hold from 3.0 to 8.5 gigabytes of multimedia data on each side of a compact disk. The large capacities and high-quality images and sound of DVD technology are expected to eventually replace CD-ROM and CD-RW technologies for data storage, and promise to accelerate the use of DVD drives for multimedia products that can be used in both computers and home entertainment systems. Thus, **DVD-ROM** is beginning to replace magnetic tape videocassettes for movies and other multimedia products, while **DVD-RAM** is being used for backup and archival storage of large data and multimedia files. See Figure 3.29.

Business Applications

One of the major uses of optical disks in mainframe and midrange systems is in **image processing,** where long-term archival storage of historical files of document images must be maintained. Mainframe and midrange computer versions of optical

Figure 3.29

Optical disk storage includes CD and DVD technologies.

Source: PhotoDisc, Inc.

disks use 12-inch plastic disks with capacities of several gigabytes, with up to 20 disks held in jukebox drive units. Financial institutions, among others, are using optical scanners to capture digitized document images and store them on **WORM** (write once, read many) versions of such optical disks as an alternative to microfilm media.

One of the major business uses of CD-ROM disks for personal computers is to provide a publishing medium for fast access to reference materials in a convenient, compact form. This includes catalogs, directories, manuals, periodical abstracts, part listings, and statistical databases of business and economic activity. Interactive multimedia applications in business, education, and entertainment are another major use of CD-ROM and DVD disks. The large storage capacities of CD-ROM and DVD disks are a natural choice for computer video games, educational videos, multimedia encyclopedias, and advertising presentations.

Thus, optical disks have become a popular storage medium for image processing and multimedia business applications, and they appear to be a promising alternative to magnetic disks and tape for very large *mass storage* capabilities for enterprises' computing systems. However, rewritable optical technologies are still maturing, and most optical disk devices are significantly slower and more expensive (per byte of storage) than magnetic disk devices. So optical disk systems are not expected to displace magnetic disk technology in the near future for many business applications.

Summary

- **Computer Systems.** Major types and trends in computer systems are summarized in Figures 3.2 and 3.3. A computer is a system of information processing components that perform input, processing, output, storage, and control functions. Its hardware components include input and output devices, a central processing unit (CPU), and primary and secondary storage devices. The major functions and hardware in a computer system are summarized in Figure 3.11.

- **Microcomputer Systems.** Microcomputers are used as personal computers, network computers, personal digital assistants, technical workstations, and information appliances. Like most computer systems today,

microcomputers are interconnected in a variety of telecommunications networks. This typically includes local area networks, client/server networks, intranets and extranets, and the Internet.

- **Other Computer Systems.** Midrange computers are increasingly used as powerful network servers, and for many multiuser business data processing and scientific applications. Mainframe computers are larger and more powerful than most midsize computers. They are usually faster, have more memory capacity, and can support more network users and peripheral devices. They are designed to handle the information processing needs of large organizations with high volumes of transaction processing, or with complex computational problems. Supercomputers are a special category of extremely powerful mainframe computer systems designed for massive computational assignments.

- **Peripheral Devices.** Refer to Figures 3.14, 3.15, 3.21, 3.24, and 3.25 to review the important trends and capabilities of peripheral devices for input, output, and storage discussed in this chapter.

Key Terms and Concepts

These are the key terms and concepts of this chapter. The page number of their first explanation is given in parentheses.

1. Binary representation (93)
2. Central processing unit (80)
3. Computer system (80)
4. Computer terminal (76)
5. Digital cameras (89)
6. Direct access (93)
7. Generations of computing (72)
8. Information appliance (76)
9. Laptop computer (73)
10. Liquid crystal displays (90)
11. Magnetic disk storage (95)
    a. Floppy disk (96)
    b. Hard disk (96)
    c. RAID (96)
12. Magnetic ink character recognition (90)
13. Magnetic stripe (89)
14. Magnetic tape (97)
15. Mainframe computer (78)
16. Microcomputer (73)
17. Microprocessor (80)
18. Midrange computer (77)
19. Minicomputer (73)
20. Network computer (74)

21. NetPC (74)
22. Network server (74)
23. Network terminal (76)
24. Offline (84)
25. Online (84)
26. Optical character recognition (88)
27. Optical disk storage (97)
    a. CD-ROM (97)
    b. CD-R (97)
    c. CD-RW (97)
    d. DVD (97)
    e. WORM disks (98)
28. Optical scanning (88)
29. Pen-based computing (86)
30. Peripheral devices (82)
31. Personal digital assistant (76)
32. Pointing devices (85)
    a. Electronic mouse (85)
    b. Pointing stick (85)
    c. Touchpad (85)
    d. Trackball (85)
33. Primary storage (81)
34. Printers (91)
35. Secondary storage (81)
36. Semiconductor memory (95)

    a. RAM (95)
    b. ROM (95)
37. Sequential access (94)
38. Smart cards (89)
39. Speech recognition (86)
40. Storage capacity elements (93)
    a. Bit (93)
    b. Byte (93)
    c. Kilobyte (93)
    d. Megabyte (93)
    e. Gigabyte (93)
    f. Terabyte (93)
41. Storage media trade-offs (91)
42. Supercomputer (79)
43. Time elements (81)
    a. Millisecond (81)
    b. Microsecond (81)
    c. Nanosecond (81)
    d. Picosecond (81)
44. Touch-sensitive screen (85)
45. Trends in computers (70)
46. Video output (90)
47. Volatility (95)
48. Wand (89)
49. Workstation (74)

Review Quiz

Match one of the previous key terms and concepts with one of the following brief examples or definitions. Try to find the best fit for answers that seem to fit more than one term or concept. Defend your choices.

_____ 1. Computers will become smaller, faster, more reliable, easier to use, and less costly.

_____ 2. Major stages in the development of computing.

_____ 3. A computer is a combination of components that perform input, processing, output, storage, and control functions.

_____ 4. The main processing component of a computer system.

_____ 5. A small, portable PC.

_____ 6. Devices for consumers to access the Internet.

_____ 7. The memory of a computer.

_____ 8. Magnetic disks and tape and optical disks perform this function.

_____ 9. Input/output and secondary storage devices for a computer system.

_____ 10. Connected to and controlled by a CPU.

_____ 11. Separate from and not controlled by a CPU.

_____ 12. Results from the presence or absence or change in direction of electric current, magnetic fields, or light rays in computer circuits and media.

_____ 13. The central processing unit of a microcomputer.

_____ 14. Can be a desktop/laptop, or hand-held computer.

_____ 15. A computer category between microcomputers and mainframes.

_____ 16. A computer that can handle the information processing needs of large organizations.

_____ 17. Hand-held microcomputers for communications and personal information management.

_____ 18. Low-cost microcomputers for use with the Internet and corporate intranets.

_____ 19. Low-cost network-enabled PCs with reduced features.

_____ 20. A terminal that depends on network servers for its software and processing power.

_____ 21. A computer that manages network communications and resources.

_____ 22. The most powerful type of computer.

_____ 23. A magnetic tape technology for credit cards.

_____ 24. One billionth of a second.

_____ 25. Roughly one billion characters of storage.

_____ 26. Includes electronic mouses, trackballs, pointing sticks, and touchpads.

_____ 27. You can write on the pressure-sensitive LCD screen of hand-held microcomputers with a pen.

_____ 28. Moving this along your desktop moves the cursor on the screen.

_____ 29. You can communicate with a computer by touching its display.

_____ 30. Produces hard copy output such as paper documents and reports.

_____ 31. Promises to be the easiest, most natural way to communicate with computers.

_____ 32. Capturing data by processing light reflected from images.

_____ 33. Optical scanning of bar codes and other characters.

_____ 34. Bank check processing uses this technology.

_____ 35. A debit card with an embedded microprocessor and memory is an example.

_____ 36. A device with a keyboard and a video display networked to a computer is a typical example.

_____ 37. Photos or video can be captured and downloaded to your PC for image processing.

_____ 38. A video output technology.

_____ 39. A hand-held device that reads bar coding.

_____ 40. Storage media cost, speed, and capacity differences.

_____ 41. You cannot erase the contents of these storage circuits.

_____ 42. The memory of most computers consists of these storage circuits.

_____ 43. The property that determines whether data are lost or retained when power fails.

_____ 44. Each position of storage can be accessed in approximately the same time.

_____ 45. Each position of storage can be accessed according to a predetermined order.

_____ 46. Microelectronic storage circuits on silicon chips.

_____ 47. Uses magnetic spots on metal or plastic disks.

_____ 48. Uses magnetic spots on plastic tape.

_____ 49. Uses a laser to read microscopic points on plastic disks.

_____ 50. Vastly increases the storage capacity and image and sound quality of optical disk technology.

Discussion Questions

1. Do you agree with the statement: "The network is the computer"? Why or why not?

2. What trends are occurring in the development and use of the major types of computer systems?

3. Refer to the Real World Case on Boeing, Monster.com, and Others in the chapter. What other criteria should be considered when buying PCs for business use?

4. Do you think that network computers (NCs) will replace personal computers (PCs) in business applications? Explain.

5. Are networks of PCs and servers making mainframe computers obsolete? Explain.

6. Refer to the Real World Case on Dresdner Bank and Wyndham International in the chapter. Does the move toward server consolidation and large servers indicate a greater role for mainframe systems in the future? Explain your reasoning.

7. What are several trends that are occurring in the development and use of peripheral devices? Why are these trends occurring?

8. When would you recommend the use of each of the following: (1) network computers, (2) NetPCs, (3) network terminals, or (4) information appliances in business applications?

9. What processor, memory, magnetic disk storage, and video display capabilities would you require for a personal computer that you would use for business purposes? Explain your choices.

10. What other peripheral devices and capabilities would you want to have for your business PC? Explain your choices.

Application Exercises

1. **Input Alternatives**
   Which method of input would you recommend for the following activities? Explain your choices.
   a. Entering data from printed questionnaires.
   b. Entering data from telephone surveys.
   c. Entering data from bank checks.
   d. Entering data from merchandise tags.
   e. Entering data from business documents.

2. **Output Alternatives**
   Which method of output would you recommend for the following information products? Explain your choices.
   a. Visual displays for portable microcomputers.
   b. Legal documents.
   c. Color photographs.
   d. Financial results for top executives.
   e. Responses for telephone transactions.

3. **Purchasing Computer Systems for Your Workgroup**
   You have been asked to get pricing information for a potential purchase of 5 PCs for the members of your workgroup. Go to the Internet to get prices for these units from at least two prominent PC suppliers.
   The list below shows the specifications for the basic system you have been asked to price and potential upgrades to each feature. You will want to get a price for the basic system described below and a separate price for each of the upgrades shown.

	Basic Unit	Upgrade
CPU (gigahertz)	1.3	1.5
Hard Drive (gigbytes)	40	80
RAM (megabytes)	256	512
CD-ROM	48 speed	8 Speed DVD
Monitor (inches)	17	21

   Network cards and modems will not be purchased with these systems. These features will be added from stock already owned by the company. Take the standard warranty and servicing coverage offered by each supplier, but be sure to note any differences in coverage.
   a. Prepare a spreadsheet summarizing this pricing information and showing the cost, from each supplier, of the following options: **a.** 5 units with the basic configuration, **b.** 3 units with the basic configuration and 2 units with all of the upgrades, **c.** 3 units with the basic configuration plus the monitor upgrade and 2 units with all upgrades, and **d.** all 5 units fully upgraded.
   b. Prepare a set of PowerPoint slides or similar presentation materials summarizing your results. Include a discussion of the warranty and servicing contract options available from each supplier.

4. **Price and Performance Trends for Computer Hardware**
   The table below shows a set of price and capacity figures for common components of personal computers. Typical prices for Microprocessors, Random Access Memory (RAM), and Hard Disk storage prices are shown. The performance of typical components has increased substantially over time, so the speed (for the microprocessor) or the capacity (for the storage devices) is also listed. Although there have been improvements in these components that are not reflected in these capacity measures, it is interesting to examine trends in these measurable characteristics.
   a. Create a spreadsheet based on the figures below and including a new column for each component showing the price per unit of capacity. (Cost per megahertz of speed for microprocessors, and cost per megabyte of storage for RAM and hard disk devices.)
   b. Create a set of graphs highlighting your results and illustrating trends in price per unit of performance (speed) or capacity.
   c. Write a short paper discussing the trends you found. How long do you expect these trends to continue? Why?

	1991	1993	1995	1997	1999	2001
Microprocessor						
Speed (Megahertz)	25	33	100	125	350	1,000
Cost	$180	$125	$275	$250	$300	$251
RAM Chip						
Megabytes per Chip	1	4	4	16	64	256
Cost	$55	$140	$120	$97	$125	$90
Hard Disk Device						
Megabytes per Disk	105	250	540	2,000	8,000	40,000
Cost	$480	$375	$220	$250	$220	$138

AMS Services, Primestream, and The Jockey Club:
The Business Case for Rack-Mounted Servers

New server strategies are supplanting traditional minirefrigerator-size pedestal servers and large, mainframe-style servers by taking advantage of rack mounting.

The Technology

Standard data center racks are 42U high (where U is a form factor measuring 1.75 inches, which is a standard PC "pizza box" size). Ordinary servers are usually 3U high, meaning a rack theoretically can hold 14 servers. However, by reducing server height to 1U, a rack can hold 42 of these pizza box servers—increasing the processing power by 50 percent to 100 percent in the same floor space. Data center managers value this increase, and indeed 1U seems to be the new standard. Major server vendors, including Compaq, Dell, Hewlett-Packard, and IBM, all offer 1U servers.

These aren't skimpy boxes, either. Each 1U server can typically handle one or two processors in the Pentium to near-gigahertz range, up to 4GB of RAM, one to three 20GB hard drives, plus at least two network ports and all the trimmings. Slip 42 of these screamers into a rack, and you're packing a punch.

However, racks can hold even more "blade servers," which are the latest and smallest form of rack-mounted server. A blade is essentially a server mounted on a card, with 6 to 12 blades mounted vertically in slots within a special 3U chassis that slips into a rack. Blade servers can typically handle one or two processors, up to 512 MB of RAM, up to three 20GB hard drives, and one or two network connections. Since standard racks can hold 14 chassis, each rack can then hold the equivalent of 336 servers. That's compact.

The Users

Joe Bartlett was facing the kind of nightmare that upper management calls a "challenge": He had to move AMS Services Inc. from zero to Internet-ready in two months. Windsor, Connecticut–based AMS is a family of companies that provides automation products and services to more than 30,000 insurance agents and carriers. TowerStreet, one part of AMS, offers online applications and business-to-business services on an application service provider basis. Bartlett, who is CIO and chief technology officer at AMS, had to ramp up server support, and he had only one 8,000 square foot facility in College Station, Texas, to do it.

Luckily, AMS already had networked storage systems in place. "Typical servers would have been overkill, since we didn't need their storage," says Bartlett. Instead, AMS chose rack-mounted servers from HP. "We needed CPUs and RAM," notes Bartlett. Using 1U servers allowed AMS to maximize the number of servers per square foot of precious data center area. The company has settled mainly on HP's LP 1000r servers with dual 2-GHz processors and either 20B (for Web processing) or 4GB (for terminal services for users) of RAM.

The AMS data center facility had an adequate power supply to support all their rack servers, but did add extra fan units to each rack to increase air circulation. To administer all those servers, the AMS data center uses HP's OpenView system performance software to monitor major system components, including processor and RAM usage.

Of course, different enterprises have different needs. For example, Miami-based Primestream Corp. provides streaming audio and video via the Internet from facilities in Argentina, Brazil, Mexico, and the United States. Primestream serves both corporate clients (with training, seminars, and earnings reports) and entertainment customers (with broadcasting that sidesteps traditional cable programming). The key statistic for Primestream is its number of simultaneous users.

"We used to support 500 connections with three racks," reports CEO Claudio Lisman. "Now we can support 1,500 connections with one rack of servers." The server configuration is vital to this capability. Primestream uses Compaq Prollant DL 360s with dual 36GB hard drives, dual 900-MHz Pentium III processors, and 512MG of RAM. Those separate onboard hard disk drives are logically clustered so that they appear as a single 720 GB drive to all servers in the rack.

The Jockey Club in Lexington, Kentucky, also has unique needs. It supports a huge database of registered racehorses, maintains a website for owners and traders to manage portfolios of holdings, and handles financial transactions.

"Our rack-mounted servers provide the middle tier of architecture," says Bobby Burch, vice president of IT. "The front end is browser-based networked PCs, while the back-end includes the database on a networked storage system." The Jockey Club's combination of applications uses a mix of Dell rack-mounted server configurations, including both one- and two-processor boxes, with 2GB of RAM each. Storage resides centrally in a storage-area network.

The Jockey Club's strategy is to consolidate more servers, if possible. "We'd like to get several applications on one box, while preserving reliability for the user," he notes. Lisman plans to expand the number of Primestream's servers from 50 to 300. Bartlett continues to add about 50 servers per month to the AMS facility, so he appreciates the modularity of the rack-mounted servers. "It's extremely scalable," Bartlett observes. "We call it LOLB: lots of little boxes." This solution is anticipated to allow the AMS data center to continue in the original facility for at least two to three more years.

Case Study Questions

1. What business benefits are driving the trend toward rack-mounted servers?

2. What potential problems can you foresee with a move to such servers? What are some possible solutions?

3. Do you believe that rack-mounted servers are going to replace large servers or mainframes? Why or why not?

Source: Adapted from Edmund DeJesus, "Server Size Matters," *Computerworld*, September 24, 2001, pp. 50, 51. Reprinted by permission.

Kmart and Staples:
Benefits and Challenges of Web Kiosks in Retail Outlets

Are you a Kmart shopper? Don't expect to find a wide selection at the cramped Kmart store in Herndon, Virginia. Instead, you can go to one of two desktop kiosks—the ones below bright BlueLight.com signs—and check out a variety of products that can be shipped in three to seven days. For Kmart Corp., the Web-connected kiosks are an effort to "save the sale," allowing customers to buy merchandise not available at stores.

This isn't new territory for Kmart. The Troy, Michigan–based discount retailer has been flirting with kiosk programs since the early 1990s, but with little success. The problem then was that maintaining a large kiosk network was expensive. "You had to hire a ton of people for maintenance, and a lot of the technology was shaky," recalled Dave Karraker, a spokesman for BlueLight.com LLC, a Kmart unit that handles Internet and kiosk sales. What's more, customers saw little need for kiosks at the time, he added. Those systems, built on each store's LAN, would often crash, and when products or a kiosk feature needed updating, technicians would have to visit each store to make the changes.

But now, Kmart has placed its bets on Web-based kiosks that mimic its BlueLight.com website. Some 3,500 kiosks occupy 1,100 U.S. stores. The new kiosks eliminate many IT department headaches by updating products and information simultaneously in all of the stores. So far, the kiosks are paying off big. Since launching the kiosks in January, 20 percent of BlueLight.com's site traffic has come through the kiosks. That's twice as much as expected, according to Karraker.

Thousands of retailers and service providers are hoping for the same results as they add kiosks through which customers can order furniture, burn custom music CDs, check in at the airport, rent cars, and even order a newborn's first photographs at the hospital. Jupiter Media Metrix Inc. in New York predicts that consumers will purchase almost $200 million in goods and services through kiosks in 2001 and $6.5 billion by 2006.

There's more to Internet-based kiosks than simply making a website available at a store location. The No. 1 IT requirement is a high-bandwidth, reliable network. Response times are also critical. Customers may be willing to tolerate slow response from a website while sitting at a home PC, but they're far less tolerant standing at a kiosk in a store. Companies that want kiosks but lack the IT staff to support them often hire hosting services, at least initially, to see how much usage and revenue the kiosks generate.

For example, Netkey in Branford, Connecticut, and Autopulse, in Raleigh, North Carolina, are jointly rolling out kiosks for Raleigh-based Lucor Inc., the nation's largest franchise of Jiffy Lube stores. NCR Corp. in Dayton, Ohio, is another kiosk-hosting provider. It claimed a tenfold increase in its Web kiosk business last year.

Retailers with robust data networks can handle kiosks themselves. In January, office supply retailer Staples Inc. installed more than 2,500 kiosks in 954 stores. The kiosks emulate the Staples.com website, but at the store customers are able to order products online and pay at a cash register.

This is possible because in the late 1990s, Staples installed a frame-relay network with circuits that carry integrated voice and data. "In a given store, there are 13 different devices that can connect into our system directly or over the net," such as cash registers, telephones, and back-office software, said Max Ward, vice president of technology at Framingham, Massachusetts–based Staples. The IT department constantly monitors the network status to avoid downtime and has trained the help desk to handle problems that might occur inside the stores.

At the Staples store in Sterling, Virginia, store manager Steve Saunders said that he has experienced few problems with the kiosks and that customers need little assistance with them. All sales associates are trained in kiosk operation, and each has to pass a test on its use, he added. If problems do occur, Staples' help desk contacts a contractor handling support and repairs for the kiosks.

Kmart's IT department maintains the hardware and Internet connections at the company's stores. The department also provides ongoing technical support through a toll-free number. Kmart associates have been trained on kiosk use and are responsible for assisting customers and keeping the keyboard and monitor clean and powered up.

So far, the most successful kiosks in business use have been ones that help consumers research or locate products, fulfill orders, or that extend shelf space by offering unusual or bulky products. But, the potential of Web kiosks is still untapped in many markets. Consumers say they're willing to rent movies, purchase event tickets, make bill payments, and create customized products at kiosks, Jupiter Media's research found. But those services will require kiosks that have card scanners, printers, and additional security features, all tied to a central host and a reliable network.

Case Study Questions

1. What technological advances and business benefits are driving the expansion in the use of kiosks in retail stores and other outlets?

2. What are the limitations of kiosks for such uses? For future uses?

3. Could a small business use kiosks profitably? Why or why not?

Source: Adapted from Stacy Collett, "Retailers, Travel Companies Deploy Thousands of Kiosks," *Computerworld*, August 6, 2001, pp. 18, 19. Reprinted by permission.

Chapter 4

Computer Software

Chapter Highlights

Section I
Application Software: End User Applications

Introduction to Software

Real World Case: Intuit, Inc.: Challenge and Innovation in Consumer and Small Business Software

Application Software for End Users

Software Suites and Integrated Packages

Web Browsers and More

Electronic Mail

Word Processing and Desktop Publishing

Electronic Spreadsheets

Database Management

Presentation Graphics and Multimedia

Personal Information Managers

Groupware

Other Business Software

Section II
System Software: Computer System Management

System Software Overview

Real World Case: Air Products, Farmers Group, and Others: Microsoft's Battle for the Enterprise Software Market

Operating Systems

Network Management Programs

Database Management Systems

Other System Management Programs

Programming Languages

Programming Software

Learning Objectives

After reading and studying this chapter, you should be able to:

1. Describe several important trends occurring in computer software.

2. Give examples of several major types of application and system software.

3. Explain the purpose of several popular software packages for end user productivity and collaborative computing.

4. Outline the functions of an operating system.

5. Describe the main uses of high-level, fourth-generation, object-oriented, and Web-oriented programming languages and tools.

Application Software: End User Applications

Introduction to Software

This chapter presents an overview of the major types of software you depend on as you work with computers and access computer networks. It discusses their characteristics and purposes and gives examples of their uses. Before we begin, let's look at an example of the changing world of software in business.

Analyzing Intuit, Inc.

Read the Real World Case on Intuit, Inc. on the next page. We can learn a lot about the development and markets for consumer and small business software from this example. See Figure 4.1.

Like many post dot-com entrepreneurs today, Scott Cook had a lot of trouble getting investors to finance his new software business after the burst of the VC software bubble of the 1980s. So he began selling his Quicken personal finance software to banks to sell to their customers, because he could not afford to market it directly to consumers. But Intuit's new product was much more consumer-tested and user friendly than its early competitors. So after enduring two years of financial hardship and near bankruptcy, Intuit's Quicken surged past its competitors to dominate the personal finance software market.

The success of Quicken was followed in the 90s by the success of Intuit's Quick-Books small business accounting software, which also has a dominant share of its market. Intuit almost missed this opportunity, because Scott and others misinterpreted their customer data that showed that half of their Quicken customers were

Figure 4.1

Scott Cook, chairman of Intuit, Inc., led his company's development and major success in the markets for personal finance, tax, and small business accounting software.

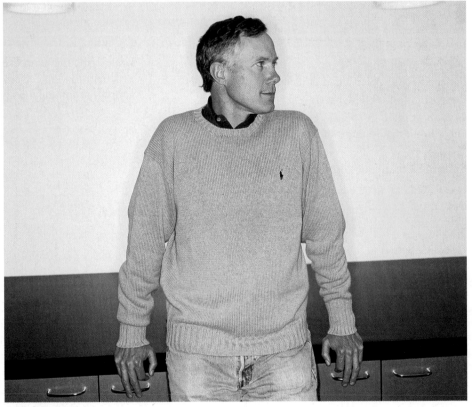

Source: Brad Hines

Intuit, Inc.:
Challenge and Innovation in Consumer and Small Business Software

Scott Cook was in his early 20s when he and his wife, Signe, arrived in Silicon Valley at the peak of the software explosion of the early 1980s. When Signe complained about doing the bills, Cook had an entrepreneur's classic "eureka!" moment: Why not create software that would handle household finances? But when Cook, a consultant with a Harvard MBA and a first job at Procter & Gamble, tried to get VC funding, he ran into a brick wall remarkably similar to the one post dot-com entrepreneurs are finding today.

Ultimately, Intuit broke through both financial and psychological barriers, barreling through recessions and a near bankruptcy, to become one of the great success stories of the late 80s and 90s. Today Intuit software products such as Quicken for personal finance, QuickBooks for small business accounting, and TurboTax for tax return preparation are by far the most popular in their markets.

FSB (Fortune Small Business) talked with Cook, now 49 and the chairman of the board's executive committee.

Were you the first to see this market? No, there were products out there. We were about the 25th company to build personal finance software, with competitors that included Home Account, Dollars & Sense, and Andrew Tobias' Managing Your Money. I bought the leading product expecting to find "Oh, they've solved this problem already." But it was horribly slow and hard to use. They were all terrible, but they sold well. And we were the first software company, to my knowledge, that did consumer testing. P&G had taught me the culture of customer-driven innovation; learning from customers and driving the product and the organization to win customers.

But if you go back to software as it was in 1983 when we started, it was generally products designed by engineers and sold to corporations. We were building a consumer product. For that, out that the disciplines required to sell to corporate customers were worthless. So when Quicken was half-built, we had groups of housewives that we recruited working with us in our labs. That's commonplace today, but we probably did it five years before others.

So you never got any VC funds? No. This was during the huge software bubble of 1982–83. Even truly stupid ideas, truly bad companies were getting money from VCs. We had our product ready for demo in 1984, and then went out to get funding. But by then, the software market collapsed.

The operating guy I brought in, Tom LaFevre, said, "Let's go talk to some rich people." I said, "I don't know any rich people." He said, "Well, I know two." They invested a total of $151,000. But we were looking for $3 million. We had to scale back our plan twentyfold. We couldn't spend any money on marketing. Instead of selling Quicken ourselves, we started selling it through banks on the suggestion of a friend I knew from consulting, the president of Wells Fargo bank.

But in May 1985, we were about out of money. We stopped paying salaries, we returned our rented computers and furniture; we stopped paying bills except for the phone and a few others. Three people left; four of us worked without pay. My marriage almost broke up. And it was my job to sell the banks. I had failed for months. Finally, in September, I started signing a bank a month. Finally it happened. We passed all our competitors in late 1987. It happened so fast, the late '80s just blew by.

How did you come up with QuickBooks? We were so busy keeping up with orders for Quicken that we didn't even see it. It's a story about what makes entrepreneurship so wonderful. It all happened by accident. We had built Quicken as a consumer home use product. When we surveyed our customers, half of them—48 percent—claimed to be a business. I ignored it; I thought, "That must be a mistake." Then we did the same research a year and a half later: 49 percent. I ignored that. It was only later that we got it.

How could you miss it? We had thought, why aren't they buying accounting software? In a nutshell, the answer was the vast majority of small businesses don't have an accountant on staff. They don't know a debit from a credit; they think "general ledger" was a World War II hero. Yet nobody made an accounting product designed just for them. It's the power of paradigm. It makes you twist and misinterpret facts to see what you want to see.

What's the biggest danger to Intuit now? Operating profits (in the year ending July 31, 2001) were up 42 percent, revenues up 15 percent. Intuit has felt some pressure from the economic downturn, but not nearly as much as other companies. Nearly half of our revenue comes from tax-related activities. You've heard that "only death and taxes are certain," and the certainty of taxes makes for a large and growing business for Intuit—and one with relatively low volatility. Our biggest danger would be if we failed to innovate. Our biggest business is providing solutions for small business people. And there is so much need there. The biggest tragedy would be if we somehow failed to innovate.

Case Study Questions

1. What lessons about how to develop and market consumer and small business software did you learn from this case?

2. Visit www.intuit.com and review Intuit's software products. Why do you think their personal finance, small business accounting, and tax return preparation software "continue to dominate their markets"?

3. Visit www.intuit.com. Is Intuit successfully meeting the challenges and opportunities to software products posed by the Internet and the Web? Explain.

Source: Adapted from Jolie Solomon, "The Secrets of His Success," *FSB: Fortune Small Business*, October 2001, pp. 35–38. 2001 Time Inc. All rights reserved.

Figure 4.2

An overview of computer software. Note the major types and examples of application and system software.

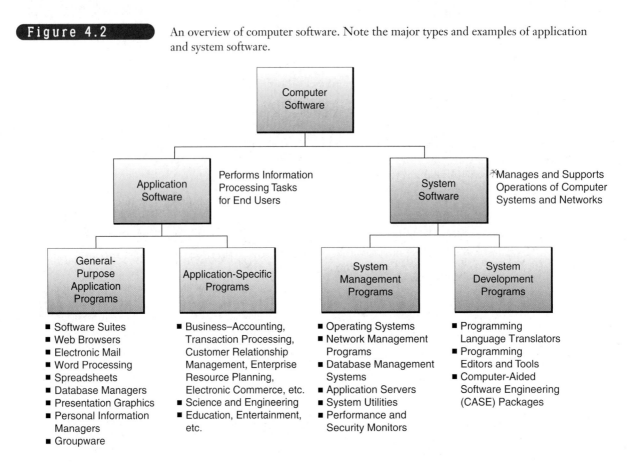

small businesses. Only after they realized that this indicated a big market for easy-to-use accounting software for nonaccountant small business owners, did they develop their successful Quickbooks product.

Software Trends

Let's begin our analysis of software by looking at an overview of the major types and functions of **application software** and **system software** available to computer users, shown in Figure 4.2. This figure summarizes the major categories of system and application software we will discuss in this chapter. Of course, this is a conceptual illustration. The types of software you will encounter depend primarily on the types of computers and networks you use, and on what specific tasks you want to accomplish.

Figure 4.3 emphasizes several major **software trends.** First, there has been a major trend away from custom-designed programs developed by the professional programmers of an organization. Instead, the trend is toward the use of off-the-shelf software packages acquired by end users from software vendors. This trend dramatically increased with the development of relatively inexpensive and easy-to-use application software packages and multipurpose *software suites* for microcomputers. The trend has accelerated recently, as software packages are designed with Web-enabled networking capabilities and collaboration features that optimize their usefulness for end users and workgroups on the Internet and corporate intranets and extranets. Also, many software packages can now be downloaded, updated, managed, and rented or leased from software companies or *application service providers* (ASPs) over the Internet and corporate intranets.

Second, there has been a steady trend away from (1) technical, machine-specific programming languages using binary-based or symbolic codes, or (2) *procedural languages,* which use brief statements and mathematical expressions to specify the sequence of instructions a computer must perform. Instead, the trend is toward the use

Figure 4.3

Trends in computer software. The trend in software is toward multipurpose, Web-enabled, expert-assisted packages with natural language and graphical user interfaces.

	FIRST GENERATION	SECOND GENERATION	THIRD (3GL) GENERATION	FOURTH (4GL) GENERATION	FIFTH GENERATION?
Trend: Toward Easy-to-Use Multipurpose Web–Enabled Application Packages for Productivity and Collaboration					
Software Trends	User-Written Programs Machine Languages	Packaged Programs Symbolic Languages	Operating Systems High-Level Languages	Database Management Systems Fourth-Generation Languages Microcomputer Packages	Natural and Object-Oriented Languages Multipurpose Graphic-Interface Network-Enabled Expert-Assisted Packages
Trend: Toward Visual or Conversational Programming Languages and Tools					

of a visual graphic interface for object-oriented programming, or toward nonprocedural *natural languages* for programming that are closer to human conversation. This trend accelerated with the creation of easy-to-use, nonprocedural *fourth-generation languages* (4GLs). It continues to grow as developments in object technology, graphics, and artificial intelligence produce natural language and graphical user interfaces that make both programming tools and software packages easier to use.

In addition, artificial intelligence features are built into many types of software packages. For example, software suites provide intelligent help features called *wizards* that help you perform common software functions like graphing parts of a spreadsheet or generating reports from a database. Other software packages use capabilities called *intelligent agents* to perform activities based on instructions from a user. For example, some electronic mail packages can use an intelligent agent capability to organize, send, and screen e-mail messages for you.

These major trends seem to be converging to produce a fifth generation of powerful, multipurpose, expert-assisted, and Web-enabled software packages with natural language and graphical interfaces to support the productivity and collaboration of both end users and IS professionals.

Application Software for End Users

Figure 4.2 showed that application software includes a variety of programs that can be subdivided into general-purpose and application-specific categories. Thousands of **application-specific** software packages are available to support specific applications of end users in business and other fields. For example, application-specific packages in business support managerial, professional, and business uses such as transaction processing, decision support, accounting, sales management, investment analysis, and electronic commerce. Application-specific software for science and engineering plays a major role in the research and development programs of industry and the design of efficient production processes for high-quality products. Other software packages help end users with personal finance and home management, or provide a wide variety of entertainment and educational products.

General-purpose application programs are programs that perform common information processing jobs for end users. For example, word processing programs, spreadsheet programs, database management programs, and graphics programs are popular with microcomputer users for home, education, business, scientific, and many other purposes. Because they significantly increase the productivity of end users, they are sometimes known as *productivity packages.* Other examples include Web browsers, electronic mail, and *groupware,* which help support communication and collaboration among workgroups and teams.

The basic program components of the top four software suites. Other programs may be included, depending on the suite edition selected.

Programs	Microsoft Office	Lotus SmartSuite	Corel WordPerfect Office	Sun StarOffice
Word Processor	Word	WordPro	WordPerfect	StarWriter
Spreadsheet	Excel	1–2–3	Quattro Pro	StarCalc
Presentation Graphics	PowerPoint	Freelance	Presentations	StarImpress
Database Manager	Access	Approach	Paradox	StarBase
Personal Information Manager	Outlook	Organizer	Corel Central	StarSchedule

Software Suites and Integrated Packages

Let's begin our discussion of popular general-purpose application software by looking at **software suites.** That's because the most widely used productivity packages come bundled together as software suites such as Microsoft Office, Lotus SmartSuite, Corel WordPerfect Office, and Sun's StarOffice. Examining their components gives us an overview of the important software tools that you can use to increase your productivity.

Figure 4.4 compares the basic programs that make up the top four software suites. Notice that each suite integrates software packages for word processing, spreadsheets, presentation graphics, database management, and personal information management. Microsoft, Lotus, Corel, and Sun bundle several other programs in each suite, depending on the version you select. Examples include programs for Internet access, e-mail, Web publishing, desktop publishing, voice recognition, financial management, electronic encyclopedias, and so on.

A software suite costs a lot less than the total cost of buying its individual packages separately. Another advantage is that all programs use a similar **graphical user interface** (GUI) of icons, tool and status bars, menus, and so on, which gives them the same look and feel, and makes them easier to learn and use. Software suites also share common tools, such as spell checkers and help wizards to increase their efficiency. Another big advantage of suites is that their programs are designed to work together seamlessly and import each other's files easily, no matter which program you are using at the time. These capabilities make them more efficient and easier to use than using a variety of individual package versions.

Of course, putting so many programs and features together in one super-size package does have some disadvantages. Industry critics argue that many software suite features are never used by most end users. The suites take up a lot of disk space, from over 100 megabytes to over 150 megabytes, depending on which version or functions you install. So such software is sometimes derisively called *bloatware* by its critics. The cost of suites can vary from as low as $100 for a competitive upgrade to over $700 for a full version of some editions of the suites.

These drawbacks are one reason for the continued use of **integrated packages** like Microsoft Works, Lotus eSuite WorkPlace, AppleWorks, and so on. Integrated packages combine some of the functions of several programs—word processing, spreadsheets, presentation graphics, database management, and so on—into one software package.

Because Works programs leave out many features and functions that are in individual packages and software suites, they cannot do as much as those packages do. However, they use a lot less disk space (less than 10 megabytes), cost less than a hundred dollars, and are frequently pre-installed on many low-end microcomputer systems. So integrated packages have proven that they offer enough functions and features for many computer users, while providing some of the advantages of software suites in a smaller package.

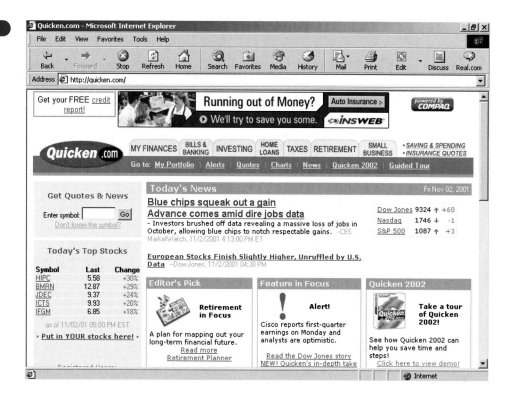

Figure 4.5

Using the Microsoft Internet Explorer Web browser to access the Quicken.com website.

Web Browsers and More

The most important software component for many computer users today is the once simple and limited, but now powerful and feature-rich, **Web browser.** A browser like Netscape Navigator or Microsoft Explorer is the key software interface you use to point and click your way through the hyperlinked resources of the World Wide Web and the rest of the Internet, as well as corporate intranets and extranets. Once limited to surfing the Web, browsers are becoming the universal software platform on which end users launch into information searches, e-mail, multimedia file transfer, discussion groups, and many other Internet, intranet, and extranet applications. See Figure 4.5.

Industry experts are predicting that the Web browser will be the model for how most people will use networked computers in the future. So now, whether you want to watch a video, make a phone call, download some software, hold a videoconference, check your e-mail, or work on a spreadsheet of your team's business plan, you can use your browser to launch and host such applications. That's why browsers are being called the *universal client*, that is, the software component installed on all of the networked computing and communications devices of the clients (users) throughout an enterprise.

Electronic Mail

The first thing many people do at work all over the world is check their e-mail. **Electronic mail** has changed the way people work and communicate. Millions of end users now depend on e-mail software to communicate with each other by sending and receiving electronic messages via the Internet or their organizations' intranets or extranets. E-mail is stored on network servers until you are ready. Whenever you want to, you can read your e-mail by displaying it on your workstations. So, with only a few minutes of effort (and a few microseconds or minutes of transmission time), a message to one or many individuals can be composed, sent, and received. See Figure 4.6.

As we mentioned earlier, e-mail software is now a component of top software suites and Web browsers. Free e-mail packages like Microsoft HotMail and Netscape WebMail are available to Internet users from online services and Internet service providers. Full-featured e-mail software like Microsoft Exchange E-Mail or Netscape Messenger can route messages to multiple end users based on predefined

Figure 4.6

Using the Microsoft
Outlook e-mail package.

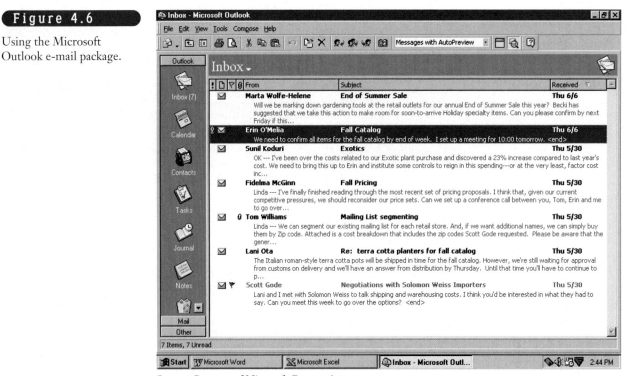

Source: Courtesy of Microsoft Corporation.

mailing lists and provide password security, automatic message forwarding, and remote user access. They also allow you to store messages in folders with provisions for adding attachments to message files. E-mail packages may also enable you to edit and send graphics and multimedia as well as text, and provide bulletin board and computer conferencing capabilities. Finally, your e-mail software may automatically filter and sort incoming messages (even news items from online services) and route them to appropriate user mailboxes and folders.

Word Processing and Desktop Publishing

Software for **word processing** has transformed the process of writing. Word processing packages computerize the creation, editing, revision, and printing of *documents* (such as letters, memos, and reports) by electronically processing your *text data* (words, phrases, sentences, and paragraphs). Top word processing packages like Microsoft Word, Lotus WordPro, and Corel WordPerfect can provide a wide variety of attractively printed documents with their desktop publishing capabilities. These packages can also convert all documents to HTML format for publication as Web pages on corporate intranets or the World Wide Web.

Word processing packages also provide advanced features. For example, a spelling checker capability can identify and correct spelling errors, and a thesaurus feature helps you find a better choice of words to express ideas. You can also identify and correct grammar and punctuation errors, as well as suggest possible improvements in your writing style, with grammar and style checker functions. Another text productivity tool is an idea processor or outliner function. It helps you organize and outline your thoughts before you prepare a document or develop a presentation. Besides converting documents to HTML format, you can also use the top packages to design and create Web pages from scratch for an Internet or intranet website. See Figure 4.7.

End users and organizations can use **desktop publishing** (DTP) software to produce their own printed materials that look professionally published. That is, they can design and print their own newsletters, brochures, manuals, and books with several type styles, graphics, photos, and colors on each page. Word processing packages and desktop publishing packages like Adobe PageMaker and QuarkXPress

Figure 4.7

Using the Microsoft Word word processing package. Note the insertion of clip art.

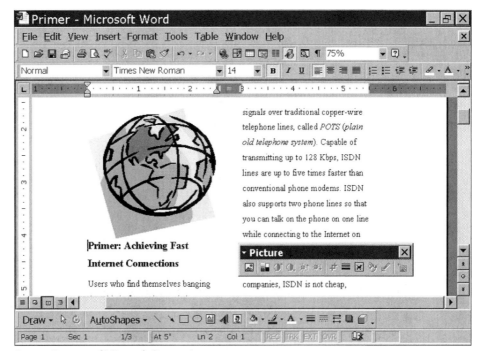

Source: Courtesy of Microsoft Corporation.

are used to do desktop publishing. Typically, text material and graphics can be generated by word processing and graphics packages and imported as text and graphics files. Optical scanners may be used to input text and graphics from printed material. You can also use files of *clip art*, which are predrawn graphic illustrations provided by the software package or available from other sources.

The heart of desktop publishing is a page design process called *page makeup* or *page composition*. Your video screen becomes an electronic pasteup board with rulers, column guides, and other page design aids. Text material and illustrations are then merged into the page format you design. The software will automatically move excess text to another column or page and help size and place illustrations and headings. Most DTP packages provide WYSIWYG (What You See Is What You Get) displays so you can see exactly what the finished document will look like before it is printed.

Electronic Spreadsheets

Electronic spreadsheet packages like Lotus 1-2-3, Microsoft Excel, and Corel QuattroPro are used for business analysis, planning, and modeling. They help you develop an *electronic spreadsheet*, which is a worksheet of rows and columns that can be stored on your PC or a network server, or converted to HTML format and stored as a Web page or *websheet* on the World Wide Web. Developing a spreadsheet involves designing its format and developing the relationships (formulas) that will be used in the worksheet. In response to your input, the computer performs necessary calculations based on the formulas you defined in the spreadsheet, and displays results immediately, whether at your workstation or website. Most packages also help you develop graphic displays of spreadsheet results. See Figure 4.8.

For example, you could develop a spreadsheet to record and analyze past and present advertising performance for a business. You could also develop hyperlinks to a similar websheet at your marketing team's intranet website. Now you have a decision support tool to help you answer *what-if questions* you may have about advertising. For example, "What would happen to market share if advertising expense increased by 10 percent?" To answer this question, you would simply change the advertising expense formula on the advertising performance worksheet you

Figure 4.8

Using an electronic spreadsheet package, Microsoft Excel. Note the use of graphics.

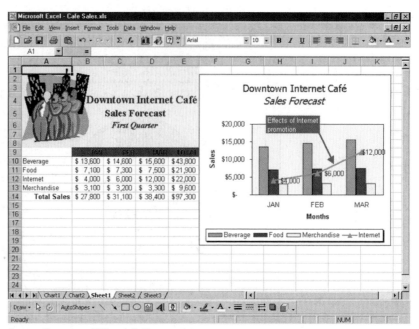

Source: Courtesy of Microsoft Corporation.

developed. The computer would recalculate the affected figures, producing new market share figures and graphics. You would then have a better insight on the effect of advertising decisions on market share. Then you could share this insight with a note on the websheet at your team's intranet website.

Database Management

Microcomputer versions of **database management** programs have become so popular that they are now viewed as general-purpose application software packages like word processing and spreadsheet packages. Database management packages such as Microsoft Access, Lotus Approach, or Corel Paradox allow you to set up and manage databases on your PC, network server, or the World Wide Web. See Figure 4.9. Most database managers can perform four primary tasks, which we will discuss further in Chapter 5.

- **Database development.** Define and organize the content, relationships, and structure of the data needed to build a database, including any hyperlinks to data on Web pages.
- **Database interrogation.** Access the data in a database to display information in a variety of formats. End users can selectively retrieve and display information and produce forms, reports, and other documents, including Web pages.
- **Database maintenance.** Add, delete, update, and correct the data in a database, including hyperlinked data on Web pages.
- **Application development.** Develop prototypes of Web pages, queries, forms, reports, and labels for a proposed business application. Use a built-in 4GL or application generator to program the application.

Presentation Graphics and Multimedia

Which type of display would you rather see: columns or rows of numbers, or a graphics display of the same information? **Presentation graphics** packages help you convert numeric data into graphics displays such as line charts, bar graphs, pie charts, and many other types of graphics. Most of the top packages also help you prepare multimedia presentations of graphics, photos, animation, and video

Figure 4.9

Using a database management package. Note how Microsoft Access lets you select and preview a variety of database files.

Source: Courtesy of Microsoft Corporation.

clips, including publishing to the World Wide Web. Not only are graphics and multimedia displays easier to comprehend and communicate than numeric data but multiple-color and multiple-media displays also can more easily emphasize key points, strategic differences, and important trends in the data. Presentation graphics has proved to be much more effective than tabular presentations of numeric data for reporting and communicating in advertising media, management reports, or other business presentations. See Figure 4.10.

Presentation graphics software packages like Microsoft PowerPoint, Lotus Freelance, or Corel Presentations give you many easy-to-use capabilities that encourage

Figure 4.10

Using a presentation graphics package, Microsoft PowerPoint.

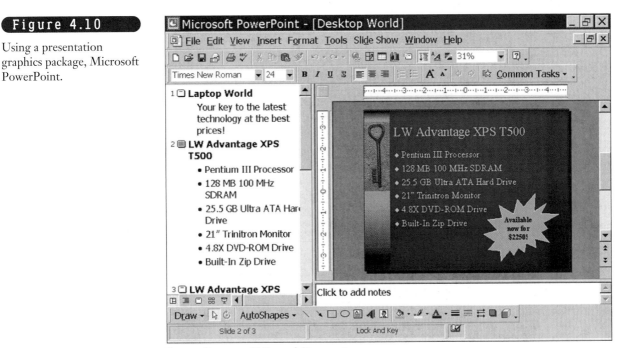

Source: Courtesy of Microsoft Corporation.

the use of graphics presentations. For example, most packages help you design and manage computer-generated and -orchestrated *slide shows* containing many integrated graphics and multimedia displays. Or you can select from a variety of predesigned *templates* of business presentations, prepare and edit the outline and notes for a presentation, and manage the use of multimedia files of graphics, photos, sounds, and video clips. And of course, the top packages help you tailor your graphics and multimedia presentation for transfer in HTML format to websites on corporate intranets or the World Wide Web.

Multimedia Software Technologies

Hypertext and hypermedia are software technologies for multimedia presentations. By definition, hypertext contains only text and a limited amount of graphics. Hypermedia are electronic documents that contain multiple forms of media, including text, graphics, video, and so on. Key topics and other presentations in hypertext or hypermedia documents are indexed by software links so that they can be quickly searched by the reader. For example, if you click your mouse button on an underlined term on a hypermedia document, your computer may instantly bring up another display using text, graphics, and sound related to that term. Once you finish viewing that presentation, you can return to what you were reading originally, or jump to another part of the document.

Hypertext and hypermedia are developed by using software packages that rely on specialized programming languages like Java and the Hypertext Markup Language (HTML), which create hyperlinks to other parts of a document or to other documents and multimedia files. Hypertext and hypermedia documents can thus be programmed to let a reader navigate through a multimedia database by

---

Figure 4.11

Examples of software technologies for multimedia productions and presentations available on the World Wide Web.

Online Multimedia Technologies
● **Liquid Audio www.liquidaudio.com** Liquid Audio's Liquid Player is a program you can download for free to play Web-based audio tracks. MP3 and Liquid Audio compressed files are reproduced with CD-quality sound. The program lets you view album art and lyrics while you listen, set up custom play lists, and purchase a copy of the music from the publisher.
● **Macromedia Shockwave and Flash www.macromedia.com** Macromedia makes some of the most popular software for jazzing up Web pages with sound and animation. If your browser doesn't have the Shockwave and Flash player plug-ins, you can download them for free here. Check out the ShockRave website (www.shockrave.com) for a sampling of what's out there.
● **MP3.com www.mp3.com** The granddaddy of MP3 sites, MP3.com provides an open marketplace for thousands of artists and their fans. Listen to free sample tracks, then buy the whole album if it appeals to you. A Net radio station, mp3radio.com, features streaming MP3s and links to purchase CDs.
● **RealNetworks www.real.com** RealNetworks software, RealPlayer G2, provides a slick user interface and much improved transmission of compressed audio and video. G2 is free, but for $29.95 you can download a copy of RealPlayer Plus G2, which offers several advanced features: an audio equalizer, fine-tuning for video, the ability to save media clips to your hard drive, phone support, a manual and CD-ROM, and one-click searches for broadcasts on the Web.
● **Winamp www.winamp.com** For Windows users, Winamp is a great shareware program—they ask for $10 to $20 if you keep using it—for playing back nearly every type of digital audio file you find online. Along with its virtual graphic equalizers, Winamp's SHOUTcast plug-in enables you to broadcast or listen to streaming MP3 radio from thousands of Net radio stations.

Source: Adapted from "Tune In," Technology Buyers Guide, *Fortune*, Winter 2000, pp. 268–72, and "Changing the Channels," Technology Buyers Guide, *Fortune*, Winter 2001, pp. 266–70.

following a chain of hyperlinks through various multimedia files. The websites on the World Wide Web of the Internet are a popular example of this technology. Thus, the use of hypertext and hypermedia software in Web browsers and other programs provides an environment for online interactive multimedia presentations. See Figure 4.11.

Personal Information Managers

The **personal information manager** (PIM) is a popular software package for end user productivity and collaboration, and is a popular application for personal digital assistant (PDA) hand-held devices. PIMs such as Lotus Organizer and Microsoft Outlook help end users store, organize, and retrieve information about customers, clients, and prospects, or schedule and manage appointments, meetings, and tasks. The PIM package will organize data you enter and retrieve information in a variety of forms, depending on the style and structure of the PIM and the information you want. For example, information can be retrieved as an electronic calendar or list of appointments, meetings, or other things to do; the timetable for a project; or a display of key facts and financial data about customers, clients, or sales prospects. See Figure 4.12.

Personal information managers are sold as independent programs or are included in software suites, and vary widely in their style, structure, and features. For example, Lotus Organizer uses a notebook with tabs format, while Microsoft Outlook organizes data about people as a continuous A–to–Z list. Most PIMs emphasize the maintenance of *contact lists*, that is, customers, clients, or prospects. Scheduling appointments and meetings and task management are other top PIM applications. PIMs are now changing to include the ability to access the World Wide Web and provide e-mail capability. Also, some PIMs use Internet and e-mail features to support team collaboration by sharing information such as contact lists, task lists, and schedules with other networked PIM users.

Groupware

Groupware is *collaboration software*, that is, software that helps workgroups and teams work together to accomplish group assignments. Groupware is a fast-growing category of general-purpose application software that combines a variety of software

---

Figure 4.12

Using a personal information manager (PIM): Microsoft Outlook.

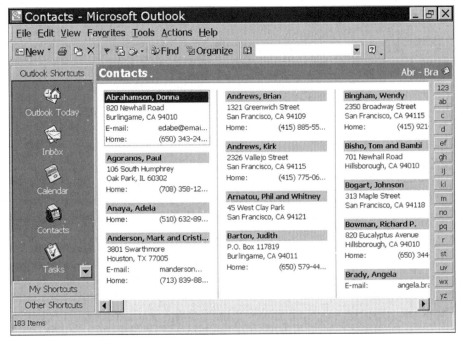

Source: Courtesy of Microsoft Corporation.

Figure 4.13

Lotus Notes is the leading corporate groupware package.

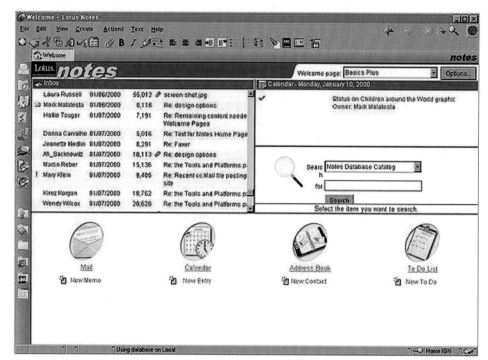

Source: Courtesy of Lotus Development Corporation.

features and functions to facilitate collaboration. For example, groupware products like Lotus Notes, Novell GroupWise, Microsoft Exchange, and Netscape Communicator support collaboration through electronic mail, discussion groups and databases, scheduling, task management, data, audio and videoconferencing, and so on. See Figure 4.13.

Groupware products are changing in several ways to meet the demand for better tools for collaboration. Groupware is now designed to use the Internet and corporate intranets and extranets to make collaboration possible on a global scale by *virtual teams* located anywhere in the world. For example, team members might use the Internet for global e-mail, project discussion forums, and joint Web page development. Or they might use corporate intranets to publish project news and progress reports, and work jointly on documents stored on Web servers.

Collaborative capabilities are also being added to other software to give them groupware features. For example, in the Microsoft Office software suite, Microsoft Word keeps track of who made revisions to each document, Excel tracks all changes made to a spreadsheet, and Outlook lets you keep track of tasks you delegate to other team members.

Other Business Software

As we mentioned earlier, there are many other types of application software used in business today. Application software packages support managerial and operational uses such as accounting, transaction processing, customer relationship management, enterprise resource planning, data warehousing and data mining, and electronic commerce, to name a few.

For example, data warehousing and data mining are discussed in Chapters 5 and 9; accounting, marketing, manufacturing, human resource management, and financial management applications are covered in Chapter 7, along with customer relationship management, enterprise resource planning, supply chain management, and electronic commerce. Decision support and data analysis applications are explored in Chapter 9. Figure 4.14 illustrates some of these major application software categories.

Figure 4.14

Some of the major application software categories in an e-business enterprise.

Source: Adapted from Ravi Kalakota and Marcia Robinson, *E-business: Roadmap for Success* (Reading, MA: Addison-Wesley, 2001), p. 243. © 2001 Addison-Wesley Publishing Company, Inc. Reprinted by permission of Addison-Wesley Longman Inc.

System Software: Computer System Management

System Software Overview

Analyzing Air Products, Farmers Group, and Others

System software consists of programs that manage and support a computer system and its information processing activities. For example, operating systems and network management programs serve as a vital *software interface* between computer networks and hardware and the application programs of end users.

Read the Real World Case on Air Products, Farmers Group, and Others on the next page. We can learn a lot about the business value of competitive developments in system software from this example. See Figure 4.15.

This case illustrates the challenges faced by many companies as Microsoft intensifies its battle for the enterprise software market, where it lags behind Sun, IBM, and Oracle. Companies like Air Products and Chemicals concentrate on the present and potential business and IT benefits of an integrated family of software products that work together. Thus they have chosen a Microsoft-centric strategy that standardizes on Microsoft software products. Farmers Group and other companies, on the other hand, are wary of the loss of control over IT costs and flexibility that may result from being locked-in to one vendor for all of their software products. This view intensified in 2001 as Microsoft began implementing a major change in its software licensing policy and fee structure that increased the costs of many corporate users. Thus, companies like Farmers Group and Green Mountain Coffee are now actively seeking alternatives to Microsoft software products. But the consensus is that the battle is only beginning, as Microsoft, IBM, and Oracle compete head-to-head in the enterprise software market.

Overview

Figure 4.16 shows that we can group system software into two major categories:

- **System management programs.** Programs that manage the hardware, software, network, and data resources of computer systems during the execution of the various information processing jobs of users. Examples of important system management programs are operating systems, network management programs, database management systems, and system utilities.

- **System development programs.** Programs that help users develop information system programs and procedures and prepare user programs for

Figure 4.15

Cecilia Claudio, CIO of Farmers Group Inc., says Microsoft's enterprise software licensing costs and policies are causing her to aggressively seek alternative software products.

Source: Seth Joel

Air Products, Farmers Group, and Others:
Microsoft's Battle for the Enterprise Software Market

Two weeks before Christmas 2000, Steve Ballmer delivered a memo to his 40,000 employees. "We have only begun to scratch the surface of competing in the market with the 'big iron' companies like Sun, Oracle, and IBM," the Microsoft CEO wrote. Ballmer recently identified the large enterprise software market as one of Microsoft's top six priorities. So far, Microsoft group manager Barry Goffe said his company's $4 billion in enterprise software revenue is a "mathematically insignificant" portion of the $150 billion enterprise software market.

Microsoft's Status. But in segment after segment, the Redmond, Washington, software giant is making a credible and sometimes even impressive showing. Analysts said it has enough momentum to overtake Lotus Development's Notes products in the messaging and collaboration market, and its Windows CE for the Pocket PC is surging in its mobile computing battle with Palm Inc. in the enterprise field. Still, there are no signs that Microsoft is approaching the market share that suggests monopoly power.

Take the server operating system market, for example. Microsoft Windows server versions have penetrated a majority of small businesses, and it has secured a solid place in midsize and large companies, especially for specific tasks: file and print serving, Web serving, and application serving. But Windows will continue to battle open-source Linux at the low end and commercial Unix at the high end, analysts say.

Even Microsoft's exalted position in the software developer community, often viewed as a critical factor in the company's success, has taken a hit. Many large corporations now write applications for Java-based application servers, and Gartner Group, Inc. predicts it will be a two-standard, Java/Microsoft world five years from now. And Microsoft's SQL Server has shaken off early ridicule to reach a solid No. 3 in the enterprise database market, but still commands only a 15 percent market share.

That's not to say that Microsoft hasn't been laying the foundation to become a major enterprise player. It has courted developers, invested big in research and development, worked hard to improve its enterprise software, and boosted its consulting capacity. Microsoft also continues to leverage one product off of another—bundling and integrating software while frustrating competitors.

Microsoft's Users. Enterprise users have mixed feelings about Microsoft. The appeal of tightly integrated products that work well together is compelling for many companies. Three years ago, Air Products and Chemicals Inc. in Allentown, Pennsylvania, decided to go Microsoft-centric for just that reason. "We can leverage our IT staff's skills and knowledge better," said Roger Gariepy, the company's chief information technologist.

But one-stop shopping can also inspire resistance among those concerned about competition. "Microsoft has incredible resources, both human and capital, so whatever they decide to dominate, they will dominate them," said Cecilia Claudio, CIO at Farmers Group Inc., a Los Angeles–based national insurance company. Claudio said she will deal with Microsoft's power and arrogance by becoming "much more aggressive" about seeking alternatives to the vendor. One reason: she said Microsoft's controversial new Software Assurance licensing policy and fee structure will increase her costs.

Several IT managers warned that they may upgrade less often or consider looking more seriously at Microsoft competitors' products rather than pony up for potentially costly licenses or upgrades. "If Microsoft continues to make my choices narrower and life tougher for me, they'll see exactly how little monopoly they really do have over this market, and we'll exercise our choices to go somewhere else," said Jim Prevo, CIO at Green Mountain Coffee, Inc., in Waterbury, Vermont. Prevo added that he had never even thought about considering alternatives until he was confronted with Microsoft's new licensing changes. Rob Enderle, an analyst at Giga Information Group Inc., said one of his firm's clients, a $2 billion insurance company, is yanking out everything but Microsoft's desktop products in response to the changes.

But Microsoft would need to jump a considerable number of hurdles to become a dominant force in the enterprise market anyway, analysts said. Many IT managers still harbor doubts about Microsoft's scalability and reliability claims for its enterprise software products. And Gartner research shows that Microsoft's software challenger to high-end Unix systems—Windows 2000 Datacenter Server—is off to a slow start, with no more than 200 deployments. But maybe a bigger hurdle is simple inertia. Large users aren't inclined to rip out their mainframes and Sun, IBM, or Oracle Unix servers that are working just fine.

For Microsoft to have a stranglehold on enterprise software, IBM and Oracle would have to fail, Gartner analyst Tom Bittman said. "Will IBM and Oracle both fail? No. They're all going to be fighting it out, and it's going to be a tooth-and-nail fight."

Case Study Questions

1. What is the business value of a Microsoft-centric enterprise software strategy for midsize to large companies? What is the downside of such a strategy?

2. What is the business value of choosing to use a mainframe or Sun, IBM, or Oracle Unix enterprise software strategy for midsize to large companies? What is the downside of this strategy?

3. What role could Linux and other open-source software play in these enterprise software strategies?

Source: Adapted from Carol Sliwa and Patrick Thibodeau, "Microsoft Makes Gains in Enterprise Markets," *Computerworld*, June 25, 2001, pp. 16, 22; and Carol Sliwa, "License Changes Anger Managers", *Computerworld*, August 20, 2001, pp. 1, 61. Reprinted by permission.

Figure 4.16

The system and application software interface between end users and computer hardware.

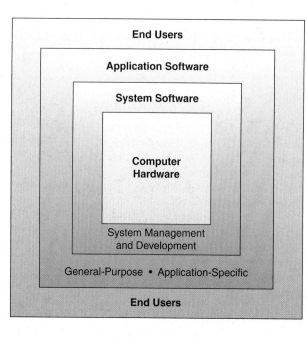

computer processing. Major development programs are programming language translators and editors, other programming tools, and CASE (computer-aided software engineering) packages.

Operating Systems

The most important system software package for any computer is its operating system. An **operating system** is an integrated system of programs that manages the operations of the CPU, controls the input/output and storage resources and activities of the computer system, and provides various support services as the computer executes the application programs of users.

The primary purpose of an operating system is to maximize the productivity of a computer system by operating it in the most efficient manner. An operating system minimizes the amount of human intervention required during processing. It helps your application programs perform common operations such as accessing a network, entering data, saving and retrieving files, and printing or displaying output. If you have any hands-on experience on a computer, you know that the operating system must be loaded and activated before you can accomplish other tasks. This emphasizes the fact that operating systems are the most indispensable components of the software interface between users and the hardware of their computer systems.

Operating System Functions

An operating system performs five basic functions in the operation of a computer system: providing a user interface, resource management, task management, file management, and utilities and support services. See Figure 4.17.

The User Interface. The **user interface** is the part of the operating system that allows you to communicate with it so you can load programs, access files, and accomplish other tasks. Three main types of user interfaces are the *command-driven, menu-driven,* and *graphical user interfaces.* The trend in user interfaces for operating systems and other software is moving away from the entry of brief end user commands, or even the selection of choices from menus of options. Instead, most software provides an easy-to-use **graphical user interface** (GUI) that uses icons, bars, buttons, boxes, and other images. GUIs rely on pointing devices like the electronic mouse or touchpad to make selections that help you get things done. See Figure 4.18.

Resource Management. An operating system uses a variety of **resource management** programs to manage the hardware and networking resources of a computer

Figure 4.17

The basic functions of an operating system include a user interface, resource management, task management, file management, and utilities and other functions.

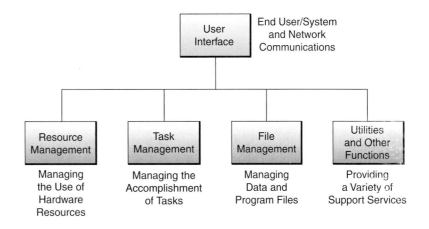

system, including its CPU, memory, secondary storage devices, telecommunications processors, and input/output peripherals. For example, memory management programs keep track of where data and programs are stored. They may also subdivide memory into a number of sections and swap parts of programs and data between memory and magnetic disks or other secondary storage devices. This can provide a computer system with a **virtual memory** capability that is significantly larger than the real memory capacity of its primary storage circuits. So, a computer with a virtual memory capability can process large programs and greater amounts of data than the capacity of its memory chips would normally allow.

File Management. An operating system contains **file management** programs that control the creation, deletion, and access of files of data and programs. File management also involves keeping track of the physical location of files on magnetic disks and other secondary storage devices. So operating systems maintain directories of information about the location and characteristics of files stored on a computer system's secondary storage devices.

Figure 4.18

The graphical user interface of Microsoft's Windows 2000 operating system.

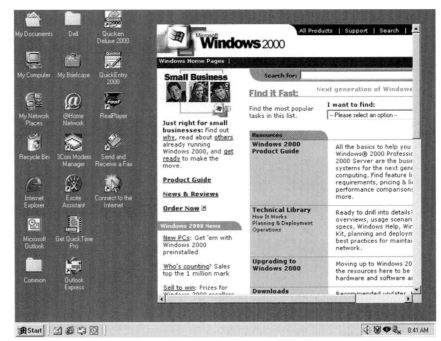

Source: Courtesy of Microsoft Corporation.

Task Management. The **task management** programs of an operating system manage the accomplishment of the computing tasks of end users. They give each task a slice of a CPU's time and interrupt the CPU operations to substitute other tasks. Task management may involve a **multitasking** capability where several computing tasks can occur at the same time. Multitasking may take the form of *multiprogramming*, where the CPU can process the tasks of several programs at the same time, or *timesharing*, where the computing tasks of several users can be processed at the same time. The efficiency of multitasking operations depends on the processing power of a CPU and the virtual memory and multitasking capabilities of the operating system it uses.

Most microcomputer, midrange, and mainframe operating systems provide a multitasking capability. With multitasking, end users can do two or more operations (e.g., keyboarding and printing) or applications (e.g., word processing and financial analysis) concurrently, that is, at the same time. Multitasking on microcomputers has also been made possible by the development of more powerful microprocessors and their ability to directly address much larger memory capacities (up to 4 gigabytes). This allows an operating system to subdivide primary storage into several large partitions, each of which can be used by a different application program.

In effect, a single computer can act as if it were several computers, or *virtual machines*, since each application program is running independently at the same time. The number of programs that can be run concurrently depends on the amount of memory that is available and the amount of processing each job demands. That's because a microprocessor (or CPU) can become overloaded with too many jobs and provide unacceptably slow response times. However, if memory and processing capacities are adequate, multitasking allows end users to easily switch from one application to another, share data files among applications, and process some applications in a *background* mode. Typically, background tasks include large printing jobs, extensive mathematical computation, or unattended telecommunications sessions.

Popular Operating Systems

Figure 4.19 compares the four top operating systems today. For many years, MS-DOS (Microsoft Disk Operating System) was the most widely used microcomputer operating system. It is a single-user, single-tasking operating system, but was given a graphical user interface and limited multitasking capabilities by combining it with Microsoft Windows. Microsoft began replacing its DOS/Windows combination in 1995 with the Windows 95 operating system, featuring a graphical user interface, true multitasking, networking, multimedia, and many other capabilities. Microsoft introduced an enhanced Windows 98 version during 1998, and a Windows Me (Millennium Edition) consumer PC system in 2000, with a Windows XP version released in 2001.

Microsoft introduced its **Windows NT** (New Technology) operating system in 1995. Windows NT is a powerful, multitasking, multiuser operating system that is installed on many network servers to manage client/server networks and on PCs with high-performance computing requirements. New Server and Workstation versions were introduced in 1997. Microsoft merged its Windows 98 and Windows NT products into the **Windows 2000** operating system during the year 2000.

Windows 2000 has four versions, including:

- *Professional:* a full-featured operating system for PC desktops and laptops.
- *Server:* a multipurpose operating system for network servers and Web servers in smaller networks.
- *Advanced Server:* a network operating system to manage large networks and websites powered by *server farms* of many servers.
- *Datacenter Server:* a high-performance network operating system for large-scale business applications, such as online transaction processing and data warehousing.

Figure 4.19   A comparison of popular operating systems.

Windows 2000 *Microsoft*	Solaris 8 UNIX *Sun Microsystems*
What's New. Improvements in reliability and the ability to manage computer networks less expensively. Handles some of the more demanding computing jobs, such as managing major websites.	**What's New.** Solaris handles servers with as many as 64 microprocessors—compared with 32 for Windows 2000. Also, eight computers can be clustered together to work as one, compared with four for Windows 2000.
Strengths. It is inexpensive. Used with servers based on Intel microprocessors, it's about one-third as expensive as UNIX-based combos from the likes of Sun.	**Strengths.** Solaris has emerged as the server operating system of choice for large websites. It's super-reliable and handles the most demanding tasks.
Weaknesses. It still can't run on most powerful servers, and many computer systems administrators don't trust it for complex computing tasks.	**Weaknesses.** It is more expensive than Windows 2000 systems, though Sun is now offering Solaris free on low-end Sun servers.
Netware 5.1 *Novell*	Linux 6.1 *Red Hat Software*
What's New. Novell's directory software now runs on Windows 2000, Solaris, and Linux servers as well as NetWare, making it easier for companies to manage complex networks.	**What's New.** It's easier to install than it used to be. Also, customers can now cluster up to eight servers—which means better reliability.
Strengths. The directory software for keeping track of computers, programs, and people on a network has proved vital to companies such as Ford and Wal-Mart, and this update keeps it ahead.	**Strengths.** Red Hat taps into tens of thousands of volunteer programmers who help out with improvements to the open-source Linux operating system. Plus, Red Hat's server package is nearly free: $149.
Weaknesses. NetWare is primarily a networking system—not able to run general applications such as databases or accounting.	**Weaknesses.** Linux is good for serving up Web pages, but isn't as effective as Windows 2000 at handling more complex jobs.

Source: Adapted from Steve Hamm, Peter Burrows, and Andy Reinhardt, "Is Windows Ready to Run E-Business?" *Business Week*, January 24, 2000, pp. 154–60. Reprinted with special permission, copyright © 2000 by The McGraw-Hill Companies, Inc.

Originally developed by AT&T, **UNIX** now is also offered by other vendors, including Solaris by Sun Microsystems and AIX by IBM. UNIX is a multitasking, multiuser, network-managing operating system whose portability allows it to run on mainframes, midrange computers, and microcomputers. UNIX is a popular choice for Web and other network servers.

Linux is a low-cost, powerful, and reliable UNIX-like operating system that is rapidly gaining market share as a high-performance operating system for network servers and Web servers in both small and large networks. Linux was developed as free or low-cost *shareware* or *open-source software* over the Internet in the 1990s by Linus Torvald of Finland and millions of programmers around the world. Linux is still being enhanced in this way, but is sold with extra features and support services by software vendors such as Red Hat, Caldera, and VA Linux. PC versions are also available, which support office software suites, Web browsers, and other application software.

The **Mac OS X** is the latest operating system from Apple for the iMac and other Macintosh microcomputers. The Mac OS X has a new graphical user interface as well as advanced multitasking and multimedia capabilities, along with a new suite of Internet services called iTools [9].

Network Management Programs

Today's information systems rely heavily on the Internet, intranets, extranets, local area networks, and other telecommunications networks to interconnect end user workstations, network servers, and other computer systems. This requires a variety of system software for **network management,** including **network operating systems,** network performance monitors, telecommunications monitors, and so on. These programs are used by network servers and other computers in a network to

A display of a network management program.

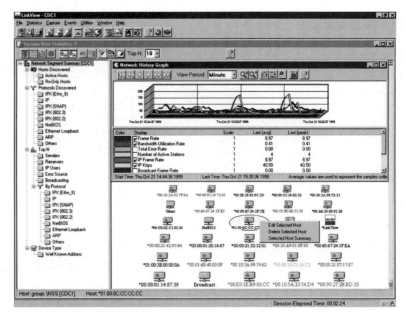

Source: Courtesy of Tinwald Corporation.

manage network performance. Network management programs perform such functions as automatically checking client PCs and video terminals for input/output activity, assigning priorities to data communications requests from clients and terminals, and detecting and correcting transmission errors and other network problems. In addition, some network management programs function as *middleware* to help diverse networks communicate with each other. See Figure 4.20.

Examples of network management programs include Novell NetWare, the most widely used network operating system for complex interconnected local area networks. Microsoft's Windows NT Server and its new Windows 2000 server versions are other popular network operating systems. IBM's telecommunications monitor CICS (Customer Identification and Control System) is an example of a widely used *telecommunications monitor* for mainframe-based wide area networks. IBM's NetView and Hewlett-Packard's OpenView are examples of network management programs for managing several mainframe-based or midrange-based computer networks.

Database Management Systems

In Section I, we discussed microcomputer database management programs like Microsoft Access, Lotus Approach, and Corel Paradox. In mainframe and midrange computer systems, a **database management system** (DBMS) is considered an important system software package that controls the development, use, and maintenance of the databases of computer-using organizations. A DBMS program helps organizations use their integrated collections of data records and files known as databases. It allows different user application programs to easily access the same database. For example, a DBMS makes it easy for an employee database to be accessed by payroll, employee benefits, and other human resource programs. A DBMS also simplifies the process of retrieving information from databases in the form of displays and reports. Instead of having to write computer programs to extract information, end users can ask simple questions in a *query language*. Thus, many DBMS packages provide *fourth-generation languages* (4GLs) and other application development features. Examples of popular mainframe and midrange packages are IBM's DB2 Universal Database and Oracle 9i by Oracle Corporation. We will discuss database management software in more detail in Chapter 5.

The Diskeeper utility is a top-rated defragmentation program that dynamically eliminates fragmented file storage (as shown here), which dramatically improves hard drive performance.

Volume	Session Status	File System	Capacity	Free Space	% Free Space
Data E (J:)		NTFS	996 MB	477 MB	47 %
Apps2 F (M:)	Defragmented	NTFS	502 MB	368 MB	73 %
NTSYSTEM (N:)		FAT	595 MB	66,112 KB	10 %
Email 1 (O:)		NTFS	392 MB	287 MB	73 %
E-mail 2 (P:)	Analyzed	NTFS	200 MB	61,899 KB	30 %

Source: Courtesy of Executive Software International.

Other System Management Programs

Several other types of system management software are marketed as separate programs or are included as part of an operating system. Utility programs, or **utilities,** are an important example. Programs like Norton Utilities perform miscellaneous housekeeping and file conversion functions. Examples include data backup, data recovery, virus protection, data compression, and file defragmentation. Most operating systems also provide many utilities that perform a variety of helpful chores for computer users. See Figure 4.21.

Other examples of system support programs include performance monitors and security monitors. **Performance monitors** are programs that monitor and adjust the performance and usage of one or more computer systems to keep them running efficiently. **Security monitors** are packages that monitor and control the use of computer systems and provide warning messages and record evidence of unauthorized use of computer resources. A recent trend is to merge both types of programs into operating systems like Microsoft's Windows 2000 Datacenter Server, or into system management software like Computer Associates' CA-Unicenter, which can manage both mainframe systems and servers in a data center.

Another important software trend is the use of system software known as **application servers,** which provide a *middleware* interface between an operating system and the application programs of users. For example, application servers like BEA's WebLogic and IBM's WebSphere help Web-based e-business and e-commerce applications run much faster and more efficiently on computers using Windows, Unix, and other operating systems.

Programming Languages

To understand computer software, you need a basic knowledge of the role that programming languages play in the development of computer programs. A **programming language** allows a programmer to develop the sets of instructions that constitute a computer program. Many different programming languages have been developed, each with its own unique vocabulary, grammar, and uses.

Machine Languages

Machine languages (or *first-generation languages*) are the most basic level of programming languages. In the early stages of computer development, all program instructions had to be written using binary codes unique to each computer. This

Examples of four levels of
programming languages.
These programming
language instructions might
be used to compute the sum
of two numbers as expressed
by the formula X = Y + Z.

Four Levels of Programming Languages	
● **Machine Languages:** Use binary coded instructions 1010 11001 1011 11010 1100 11011	● **High-Level Languages:** Use brief statements or arithmetic notations BASIC: X = Y + Z COBOL: COMPUTE X = Y + Z
● **Assembler Languages:** Use symbolic coded instructions LOD Y ADD Z STR X	● **Fourth-Generation Languages:** Use natural and nonprocedural statements SUM THE FOLLOWING NUMBERS

type of programming involves the difficult task of writing instructions in the form of strings of binary digits (ones and zeros) or other number systems. Programmers must have a detailed knowledge of the internal operations of the specific type of CPU they are using. They must write long series of detailed instructions to accomplish even simple processing tasks. Programming in machine language requires specifying the storage locations for every instruction and item of data used. Instructions must be included for every switch and indicator used by the program. These requirements make machine language programming a difficult and error-prone task. A machine language program to add two numbers together in the CPU of a specific computer and store the result might take the form shown in Figure 4.22.

Assembler Languages

Assembler languages (or *second-generation languages*) are the next level of programming languages. They were developed to reduce the difficulties in writing machine language programs. The use of assembler languages requires language translator programs called *assemblers* that allow a computer to convert the instructions of such language into machine instructions. Assembler languages are frequently called symbolic languages because symbols are used to represent operation codes and storage locations. Convenient alphabetic abbreviations called *mnemonics* (memory aids) and other symbols represent operation codes, storage locations, and data elements. For example, the computation X = Y + Z in an assembler language might take the form shown in Figure 4.22.

Assembler languages are still used as a method of programming a computer in a machine-oriented language. Most computer manufacturers provide an assembler language that reflects the unique machine language instruction set of a particular line of computers. This feature is particularly desirable to *system programmers*, who program system software (as opposed to application programmers, who program application software), since it provides them with greater control and flexibility in designing a program for a particular computer. They can then produce more efficient software, that is, programs that require a minimum of instructions, storage, and CPU time to perform a specific processing assignment.

High-Level Languages

High-level languages (or *third-generation languages*) use instructions, which are called *statements* that use brief statements or arithmetic expressions. Individual high-level language statements are actually *macroinstructions*; that is, each individual statement generates several machine instructions when translated into machine language by high-level language translator programs called *compilers* or *interpreters*. High-level language statements resemble the phrases or mathematical expressions required to express the problem or procedure being programmed. The *syntax* (vocabulary, punctuation, and grammatical rules) and the *semantics* (meanings) of such statements do

Figure 4.23

Highlights of several important high-level languages.

High-Level Programming Languages
Ada: Named after Augusta Ada Byron, considered the world's first computer programmer. Developed for the U.S. Department of Defense as a standard "high-order language" to replace COBOL and FORTRAN.
BASIC: (Beginner's All-Purpose Symbolic Instruction Code). A simple procedure-oriented language designed for end user programming.
C: A mid-level structured language developed as part of the UNIX operating system. It resembles a machine-independent assembler language.
COBOL: (COmmon Business Oriented Language). An Englishlike language widely used for programming business applications.
FORTRAN: (FORmula TRANslation). A high-level language designed for scientific and engineering applications.
Pascal: Named after Blaise Pascal. Developed specifically to incorporate structured programming concepts.

not reflect the internal code of any particular computer. For example, the computation $X = Y + Z$ would be programmed in the high-level languages of BASIC and COBOL as shown in Figure 4.22.

A high-level language is easier to learn and program than an assembler language, since it has less-rigid rules, forms, and syntaxes. However, high-level language programs are usually less efficient than assembler language programs and require a greater amount of computer time for translation into machine instructions. Since most high-level languages are machine independent, programs written in a high-level language do not have to be reprogrammed when a new computer is installed, and programmers do not have to learn a different language for each type of computer. Figure 4.23 highlights some of the major high-level languages still being used in some form today.

Fourth-Generation Languages

The term **fourth-generation language** describes a variety of programming languages that are more nonprocedural and conversational than prior languages. These languages are called fourth-generation languages (4GLs) to differentiate them from machine languages (first generation), assembler languages (second generation), and high-level languages (third generation).

Most fourth-generation languages are **nonprocedural languages** that encourage users and programmers to specify the results they want, while the computer determines the sequence of instructions that will accomplish those results. Thus, fourth-generation languages have helped simplify the programming process. **Natural languages** are 4GLs that are very close to English or other human languages. Research and development activity in artificial intelligence (AI) is developing programming languages that are as easy to use as ordinary conversation in one's native tongue. For example, INTELLECT, a natural language 4GL, would use a statement like, "What are the average exam scores in MIS 200?" to program a simple average exam score task.

The ease of use of 4GLs is gained at the expense of some loss in flexibility. It is frequently difficult to override some of the prespecified formats or procedures of 4GLs. Also, the machine language code generated by a program developed by a 4GL is frequently much less efficient (in terms of processing speed and amount of storage capacity needed) than a program written in a language like COBOL. Thus, some large transaction processing applications programmed in a 4GL have not provided reasonable response times when faced with a large amount of real-time transaction processing and end user inquiries. However, 4GLs have shown great success in business applications that do not have a high volume of transaction processing.

Figure 4.24

An example of a bank savings account object. This object consists of data about a customer's account balance and the basic operations that can be performed on those data.

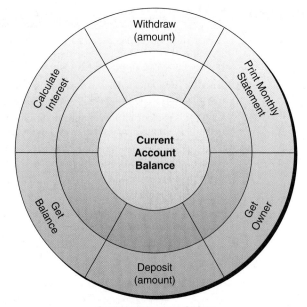

Savings Account Object

Object-Oriented Languages

Object-oriented programming (OOP) languages like Visual Basic, C++, and Java have become major tools of software development. Briefly, while most other programming languages separate data elements from the procedures or actions that will be performed upon them, OOP languages tie them together into **objects.** Thus, an object consists of data and the actions that can be performed on the data. For example, an object could be a set of data about a bank customer's savings account, and the operations (such as interest calculations) that might be performed upon the data. Or an object could be data in graphic form such as a video display window, plus the display actions that might be used upon it. See Figure 4.24.

In procedural languages, a program consists of procedures to perform actions on each data element. However, in object-oriented systems, objects tell other objects to perform actions on themselves. For example, to open a window on a computer video display, a beginning menu object could send a window object a message to open and a window will appear on the screen. That's because the window object contains the program code for opening itself.

Object-oriented languages are easier to use and more efficient for programming the graphics-oriented user interfaces required by many applications. Also, once objects are programmed, they are reusable. Therefore, reusability of objects is a major benefit of object-oriented programming. For example, programmers can construct a user interface for a new program by assembling standard objects such as windows, bars, boxes, buttons, and icons. Therefore, most object-oriented programming packages provide a GUI that supports a "point and click," "drag and drop" visual assembly of objects known as *visual programming.* Figure 4.25 shows a display of the Visual Basic object-oriented programming environment. Object-oriented technology is discussed further in the coverage of object-oriented databases in Chapter 5.

HTML, XML, and Java

HTML, XML, and Java are three programming languages that are important tools for building multimedia Web pages, websites, and Web-based applications.

HTML (Hypertext Markup Language) is a page description language that creates hypertext or hypermedia documents. HTML inserts control codes within a document at points you can specify that create links *(hyperlinks)* to other parts of the document or to other documents anywhere on the World Wide Web.

Figure 4.25   The Visual Basic object-oriented programming environment.

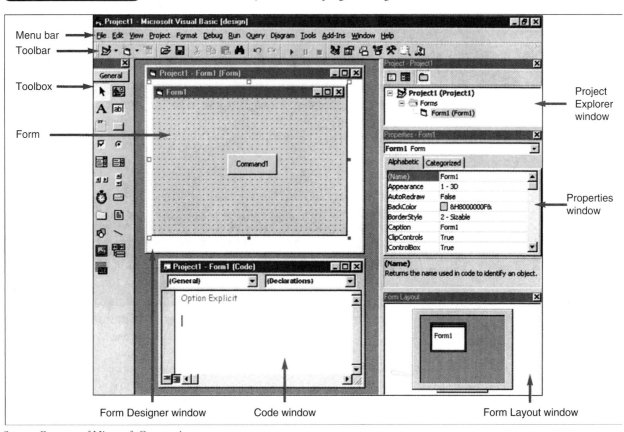

Source: Courtesy of Microsoft Corporation.

HTML embeds control codes in the ASCII text of a document that designate titles, headings, graphics, and multimedia components, as well as hyperlinks within the document.

As we mentioned earlier, several of the programs in the top software suites will automatically convert documents into HTML formats. These include Web browsers, word processing and spreadsheet programs, database managers, and presentation graphics packages. These and other specialized *Web publishing* programs like Microsoft FrontPage and Lotus FastSite provide a range of features to help you design and create multimedia Web pages without formal HTML programming.

XML (eXtensible Markup Language) is not a Web page format description language like HTML. Instead, XML describes the contents of Web pages by applying identifying tags or *contextual labels* to the data in Web documents. For example, a travel agency Web page with airline names and flight times would use hidden XML tags like "airline name" and "flight time" to categorize each of the airline flight times on that page. Or product inventory data available at a website could be labeled with tags like "brand," "price," and "size." By classifying data in this way, XML makes website information a lot more searchable, sortable, and easier to analyze.

For example, XML-enabled search software could easily find the exact product you specify if the product data at a website had been labeled with identifying XML tags. And a website that used XML could more easily determine what Web page features its customers used and what products they investigated. Thus XML

Figure 4.26

The benefits and limitations of XML.

Pros and Cons of XML	
Why XML is a good idea:	**Why XML may not be such a good idea:**
• Its self-describing tags identify what your content is all about	• Majority of online browsers still see only HTML; you will need to add an XML-to-HTML translator
• Data is easily repurposed via tags	• Performance is still slower than equivalent HTML documents
• Creating, using and reusing tags is easy, making XML highly extensible	• The XML-tagged document is still rare; you will likely be doing a lot of conversion of older data
• XML data types map easily among different applications, so it's very interoperable	• Standard tag sets for different applications and industries aren't in widespread use yet
• It makes transferring data easy; simply give it XML tags	

Source: Amy Helen Johnson, "XML Xtends Its Reach." *Computerworld*, October 18, 1999, p. 80. Copyright 1999 by Computerworld, Inc., Framingham, MA 01701. Reprinted from *Computerworld*.

promises to make electronic commerce a lot easier and more efficient by supporting the automatic electronic exchange of business data between companies and their customers, suppliers, and other business partners. Figure 4.26 outlines some of the pros and cons of XML [5, 6].

Java is an object-oriented programming language created by Sun Microsystems that is revolutionizing the programming of applications for the World Wide Web and corporate intranets and extranets. Java is related to the C++ and Objective C programming languages, but is much simpler and secure, and is computing platform independent. Java is also specifically designed for real-time, interactive, Web-based network applications. So Java applications consisting of small application programs, called *applets*, can be executed by any computer and any operating system anywhere in a network.

The ease of creating Java applets and distributing them from network servers to client PCs and network computers is a major reason for Java's popularity. Applets can be small special-purpose application programs or small modules of larger application programs. Applets can reside at websites on a network server until needed by client systems, and are easy to distribute over the Internet or intranets and extranets. Applets are platform independent too—they can run on Windows, UNIX, and Macintosh systems without modification. Java continues to improve its speed of execution (which has been a major limitation), and thus is becoming the alternative to Microsoft's Active X language for many organizations intent on capitalizing on the business potential of the Internet, as well as their own intranets and extranets [10].

Programming Software

A variety of software packages are available to help programmers develop computer programs. For example, *programming language translators* are programs that translate other programs into machine language instruction codes that computers can execute. Other software packages, such as programming language editors, are called *programming tools* because they help programmers write programs by providing a variety of program creation and editing capabilities. See Figure 4.27.

Language Translator Programs

Computer programs consist of sets of instructions written in programming languages that must be translated by a **language translator** into the computer's own machine language before they can be processed, or executed, by the CPU. Programming language translator programs (or *language processors*) are known by a variety of names. An **assembler** translates the symbolic instruction codes of programs written in an

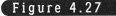

Figure 4.27

Using the graphical programming interface of a Java programming tool, Forte for Java, by Sun Microsystems.

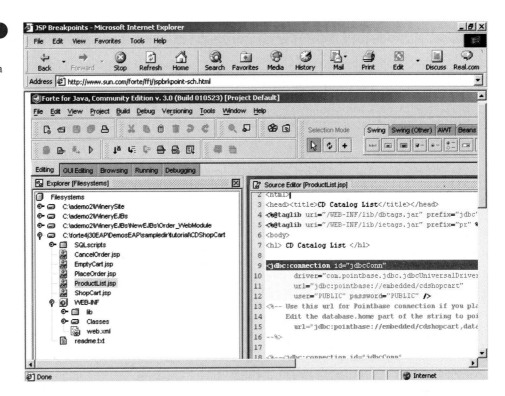

assembler language into machine language instructions, while a **compiler** translates high-level language statements.

An **interpreter** is a special type of compiler that translates and executes each statement in a program one at a time, instead of first producing a complete machine language program, as compilers and assemblers do. Java is an example of an interpreted language. Thus, the program instructions in Java applets are interpreted and executed *on-the-fly* as the applet is being executed by a client PC.

Programming Tools

Software development and the computer programming process have been enhanced by adding *graphical programming interfaces* and a variety of built-in development capabilities. Language translators have always provided some editing and diagnostic capabilities to identify programming errors or *bugs*. However, most software development programs now include powerful graphics-oriented *programming editors* and *debuggers*. These programmining tools help programmers identify and minimize errors while they are programming. Such programming tools provide a computer-aided programming *environment* or *workbench*. This decreases the drudgery of programming while increasing the efficiency and productivity of software developers. Other programming tools include diagramming packages, code generators, libraries of reusable objects and program code, and prototyping tools. Many of these tools may be part of the toolkit provided by *computer-aided software engineering* (CASE) packages.

Summary

- **Software.** Computer software consists of two major types of programs: (1) application software that directs the performance of a particular use, or application, of computers to meet the information processing needs of users, and (2) system software that controls and supports the operations of a computer system as it performs various information processing tasks. Refer to Figure 4.2 for an overview of the major types of software.

- **Application Software.** Application software includes a variety of programs that can be segregated into general-purpose and application-specific categories. General-purpose application programs perform common information processing jobs for end users. Examples are word processing, electronic spreadsheet, database management, telecommunications, and presentation graphics programs. Application-specific programs accomplish information processing tasks that support specific business functions or processes, scientific or engineering applications, and other computer applications in society.

- **System Software.** System software can be subdivided into system management programs and system development programs. System management programs manage the hardware, software, network, and data resources of a computer system during its execution of information processing jobs. Examples of system management programs are operating systems, network management programs, database management systems, system utilities, performance monitors, and security monitors. Network management programs support and manage telecommunications activities and network performance telecommunications networks. Database management systems control the development, integration, and maintenance of databases. Utilities are programs that

perform routine computing functions, such as backing up data or copying files, as part of an operating system or as a separate package. System development programs help IS specialists and end users develop computer programs and information system procedures. Major development programs are language translators, programming editors, and other programming tools.

- **Operating Systems.** An operating system is an integrated system of programs that supervises the operation of the CPU, controls the input/output storage functions of the computer system, and provides various support services. An operating system performs five basic functions: (1) a user interface for system and network communications with users, (2) resource management for managing the hardware resources of a computer system, (3) file management for managing files of data and programs, (4) task management for managing the tasks a computer must accomplish, and (5) utilities and other functions that provide miscellaneous support services.

- **Programming Languages.** Programming languages are a major category of system software. They require the use of a variety of programming packages to help programmers develop computer programs, and language translator programs to convert programming language instructions into machine language instruction codes. The five major levels of programming languages are machine languages, assembler languages, high-level languages, fourth-generation languages, and object-oriented languages. Object-oriented languages like Java and special-purpose languages like HTML and XML are being widely used for Web-based business applications.

Key Terms and Concepts

These are the key terms and concepts of this chapter. The page number of their first explanation is given in parentheses.

1. Application server (127)
2. Application software (108)
3. Application-specific programs (109)
4. Assembler language (128)
5. Database management software (114)
6. Desktop publishing (112)
7. Electronic mail (111)
8. Electronic spreadsheet software (113)
9. File management (123)
10. Fourth-generation language (129)
11. General-purpose application programs (109)
12. Graphical user interface (122)
13. Groupware (117)
14. High-level language (128)
15. HTML (130)
16. Integrated package (110)
17. Java (132)
18. Language translator program (132)
19. Machine language (127)
20. Multitasking (124)
21. Natural language (129)
22. Network management programs (125)
23. Network operating systems (125)
24. Nonprocedural language (129)
25. Object-oriented language (130)
26. Operating system (122)
27. Personal information manager (117)
28. Presentation graphics software (114)
29. Programming tools (132)
30. Resource management (122)

31. Software suites (110)

32. System management programs (120)

33. System software (108)

34. Task management (124)

35. Trends in software (109)

36. User interface (122)

37. Utility programs (127)

38. Virtual memory (123)

39. Web browser (111)

40. Word processing software (112)

Review Quiz

Match one of the previous key terms and concepts with one of the brief examples or definitions that follow. Try to find the best fit for answers that seem to fit more than one term or concept. Defend your choices.

____ 1. Programs that manage and support the operations of computers.

____ 2. Programs that direct the performance of a specific use of computers.

____ 3. A system of programs that manages the operations of a computer system.

____ 4. Managing the processing of tasks in a computer system.

____ 5. Managing the use of CPU time, primary and secondary storage, telecommunications processors, and input/output devices.

____ 6. Managing the input/output, storage, and retrieval of files.

____ 7. The function that provides a means of communication between end users and an operating system.

____ 8. The use of icons, bars, buttons, and other image displays to help you get things done.

____ 9. Provides a greater memory capability than a computer's actual memory capacity.

____ 10. Programs that manage and support the performance of networks.

____ 11. Software that manages telecommunications in complex local area networks.

____ 12. Manages and supports the maintenance and retrieval of data stored in databases.

____ 13. Translates high-level instructions into machine language instructions.

____ 14. Performs housekeeping chores for a computer system.

____ 15. A category of application software that performs common information processing tasks for end users.

____ 16. Software available for the specific applications of end users in business, science, and other fields.

____ 17. Helps you surf the Web.

____ 18. Use your networked computer to send and receive messages.

____ 19. Creates and displays a worksheet for analysis.

____ 20. Allows you to create and edit documents.

____ 21. You can produce your own brochures and newsletters.

____ 22. Helps you keep track of appointments and tasks.

____ 23. A program that performs several general-purpose applications.

____ 24. A combination of individual general-purpose application packages that work easily together.

____ 25. Software to support the collaboration of teams and workgroups.

____ 26. Uses instructions in the form of coded strings of ones and zeros.

____ 27. Uses instructions consisting of symbols representing operation codes and storage locations.

____ 28. Uses instructions in the form of brief statements or the standard notation of mathematics.

____ 29. Might take the form of query languages and report generators.

____ 30. Languages that tie together data and the actions that will be performed upon the data.

____ 31. You don't have to tell the computer how to do something, just what result you want.

____ 32. As easy to use as one's native tongue.

____ 33. Includes programming editors, debuggers, and code generators.

____ 34. Produces hyperlinked multimedia documents for the Web.

____ 35. A popular object-oriented language for Web-based applications.

____ 36. Middleware that helps Web-based application programs run faster and more efficiently.

____ 37. Toward powerful, integrated, network-enabled, expert-assisted packages with easy-to-use graphic and natural language interfaces for productivity and collaboration.

Discussion Questions

1. What major trends are occurring in software? What capabilities do you expect to see in future software packages?

2. How do the different roles of system software and application software affect you as a business end user? How do you see this changing in the future?

3. Refer to the Real World Case on Intuit, Inc. in the chapter. What consumer or business software products that you use are most in need of customer-driven alternatives or revisions? Explain your choices.

4. Why is an operating system necessary? That is, why can't an end user just load an application program in a computer and start computing?

5. Should a Web browser be integrated into an operating system? Why or why not?

6. Refer to the Real World Case on Air Products, Farmers Group, and Others in the chapter. How might the enterprise software alternatives discussed in this case relate to the software challenges of small businesses?

7. Are software suites, Web browsers, and groupware merging together? What are the implications for a business and its end users?

8. How are HTML, XML, and Java affecting business applications on the Web?

9. Do you think Windows 2000 and Linux will surpass Unix and Netware as operating systems for network and Web servers? Why or why not?

10. Which application software packages are the most important for a business end user to know how to use? Explain the reasons for your choices.

Application Exercises

Complete the following exercises as individual or group projects that apply chapter concepts to real world business situations.

1. **ABC Department Stores: Software Selection**
   ABC Department Stores would like to acquire software to do the following tasks. Identify what software packages they need.
   a. Surf the Web and their intranets and extranets.
   b. Send messages to each others' computer workstations.
   c. Help employees work together in teams.
   d. Use a group of productivity packages that work together easily.
   e. Help sales reps keep track of meetings and sales calls.
   f. Type correspondence and reports.
   g. Analyze rows and columns of sales figures.
   h. Develop a variety of graphical presentations.

2. **Evaluating Software Packages**
   Which of the software packages mentioned in this chapter have you used?

   a. Briefly describe the advantages and disadvantages of one of these packages.
   b. How would such a package help you in a present or future job situation?
   c. How would you improve the package you used?

3. **Tracking Employee Software Training**
   You have the responsibility for managing software training for Sales, Accounting, and Operations Department workers in your organization. The data below presents summary information about training sessions held in the last quarter. You want to record this information in a database table and use that table to record information about all future training sessions as they occur.
   a. Create a database table to store this information and enter the ten records shown below. Session ID can serve as the primary key. Print out a listing of your table.

Session ID	Hours	Title	Category	Sales Attendees	Accounting Attendees	Operations Attendees
100	16	Spreadsheet Fundamentals	SS	5	3	8
101	24	Database Fundamentals	DB	4	6	4
102	12	Using Presentation Graphics	PR	9	2	3
103	16	Advanced Spreadsheet	SS	1	9	6
104	24	Database Fundamentals	DB	3	8	4
105	12	Using Presentation Graphics	PR	10	1	3
106	16	Advanced Database Features	DB	0	8	4
107	8	Enliven Your Presentations	PR	9	0	2
108	16	Spreadsheet Fundamentals	SS	2	7	7
109	16	Advanced Spreadsheet	SS	1	6	4

b. Create and print the results of queries showing: **a.** Average attendance at Database Fundamentals Classes, **b.** the total number of hours of spreadsheet, SS, class attendance by workers in each department, and **c.** the average attendance for each course (Title).

c. Generate a report Grouped by Category and showing the number of sessions, average attendance, and total hours of training provided for each course title. Your report should include subtotal and grand total figures as well.

d. If the number of hours and category for a particular course title are always the same, e.g., the Spreadsheet Fundamentals class is always 16 hours long and in the SS Category, can you see any problems caused by recording the hours and category as an attribute of this table? (Be sure to keep a copy of your work for this project because it is used again in a later exercise.)

4. **Matching Training to Software Use**

As in the previous exercise, You have responsibility for managing software training for Sales, Accounting, and

a. Create a spreadsheet that will emphasize the average use and training per worker of each type of package and make it easy to compare the usage across departments. To do this you will first enter the data shown above. Next perform a query on the data of the previous application exercise to determine the total hours of training on each type of package for each department and add these results to your spreadsheet. Be sure to add overall use and training categories to show overall use and training across packages. Compute the average weekly use per worker by dividing hours by the number of workers in the department. Compute a similar figure for training hours by dividing by the number of workers and then dividing by 13 to convert the quarterly data to a weekly basis.

b. Create a set of graphs summarizing your results. Be sure to include a graph comparing training hours per package and usage hours per package in some way.

c. A committee has been formed to schedule future software training classes at your company. You have been asked to present the results of your analysis as a

Department	Employees	Spreadsheet	Database	Presentation
Sales	225	410	1100	650
Operations	195	820	520	110
Accounting	235	1050	1225	190

Operations Department workers in your organization. You have surveyed the workers to get a feel for the amount of time spent using various packages and the results are shown below. The values shown are the total number of workers in each department and the total weekly hours of use of each type of package. You have been asked to prepare a spreadsheet summarizing this data and comparing the use of the various packages across departments, and relating these data to the training data from the previous exercise.

starting point for this committee's work. Using presentation software, produce a brief summary highlighting key results and including related spreadsheet pages and graphs needed to support your findings.

First Union, Martins & Demotses, and Others: Peer-to-Peer Applications for Large and Small Business

First Union Corp. has found a way to dramatically cut the cost of performing heavy-duty number crunching by taking advantage of peer-to-peer (P2P) computing. Large financial services firms that need to crunch numbers have traditionally had two options: They could run the application on a high-end server, which typically costs somewhere in the vicinity of $300,000 and can take eight hours every night; or they could do the computation in real time on a dedicated server farm that can cost 10 times as much when the programming time is factored in. But banks are finding that there's a cost-saving alternative: running the application over existing PCs by using P2P software to slice up the computational work and spread it out among the hundreds of workstations that sit idle for some parts of each day.

According to Charlotte, North Carolina–based First Union, the P2P computing alternative costs roughly as much as buying one server yet produces nearly realtime computations. Joe Belciglio, First Union's managing director of trading technology, said last week that the bank has taken the P2P approach with an application for analyzing portfolio risk that integrated easily and unobtrusively with existing systems.

The software and development work was provided by New York–based DataSynapse Inc., which says it has eight other Wall Street customers. But not every application is suitable for the P2P approach, said DataSynapse CEO, Peter Lee. Lee said the applications that work best are those in which computations can be done in parallel—for example, the risk associated with one investment portfolio can be calculated at a separate place or time from that of another. Lee said DataSynapse has already developed all the middleware it requires, so converting an application to a P2P format can be accomplished in two weeks or less.

Small Business P2P

It was just a coincidence that Charles Martins started up his two-man law firm at the same time that a friend (and Groove Networks employee) persuaded him to download Groove's new P2P software last October from www.groove.net. (Peer-to-peer is a type of network that lets a group of computer users with the same software connect directly with one another [typically via the Internet], to access files from one another's hard drive.)

Initially Martins just thought he was being a good friend, a guinea pig. Instead, he and partner James Demotses liked Groove's free software so much—it allows them to work on legal briefs simultaneously online—that today they run their daily online operations with it. The only problem? Getting their small business clients—who also have to download the Groove software if they want to communicate with the firm—to try it as well. Martins & Demotses LLP, based in Peabody, Massachusetts, are enthusiastic early adopters. But

their reluctant clients are the norm when thinking about today's state of P2P software for small business.

It's true that the business use of P2P, which was introduced to the masses by the explosion of music-sharing Napster early in 2000, could allow remote workers to access data more readily, cheaply, and securely. But right now the feeling among industry experts seems to be: We're almost there, but not quite yet. However, "the wicked and dirty secret is that P2P is inevitable," says Tim O'Reilly, founder of high-tech book publisher O'Reilly & Associates. "Napster woke us up to its potential."

That said, small companies can't afford and don't need the capacity of huge, network-replaceable software applications made by companies like Groove. But they are experimenting with more narrowly focused P2P applications—primarily file sharing—which promotes working together. For example, Stagecast, a company based in Burlingame, California, that makes software to enable children to create their own video games, uses P2P software and services from New York–based Softwax to improve its customers' experience. Stagecast's customers can post and view games directly without the seven staffers at Stagecast having to screen each submission. But Stagecast still has the ability to go in and block anything inappropriate. "It was such a burden to have to review each game," says Stagecast founder Larry Tesler. "Now, in just two seconds we can make a submission unsharable."

Tom Gora, the director of information services at Ginsburg Development Corp., a condominium builder and developer based in Hawthorne, New York, needed to give his employees an alternative way to communicate because the company's projects were taking place farther away from the central office and the price of frame-relay circuits was becoming prohibitive. He chose Mangosoft (www.mangosoft.com) of Westborough, Massachusetts, whose P2P software provides its customers with shareable encrypted virtual hard drives (50 MB for $15 per month for up to five users) that let employees access one another's documents, spreadsheets, and so on. "It beats the pants off a virtual private network because of its speed," says Gora.

Case Study Questions

1. What is the business value of P2P software used for parallel computing applications?

2. What is the business value of P2P software like Groove for both large and small businesses? Check out their website to help you answer.

3. What other business or consumer applications besides Napster-like music file sharing can you envision? Explain the business value of one of your proposals.

Source: Adapted from Maria Tombley, "Peer-to-Peer Makes Inroads on Wall Street," *Computerworld*, April 30, 2001, p. 12; and Maggie Overfelt, "Too Soon for P2P?" *FSB:Fortune Small Business*, October 2001, p. 83. 2001 Time Inc. All rights reserved.

Fidelity Investments:
Challenges and Benefits of Converting to XML

Fidelity Investments completed a retrofit during October 2001 of its corporate data to an XML format in an effort that has already allowed it to eliminate a significant amount of hardware, proprietary databases, and Web and transactional protocols. Analysts say the project is the largest of its kind and estimate that it could cost the investment firm tens of millions of dollars. "When looking at the multitude of data required to be made XML-compatible within an institution the size of Fidelity, it's mind-boggling," said Sara Ablett, a research analyst at Meridien Research Inc. in Newton, Massachusetts.

XML has become an important software development language as more and more companies, big and small, want to link both internal and external data sources and applications for use on their websites. These same companies will then need XML to help integrate the resulting data flows with their back office applications, says Payet Guilleromo, president and CTO of the Ocean Group IT consulting firm in Santa Cruz, California. And they'll soon be needing XML to support all of the transactions and services they hope to offer on the business-to-business extranets that many will probably be implementing, says Guilleromo.

But XML has a dark side, posing a new set of security vulnerabilities, which XML standards bodies and proponents like Microsoft and IBM are still working to solve. The powerful capabilities of XML data sets and dynamic links open up a whole new security can of worms because the code defined by XML could carry virtually any payload unchecked through a fire wall. "Just as there are a bunch of hackers that use malformed HTML and Java to crash your browser or take control of your machine, we'll probably see the same types of attacks aimed at XML software engines and the applications using XML data," says Guillermo.

Fidelity's Conversion

Two years ago, Fidelity started looking for a way to simplify communications between consumer Web applications and back-end systems. During the past decade, the Boston-based mutual funds giant had installed a plethora of proprietary messaging formats, remote procedure calls, interfaces, and commercial middleware applications, such as Sybase Enterprise Connect, to support its various e-commerce and e-business iniatives. By using XML as its core communications connection to translate data among its website, its Unix and Windows NT servers, and its back-office mainframes, Fidelity was able to eliminate a glut of translation protocols and message buffers and 75 of its 85 midtier network servers.

Bill Stangel, XML team leader and an enterprise architect at Fidelity, said a common language has also allowed the company's IT managers to redeploy programmers who were tied up writing interfaces, to work on more important business functions. The conversion should also improve time to

market for applications, he said. "It's simplified our environment significantly," Stangel said. "Instead of us having to invent our own messaging, we can now use XML as the common language. We can buy a book on it and give it to our programmers and say, 'You can use this instead of inventing a new interface.'"

Getting the project off the ground was difficult, said Stangel, "but once the culture kicked in, we didn't have to explain why XML is a good thing. People picked up on it and realized if we can reduce the complexity of our systems, we can have a real competitive advantage."

While it's not unusual for financial services firms to develop XML formats for future or even current information, it's somewhat rare for a company to spend the amount of money Fidelity is believed to have invested to retrofit all of its internal information, said Neal Goldman, an analyst at The Yankee Group in Boston. Fidelity officials declined to comment on the specific costs or savings associated with the project.

Several XML standards compete in the financial services industry, including Financial Information Exchange (FIX), a protocol used by a group of asset management and brokerage firms for the realtime exchange of securities transactions. Currently, FIX developers must write application-level code to validate the structure of FIX messages. Instead of going with one of several proposed XML standards, Fidelity settled on its own proprietary version of XML, because of the early adoption of the technology and the fit with its investment business.

As Fidelity looks to convert its external systems to XML, Stangel said the firm will consider evolving standards such as FIXML for FIX messages or RIXML which makes it easier for investors to share information about companies. "Our work upfront has put us in a good position to now take advantage of these next-generation XML standards as we move forward," Stangel said. "We probably won't move to one of the evolving proposed standards like ebXML. That doesn't fit our business. But we will take advantage of the next part of that standard, such as data structures and those types of things, instead of us having to invent those components."

Case Study Questions

1. What is the business value of XML for companies like Fidelity?

2. What business risks are posed by the use of a new language like XML?

3. How would you advise a business that is considering the use of XML in its e-business and e-commerce applications? Explain your recommendations.

Source: Adapted from Deborah Radcliff, "The Threat of XML," *Computerworld*, July 9, 2001, pp. 36, 37; Deborah Radcliff, "XML Survivors," *Computerworld*, September 10, 2001, p. 42; and Lucas Mearian, "Fidelity Makes Big XML Conversion," *Computerworld*, October 1, 2001, p. 12. Reprinted by permission.

Chapter 5

Data Resource Management

Chapter Highlights

Learning Objectives

After reading and studying this chapter, you should be able to:

1. Explain the importance of implementing data resource management processes and technologies in an organization.

2. Outline the advantages of a database management approach to managing the data resources of a business.

3. Explain how database management software helps business professionals and supports the operations and management of a business.

4. Provide examples to illustrate each of the following concepts:

   a. Major types of databases.

   b. Data warehouses and data mining.

   c. Logical data elements.

   d. Fundamental database structures.

   e. Database access methods.

   f. Database development.

Managing Data Resources

Data Resource Management

Data are a vital organizational resource that need to be managed like other important business assets. Today's e-business enterprises cannot survive or succeed without quality data about their internal operations and external environment.

> *With each online mouse click, either a fresh bit of data is created or already-stored data are retrieved from all those e-commerce websites, filled with data-rich photos, stock graphs, and music videos. And the thousands of new Web pages created each day need a safe, stable managed environment to hang out. All that's on top of the heavy demand for industrial-strength data storage already in use by scores of big corporations. What's driving the growth is a crushing imperative for corporations to analyze every bit of information they can extract from their huge data warehouses for competitive advantage. That has turned the data storage and management function into a key strategic role of the information age [9].*

That's why organizations and their managers need to practice **data resource management,** a managerial activity that applies information systems technologies like *database management, data warehousing,* and other data management tools to the task of managing an organization's data resources to meet the information needs of their business stakeholders. This chapter will show you the managerial implications of using data resource management technologies and methods to manage an organization's data assets to meet the information requirements of e-business companies.

Analyzing Oracle, IBM, and Others

Read the Real World Case on Oracle, IBM, and Others on the next page. We can learn a lot from this case about the major choices companies face in selecting database and applications software. See Figure 5.1.

Figure 5.1

IBM Chairman and CEO Lou Gerstner (left) and Oracle CEO Larry Ellison are implementing opposing strategies as their companies battle for the enterprise database and applications software market.

Source: James Leynse/Corbis/SABA

Source: Tim Sharp/AP Wide World

Oracle, IBM, and Others:
The Battle for the Enterprise Database and Applications Market

Ask Oracle CEO Lawrence Ellison what keeps him up at night, and the answer might surprise you. It's not his longtime nemesis, Microsoft. It's not up-and-comer Siebel Systems. It's IBM, the awakening tech giant. "He has stopped with that 'Microsoft is the devil' stuff," says Steve Mills, IBM's software head. "He has moved on to us."

With good reason. Whoever wins in this face-off will grab the lion's share of the $50 billion corporate-software market for years. For every Oracle product, IBM has a counterpunch: databases, applications, and e-business foundation software. At the same time, the companies' philosophies are strikingly different. Oracle's strategy is to offer customers a complete and tightly integrated package of software—everything a company needs to manage its financials, manufacturing, sales force, logistics, e-commerce, and suppliers. In contrast, IBM Chairman and CEO Louis Gerstner is backing a "best-of-breed" approach in which IBM stitches together a quilt of enterprise resource planning (ERP), customer relationship management (CRM), and other software from various companies, including itself.

The outcome of this battle has huge implications for the software industry. If IBM's partnering strategy carries the day, it means there will be plenty of breathing room for major application software makers such as SAP, Siebel, and PeopleSoft, and for countless upstarts that are bringing Internet-based application programs to market. If Oracle gains the upper hand, it will be pushing its own applications, leaving less room for other players.

To get ahead, IBM is targeting what it sees as Oracle's chief vulnerability: Oracle competes in the applications software market with the same software makers it relies on to help sell its databases. IBM has an advantage because it doesn't sell applications software of its own. So, by setting itself up as a neutral party, IBM is able to gain those companies as allies. That boosts its database software sales, since application companies often recommend to customers which database they think should be used with their software. IBM's consultants then sew the software together.

IBM's momentum is undeniable. Take Oracle's flagship database business. Sure, Oracle is still in the lead in the non-mainframe piece of the market, with a 50 percent share, according to AMR Research. But Oracle's database sales have stagnated over the past two quarters, while IBM's are surging. In the most recent quarter, IBM's DB2 database sales on high-end computers running the Unix operating system jumped 36 percent, while Oracle's grew just 6 percent. And thanks in part to the recent $1 billion acquisition of database software company Informix Corp., IBM, which practically owns the mainframe database market, is now the second-largest maker of nonmainframe database software, with a 25 percent share.

Ellison, however, is worried about more than databases. Consider the e-business software dubbed "application servers"—a foundation of e-commerce software that processes transactions and connects to back-end programs such as databases. As a result of an early jump in the business, IBM owns 30 percent of the market—three times Oracle's share—according to Giga Information Group.

And in the past 18 months, IBM has signed 59 alliances with application software makers such as Siebel Systems, Ariba, and PeopleSoft—all Oracle rivals. Many of them, long under Oracle's thumb, are happy to align with a company they don't compete with. "I will not help Oracle make a single dime that I don't have to," says Rick Berquist, a senior vice president at PeopleSoft.

In fall 2000, Oracle began selling an "e-business suite," which includes all of its enterprise application software tied to its database in one comprehensive package. Sound familiar? SAP, by far the largest provider of enterprise applications, tried something similar and failed. As recently as two years ago SAP was plugging its ERP and other applications as a one-size-fits-all solution, scornfully dismissing the wares of just about every other software maker. But getting the software working proved hugely expensive, and SAP often made connecting with non-SAP products unnecessarily difficult. Co-CEO Hasso Plattner now concedes, "No one will ever standardize solely on SAP. The future will be cooperation between different software applications."

Bruce Richardson, AMR Research's longtime enterprise-software sage agrees, saying that companies won't want to rip out software they've already laboriously installed, nor will competitive advantage be achieved by using the exact same Oracle software as everyone else. Adds Byron Miller, a technology analyst at Giga Group, "The major vendors have to get out of this mentality that they can provide it all."

Case Study Questions

1. What is the business case for both Oracle's and IBM's approach to enterprise database and applications software?

2. Which one of these two approaches would you recommend to a company today? Why?

3. If you were advising Oracle or IBM, what would you recommend to each of them to strengthen their position in the enterprise database and applications market? Why?

Source: Adapted from Jim Kersteter and Spencer Ante, "IBM vs. Oracle: It Could Get Bloody," *Business Week*, May 28, 2001, pp. 65–66. © 2001 McGraw-Hill Companies. Reprinted by permission. "Larry to Everyone: King Me!" FORTUNE, June 25, 2001, p. 53. © 2001 Time Inc. All rights reserved; and Dan Verton, "IBM Enlists ISVs in War Against Oracle," *Computerworld*, August 27, 2001, p. 6. Reprinted by permission.

This case illustrates two classic competing software strategies that are being implemented by Oracle, IBM, Microsoft, and other software companies. Oracle is now offering large and medium-sized companies its "e-business suite," a tightly integrated package of database and applications software. In contrast, IBM is countering with a "best-of-breed" approach, in which it offers a mix of software that includes its database, application server, and e-commerce software, along with applications software (enterprise resource management and customer relationship management, for example), offered by companies like SAP, PeopleSoft, and Siebel Systems. IBM then offers companies its consulting services to help implement this mix of software products. Now many of the applications software companies prefer to deal with IBM, which does not offer applications software of its own, rather than Oracle, which competes with them in the same applications software market. Thus IBM has been gaining ground on Oracle in the enterprise database market, though the outcome in the battle for the e-business application software market is just beginning.

Foundation Data Concepts

Before we go any further, let's review some fundamental concepts about how data are organized in information systems. As we first mentioned in Chapter 1, a hierarchy of several levels of data has been devised that differentiates between different groupings, or elements, of data. Thus, data may be logically organized into characters, fields, records, files, and databases, just as writing can be organized in letters, words, sentences, paragraphs, and documents. Examples of these logical data elements are shown in Figure 5.2.

Character

The most basic logical data element is the **character,** which consists of a single alphabetic, numeric, or other symbol. One might argue that the bit or byte is a more elementary data element, but remember that those terms refer to the physical storage elements provided by the computer hardware, discussed in Chapter 3. From a user's point of view (that is, from a *logical* as opposed to a physical or hardware view of data), a character is the most basic element of data that can be observed and manipulated.

Figure 5.2

Examples of the logical data elements in information systems. Note especially the examples of how data fields, records, files, and databases are related.

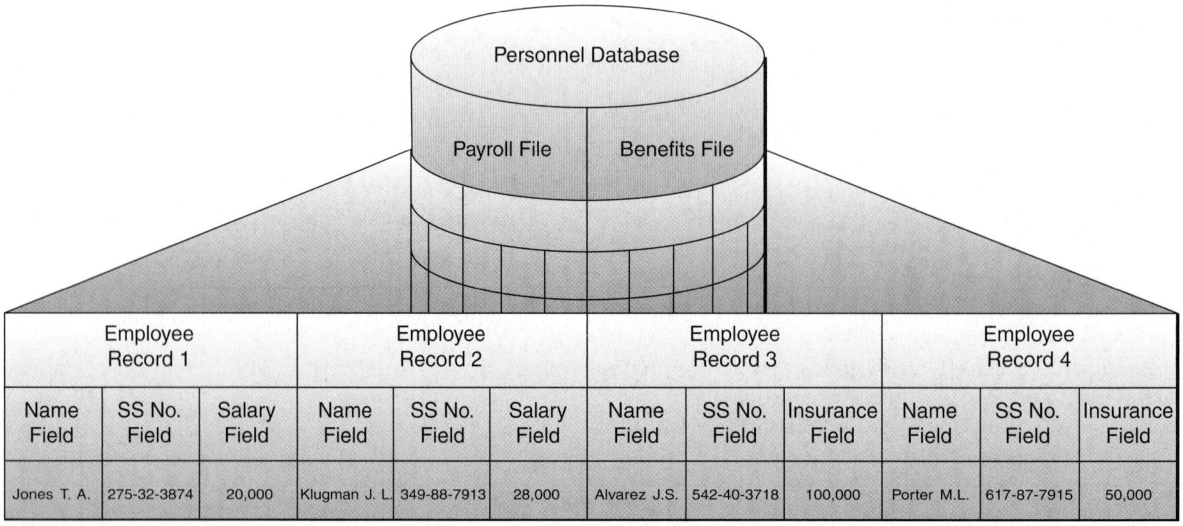

Employee Record 1			Employee Record 2			Employee Record 3			Employee Record 4		
Name Field	SS No. Field	Salary Field	Name Field	SS No. Field	Salary Field	Name Field	SS No. Field	Insurance Field	Name Field	SS No. Field	Insurance Field
Jones T. A.	275-32-3874	20,000	Klugman J. L.	349-88-7913	28,000	Alvarez J.S.	542-40-3718	100,000	Porter M.L.	617-87-7915	50,000

Field	The next higher level of data is the **field,** or data item. A field consists of a grouping of characters. For example, the grouping of alphabetic characters in a person's name forms a name field, and the grouping of numbers in a sales amount forms a sales amount field. Specifically, a data field represents an **attribute** (a characteristic or quality) of some **entity** (object, person, place, or event). For example, an employee's salary is an attribute that is a typical data field used to describe an entity who is an employee of a business.
Record	Related fields of data are grouped to form a **record.** Thus, a record represents a collection of *attributes* that describe an *entity*. An example is the payroll record for a person, which consists of data fields describing attributes such as the person's name, Social Security number, and rate of pay. *Fixed-length* records contain a fixed number of fixed-length data fields. *Variable-length* records contain a variable number of fields and field lengths.
File	A group of related records is a data **file,** or *table*. Thus, an employee file would contain the records of the employees of a firm. Files are frequently classified by the application for which they are primarily used, such as a *payroll file* or an *inventory file*, or the type of data they contain, such as a *document file* or a *graphical image file*. Files are also classified by their permanence, for example, a payroll *master file* versus a payroll weekly *transaction file*. A transaction file, therefore, would contain records of all transactions occurring during a period and might be used periodically to update the permanent records contained in a master file. A *history file* is an obsolete transaction or master file retained for backup purposes or for long-term historical storage called *archival storage*.
Database	A **database** is an integrated collection of logically related data elements. A database consolidates records previously stored in separate files into a common pool of data elements that provides data for many applications. The data stored in a database are independent of the application programs using them and of the type of storage devices on which they are stored. Thus, databases contain data elements describing entities and relationships among entities. For example, Figure 5.3 outlines some of the entities and relationships in a database for an electric utility. Also shown are some of the business applications (billing, payment processing) that depend on access to the data elements in the database.

Figure 5.3

Some of the entities and relationships in a simplified electric utility database. Note a few of the business applications that access the data in the database.

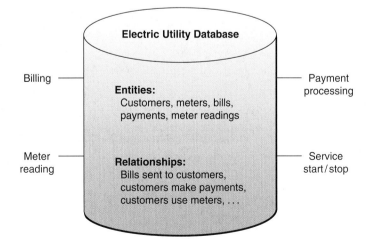

Source: Adapted from Michael V. Mannino, *Database Application Development and Design* (Burr Ridge, IL: McGraw-Hill/Irwin, 2001), p. 6.

The Database Management Approach

The development of databases and database management software is the foundation of modern methods of managing organizational data. The **database management approach** consolidates data records and objects into databases that can be accessed by many different application programs. In addition, an important software package called a *database management system* (DBMS) serves as a software interface between users and databases. This helps users easily access the records in a database. Thus, database management involves the use of database management software to control how databases are created, interrogated, and maintained to provide information needed by end users and their organizations.

For example, customer records and other common types of data are needed for several different applications in banking, such as check processing, automated teller systems, bank credit cards, savings accounts, and installment loan accounting. These data can be consolidated into a common *customer database*, rather than being kept in separate files for each of those applications. See Figure 5.4.

Thus, the database management approach involves three basic activities:

- Updating and maintaining common databases to reflect new business transactions and other events requiring changes to an organization's records.

- Providing information needed for each end user's application by using application programs that share the data in common databases. This sharing of data is supported by the common software interface provided by a database management system package. Thus, end users and programmers do not have to know where or how data are physically stored.

- Providing an inquiry/response and reporting capability through DBMS software so that end users can use Web browsers and the Internet or corporate intranets to easily interrogate databases, generate reports, and receive quick responses to their ad hoc requests for information. Let's look at a real world example.

Figure 5.4

An example of a database management approach in a banking information system. Note how the savings, checking, and installment loan programs use a database management system to share a customer database. Note also that the DBMS allows a user to make a direct, ad hoc interrogation of the database without using application programs.

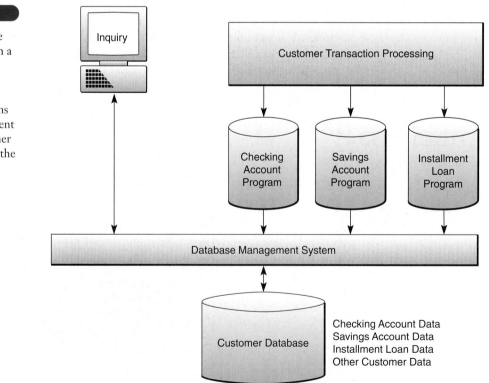

Borders.com: Website Database Management	Borders' online store, located at www.borders.com, offers more than 10 million books, audio books, CDs, cassettes, and videos—all available to ship from stock to any home or business. Borders.com is driven by the IBM Net Commerce suite of e-business software and IBM's popular DB2 database management system.

Borders' online store, located at www.borders.com, offers more than 10 million books, audio books, CDs, cassettes, and videos—all available to ship from stock to any home or business. Borders.com is driven by the IBM Net Commerce suite of e-business software and IBM's popular DB2 database management system.

If you want to find a particular book, CD, audiocassette, or video, a search engine based on a DB2 module rapidly returns the results you want in a format most conducive to making a purchasing decision. As simple as they may seem, these searches are no trivial feat for a database management system. Just searching for a specific title takes three queries to three different database tables, each of which has about 20 million rows. But thanks to Borders' unique database design and DB2's fast indexing scheme, the Borders search engine can return results for most searches in about four-tenths of a second.

DB2 manages a huge database that stores information on all of the items offered on the site, as well as customer registration, order, inventory, shipping, and other information required to manage the online store. Net Data Web and database connectivity software enable Net Commerce software to provide access to the Borders.com database from any Web browser [5].

Using Database Management Software

Let's take a closer look at the capabilities provided by database management software. A **database management system** (DBMS) is a set of computer programs that controls the creation, maintenance, and use of the databases of an organization and its end users. As we said in Chapter 4, database management packages are available for micro, midrange, and mainframe computer systems. The four major uses of a DBMS are illustrated in Figure 5.5; common DBMS software components and functions are summarized in Figure 5.6.

Database Development

Database management packages like Microsoft Access or Lotus Approach allow end users to easily develop the databases they need. However, large organizations with client/server or mainframe-based systems usually place control of enterprisewide database development in the hands of **database administrators** (DBAs) and other database specialists. This improves the integrity and security of organizational databases. Database developers use the *data definition language* (DDL) in database management systems like Oracle 9i or IBM's DB2 to develop and specify the data contents, relationships, and structure of each database, and to modify these database specifications when necessary. Such information is cataloged and stored in a database of data definitions and specifications called a *data dictionary*,

Figure 5.5

The four major uses of a DBMS package are database development, database interrogation, database maintenance, and application development.

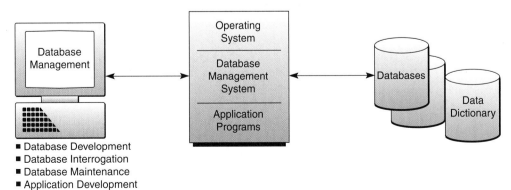

Database Management

Operating System

Database Management System

Application Programs

Databases

Data Dictionary

- Database Development
- Database Interrogation
- Database Maintenance
- Application Development

Common software components and functions of a database management system.

Common DBMS Software Components	
● **Database definition**	Language and graphical tools to define entities, relationships, integrity constraints, and authorization rights
● **Nonprocedural access**	Language and graphical tools to access data without complicated coding
● **Application development**	Graphical tools to develop menus, data entry forms, and reports
● **Procedural language interface**	Language that combines nonprocedural access with full capabilities of a programming language
● **Transaction processing**	Control mechanisms to prevent interference from simultaneous users and recover lost data after a failure
● **Database tuning**	Tools to monitor and improve database performance

Source: Adapted from Michael V. Mannino, *Database Application Development and Design* (Burr Ridge, IL: McGraw-Hill/Irwin, 2001), p. 7.

which is maintained by the DBA. We will discuss database development further in Section II of this chapter.

The Data Dictionary. Data dictionaries are another tool of database administration. A data dictionary is a computer-based catalog or directory containing **metadata,** that is, data about data. A data dictionary includes a software component to manage a database of data definitions, that is, metadata about the structure, data elements, and other characteristics of an organization's databases. For example, it contains the names and descriptions of all types of data records and their interrelationships, as well as information outlining requirements for end users' access and use of application programs, and database maintenance and security.

Data dictionaries can be queried by the database administrator to report the status of any aspect of a firm's metadata. The administrator can then make changes to the definitions of selected data elements. Some *active* (versus *passive*) data dictionaries automatically enforce standard data element definitions whenever end users and application programs use a DBMS to access an organization's databases. For example, an active data dictionary would not allow a data entry program to use a nonstandard definition of a customer record, nor would it allow an employee to enter a name of a customer that exceeded the defined size of that data element.

Database Interrogation

The database interrogation capability is a major benefit of a database management system. End users can use a DBMS by asking for information from a database using a *query language* or a *report generator*. They can receive an immediate response in the form of video displays or printed reports. No difficult programming is required. The **query language** feature lets you easily obtain immediate responses to ad hoc data requests: You merely key in a few short inquiries. The **report generator** feature allows you to quickly specify a report format for information you want presented as a report. Figure 5.7 illustrates the use of a DBMS report generator.

SQL Queries. SQL, or Structured Query Language, is a query language found in many database management packages. The basic form of an SQL query is:

SELECT . . . FROM . . . WHERE . . .

After SELECT you list the data fields you want retrieved. After FROM you list the files or tables from which the data must be retrieved. After WHERE you specify conditions that limit the search to only those data records in which you are interested. Figure 5.8 compares an SQL query to a natural language query for information on customer orders.

Figure 5.7

Using the report generator of Microsoft Access.

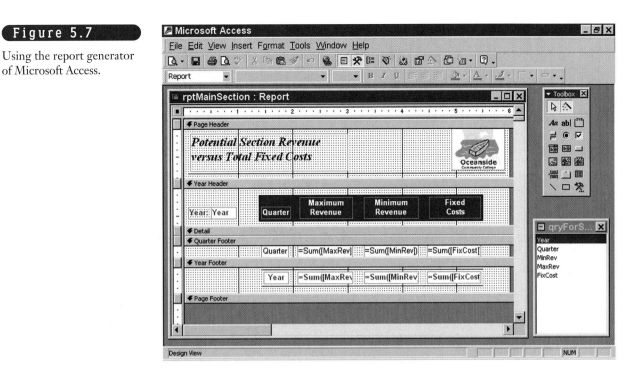

Figure 5.7

Using the report generator of Microsoft Access.

Graphical and Natural Queries. Many end users (and IS professionals) have difficulty correctly phrasing SQL and other database language queries. So most end user database management packages offer GUI (graphical user interface) point-and-click methods, which are easier to use and are translated by the software into SQL commands. See Figure 5.9. Other packages are available that use *natural language* query statements similar to conversational English (or other languages), as illustrated in Figure 5.8.

Database Maintenance

The databases of an organization need to be updated continually to reflect new business transactions and other events. Other miscellaneous changes must also be made to ensure accuracy of the data in the databases. This **database maintenance** process is accomplished by transaction processing programs and other end user application packages, with the support of the DBMS. End users and information specialists can also employ various utilities provided by a DBMS for database maintenance.

Application Development

DBMS packages play a major role in **application development.** End users, systems analysts, and other application developers can use the internal 4GL programming language and built-in software development tools provided by many DBMS

Figure 5.8

Comparing a natural language query with an SQL query.

A Sample Natural Language-to-SQL Translation for Microsoft Access

Natural Language

WHAT CUSTOMERS DIDN'T HAVE ANY ORDERS LAST MONTH?

SQL

SELECT [Customers].[Company Name],[Customers].[Contact Name]

FROM [Customers]

WHERE not Exists {SELECT [Ship Name] FROM [Orders]

WHERE Month {[Order Date]}=1 and Year {[Order Date]}=2000 and
[Customers].[Customer ID]=[Orders].{[Customer ID]}

Figure 5.9

Using the Query Wizard of the Microsoft Access database management package to develop a query.

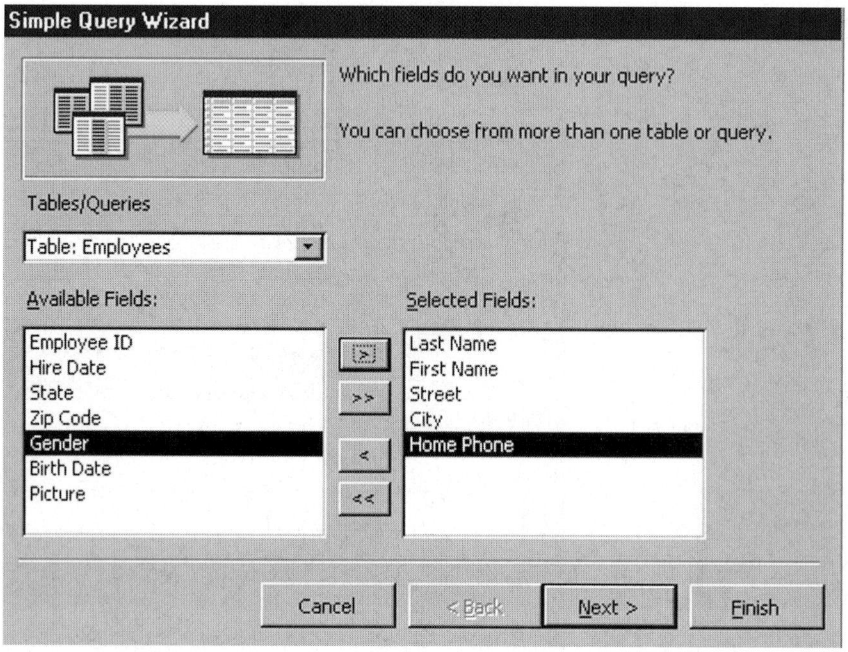

packages to develop custom application programs. For example, you can use a DBMS to easily develop the data entry screens, forms, reports, or Web pages of a business application. A DBMS also makes the job of application programmers easier, since they do not have to develop detailed data-handling procedures using a conventional programming language every time they write a program. Instead, they can include *data manipulation language* (DML) statements in their programs that call on the DBMS to perform necessary data-handling activities.

Types of Databases

Continuing developments in information technology and its business applications have resulted in the evolution of several major types of databases. Figure 5.10 illustrates several major conceptual categories of databases that may be found in many organizations.

Operational Databases

These databases store detailed data needed to support the business processes and operations of the e-business enterprise. They are also called *subject area databases* (SADB), *transaction databases,* and *production databases.* Examples are a customer database, human resource database, inventory database, and other databases containing data generated by business operations. This includes databases of Internet and electronic commerce activity, such as *click stream data* describing the online behavior of customers or visitors to a company's website.

Distributed Databases

Many organizations replicate and distribute copies or parts of databases to network servers at a variety of sites. These distributed databases can reside on network servers on the World Wide Web, on corporate intranets or extranets, or on other company networks. Distributed databases may be copies of operational or analytical databases, hypermedia or discussion databases, or any other type of database. Replication and distribution of databases is done to improve database performance and security. Ensuring that all of the data in an organization's distributed databases are consistently and concurrently updated is a major challenge of distributed database management.

External Databases

Access to a wealth of information from external databases is available for a fee from commercial online services, and with or without charge from many sources on the Internet, especially the World Wide Web. Websites provide an endless variety of

Figure 5.10   Examples of the major types of databases used by organizations and end users.

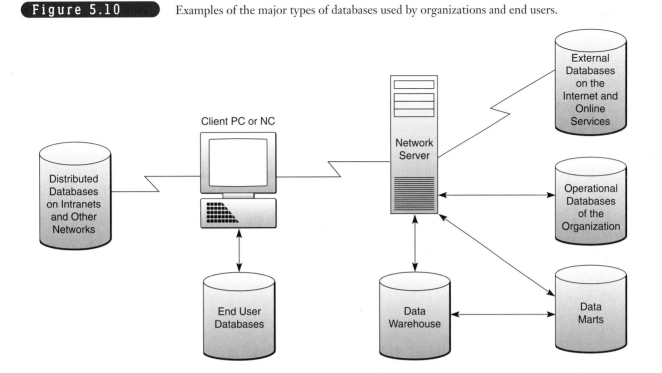

hyperlinked pages of multimedia documents in *hypermedia databases* for you to access. Data are available in the form of statistics on economic and demographic activity from *statistical* data banks. Or you can view or download abstracts or complete copies of hundreds of newspapers, magazines, newsletters, research papers, and other published material and other periodicals from *bibliographic* and *full text* databases.

Data Warehouses and Data Mining

A **data warehouse** stores data that have been extracted from the various operational, external, and other databases of an organization. It is a central source of the data that have been cleaned, transformed, and cataloged so they can be used by managers and other business professionals for data mining, online analytical processing, and other forms of business analysis, market research, and decision support. Data warehouses may be subdivided into **data marts,** which hold subsets of data from the warehouse that focus on specific aspects of a company, such as a department or a business process.

Figure 5.11 illustrates the components of a complete data warehouse system. Notice how data from various operational and external databases are captured, cleaned, and transformed into data that can be better used for analysis. This acquisition process might include activities like consolidating data from several sources, filtering out unwanted data, correcting incorrect data, converting data to new data elements, and aggregating data into new data subsets.

This data is then stored in the enterprise data warehouse, from where it can be moved into data marts or to an *analytical data store* that holds data in a more useful form for certain types of analysis. Metadata that defines the data in the data warehouse is stored in a metadata repository and cataloged by a metadata directory. Finally, a variety of analytical software tools can be provided to query, report, mine, and analyze the data for delivery to business end users via Internet and intranet Web systems or other networks.

Data Mining

Data mining is a major use of data warehouse databases. In data mining, the data in a data warehouse are analyzed to reveal hidden patterns and trends in historical

Figure 5.11 The components of a complete data warehouse system.

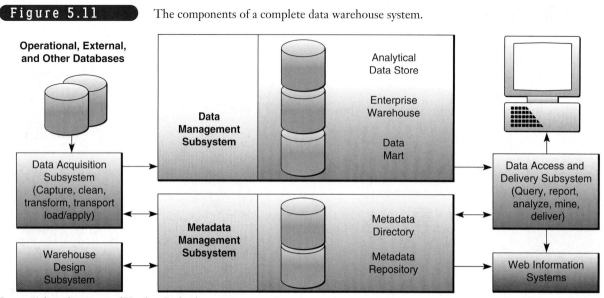

Source: Adapted courtesy of Hewlett-Packard.

business activity. This can be used to help managers make decisions about strategic changes in business operations to gain competitive advantages in the marketplace. See Figure 5.12.

Data mining can discover new correlations, patterns, and trends in vast amounts of business data (frequently several terabytes of data), stored in data warehouses. Data mining software uses advanced pattern recognition algorithms, as well as a variety of mathematical and statistical techniques to sift through mountains of data to extract previously unknown strategic business information. We discuss data mining, online analytical processing (OLAP), and other technologies that analyze the data in databases and data warehouses to provide vital support for business decisions in Chapter 9. Let's look at a real world example.

Bank of America: Mining a Data Warehouse	The Bank of America (BofA) is using a data warehouse and data mining software to develop more accuracy in marketing and pricing financial products, such as home equity loans. BofA's data warehouse is so large—for some customers, there are 300 data points—that traditional analytic approaches are overwhelmed. For each market, BofA can offer a variety of tailored product packages by adjusting fees, interest rates, and features. The result is a staggering number of potential strategies for reaching profitable customers. Sifting through the vast number of combinations requires the ability to identify very fine opportunity segments.

Data extracted from the data warehouse were analyzed by data mining software to discover hidden patterns. For example, the software discovered that a certain set of customers were 15 times more likely to purchase a high-margin lending product. The bank also wanted to determine the sequence of events leading to purchasing. They fed the parameters to the Discovery software from HYPERparallel and built a model for finding other customers. This model proved to be so accurate that it discovered people already in the process of applying and being approved for the lending product. Using this profile, a final list of quality prospects for solicitation was prepared. The resulting direct marketing response rates have dramatically exceeded past results [14].

| Figure 5.12 | How data mining extracts business knowledge from a data warehouse. |

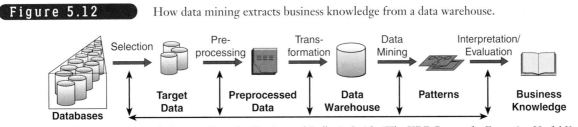

Source: Adapted from Usama Fayyad, Gregory Piatetsky-Shapiro, and Padhraic Smith, "The KDD Process for Extracting Useful Knowledge from Volumes of Data," *Communications of the ACM*, November 1996, p. 29. Copyright © 1996, Association of Computing Machinery. Used by permission.

Hypermedia Databases on the Web

The most compelling business driver today is the Internet. Because so much of the information flying across the Internet is [multimedia], companies need databases that can store, retrieve, and manage other data types, particularly documents, video, and sound [17].

The rapid growth of websites on the Internet and corporate intranets and extranets has dramatically increased the use of databases of hypertext and hypermedia documents. A website stores such information in a **hypermedia database** consisting of hyperlinked pages of multimedia (text, graphic, and photographic images, video clips, audio segments, and so on). That is, from a database management point of view, the set of interconnected multimedia pages at a website is a database of interrelated hypermedia page elements, rather than interrelated data records [3].

Figure 5.13 shows how you might use a Web browser on your client PC to connect with a Web network server. This server runs Web server software to access and transfer the Web pages you request. The website illustrated in Figure 5.13 uses a hypermedia database consisting of Web page content described by HTML (Hypertext Markup Language) code or XML (Extended Markup Language) labels, image files, video files, and audio. The Web server software acts as a database management system to manage the transfer of hypermedia files for downloading by the multimedia plug-ins of your Web browser.

Implementing Data Resource Management

Propelled by the Internet, intranets, a flood of multimedia information, and applications such as data warehousing and data mining, data storage at most companies is growing faster than ever. That has information technology managers in the most information-intensive industries wondering if technology can keep up with the surging tide—and, if it can, whether they can manage it [2].

| Figure 5.13 | The components of a Web-based information system include Web browsers, servers, and hypermedia databases. |

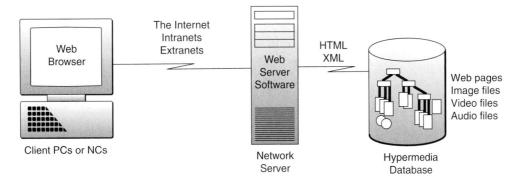

Figure 5.14   Data resource management includes database administration, data planning, and data administration activities.

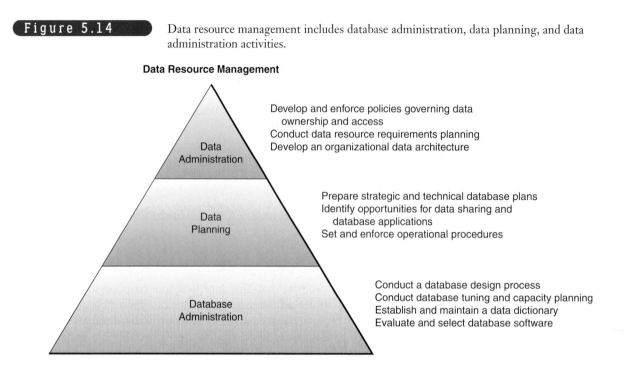

Data Resource Management

Data Administration
- Develop and enforce policies governing data ownership and access
- Conduct data resource requirements planning
- Develop an organizational data architecture

Data Planning
- Prepare strategic and technical database plans
- Identify opportunities for data sharing and database applications
- Set and enforce operational procedures

Database Administration
- Conduct a database design process
- Conduct database tuning and capacity planning
- Establish and maintain a data dictionary
- Evaluate and select database software

Managers and business professionals need to view data as an important resource that they must manage properly to ensure the success and survival of their organizations. But this is easier said than done. For example, database management is an important application of information technologies to the management of a firm's data resources. However, other major data resource management efforts are needed in order to supplement the solutions provided by a database management approach. Those are (1) database administration, (2) data planning, and (3) data administration. See Figure 5.14.

Database administration is an important data resource management function responsible for the proper use of database management technology. Database administration includes responsibility for developing and maintaining the organization's data dictionary, designing and monitoring the performance of databases, and enforcing standards for database use and security. Database administrators and analysts work with systems developers and end users to provide their expertise to major systems development projects.

Data planning is a corporate planning and analysis function that focuses on data resource management. It includes the responsibility for developing an overall data architecture for the firm's data resources that ties in with the firm's strategic mission and plans, and the objectives and processes of its business units. Data planning is done by organizations that have made a formal commitment to long-range planning for the strategic use and management of their data resources.

Data administration is another vital data resource management function. It involves administering the collection, storage, and dissemination of all types of data in such a way that data become a standardized resource available to all end users in the organization. The focus of data administration is the support of an organization's business processes and strategic business objectives. Data administration may also include responsibility for developing policies and setting standards for corporate database design, processing, and security arrangements.

Challenges of Data Resource Management

The data resource management approach provides business managers and professionals with several important benefits. Database management reduces the duplication of data and integrates data so that they can be accessed by multiple programs and users. Software is not dependent on the format of the data or the type of secondary storage hardware being used. Business professionals can use inquiry/response and reporting capabilities to easily obtain information they need from databases, data warehouses, or data marts, without complex programming. Software development is simplified, because programs are not dependent on either the logical format of the data or their physical storage location. Finally, the integrity and security of data are increased, since access to data and modification of data are controlled by data management software, data dictionaries, and a data administration function.

The challenge of data resource management arises from its technological complexity and the vast amounts of business data that need to be managed. Developing large databases of complex data types and installing data warehouses can be difficult and expensive. More hardware capability is required, since storage requirements for the organization's data, overhead control data, and the database management or data warehouse software are greater. Longer processing times may result from this additional data and software complexity. Finally, if an organization relies on centralized databases, its vulnerability to errors, fraud, and failures is increased. Yet problems of inconsistency of data can arise if a distributed database approach is used. Therefore, supporting the security and integrity of their databases and data warehouses is a major objective of data resource management for e-business enterprises.

Section II

Technical Foundations of Database Management

Database Management

Just imagine how difficult it would be to get any information from an information system if data were stored in an unorganized way, or if there was no systematic way to retrieve it. Therefore, in all information systems, data resources must be organized and structured in some logical manner so that they can be accessed easily, processed efficiently, retrieved quickly, and managed effectively. Thus, data structures and access methods ranging from simple to complex have been devised to efficiently organize and access data stored by information systems. In this section, we will explore these concepts, as well as more technical concepts of database management.

Analyzing Aetna and Boeing

Read the Real World Case on Aetna and Boeing on the next page. We can learn a lot about storage management software, functions, and strategies that are an important part of data resource management from this case. See Figure 5.15.

Companies today are faced with major data resource management challenges as they try to deal with the massive flood of data generated by their e-business and e-commerce activities. Aetna's biggest concerns are the integrity, backup, security, and availability of the mountains of corporate data stored on thousands of disk drives connected to the mainframes and midrange computers in their four interconnected data centers. Aetna uses data resource management tools that include IBM, Oracle, and Sybase database management software, system performance monitors, load balancing software for Web servers, and data modeling software tools. Boeing uses IBM, Microsoft, and Oracle database management software and a variety of backup and restore utilities as some of the software tools it depends on to manage the reliability and security of its massive and diverse data resources spread across 27 states and several overseas locations.

Figure 5.15

Michael Mathias, Nancy Tillberg, and Renee Zaugg are responsible for implementing Aetna's management strategies for the integrity, security, and availability of its data resources.

Source: Amy Etra

Aetna and the Boeing Co.: Challenges of Data Resource Management

How does an enterprise deal gracefully and effectively with unwieldy mountains of information? We asked two data-intensive companies—Aetna Inc. and the Boeing Co. to tell us about the problems they faced in managing massive data stores and how they solved them. For each company, data is a significant corporate asset resulting from huge investments of time and effort. The data is also the source of many trials and tribulations for the employees who keep vigilant watch over it.

Aetna Inc. On a daily basis, Renee Zaugg, operations manager in the operational services central support area at Aetna, is responsible for 174.6 terabytes (TB) of data. She says 119.2TB reside on mainframe-connected disk drives, while the remaining 55.4TB sit on disks attached to midrange computers running Unix by IBM or Sun. Almost all of this data is located in the company's headquarters in Hartford, Connecticut. Most of the information is in relational databases, handled by IBM's DB2 Universal Database, Oracle8, or Sybase. To make matters even more interesting, Zaugg adds, outside customers have access to about 20TB of the information. Four interconnected data centers contain 14 mainframes and more than 4,100 direct-access storage devices to hold Aetna's key databases.

Nancy Tillberg, head of strategic data planning, says: "Data integrity, backup, security, and availability are our biggest concerns." So Zaugg says that her data handling software tools, procedures, and operations schedules have to stay ahead of not only the normal growth that results from the activities of the sales, underwriting, and claims departments but also growth from corporate acquisitions and mergers.

She adds that Aetna has a server consolidation effort under way to reduce the effort necessary to manage data on the midrange machines. For its Web servers, Aetna uses Resonate's Global Dispatch load balancing software to distribute Web data traffic to the nearest available server that's least busy. Tillberg also says the company is increasing its use of storage-area networks to centralize and streamline the management of that data. She points out that Aetna uses Global Enterprise Management performance monitor software from Tivoli Systems to monitor the network, distribute files, and track database usage.

Aetna's database administrators maintain the more than 15,000 database table definitions with the ERWin data modeling tool, according to Michael Mathias, an information systems data storage expert at Aetna. Manual upkeep of the table definitions became impossible years ago, he says. Mathias sees the importance of viewing the maintenance of large amounts of data from a logical perspective. While the physical management of large data stores is certainly a nontrivial effort, Mathias says that failing to keep the data organized leads inexorably to user workflow problems, devaluation of the data as a corporate asset and, eventually, customer complaints.

Boeing Co. LeaAnne Armstrong, director of distributed servers at the Boeing Co., makes sure the approximately 50TB to 150TB of data the company owns remains as reliable and safe as the aircraft and spacecraft the company builds. She says the 50TB to 150TB estimate reflects Boeing's inability to know exactly how much data exists on its 150,000 desktop computers. Users don't necessarily store their data files on a server, which makes quantifying Boeing's data stores difficult, she says.

Like Aetna, Boeing has tens of mainframes and thousands of midrange servers running Unix and Windows NT. "Much of the data exists in relational form," Armstrong says, "but across the enterprise, Boeing's files run the gamut from document images to computer-aided design and manufacturing machine and part descriptions." The relational database software used includes IBM's DB2 on the mainframes, Oracle on the Unix midrange machines, and Microsoft's SQL Server on the smaller Intel-based Windows NT computers.

Boeing's data stores are spread out across 27 states and a few overseas locations, but most computing takes place in the Puget Sound area of Washington. Armstrong says the company currently has dozens of different backup and restore software utilities. Each department buys its own backup media and performs its own backup and restore operations. A major data loss hasn't happened yet, says Armstrong, but she's aware of the risks, and plans to centralize the backing up and restoring of files in the future.

Although hard disks are inexpensive these days, Armstrong says data management costs on a per-disk or per-tape basis are high enough that she wants to significantly reduce the amount of unused disk and tape space on the media that Boeing uses. Thus she wishes that all Boeing's tapes and disks were based on a "storage-on-demand" model, whereby Boeing could simply rent whatever capacity it needed from an outside vendor and not have to worry about running out of space.

Case Study Questions

1. What are the most important challenges facing the data resource managers of Aetna and Boeing? How do they meet these challenges?

2. What business benefits could be gained, and business risks minimized, by the data resource management efforts displayed by these companies?

3. What can small businesses learn from the data resource management tactics of these two large companies?

Source: Adapted from Barry Nance, "Managing Tons of Data," *Computerworld*, April 23, 2001, pp. 62–64; and Robert Schier, "The Data Squeeze," *Computerworld*, October 15, 2001, pp. 36–38. Reprinted by permission.

Database Structures

The relationships among the many individual records stored in databases are based on one of several logical data structures, or models. Database management system packages are designed to use a specific data structure to provide end users with quick, easy access to information stored in databases. Five fundamental database structures are the hierarchical, network, relational, object-oriented, and multidimensional models. Simplified illustrations of the first three database structures are shown in Figure 5.16.

Hierarchical Structure

Early mainframe DBMS packages used the **hierarchical structure,** in which the relationships between records form a hierarchy or treelike structure. In the traditional hierarchical model, all records are dependent and arranged in multilevel structures, consisting of one *root* record and any number of subordinate levels. Thus, all of the

Figure 5.16

Example of three fundamental database structures. They represent three basic ways to develop and express the relationships among the data elements in a database.

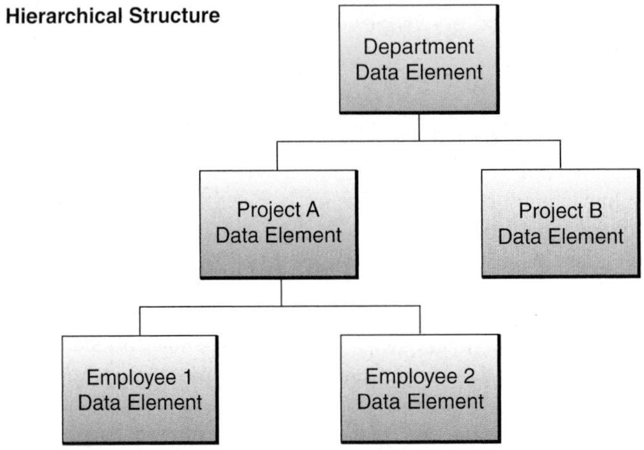

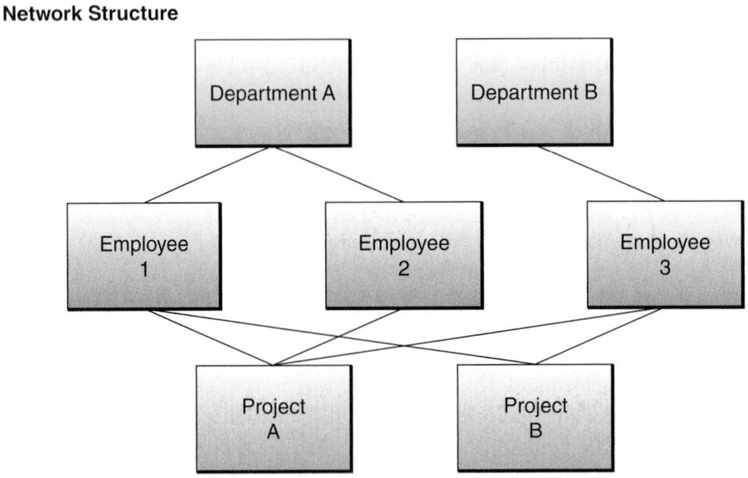

Hierarchical Structure

Network Structure

Relational Structure

Department Table

Deptno	Dname	Dloc	Dmgr
Dept A			
Dept B			
Dept C			

Employee Table

Empno	Ename	Etitle	Esalary	Deptno
Emp 1				Dept A
Emp 2				Dept A
Emp 3				Dept B
Emp 4				Dept B
Emp 5				Dept C
Emp 6				Dept B

relationships among records are *one-to-many*, since each data element is related to only one element above it. The data element or record at the highest level of the hierarchy (the department data element in this illustration) is called the root element. Any data element can be accessed by moving progressively downward from a root and along the branches of the tree until the desired record (for example, the employee data element) is located.

Network Structure

The **network structure** can represent more complex logical relationships, and is still used by some mainframe DBMS packages. It allows *many-to-many* relationships among records; that is, the network model can access a data element by following one of several paths, because any data element or record can be related to any number of other data elements. For example, in Figure 5.16, departmental records can be related to more than one employee record, and employee records can be related to more than one project record. Thus, one could locate all employee records for a particular department, or all project records related to a particular employee.

Relational Structure

The **relational model** has become the most popular of the three database structures. It is used by most microcomputer DBMS packages, as well as by most midrange and mainframe systems. In the relational model, all data elements within the database are viewed as being stored in the form of simple **tables.** Figure 5.16 illustrates the relational database model with two tables representing some of the relationships among departmental and employee records. Other tables, or **relations,** for this organization's database might represent the data element relationships among projects, divisions, product lines, and so on. Database management system packages based on the relational model can link data elements from various tables to provide information to users. For example, a DBMS package could retrieve and display an employee's name and salary from the employee table in Figure 5.16, and the name of the employee's department from the department table, by using their common department number field (Deptno) to link or join the two tables.

Multidimensional Structure

The multidimensional database structure is a variation of the relational model that uses multidimensional structures to organize data and express the relationships between data. You can visualize multidimensional structures as cubes of data and cubes within cubes of data. Each side of the cube is considered a dimension of the data. Figure 5.17 is an example that shows that each dimension can represent a different category, such as product type, region, sales channel, and time [7].

Each cell within a multidimensional structure contains aggregated data related to elements along each of its dimensions. For example, a single cell may contain the total sales for a product in a region for a specific sales channel in a single month. A major benefit of multidimensional databases is that they are a compact and easy-to-understand way to visualize and manipulate data elements that have many interrelationships. So multidimensional databases have become the most popular database structure for the analytical databases that support *online analytical processing* (OLAP) applications, in which fast answers to complex business queries are expected. We discuss OLAP applications in Chapter 9.

Object-Oriented Structure

The **object-oriented** database model is considered to be one of the key technologies of a new generation of multimedia Web-based applications. We introduced the concept of objects when we discussed object-oriented programming in Chapter 4. As Figure 5.18 illustrates, an **object** consists of data values describing the attributes of an entity, plus the operations that can be performed upon the data. This *encapsulation* capability allows the object-oriented model to better handle more complex types of data (graphics, pictures, voice, text) than other database structures.

Figure 5.17 An example of the different dimensions of a multidimensional database.

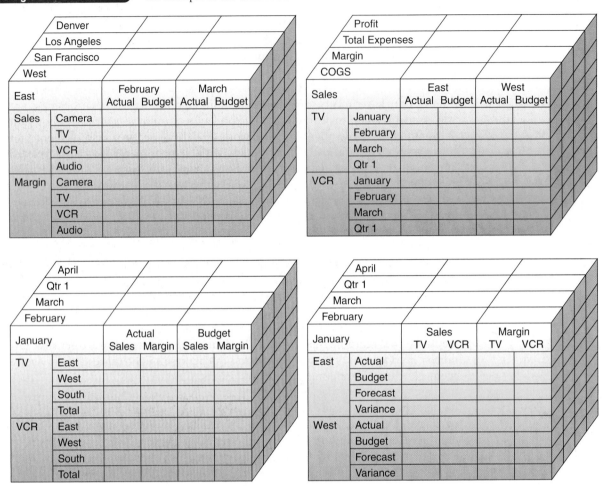

The object-oriented model also supports *inheritance;* that is, new objects can be automatically created by replicating some or all of the characteristics of one or more *parent* objects. Thus, in Figure 5.18, the checking and savings account objects can both inherit the common attributes and operations of the parent bank account object. Such capabilities have made *object-oriented database management systems* (OODBMS) popular in computer-aided design (CAD) and in a growing number of applications. For example, object technology allows designers to develop product designs, store them as objects in an object-oriented database, and replicate and modify them to create new product designs. In addition, multimedia Web-based applications for the Internet and corporate intranets and extranets have become a major application area for object technology, as we will discuss shortly.

Evaluation of Database Structures

The hierarchical data structure was a natural model for the databases used for the structured, routine types of transaction processing that was a characteristic of many business operations. Data for these operations can easily be represented by groups of records in a hierarchical relationship. However, there are many cases where information is needed about records that do not have hierarchical relationships. For example, it is obvious that, in some organizations, employees from more than one department can work on more than one project (refer back to Figure 5.16). A network data structure could easily handle this many-to-many relationship. It is thus

Figure 5.18

The checking and savings account objects can inherit common attributes and operations from the bank account object.

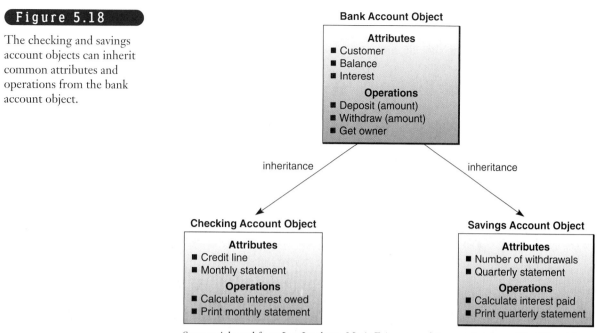

Source: Adapted from Ivar Jacobsen, Maria Ericsson, and Ageneta Jacobsen, *The Object Advantage: Business Process Reengineering with Object Technology* (New York: ACM Press, 1995), p. 65. Copyright © 1995, Association for Computing Machinery. By permission.

more flexible than the hierarchical structure in support of databases for many types of business operations. However, like the hierarchical structure, because its relationships must be specified in advance, the network model cannot easily handle ad hoc requests for information.

Relational databases, on the other hand, allow an end user to easily receive information in response to ad hoc requests. That's because not all of the relationships between the data elements in a relationally organized database need to be specified when the database is created. Database management software (such as Oracle 9i, DB2, Access, and Approach) creates new tables of data relationships using parts of the data from several tables. Thus, relational databases are easier for programmers to work with and easier to maintain than the hierarchical and network models.

The major limitation of the relational model is that relational database management systems cannot process large amounts of business transactions as quickly and efficiently as those based on the hierarchical and network models, or complex, high-volume applications as well as the object-oriented model. This performance gap has narrowed with the development of advanced relational DBMS software with object-oriented extensions. The use of database management software based on the object-oriented and multidimensional models is growing steadily, as these technologies are playing a greater role for OLAP and Web-based applications.

Object Technology and the Web

Object-oriented database software is finding increasing use in managing the hypermedia databases and Java applets on the World Wide Web and corporate intranets and extranets. Industry proponents predict that object-oriented database management systems will become the key software component that manages the hyperlinked multimedia pages and other types of data that support corporate websites. That's because an OODBMS can easily manage the access and storage of objects such as document and graphic images, video clips, audio segments, and other subsets of Web pages.

Object technology proponents argue that an object-oriented DBMS can work with such *complex data types* and the Java applets that use them much more efficiently than relational database management systems. However, major relational DBMS vendors have countered by adding object-oriented modules to their relational software. Examples include multimedia object extensions to IBM's DB2, and Oracle's object-based "cartridges" for Oracle 9i. See Figure 5.19. Let's look at another real world example.

Enron Energy Services: Object versus Relational

Houston-based Enron Energy Services, a unit of Enron Corp., found that its Oracle relational database billing application was running out of gas. Depending on local contracts and regulations in more than 100 markets nationwide, Enron may act as an energy wholesaler or energy retailer. Different customer types are charged different rates, pay different taxes, or get billing information in different formats.

Enron originally wrote its billing application to access an Oracle relational database that contained three dozen tables for billing alone. But performance was unacceptable. Asking the relational DBMS to perform the complex queries necessary to produce the customized bills "was like assembling an automobile from scratch" tens of thousands of times per day, according to senior developer Tom Dahl.

Enron didn't replace Oracle but instead added an ObjectStore database management system to create an object database that serves as a buffer. The daily joins are performed in Oracle, but the results are stored in an ObjectStore database, which produces the data needed to create the actual bill. Performance is faster and maintenance is easier with the new relational/object approach. Enron estimates that the new system can handle tens of thousands of transactions per day [4].

Figure 5.19

This management alert display provided by the BizWorks enterprise portal is powered by the Jasmineii object oriented database management system of Computer Associates.

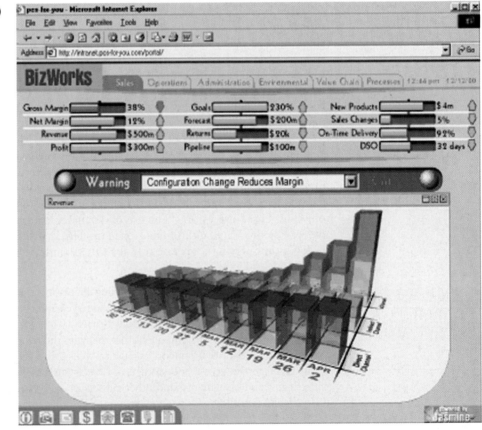

Accessing Databases

Efficient access to data is important. In database maintenance, records or objects have to be continually added, deleted, or updated to reflect business transactions. Data must also be accessed rapidly so information can be produced in response to end user requests.

Key Fields

That's why all data records usually contain one or more identification fields, or *keys*, that identify the record so it can be located. For example, the Social Security number of a person is often used as a *primary* **key field** that uniquely identifies the data records of individuals in student, employee, and customer files and databases. Other methods also identify and link data records stored in several different database files. For example, hierarchical and network databases may use *pointer fields*. These are fields within a record that indicate (point to) the location of another record that is related to it in the same file, or in another file. Hierarchical and network database management systems use this method to link records so they can retrieve information from several different database files.

Relational database management packages use primary keys to link records. Each table (file) in a relational database must contain a primary key. This field (or fields) uniquely identifies each record in a file and must also be found in other related files. For example, in Figure 5.16, department number (Deptno) is the primary key in the Department table and is also a field in the Employee table. As we mentioned earlier, a relational database management package could easily provide you with information from both tables by joining the tables and retrieving the information you want. See Figure 5.20.

Sequential Access

One of the original and basic ways to access data is by **sequential access.** This method uses a *sequential organization*, in which records are physically stored in a specified order according to a key field in each record. For example, payroll records could be placed in a payroll file in a numerical order based on employee Social Security numbers. Sequential access is fast and efficient when dealing with large volumes of data that need to be processed periodically. However, it requires that all new transactions be sorted into the proper sequence for sequential access processing. Also, most of the database or file may have to be searched to locate, store, or modify even a small number of data records. Thus, this method is too slow to handle applications requiring immediate updating or responses.

Direct Access

When using **direct access** methods, records do not have to be arranged in any particular sequence on storage media. However, the computer must keep track of the storage location of each record using a variety of *direct organization* methods so that data can be retrieved when needed. New transactions data do not have to be sorted, and processing that requires immediate responses or updating is easily handled. There are a number of ways to directly access records in the direct organization method. Let's take a brief look at three widely used methods to accomplish such direct access processing.

Figure 5.20

Joining the Employee and Department tables in a relational database enables you to selectively access data in both tables at the same time.

Department Table

Deptno	Dname	Dloc	Dmgr
Dept A			
Dept B			
Dept C			

Employee Table

Empno	Ename	Etitle	Esalary	Deptno
Emp 1				Dept A
Emp 2				Dept A
Emp 3				Dept B
Emp 4				Dept B
Emp 5				Dept C
Emp 6				Dept B

One common technique of direct access is **key transformation.** This method performs an arithmetic computation on a key field of record (such as a product number or Social Security number) and uses the number that results from that calculation as an address to store and access that record. Thus, the process is called key transformation because an arithmetic operation is applied to a key field to transform it into the storage location address of a record. Another direct access method used to store and locate records involves the use of an **index** of record keys and related storage addresses. A new data record is stored at the next available location, and its key and address are placed in an index. The computer uses this index whenever it must access a record.

In the **indexed sequential access method** (ISAM), records are stored in a sequential order on a magnetic disk or other direct access storage device based on the key field of each record. In addition, each database contains an index that references one or more key fields of each data record to its storage location address. Thus, an individual record can be directly located by using its key fields to search and locate its address in the database index, just as you can locate key topics in this book by looking them up in its index. As a result, if a few records must be processed quickly, the index is used to directly access the record needed. However, when large numbers of records must be processed periodically, the sequential organization provided by this method is used. For example, processing the weekly payroll for employees or producing monthly statements for customers could be done using sequential access processing of the records in the database.

Database Development

Developing small, personal databases is relatively easy using microcomputer database management packages. See Figure 5.21. However, developing a large database of complex data types can be a complex task. In many companies, developing and managing large corporate databases are the primary responsibility of the database administrator and database design analysts. They work with end users and systems analysts to model business processes and the data they require. Then they determine (1) what data definitions should be included in the database and (2) what structure or relationships should exist among the data elements.

Data Planning and Database Design

As Figure 5.22 illustrates, database development may start with a top-down **data planning process.** Database administrators and designers work with corporate and end user management to develop an *enterprise model* that defines the basic business

---

Creating a database using the Database Wizard of Microsoft Access.

Figure 5.22

Database development
involves data planning and
database design activities.
Data models that support
business processes are used
to develop databases that
meet the information needs
of users.

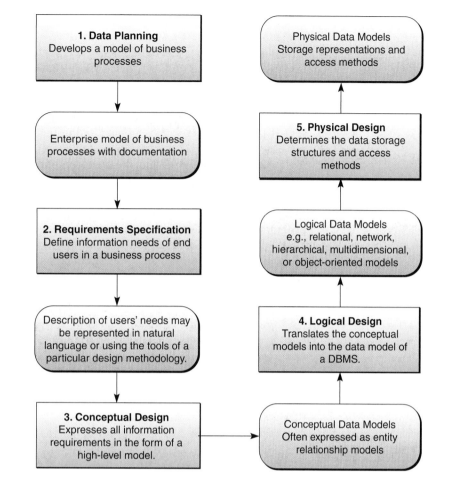

process of the enterprise. Then they define the information needs of end users in a
business process, such as the purchasing/receiving process that all businesses
have [18].

Next, end users must identify the key data elements that are needed to perform
their specific business activities. This frequently involves developing *entity relationship diagrams* (ERDs) that model the relationships among the many entities involved
in business processes. For example, Figure 5.23 illustrates some of the relationships
in a purchasing/receiving process. End users and database designers could use ERD
models to identify what supplier and product data are required to automate their
purchasing/receiving and other business processes using enterprise resource management (ERP) or supply chain management (SCM) software.

Figure 5.23

This entity relationship
diagram illustrates some of
the relationships among
entities in a purchasing/
receiving business process.

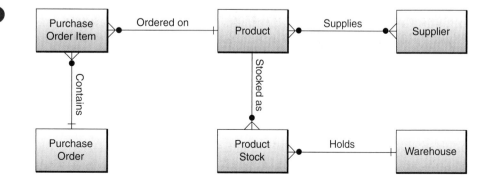

Such user views are a major part of a **data modeling** process where the relationships between data elements are identified. Each data model defines the logical relationships among the data elements needed to support a basic business process. For example, can a supplier provide more than one type of product to us? Can a customer have more than one type of account with us? Can an employee have several pay rates or be assigned to several project workgroups?

Answering such questions will identify data relationships that have to be represented in a data model that supports a business process. These data models then serve as logical frameworks (called *schemas and subschemas*) on which to base the *physical design* of databases and the development of application programs to support the business processes of the organization. A schema is an overall logical view of the relationships among the data elements in a database, while the subschema is a logical view of the data relationships needed to support specific end user application programs that will access that database.

Remember that data models represent *logical views* of the data and relationships of the database. Physical database design takes a *physical view* of the data (also called the internal view) that describes how data are to be physically stored and accessed on the storage devices of a computer system. For example, Figure 5.24 illustrates these different database views and the software interface of a bank database processing system. In this example, checking, savings, and installment lending are the business processes whose data models are part of a banking services data model that serves as a logical data framework for all bank services.

Figure 5.24 Examples of the logical and physical database views and the software interface of a banking services information system.

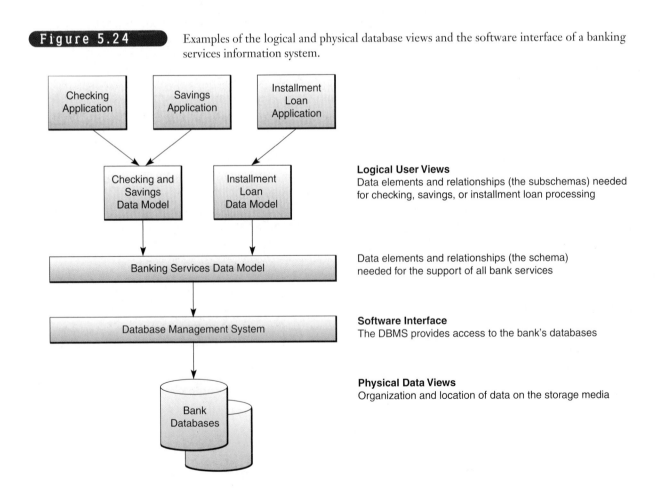

Summary

- **Data Resource Management.** Data resource management is a managerial activity that applies information systems technology and management tools to the task of managing an organization's data resources. It includes the database administration function that focuses on developing and maintaining standards and controls for an organization's databases. Data administration, however, focuses on the planning and control of data to support business functions and strategic organizational objectives. This includes a data planning effort that focuses on developing an overall data architecture for a firm's data resources.

- **Database Management.** The database management approach affects the storage and processing of data. The data needed by different applications are consolidated and integrated into several common databases, instead of being stored in many independent data files. Also, the database management approach emphasizes updating and maintaining common databases, having users' application programs share the data in the database, and providing a reporting and an inquiry/response capability so end users can easily receive reports and quick responses to requests for information.

- **Database Software.** Database management systems are software packages that simplify the creation, use, and maintenance of databases. They provide software tools so end users, programmers, and database administrators can create and modify databases, interrogate a database, generate reports, do application development, and perform database maintenance.

- **Types of Databases.** Several types of databases are used by business organizations, including operational, distrib-

uted, and external databases. Data warehouses are a central source of data from other databases that have been cleaned, transformed and cataloged for business analysis and decision support applications. That includes data mining, which attempts to find hidden patterns and trends in the warehouse data. Hypermedia databases on the World Wide Web and corporate intranets and extranets store hyperlinked multimedia pages at a website. Web server software can manage such databases for quick access and maintenance of the Web database.

- **Database Development.** The development of databases can be easily accomplished using microcomputer database management packages for small end user applications. However, the development of large corporate databases requires a top-down data planning effort. This may involve developing enterprise and entity relationship models, subject area databases, and data models that reflect the logical data elements and relationships needed to support the operation and management of the basic business processes of the organization.

- **Data Access.** Data must be organized in some logical manner on physical storage devices so that they can be efficiently processed. For this reason, data are commonly organized into logical data elements such as characters, fields, records, files, and databases. Database structures, such as the hierarchical, network, relational, and object-oriented models, are used to organize the relationships among the data records stored in databases. Databases and files can be organized in either a sequential or direct manner and can be accessed and maintained by either sequential access or direct access processing methods.

Key Terms and Concepts

These are the key terms and concepts of this chapter. The page number of their first explanation is in parentheses.

1. Data dictionary (148)
2. Data mining (151)
3. Data modeling (166)
4. Data planning (154)
5. Data resource management (142)
6. Database access (163)
   a. Direct (163)
   b. Sequential (163)
7. Database administration (154)
8. Database administrator (154)
9. Database management approach (146)
10. Database management system (147)
11. Database structures (158)

    a. Hierarchical (158)
    b. Multidimensional (159)
    c. Network (159)
    d. Object-oriented (159)
    e. Relational (159)
12. DBMS uses (147)
    a. Application development (149)
    b. Database development (147)
    c. Database interrogation (148)
    d. Database maintenance (149)
13. Key field (163)
14. Logical data elements (144)
    a. Character (144)

    b. Field (145)
    c. Record (145)
    d. File (145)
    e. Database (145)
15. Metadata (148)
16. Query language (148)
17. Report generator (148)
18. Types of databases (150)
    a. Data warehouse (151)
    b. Distributed (150)
    c. External (150)
    d. Hypermedia (153)
    e. Operational (150)

Review Quiz

Match one of the key terms and concepts listed previously with one of the brief examples or definitions that follow. Try to find the best fit for answers that seem to fit more than one term or concept. Defend your choices.

_____ 1. The use of integrated collections of data records and files for data storage and processing.

_____ 2. A DBMS allows you to create, interrogate, and maintain a database, create reports, and develop application programs.

_____ 3. A specialist in charge of the databases of an organization.

_____ 4. This DBMS feature allows users to easily interrogate a database.

_____ 5. Defines and catalogs the data elements and data relationships in an organization's database.

_____ 6. Helps you specify and produce reports from a database.

_____ 7. The main software package that supports a database management approach.

_____ 8. Databases are dispersed to the Internet and corporate intranets and extranets.

_____ 9. Databases that organize and store data as objects.

_____ 10. Databases of hyperlinked multimedia documents on the Web.

_____ 11. The management of all the data resources of an organization.

_____ 12. Developing databases and maintaining standards and controls for an organization's databases.

_____ 13. Processing data in a data warehouse to discover key business factors and trends.

_____ 14. Enterprise planning that ties database development to the support of basic business processes.

_____ 15. Developing conceptual views of the relationships among data in a database.

_____ 16. A customer's name.

_____ 17. A customer's name, address, and account balance.

_____ 18. The names, addresses, and account balances of all of your customers.

_____ 19. An integrated collection of all of the data about your customers.

_____ 20. An identification field in a record.

_____ 21. A treelike structure of records in a database.

_____ 22. A tabular structure of records in a database.

_____ 23. Records are organized as cubes within cubes in a database.

_____ 24. Transactions are sorted in ascending order by Social Security number before processing.

_____ 25. Unsorted transactions can be used to immediately update a database.

_____ 26. Databases that support the major business processes of an organization.

_____ 27. A centralized and integrated database of current and historical data about an organization.

_____ 28. Databases available on the Internet or provided by commercial information services.

Discussion Questions

1. How should an e-business enterprise store, access, and distribute data and information about their internal operations and external environment?

2. What roles do database management, data administration, and data planning play in managing data as a business resource?

3. What are the advantages of a database management approach to organizing, accessing, and managing an organization's data resources? Give examples to illustrate your answer.

4. Refer to the Real World Case on Oracle and IBM in the chapter. What strategies do you think Microsoft will take in the battle for the enterprise database and applications software market? How might this affect the other software companies involved and the companies who use such products?

5. What is the role of a database management system in an e-business information system?

6. Databases of information about a firm's internal operations were formerly the only databases that were considered to be important to a business. What other kinds of databases are important for a business today?

7. Refer to the Real World Case on Aetna and Boeing in the chapter. Is there a business case and a technology solution for reducing the swiftly expanding amounts of data being captured and stored from the Internet and Web activities of many companies today? Explain.

8. What are the benefits and limitations of the relational database model for business applications today?

9. Why is the object-oriented database model gaining acceptance for developing applications and managing the hypermedia databases at business websites?

10. How have the Internet, intranets, extranets, and the World Wide Web affected the types and uses of data resources available to business end users?

Application Exercises

Complete the following exercises as individual or group projects that apply chapter concepts to real world business situations.

1. Calculating Training Costs

Database systems typically involve multiple tables that are related to each other and can be combined on the basis of their logical relationship.

The data below describe a set of training classes that are available to workers in the Sales, Accounting, and Operations departments. For each course there is a title which can be used to identify it (Title), the duration of the class in hours (Hours), the fixed costs of an instructor and room for the class (Fixed Cost) and a per student cost for materials (Unit Cost).

Title	Category	Hours	Fixed_ Cost	Unit_ Cost
Advanced Database Features	DB	16	$3,250.00	$120.00
Advanced Spreadsheet	SS	16	$3,000.00	$90.00
Database Fundamentals	SS	24	$4,000.00	$100.00
Enliven Your Presentations	PR	8	$1,000.00	$30.00
Spreadsheet Fundamentals	SS	16	$2,500.00	$65.00
Using Presentation Graphics	PR	12	$1,500.00	$40.00

a. If you have not completed **Application Exercise 4–3** complete part A of that exercise now. For this exercise, we will delete the Hours and Category columns from the existing table because they are characteristics of the course and not a particular session, so delete those columns now. Next create a course table with the structure and data shown in the example above. Make sure that the Title column in this new table has exactly the same data type and length that you used for the Title column on the previous table. Create and print a listing of a query that joins the two tables based on the common Title column and displays all columns of both tables.

b. Create a report that could be used to bill the costs of each session to the appropriate departments. Each department will be billed only for Unit Costs, so join the tables and multiply unit cost by the number of attendees from each department to get the billing for that department. Include a total to be billed to each department across all training sessions that have been held.

c. Create a report grouped by Course and Category that shows the total cost of each session (Fixed cost + unit Cost * total attendees) and cost per attendee (the above divided by total attendees).

2. Tracking Project Work at AAA Systems

You are responsible for managing information systems development projects at AAA Systems. To better track progress in completing projects you have decided to maintain a simple database table to track the time your employees spend on various tasks and the projects with which they are associated. It will also allow you to keep track of employee billable hours each week. A sample set of data for this table is shown below.

a. Build a database table to store the data shown below and enter the records shown as a set of sample data. (Note that this table has no natural unique identifier. A combination of the project name, task name, employee ID and production week is required to uniquely identify a row in this table.

b. Create a query that will list the hours worked for all workers who worked more than 40 hours during production week 20.

c. Create a report grouped by project that will show the number of hours devoted to each task on the project and the total number of hours devoted to each project as well as a grand total of hours worked.

d. Create a report grouped by employee that will show their hours worked on each task and total hours worked. The user should be able to select a production week and have data for just that week presented.

Project_Name	Task_Name	Employee_Id	Production_Week	Hours_worked
Fin-Goods-Inv	App. Devel.	456	21	40
Fin-Goods-Inv	DB Design	345	20	20
Fin-Goods-Inv	UI Design	234	20	16
HR	Analysis	234	21	24
HR	Analysis	456	20	48
HR	UI Design	123	20	8
HR	UI Design	123	21	40
HR	UI Design	234	21	32
Shipmt-Tracking	DB Design	345	20	24
Shipmt-Tracking	DB Design	345	21	16
Shipmt-Tracking	DB Development	345	21	20
Shipmt-Tracking	UI Design	123	20	32
Shipmt-Tracking	UI Design	234	20	24

Trimac Corp. and Sallie Mae: Using Data Warehouses for Business Intelligence

It wasn't always easy for Trimac Corp.'s internal users to access critical data for their reporting needs without contacting the IT department. Although Trimac kept data about its day-to-day operations, it didn't have a database that could consolidate all of the business information from various sources within the company and provide a multidimensional view of that data so employees could analyze business conditions.

The problem affected users' ability to perform key analyses such as trip standards and analysis, which examine factors like profitability based on equipment or a particular customer by reviewing variables such as load time, loaded miles traveled, and gross vehicle weight. Financial reporting in areas such as accounts payable and accounts receivable was also fragmented.

So Trimac, a bulk hauling and trucking firm based in Calgary, Alberta, Canada, turned to Toronto-based enterprise software company Hummingbird's universal data-exchange product, Genio Suite, to help improve access to corporate data from across the organization. "We initiated this with our Business Intelligence Project," says Len Mori, project manager for infrastructure at Trimac. "One of the tasks was to deliver reports to different departments. To do that, we had to build a data warehouse. We didn't have the tools to do that, so we started looking around for a solution that gave us a fast turnaround to implementation."

That's where data warehousing and access tool suites come in. "This technology facilitates the implementation of data marts used for trip analysis, haul analysis, and profitability, either by customer or equipment," says Martin Zardecki, business intelligence manager at Trimac.

Mori says Trimac decided on the Genio Suite after looking at several other products. "We had three software products demonstrated for us," Mori explains. "Genio Suite was the most mature product we saw. And Genio was a breeze to install and set up." Genio automates many tasks that normally require time-consuming programming, letting users rapidly develop data-transformation routines.

Genio Suite is a data extract, transform, and load (ETL) software tool that pulls data from its original database, converts the data into the right format for analysis and loads it into a central repository, or target database. Trimac implemented Genio Suite on its Solaris Unix servers to populate its data warehouse with clean, accurate data from various financial and human resources applications.

The tool lets Trimac's IT department cost-effectively and easily design, deploy, and maintain data transformation and exchange processes, according to Mori. This dramatically simplified Trimac's internal systems and ensured the consistency of data, he says. The company uses PeopleSoft financial and human resources applications running on an Oracle database. Business intelligence tools from Ottawa-based Cognos deliver querying, reporting, and online analytical processing capabilities to users. Using Genio, Trimac is able to extract data from its various applications and populate the data warehouse.

Several data marts are created for use with the Cognos tools for multidimensional analysis of data such as account information, products, customers, and schedules, as well as accounts payable and receivable information. To gain an edge in nabbing profitable clients, savvy companies often use segmentation techniques to slice and dice customer data in an effort to match the best sales prospects to specific products and services.

"The trend has been quicker and easier access to the information, creating a dashboard for a senior executive to look at on the fly," says Kaenan Hertz, director of CRM digital intelligence at the Student Loan Marketing Association, or Sallie Mae, in Reston, Virginia. He says enterprise managers now prefer to keep that data in house, merge it with accounting and sales figures, store it in a data warehouse, and run queries from their own desktops.

Historically, data at Sallie Mae was stored in a single mainframe, which made it difficult for employees to access the information and run their own segmentation queries. To remedy that, Sallie Mae recently formed a special team to place the CRM data in a data mart that was Web-accessible to end users throughout the company. Extracting the data and making sure it was valid required significant customization work, says Hertz.

The key challenges that Sallie Mae has faced since then include limiting access to specific data for certain employees and ensuring that the segmentation programs run fast enough across millions of cross-referenced records, according to Hertz. The company factors in not only the age and sex of the borrower when running a query, but also what school he went to and for how many years. So Sallie Mae recently installed software from E.piphany Inc. in San Mateo, California to help segment customer data and run more efficient e-mail marketing campaigns.

Case Study Questions

1. What is the business value of a data warehouse approach to data resource management for the companies in this case?

2. What are the business benefits of the software tools they use for business intelligence?

3. How do e-business and e-commerce provide both opportunities and problems that need the data resource management and reporting technologies mentioned in this case?

Source: Adapted from Linda Rosencrance, "Data Warehouse Gives Trimac Information for the Long Haul," *Computerworld*, July 30, 2001, p. 42. Reprinted by permission.

Merrill Lynch and Terra Lycos:
The Business Case for Outsourcing Data Storage

According to research conducted last year by the University of California at Berkeley, the amount of digital information produced in the world is doubling as often as every two years. At many companies the growth is even faster, with data doubling each year, thanks to the reams of information generated by the Web. All those e-business tools—databases, customer-relationship management systems, and personalization servers, not to mention website content, graphics, and audio and video files—are kicking up a veritable tsunami of data.

Data storage is fast becoming the biggest expense in large companies' IT budgets, gobbling up as much as 30 percent of capital expenditures. Which means that if you need to hold down IT costs, storage should be the first place you look. When you consider that you might be able to cut 10 to 30 percent of your budget by outsourcing your storage needs, you may begin to see the allure.

What's a budget-conscious company to do? My vote: Outsource the whole mess to a storage service provider (SSP) such as IBM Global Services, EDS, Compaq, or newcomer StorageNetworks. SSPs provide storage capacity and manage it for you, either in your own data center, in the co-location facility where your site is hosted, or at the SSP's own data center. In return you pay only for what you use—typically $20 to $70 per gigabyte per month, depending on how much data you have, what kind of backups you need, and how much bandwidth you connect to your data.

Outsourcing data storage is a relatively new option, but the industry is growing fast. The reason is that outsourcing storage is faster to deploy, easier to manage, and often much cheaper. However, it doesn't make sense to outsource unless you have a huge amount of data to deal with, at which point volume discounts will bring your monthly cost per gigabyte down to less than the cost of doing it yourself. Right now, that minimum level is about 8 terabytes, reckons StorageNetworks co-founder and CTO Bill Miller, although it may drop as the cost of outsourced storage does.

Merrill Lynch. Merrill Lynch & Co.'s senior technology officer, Chris Corrado, was juggling an enormous server consolidation at the brokerage's New York headquarters. At the same time, he was migrating its business data to a storage subnetwork, so the last thing he wanted to do was worry about what storage technology would work best. The answer for Corrado, and an increasing number of other Global 2,000 IT executives, was to outsource his storage-area network (SAN).

While Merrill Lynch's IT staff could have built the SAN in-house, Corrado said he expects to save 20 percent on the total cost of ownership of the storage network by having Waltham, Massachusetts–based, StorageNetworks, Inc., build and then remotely manage the SAN. The effort began in January, and Corrado expects the project to be completed within the next year.

To date, Merrill Lynch has been using just 40 percent of the storage capacity of its direct-attached storage system. Meanwhile, maintenance and upgrade costs have been steadily increasing. The world's largest brokerage house is taking a cautious approach to migrating its business and mission-critical data to a SAN over the next few years. Currently, about 15 to 20 percent of the firm's data resides on the SAN. "This is a long process. You can try to do it fast—if you're suicidal," Corrado said.

Corrado cautioned those entering into contracts with SSPs to read the fine print of any service-level agreement and make it work to their advantage. "You have to force these guys to pass along not only hardware costs savings over the years but productivity costs, considering storage software will get better as well," Corrado said.

Part of the impetus behind Merrill Lynch's outsourcing deal: the firm's IT staffers are busy consolidating about 2,500 servers at its New York headquarters down to 250 to 300 machines over the next year. Corrado said that if Merrill Lynch's outsourcing project didn't reduce costs by at least 10 percent, he wouldn't do it. "It's just not worth the risk," he said.

Terra Lycos. When web portal Terra Lycos needed to move 5.5 terabytes of data—spread across 30 network-attached storage devices—from its Tripod subsidiary in Jersey City, New Jersey, to company headquarters in Waltham, Massachusetts, CTO/CIO Tim Wright knew that his team couldn't handle it alone. The difficulty and expense of buying hardware, deploying it, and then transferring all the data was, as he puts it, "daunting." Instead, he turned the whole project over to StorageNetworks, which built a new storage infrastructure for Tripod, and then moved all their data in just three hours.

Wright has found that the outsourced storage system is indeed faster and cheaper than the old system. The Terra Lycos data handled by StorageNetworks has since swelled to 20 terabytes, yet Wright estimates that he has shaved 10 percent off his storage costs while improving the overall performance of Terra Lycos websites.

Case Study Questions

1. What data resource management challenges are resulting from the growth of e-business and e-commerce?

2. What storage management alternatives should be considered by a company to meet such challenges?

3. What are the business benefits and risks of outsourcing data storage for Merrill Lynch and Terra Lycos?

Source: Adapted from Dylan Tweeney, "How to Beat the High Cost of Storage," *eCompany Now*, July 2001, pp. 84–85. © 2001 Time Inc. All rights reserved; and Lucas Mearian, "Merrill Lynch Hands over SAN Management," *Computerworld*, August 20, 2001, p. 8. Reprinted by permission.

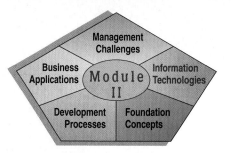

Management Challenges

Business Applications   Module II   Information Technologies

Development Processes   Foundation Concepts

Chapter 6

Telecommunications

and Networks

Chapter Highlights

Learning Objectives

After reading and studying this chapter; you should be able to:

1. Identify several major developments and trends in the industries, technologies, and business applications of telecommunications and Internet technologies.

2. Provide examples of the business value of Internet, intranet, and extranet applications.

3. Identify the basic components, functions, and types of telecommunications networks used in business.

4. Explain the functions of major types of telecommunications network hardware, software, media, and services.

The Internetworked Enterprise

Internetworking the Enterprise

When computers are networked, two industries—computing and communications—converge, and the result is vastly more than the sum of the parts. Suddenly, computing applications become available for business-to-business coordination and commerce, and for small as well as large organizations. The global Internet creates a public place without geographic boundaries—cyberspace—where ordinary citizens can interact, publish their ideas, and engage in the purchase of goods and services. In short, the impact of both computing and communications on our society and organizational structures is greatly magnified [15].

Thus, telecommunications and network technologies are internetworking and revolutionizing business and society. Businesses have become **internetworked enterprises.** The Internet, the Web, and intranets and extranets are networking business processes and employees together, and connecting them to their customers, suppliers, and other business stakeholders. Companies and workgroups can thus collaborate more creatively, manage their business operations and resources more effectively, and compete successfully in today's fast-changing global economy. This chapter presents the telecommunications and network foundations for these developments.

Analyzing Sears and UPS

Read the Real World Case on Sears and UPS on the next page. We can learn a lot about the role that wireless telecommunications technologies can play in e-business and e-commerce. See Figure 6.1.

Figure 6.1

Robert Conner is senior director of interactive marketing at UPS and leads their wireless e-commerce initiatives.

Source: Ann States/SABA.

Sears and UPS:
Challenges and Benefits of Wireless e-Business and e-Commerce

E-business wireless applications that dispatch information to field service technicians or connect embedded factory machines to one another have caught on bigtime. E-commerce wireless applications (M-commerce or mobile commerce), in which consumers use wireless devices to obtain product information or make purchases, have fizzled. Still, analysts say it's premature to sound the death knell for M-commerce.

"M-commerce to banks and airlines still makes sense because their customers see time as critically important, " notes Ken Dulaney, an analyst at Gartner, Inc. But Dulaney says the projects with the biggest paybacks have been "unsexy" and industry-related, in field service or factory settings.

By contrast, consumers have given dismal responses to recent M-commerce initiatives, due in part to the hassle of having to navigate the small screens of PDAs and Web-enabled cell phones. Such applications use the Wireless Application Protocol (WAP) and run various much-hyped wireless Web applications, from e-retailer transactions to stock trading. "WAP access has been a miserable experience, and wireless Web is an oxymoron, says William Crawford, an analyst at U.S. Bancorp Piper Jaffray Inc.

Instead, most of the corporate interest surrounding wireless fits into three e-business categories: messaging (business e-mail, including field service applications), wireless LANs, and wireless embedded devices. "For now, messaging is the killer application, given the widespread interest in it for a variety of business needs," Crawford says.

One of the pioneering applications reflects just how valuable wireless field service programs can be. In 1997, Sears Roebuck and Co. spent $40 million to arm its 12,500 field service technicians nationwide with wireless-ready laptops and saw a return on investment within one year, company officials say.

Each night, Sears technicians download the next day's service orders via phone line to ruggedized laptops at their homes or Sears service center. They then use a variety of wireless data networks while in the field to access realtime updates on arrival, departure, and repair parts information on the scheduled day of service, according to William P. Miller, program manager at Sears. Since the initiative was launched, the number of phone calls placed by Sears field technicians for service order information has dropped by 75 percent, saving the company $7 million over three years while improving customer service, Miller says.

Atlanta-based UPS uses wireless as part of UPScan, a companywide, global initiative to streamline and standardize all in-building scanning hardware and software used in their package distribution centers. For package tracking, UPScan will consolidate multiple scanning applications into one wireless LAN application, while maintaining interfaces with critical control and repository systems. The project is part of a $100 million upgraded and expanded effort throughout the decade.

As part of its latest initiative, UPS is also consolidating 18 hardware terminals, each running different software. The consolidation of devices alone will deliver significant business benefits, including simplified operations, lower costs, faster application development, lower support requirements, and improved data integrity, which will lead to increased customer satisfaction, notes David Salzman, a UPS program manager.

UPS will use Bluetooth, a short-range wireless networking protocol for communications with cordless peripherals (such as ring-mounted wireless manual scanners), linked to wireless LANs, which communicate with corporate systems. The project calls for fixed-mount, wearable, and portable devices, which are expected to serve most UPS applications, from package tracking to equipment monitoring to two-way communications, Salzman says. UPS will also install advanced wireless LANs at all of its 2,000 facilities worldwide.

UPS had already developed application programming interfaces (APIs) in-house to link its legacy tracking systems to business customers, such as retailers that wanted to provide order-status information on their websites from UPS to their customers. When UPS decided to offer its customers shipment tracking as part of a mobile information services package, it hired Air2Web, Inc., a wireless application service provider in Atlanta. The company used the existing APIs to link UPS applications to multiple types of wireless networks from different providers and configure them for a range of wireless devices.

"Speed to market, customer satisfaction, and dealing with the issues of a wireless network environment were our main concerns," says Robert Conner, senior director of interactive marketing at UPS. Explains Conner: "The learning curve for wireless was too stiff, and the technology is too vast. Air2Web had the expertise, and they deployed the application in four months."

Case Study Questions

1. What do you think needs to be done to encourage sufficient customer participation in wireless e-commerce services to make them a success?

2. What are the business benefits of the Sears and UPS wireless e-business applications?

3. Why do wireless e-business applications seem to be more successful than wireless e-commerce services?

Source: Adapted from Matt Hamblen, "In Search of the Killer App," *Computerworld*, September 17, 2001, pp. 24–26; Julie Sartan, "Quick, Get Me Wireless," *Computerworld*, September 17, 2001, pp. 42–44; and Alan Radding, "Leading the Way," *Computerworld ROI*, September/October 2001, pp. 21, 22. Reprinted by permission.

While wireless e-business applications have been successful for several years, wireless e-commerce (mobile commerce or M-commerce), has not done well at all. Analysts say part of the problem is the hassle of navigating small screens on Web-enabled PDAs and cell phones. But e-business applications such as wireless e-mail and field services, wireless LANs, and wireless embedded business devices are becoming an essential component of many businesses today. For example, Sears has found major cost savings and customer service benefits in its program to arm its field technicians with wireless-ready laptops. And UPS is spending massive amounts to employ wireless LANs and wireless embedded devices like ring-mounted manual scanners to consolidate and streamline all scanning operations in its huge package distribution centers.

Trends in Telecommunications

Telecommunications is the exchange of information in any form (voice, data, text, images, audio, video) over computer-based networks. Major trends occurring in the field of telecommunications have a significant impact on management decisions in this area. You should thus be aware of major trends in telecommunications industries, technologies, and applications that significantly increase the decision alternatives confronting business managers and professionals. See Figure 6.2.

Industry Trends

The competitive arena for telecommunications service has changed dramatically in many countries in recent years. The telecommunications industry has changed from government-regulated monopolies to a deregulated market with fiercely competitive suppliers of telecommunications services. Numerous companies now offer businesses and consumers a choice of everything from local and global telephone services to communications satellite channels, mobile radio, cable TV, cellular phone services, and Internet access. See Figure 6.3.

The explosive growth of the Internet and the World Wide Web has spawned a host of new telecommunications products, services, and providers. Driving and responding to this growth, business firms have dramatically increased their use of the Internet and the Web for electronic commerce and collaboration. Thus, the service and vendor options available to meet a company's telecommunications needs have increased significantly, as have a business manager's decision-making alternatives.

Figure 6.2

Major trends in business telecommunications.

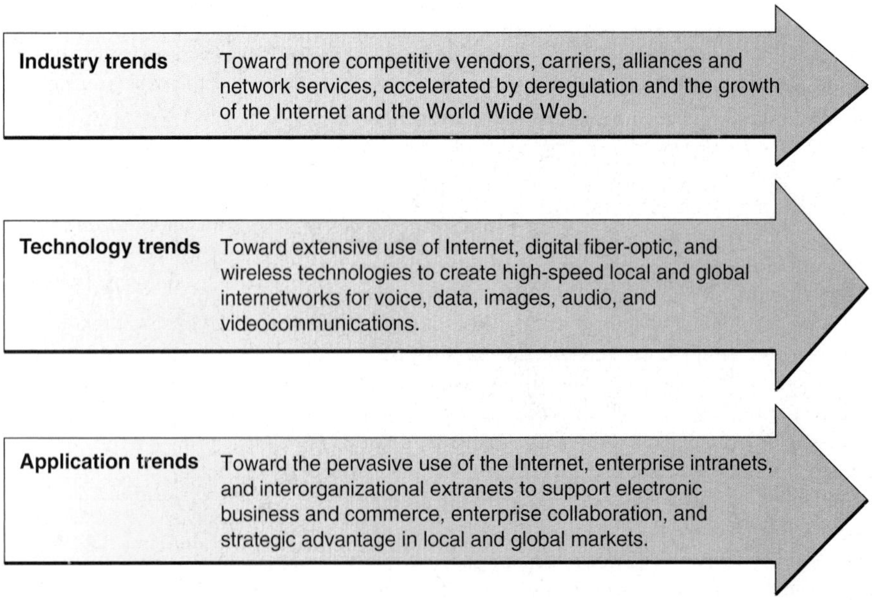

Industry trends Toward more competitive vendors, carriers, alliances and network services, accelerated by deregulation and the growth of the Internet and the World Wide Web.

Technology trends Toward extensive use of Internet, digital fiber-optic, and wireless technologies to create high-speed local and global internetworks for voice, data, images, audio, and videocommunications.

Application trends Toward the pervasive use of the Internet, enterprise intranets, and interorganizational extranets to support electronic business and commerce, enterprise collaboration, and strategic advantage in local and global markets.

Figure 6.3

The spectrum of telecommunications-based services available today.

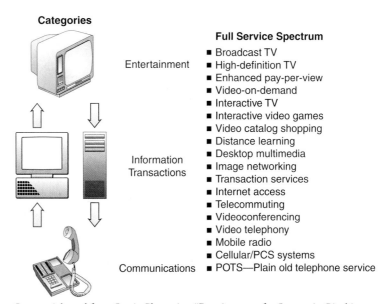

Categories

Entertainment

Information Transactions

Communications

Full Service Spectrum
- Broadcast TV
- High-definition TV
- Enhanced pay-per-view
- Video-on-demand
- Interactive TV
- Interactive video games
- Video catalog shopping
- Distance learning
- Desktop multimedia
- Image networking
- Transaction services
- Internet access
- Telecommuting
- Videoconferencing
- Video telephony
- Mobile radio
- Cellular/PCS systems
- POTS—Plain old telephone service

Source: Adapted from Samir Chatterjee, "Requirements for Success in Gigabit Networking," *Communications of the ACM*, July 1997, p. 64. Copyright © 1997, Association of Computing Machinery. By permission.

Technology Trends

Open systems with unrestricted connectivity, using **Internet networking technologies** as their technology platform, are today's primary telecommunications technology drivers. Web browser suites, HTML Web page editors, Internet and intranet servers and network management software, TCP/IP Internet networking products, and network security fire walls are just a few examples. These technologies are being applied in Internet, intranet, and extranet applications, especially those for electronic commerce and collaboration. This trend has reinforced previous industry and technical moves toward building client/server networks based on an open systems architecture.

Open systems are information systems that use common standards for hardware, software, applications, and networking. Open systems, like the Internet and corporate intranets and extranets, create a computing environment that is open to easy access by end users and their networked computer systems. Open systems provide greater **connectivity,** that is, the ability of networked computers and other devices to easily access and communicate with each other and share information. Any open systems architecture also provides a high degree of network **interoperability.** That is, open systems enable the many different applications of end users to be accomplished using the different varieties of computer systems, software packages, and databases provided by a variety of interconnected networks. Frequently, software known as *middleware* may be used to help diverse systems work together.

Telecommunications is also being revolutionized by the rapid change from analog to **digital network technologies.** Telecommunication systems have always depended on voice-oriented analog transmission systems designed to transmit the variable electrical frequencies generated by the sound waves of the human voice. However, local and global telecommunications networks are rapidly converting to digital transmission technologies that transmit information in the form of discrete pulses, as computers do. This provides (1) significantly higher transmission speeds, (2) the movement of larger amounts of information, (3) greater economy, and (4) much lower error rates than analog systems. In addition, digital technologies allow telecommunications networks to carry multiple types of communications (data, voice, video) on the same circuits.

Another major trend in telecommunications technology is a change from reliance on copper wire-based media and land-based microwave relay systems to fiber-optic lines and cellular, PCS, communications satellite, and other **wireless technologies.** Fiber-optic transmission, which uses pulses of laser-generated light, offers significant advantages in terms of reduced size and installation effort, vastly greater communication capacity, much faster transmission speeds, and freedom from electrical interference. Satellite transmission offers significant advantages for organizations that need to transmit massive quantities of data, audio, and video over global networks, especially to isolated areas. Cellular, PCS, mobile radio, and other wireless systems are connecting cellular and PCS phones, PDAs, and other wireless appliances to the Internet and corporate networks.

Business Application Trends

The changes in telecommunications industries and technologies just mentioned are causing a significant change in the business use of telecommunications. The trend toward more vendors, services, Internet technologies, and open systems, and the rapid growth of the Internet, the World Wide Web, and corporate intranets and extranets dramatically increase the number of feasible telecommunications applications. Thus, telecommunications networks are now playing vital and pervasive roles in electronic commerce, enterprise collaboration, and other e-business applications that support the operations, management, and strategic objectives of both large and small business enterprises.

An organization's local and global computer networks can dramatically cut costs, shorten business lead times and response times, support electronic commerce, improve the collaboration of workgroups, develop online operational processes, share resources, lock in customers and suppliers, and develop new products and services. This makes telecommunications a more complex and important decision area for businesses that must increasingly find new ways to compete in both domestic and global markets.

The Business Value of Telecommunications Networks

What *business value* is created by the trends in business applications of telecommunications we have identified? A good way to summarize the answer to this question is shown in Figure 6.4. Information technology, especially in telecommunications-based business applications, helps a company overcome geographic, time, cost, and structural barriers to business success. Figure 6.4 outlines examples of the business value of these four strategic capabilities of telecommunications networks. This figure emphasizes how several applications of electronic commerce can help a firm capture

Figure 6.4   Examples of the business value of e-business applications of telecommunications networks.

Strategic Capabilities	e-Business Examples	Business Value
Overcome geographic barriers: Capture information about business transactions from remote locations	Use the Internet and extranets to transmit customer orders from traveling salespeople to a corporate data center for order processing and inventory control	Provides better customer service by reducing delay in filling orders and improves cash flow by speeding up the billing of customers
Overcome time barriers: Provide information to remote locations immediately after it is requested	Credit authorization at the point of sale using online POS networks	Credit inquiries can be made and answered in seconds
Overcome cost barriers: Reduce the cost of more traditional means of communication	Desktop videoconferencing between a company and its business partners using the Internet, intranets, and extranets	Reduces expensive business trips; allows customers, suppliers, and employees to collaborate, thus improving the quality of decisions reached
Overcome structural barriers: Support linkages for competitive advantage	Business-to-business electronic commerce websites for transactions with suppliers and customers using the Internet and extranets	Fast, convenient services lock in customers and suppliers

and provide information quickly to end users at remote geographic locations at reduced costs, as well as supporting its strategic organizational objectives.

For example, traveling salespeople and those at regional sales offices can use the Internet, extranets, and other networks to transmit customer orders from their laptop or desktop PCs, thus breaking geographic barriers. Point-of-sale terminals and an online sales transaction processing network can break time barriers by supporting immediate credit authorization and sales processing. Teleconferencing can be used to cut costs by reducing the need for expensive business trips since it allows customers, suppliers, and employees to participate in meetings and collaborate on joint projects. Finally, business-to-business electronic commerce websites are used by the business to establish strategic relationships with their customers and suppliers by making business transactions fast, convenient, and tailored to the needs of the business partners involved.

The Internet Revolution

The explosive growth of the **Internet** is a revolutionary phenomenon in computing and telecommunications. The Internet has become the largest and most important network of networks today, and has evolved into a global *information superhighway.* The Internet is constantly expanding, as more and more businesses and other organizations and their users, computers, and networks join its global web. Thousands of business, educational, and research networks now connect millions of computer systems and users in more than 200 countries to each other. The Internet has also become a key platform for a rapidly expanding list of information and entertainment services and business applications, including enterprise collaboration and electronic commerce systems.

The Net doesn't have a central computer system or telecommunications center. Instead, each message sent has a unique address code so any Internet server in the network can forward it to its destination. Also, the Internet does not have a headquarters or governing body. International standards groups of individual and corporate members (such as the World Wide Web Consortium), promote use of the Internet and the development of new communications standards. These common standards are the key to the free flow of messages among the widely different computers and networks of the many organizations and *Internet service providers* (ISPs) in the system.

Internet Applications

The most popular Internet applications are e-mail, browsing the sites on the World Wide Web, and participating in *newsgroups* and *chat rooms.* Internet e-mail messages usually arrive in seconds or a few minutes anywhere in the world, and can take the form of data, text, fax, and video files. Internet browser software like Netscape Navigator and Microsoft Explorer enables millions of users to *surf* the World Wide Web by clicking their way to the multimedia information resources stored on the hyperlinked pages of businesses, government, and other websites. Websites offer information and entertainment, and are the launch sites for electronic commerce transactions between businesses and their suppliers and customers. As we will discuss in Chapter 8, e-commerce websites offer all manner of products and services via online retailers, wholesalers, service providers, and online auctions. See Figure 6.5.

The Internet provides electronic discussion forums and bulletin board systems formed and managed by thousands of special-interest newsgroups. You can participate in discussions or post messages on thousands of topics for other users with the same interests to read and respond to. Other popular applications include downloading software and information files and accessing databases provided by thousands of business, government, and other organizations. You can make online searches for information at websites in a variety of ways, using search sites and search engines such as Yahoo!, Google, and Fast Search. Logging on to other computers

Figure 6.5

Popular uses of the Internet.

- **Surf.** Point and click your way to thousands of hyperlinked websites and resources for multimedia information, entertainment, or electronic commerce.
- **e-Mail.** Exchange electronic mail with millions of Internet users.
- **Discuss.** Participate in discussion forums or post messages on bulletin board systems formed by thousands of special-interest newsgroups.
- **Chat.** Hold real-time text conversations in website chat rooms with Internet users around the world.
- **Buy and Sell.** You can buy and sell practically anything via e-commerce retailers, wholesalers, service providers, and online auctions.
- **Download.** Transfer data files, software, reports, articles, pictures, music, videos, and other types of files to your computer system.
- **Compute.** Log on to and use thousands of Internet computer systems around the world.
- **Other Uses:** Make long-distance phone calls, hold desktop videoconferences, listen to radio programs, watch television, play video games, explore virtual worlds, etc.

on the Internet and holding real-time conversations with other Internet users in *chat rooms* are also popular uses of the Internet.

Business Use of the Internet

As Figure 6.6. illustrates, business use of the Internet has expanded from an electronic information exchange to a broad platform for strategic business applications. Notice how applications like collaboration among business partners, providing customer and vendor support, and electronic commerce have become major business uses of the Internet. Companies are also using Internet technologies for marketing, sales, and customer relationship management applications, as well as cross-functional business applications, and applications in engineering, manufacturing, human resources, and accounting. Let's look at a real world example.

GE Power Systems: Using the Internet

General Electric Co. (GE) provides a fascinating glimpse of how the Net changes things. At GE Power Systems, customers and designers can use intranets, extranets, the Internet, and project collaboration technology to help construct a power plant from the ground up on the Web, says Jose A. Lopez, the subsidiary's general manager of e-business.

GE and customer engineers can now hold virtual meetings in which blueprints can be exchanged and manipulated in real time. Then customers can use the Web to watch from anywhere in the world as a turbine is built and moves down the production line, ordering last-minute changes as needed. Because the turbines cost an average of $35 million each and contain about 18,000 parts, catching changes—and errors—early is priceless. And after the turbine is delivered, a new Net-powered system called the Turbine Optimizer lets both customers and GE compare the performances of the turbines with other GE turbines around the world.

While GE's new systems should give the company a 20 percent to 30 percent reduction in the time it takes to build a turbine and could improve the annual output of each turbine by 1 percent to 2 percent, that's just the beginning. "Sure, there are productivity gains for us, but this is mainly a competetive advantage," says Lopez. "If customers find this helps them, they'll come back." So far, so good: Sales at GE Power Systems increased to about $13 billion in 2000, up 30 percent from 1999 [21].

Figure 6.6   Examples of how a company can use the Internet for business.

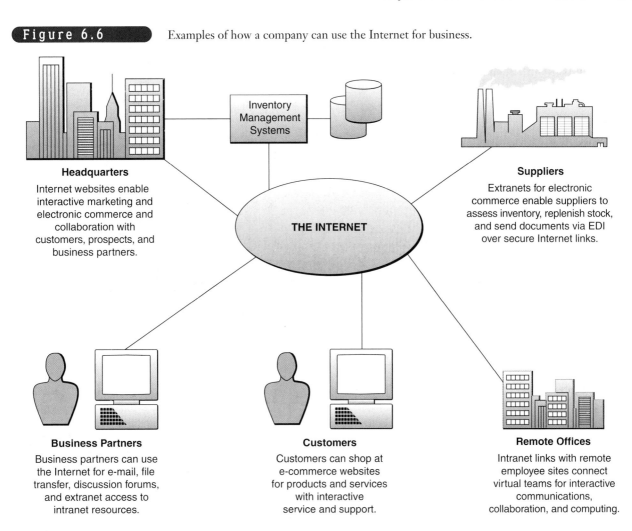

Headquarters
Internet websites enable interactive marketing and electronic commerce and collaboration with customers, prospects, and business partners.

Suppliers
Extranets for electronic commerce enable suppliers to assess inventory, replenish stock, and send documents via EDI over secure Internet links.

Business Partners
Business partners can use the Internet for e-mail, file transfer, discussion forums, and extranet access to intranet resources.

Customers
Customers can shop at e-commerce websites for products and services with interactive service and support.

Remote Offices
Intranet links with remote employee sites connect virtual teams for interactive communications, collaboration, and computing.

The Business Value of the Internet

The Internet provides a synthesis of computing and communication capabilities that adds value to every part of the business cycle [5].

What business value do companies derive from their business applications on the Internet? Figure 6.7 summarizes how many companies perceive the business value of the Internet for electronic commerce. Substantial cost savings can arise because applications that use the Internet and Internet-based technologies (like intranets and extranets) are typically less expensive to develop, operate, and maintain than traditional systems. For example, American Airlines saves money every time customers use their website instead of their customer support telephone system.

Other primary reasons for business value include attracting new customers with innovative marketing and products, and retaining present customers with improved customer service and support. Of course, generating revenue through electronic commerce applications is a major source of business value, which we will discuss in Chapter 8. To summarize, most companies are building e-commerce websites to achieve six major business values:

- Generate new revenue from online sales.
- Reduce costs through online sales and customer support.
- Attract new customers via Web marketing and advertising and online sales.
- Increase the loyalty of existing customers via improved Web customer service and support.

Figure 6.7

How companies are deriving business value from their e-commerce applications.

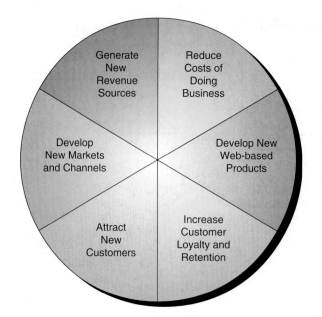

- Develop new Web-based markets and distribution channels for existing products.
- Develop new information-based products accessible on the Web [11].

The Role of Intranets

Many companies have sophisticated and widespread intranets, offering detailed data retrieval, collaboration tools, personalized customer profiles, and links to the Internet. Investing in the intranet, they feel, is as fundamental as supplying employees with a telephone [18].

Before we get any futher, let's redefine the concept of an intranet, to specifically emphasize how intranets are related to the Internet and extranets. An **intranet** is a network inside an organization that uses Internet technologies (such as Web browsers and servers, TCP/IP network protocols, HTML hypermedia document publishing and databases, and so on) to provide an Internet-like environment within the enterprise for information sharing, communications, collaboration, and the support of business processes. An intranet is protected by security measures such as passwords, encryption, and fire walls, and thus can be accessed by authorized users through the Internet. A company's intranet can also be accessed through the intranets of customers, suppliers, and other business partners via *extranet* links.

The Business Value of Intranets

Organizations of all kinds are implementing a broad range of intranet uses. One way that companies organize intranet applications is to group them conceptually into a few user services categories that reflect the basic services that intranets offer to their users. These services are provided by the intranet's portal, browser, and server software, as well as by other system and application software and groupware that are part of a company's intranet software environment. Figure 6.8 illustrates how intranets provide an *enterprise information portal* that supports communication and collaboration, Web publishing, business operations and management, and intranet portal management. Notice also how these applications can be integrated with existing IS resources and applications, and extended to customers, suppliers, and business partners via the Internet and extranets.

Communications and Collaboration. Intranets can significantly improve communications and collaboration within an enterprise. For example, you can use your intranet

Figure 6.8

Intranets can provide an enterprise information portal for applications in communication and collaboration, business operations and management, Web publishing, and intranet portal management.

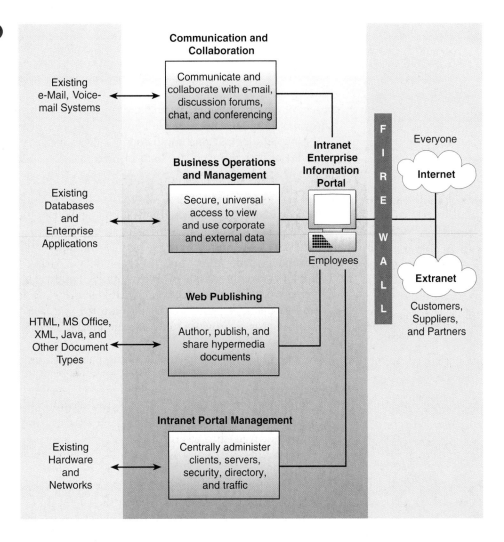

browser and your PC or NC workstation to send and receive e-mail, voicemail, paging, and faxes to communicate with others within your organization, and externally through the Internet and extranets. You can also use intranet groupware features to improve team and project collaboration with services such as discussion groups, chat rooms, and audio- and videoconferencing.

Web Publishing. The advantages of developing and publishing hyperlinked multimedia documents to hypermedia databases accessible on World Wide Web servers has moved to corporate intranets. The comparative ease, attractiveness, and lower cost of publishing and accessing multimedia business information internally via intranet websites have been the primary reasons for the explosive growth in the use of intranets in business. For example, information products as varied as company newsletters, technical drawings, and product catalogs can be published in a variety of ways, including hypermedia Web pages, e-mail, and net broadcasting, and as part of in-house business applications. Intranet software browsers, servers, and search engines can help you easily navigate and locate the business information you need.

Business Operations and Management. Intranets have moved beyond merely making hypermedia information available on Web servers, or pushing it to users via net broadcasting. Intranets are also being used as the platform for developing and deploying critical business applications to support business operations and managerial decision making across the internetworked enterprise. For example, many companies are developing custom applications like order processing, inventory control, sales management, and enterprise information portals that can be implemented on intranets, extranets, and the Internet. Many of these applications are designed to interface with, and access, existing company databases and legacy systems. The software for such business uses is then installed on intranet Web servers. Employees within the company, or external business partners, can access and run such applications using Web browsers from anywhere on the network whenever needed.

Now let's look at one company's use of an intranet in more detail to get a better idea of how intranets are used in business.

Cadence OnTrack: Business Value of an Intranet	Cadence Design Systems is the leading supplier of electronic design automation (EDA) software tools and professional services for managing the design of semiconductors, computer systems, networking and telecommunications equipment, consumer electronics, and other electronics-based products. The company employs more than 3,000 people in offices worldwide to support the requirements of the world's leading electronics manufacturers. Cadence developed an intranet for 500 managers, sales reps, and customer support staff. Called OnTrack, the intranet project provides sales support for a Cadence product line of over 1,000 products and services.

The OnTrack system uses a home page with links to other pages, information sources, and other applications to support each phase of the sales process with supporting materials and reference information. For example, at any point in the sales process, such as one called "Identify Business Issues," a sales rep can find customer presentations, sample letters, and the internal forms needed to move effectively through this step.

With OnTrack, sales reps now use the intranet as a single enterprise information portal that provides all of the information and data needed to go through the sales process, from prospecting, to closing a deal, to account management. In addition, global account teams have their own home page where they can collaborate and share information. Information on customers or competitors is now available instantly through access to an outside provider of custom news. The sales rep simply searches using a company name to get everything from financial information to recent news articles and press releases about the customer or competitor [4].

The Role of Extranets

As businesses continue to use open Internet technologies [extranets] to improve communication with customers and partners, they can gain many competitive advantages along the way—in product development, cost savings, marketing, distribution, and leveraging their partnerships [2].

As we have explained earlier, **extranets** are network links that use Internet technologies to interconnect the intranet of a business with the intranets of its customers, suppliers, or other business partners. Companies can establish direct private network links between themselves, or create private secure Internet links between them called *virtual private networks*. Or a company can use the unsecured Internet as the extranet link between its intranet and consumers and others, but rely on encryption of sensitive data and its own fire wall systems to provide adequate security. Thus, extranets enable customers, suppliers, consultants, subcontractors, business prospects, and others to access selected intranet websites and other company databases. See Figure 6.9.

Business Value of Extranets

The business value of extranets is derived from several factors. First, the Web browser technology of extranets makes customer and supplier access of intranet resources a lot easier and faster than previous business methods. Second, as you will

Figure 6.9

Extranets connect the internetworked enterprise to consumers, business customers, suppliers, and other business partners.

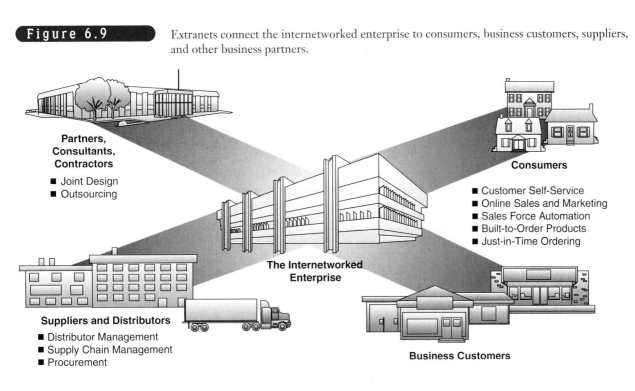

Partners, Consultants, Contractors
- Joint Design
- Outsourcing

Consumers
- Customer Self-Service
- Online Sales and Marketing
- Sales Force Automation
- Built-to-Order Products
- Just-in-Time Ordering

The Internetworked Enterprise

Suppliers and Distributors
- Distributor Management
- Supply Chain Management
- Procurement

Business Customers

see in two upcoming examples, extranets enable a company to offer new kinds of interactive Web-enabled services to their business partners. Thus, extranets are another way that a business can build and strengthen strategic relationships with its customers and suppliers. Also, extranets can enable and improve collaboration by a business with its customers and other business partners. Extranets facilitate an online, interactive product development, marketing, and customer-focused process that can bring better-designed products to market faster.

Countrywide and Snap-on: Extranet Examples

Countrywide Home Loans has created an extranet called Platinum Lender Access for its lending partners and brokers. About 500 banks and mortgage brokers can access Countrywide's intranet and selected financial databases. The extranet gives them access to their account and transaction information, status of loans, and company announcements. Each lender or broker is automatically identified by the extranet and provided with customized information on premium rates, discounts, and any special business arrangements they have negotiated with Countrywide [1].

Snap-on Incorporated spent $300,000 to create an extranet link to their intranet called the Franchise Information Network. The extranet lets Snap-on's 4,000 independent franchises for automotive tools access a secured intranet website for customized information and interactive communications with Snap-on employees and other franchisees. Franchisers can get information on sales plus marketing updates. Tips and training programs about managing a franchise operation and discussion forums for employees and franchisees to share ideas and best practices are also provided by the extranet. Finally, the Franchise Information Network provides interactive news and information on car racing and other special events sponsored by Snap-on, as well as corporate stock prices, business strategies, and other financial information [19].

Telecommunications Network Alternatives

Telecommunications Alternatives

Telecommunications is a highly technical, rapidly changing field of information systems technology. Most business professionals do not need a detailed knowledge of its technical characteristics. However, it is necessary that you understand some of the important characteristics of the basic components of telecommunications networks. This understanding will help you participate effectively in decision making regarding telecommunications alternatives.

Analyzing Welch Packaging and Gorman Uniform Service

Read the Real World Case on Welch Packaging and Gorman Uniform Service on the next page. We can learn a lot about the business impact of wireless-based telecommunications alternatives from this case. See Figure 6.10.

Companies in both urban areas and more remote areas of the country are turning to wireless technologies for broadband Internet access, because many alternatives

Figure 6.10

Jim Williams, IT manager at Welch Packaging, managed their implementation of a wireless broadband Internet service and wireless LANs to network their business locations.

Source: Marc Berlow.

Welch Packaging and Gorman Uniform Service: Evaluating Broadband Internet Access Alternatives

Back in 1999, Jim Williams, IT manager at Welch Packaging Group in Elkhart, Indiana, found that a speedy, cost-effective wired connection to the Internet simply wasn't available. So, like people at hundreds of other small and midsize businesses, Williams turned to a fixed wireless technology to bridge that last mile between his business and the Internet access that he felt was essential to run his company.

Williams explored a range of services, including ordinary wired telephone dial-up service, and a leased 1.54 MBPS T1 line, but found the former too slow and the latter too expensive. Finally, he elected to use a local Internet service provider that offers wireless access from cellular antenna towers using the 11M bit/sec. Wi-Fi (802 llb) wireless LAN standard. The service, from MicroVillage Internet Services in Mishawaka, Indiana, operates in the 1.4 GHz frequency spectrum to link business users and consumers in a two-county area to an Internet backbone network.

Dial-up Internet access via Digital Subscriber Line (DSL) wasn't an option for his company, Williams explains. "We were too far from the central office of the telephone company for DSL, and even a partial T1 line was going to run us over $500 per month. Wireless was cheaper," Williams says. "And it gave us more bandwidth than leasing a partial T1 line." Williams pays $450 a month for his service and is guaranteed a transfer rate of 128K bit/sec. But he notes that average throughput is much higher, as he regularly gets burst speeds of up to 3.5M bit/sec.

Reliability was at first a little problematic, Williams says, because the 2.4-GHz signal must have a clear line of sight. But erecting an 80-foot tower solved the problem and provided the antenna platform for a wireless LAN based on Aironet technology from Cisco Systems. The wireless LAN connects the main Welch plant with two other nearby packaging plants that Welch obtained when it acquired another company.

Welch's fixed wireless setup uses an unlicensed spectrum, which is a little risky because there are no regulations against interference from other devices, such as microwave ovens and portable phones that use the same frequencies, says Lisa Pierce, an analyst at Giga Information Group. Still, MicroVillage officials say they haven't experienced any major interference problems. Chris Brewer, MicroVillage's network operations manager, says he has one wireless access customer that's seven and a half miles from the nearest tower, but he prefers to limit transmission distances to no more than four miles. The cost of installation is $400 for business customers.

Distance from the telecom service provider's antenna is less of an issue for wireless users like Todd Gorman, operations manager at Gorman Uniform Service, a uniform rental business in Houston, Texas. Gorman contracted with Sprint Corp. to provide MMDS (Multichannel Multipoint Distribution System) broadband wireless to his business. MMDS operates over a licensed wireless spectrum at 2.6 GHz, which was originally used by local "wireless cable TV" operators to send signals to subscribers' homes. The wireless TV application, however, ultimately lost out to coaxial cable.

Now Sprint and WorldCom are using the 2.6 GHz spectrum to provide broadband wireless network connections. Sprint is the most aggressive in this sector, says analyst Lindsay Schroth of the Yankee Group. WorldCom seems to be waiting for Sprint to work out any kinks in the technology before it presses ahead, she says. Sprint's MMDS service is now available in 14 large markets including Chicago, Denver, and Phoenix, says the company's vice president of wireless operations, Cameron Rejali. A central MMDS antenna like the one Sprint has placed on top of the Sears Tower in Chicago can reach customers within a radius of 35 miles, Rejali says.

Gorman chose MMDS wireless even through he had access to DSL and T1 services. Why? "Sprint wireless service was the cheapest for the speeds we got," he says. The MMDS service, which Gorman says costs him $149 per month, is comparable in speed to a T1 line that XO Communications of Reston, Virginia, offered him for $700. Both have burst speeds of up to 1.5M bit/sec., Gorman says.

Wireless access was an even better deal than wired DSL, according to Gorman. He says the local telecommunications provider, Southwestern Bell Telephone in San Antonio, wanted $300 to $400 a month to provide DSL lines. Gorman has been using the Sprint MMDS service for five months and says it's been very reliable, with one exception: The Internet proxy server that caches Web content and is located between the uniform company's network hub and the Sprint MMDS modem has gone down a few times. "When that happens, I reset my Internet Protocol addresses on the server to restore the service," he explains.

Case Study Questions

1. What are the benefits and limitations of Wi-Fi wireless Internet access for Welch Packaging compared to their DSL and T1 alternatives?

2. Do you agree with Gorman Uniform Service's selection of MMDS wireless Internet access over competing technologies? Why or why not?

3. What Internet access technology would you recommend for a small business? Explain the reasons for your recommendation?

Source: Adapted from James Cope, "Bridging the Long Last Mile," *Computerworld*, September 17, 2001, pp. 34, 35. Reprinted by permission

Figure 6.11

Key telecommunications
network components and
alternatives.

Network Alternative	Examples of Alternatives
Networks	Internet, intranet, extranet, wide area, local area, client/server, network computing, peer-to-peer
Media	Twisted-pair wire, coaxial cable, fiber optics, microwave radio, communications satellites, cellular and PCS systems, wireless mobile and LAN systems
Processors	Modems, multiplexers, switches, routers, hubs, gateways, front-end processors, private branch exchanges
Software	Network operating systems, telecommunications monitors, Web browsers, middleware
Channels	Analog/digital, switched/nonswitched, circuit/message/packet/cell switching, bandwidth alternatives
Topology/architecture	Star, ring, and bus topologies, OSI and TCP/IP architectures and protocols

being offered by telecommunications companies are too costly or not available. Thus, when Welch Packaging's location made wire-based Internet access cost-prohibitive, the company turned to a Wi-Fi wireless service using cellular antenna towers and a wireless LAN to connect its business locations. And though Gorman Uniform Service is located in an urban area, it turned to a "wireless cable TV" technology called MMDS from Sprint Corp. for broadband Internet access because it was faster and cheaper than alternatives like T1 lines or DSL connections.

Figure 6.11 outlines key telecommunications components and alternatives. Remember, a basic understanding and appreciation, not a detailed knowledge, are sufficient for most business professionals.

A Telecommunications Network Model

Before we begin our discussion of telecommunications network alternatives, we should understand the basic components of a **telecommunications network.** Generally, a *communications network* is any arrangement where a *sender* transmits a message to a *receiver* over a *channel* consisting of some type of *medium*. Figure 6.12 illustrates a simple conceptual model of a telecommunications network, which shows that it consists of five basic categories of components:

- **Terminals,** such as networked personal computers, network computers, or information appliances. Any input/output device that uses telecommunications networks to transmit or receive data is a terminal, including telephones and the various computer terminals discussed in Chapter 3.

Figure 6.12

The five basic components in a telecommunications network: (1) terminals, (2) telecommunications processors, (3) telecommunications channels, (4) computers, and (5) telecommunications software.

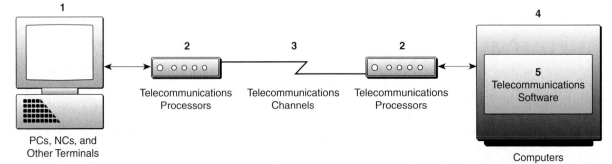

- **Telecommunications processors,** which support data transmission and reception between terminals and computers. These devices, such as modems, switches, and routers, perform a variety of control and support functions in a telecommunications network. For example, they convert data from digital to analog and back, code and decode data, and control the speed, accuracy, and efficiency of the communications flow between computers and terminals in a network.

- **Telecommunications channels** over which data are transmitted and received. Telecommunications channels may use combinations of **media,** such as copper wires, coaxial cables, or fiber-optic cables, or use wireless systems like microwave, communications satellite, radio, and cellular systems to interconnect the other components of a telecommunications network.

- **Computers** of all sizes and types are interconnected by telecommunications networks so that they can carry out their information processing assignments. For example, a mainframe computer may serve as a *host computer* for a large network, assisted by a midrange computer serving as a *front-end processor*, while a microcomputer may act as a *network server* in a small network.

- **Telecommunications control software** consists of programs that control telecommunications activities and manage the functions of telecommunications networks. Examples include network management programs of all kinds, such as *telecommunications monitors* for mainframe host computers, *network operating systems* for network servers, and *Web browsers* for microcomputers.

No matter how large and complex real world telecommunications networks may appear to be, these five basic categories of network components must be at work to support an organization's telecommunications activities. This is the conceptual framework you can use to help you understand the various types of telecommunications networks in use today.

Types of Telecommunications Networks

Many different types of networks serve as the telecommunications infrastructure for the Internet and the intranets and extranets of internetworked enterprises. However, from an end user's point of view, there are only a few basic types, such as wide area and local area networks and client/server, network computing, and peer-to-peer networks.

Wide Area Networks

Telecommunications networks covering a large geographic area are called **wide area networks** (WANs). Networks that cover a large city or metropolitan area *(metropolitan area networks)* can also be included in this category. Such large networks have become a necessity for carrying out the day-to-day activities of many business and government organizations and their end users. For example, WANs are used by many multinational companies to transmit and receive information among their employees, customers, suppliers, and other organizations across cities, regions, countries, and the world. Figure 6.13 illustrates an example of a global wide area network for a major multinational corporation.

Local Area Networks

Local area networks (LANs) connect computers and other information processing devices within a limited physical area, such as an office, classroom, building, manufacturing plant, or other work site. LANs have become commonplace in many organizations for providing telecommunications network capabilities that link end users in offices, departments, and other workgroups.

LANs use a variety of telecommunications media, such as ordinary telephone wiring, coaxial cable, or even wireless radio and infrared systems, to interconnect

Figure 6.13   A global wide area network (WAN): The Chevron MPI (Multi-Protocol Internetwork).

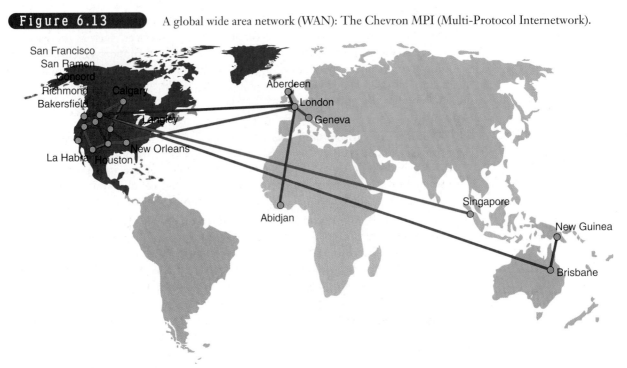

Source: Courtesy of Cisco Systems, Inc.

microcomputer workstations and computer peripherals. To communicate over the network, each PC usually has a circuit board called a *network interface card*. Most LANs use a more powerful microcomputer having a large hard disk capacity, called a *file server* or **network server,** that contains a **network operating system** program that controls telecommunications and the use and sharing of network resources. For example, it distributes copies of common data files and software packages to the other microcomputers in the network and controls access to shared laser printers and other network peripherals. See Figure 6.14.

Figure 6.14

A local area network (LAN). Note how the LAN allows users to share hardware, software, and data resources.

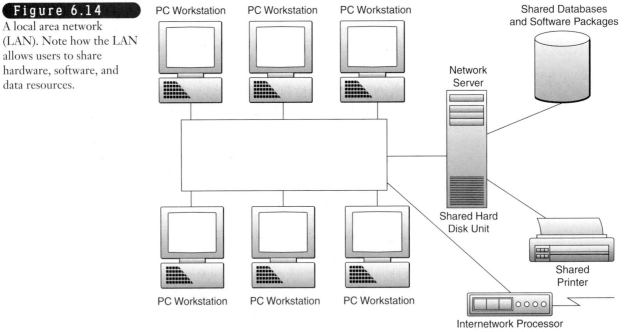

Virtual Private Networks

Many organizations use *virtual private networks* (VPNs) to establish secure intranets and extranets. A **virtual private network** is a secure network that uses the Internet as its main *backbone network*, but relies on the fire walls and other security features of its Internet and intranet connections and those of participating organizations. Thus, for example, VPNs would enable a company to use the Internet to establish secure intranets between its distant branch offices and manufacturing plants, and secure extranets between itself and its customers and suppliers. See Figure 6.15. Let's look at a real world example.

On Command Corporation: Benefits of a VPN

On Command Corporation has replaced its low-speed private-line network with a quicker virtual private network (VPN) so it can provide faster customer service to hotels worldwide that have bought its in-room TV. The VPN service is managed by Internet service provider Concentrick Networks Corporation. The virtual network has slashed the time it takes agents to access data from customer support systems from several minutes to just seconds. The virtual net links 12 far-flung regional offices with the $225 million firm's San Jose, California, headquarters.

Because VPN links are much cheaper than dedicated connections, On Command was able to afford much higher bandwidth—24 times the bandwidth of its 56K bit/sec. private-line network—for about the same price: $1,200 per site per month. The 1.544M bit/sec. lines that On Command now use give its agents access to technical data, information on trouble tickets, and contracts to handle customer inquiries faster. Before the virtual network, agents had to take information from customers, hang up, wait several minutes for the data to arrive, and then call customers back to answer their questions. Now the data arrives in a matter of seconds [24].

Figure 6.15

An example of a virtual private network.

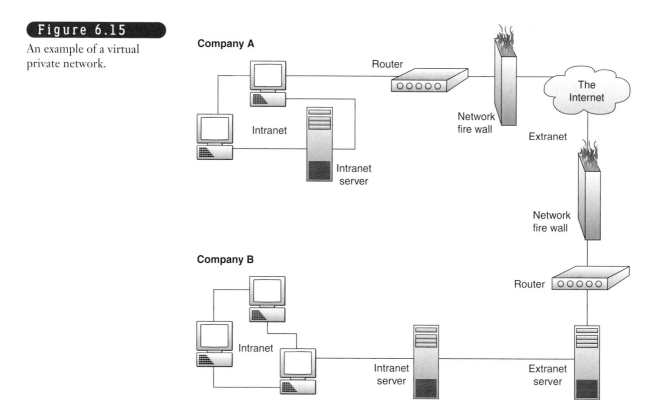

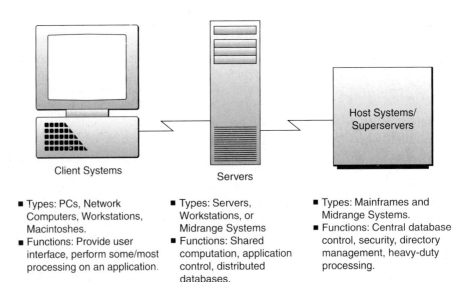

Figure 6.16

The functions of the computer systems in client/server networks.

Client Systems

- Types: PCs, Network Computers, Workstations, Macintoshes.
- Functions: Provide user interface, perform some/most processing on an application.

Servers

- Types: Servers, Workstations, or Midrange Systems
- Functions: Shared computation, application control, distributed databases.

Host Systems/ Superservers

- Types: Mainframes and Midrange Systems.
- Functions: Central database control, security, directory management, heavy-duty processing.

Client/Server Networks

Client/server networks have become the predominant information architecture of enterprisewide computing. In a client/server network, end user PC or NC workstations are the **clients.** They are interconnected by local area networks and share application processing with network **servers,** which also manage the networks. (This arrangement of clients and servers is sometimes called a *two-tier* client/server architecture.) Local area networks are also interconnected to other LANs and wide area networks of client workstations and servers. Figure 6.16 illustrates the functions of the computer systems that may be in client/server networks, including optional host systems and superservers.

A continuing trend is the **downsizing** of larger computer systems by replacing them with client/server networks. For example, a client/server network of several interconnected local area networks may replace a large mainframe-based network with many end user terminals. This typically involves a complex and costly effort to install new application software that replaces the software of older, traditional mainframe-based business information systems, now called **legacy systems.** Client/server networks are seen as more economical and flexible than legacy systems in meeting end user, workgroup, and business unit needs, and more adaptable in adjusting to a diverse range of computing workloads.

Network Computing

The growing reliance on the computer hardware, software, and data resources of the Internet, intranets, extranets, and other networks has emphasized that for many users, "the network is the computer." This **network computing** or *network-centric* concept views networks as the central computing resource of any computing environment.

Figure 6.17 illustrates that in network computing, **network computers** and other *thin clients* provide a browser-based user interface for processing small application programs called *applets.* Thin clients include network computers, Net PCs, and other low-cost network devices or information appliances. Application and database servers provide the operating system, application software, applets, databases, and database management software needed by the end users in the network. Network computing is sometimes called a *three-tier* client/server model, since it consists of thin clients, application servers, and database servers.

Peer-to-Peer Networks

Peer-to-peer networking is a civilization-altering event for the media industry. Every consumer now is a producer, distributor, and marketer . . . of intellectual property and information content . . . a "human node" with vast new powers [3].

Figure 6.17

The functions of the computer systems in network computing.

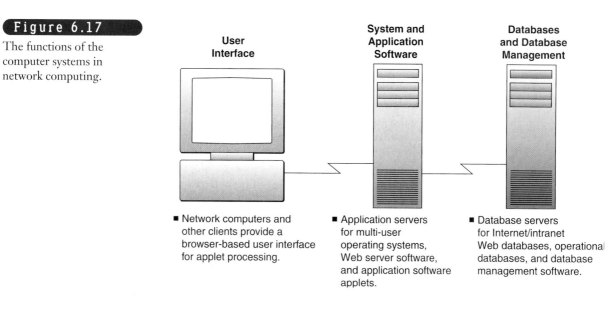

User Interface

System and Application Software

Databases and Database Management

- Network computers and other clients provide a browser-based user interface for applet processing.

- Application servers for multi-user operating systems, Web server software, and application software applets.

- Database servers for Internet/intranet Web databases, operational databases, and database management software.

The emergence of peer-to-peer (P2P) networking technologies and applications is being hailed as a development that will revolutionize e-business and e-commerce and the Internet itself. Whatever the merits of such claims, it is clear that peer-to-peer networks are a powerful telecommunications networking tool for many business applications.

Figure 6.18 illustrates two major models of **peer-to-peer networking** technology. In the Napster architecture, P2P file-sharing software connects your PC to a central server that contains a directory of all of the other users *(peers)* in the network. When you request a file, the software searches the directory for any other users who have that file and are online at that moment. It then sends you a list of user names

Figure 6.18   The two major forms of peer-to-peer networks.

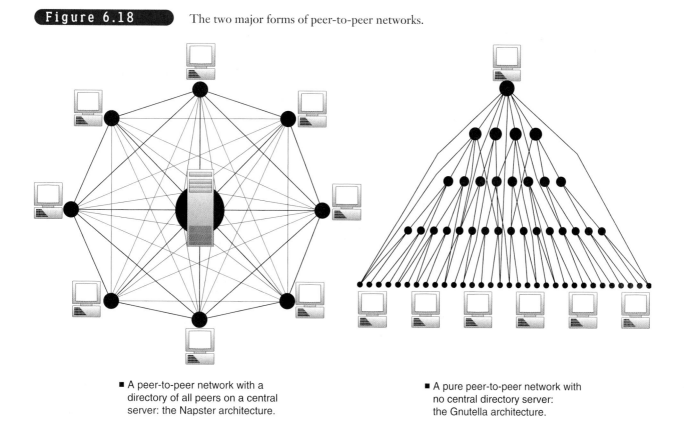

- A peer-to-peer network with a directory of all peers on a central server: the Napster architecture.

- A pure peer-to-peer network with no central directory server: the Gnutella architecture.

that are active links to all such users. Clicking on one of these user names prompts the software to connect your PC to their PC (making a *peer-to-peer* connection) and automatically transfers the file you want from their hard drive to yours.

The Gnutella architecture is a *pure* peer-to-peer network, since there is no central directory or server. First, the file-sharing software in a Gnutella-style P2P network connects your PC with one of the online users in the network. Then an active link to your user name is transmitted from peer to peer to all the online users in the network that the first user (and the other online users) encountered in previous sessions. In this way, active links to more and more peers spread throughout the network the more it is used. When you request a file, the software searches every online user and sends you a list of active file names related to your request. Clicking on one of these automatically transfers the file from their hard drive to yours.

One of the major advantages and limitations of the Napster architecture is its reliance on a central directory and server. The directory server can be slowed or overwhelmed by too many users or technical problems. However, it also provides the network with a platform that can better protect the integrity and security of the content and users of the network. Some applications of Gnutella P2P networks, on the other hand, have been plagued by slow response times and bogus and corrupted files containing viruses, junk, static, and empty code [3, 12].

Napster.com: Challenges and Promises	Napster is an Internet-based business in San Mateo, Calif., founded by then 19-year-old Shawn Fanning and 20-year-old Sean Parker in September, 1999. Napster developed software that lets people trade music files over the Internet with astonishing ease and at an unbeatable price—free. Since then Napster managed to turn the music industry inside out, igniting an ugly legal battle with the Recording Industry Association of America, which is fighting to keep people from making copies of songs without paying for them. Napster lost a crucial court decision and is trying to develop payment-based services to stay in business.

But Napster's import goes far beyond the balance of power in the music business. Napster represents a new idea, a peer-to-peer architecture for exchanging information. No one can say yet how important the idea will become or how it will change things. It could, for instance, change the way the Internet works, lessening its role as a repository of information and making it a conduit that lets any PC owner reach into any other wired hard drive in the world. Napster-like services could emerge as the next killer app, creating a hunger for greater bandwidth and ever more powerful PCs. The invasive nature of these services could force us to rethink our attitude toward privacy in a wired world too [12]. |

Telecommunications Media

Telecommunications channels make use of a variety of **telecommunications media.** These include twisted-pair wire, coaxial cables, and fiber-optic cables, all of which physically link the devices in a network. Also included are terrestrial microwave, communications satellites, cellular phone systems, and packet and LAN radio, all of which use microwave and other radio waves. In addition, there are infrared systems, which use infrared light to transmit and receive data.

Twisted-Pair Wire

Ordinary telephone wire, consisting of copper wire twisted into pairs (**twisted-pair wire**), is the most widely used medium for telecommunications. These lines are used in established communications networks throughout the world for both voice and data transmission. Thus, twisted-pair wiring is used extensively in home and office telephone systems and many local area networks and wide area networks.

Coaxial Cable

Coaxial cable consists of a sturdy copper or aluminum wire wrapped with spacers to insulate and protect it. The cable's cover and insulation minimize interference and distortion of the signals the cable carries. Groups of coaxial cables may be bundled together in a big cable for ease of installation. These high-quality lines can be placed underground and laid on the floors of lakes and oceans. They allow high-speed data transmission and are used instead of twisted-pair wire lines in high-service metropolitan areas, for cable TV systems, and for short-distance connection of computers and peripheral devices. Coaxial cables are also used in many office buildings and other work sites for local area networks.

Fiber Optics

Fiber optics uses cables consisting of one or more hair-thin filaments of glass fiber wrapped in a protective jacket. They can conduct pulses of visible light elements (*photons*) generated by lasers at transmission rates as high as 320 billion bits per second. This is about 640 times greater than coaxial cable and 32,000 times better than twisted-pair wire lines. Fiber-optic cables provide substantial size and weight reductions as well as increased speed and greater carrying capacity. A half-inch-diameter fiber-optic cable can carry over 500,000 channels, compared to about 5,500 channels for a standard coaxial cable.

Fiber-optic cables are not affected by and do not generate electromagnetic radiation; therefore, multiple fibers can be placed in the same cable. Fiber-optic cables have less need for repeaters for signal retransmissions than copper wire media. Fiber optics also has a much lower data error rate than other media and is harder to tap than electrical wire and cable. Fiber-optic cables have already been installed in many parts of the world, and they are expected to replace other communications media in many applications.

New optical technologies such as *dense wave division multiplexing* (DWDM) can split a strand of glass fiber into 40 channels, which enables each strand to carry 5 million calls. In the future, DWDM technology is expected to split each fiber into 1,000 channels, enabling each strand to carry up to 122 million calls. In addition, newly developed *optical routers* will be able to send optical signals up to 2,500 miles without needing regeneration, thus eliminating the need for repeaters every 370 miles to regenerate signals [17, 22].

Wireless Technologies

Wireless telecommunications technologies rely on radio wave, microwave, infrared, and visible light pulses to transport digital communications without wires between communications devices. Wireless technologies include terrestrial microwave, communications satellites, cellular and PCS telephone and pager systems, mobile data radio, wireless LANs, and various wireless Internet technologies. Each technology utilizes specific ranges (in megahertz) of electromagnetic frequencies that are specified by national regulatory agencies to minimize interference and encourage efficient telecommunications. Let's briefly review some of these major wireless communications technologies. See Figure 6.19.

Terrestrial Microwave

Terrestrial microwave involves earthbound microwave systems that transmit high-speed radio signals in a line-of-sight path between relay stations spaced approximately 30 miles apart. Microwave antennas are usually placed on top of buildings, towers, hills, and mountain peaks, and they are a familiar sight in many sections of the country. They are still a popular medium for both long-distance and metropolitan area networks. *transfer interference is high*

Communications Satellites

Communications satellites also use microwave radio as their telecommunications medium. Many communications satellites are placed in stationary geosynchronous orbits approximately 22,000 miles above the equator. Satellites are powered by solar panels and can transmit microwave signals at a rate of several hundred million bits

Figure 6.19

The Palm VII PDA gives users wireless Internet access for e-mail and website services.

Source: Fisher/Thatcher/Stone.

per second. They serve as relay stations for communications signals transmitted from earth stations. Earth stations use dish antennas to beam microwave signals to the satellites that amplify and retransmit the signals to other earth stations thousands of miles away.

While communications satellites were used initially for voice and video transmission, they are now also used for high-speed transmission of large volumes of data. Because of time delays caused by the great distances involved, they are not suitable for interactive, real-time processing. Communications satellite systems are operated by several firms, including Comsat, American Mobile Satellite, and Intellsat.

A variety of other satellite technologies are being implemented to improve global business communications. For example, many companies use networks of small satellite dish antennas known as VSAT (very-small-aperture terminal) to connect their stores and distant work sites via satellite. Other satellite networks use many low-earth orbit (LEO) satellites orbiting at an altitude of only 500 miles above the earth. Companies like Globalstar offer cellular phone, paging, and messaging services to users anywhere on the globe.

Cellular and PCS Systems

Cellular and PCS telephone and pager systems use several radio communications technologies. However, all of them divide a geographic area into small areas, or *cells*, typically from one to several square miles in area. Each cell has its own low-power transmitter or radio relay antenna device to relay calls from one cell to another. Computers and other communications processors coordinate and control the transmissions to and from mobile users as they move from one area to another.

Cellular phone systems have long used analog communications technologies operating at frequencies in the 800 to 900 MHz cellular band. Newer cellular systems use digital technologies, which provide greater capacity and security, and additional services such as voice mail, paging, messaging, and caller ID. These capabilities are also available with the new PCS (Personal Communications Services) phone systems. PCS operates at 1,900 MHz frequencies using digital technologies that are related to digital cellular. However, PCS phone systems cost substantially less to operate and use than cellular systems and have lower power consumption requirements [20].

Wireless LANs

Wiring an office or a building for a local area network is often a difficult and costly task. Older buildings frequently do not have conduits for coaxial cables or additional twisted-pair wire, and the conduits in newer buildings may not have enough room to pull additional wiring through. Repairing mistakes and damages to wiring is often difficult and costly, as are major relocations of LAN workstations and other components. One solution to such problems is installing a **wireless LAN,** using one of several wireless technologies. Examples include a high-frequency radio technology similar to digital cellular, and a low-frequency radio technology called *spread spectrum.* The other wireless LAN technology is called infrared because it uses beams of infrared light to establish network links between LAN components.

The use of wireless LANs is growing rapidly as new high-speed technologies are implemented. A prime example is a new open-standard wireless radio-wave technology technically known as IEEE 802.11b, or more popularly as Wi-Fi (for wireless fidelity). Wi-Fi is faster and less expensive than Standard Ethernet and other common wire-based LAN technologies. Thus, Wi-Fi wireless LANs enable laptop PCs and other devices with Wi-Fi modems to easily connect to the Internet and other networks in a rapidly increasing number of business, public, and home environments [23].

The Wireless Web

Wireless access to the Internet, intranets, and extranets is growing as more Web-enabled information appliances proliferate. Smart telephones, pagers, PDAs, and other portable communications devices have become *very thin clients* in wireless networks. Agreement on a standard *wireless application protocol* (WAP) has encouraged the development of many wireless Web applications and services. The telecommunications industry continues to work on *third generation* (3G) wireless technologies whose goal is to raise wireless transmission speeds to enable streaming video and multimedia applications on mobile devices.

For example, the Palm VII PDA shown in Figure 6.19 can send and receive e-mail and provides Web access via a "Web clipping" technology that generates custom-designed Web pages from many popular financial, securities, travel, sport, entertainment, and e-commerce websites. Another example is the Sprint PCS Wireless Web phone, which delivers similar Web content and e-mail services via a Web-enabled PCS phone [7].

Figure 6.20 illustrates the wireless application protocol that is the foundation of wireless mobile Internet and Web applications. The WAP standard specifies how Web pages in HTML or XML are translated into a *wireless markup language* (WML)

Figure 6.20

The wireless application protocol (WAP) architecture for wireless Internet services to mobile information appliances.

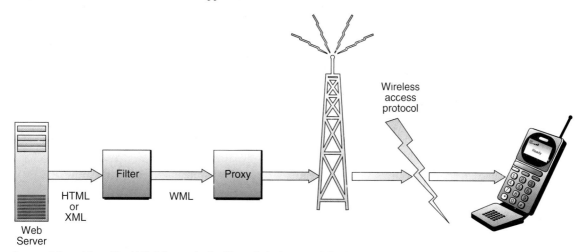

Source: Adapted from David G. Messerschmitt, *Network Applications: A Guide to the New Computing Infrastructure* (San Francisco: Morgan Kaufmann Publishers, 1999), p. 350.

by *filter* software and preprocessed by *proxy* software to prepare the Web pages for wireless transmission from a Web server to a Web-enabled wireless device [15].

Telecommunications Processors

Telecommunications processors such as modems, multiplexers, switches, and routers perform a variety of support functions between the computers and other devices in a telecommunications network. Let's take a look at some of these processors and their functions. See Figure 6.21.

Modems

Modems are the most common type of communications processor. They convert the digital signals from a computer or transmission terminal at one end of a communications link into analog frequencies that can be transmitted over ordinary telephone lines. A modem at the other end of the communications line converts the transmitted data back into digital form at a receiving terminal. This process is known as *modulation* and *demodulation*, and the word *modem* is a combined abbreviation of those two words. Modems come in several forms, including small stand-alone units, plug-in circuit boards, and removable modem cards for laptop PCs. Most modems also support a variety of telecommunications functions, such as transmission error control, automatic dialing and answering, and a faxing capability.

Modems are used because ordinary telephone networks were first designed to handle continuous analog signals (electromagnetic frequencies), such as those generated by the human voice over the telephone. Since data from computers are in digital form (voltage pulses), devices are necessary to convert digital signals into appropriate analog transmission frequencies and vice versa. However, digital communications networks that use only digital signals and do not need analog/digital conversion are becoming commonplace. Since most modems also perform a variety

Figure 6.21   The communications processors involved in a typical Internet connection.

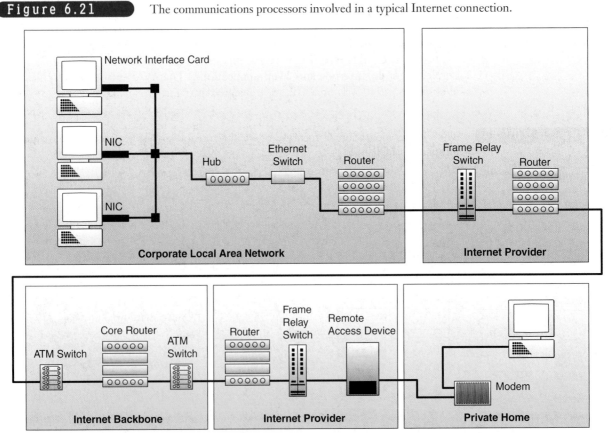

Figure 6.22

Comparing modem and telecommunications technologies for Internet and other network access.

Modem (56K bit/sec)	DSL (Digital Subscriber Line) Modem
• Receives at 56K bit/sec.	• Receives at up to 256K bit/sec.
• Sends at 28.8K bit/sec.	• Sends at 64K bit/sec.
• Slowest technology	• Users must be near switching centers
ISDN (Integrated Services Digital Network)	**Cable Modem**
• Sends and receives at 128K bit/sec.	• Receives at 1.5 to 3M bit/sec.
• Users need extra lines	• Sends at 128K bit/sec.
• Becoming obsolete	• Cable systems need to be upgraded
Home Satellite	**Local Microwave**
• Receives at 400K bit/sec.	• Sends and receives at 512K to 1.4M bit/sec.
• Sends via phone modem	• Higher cost alternative
• Slow sending, higher cost	• May require line of sight to base antenna

of telecommunications support functions, devices called digital modems are still used in digital networks. Figure 6.22 compares several new modem and telecommunications technologies for access to the Internet and other networks by home and business users [16].

Multiplexers

A **multiplexer** is a communications processor that allows a single communications channel to carry simultaneous data transmissions from many terminals. Thus, a single communications line can be shared by several terminals. Typically, a multiplexer merges the transmissions of several terminals at one end of a communications channel, while a similar unit separates the individual transmissions at the receiving end.

This is accomplished in two basic ways. In *frequency division multiplexing* (FDM), a multiplexer effectively divides a high-speed channel into multiple slow-speed channels. In *time division multiplexing* (TDM), the multiplexer divides the time each terminal can use the high-speed line into very short time slots, or time frames. The most advanced and popular type of multiplexer is the *statistical time division multiplexer,* most commonly referred to as a statistical multiplexer. Instead of giving all terminals equal time slots, it dynamically allocates time slots only to active terminals according to priorities assigned by a telecommunications manager.

Internetwork Processors

Telecommunications networks are interconnected by special-purpose communications processors called **internetwork processors** such as switches, routers, hubs, and gateways. A *switch* is a communications processor that makes connections between telecommunications circuits in a network so a telecommunications message can reach its intended destination. A *router* is a more intelligent communications processor that interconnects networks based on different rules or *protocols,* so a telecommunications message can be routed to its destination. A *hub* is a port switching communications processor. Advanced versions of hubs provide automatic switching among connections called *ports* for shared access to a network's resources. Workstations, servers, printers, and other network resources are connected to ports, as are switches and routers provided by the hub to other networks. Networks that use different communications architectures are interconnected by using a communications processor called a *gateway.* All these devices are essential to providing connectivity and easy access between the multiple LANs and wide area networks that are part of the intranets and client/server networks in many organizations.

Telecommunications Software

Software is a vital component of all telecommunications networks. In Chapter 4, we discussed telecommunications and network management software, which may reside in PCs, servers, mainframes, and communications processors like multiplexers and routers. For example, mainframe-based wide area networks frequently use *telecommunications monitors or teleprocessing* (TP) monitors. CICS (Customer Identification Control System) for IBM mainframes is a typical example. Servers in local area networks frequently rely on Novell NetWare, Sun's Solaris, UNIX, Linux, or Microsoft Windows 2000 Servers.

Telecommunications functions built into Microsoft Windows and other operating systems provide a variety of communications support services. For example, they work with a communications processor (such as a modem) to connect and disconnect communications links and establish communications parameters such as transmission speed, mode, and direction.

Corporate intranets use network management software like the iPlanet Portal Server, which is one of several programs for network management, electronic commerce, and application development in Sun Microsystems and Netscape's iPlanet software servers for the Internet, intranets, and extranets. Many software vendors also offer telecommunications software known as *middleware*, which can help diverse networks communicate with each other.

Network Management

Network management packages such as network operating systems and telecommunications monitors determine transmission priorities, route (switch) messages, poll terminals in the network, and form waiting lines (queues) of transmission requests. They also detect and correct transmission errors, log statistics of network activity, and protect network resources from unauthorized access. See Figure 6.23.

Examples of major **network management** functions include:

● **Traffic management.** Manage network resources and traffic to avoid congestion and optimize telecommunications service levels to users.

Figure 6.23

Network management software monitors and manages network performance. This CA Unicenter display shows a group of Web servers and their relationships.

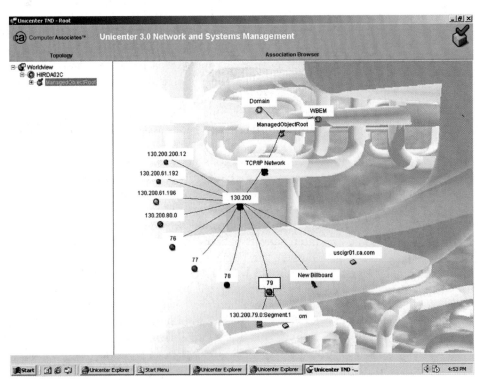

Source: Computer Associates

- **Security.** Provide authentication, encryption, and auditing functions, and enforce security policies.
- **Network monitoring.** Troubleshoot and watch over the network, informing network administrators of potential problems before they occur.
- **Capacity planning.** Survey network resources and traffic patterns and users' needs to determine how best to accommodate the needs of the network as it grows and changes.

Network Topologies

There are several basic types of network *topologies*, or structures, in telecommunications networks. Figure 6.24 illustrates three basic topologies used in wide area and local area telecommunications networks. A *star* network ties end user computers to a central computer. A *ring* network ties local computer processors together in a ring on a more equal basis. A *bus* network is a network in which local processors share the same bus, or communications channel. A variation of the ring network is the *mesh* network. It uses direct communications lines to connect some or all of the computers in the ring to each other. Another variation is the *tree* network, which joins several bus networks together.

Client/server networks may use a combination of star, ring, and bus approaches. Obviously, the star network is more centralized, while ring and bus networks have a more decentralized approach. However, this is not always the case. For example, the central computer in a star configuration may be acting only as a *switch*, or message-switching computer, that handles the data communications between autonomous local computers. Star, ring, and bus networks differ in their performances, reliabilities, and costs. A pure star network is considered less reliable than a ring network, since the other computers in the star are heavily dependent on the central host computer. If it fails, there is no backup processing and communications capability, and the local computers are cut off from each other. Therefore, it is essential that the host computer

---

Figure 6.24   The ring, star, and bus network topologies.

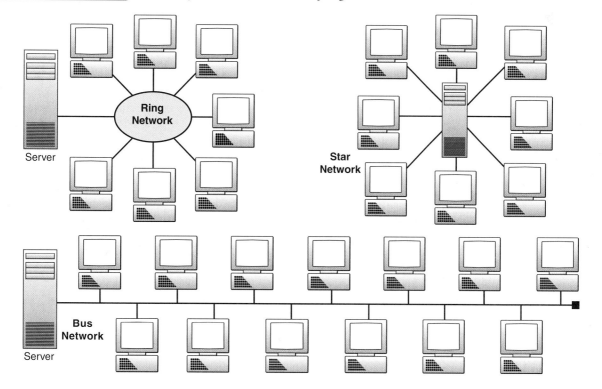

be highly reliable. Having some type of multiprocessor architecture to provide a fault tolerant capability is a common solution.

Ring and bus networks are most common in local area networks. Ring networks are considered more reliable and less costly for the type of communications in such networks. If one computer in the ring goes down, the other computers can continue to process their own work as well as to communicate with each other.

Network Architectures and Protocols

Until quite recently, there was a lack of sufficient standards for the interfaces between the hardware, software, and communications channels of telecommunications networks. This situation hampered the use of telecommunications, increased its costs, and reduced its efficiency and effectiveness. In response, telecommunications manufacturers and national and international organizations have developed standards called *protocols* and master plans called *network architectures* to support the development of advanced data communications networks.

Protocols. A **protocol** is a standard set of rules and procedures for the control of communications in a network. However, these standards may be limited to just one manufacturer's equipment, or to just one type of data communications. Part of the goal of communications network architectures is to create more standardization and compatibility among communications protocols. One example of a protocol is a standard for the physical characteristics of the cables and connectors between terminals, computers, modems, and communications lines. Other examples are the protocols that establish the communications control information needed for *handshaking*, which is the process of exchanging predetermined signals and characters to establish a telecommunications session between terminals and computers. Other protocols deal with control of data transmission reception in a network, switching techniques, internetwork connections, and so on.

Network Architectures. The goal of network architectures is to promote an open, simple, flexible, and efficient telecommunications environment. This is accomplished by the use of standard protocols, standard communications hardware and software interfaces, and the design of a standard multilevel interface between end users and computer systems.

The OSI Model

The International Standards Organization (ISO) has developed a seven-layer Open Systems Interconnection (OSI) model to serve as a standard model for network architectures. Dividing data communications functions into seven distinct layers promotes the development of modular network architectures, which assists the development, operation, and maintenance of complex telecommunications networks. Figure 6.25 illustrates the functions of the seven layers of the OSI model architecture.

The Internet's TCP/IP

The Internet uses a system of telecommunications protocols that has become so widely used that it is equivalent to a network architecture. The Internet's protocol suite is called Transmission Control Protocol/Internet Protocol and is known as TCP/IP. As Figure 6.25 shows, TCP/IP consists of five layers of protocols that can be related to the seven layers of the OSI architecture. TCP/IP is used by the Internet and by all intranets and extranets. Many companies and other organizations are thus converting their client/server networks to TCP/IP technology, which are now commonly called IP networks.

Bandwidth Alternatives

The communications speed and capacity of telecommunications networks can be classified by **bandwidth.** This is the frequency range of a telecommunications channel; it determines the channel's maximum transmission rate. The speed and capacity of

Figure 6.25

The seven layers of the OSI communications network architecture, and the five layers of the Internet's TCP/IP protocol suite.

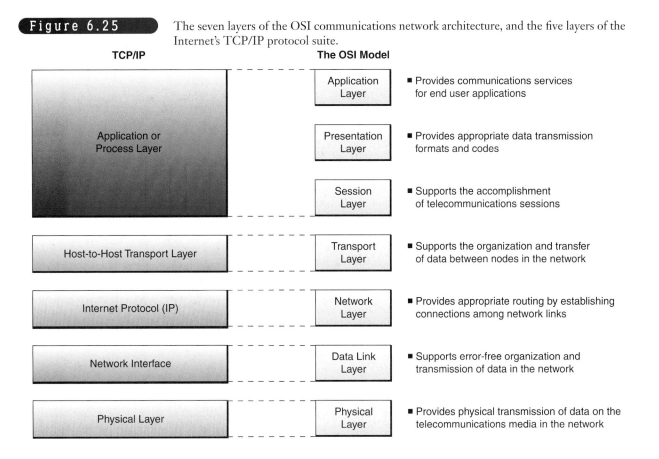

data transmission rates are typically measured in bits per second (BPS). This is sometimes referred to as the *baud* rate, though baud is more correctly a measure of signal changes in a transmission line.

Narrow-band channels typically provide low-speed transmission rates up to 64K BPS, but can now handle up to 2 million BPS. They are usually unshielded twisted-pair lines commonly used for telephone voice communications, and for data communications by the modems of PCs and other devices. Medium-speed channels *(medium-band)* use shielded twisted-pair lines for transmission speeds up to 100 MBPS.

Broadband channels provide high-speed transmission rates at intervals from 256,000 BPS to several billion BPS. Typically, they use microwave, fiber optics, or satellite transmission. Examples are 1.54 million BPS for T1 and 45M BPS for T3 communications channels, up to 100 MBPS for communications satellite channels, and between 52 MBPS and 10 GBPS for fiber-optic lines. See Figure 6.26.

Switching Alternatives

Regular telephone service relies on *circuit switching*, in which a switch opens a circuit to establish a link between a sender and receiver; it remains open until the communication session is completed. In message switching, a message is transmitted a block at a time from one switching device to another.

Packet switching involves subdividing communications messages into fixed or variable groups called packets. For example, in the X.25 protocol, packets are 128 characters long, while they are of variable length in the *frame relay* technology. Packet switching networks are frequently operated by *value-added carriers* who use computers and other communications processors to control the packet switching process and transmit the packets of various users over their networks.

Figure 6.26

Examples of telecommunications transmission speeds by type of media and network technology.

Type of Media	Maximum BPS
Twisted pair—unshielded/shielded	2M/100M
Coaxial cable—baseband/broadband	264M/550M
Satellite/terrestrial microwave	200M
Wireless LAN: radio wave	11M
Wireless LAN: infrared	4M
Fiber-optic cable	320G

Network Technologies	Typical-Maximum BPS
Standard Ethernet or token ring	10–16M
High-speed Ethernet	100M–1G
FDDI: fiber distributed data interface	100M
DDN: digital data network	2.4K–2M
PSN: packet switching network	2.4K–64K
Frame relay network	1.5M–45M
ISDN: integrated services digital network	64K/128K–2M
ATM: asynchronous transfer mode	25/155M–2.4G
OC: Optical Carrier	52M–10G

KBPS = thousand BPS or kilobits per second. GBPS = billion BPS or gigabits per second.
MBPS = million BPS or megabits per second.

Early packet switching networks were X.25 networks. The X.25 protocol is an international set of standards governing the operations of widely used, but relatively slow, packet switching networks. *Frame relay* is another popular packet switching protocol, and is used by many large companies for their wide area networks. Frame relay is considerably faster than X.25, and is better able to handle the heavy telecommunications traffic of interconnected local area networks within a company's wide area client/server network. ATM *(asynchronous transfer mode)* is an emerging high-capacity *cell switching* technology. An ATM switch breaks voice, video, and other data into fixed cells of 53 bytes (48 bytes of data and 5 bytes of control information) and routes them to their next destination in the network. ATM networks are being developed by many companies needing their fast, high-capacity multimedia capabilities for voice, video, and data communications. See Figure 6.27.

Figure 6.27

Why four large retail chains chose different network technologies to connect their stores.

Company	Technology	Why
Sears	Frame relay	Reliable, inexpensive, and accommodates mainframe and Internet protocols
Rack Room	VSAT	Very inexpensive way to reach small markets and shared satellite dishes at malls
Hannaford	ATM	Very high bandwidth; combines voice, video, and data
7-Eleven	ISDN	Can use multiple channels to partition traffic among different uses

Source: Adapted from David Orenstein, "Price, Speed, Location All Part of Broadband Choice," *Computerworld*, July 26, 1999, p. 62. Copyright 1999 by Computerworld, Inc., Framingham, MA 01701. Reprinted from *Computerworld*.

Summary

- **Telecommunications Trends.** Organizations are becoming internetworked enterprises that use the Internet, intranets, and other telecommunications networks to support e-business operations and collaboration within the enterprise, and with their customers, suppliers, and other business partners. Telecommunications has entered a deregulated and fiercely competitive environment with many vendors, carriers, and services. Telecommunications technology is moving toward open, internetworked digital networks for voice, data, video, and multimedia. A major trend is the pervasive use of the Internet and its technologies to build interconnected enterprise and global networks, like intranets and extranets, to support enterprise collaboration, electronic commerce, and other e-business applications.

- **The Internet Revolution.** The explosive growth of the Internet and the use of its enabling technologies have revolutionized computing and telecommunications. The Internet has become the key platform for a rapidly expanding list of information and entertainment services and business applications, including enterprise collaboration and electronic commerce systems. Open systems with unrestricted connectivity using Internet technologies are the primary telecommunications technology drivers in e-business systems. Their primary goal is to promote easy and secure access by business professionals and consumers to the resources of the Internet, enterprise intranets, and interorganizational extranets.

- **The Business Value of the Internet.** Companies are deriving strategic business value from the Internet, which enables them to disseminate information globally, communicate and trade interactively with customized information and services for individual customers, and foster collaboration of people and integration of business processes within the enterprise and with business partners. These capabilities allow them to generate cost savings from using Internet technologies, revenue increases from electronic commerce, and better customer service and relationships through interactive marketing and customer relationship management.

- **The Role of Intranets.** Businesses are installing and extending intranets throughout their organizations (1) to improve communications and collaboration among individuals and teams within the enterprise; (2) to pub-

lish and share valuable business information easily, inexpensively, and effectively via enterprise information portals and intranet websites and other intranet services; and (3) to develop and deploy critical applications to support business operations and decision making.

- **The Role of Extranets.** The primary role of extranets is to link the intranet resources of a company to the intranets of its customers, suppliers, and other business partners. Extranets can also provide access to operational company databases and legacy systems to business partners. Thus, extranets provide significant business value by facilitating and strengthening the business relationships of a company with customers and suppliers, improving collaboration with its business partners, and enabling the development of new kinds of Web-based service for its customers, suppliers, and others.

- **Telecommunications Networks.** The major generic components of any telecommunications network are (1) terminals, (2) telecommunications processors, (3) communications channels, (4) computers, and (5) telecommunications software. There are several basic types of telecommunications networks, including wide area networks (WANs) and local area networks (LANs). Most WANs and LANs are interconnected using client/server, network computing, peer-to-peer, and Internet networking technologies.

- **Network Alternatives.** Key telecommunications network alternatives and components are summarized in Figure 6.11 for telecommunications media, processors, software, channels, and network architectures. A basic understanding of these major alternatives will help business end users participate effectively in decisions involving telecommunications issues. Telecommunications processors include modems, multiplexers, internetwork processors, and various devices to help interconnect and enhance the capacity and efficiency of telecommunications channels. Telecommunications networks use such media as twisted-pair wire, coaxial cables, fiber-optic cables, terrestrial microwave, communications satellites, cellular and PCS systems, wireless LANs, and other wireless technologies. Telecommunications software, such as network operating systems and telecommunications monitors, controls and manages the communications activity in a telecommunications network.

Key Terms and Concepts

These are the key terms and concepts of this chapter. The page number of their first explanation is in parentheses.

1. Bandwidth alternatives (202)
2. Business applications of the Internet (180)
3. Business value of the Internet (181)
4. Business value of telecommunications networks (178)
5. Cellular phone systems (196)
6. Client/server networks (192)

7. Coaxial cable (195)

8. Communications satellites (195)

9. Downsizing (192)

10. Extranets (184)

11. Fiberoptics (195)

12. Internet revolution (179)

13. Internet technologies (177)

14. Internetwork processors (199)

15. Intranets (182)

16. Legacy systems (192)

17. Local area network (189)

18. Modem (198)

19. Multiplexer (199)

21. Network architectures (202)
   a. OSI (202)
   b. TCP/IP (202)

22. Network computing (192)

23. Network management (200)

24. Network operating system (190)

25. Network server (190)

26. Network topologies (201)

27. Open systems (177)

28. Peer-to-peer networks (193)

29. Protocol (202)

30. Switching alternatives (203)

31. Telecommunications channels (189)

32. Telecommunications media (189)

33. Telecommunications network components (188)

34. Telecommunications processors (189)

35. Telecommunications software (189)

36. Trends in telecommunications (176)

37. Virtual private network (191)

38. Wide area network (189)

39. Wireless LAN (197)

40. Wireless technologies (195)

Review Quiz

Match one of the key terms and concepts listed previously with one of the brief examples or definitions that follow. Try to find the best fit for answers that seem to fit more than one term or concept. Defend your choices.

_____ 1. Fundamental changes have occurred in the competitive environment, the technology, and the application of telecommunications.

_____ 2. Telecommunications networks help companies overcome geographic, time, cost, and structural barriers to business success.

_____ 3. Companies are using the Internet for electronic commerce and enterprise collaboration.

_____ 4. Companies are cutting costs, generating revenue, improving customer service, and forming strategic business alliances via the Internet.

_____ 5. The rapid growth in the business and consumer use of the Internet, and the use of its technologies in internetworking organizations.

_____ 6. Internet-like networks that improve communications and collaboration, publish and share information, and develop applications to support business operations and decision making within an organization.

_____ 7. Provide Internet-like access to a company's operational databases and legacy systems by its customers and suppliers.

_____ 8. Includes terminals, telecommunications processors, channels, computers, and control software.

_____ 9. A communications network covering a large geographic area.

_____ 10. A communications network in an office, a building, or other work site.

_____ 11. Communications data move in these paths using various media in a network.

_____ 12. Coaxial cable, microwave, and fiber optics are examples.

_____ 13. A communications medium that uses pulses of laser light in glass fibers.

_____ 14. A wireless mobile telephone technology.

_____ 15. Includes modems, multiplexers, and internetwork processors.

_____ 16. Includes programs such as network operating systems and Web browsers.

_____ 17. A common communications processor for microcomputers.

_____ 18. Helps a communications channel carry simultaneous data transmissions from many terminals.

_____ 19. Star, ring, and bus networks are examples.

_____ 20. Cellular and PCS systems can connect mobile information appliances to the Internet.

_____ 21. A computer that handles resource sharing and network management in a local area network.

_____ 22. Intranets and extranets can use their network fire walls and other security features to establish secure Internet links within an enterprise or with its trading partners.

_____ 23. The software that manages a local area network.

_____ 24. Standard rules or procedures for control of communications in a network.

_____ 25. An international standard, multilevel set of protocols to promote compatibility among telecommunications networks.

_____ 26. The standard suite of protocols used by the Internet, intranets, extranets, and some other networks.

_____ 27. Information systems with common hardware, software, and network standards that provide easy access for end users and their networked computer systems.

_____ 28. Interconnected networks need communications processors such as switches, routers, hubs, and gateways.

_____ 29. Websites, Web browsers, HTML documents, hypermedia databases, and TCP/IP networks are examples.

_____ 30. Networks where end user PCs are tied to network servers to share resources and application processing.

_____ 31. Network computers provide a browser-based interface for software and databases provided by servers.

_____ 32. End user computers connect directly with each other to exchange files.

_____ 33. Replacing mainframe-based systems with client/server networks.

_____ 34. Older, traditional mainframe-based business information systems.

_____ 35. Telecommunications networks come in a wide range of speed and capacity capabilities.

_____ 36. Examples are packet switching using frame relay and cell switching using ATM technologies.

_____ 37. Provides wireless network access for laptop PCs in business settings.

_____ 38. Monitoring and optimizing network traffic and service.

Discussion Questions

1. The Internet is the driving force behind developments in telecommunications, networks, and other information technologies. Do you agree or disagree? Why?

2. How is the trend toward open systems, connectivity, and interoperability related to business use of the Internet, intranets, and extranets?

3. Refer to the Real World Case on Sears and UPS in the chapter. Which applications do you think have the most promise to bring success to wireless e-commerce? Why?

4. How will wireless information appliances and services affect the business use of the Internet and the Web? Explain.

5. What are some of the business benefits and management challenges of client/server networks? Network computing? Peer-to-peer networks?

6. What is the business value driving so many companies to rapidly install and extend intranets throughout their organizations?

7. What strategic competitive benefits do you see in a company's use of extranets?

8. Refer to the Real World Case on Welch Packaging and Gorman Uniform Service in the chapter. Should a company only rely on the Internet to network its business operations and stakeholders? Why or why not?

9. Do you think that business use of the Internet, intranets, and extranets has changed what businesspeople expect from information technology in their jobs? Explain.

10. The insatiable demand for everything wireless, video, and Web-enabled everywhere will be the driving force behind developments in telecommunications, networking, and computing technologies for the forseeable future. Do you agree or disagree? Why?

Application Exercises

Complete the following exercises as individual or group projects that apply chapter concepts to real world business situations.

1. Evaluating Online Trading Websites

It's as voyeuristic as Internet sex sites, more addictive than video games, and a lot easier to play—and you can win (or lose) big money! It's online investing, one of the hottest destinations in cyberspace. Once the preserve of a few computer-literate plungers, online trading could one day account for much of the hundreds of millions in securities transactions each year. See Figure 6.28.

Figure 6.28

Datek is one of the top online investment websites.

Some top sites:
- **Charles Schwab & Co.** (www.schwab.com). The one to beat. Leverages its huge customer base to gain the lead on the Web.
- **E*Trade** (www.etrade.com). A brash upstart whose ad push and emphasis on low prices catapulted it into the top players.
- **Datek Online** (www.datek.com). Active daytraders' paradise. Real-time quotes and trades. Refund if order not completed in a minute.

a. Surf to the online trading sites shown above. Evaluate and rank them based on ease of use, speed, cost, and quality of investment research and help provided.

b. Write up the results of your evaluations in a one- or two-page report. Which is your favorite online trading site? Why? Your least favorite? Explain.

Source: Adapted from Nelson D. Schwartz, "Can't Keep a Good Day Trader Down," *Fortune*, February 19, 2001, p. 146–150. © 2001 Time Warner Inc. All rights reserved.

2. Evaluating Online Banking Websites

On the Web, banking has been less popular than stock trading, mainly because of some limitations of the technology. You can't withdraw cash using a PC. But some of the biggest players want your business, and options for managing your accounts and paying bills have improved.

American Express
(www.americanexpress.com/banking).
Why leave home? Amex offers very attractive interest rates on deposits, lots of personal finance information, and links to online trading.

Bank of America
(www.bankofamerica.com).
Sleek, no-nonsense design is pitched to retail and business customers alike. Interesting advertising of international business services in Asia on the home page during the Olympics in Sydney.

CompuBank
(www.compubank.com).
All Net, all the time. CompuBank's website gets kudos for detailed account information and security. Ranks among the low-price leaders in fees, while paying among the highest rates on deposits.

My Citi
(www.myciti.com).
Citigroup wants to help you round up all your financial activity and park it here. The site updates your finances to include your latest credit card bill, for instance. Security is top-notch.

Wells Fargo
(www.wellsfargo.com).
This West Coast innovator has taken its act national. Good design aimed at both consumers and commercial accounts. Color scheme looks odd unless you're a San Francisco 49ers fan.

Wingspan
(www.wingspanbank.com).
After a recent overhaul, Wingspan's site makes online banking relatively painless. A good comeback for the online unit of troubled BankOne's First USA subsidiary.

a. Check out several of these online banking sites. Evaluate and rank them based on ease of use, speed, banking fees and other costs, and the amount and quality of their online banking services.

b. Write up the results of your evaluations in a one- or two-page report. Which is your favorite banking site? Why? Your least favorite? Explain.

c. How would you improve the sites you visited? Include your recommendations in your report.

Source: Adapted from "Stake Your Claim to Wealth," Technology Buyers Guide, *Fortune*, Winter 2001, p. 252.

3. MNO Incorporated Communications Network

MNO Incorporated is considering acquiring its own leased lines to handle its voice and data communications between its 14 distribution sites in three regions around the country. The peak load of communications for each site is expected to be a function of the number of phone lines and the number of computers at that site. You have been asked to gather this information, as shown in the first table below, and place it in a database file.

a. Create a database table with an appropriate structure to store the data above. Site Location can serve as the primary key for this table. Enter the records shown above and get a printed listing of your table.

b. Survey results suggest that the peak traffic to and from a site will be approximately 2 kilobits per second for each phone line plus 10 kilobits per second for each computer. Create a report showing the estimated peak demand for the telecommunications system at each site in kilobits. Create a second report grouped by region and showing regional subtotals and a total for the system as a whole.

4. Prioritizing Calls to Service Centers

ABC Products International has over 100 offices worldwide and has 12 service centers worldwide which handle computer-related problems of the company's employees. Each center is open only about 10 hours a day and calls can be placed to other centers around the globe to provide 24-hour service. You are assigned to the New Orleans office and have been asked to develop a database that will list all available service centers at a particular time of day and sort them so that the center with the lowest communications cost appears first.

The second table below summarizes this information with the hours shown reflecting local New Orleans time.

a. Create a database table structure to store the data shown in the table, and enter the set of records. (Use the short time format and a 24-hour clock for the Opening Hour and Closing Hour figures.) Print out a listing of this table.

b. Create a query that will allow the user to enter the current time and will display a list of the locations and phone numbers of service centers that are open, sorted so that the location with the lowest communication cost per minute is listed first. Test your query to be sure that it works across all hours of the day. Print out results for 3:00, 10:00, 18:00, and 23:00. (Note that centers open through midnight have a closing hour that is earlier than their opening hour and require different treatment. Hint: Centers that open after 14:00 close at times earlier than their opening time. Literal time values can be entered in Access by placing # around the values, e.g. #14:00#.)

Site Location	Region	Phone Lines	Computers
Boston	East	228	95
New York	East	468	205
Richmond	East	189	84
Atlanta	East	192	88
Detroit	East	243	97
Cincinnati	East	156	62
New Orleans	Central	217	58
Chicago	Central	383	160
Saint Louis	Central	212	91
Houston	Central	238	88
Denver	West	202	77
Los Angeles	West	364	132
San Francisco	West	222	101
Seattle	West	144	54

Site Location	Phone No	Opening Hour	Closing Hour	Comm. Cost Per Minute
Berlin	49 348281723	15:00	1:00	$0.24
Boston	617 6792814	9:00	19:00	$0.12
Cairo	20 33721894	16:00	2:00	$0.30
Honolulu	808 373-1925	4:00	14:00	$0.18
London	44 4622649172	14:00	0:00	$0.20
Mexico City	52 273127901	8:00	18:00	$0.25
New Delhi	91 7432631952	19:00	5:00	$0.32
Rio De Janeiro	55 8202131485	11:00	21:00	$0.32
San Francisco	650 212-9047	6:00	16:00	$0.13
Seoul	82 164195023	22:00	8:00	$0.28
St. Petersburg	7 4837619103	16:00	2:00	$0.30
Sydney	61 934816120	0:00	10:00	$0.27

Bob Evans Farms:
The Business Case for Communications Satellite Networks

The network connecting the Bob Evans Farms, Inc., 459 restaurants and six food production plants to each other and the Internet runs via satellite, a technology choice that came as something of a surprise to company executives. "Truthfully, we didn't want to do satellite at first," says Bob Evans Farms CIO Larry Beckwith. The company looked at frame relay, ISDN lines, a virtual private network over the Internet, and DSL services. "Heck, we even looked at microwave," he says.

Rightly so, says Brownlee Thomas, a Giga Information Group analyst in Montreal. "Terrestrial will always be a better technology, where you can get it." But a VSAT (very small aperture terminal) communications satellite network was the only technology that supported Bob Evans' goals, was available at all sites, and was cost-effective, Beckwith says.

One reason is that satellite companies are hungry for the broadband Internet access market, and are planning to play an even bigger role in the next few years. Even Quest, the third largest carrier of Internet traffic in the United States, concedes that satellites have an important role to play in providing an Internet on-ramp. Already, satellite use for Internet access is growing. "Five years ago, there was no Internet service provider for satellite companies; today, eleven percent of ISPs are using satellite to extend their reach," says David Hartshorn, secretary-general of the Global VSAT Forum, a London-based trade group. And Hughes Network Systems is planning to launch eight GEO (geostationary earth orbit) satellites in 2002 that will offer data transfer rates as high as 10 GBPs, as Hughes aims right at the global Internet access market.

But until last year, the computers at Bob Evans restaurants dialed in daily over ordinary phone lines to the Columbus, Ohio, headquarters to report sales, payroll, and other data. That worked well enough, Beckwith says. Credit card authorization, especially on busy weekend mornings, was another story. "With dial-up, every time you swipe a credit card, a modem dials the credit card authorization site, makes the connection, then verifies the card, which takes another 15 seconds," Beckwith says. If the connection fails, it restarts after timing out for 30 seconds, "a long time when you've got a line of people waiting to pay. We needed a persistent IP connection."

Satellite would give the restaurants the connection and sufficient bandwidth—8M bit/second outbound from remote sites, and 153K bit/second inbound. After talks with satellite network vendors, Beckwith ran tests for two months, first in the lab, then in one restaurant, on a Skystar Advantage system from Spacenet Inc., a subsidiary of Israel-based Gilat Satellite Networks Ltd. Only after a further month-long pilot with 10 stores was Beckwith sold on satellite. During the next five weeks, Spacenet rolled out earth stations to 440 stores, and the network went live in September 2000.

"Average time to do a credit card authorization is about three seconds now, including getting your printed receipt," Beckwith says. Also running over satellite are nightly automatic polling of financial data from the point-of-sale (POS) systems, Lotus Notes e-mail to managers, and online manuals of restaurant procedures, restaurant POS systems, facilities and physical plant maintenance, "things the restaurants never had live access to before," Beckwith says.

To use its VSAT network to collect sales data from its 459 restaurants, Bob Evans headquarters initiates a request that travels via a T1 line to the master Earth station at a Spacenet hub. The hub sends it to a satellite, which is both a wireless receiver and transmitter, and then to Earth stations at each of the restaurants. A three- to five-foot diameter dish antenna mounted on the roof of each restaurant sends the message to the indoor unit, which provides the interface to an NT server. The server polls the restaurant's POS terminals and sends the data back along the same route.

The benefits mentioned earlier, and savings from dropping one phone line per store, justify the costs of the satellite network, Beckwith says. And "we haven't given up anything. Sometimes we see a little 'rain fade,' and we might lose a store for . . . a minute, but nothing significant. We put software on the servers that would use the phone lines as backup, but we've only used them a couple of times," he says. Also important for Bob Evans Farms was the ability to easily add stores or applications. "We open about 30 new restaurants a year," Beckwith says.

New applications planned for this year include online inventory management, with XML-based electronic ordering to follow. In-store audio for music and promotional messages, and video broadcasting for employee training and corporate communications (Skystar supports IP multicasting) are also in the works for the near future.

Case Study Questions

1. What are the benefits and limitations of communications satellite networks for Internet access?

2. What are the business benefits of a VSAT communications satellite network for Bob Evans Farms?

3. When would you recommend a communications satellite network to a company as a way to network their business locations? To gain Internet access?

Source: Adapted from Christopher Locke, "Hughes: The Boss," *Red Herring*, January 30, 2001, pp. 84, 85; and Sami Lais, "Satellites Link Bob Evans Farms," *Computerworld*, July 2, 2001, p. 51. Reprinted by permission.

Beema, Inc. and Ignition State:
Evaluating Internet Telephony for Small Business

Beema, Inc. has just eight employees, but those staffers are spread out among four offices: three in California, and one in Cincinnati, where their IT guy David Lemmink resides. Company president and CEO Steven C. Toy, who works in the multimedia production company's Campbell, California, headquarters, says that the company's phone bills would be $2,000 to $3,000 a month, were it not for Lemmink's technical wizardry. Lemmink took the high-speed lines the offices were already using for Internet access and pressed them into double duty as phone lines. As a result "we pay no charges to any telephone company for calls between our offices," Toy says. That's right: Beeman's interoffice phone bill is a big fat zero.

Sounds like a good deal, right? However, setting up this mini-Internet telephone network cost Beema $10,000 in modifications. Even if such a system were to pay off in the long run, not every small business could afford that kind of hit up front—and not every small company has a David Lemmink.

Several Web-based services now offer an alternative to buying and installing your own telephony equipment and software on your PC. These sites—which include Net2Phone.com, iConnectHere.com, Dialpad.com, and PhoneFree.com—offer free or inexpensive local and long-distance service and very competitive international rates. International calling is the killer app for these sites. Doing business in China? iConnectHere.com will put your call through for 25¢ a minute, compared with the $2 that regular phone companies charge, says Noam Bardin, CEO and president of Deltathree, the company that runs iConnectHere.com, based in New York City. Some downsides: Calls aren't always of "pin drop" quality, and such business telephone services as internal call routing simply aren't available.

With Internet telephony, also called Voice Over Internet Protocol, or VOIP, calls that start at your office jump onto the Internet and then reconnect with the phone system at the very last stop—the office of the person you are calling. You may not know it, but you've probably already used a version of VOIP. Many office phone systems send calls through digital switches before kicking them out to the traditional phone network, and some long-distance carriers route calls through chunks of the Internet to save themselves money.

The first VOIP calls were computer to computer, with the callers speaking into microphones on their PCs. Later, callers that used their computers to connect could speak to one another on the telephone. But calls were plagued by "latency" (that weird delay when you can hear your own voice after you've already finished, "jitter" (when your voice sounds as of it's quivering), and connection problems. "Sometimes calls traveling across the public Internet just got lost," says Aurica Yen, an analyst at the Yankee Group.

Today industry competitors have improved call quality considerably. The latest advances are Internet phones, appliances that plug into a phone jack. Such devices, like the $199 Aplio/Phone, eliminate the need for a computer altogether for folks who might balk at talking to their PCs all day. (Internet phones are hardly perfect yet: Both the Aplio caller and the call's recipient must have an Aplio/Phone, for instance, in order for the call to go through.)

Adding to their offering of cheap calls, Internet telephony providers are courting small businesses with services like unified messaging and live-calling software for consumer websites. For example, ISPs that partner with Deltathree offer voice-mail services for 80 percent less than the cost of traditional voice-mail service, says Deltathree's Bardin. "And that includes faxes and the ability to access it all online," he adds.

That's why Sheri Harris, a business strategist at Ignition State, a Chicago-based Internet consulting firm, became interested in VOIP last summer. The draw: those cheap international calls. Many of Ignition State's 40 employees visit clients in Europe and make costly calls back to the home office. Harris tried several services before settling on Go2Call.com, in nearby Evanston, Illinois. She likes Go2Call's voice quality and general ease of use. (Unlike most services, Go2Call can be used from any computer without downloading software.) Now Ignition State consultants traveling to Europe pack headsets that they plug into PCs at their clients' offices. As a result of using the new service, the company has cut its international phone bill in half. "We can do business better and more efficiently when we don't have to worry about passing those expenses on to the clients," says Harris.

Despite the lure of cheap calls and new business-focused services, small companies are hardly flocking to VOIP websites. Instead, companies like Beema, Inc., who can afford custom business network installations seem to prefer them. One reason: the Internet telephony websites can't handle inbound toll-free calls. Nor can they route calls around an office. "Most of these providers really are not business-class yet," says Lisa Pierce at Giga Information Group.

Case Study Questions

1. What are the benefits and limitations of Internet telephony for business use?

2. Why are Beema, Inc., and Ignition State happy with their use of Internet telephone service?

3. Evaluate the products and services offered at the websites of Go2Call and several other Internet telephone companies mentioned in this case. Which services and company would you recommend to a small business? Why?

Management
Challenges

Business
Applications

Module
III

Information
Technologies

Development
Processes

Foundation
Concepts

Module III

Business Applications

How do Internet technologies and other forms of IT support electronic business operations, electronic commerce, and business decision making? The three chapters of this module show you how such e-business applications of information systems are accomplished in today's internetworked enterprises.

- **Chapter 7: Electronic Business Systems,** describes how information systems integrate and support enterprisewide business processes and the business functions of marketing, manufacturing, human resource management, accounting, and finance.

- **Chapter 8: Electronic e-Commerce Systems,** introduces the basic process components of e-commerce systems, and discusses important trends, applications, and issues in e-commerce.

- **Chapter 9: Decision Support Systems,** shows how management information systems, decision support systems, executive information systems, expert systems, and artificial intelligence technologies can be applied to decision-making situations faced by business managers and professionals in today's e-business environment.

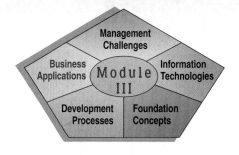

Management
Challenges

Business
Applications

Module
III

Information
Technologies

Development
Processes

Foundation
Concepts

Chapter 7

Electronic Business Systems

Chapter Highlights

Learning Objectives

*After reading and studying this chapter, you should be
able to:*

1. Identify each of the following cross-functional
   e-business systems and give examples of how they
   can provide significant business value to a company and its customers and business partners.

   a. Enterprise resource planning

   b. Customer relationship management

   c. Enterprise application integration

   d. Supply chain management

   e. Online transaction processing

   f. Enterprise collaboration

2. Give examples of how Internet and other information technologies support business processes
   within the business functions of accounting,
   finance, human resource management, marketing,
   and production and operations management.

Cross-Functional e-Business Systems

e-Business Applications

It's happening right before our eyes: a vast and quick reconfiguration of commerce on an evolving e-business foundation. What is the difference between e-commerce and e-business? We define e-commerce as buying and selling over digital media. E-business, in addition to encompassing e-commerce, includes both front- and back-office applications that form the engine for modern business. E-business is not just about e-commerce transactions; it's about redefining old business models, with the aid of technology, to maximize customer value [19].

This chapter explores the fast-changing world of electronic business applications of information technology. Remember that **e-business** is the use of the Internet and other networks and information technologies to support electronic commerce, enterprise communications and collaboration, and Web-enabled business processes both within an internetworked enterprise, and with its customers and business partners.

In this chapter, we will spotlight some of the major applications of e-business. We will focus on examples of cross-functional e-business applications like enterprise resource planning and enterprise application integration in Section I, and more traditional e-business applications that support activities in the functional areas of business in Section II.

Analyzing Netro Corp. and Lightwave Microsystems

Read the Real World Case on Netro Corp. and Lightwave Microsystems on the next page. We can learn a lot from this case about how information technologies are transforming and improving the management of the manufacturing processes of e-business enterprises. See Figure 7.1.

Figure 7.1

Mannon Wong, vice president of operations for Netro Corp., says companies must rely on Web-based manufacturing systems to be responsive to customer demands during the production process.

Source: © Seth Affoumado

Netro Corp. and Lightwave Microsystems: The Business Value of Web-Based Manufacturing Systems

Once upon a time, manufacturers operated on a simple build-to-stock model. They built 100 or 100,000 of an item and sold them via distribution networks. They kept track of the stock of inventory and made more of the item once inventory levels dipped below a threshold. Rush jobs were both rare and expensive, and configuration options limited. Things have changed. Concepts like just-in-time inventory, build-to-order (BTO) manufacturing, end-to-end supply chain visibility, the explosion in contract manufacturing, and the development of Web-based e-business tools for collaborative manufacturing have revolutionized plant management.

"We can have goods en route to the airport, and the customer calls us requesting a change," says Mannon Wong, vice president of operations at San Jose–based Netro Corp., a manufacturer of broadband wireless access systems. "These days, you have to go out of your way to accommodate such requests." Netro copes with the need to incorporate that kind of flexibility into its manufacturing processes by using a Web-based manufacturing execution system (MES) from Datasweep Inc. The MES helps the company maintain tight control over an operation in which 99 percent of manufacturing is outsourced and which was designed to let customers adjust hundreds of possible product configurations up until final delivery.

MES evolved during the 1980s and 90s as a staple of semiconductor fabrication plants and big aerospace and pharmaceutical concerns. Then, a series of changes pushed MES into the background: The move from build-to-stock to build-to-order placed attention on the order end of the manufacturing equation, driving the broad adoption of enterprise resource planning (ERP) and customer relationship management (CRM) systems. An increasing dependency on contract manufacturing necessitated tight integration with suppliers using supply chain management (SCM) software; and the arrival of the Internet sent companies scurrying to develop a Web presence and Web-enabled business systems.

But now, there's a revival of interest in MES technology. All the attention on the order-taking side created an imbalance. Companies could now accept orders, coordinate supply chain logistics, and communicate with customers like never before. But this exposed the weakest link—visibility of the manufacturing floor. And that's where MES comes in.

MES has evolved from an inflexible, monolithic offering for the elite few into a Web-enabled e-business tool that reaches beyond the walls of a single factory. It exposes shop-floor data from any of a company's manufacturing plants to anyone in the supply chain who has been given intranet or extranet access to monitor manufacturing processes.

For example, customers such as Lucent Technologies and Nokia Corp. hold Netro accountable for constant changes in orders for goods that aren't even produced on its premises. Such a BTO model requires that manufacturers have a clear and detailed picture of each order and of the in-dividual products within the order as they move through the production cycle. Only with that knowledge is it possible to make changes to configurations on short notice. Without MES, companies like Netro don't have the ability to respond at the pace demanded by today's customers.

But MES isn't just attractive to virtual manufacturers with widely dispersed operations. Almost anyone in build-to-order manufacturing will find MES attractive, particularly since MES module pricing has dropped to less than $100,000 for small plants.

"We needed MES to gain immediate visibility into operations for realtime inventory control, yield improvements, and cycle-time reduction," says Doug Barnes, IT manager at Lightwave Microsystems in San Jose. Lightwave manufactures lightwave circuits and integrated devices for optical communications systems. It uses InSite, a modular Web-based MES application from Camstar Systems, for manufacturing process data collection, traceability, process control, yield management, and work-in-process tracking.

Lightwave previously used a homegrown engineering database application with simple tracking capabilities. Supervisors had to walk onto the plant floor, inspect the production line, update the sheets daily, and manually enter numbers into the database. "As everything was manual, we tended to question the validity of data, rather than act on it," says Barnes. "Management was largely in the dark." So the company asked IT consultants to modify and extend Lightwave's ERP system to contain product and bill-of-material data and feed this to the MES system via a custom software interface. Result: a 15 percent increase in line yield, 20 percent better chip yield, and a doubling of on-time delivery.

"The visibility we're getting into our operations represents an enormous competitive advantage," says Barnes. "Now, we can make better business decisions by looking directly at our work-in-process inventory status, increase yields by identifying and classifying failure mechanisms, and detect bottlenecks that may have been preventing us from achieving maximum manufacturing throughout."

Case Study Questions

1. Why have manufacturing execution systems become an important e-business tool for managing today's manufacturing processes?

2. How does Netro's Web-based manufacturing execution system help them deal with their customers, suppliers, and subcontractors? What business benefits result?

3. Do you agree that Lightwave's MES gives them "an enormous competitive advantage"? Why or why not?

Source: Adapted from Drew Robb, "Rediscovering Efficiency," *Computerworld*, July 16, 2001, pp. 54, 55. Reprinted by permission.

Figure 7.2

This e-business application architecture presents an overview of e-business applications and their interrelationships within an e-business enterprise.

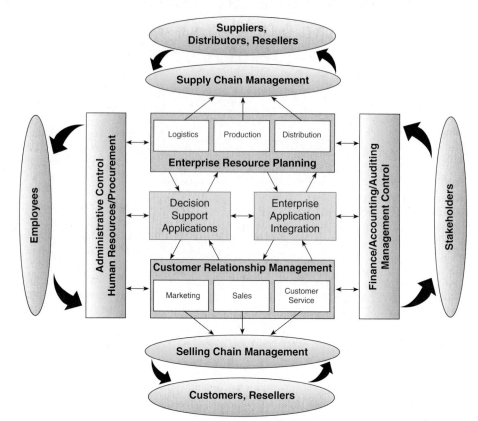

Source: Adapted from Ravi Kalakota and Marcia Robinson, *E-Business 2.0: Roadmap for Success* (Reading, MA: Addison-Wesley, 2001), p. 164. © 2001 Addison-Wesley Publishing Company, Inc. Reprinted by permission of Addison-Wesley Longman, Inc.

The days of manufacturing products and placing them in inventory are withering, as more and more companies switch from that build-to-stock model to a build-to-order manufacturing environment, where products are custom-built or assembled to specific customer orders. Thus, companies like Netro Corp. and Lightwave Microsystems are relying on Web-based manufacturing execution systems and other collaborative e-business applications to support a detailed online view of the status of manufacturing processes that is shared among a company's employees, suppliers, and customers. This enables agile manufacturing companies to be responsive to changing customer requirements during the production process, and make realtime adjustments to improve the efficiency and quality of manufacturing processes.

e-Business Application Architecture

The world-class enterprise of tomorrow is built on the foundation of world-class application clusters implemented today. [19]

Figure 7.2 presents an **e-business application architecture,** which illustrates the application components, interrelationships, and interfaces with customers, employees, business partners, and other stakeholders of an e-business enterprise. Notice how many e-business applications are integrated into cross-functional *enterprise application clusters* like enterprise resource planning, customer relationship management, decision support, supply chain management, and selling chain management. We will discuss such applications in this section and in Chapters 8 and 9. Other applications fall into more traditional clusters, like management control (finance, accounting, and auditing) and administrative control (human resource management and procurement), which we will cover in Section II. Thus, Figure 7.2 gives you a good

Figure 7.3   The new product development process in a manufacturing company. This business process must be supported by cross-functional information systems that cross the boundaries of several business functions.

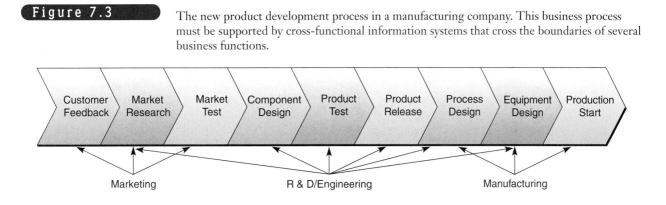

overview of the interrelatedness, interdependence, and integration of the e-business applications that are vital components of the successful operations and management of an e-business enterprise.

Cross-Functional Enterprise Systems

Integration of the enterprise has emerged as a critical issue for organizations in all business sectors striving to maintain competitive advantage. Integration is the key to success. It is the key to unlocking information and making it available to any user, anywhere, anytime [19].

As we emphasized in Chapter 1, information systems in the real world typically are integrated combinations of cross-functional business systems. Such systems support **business processes,** such as product development, production, distribution, order management, customer support, and so on. Many organizations are using information technology to develop integrated **cross-functional enterprise systems** that cross the boundaries of traditional **business functions** (such as marketing and finance), in order to reengineer and improve vital business processes all across the enterprise [3]. These organizations view cross-functional enterprise systems as a strategic way to use IT to share information resources and improve the efficiency and effectiveness of business processes, thus helping an e-business attain its strategic objectives. See Figure 7.3.

For example, as we have seen in the Real World Cases in previous chapters, business firms are turning to Internet technologies to help them reengineer and integrate the flow of information among their internal business processes and their customers and suppliers. Companies are using the World Wide Web and their intranets and extranets as a technology platform for their cross-functional and interorganizational enterprise systems.

In addition, many companies have moved from functional mainframe-based *legacy systems* to integrated cross-functional *client/server* applications. This typically has involved installing *enterprise resource planning* (ERP), *supply chain management* (SCM), or *customer relationship management* (CRM) software from SAP America, Baan, PeopleSoft, Oracle, and others. Instead of focusing on the information processing requirements of business functions, such enterprise software focuses on supporting integrated clusters of business processes involved in the operations of a business.

Enterprise Resource Planning

ERP is the backbone of e-business. In other words, ERP is a business operating system, the equivalent of the Windows operating system for back-office operations [19].

Enterprise resource planning (ERP) is a cross-functional enterprise system that serves as a framework to integrate and automate many of the business processes that must be accomplished within the manufacturing, logistics, distribution, accounting,

Figure 7.4

The major application components of enterprise resource planning demonstrate the cross-functional approach of ERP systems.

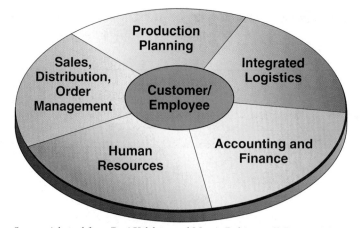

Source: Adapted from Ravi Kalakota and Marcia Robinson, *E-Business 2.0: Roadmap for Success* (Reading, MA: Addison-Wesley, 2001), p. 243. © 2001 Addison-Wesley Publishing Company, Inc. Reprinted by permission of Addison-Wesley Longman, Inc.

finance, and human resources functions of a business. ERP software is a family of software modules that supports the business activities involved in these vital *back-office* processes. For example, ERP software for a manufacturing company will typically track the status of sales, inventory, shipping, and invoicing, as well as forecast raw material and human resource requirements. Figure 7.4 illustrates the major application components of an ERP system.

Many companies began installing ERP systems as a vital conceptual foundation for reengineering their business processes, and as the software engine required to accomplish these new cross-functional processes. Now ERP is being recognized as a necessary ingredient for the efficiency, agility, and responsiveness to customers and suppliers that an e-business enterprise needs to succeed in the dynamic world of e-commerce. Companies are finding major business value in installing ERP software in two major ways:

Figure 7.5

Some of the enterprise process flows and customer and supplier information flows supported by cross-functional ERP systems.

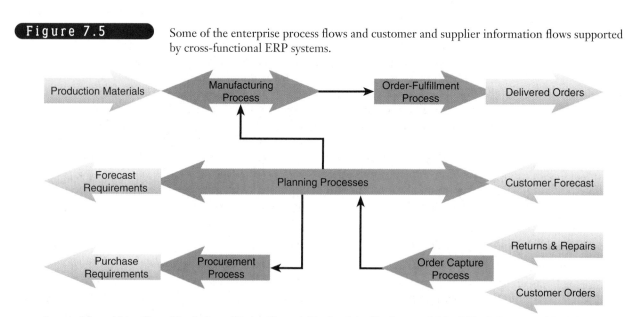

Source: Adapted from Grant Norris, James Hurley, Kenneth Hartley, John Dunleavy, and John Balls, *E-Business and ERP: Transforming the Enterprise*, p. 83. Copyright © 2000 by John Wiley & Sons, Inc. Reprinted by permission.

- ERP creates a framework for integrating and improving their back-office systems that results in major improvements in customer service, production, and distribution efficiency.

- ERP provides vital cross-functional information quickly on business performance to managers to significantly improve their ability to make better business decisions across the enterprise [19, 22, 27].

Figure 7.5 illustrates some of the cross-functional business processes and supplier and customer information flows supported by ERP systems. As we will see several times in this text, installing ERP systems successfully is not an easy task because of the major changes to a company's business processes required by ERP software. Now let's look at how a global corporation views the business value of ERP systems.

Colgate-Palmolive: The Benefits of ERP	Colgate-Palmolive is a global consumer products company that implemented the SAP R/3 enterprise resource planning system. Colgate embarked on an implementation of SAP R/3 to allow the company to access more timely and accurate data, get the most out of working capital, and reduce manufacturing costs. An important factor for Colgate was whether it could use the software across the entire spectrum of the business. Colgate needed the ability to coordinate globally and act locally. The implementation of SAP across the Colgate supply chain contributed to increased profitability. Now installed in operations that produce most of Colgate's worldwide sales, SAP will be expanded to all Colgate divisions worldwide by 2001. Global efficiencies in purchasing—combined with product and packaging standardization—also produced large savings.

- Before ERP, it took Colgate U.S. anywhere from one to five days to acquire an order, and another one to two days to process the order. Now, order acquisition and processing combined takes four hours, not up to seven days. Distribution planning and picking used to take up to four days; today, it takes 14 hours. In total, the order-to-delivery time has been cut in half.

- Before ERP, on-time deliveries used to occur only 91.5 percent of the time, and cases ordered were delivered correctly 97.5 percent of the time. After R/3 the figures are 97.5 percent and 99.0 percent, respectively.

- After ERP, domestic inventories have dropped by one-third and receivables outstanding have dropped to 22.4 days from 31.4. Working capital as a percentage of sales has plummeted to 6.3 percent from 11.3 percent. Total delivered cost per case has been reduced by nearly 10 percent [19].

Customer Relationship Management

- *It costs six times more to sell to a new customer than to sell to an existing one.*
- *A typical dissatisfied customer will tell eight to ten people about his or her experience.*
- *A company can boost its profits 85 percent by increasing its annual customer retention by only 5 percent.*
- *The odds of selling a product to a new customer are 15 percent, whereas the odds of selling a product to an existing customer are 50 percent.*
- *Seventy percent of complaining customers will do business with the company again if it quickly takes care of a service snafu.*
- *More than 90 percent of existing companies don't have the necessary sales and service integration to support e-commerce [19].*

Figure 7.6

The major application
clusters in customer
relationship management.

Source: Adapted from Ravi Kalakota and Marcia Robinson, *E-Business 2.0: Roadmap for Success*
(Reading, MA: Addison-Wesley, 2001), p. 180. © 2001 Addison-Wesley Publishing Company,
Inc. Reprinted by permission of Addison-Wesley Longman, Inc.

That's why businesses are turning to **customer relationship management**
(CRM) as a major *customer-centric* business strategy. CRM uses information technology to create a cross-functional enterprise system that integrates and automates
many of the *customer serving* processes in sales, marketing, and product services
that interact with a company's customers. CRM systems also create an IT framework that integrates all of these processes with the rest of a company's business
operations. CRM systems consist of a family of software modules that perform the
business activities involved in such *front office* processes. CRM software provides
the tools that enable a business and its employees to provide fast, convenient,
dependable, and consistent service to its customers. Figure 7.6 illustrates some of
the major application components of a CRM system.

For example, CRM programs typically include:

- **Sales.** CRM software tracks customer contacts and other business and life
  cycle events of customers for cross-selling and up-selling. For example, CRM
  would alert a bank sales rep to call customers who make large deposits to sell
  them premier credit programs or investment services.

- **Direct Marketing and Fulfillment.** CRM software can automate tasks such
  as qualifying leads, managing responses, scheduling sales contacts, and providing information to prospects and customers.

- **Customer Service and Support.** CRM helps customer service managers
  quickly create, assign, and manage service requests. *Help desk* software assists
  customer service reps in helping customers who are having problems with a
  product or service, by providing relevant service data and suggestions for
  resolving problems.

The business benefits of customer relationship management are many. For example,
CRM allows a business to identify and target their best customers, those who are
the most profitable to the business, so they can be retained as lifelong customers for
greater and more profitable services. It enables real-time customization and personalization of products and services based on customer wants, needs, buying habits,
and life cycles. CRM can also keep track of when a customer contacts the company,
regardless of the contact point. And CRM enables a company to provide a consistent customer experience and superior service and support across all the contact

points a customer chooses. All of these benefits provide strategic business value to a company and major customer value to its customers [14, 17, 18].

Telstra Corporation: The Business Value of CRM

Australia's Telstra Corporation provides fixed, wireless, and e-commerce services to a customer base in nineteen countries. In addition, Telstra offers voice, data, Internet, multimedia, managed communications services, and customer-contact center solutions globally through its strategic alliances and partnerships. The Melbourne company is Australia's largest communications carrier and the clear market leader, with annual revenues of U.S. $9.5 billion.

To succeed in transforming its relationship with its customers, Telstra determined that it needed a CRM solution that would provide both its customer-facing employees and channel partners a single view of each customer relationship. The solution would also require the integration of more than twenty core legacy billing and operations databases across all of its product lines. After exploring several options, Telstra chose a variety of Siebel Systems products to provide its e-business solution.

For its initial deployment, Telstra rolled out a Siebel Call Center to more than 250 telesales representatives and 150 telephone account managers in its outbound call centers, which are geographically dispersed throughout Australia. "This was where we could most quickly impact our business," explains Ross Riddoch, General Manager of Retail Technology Products. "We rolled out account, contact, and opportunity management modules." This Siebel CRM product was deployed in approximately three months, on time and on budget.

User acceptance and business benefits quickly followed "Users found Siebel Call Center's Web-based interface to be extremely intuitive and easy to use," says Riddoch. "This enabled us to reduce our training time and get our users up to speed in record time. Within four months of employing Siebel Call Center, our account management team doubled its weekly revenue, and we achieved a threefold gain in employee productivity" [4].

Enterprise Application Integration

Enterprise application integration (EAI) software is becoming available which interconnects several e-business application clusters. See Figure 7.7. EAI software enables users to model the business processes involved in the interactions that should occur between business applications. EAI also provides *middleware* that performs data conversion and coordination, application communication and messaging services, and access to the application interfaces involved. Thus, EAI software can integrate a variety of enterprise application clusters by letting them exchange data according to rules derived from the business process models developed by users. For example, a typical rule might be:

Figure 7.7

Enterprise application integration software interconnects front-office and back-office applications clusters like customer relationship management and enterprise resource planning.

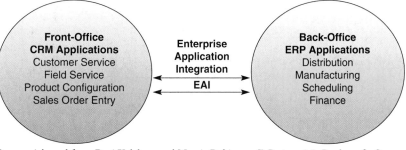

Source: Adapted from Ravi Kalakota and Marcia Robinson, *E-Business 2.0: Roadmap for Success* (Reading, MA: Addison-Wesley, 2001), p. 160. © 2001 Addison-Wesley Publishing Company, Inc. Reprinted by permission of Addison-Wesley Longman, Inc.

When an order is complete, have the order application tell the accounting system to send a bill and alert shipping to send out the product.

Thus, as Figure 7.7 illustrates, EAI software can integrate the front-office and back-office applications of an e-business so they work together in a seamless, integrated way. This is a vital capability that provides real business value to an e-business enterprise that must respond quickly and effectively to business events and customer demands. For example, the integration of enterprise application clusters has been shown to dramatically improve customer call center responsiveness and effectiveness. That's because EAI integrates access to all of the customer and product data customer reps need to quickly serve customers. EAI also streamlines sales order processing so products and services can be delivered faster. Thus, EAI improves customer and supplier experience with the business because of its responsiveness [10, 19, 24].

Dell Computer: Enterprise Application Integration	In a survey of just 75 companies it deals with, Dell Computer found they used 18 different software packages, says Terry Klein, vice president of e-business for Dell's "relationship group." This lack of integration means that companies aren't getting the seamless processing that reduces costs and speeds up customer responsiveness.
	Dell knew that figuring out how to get its system to talk to each of those eighteen different systems in its partners' back offices, one at a time, would be impractical, to say the least. Instead Dell used WebMethods enterprise application integration software to build links to 40 or so of its biggest customers, allowing a customer to buy, say, a truckload of new laptops online while Dell simultaneously enters the order for those laptops into the customer's procurement system. Think of it as one-click shopping for corporate buyers. Just as Amazon.com automates the process of entering credit card information to speed purchases by consumers, Dell is able to update its customers' procurement tracking systems every time they make a purchase [3].

Supply Chain Management

Legacy supply chains are clogged with unnecessary steps and redundant stockpiles. For instance, a typical box of breakfast cereal spends an incredible 104 days getting from factory to supermarket, struggling its way through an unbelievable maze of wholesalers, distributors, brokers, and consolidators, each of which has a warehouse.

The e-commerce opportunity lies in the fusing of each company's internal systems to those of its suppliers, partners, and customers. This fusion forces companies to better integrate interenterprise supply chain processes to improve manufacturing efficiency and distribution effectiveness [19].

So that's why many companies are making **supply chain management** (SCM) a top strategic objective of their e-business initiatives. Its an absolute requirement if they want to meet their e-commerce customer value imperative: *what the customer wants, when and where it's wanted, at the lowest possible cost.* Companies are reengineering their supply chain processes, aided by Internet technologies and supply chain management software. See Figure 7.8.

What is a company's supply chain? Let's suppose a company wants to build and sell a product to other businesses. Then it must buy raw materials and a variety of contracted services from other companies. The interrelationships with other businesses needed to build and sell a product make up a network of business relationships that is called the **supply chain.** Cross-functional e-business systems like supply chain management reengineer and streamline traditional supply chain processes.

Internet technologies and supply chain management software can help companies reengineer and integrate the functional processes in the supply chain life cycle.

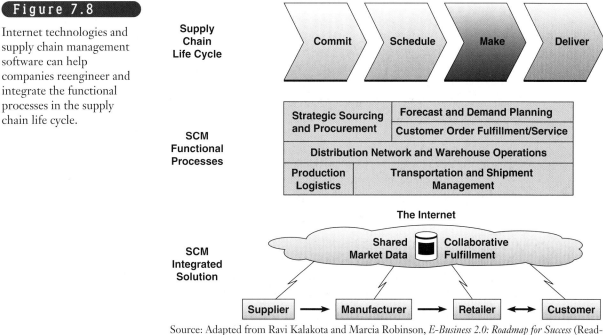

Source: Adapted from Ravi Kalakota and Marcia Robinson, *E-Business 2.0: Roadmap for Success* (Reading, MA: Addison-Wesley, 2001) pp. 280–289. © 2001 Addison-Wesley Publishing Company, Inc. Reprinted by permission of Addison-Wesley Longman, Inc.; and Craig Fellenstein and Ron Wood, *Exploring E-commerce, Global E-business, and E-societies* (Upper Saddle River, NJ: Prentice-Hall, 2000), p. 192.

For example, the demands of e-commerce are pushing manufacturers to use their intranets, extranets, and e-commerce Web portals to help them reengineer their relationships with their suppliers, distributors, and retailers. The objective is to significantly reduce costs, increase efficiency, and improve their supply chain cycle times. SCM software can also help to improve interenterprise coordination among supply chain process players. The result is much more effective distribution and channel networks among business partners. All of the objectives of supply chain management are aimed at achieving agility and responsiveness in meeting the demands of a company's customers and the needs of their business partners [2, 8, 19]. See Figure 7.9.

Achieving the objectives of supply chain management enables a company to reach its e-business and customer value goals.

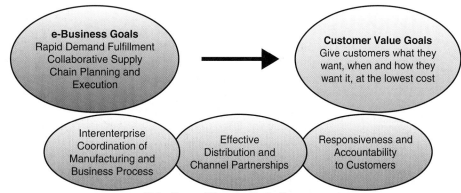

Objectives of Supply Chain Management

Source: Adapted from Ravi Kalakota and Marcia Robinson, *E-Business 2.0: Roadmap for Success* (Reading, MA: Addison-Wesley, 2001), pp. 273–79. © 2001 Addison-Wesley Publishing Company, Inc. Reprinted by permission of Addison-Wesley Longman, Inc.

Sun Microelectronics is a division of $116.5 billion Sun Microsystems. It custom-orders processors, chips, and circuit boards for Sun's desktop, server, and storage products. Sun doesn't actually *make* any of its microelectronic gear itself. As a "fabless" manufacturer, Sun contracts equipment fabrication to outside manufacturers, who in turn rely on components from their own subcontracted suppliers. All told, it's a supply chain with 150 "links"—suppliers in places such as Canada, Japan, Taiwan, and the United Kingdom. Somehow, no hard goods ever sit in Sun's inventory or touch the hands of any one of Sun's 29,000 employees.

Here's how it works: The microelectronics division gathers chip demand forecasts based on projected sales and Sun's internal demands, and loads them into i2 Technologies' Web-based supply chain management software. Instantly, every supplier has access to those forecasts via Sun's extranet. Contract manufacturers check Sun's demand against inventory and capacity, then enter components and materials needs into the system. That lets so-called second-tier suppliers (of memory and CPUs) see exactly what they must deliver to manufacturers. Once Sun places its demands online, each supplier's commitment to deliver materials or chips propagates back through the supply chain, giving Sun a picture of its upcoming product flow.

By entrusting its supply chain and fulfillment needs to i2's SCM software, Sun expects to lower operations costs by reducing the planning staff headcount, squeeze the most efficient production out of its manufacturing contractors, and shorten product cycles [7].

Online Transaction Processing

Transaction processing systems (TPS) are cross-functional information systems that process data resulting from the occurrence of business transactions. We introduced transaction processing systems in Chapter 1 as one of the major application categories of information systems in business.

Transactions are events that occur as part of doing business, such as sales, purchases, deposits, withdrawals, refunds, and payments. Think, for example, of the data generated whenever a business sells something to a customer on credit, whether in a retail store or at an e-commerce site on the Web. Data about the customer, product, salesperson, store, and so on, must be captured and processed. This in turn causes additional transactions, such as credit checks, customer billing, inventory changes, and increases in accounts receivable balances, that generate even more data. Thus, transaction processing activities are needed to capture and process such data, or the operations of a business would grind to a halt. Therefore, transaction processing systems play a vital role in supporting the operations of an e-business enterprise.

Online transaction processing systems play a strategic role in electronic commerce. Many firms are using the Internet, extranets, and other networks that tie them electronically to their customers or suppliers for online transaction processing (OLTP). Such *realtime* systems, which capture and process transactions immediately, can help firms provide superior service to customers and other trading partners. This capability adds value to their products and services, and thus gives them an important way to differentiate themselves from their competitors.

For example, Figure 7.10 illustrates an online transaction processing system for cable pay-per-view systems developed by Syntellect Interactive Services. Cable TV viewers can select pay-per-view events offered by their cable companies using the phone or the World Wide Web. The pay-per-view order is captured by

Figure 7.10   The Syntellect pay-per-view online transaction processing system.

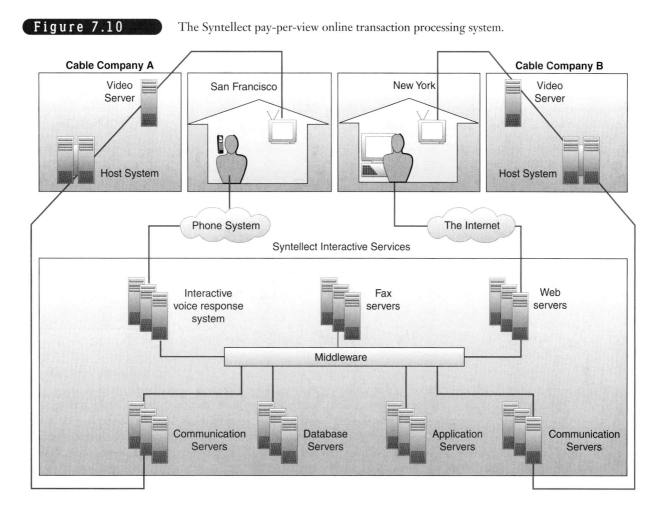

Syntellect's interactive voice response system or Web server, then transported to Syntellect database application servers. There the order is processed, customer and sales databases are updated, and the approved order is relayed back to the cable company's video server, which transmits the video of the pay-per-view event to the customer. Thus, Syntellect teams with over 700 cable companies to offer a very popular and very profitable service [30].

The Transaction Processing Cycle

Transaction processing systems, such as Syntellect's, capture and process data describing business transactions, update organizational databases, and produce a variety of information products. You should understand this as a **transaction processing cycle** of several basic activities, as illustrated in Figure 7.11.

- **Data Entry.** The first step of the transaction processing cycle is the capture of business data. For example, transaction data may be collected by point-of-sale terminals using optical scanning of bar codes and credit card readers at a retail store or other business. Or transaction data can be captured at an electronic commerce website on the Internet. The proper recording and editing of data so they are quickly and correctly captured for processing is one of the major design challenges of information systems discussed in Chapter 10.

- **Transaction Processing.** Transaction processing systems process data in two basic ways: (1) **batch processing,** where transaction data are accumulated

Figure 7.11

The transaction processing cycle. Note that transaction processing systems use a five-stage cycle of data entry, transaction processing, database maintenance, document and report generation, and inquiry processing activities.

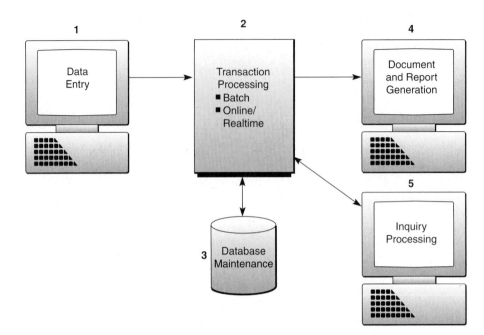

over a period of time and processed periodically, and (2) **realtime processing** (also called online processing), where data are processed immediately after a transaction occurs. All online transaction processing systems incorporate realtime processing capabilities. Many online systems also depend on the capabilities of *fault tolerant* computer systems that can continue to operate even if parts of the system fail. We will discuss this fault tolerant concept in Chapter 11.

- **Database Maintenance.** An organization's database must be maintained by its transaction processing systems so that they are always correct and up-to-date. Therefore, transaction processing systems update the corporate databases of an organization to reflect changes resulting from day-to-day business transactions. For example, credit sales made to customers will cause customer account balances to be increased and the amount of inventory on hand to be decreased. Database maintenance ensures that these and other changes are reflected in the data records stored in the company's databases.

- **Document and Report Generation.** Transaction processing systems produce a variety of documents and reports. Examples of transaction documents include purchase orders, paychecks, sales receipts, invoices, and customer statements. Transaction reports might take the form of a transaction listing such as a payroll register, or edit reports that describe errors detected during processing.

- **Inquiry Processing.** Many transaction processing systems allow you to use the Internet, intranets, extranets, and Web browsers or database management query languages to make inquiries and receive responses concerning the results of transaction processing activity. Typically, responses are displayed in a variety of prespecified formats or screens. For example, you might check on the status of a sales order, the balance in an account, or the amount of stock in inventory and receive immediate responses at your PC.

Enterprise Collaboration

The Internet phenomenon has permanently changed the computing mentality of businesspeople. Today's users expect any computing experience to include on-demand Internet access and tools for collaborating with other people [25].

Most of us have to interact with others to get things done. And as you already know, information technology is changing the way we work together. Information technology, especially Internet technologies, provides tools to help us collaborate—to communicate ideas, share resources, and coordinate our cooperative work efforts as members of the many formal and informal process and project teams and workgroups that make up many of today's organizations.

The goal of **enterprise collaboration systems** is to enable us to work together more easily and effectively by helping us to:

- **Communicate:** Sharing information with each other.
- **Coordinate:** Coordinating our individual work efforts and use of resources with each other.
- **Collaborate:** Working together cooperatively on joint projects and assignments.

We introduced enterprise collaboration systems (ECS) in Chapter 1 as cross-functional e-business systems that enhance communication, coordination, and collaboration among the members of business teams and workgroups. For example, engineers, business specialists, and external consultants may form a virtual team for a project. The team may rely on intranets and extranets to collaborate via e-mail, videoconferencing, discussion forums, and a multimedia database of work-in-progress information at a project website. The enterprise collaboration system may use PC workstations networked to a variety of servers on which project, corporate, and other databases are stored. In addition, network servers may provide a variety of software resources, such as Web browsers, groupware, and application packages, to assist the team's collaboration until the project is completed.

Tools for Enterprise Collaboration

Many industry analysts believe that the capabilities and potential of the Internet, as well as intranets and extranets, are driving the demand for enterprise collaboration tools in business. On the other hand, it is Internet technologies like Web browsers and servers, hypermedia documents and databases, and intranets and extranets that are providing the hardware, software, data, and network platforms for many of the groupware tools for enterprise collaboration that business users want. Figure 7.12 provides an overview of some of the software tools for electronic communication, electronic conferencing, and collaborative work management.

Electronic communications, conferencing, and collaborative work software tools enhance enterprise collaboration.

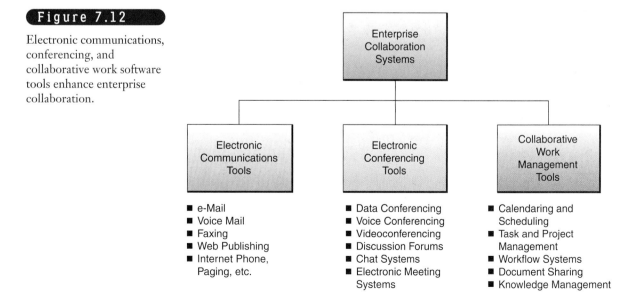

Electronic communication tools include electronic mail, voice mail, faxing, Web publishing, bulletin board systems, paging, and Internet phone systems. These tools enable you to electronically send messages, documents, and files in data, text, voice, or multimedia over computer networks. This helps you share everything from voice and text messages to copies of project documents and data files with your team members, wherever they may be. The ease and efficiency of such communications are major contributors to the collaboration process.

Electronic conferencing tools help people communicate and collaborate while working together. A variety of conferencing methods enables the members of teams and workgroups at different locations to exchange ideas interactively at the same time, or at different times at their convenience. These include data and voice conferencing, videoconferencing, chat systems, discussion forums, and electronic meeting systems. Electronic conferencing options also include *electronic meeting systems*, where team members can meet at the same time and place in a *decision room* setting.

Collaborative work management tools help people accomplish or manage group work activities. This category of software includes calendaring and scheduling tools, task and project management, workflow systems, and knowledge management tools. Other tools for joint work, such as joint document creation, editing, and revision, are found in the software suites discussed in Chapter 4. Figure 7.13 summarizes the software tools for electronic communications, conferencing, and collaborative work management that are vital components of today's enterprise collaboration systems.

Figure 7.13 A summary of the major categories of software tools used in enterprise collaboration systems.

Electronic Communication Tools

Electronic communication tools help you to communicate and collaborate with others by electonically sending messages, documents, and files in data, text, voice, or multimedia over the Internet, intranets, extranets, and other computer networks.

- **Electronic Mail.** Widely used to send and receive text messages between networked PCs over telecommunications networks. E-mail can also include data files, software, and multimedia messages and documents as attachments.

- **Voice Mail.** Unanswered telephone messages are digitized, stored, and played back to you by a voice messaging computer.

- **Faxing.** Transmitting and receiving images of documents over telephone or computer networks using PCs or fax machines.

- **Web Publishing.** Creating, converting, and storing hyperlinked documents and other material on Internet or intranet Web servers so they can easily be shared via Web browsers or netcasting with teams, workgroups, or the enterprise.

Electronic Conferencing Tools

Electronic conferencing tools help networked computer users share information and collaborate while working together on joint assignments, no matter where they are located.

- **Data Conferencing.** Users at networked PCs can view, mark up, revise, and save changes to a shared whiteboard of drawings, documents, and other material.

- **Voice Conferencing.** Telephone conversations shared among several participants via speaker phones or networked PCs with *Internet telephone* software.

- **Videoconferencing.** Realtime video- and audioconferencing (1) among users at networked PCs (desktop videoconferencing) or (2) among participants in conference rooms or auditoriums in different locations (teleconferencing). Videoconferencing can also include whiteboarding and document sharing.

- **Discussion Forums.** Provide a computer network discussion platform to encourage and manage online text discussions over a period of time among members of special interest groups or project teams.

- **Chat Systems.** Enable two or more users at networked PCs to carry on online, realtime text conversations.

- **Electronic Meeting Systems.** Using a meeting room with networked PCs, a large-screen projector, and EMS software to facilitate communication, collaboration, and group decision making in business meetings.

Collaborative Work Management Tools

Collaborative work management tools help people accomplish or manage joint work activities.

- **Calendaring and Scheduling**. Using electronic calendars and other groupware features to automatically schedule, notify, and remind the computer networked members of teams and workgroups of meetings, appointments, and other events.

- **Task and Project Management.** Managing team and workgroup projects by scheduling, tracking, and charting the completion status of tasks within a project.

- **Workflow Systems.** Helping networked knowledge workers collaborate to accomplish and manage the flow of structured work tasks and electronic document processing within a business process.

- **Knowledge Management.** Organizing and sharing the diverse forms of business information created within an organization. Includes managing and providing personalized access to project and enterprise document libraries, discussion databases, hypermedia website databases, and other types of knowledge bases.

Functional e-Business Systems

Functional Business Systems

Business managers are moving from a tradition where they could avoid, delegate, or ignore decisions about IT to one where they cannot create a marketing, product, international, organization, or financial plan that does not involve such decisions [20].

There are as many ways to use information technology in business as there are business activities to be performed, business problems to be solved, and business opportunities to be pursued. As a business professional, you should have a basic understanding and appreciation of the major ways information systems are used to support each of the functions of business. Thus, in this section, we will discuss **functional business systems,** that is, a variety of types of information systems (transaction processing, management information, decision support, etc.) that supports the business functions of accounting, finance, marketing, operations management, and human resource management.

Analyzing Charles Schwab and Others

Read the Real World Case on Charles Schwab and Others on the next page. We can learn a lot from this case about how companies are using e-business systems to support a variety of human resource management applications. See Figure 7.14.

This case illustrates how Web-based human resource management systems are revolutionizing the provision of HR services to a company's employees and

Figure 7.14

Anne Barr is a vice president and leader of Charles Schwab's human resources intranet initiative.

Source: © Seth Affoumado

Charles Schwab and Others:
The Business Value of Web-Based Human Resource Systems

Web-based human resources management systems can free HR professionals from time-consuming tasks like running weekly reports, drafting employee handbooks, orienting new hires, and even tracking vacation time. Better yet, employees can take control of their own benefits—without ever contacting the HR department, and HR staff can concentrate on more strategic tasks, such as recruiting people with needed skills and professional development of employees. Let's take a look at the HR systems at a large corporation and several small companies.

Charles Schwab & Co. It receives 1.3 million page views per day, but it's not Yahoo or America Online or even CNN.com. It's an intranet created by Charles Schwab & Co. that enables Schwab's 23,000 employees to access detailed HR information about benefits, training, computer support, and scads of company information.

"As a company, we're very committed to using technology to benefit our customers and to provide good services to our employees," says Anne Barr, vice president of the intranet initiative known throughout the company as the "Schweb." The Schweb provides managers with online access to accurate information about employees. Because the directory is online, it's a lot easier to update and maintain than a set of desktop applications, notes Barr.

The intranet provides employees with more personalized information about themselves, their roles, and the organization than they'd otherwise be able to obtain from the company's human resources department. "The other benefit is that it helps employees find the information they need faster and serve customers faster, more effectively," says Barr. There are now 30 HR applications that link into the Schweb, including the Learning Intranet, an application that helps manage training for Schwab's 24,000 customer-facing employees, and eTimesheets, which employees use to manage their own vacation time.

The productivity benefits alone from the use of the Schweb are huge. Schwab is saving hundreds of thousands of dollars annually by having employees fill out benefit forms online using an application called eForms, says Barr.

Small Business. While the number of businesses using Web-based human resources systems is still relatively small, some companies, such as OneWorkplace, an office space design firm and furniture retailer in Milpitas, California, are catching on to their benefits. "We've reduced our administrative workloads by about 65 percent," says Jeffrey Crocker, executive director of human resources. "Now we can focus on more proactive tasks, such as developing training profiles for each position in our organization. I'm paying good wages to our HR people to do senior-level work and now I'm letting them do that, rather than forcing them to focus on boring paperwork."

What's more, when an employee leaves the company, an HR system can expedite the paper-intensive process, including issuing final paychecks and tallying vacation compensation. For example, when a claim comes in from COBRA—an insurance extension program—One Workplace's Crocker doesn't need to search his files. The company's MyHRIS system takes care of it. "The idea of not having to remember—if I called this manager, made sure I got this letter back, and signed off on this or that—is so reassuring," he says.

Web-based HR solutions offer more advanced options by transferring tedious paperwork online. Julie Boisselle, office manager for Genalytics, an e-commerce marketing software firm in Newburyport, Massachusetts, used to keep a spreadsheet to track employees' vacation time—a method she admits wasn't working. "We kept having the problem of people using up more vacation time than they'd accrued and then leaving the company," she says. But with help from eBenefits' VirtualHR service, Genalytics' employees no longer vacation on borrowed time. "Now the system automatically calculates vacation time each month and my only job is to deduct time when they take it," she says.

Web-based tools also update managers on key employee development milestones. For example, at BuildNet, a construction management software developer in Research Triangle Park, North Carolina, when an employee is due for a raise, the reporting tools in NuView Systems' MyHRIS notify the correct supervisor. "Before, when using an Excel spreadsheet, it involved a lot of tracking employees down to ask them questions and filling out forms," says David Russo, executive vice president of human resources. "Now it's much more click-and-go because there's just one place to input and manage all your HR information—it's like having an extra, efficient employee."

Case Study Questions

1. What key HR applications are provided by the Web-based systems for the companies in this case? What are some other Web-based HR applications that they might implement?

2. What is the business value of the Schweb intranet to Charles Schwab & Co.?

3. What are the business benefits of the Web-based HR applications used by the three small companies in this case?

Source: Adapted from Thomas Hoffman, "Intranet Helps Workers Navigate Corporate Maze," *Computerworld*, June 4, 2001, pp. 34, 35; and Joyce Slaton, "Give Yourself a Raise," *Ziff Davis Smart Business*, September 2001. Reprinted by permission.

freeing HR professionals for tasks with more strategic business value. For example, Charles Schwab's HR intranet provides employees with personalized benefits information and HR tools. Small companies like OneWorkplace, Genalytics, and BuildNet are using Web-based HR applications to make major reductions in paperwork for employees and HR staff, and provide more and better HR services to employees.

IS in Business

As a business professional, it is important that you have a specific understanding of how information systems affect a particular business function—marketing, for example—or a particular industry (e.g., banking) that is directly related to your career objectives. For example, someone whose career objective is a marketing position in banking should have a basic understanding of how information systems are used in banking and how they support the marketing activities of banks and other firms.

Figure 7.15 illustrates how information systems can be grouped into business function categories. Thus, information systems in this section will be analyzed according to the business function they support to give you an appreciation of the variety of functional business systems that both small and large business firms may use.

Marketing Systems

The business function of marketing is concerned with the planning, promotion, and sale of existing products in existing markets, and the development of new products and new markets to better serve present and potential customers. Thus, marketing performs a vital function in the operation of a business enterprise. Business firms have increasingly turned to information technology to help them perform vital marketing functions in the face of the rapid changes of today's environment.

Figure 7.15   Examples of functional business information systems. Note how they support the major functional areas of business.

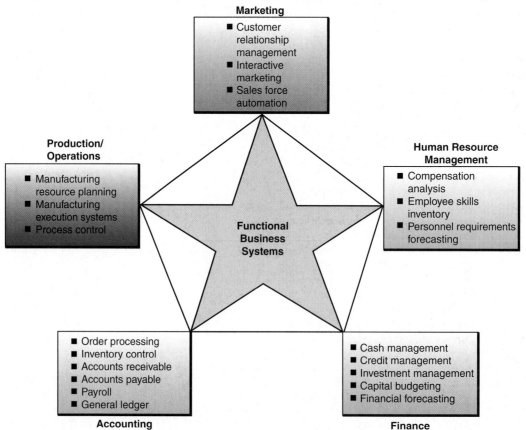

Marketing information systems provide information technologies to support major components of the marketing function.

Figure 7.16 illustrates how **marketing information systems** provide information technologies that support major components of the marketing function. For example, Internet/intranet websites and services make an *interactive marketing* process possible where customers can become partners in creating, marketing, purchasing, and improving products and services. *Sales force automation* systems use mobile computing and Internet technologies to automate many information processing activities for sales support and management. Other marketing information systems assist marketing managers in customer relationship management, product planning, pricing, and other product management decisions, advertising, sales promotion, and targeted marketing strategies, and market research and forecasting. Let's take a closer look at some of the newer marketing applications.

Interactive Marketing

The term **interactive marketing** has been coined to describe a customer focused marketing process that is based on using the Internet, intranets, and extranets to establish two-way transactions between a business and its customers or potential customers. The goal of interactive marketing is to enable a company to profitably use those networks to attract and keep customers who will become partners with the business in creating, purchasing, and improving products and services.

In interactive marketing, customers are not just passive participants who receive media advertising prior to purchase, but are actively engaged in a network-enabled proactive and interactive processes. Interactive marketing encourages customers to become involved in product development, delivery, and service issues. This is enabled by various Internet technologies, including chat and discussion groups, Web forms and questionnaires, and e-mail correspondence. Finally, the expected outcomes of interactive marketing are a rich mixture of vital marketing data, new product ideas, volume sales, and strong customer relationships.

Targeted Marketing

Targeted marketing has become an important tool in developing advertising and promotion strategies for a company's electronic commerce websites. As illustrated in Figure 7.17, targeted marketing is an advertising and promotion management concept that includes five targeting components.

- **Community.** Companies can customize their Web advertising messages and promotion methods to appeal to people in specific communities. These can be *communities of interest*, such as *virtual communities* of online sporting enthusiasts or arts and crafts hobbyists, or geographic communities formed by the websites of a city or local newspaper.

- **Content.** Advertising such as electronic billboards or banners can be placed on various website pages, in addition to a company's home page. These messages reach the targeted audience. An ad for a movie on the opening page of an Internet search engine is a typical example.

Figure 7.17

The five major components of targeted marketing for electronic commerce on the World Wide Web.

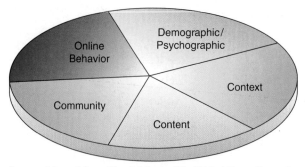

Source: Adapted from Chuck Martin, *The Digital Estate: Strategies for Competing, Surviving, and Thriving in an Internetworked World* (New York: McGraw-Hill, 1997), pp. 124–25, 206.

- **Context.** Advertising appears only in Web pages that are relevant to the content of a product or service. So advertising is targeted only at people who are already looking for information about a subject matter (vacation travel, for example) that is related to a company's products (car rental services, for example).

- **Demographic/Psychographic.** Marketing efforts can be aimed only at specific types or classes of people: unmarried, twenty-something, middle income, male college graduates, for example.

- **Online Behavior.** Advertising and promotion efforts can be tailored to each visit to a site by an individual. This strategy is based on a variety of tracking techniques, such as "Web cookie" files recorded on the visitor's disk drive from previous visits. This enables a company to track a person's online behavior at a website so marketing efforts can be instantly developed and targeted to that individual at each visit to their website.

Sales Force Automation

Increasingly, computers and networks are providing the basis for **sales force automation.** In many companies, the sales force is being outfitted with notebook computers, Web browsers, and sales contact management software that connect them to marketing websites on the Internet, extranets, and their company intranets. This not only increases the personal productivity of salespeople, but dramatically speeds up the capture and analysis of sales data from the field to marketing managers at company headquarters. In return, it allows marketing and sales management to improve the delivery of information and the support they provide to their salespeople. Therefore, many companies are viewing sales force automation as a way to gain a strategic advantage in sales productivity and marketing responsiveness. See Figure 7.18.

For example, salespeople use their PCs to record sales data as they make their calls on customers and prospects during the day. Then each night, sales reps in the field can connect their computers by modem and telephone links to the Internet and extranets, which can access intranet or other network servers at their company. Then, they can upload information on sales orders, sales calls, and other sales statistics, as well as send electronic mail messages and access website sales support information. In return, the network servers may download product availability data, prospect lists of information on good sales prospects, and e-mail messages.

Manufacturing Systems

Manufacturing information systems support the *production/operations* function that includes all activities concerned with the planning and control of the processes producing goods or services. Thus, the production/operations function is concerned with the management of the operational processes and systems of all business firms. Information systems used for operations management and transaction processing support all firms that must plan, monitor, and control

This Web-based sales force automation package supports sales lead management of qualified prospects, and management of current customer accounts.

Source: Courtesy of SalesForce.com.

inventories, purchases, and the flow of goods and services. Therefore, firms such as transportation companies, wholesalers, retailers, financial institutions, and service companies must use production/operations information systems to plan and control their operations. In this section, we will concentrate on computer-based manufacturing applications to illustrate information systems that support the production/operations function.

Computer-Integrated Manufacturing

A variety of manufacturing information systems are used to support **computer-integrated manufacturing** (CIM). See Figure 7.19. CIM is an overall concept that stresses that the objectives of computer-based systems in manufacturing must be to:

- **Simplify** (reengineer) production processes, product designs, and factory organization as a vital foundation to automation and integration.

- **Automate** production processes and the business functions that support them with computers, machines, and robots.

- **Integrate** all production and support processes using computers, telecommunications networks, and other information technologies.

The overall goal of CIM and such manufacturing information systems is to create flexible, agile, manufacturing processes that efficiently produce products of the highest quality. Thus, CIM supports the concepts of *flexible manufacturing systems*, *agile manufacturing*, and *total quality management*. Implementing such manufacturing concepts enables a company to quickly respond to and fulfill customer requirements with high-quality products and services.

Manufacturing information systems help companies simplify, automate, and integrate many of the activities needed to produce products of all kinds. For example, computers are used to help engineers design better products using both *computer-aided engineering* (CAE) and *computer-aided design* (CAD) systems, and better production processes with *computer-aided process planning*. They are also used to

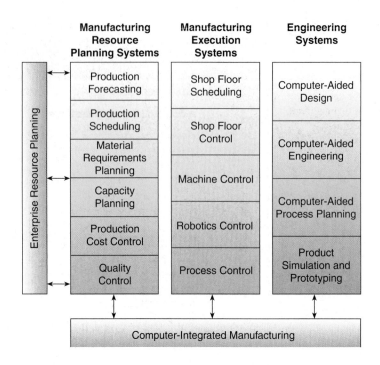

Figure 7.19

Manufacturing information systems support computer-integrated manufacturing. Note that manufacturing resources planning systems are one of the application clusters in an ERP system.

help plan the types of material needed in the production process, which is called *material requirements planning* (MRP), and to integrate MRP with production scheduling and shop floor operations, which is known as *manufacturing resource planning.* Many of the processes within manufacturing resource planning systems are included in the manufacturing module of enterprise resource planning (ERP) software discussed earlier.

Computer-aided manufacturing (CAM) systems are those that automate the production process. For example, this could be accomplished by monitoring and controlling the production process in a factory (manufacturing execution systems) or by directly controlling a physical process (process control), a machine tool (machine control), or machines with some humanlike work capabilities (robots).

Manufacturing execution systems (MES) are performance monitoring information systems for factory floor operations. They monitor, track, and control the five essential components involved in a production process: materials, equipment, personnel, instructions and specifications, and production facilities. MES includes shop floor scheduling and control, machine control, robotics control, and process control systems. These manufacturing systems monitor, report, and adjust the status and performance of production components to help a company achieve a flexible, high-quality manufacturing process.

Process Control

Process control is the use of computers to control an ongoing physical process. Process control computers control physical processes in petroleum refineries, cement plants, steel mills, chemical plants, food product manufacturing plants, pulp and paper mills, electric power plants, and so on. Many process control computers are special-purpose minicomputer systems. A process control computer system requires the use of special sensing devices that measure physical phenomena such as temperature or pressure changes. These continuous physical measurements are converted to digital form by analog-to-digital converters and relayed to computers for processing.

Process control software uses mathematical models to analyze the data generated by the ongoing process and compare them to standards or forecasts of required results. Then the computer directs the control of the process by adjusting control devices such as thermostats, valves, switches, and so on. The process control system also provides messages and displays about the status of the process so a human operator can take appropriate measures to control the process. See Figure 7.20.

Alcoa: Realtime Manufacturing Networks

How did Alcoa reduce inventories by more than a quarter of a billion dollars in one year, while increasing sales by just under $1 billion? Credit goes to the Alcoa Business System, an e-business adaptation of Toyota's production methods that took more than $1.1 billion out of the aluminum maker's cost base. A big piece of it: getting Alcoa, as much as possible, to operate in real time.

Managing in real time—making decisions now, on the basis of accurate, live information delivered via the Internet and corporate intranets and extranets; eliminating filters and emptying catch basins for information and resources; producing to actual demand rather that to forecast or budget—is changing how business works.

Alcoa, already the aluminum industry's cost leader, began rolling out its new manufacturing methods in 1998, aiming to cut costs and improve responsiveness. "We were ill-prepared to meet customers' needs," says executive vice president P. Keith Turnbull, who leads the efforts. "We'd ship out a pile of dead stuff"—inventory—"and if we didn't have what the customer wanted, we'd make the pile bigger. Inventories are a hedge against inefficiency, your own or that of your supplier or customer." Alcoa CEO Alain Belda calls them "monuments to incompetence." But now, managing in real time is central to Alcoa's process.

The results show up all over the company. A plant in Sorocaba, Brazil turns its inventory 60 times a year. A Hernando, Mississippi extrusion plant, a money loser when it was acquired in 1998, delivers custom orders in two days (versus three weeks previously) and makes money. In Portland, Australia, producing molten metal to realtime demand from an adjacent ingot mill raised asset utilization so much that the plan eliminated ten of twenty-four vacuum crucibles, saving about $60 million a year. All this—$832 million so far toward the $1.1 billion target—has taken just over two years [28].

Figure 7.20

This production control specialist monitors aluminum refining processes from an automated control room that overlooks the production areas of an aluminum mill.

Source: Charles Thatcher/Stone.

Machine Control

Machine control is the use of a computer to control the actions of a machine. This is also popularly called *numerical control*. The control of machine tools in factories is a typical numerical control application, though it also refers to the control of typesetting machines, weaving machines, and other industrial machinery.

Numerical control computer programs for machine tools convert geometric data from engineering drawings and machining instructions from process planning into a numerical code of commands that control the actions of a machine tool. Machine control may involve the use of special-purpose microcomputers called programmable logic controllers (PLCs). These devices operate one or more machines according to the directions of a numerical control program. Manufacturing engineers use computers to develop numerical control programs, analyze production data furnished by PLCs, and fine-tune machine tool performance.

Robotics

An important development in machine control and computer-aided manufacturing is the creation of smart machines and robots. These devices directly control their own activities with the aid of microcomputers. **Robotics** is the technology of building and using machines (robots) with computer intelligence and computer-controlled humanlike physical capabilities (dexterity, movement, vision, etc.). Robotics has also become a major field of artificial intelligence (AI), which we will cover in Chapter 9.

Robots are used as "steel-collar workers" to increase productivity and cut costs. For example, a robot might assemble compressor valves with 12 parts at the rate of 320 units per hour, which is 10 times the rate of human workers. Robots are also particularly valuable for hazardous areas or work activities. Robots follow programs distributed by servers and loaded into separate or on-board special-purpose microcomputers. Input is received from visual and/or tactile sensors, processed by the microcomputer, and translated into movements of the robot. Typically, this involves moving its arms and hands to pick up and load items or perform some other work assignment such as painting, drilling, or welding. Robotics developments are expected to make robots more intelligent, flexible, and mobile by improving their computing, visual, tactile, and navigational capabilities.

Human Resource Systems

The human resource management (HRM) function involves the recruitment, placement, evaluation, compensation, and development of the employees of an organization. The goal of human resource management is the effective and efficient use of the human resources of a company. Thus, **human resource information systems** are designed to support (1) planning to meet the personnel needs of the business, (2) development of employees to their full potential, and (3) control of all personnel policies and programs. Originally, businesses used computer-based information systems to (1) produce paychecks and payroll reports, (2) maintain personnel records, and (3) analyze the use of personnel in business operations. Many firms have gone beyond these traditional *personnel management* functions and have developed human resource information systems (HRIS) that also support (1) recruitment, selection, and hiring; (2) job placement; (3) performance appraisals; (4) employee benefits analysis; (5) training and development; and (6) health, safety, and security. See Figure 7.21.

HRM and the Internet

The Internet has become a major force for change in human resource management. For example, online HRM systems may involve recruiting for employees through recruitment sections of corporate websites. Companies are also using commercial recruiting services and databases on the World Wide Web, posting messages in selected Internet newsgroups, and communicating with job applicants via e-mail.

The Internet has a wealth of information and contacts for both employers and job hunters. Top websites for job hunters and employers on the World Wide Web include Monster.com, CareerPath.com, FreeAgent.com, and Jobweb.org. These websites are full of reports, statistics, and other useful HRM information, such as

Figure 7.21 Human resource information systems support the strategic, tactical, and operational use of the human resources of an organization.

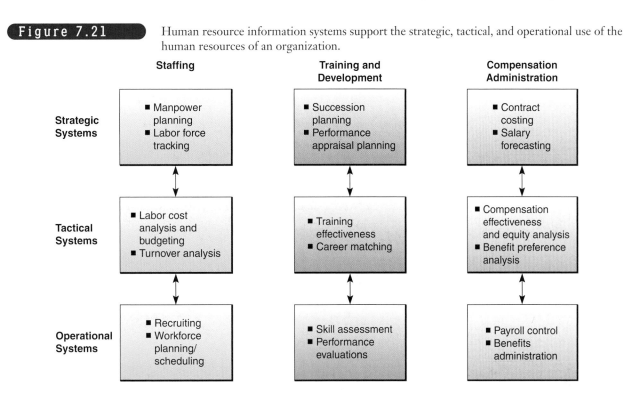

	Staffing	Training and Development	Compensation Administration
Strategic Systems	■ Manpower planning ■ Labor force tracking	■ Succession planning ■ Performance appraisal planning	■ Contract costing ■ Salary forecasting
Tactical Systems	■ Labor cost analysis and budgeting ■ Turnover analysis	■ Training effectiveness ■ Career matching	■ Compensation effectiveness and equity analysis ■ Benefit preference analysis
Operational Systems	■ Recruiting ■ Workforce planning/ scheduling	■ Skill assessment ■ Performance evaluations	■ Payroll control ■ Benefits administration

job reports by industry, or listings of the top recruiting markets by industry and profession. Of course, you may also want to access the job listings and resource databases of commercial recruiting companies on the Web.

HRM and Corporate Intranets

Intranet technologies allow companies to process most common HRM applications over their corporate intranets. Intranets allow the HRM department to provide around-the-clock services to their customers: the employees. They can also disseminate valuable information faster than through previous company channels. Intranets can collect information online from employees for input to their HRM files, and they can enable employees to perform HRM tasks with little intervention by the HRM department.

For example, *employee self-service (ESS)* intranet applications allow employees to view benefits, enter travel and expense reports, verify employment and salary information, access and update their personal information, and enter data that has a time constraint to it. Through this completely electronic process, employees can use their Web browsers to look up individual payroll and benefits information online, right from their desktop PCs, mobile computers, or intranet kiosks located around a work site.

Another benefit of the intranet is that it can serve as a superior training tool. Employees can easily download instructions and processes to get the information or education they need. In addition, employees using new technology can view training videos over the intranet on demand. Thus, the intranet eliminates the need to loan out and track training videos. Employees can also use their corporate intranets to produce automated paysheets, the online alternative to time cards. These electronic forms have made viewing, entering, and adjusting payroll information easy for both employees and HRM professionals [17].

Staffing the Organization

The staffing function must be supported by information systems that record and track human resources within a company to maximize their use. For example, a personnel record-keeping system keeps track of additions, deletions, and other changes to the records in a personnel database. Changes in job assignments and compensation, or hirings and terminations, are examples of information that would be used to update

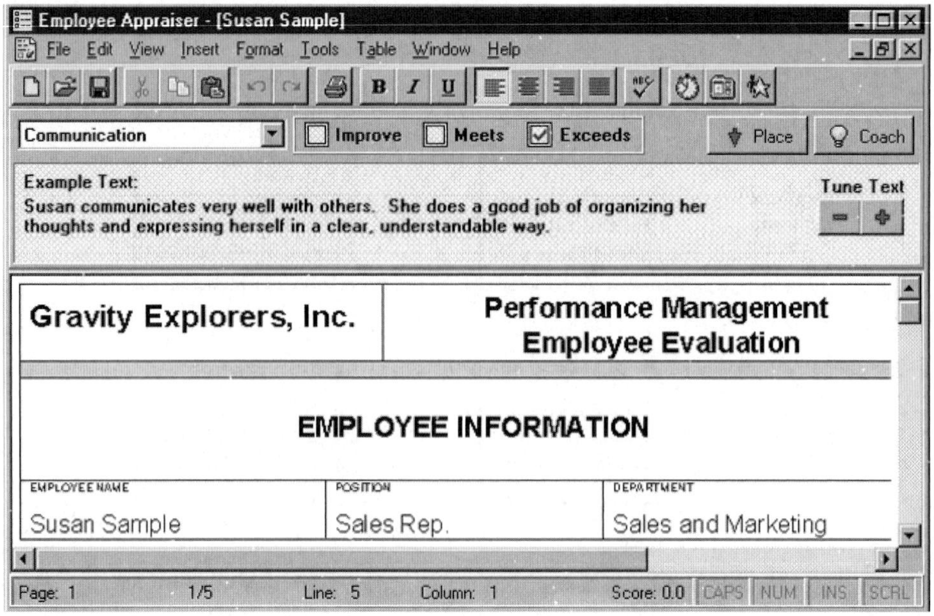

Figure 7.22

An example of a performance evaluation display for a manager.

the personnel database. Another example is an employee skills inventory system that uses the employee skills data from a personnel database to locate employees within a company who have the skills required for specific assignments and projects.

Training and Development

HRM systems can help human resource managers plan and monitor employee recruitment, training, and development programs by analyzing the success history of present programs. They also analyze the career development status of each employee to determine whether development methods such as training programs and periodic performance appraisals should be recommended. Computer-based multimedia training programs and appraisals of employee job performance are available to help support this area of human resource management. See Figure 7.22.

Accounting Systems

Accounting information systems are the oldest and most widely used information systems in business. They record and report business transactions and other economic events. Accounting information systems are based on the double-entry bookkeeping concept, which is hundreds of years old, and other, more recent accounting concepts such as responsibility accounting and activity-based costing. Computer-based accounting systems record and report the flow of funds through an organization on a historical basis and produce important financial statements such as balance sheets and income statements. Such systems also produce forecasts of future conditions such as projected financial statements and financial budgets. A firm's financial performance is measured against such forecasts by other analytical accounting reports.

Operational accounting systems emphasize legal and historical record-keeping and the production of accurate financial statements. Typically, these systems include transaction processing systems such as order processing, inventory control, accounts receivable, accounts payable, payroll, and general ledger systems. Management accounting systems focus on the planning and control of business operations. They emphasize cost accounting reports, the development of financial budgets and projected financial statements, and analytical reports comparing actual to forecasted performance.

Figure 7.23 illustrates the interrelationships of several important accounting information systems commonly computerized by both large and small businesses.

Figure 7.23   Important accounting information systems for transaction processing and financial reporting. Note how they are related to each other in terms of input and output flows.

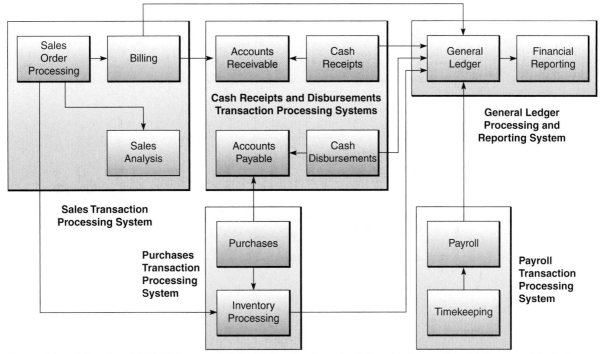

Source: Adapted from Joseph W. Wilkinson and Michael J. Cerullo, *Accounting Information Systems: Essential Concepts and Applications,* 3rd ed., p. 10. Copyright © 1997 by John Wiley & Sons, Inc. Reprinted by permission.

Many accounting software packages are available for these applications. Let's briefly review how several of these systems support the operations and management of a business firm. Figure 7.24 summarizes the purpose of six common, but important, accounting information systems.

Figure 7.24   A summary of six widely used accounting information systems.

Common Business Accounting Systems
● **Order Processing**   Captures and processes customer orders and produces data for inventory control and accounts receivable.
● **Inventory Control**   Processes data reflecting changes in inventory and provides shipping and reorder information.
● **Accounts Receivable**   Records amounts owed by customers and produces customer invoices, monthly customer statements, and credit management reports.
● **Accounts Payable**   Records purchases from, amounts owed to, and payments to suppliers, and produces cash management reports.
● **Payroll**   Records employee work and compensation data and produces paychecks and other payroll documents and reports.
● **General Ledger**   Consolidates data from other accounting systems and produces the periodic financial statements and reports of the business.

Figure 7.25

Using the sales order processing of MYOB, a popular accounting package.

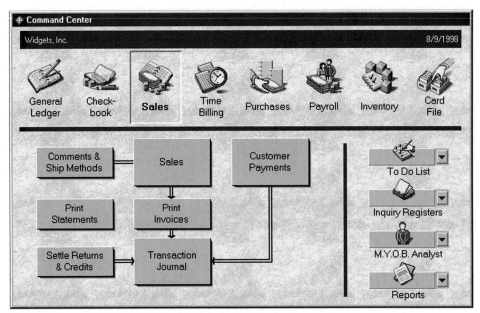

Source: Courtesy of MYOB US, Inc.

Online Accounting Systems

It should come as no surprise that the accounting information systems illustrated in Figures 7.23 and 7.24 are being affected by Internet technologies. Using the Internet, intranets, extranets, and other networks changes how accounting information systems monitor and track business activity. The online, interactive nature of such networks calls for new forms of transaction documents, procedures, and controls. This particularly applies to systems like order processing, inventory control, accounts receivable, and accounts payable. These systems are directly involved in the processing of transactions between a business and its customers and suppliers. So naturally, many companies are using Internet and other network links to these trading partners for such online transaction processing systems, as discussed in Section I.

Order Processing

Order processing, or sales order processing, is an important transaction processing system that captures and processes customer orders and produces data needed for sales analysis and inventory control. In many firms, it also keeps track of the status of customer orders until goods are delivered. Computer-based sales order processing systems provide a fast, accurate, and efficient method of recording and screening customer orders and sales transactions. They also provide inventory control systems with information on accepted orders so they can be filled as quickly as possible. See Figure 7.25.

Inventory Control

Inventory control systems process data reflecting changes to items in inventory. Once data about customer orders are received from an order processing system, a computer-based inventory control system records changes to inventory levels and prepares appropriate shipping documents. Then it may notify managers about items that need reordering and provide them with a variety of inventory status reports. Computer-based inventory control systems thus help a business provide high-quality service to customers while minimizing investment in inventory and inventory carrying costs.

Accounts Receivable

Accounts receivable systems keep records of amounts owed by customers from data generated by customer purchases and payments. They produce invoices to customers, monthly customer statements, and credit management reports. Computer-based accounts receivable systems stimulate prompt customer payments by preparing accurate and timely invoices and monthly statements to credit customers. They provide managers with reports to help them control the amount of credit extended and the collection of money owed. This activity helps to maximize profitable credit sales while minimizing losses from bad debts.

Accounts Payable

Accounts payable systems keep track of data concerning purchases from and payments to suppliers. They prepare checks in payment of outstanding invoices and produce cash management reports. Computer-based accounts payable systems help ensure prompt and accurate payment of suppliers to maintain good relationships, ensure a good credit standing, and secure any discounts offered for prompt payment. They provide tight financial control over all cash disbursements of the business. They also provide management with information needed for the analysis of payments, expenses, purchases, employee expense accounts, and cash requirements.

Payroll

Payroll systems receive and maintain data from employee time cards and other work records. They produce paychecks and other documents such as earning statements, payroll reports, and labor analysis reports. Other reports are also prepared for management and government agencies. Computer-based payroll systems help businesses make prompt and accurate payments to their employees, as well as reports to management, employees, and government agencies concerning earnings, taxes, and other deductions. They may also provide management with reports analyzing labor costs and productivity.

General Ledger

General ledger systems consolidate data received from accounts receivable, accounts payable, payroll, and other accounting information systems. At the end of each accounting period, they close the books of a business and produce the general ledger trial balance, the income statement and balance sheet of the firm, and various income and expense reports for management. Computer-based general ledger systems help businesses accomplish these accounting tasks in an accurate and timely manner. They typically provide better financial controls and management reports and involve fewer personnel and lower costs than manual accounting methods.

Financial Management Systems

Computer-based **financial management systems** support financial managers in decisions concerning (1) the financing of a business and (2) the allocation and control of financial resources within a business. Major financial management system categories include cash and investment management, capital budgeting, financial forecasting, and financial planning. See Figure 7.26.

Cash Management

Cash management systems collect information on all cash receipts and disbursements within a company on a realtime or periodic basis. Such information allows businesses to deposit or invest excess funds more quickly, and thus increase the income generated by deposited or invested funds. These systems also produce daily, weekly, or monthly forecasts of cash receipts or disbursements (cash flow forecasts) that are used to spot future cash deficits or surpluses. Mathematical models frequently can determine optimal cash collection programs and determine alternative financing or investment strategies for dealing with forecasted cash deficits or surpluses.

Figure 7.26

Examples of important financial management systems.

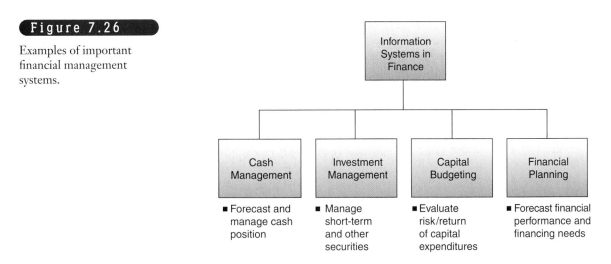

Figure 7.27

The Red Herring online investment site offers free securities and portfolio analysis and charting tools.

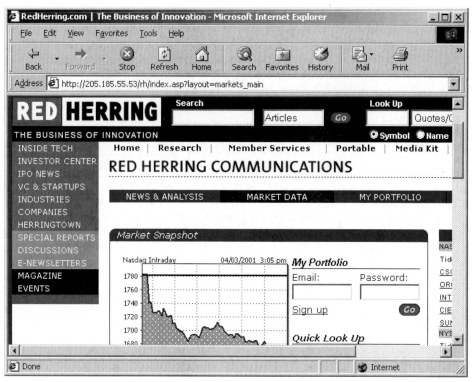

Source: Courtesy of Red Herring.

Online Investment Management

Many businesses invest their excess cash in short-term low-risk marketable securities (such as U.S. Treasury bills, commercial paper, or certificates of deposit) or in higher-return/higher-risk alternatives, so that investment income may be earned until the funds are required. The portfolio of such securities can be managed with the help of portfolio management software packages. Investment information and securities trading are available from hundreds of online sources on the Internet and other networks. Online investment management services help a financial manager make buying, selling, or holding decisions for each type of security so that an optimum mix of securities is developed that minimizes risk and maximizes investment income for the business. See Figure 7.27.

Capital Budgeting

The **capital budgeting** process involves evaluating the profitability and financial impact of proposed capital expenditures. Long-term expenditure proposals for plants and equipment can be analyzed using a variety of techniques. This application makes heavy use of spreadsheet models that incorporate present value analysis of expected cash flows and probability analysis of risk to determine the optimum mix of capital projects for a business.

Financial Forecasting and Planning

Financial analysts typically use electronic spreadsheets and other **financial planning** software to evaluate the present and projected financial performance of a business. They also help determine the financing needs of a business and analyze alternative methods of financing. Financial analysts use financial forecasts concerning the economic situation, business operations, types of financing available, interest rates, and stock and bond prices to develop an optimal financing plan for the business. Electronic spreadsheet packages, DSS software, and Web-based groupware can be used to build and manipulate financial models. Answers to what-if and goal-seeking questions can be explored as financial analysts and managers evaluate their financing and investment alternatives. We will discuss such applications further in Chapter 9.

Summary

- **Cross-Functional e-Business Applications.** Major e-business applications and their interrelationships are summarized in the e-business application architecture of Figure 7.2. Many e-business applications are integrated into cross-functional enterprise application clusters like enterprise resource planning (ERP), customer relationship management (CRM), and supply chain management (SCM), which also reengineer the business processes involved. Thus, ERP integrates and automates many of the business processes within the manufacturing, logistics, distribution, accounting, finance, and human resources functions of a business. CRM integrates and automates many of the customer serving processes in sales, marketing, and product services that interact with a company's customers, while SCM reengineers and automates many traditional supply chain processes. And enterprise collaboration systems (ECS) support and enhance communication and collaboration among the teams and workgroups in an organization.

  In addition, these clusters themselves are being interconnected with enterprise application integration (EAI) software so that the business users of these applications can more easily access all the information resources they need to support the needs of customers and the management of an e-business enterprise. Refer to Figures 7.4, 7.6, 7.7, and 7.8 for summary views of the e-business application in EAI, ERP, CRM, and SCM systems, and 7.12 and 7.13 for enterprise collaboration systems.

- **Online Transaction Processing.** Online transaction processing systems play a vital role in e-commerce. Transaction processing involves the basic activities of (1) data entry, (2) transaction processing, (3) database maintenance, (4) document and report generation, and (5) inquiry processing. Many firms are using the Internet, intranets, extranets, and other networks for online transaction processing to provide superior service to their customers and suppliers. See Figure 7.11.

- **Functional Business Systems.** Functional business information systems support the business functions of marketing, production/operations, accounting, finance, and human resource management through a variety of e-business operational and management information systems summarized in Figure 7.15.

- **Marketing.** Marketing information systems support traditional and e-commerce processes and management of the marketing function. Major types of marketing information systems include interactive marketing at e-commerce websites, sales force automation, customer relationship management, sales management, product management, targeted marketing, advertising and promotion, and market research. Thus, marketing information systems assist marketing managers in electronic commerce product development and customer relationship decisions, as well as in planning advertising and sales promotion strategies and developing the e-commerce potential of new and present products, and new channels of distribution.

- **Manufacturing.** Computer-based manufacturing information systems help a company achieve computer-integrated manufacturing (CIM), and thus simplify, automate, and integrate many of the activities needed to quickly produce high-quality products to meet changing customer demands. For example, computer-aided design using collaborative manufacturing networks helps engineers collaborate on the design of new products and processes. Then manufacturing resource planning systems help plan the types of resources needed in the production process. Finally, manufacturing execution systems monitor and control the manufacture of products on the factory floor through shop floor scheduling and control systems, controlling a physical process (process control), a machine tool (numerical control), or machines with some humanlike work capabilities (robotics).

- **Human Resource Management.** Human resource information systems support human resource management in organizations. They include information systems for staffing the organization, training and development, and compensation administration. HRM websites on the Internet or corporate intranets have become important tools for providing HR services to present and prospective employees.

- **Accounting and Finance.** Accounting information systems record, report, and analyze business transactions and events for the management of the business enterprise. Examples of common accounting information systems include order processing, inventory control, accounts receivable, accounts payable, payroll, and general ledger systems. Information systems in finance support financial managers in decisions regarding the financing of a business and the allocation of financial resources within a business. Financial information systems include cash management, online investment management, capital budgeting, and financial forecasting and planning.

Key Terms and Concepts

These are the key terms and concepts of this chapter. The page number of their first explanation is in parentheses.

1. Accounting systems (240)
2. Accounts payable (243)
3. Accounts receivable (242)
4. Batch processing (225)
5. Computer-aided manufacturing (236)

6. Computer-integrated manufacturing (235)

7. Cross-functional enterprise systems (217)

8. Customer relationship management (220)

9. E-business (214)

   a. Application architecture (216)

10. Enterprise application integration (221)

11. Enterprise collaboration systems (227)

12. Enterprise resource planning (217)

13. Financial management systems (243)

14. Functional business systems (230)

15. General ledger (243)

16. Human resource systems (238)

17. Interactive marketing (233)

18. Inventory control (242)

19. Machine control (238)

20. Manufacturing execution systems (236)

21. Manufacturing systems (234)

22. Marketing systems (232)

23. Online accounting systems (242)

24. Online HRM systems (238)

25. Online investment systems (244)

26. Online transaction processing systems (224)

27. Order processing (242)

28. Payroll (243)

29. Process control (236)

30. Realtime processing (226)

31. Robotics (238)

32. Sales force automation (234)

33. Supply chain (222)

34. Supply chain management (222)

35. Targeted marketing (233)

36. Transaction processing cycle (225)

Review Quiz

Match one of the key terms and concepts listed previously with one of the brief examples or definitions that follow. Try to find the best fit for the answers that seem to fit more than one term or concept. Defend your choices.

_____ 1. Using the Internet and other networks for e-commerce, collaboration, and business processes.

_____ 2. Information systems that cross the boundaries of the functional areas of a business in order to integrate and automate business processes.

_____ 3. Information systems that support marketing, production, accounting, finance, and human resource management.

_____ 4. E-business applications can be grouped into clusters of cross-functional enterprise applications.

_____ 5. Software that interconnects enterprise application clusters.

_____ 6. A cross-functional enterprise application that integrates and automates key back-office processes.

_____ 7. Information systems for customer relationship management, sales management, and promotion management.

_____ 8. Collaborating interactively with customers in creating, purchasing, servicing, and improving products and services.

_____ 9. Using mobile computing networks to support salespeople in the field.

_____ 10. A cross-functional enterprise system that integrates and automates many customer serving-processes.

_____ 11. Information systems that support manufacturing operations and management.

_____ 12. A conceptual framework for simplifying and integrating all aspects of manufacturing automation.

_____ 13. Using computers in a variety of ways to help manufacture products.

_____ 14. Use electronic communications, conferencing, and collaborative work tools to support and enhance collaboration among teams and workgroups.

_____ 15. Using computers to operate a petroleum refinery.

_____ 16. Using computers to help operate machine tools.

_____ 17. Computerized devices with work capabilities that enable them to take over some production activities from human workers.

_____ 18. Information systems to support staffing, training and development, and compensation administration.

_____ 19. Using the Internet for recruitment and job hunting is an example.

_____ 20. Accomplishes legal and historical record-keeping and gathers information for the planning and control of business operations.

_____ 21. An example is using the Internet and extranets to do accounts receivable and accounts payable activities.

_____ 22. Handles sales orders from customers.

_____ 23. Keeps track of items in stock.

_____ 24. Keeps track of amounts owed by customers.

_____ 25. Keeps track of purchases from suppliers.

_____ 26. Produces employee paychecks.

_____ 27. Produces the financial statements of a firm.

_____ 28. Information systems for cash management, investment management, capital budgeting, and financial forecasting.

_____ 29. Using the Internet and other networks for investment research and trading.

_____ 30. Performance monitoring and control systems for factory floor operations.

_____ 31. Customizing advertising and promotion methods to fit their intended audience.

_____ 32. Data entry, transaction processing, database maintenance, document and report generation, and inquiry processing.

_____ 33. Collecting and periodically processing transaction data.

_____ 34. Processing transaction data immediately after they are captured.

_____ 35. Systems that immediately capture and process transaction data and update corporate databases.

_____ 36. A network of business relationships between a business that produces a product or service and business partners involved in the processes that are required.

_____ 37. Integrates the management functions involved in promoting efficient and effective supply chain processes.

Discussion Questions

1. How is e-business "redefining old business models, with the aid of technology, to maximize customer value"?

2. Why is there a trend toward cross-functional integrated enterprise systems in business?

3. Do you agree that "ERP is the backbone of e-business"? Why or why not?

4. Refer to the Real World Case on Charles Schwab and Others in this chapter. What are the most important HR applications a company should offer to its employees via a Web-based system? Why?

5. How do you think sales force automation affects salesperson productivity, marketing management, and competitive advantage?

6. How can Internet technologies be involved in improving a process in one of the functions of business? Choose one example and evaluate its business value.

7. How can Internet technologies improve customer relationships and service for a business?

8. Refer to the Real World Case on Harrah's, DuPont, and Otis in the chapter. What are several e-business applications that you might recommend to a small company to help it survive and succeed in challenging economic times? Why?

9. Which of the 14 tools for enterprise collaboration summarized in Figure 7.13 do you feel are essential for any business to have today? Which of them do you feel are optional, depending on the type of business or other factor? Explain.

10. What is the role and the business value of using Internet technologies in supply chain management?

Application Exercises

Complete the following exercises as individual or group projects that apply chapter concepts to real world business situations.

1. **Apps.com and Smart Online: Online Business Applications**

Why build a power plant when you can pay someone else for electricity? This is the logic behind the recent emergence of Web-based software companies known as application service providers, or ASPs, that hope to become an essential part of the Internet economy. Instead of providing electric power, ASPs aim to deliver software applications over the Internet for monthly or per-user fees.

Today's ASPs provide browser-based, Web-native applications—meaning the software and data existing on the Web—and generally require high-speed Internet access. Service providers create enterprise-level software and charge customers a monthly per-user service fee, which includes all installations, upgrades, and maintenance, so small businesses can automate

such critical functions as accounting, human resources, and customer management.

Apps.com (www.apps.com) lists and rates online software application sites for businesses in categories such as business research, human resources, and ASPs. Each application is given a brief description and rated on a five-star scale. See Figure 7.28.

Smart Online (www.smartonline.com) provides online services in four areas—finance, legal, human resources, and sales and marketing. The apps can help you create a business plan or conduct market research. There are also lots of standard forms for contracts, letters, etc.

a. Check out Apps.com and several online application software websites such as Smart Online that are rated by Apps.com.

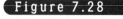

Figure 7.28

Apps.com provides a variety of information services, including ratings for business application software.

Source: Courtesy of Apps.com.

b. Do you agree with Apps.com's evaluations? Use Smart Online or another online application service provider (ASP) to illustrate your answer.

c. Would you use or recommend any of the online application services to a small business? Why or why not?

Source; "Apps on Tap," Technology Buyers Guide, *Fortune*, Winter 2001, pp. 217–218.

2. eLance.com and Others: Online Job Matching and Auctions

The online job boards are keeping pace with the Internet-time needs of recruiters and job hunters alike. "Custom-tailored" is the catch phrase characterizing what many of the sites provide: Applicants are well screened to meet job requirements and to ensure that all parties find what they are looking for.

Thousands of opportunities await those who troll the big job boards, the free-agent sites, the auction services where applicants bid for projects, and the niche sites for specialized jobs and skills. Wherever they may be, employers are electronically privy to a bountiful workforce and job seekers have the work world at their fingertips. Examples of top job matching and auction sites are eWork Exchange and eLance.com.

eWork Exchange (www.eworkexchange.com). No more sifting through irrelevant search results: Fill out a list of your skills and let eWork Exchange's proprietary technology find the most suitable projects for you—no bidding required.

eLance.com (www.elance.com). This global auction marketplace covers more than just IT jobs; it runs the gamut from astrology and medicine to corporate work and cooking projects. Register a description of your services or go straight to browsing the listings of open projects—and then start bidding. A feedback section lets both employers and freelancers rate one another.

a. Check out eWork Exchange and eLance, and other online job sites on the Web.

b. Evaluate several sites based on their ease of use and their value to job seekers and employers.

c. Which website was your favorite? Why?

Source: "Browse, Click, Career," Technology Buyers Guide, *Fortune*, Winter 2001, pp. 224–226.

3. Job Search Database

a. Create a database table to store key characteristics of jobs. Include all of the job characteristics shown in the list and sample record below as fields in your table, but feel free to add additional fields of interest to you. Use websites like Monster.com and others mentioned in the chapter to gather information about available jobs. Look up and record the relevant data for at least 10 current job openings that are of interest to you or that meet criteria provided by your instructor. If data are not available for some fields (such as, salary range) for a particular job, leave that field blank.

b. Write queries that will enable you to retrieve **(a)** just those jobs in a specified location, and **(b)** just those jobs in a specified job category.

c. Create a report that groups jobs by Location and sorts jobs within each group by Job category.

List of Fields for the Job Search Database

Job Title:	Systems Analyst
Employer:	Techron Inc.
Location:	Springfield, MA
Job Category:	Data and Information Services
Job Description:	Work with team to analyze, design, and develop e-commerce systems. Skills in systems analysis, relation database design, and Programming in Java are required.
Qualifications:	Bachelors degree in Information Systems or Computer Science
Salary Range:	$48,000–$60,000 depending on experience.

4. Performing an Industry Financial Analysis

Select an industry of interest to you and at least three prominent firms in that industry that you would like to investigate. Go to an online investment management website (as illustrated in Figure 7.27) and/or the websites of the firms you are investigating and obtain information about financial operations including at least net sales (or net revenue) and net after-tax income for the three most recent years available. Also, search the Web for current information affecting your firms and the industry.

a. Create a simple spreadsheet of the net sales and aftertax income data you collected. Your spreadsheet should include percentage changes between years to facilitate comparisons between companies that are of unequal size. Also, you should show the rate of after-tax income as a percentage of net sales. Add charts comparing trends in net revenue and net income for the firms you are investigating. Include a projection for net revenue and net income for the next year.

b. Write a brief report describing the income statistics of your spreadsheet, discussing current trends affecting your firms, and justifying your projections for the upcoming year.

Harrah's, DuPont, and Otis: Capitalizing on e-Business Initiatives in Challenging Times

As the USA stood still in the wake of the September 11 attacks of 2001, casino and hotel operator, Harrah's Entertainment Inc., faced a sharp downturn in business. The country was in no mood for a party, and few people were willing to hop a flight to Las Vegas. Occupancy rates at Harrah's flagship hotel soon dropped by more than 25 percent. So on September 14, Harrah's launched a small counteroffensive: The company sent out targeted e-mails to thousands of customers it thought might want to take a trip to the tables and slots. The gambit worked, helping to fill nearly 4,000 rooms that otherwise would have gone empty. By September 30, the hotel was back near 100 percent occupancy. "We were able to get our message out immediately over the Internet," says Harrah's Chairman Philip G. Satre.

The key to Harrah's success: That summer, the company linked its database of 24 million gamblers to its website and e-mail marketing system. A year ago, Harrah's wouldn't have been able to seize the day. It has long known who the highest rollers are, based on its records of customer habits. Many avid gamblers participate in a rewards program that allows the company to track their playing, using cards that can be plugged into slot machines or presented to pit bosses. Until this summer, though, reaching those players with targeted pitches required bulk mailings via snail mail. Now, when a customer clicks to Harrah's website from an e-mailed sales pitch, the company knows how much the player spends and can offer a tailored deal. The customer can then immediately book the room and a flight to get there, and reserve a seat for a show.

The September 11 attacks instantly made the toughest economic environment in a decade even worse. But for companies such as Harrah's that have spent the time and the money to beef up their e-business capabilities, the sting may not be as bad. With its innovative e-business marketing, Harrah's rebounded more quickly after September 11 than other big casinos in Vegas.

Companies in a sales squeeze are looking to the Net as a tool for cutting costs, generating new revenue streams, trimming inventories, and serving customers and employees more efficiently. The e-business projects getting the green light are those with proven track records for delivering results. Companies are putting human resources and customer service online so they can reduce the number of call-center employees. They're pressing ahead with supplychain management initiatives—although often in smaller pieces than two years ago. And they're moving all aspects of purchasing to the Web allowing them to slash internal costs or wring deeper discounts from suppliers.

At DuPont, for example, purchasing on the Web has cut the cost of buying supplies by $200 million—a 4 percent reduction in the first year of the $15 million e-business project. Better yet, the chemical giant expects another $200 million in annual savings by 2003—numbers that sound pretty good at DuPont, where analysts expect to see profits slide by half this year. Before the system was in place, employees ordered supplies, such as pipe fittings and lab chemicals, using phone calls, faxes, or by simply running out and picking stuff up. Now employees log onto a website to buy virtually everything. DuPont can better control what gets bought—and can funnel orders to vendors who promise price breaks.

Otis Elevator Co. is increasing its spending on e-business initiatives, says Ron Beaver, vice-president for information systems. In 2001, it more than doubled its e-business budget and expects a 50 percent increase in 2002. The bulk of the new money will go to an effort linking Otis with its suppliers and customers via the Web to streamline the way parts move in and out of its factories. Beaver estimates that half the elevator parts Otis sends out to construction sites arrive before they're needed, and end up sitting around for weeks or months, meaning the company carries them as inventory much longer than necessary. The new Web system should help the company better monitor whether a cable, a cab, or a carton of call buttons is ready to ship, because it will be in constant contact with its suppliers. And with progress reports available online, Otis will know what stage the builder has reached and when it's ready for each part.

Otis also is tapping the Net to slash repair bills. The company has a system that allows technicians at 10 centers around the globe to monitor elevators via an Internet link. When a door sticks or the car doesn't stop at floor level, the elevator zips off a signal alerting Otis to send someone to fix it. Today, some 20 percent of elevators Otis maintains worldwide use the system—a number it hopes to nearly double by the end of next year. The payoff is huge. Since Otis no longer has to dispatch repair staff as often to check for problems, elevators with remote monitoring require only one-third the number of visits as those without the system. That has helped Otis keep its North American repair staff steady while increasing the number of elevators it services by 10 percent, to 120,000 over the last year.

Case Study Questions

1. Why can e-business initiatives help companies survive and succeed in challenging economic times? Give an example from this case to illustrate your answer.

2. Why do you think companies like DuPont are just now implementing e-procurement systems that can save them hundreds of millions of dollars?

3. Why is Otis Elevator dramatically increasing its spending on e-business initiatives over two years? What business benefits may result?

Source: Adapted from David Rocks, "The Net as a Lifeline," *Business Week E-Biz*, October 29, 2001, pp. 16–20. © 2001 McGraw-Hill Companies. Reprinted by permission.

Cardinal Glass, Hunt Corp., and K&G: The Business Case for Supply Chain Event Management

Two-and-a-half years ago, Cardinal Glass's legacy systems were making it a weak link in one of its key customer's supply chain. The system, a hodgepodge of custom and purchased applications, caused so many errors that it was "shameful and embarrassing," says Dan Peterson, director or corporate information systems at the Minneapolis-based maker of glass products. So when the customer decided that its products required delivery on a just-in-time basis, with lead times of just hours, there was no way the existing supply chain management applications could keep up the pace.

Luckily, Cardinal found that by installing supply chain event management (SCEM) applications from Minneapolis-based HighJump Software, it could deliver products at nearly 100 percent accuracy. "We probably cut the error rate by 90 percent," Peterson says.

SCEM applications let companies see—in realtime, or as close as possible—if their existing supply chain management (SCM) systems are working. The applications are attached to an SCM server and get updates on supply chain activity through middleware connectors. Depending on preset rules and benchmarks, SCEM software can monitor SCM applications, run simulations of supply chain scenarios, automatically take control of supply chain processes or send out alerts to customers, suppliers, and company management. Anomalies, such as a discrepancy in an order, will trigger appropriate alert and order fulfillment responses, making the system more sensitive to realtime needs.

Cardinal did contemplate replacing its legacy enterprise resources planning (ERP) system, but Cardinal officials decided that they needed software that would address errors in the system on the fly, he explains—something traditional supply chain management and ERP systems wouldn't be able to do.

At Cardinal, when an order is received, inventory is checked immediately for availability. If a shortage is detected, the HighJump SCEM system will send alerts via e-mail to the customer and appropriate Cardinal managers. This speeds up the supply chain, reducing lead times, and meeting their customer responsiveness goals, says Peterson. There were bottom-line benefits, too. The new system cut by about two-thirds the amount of manpower needed to compensate for errors such as inventory erroneously being marked "in" when it wasn't there, or shipments being sent incorrectly.

The cost of SCEM software varies depending on the size of the implementation, but it typically starts in the hundreds of thousands of dollars and will "probably make you choke before you finish," says Sharon Ward, an analyst at Hurwitz Group. But firms with unpredictability in their supply chains, such as those that make consumer goods or fashion products, find SCEM products especially worth the price. That's because their greatest usefulness is their ability to respond to unplanned events and anomalies in a supply chain operation, says Ward.

One company that's relying on supply chain vigilance is Hunt Corp., a Statesville, North Carolina–based maker and distributor of office supplies and graphics products. "We constantly monitor critical success factors within the supply chain to ensure that we are meeting both our and our customers' objectives," says Ted Raiman, director of supply chain logistics at Hunt. Since 1998, the firm has relied on MFG/Pro software from QAD Inc., for procurement and supply chain automation.

"Without the capability to monitor critical supply chain processes, we could never achieve our objectives to improve productivity, lower costs, and improve service," Raiman says. Hunt is investigating attaching decision support software to its systems as well. The company relies on a few software tools that periodically capture data about days to ship, inventory turns, and purchase price variations.

Such a responsive system is key at K&G Mens Center, Inc., a high-volume clothing retailer with 63 warehouses nationwide. Before K&G started using an SCEM system, resolving problems such as ordering discrepancies could take as long as two weeks. Scott Saban, president of operations and information systems at K&G, says the system the company recently deployed can handle exceptions within 48 hours.

Using the Connected Store SCEM application from STS Systems, of Quebec, Canada, K&G monitors its receipts daily and generates flags when it detects anomalies. By flagging problems right from the store floor, the company has saved about $100,000 by not having to do emergency drop shipments. Connected Store, installed this past year, links to the company's core STS R12 merchandise purchasing system, which handles purchase orders, automatically matches invoices, and prepares the checks.

K&G can resolve almost 100 percent of problems on the spot. Saban says he expects to see a reduction of $250,000 in inventory costs and about 100 days of saved time for merchandise receiving processes in 2001.

Case Study Questions

1. What is the business value of supply chain event management systems? Are they worth their high cost?

2. Why can't present enterprise resource planning and supply chain management systems do the job done by SCEM software?

3. How could new ERP, CRM, and SCM systems work together to do the job being done by SCEM software?

Source: Adapted from Marc Songini, "Policing the Supply Chain," *Computerworld*, April 30, 2001, pp. 54, 55; and "Supply Chain Apps Target Complex Orders," *Computerworld*, October 22, 2001, p. 18. Reprinted by permission.

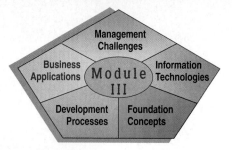

Management Challenges

Business Applications

Module III

Information Technologies

Development Processes

Foundation Concepts

Chapter 8

Electronic Commerce Systems

Chapter Highlights

Learning Objectives

After reading and studying this chapter, you should be able to:

1. Identify the major categories and trends of e-commerce applications.

2. Identify the essential processes of an e-commerce system, and give examples of how they are implemented in e-commerce applications.

3. Identify and give examples of several key factors and Web store requirements needed to succeed in e-commerce.

4. Identify and explain the business value of several types of e-commerce marketplaces.

5. Discuss the benefits and trade-offs of several e-commerce clicks and bricks alternatives.

Electronic Commerce Fundamentals

Introduction to e-Commerce

Few concepts have revolutionized business more profoundly than e-commerce. E-commerce is changing the shape of competition, the speed of action, and the nature of leadership. Simply put, the streamlining of interactions, products, and payments from customers to companies and from companies to suppliers is causing an earthquake in many boardrooms [17].

For e-business enterprises in the age of the Internet, electronic commerce is more than just buying and selling products online. Instead, it encompasses the entire online process of developing, marketing, selling, delivering, servicing, and paying for products and services transacted on internetworked, global marketplaces of customers, with the support of a worldwide network of business partners. As we will see in this chapter, electronic commerce systems rely on the resources of the Internet, intranets, extranets, and other technologies to support every step of this process.

Analyzing Orvis, Supergo, and ComfortLiving

Read the Real World Case on Orvis, Supergo, and ComfortLiving on the next page. We can learn a lot about the challenges and opportunities of retail electronic commerce from this example. See Figure 8.1.

Figure 8.1

Steven Laff, Web developer for Supergo Bike Shops, recorded a 27 percent increase in online sales after adding software to enable personalized recommendations on their website.

Source: © Zen Sekizawa.

Orvis, Supergo, and ComfortLiving: Improving e-Commerce Web Store Performance

It's been a tough 12 months for Web retailers, but that's not to say customers aren't spending money online. Online retail sales in 2001 are expected to increase by 45 percent over 2000, according to a study conducted by the Boston Consulting Group. But for e-tailers, stiffer competition—and leaner times—means you have to step up efforts to bring customers to your site and encourage them to buy. But you don't have to spend a fortune. Adding some key features can give your Web store an instant lift.

Catalog Management. Sometimes the only incentive to buy your customers need is a better view of the products in your online catalog. Just ask John Rogers, director of e-commerce for Orvis, a national outdoor outfitter headquartered in Manchester, Vermont. Although the company generates $300 million in annual sales—mostly through mail order—Rogers suspected that a dynamic online catalog feature could encourage sales of Orvis' high-end fishing gear. But he didn't want to spend a lot of time and money integrating complex 3-D imaging software into his existing Web catalog.

Point Cloud, a 3-D image-hosting service, offered to take care of that. "They had the technology to shoot the products for us and serve the images up to our customers," Roger says. "All we had to do was link to their site." With Point Cloud, Orvis.com shoppers can see selected products from any viewing angle, zooming in and out on fine details. The service offers two options: Photograph the products from several angles yourself, or let Point Cloud take care of it in about five working days. Then add the links for the 3-D product shots to your site. Point Cloud charges $8.50 per hosted image per month; it also offers a revenue-sharing pricing model.

Rogers now uses Point Cloud to showcase 70 to 100 Orvis catalog products. Though load times can be slower for shoppers with dial-up connections, Rogers isn't disappointed. "The products with the biggest lift in sales are detailed products like expensive fly reels or specialty waders where people want to see the extra features," he says.

Personalization. If you're looking to give your customers a unique experience at your e-store, Bselect by Be Free offers a personalization service at affordable prices. Setup costs around $5,000; after that you pay $5,000 per month, plus 15 cents every time someone buys a suggested sale item. Bselect works by tagging and tracking each page of your site. Frequent guests to your online store see products based on where they've been in the past and what they've bought. Bselect saves profile information by key, not a name or address. The system tracks customers anonymously, and they can delete profile details or opt out of future profiles through an online control panel (although Bselect saves customer purchase information indefinitely).

Steven Laff, Web developer for Santa Monica, California–based Supergo Bike Shops, started using Bselect about a year ago for the company's e-commerce site,

Supergo.com. Before that Laff had developed his own recommendation tool, which didn't allow him to keep track of sale items. "If you have 600 items, manually recommending something becomes a nightmare," he says. "Bselect is ingenious. It doesn't recommend the same thing twice, and if it's a consumable product, you can set it up to be recommended again. Best of all, Bselect pays for itself 5, 10, 15 times over per month." Before Bselect, e-commerce orders made up only 33 percent of Supergo's overall mail-order sales; now they make up 60 percent.

Search Management. ComfortLiving.com, a personal care products site, offered its customers more than 3,000 items to choose from—but no search button. After receiving one too many complaints, Webmaster Joe Elbaum knew something had to be done before his Emeryville, California–based company started losing customers. Atomz Search turned out to be the solution Elbaum was looking for. "We went from nothing to a full-site search in 20 minutes," he says. "It literally took just a few minutes to get up and running, including customizing the look and feel of the search results page and integrating it with our existing site."

Small businesses can afford Atomz Search, since it starts at $100 per year for a 50-page website. Large companies can shell out between $30,000 and $100,000 per year for more than 1,000 pages of e-commerce offerings.

Atomz Search's advanced options include synonym searches, automatic word endings, and the ability to push specific products or documents to a customer in response to certain key words. The system also indexes your entire website. And you can keep tabs on buying trends with a reports feature. For example, search patterns on ComfortLiving revealed that customers wanted a brand of air cleaners and filters that the site didn't carry. "As soon as we started stocking that particular line of products, they quickly became some of our best-selling items," says Elbaum.

Case Study Questions

1. What are several ways that better catalog management might increase online sales? Visit www.orvis.com and www.pointcloud.com to help you answer.

2. Which personalization features might have the greatest positive impact on sales at an e-commerce website? Visit www.supergo.com and www.befree.com to help you answer.

3. Why might a search management capability increase online customer purchases and improve Web store management? Visit www.comfortliving.com and www.atomz.com to help you answer.

Web retailers are responding to challenging economic times and greater competition by adding key capabilities to their websites to make them more attractive and encourage more purchases by online customers. For example, the Orvis Company added 3-D imaging to display high-end products in their Web catalog and increased their online sales. Supergo Bike Company added a personalized product recommendation capability and saw online sales gains of 27 percent. And ComfortLiving added a search management capability to their Web store to address customer complaints and has experienced increased sales on products added by evaluating reports of search product requests.

The Scope of e-Commerce

Figure 8.2 illustrates the range of business processes involved in the marketing, buying, selling, and servicing of products and services in companies that engage in e-commerce. Companies involved in e-commerce as either buyers or sellers rely on Internet-based technologies, and e-commerce applications and services to accomplish marketing, discovery, transaction processing, and product and customer service processes. For example, electronic commerce can include interactive marketing, ordering, payment, and customer support processes at e-commerce catalog and auction sites on the World Wide Web, extranet access of inventory databases by customers and suppliers, intranet access of customer relationship management systems by sales and customer service reps, and customer collaboration in product development via e-mail exchanges and Internet newsgroups.

Many companies today are participating in or sponsoring three basic categories of electronic commerce applications: business-to-consumer, business-to-business, and consumer-to-consumer e-commerce. Note: We will not explicitly cover business-to-government (B2G) and *e-government* applications in this text. However, many e-commerce concepts apply to such applications.

Business-to-Consumer (B2C) e-Commerce. In this form of electronic commerce, businesses must develop attractive electronic marketplaces to entice and sell products and services to consumers. For example, many companies offer e-commerce websites that provide virtual storefronts and multimedia catalogs, interactive order processing, secure electronic payment systems, and online customer support.

Business-to-Business (B2B) e-Commerce. This category of electronic commerce involves both electronic business marketplaces and direct market links

---

Figure 8.2 E-commerce involves accomplishing a range of business processes to support the electronic buying and selling of goods and services.

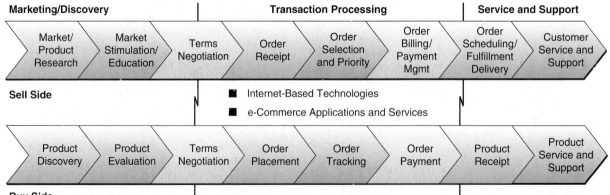

Source: Adapted from Craig Fellenstein and Ron Wood, *Exploring E-Commerce, Global E-Business, and E-Societies* (Upper Saddle River, N J Prentice-Hall, 2000) p. 28.

between businesses. For example, many companies offer secure Internet or extranet e-commerce catalog websites for their business customers and suppliers. Also very important are B2B e-commerce portals that provide auction and exchange marketplaces for businesses. Others may rely on electronic data interchange (EDI) via the Internet or extranets for computer-to-computer exchange of e-commerce documents with their larger business customers and suppliers.

Consumer-to-Consumer (C2C) e-Commerce. The huge success of online auctions like eBay, where consumers (as well as businesses) can buy and sell with each other in an auction process at an auction website, makes this e-commerce model an important e-commerce business strategy. Thus, participating in or sponsoring consumer or business auctions is an important e-commerce alternative for B2C or B2B e-commerce. Electronic personal advertising of products or services to buy or sell by consumers at electronic newspaper sites, consumer e-commerce portals, or personal websites is also an important form of C2C e-commerce.

Figure 8.3

The software components and functions of an integrated e-commerce system. This architecture would enable a business to use the Internet, intranets, and extranets to accomplish e-commerce transactions with consumers, business customers, and business partners.

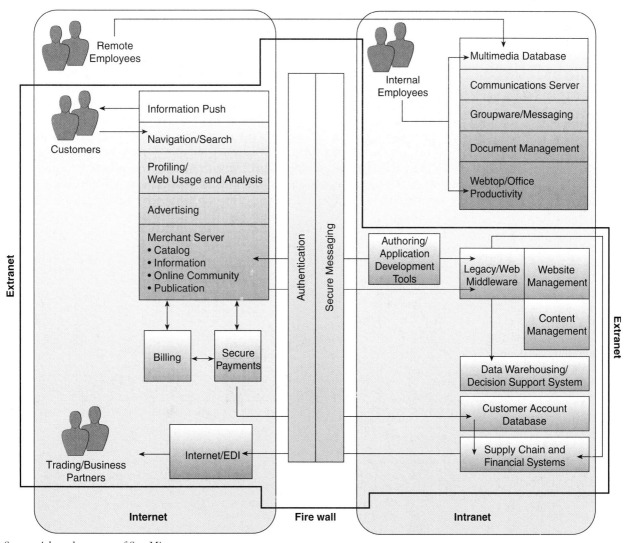

Source: Adapted courtesy of Sun Microsystems.

Electronic Commerce Technologies

What technologies are necessary for electronic commerce? The short answer is that most information technologies and Internet technologies that we discuss in this text are involved in electronic commerce systems. A more specific answer is illustrated in Figure 8.3.

Figure 8.3 illustrates an electronic commerce architecture developed by Sun Microsystems and its business partners. This architecture emphasizes that:

- The Internet, intranets, and extranets are the network infrastructure or foundation of electronic commerce.

- Customers must be provided with a range of secure information, marketing, transaction processing, and payment services.

- Trading and business partners rely on the Internet and extranets to exchange information and accomplish secure transactions, including electronic data interchange (EDI) and other supply chain and financial systems and databases.

- Company employees depend on a variety of Internet and intranet resources to communicate and collaborate in support of their EC work activities.

- IS professionals and end users can use a variety of software tools to develop and manage the content and operations of the websites and other EC resources of a company.

Figure 8.4 is an example of the technology resources required by e-commerce systems. The figure illustrates some of the hardware, software, data, and network components used by a company to provide e-commerce services.

Essential e-Commerce Processes

The essential **e-commerce processes** required for the successful operation and management of e-commerce activities are illustrated in Figure 8.5. This figure outlines the nine key components of an *e-commerce process architecture* that is the foundation of the e-commerce initiatives of many companies today [15]. We will concentrate on the role these processes play in e-commerce systems, but you should recognize that many of these components may also be used in internal, noncommerce e-business applications. An example would be an intranet-based human resource system used by a company's employees, which might use all but the catalog management and product payment processes shown in Figure 8.5. Let's take a brief look at each essential process category.

Figure 8.4

The e-commerce technology architecture of the Holt Educational Outlet (holt.com), a top retailer of educational toys with over 20,000 products online.

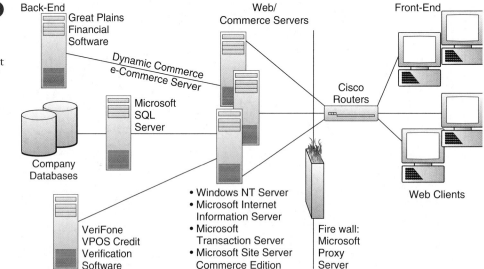

Source: Adapted from Steffano Korper and Juanita Ellis, *The E-Commerce Book: Building the E-Empire* (San Diego: Academic Press, 2000), p. 114.

Figure 8.5

This e-commerce process architecture highlights nine essential categories of e-commerce processes.

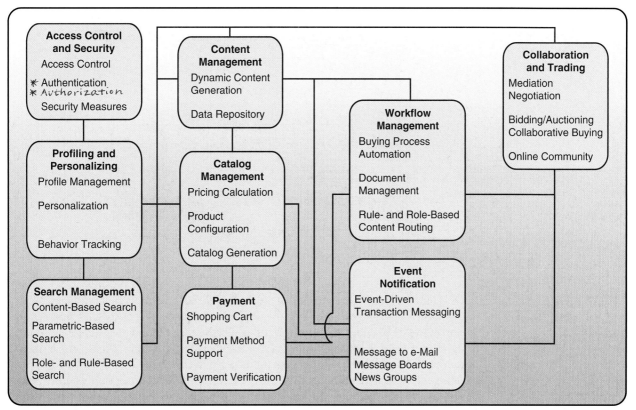

Source: Adapted from Faisal Hoque, *E-Enterprise: Business Models, Architecture, and Components* (Cambridge, UK: Cambridge University Press, 2000), p. 207.

Access Control and Security

E-commerce processes must establish mutual trust and secure access between the parties in an e-commerce transaction by authenticating users, authorizing access, and enforcing security features. For example, these processes establish that a customer and e-commerce site are who they say they are through user names and passwords, encryption keys, or digital certificates and signatures. The e-commerce site must then authorize access to only those parts of the site that an individual user needs to accomplish his or her particular transactions. Thus, you usually will be given access to all resources of an e-commerce site except for other people's accounts, restricted company data, and webmaster administration areas. Other security processes protect the resources of an e-commerce site from threats such as hacker attacks, theft of passwords or credit card numbers, and system failures. We discuss some of these security threats and features in Chapter 11.

Profiling and Personalizing

Once you have gained access to an e-commerce site, profiling processes can occur that gather data on you and your website behavior and choices, and build electronic profiles of your characteristics and preferences. User profiles are developed using profiling tools such as user registration, cookie files, website behavior tracking software, and user feedback. These profiles are then used to recognize you as an individual user and provide you with a personalized view of the contents of the site, as well as product recommendations and personalized Web advertising as part of a *one-to-one marketing* strategy. Profiling processes are also used to help authenticate your identity for account management and payment purposes, and to gather data for customer relationship management, marketing planning, and website management. Some of the ethical issues in user profiling are discussed in Chapter 11. See Figure 8.6.

Figure 8.6

E.piphany's E.4 software gathers and analyzes the behavior of visitors to a website to help companies personalize a customer's Web shopping experience.

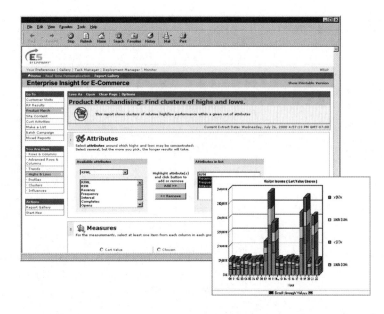

E.piphany Corporation: Personalizing e-Commerce

One of the main drawbacks of replacing brick-and-mortar commerce with e-commerce is that websites lack the personal assistance of a floor salesperson who can guide customers to appropriate products. E.piphany (www.epiphany.com) developed an E.4 software suite that is used by many e-commerce companies to reduce this problem. E.4 helps companies to personalize the online shopping experience through a realtime analysis of each customer's website inquiries and transactions. So E.4 analyzes all kinds of customer data to let companies know who their customers are and how they navigate their websites. This analysis combines Web sales data, purchase history information, and click stream data with marketing, operational, and supplier information. Also, the 16 Web-based modules of E.4 are compatible with leading database software and customer relationship management applications, so e-commerce data from E.4 can be integrated into a company's e-business processes [21].

Search Management

Efficient and effective search processes provide a top e-commerce website capability that helps customers find the specific product or service they want to evaluate or buy. E-commerce software packages can include a website search engine component, or a company may acquire a customized e-commerce search engine from search technology companies like Excite and Requisite Technology. Search engines may use a combination of search techniques, including searches based on content (a product description, for example), or by parameters (above, below, or between a range of values for multiple properties of a product, for example).

Content and Catalog Management

Content management software helps e-commerce companies develop, generate, deliver, update, and archive text data and multimedia information at e-commerce websites. For example, German media giant Bertelsmann, part owner of Barnes-andNoble.com, uses StoryServer content manager software to generate Web page templates that enable online editors from six international offices to easily publish and update book reviews and other product information, which are sold (syndicated) to other e-commerce sites.

E-commerce content frequently takes the form of multimedia catalogs of product information. So generating and managing catalog content is a major subset of content management. For example, W.W. Grainger & Co., a multibillion-dollar industrial parts distributor, uses the CenterStage catalog management software suite to retrieve data from more than 2,000 supplier databases, standardize the data and translate it into HTML or XML for Web use, and organize and enhance the data for speedy delivery as multimedia Web pages at their www.grainger.com website.

Content and catalog management software work with the profiling tools we mentioned earlier to personalize the content of Web pages seen by individual users. For example, Travelocity.com uses OnDisplay content manager software to push personalized promotional information about other travel opportunities to users while they are involved in an online travel-related transaction.

Finally, content and catalog management may be expanded to include *product configuration* processes that support Web-based customer self-service and the *mass customization* of a company's products. Configuration software helps online customers select the optimum feasible set of product features that can be included in a finished product. For example, both Dell Computer and Cisco Systems use configuration software to sell build-to-order computers and network processors to their online customers [6].

Cabletron Systems: e-Commerce Configuration	When $3 billion network equipment maker Cabletron Systems began selling its wares online, its sales reps knew full well that peddling made-to-order routers was not as simple as the mouse-click marvel of online book selling. Cabletron's big business customers—whether ISP EarthLink or motorcycle maker Harley-Davidson—did not have the technical expertise to build their own router (which can be as small as a breadbox or as large as a television, depending upon the customer, and can include hundreds of components). Worse, Cabletron's website listed thousands of parts that presented users with nearly infinite combinations, most of which would work only when assembled in a certain way.

That's why part of Cabletron's new online sales team consists of a set of complex Web-based product configuration tools made by Calico Commerce of San Jose, California. Called eSales Configuration Workbench, it prompts customers the same way a salesperson might: It walks them through product features; analyzes their needs, budgets, and time constraints; and considers only components and options compatible with existing systems. The configurator also suggests various options—different kinds of backup power, the number of parts, types of connecting wires—and generates price quotes for up to 500 concurrent online users. When a customer clicks the Buy button, the configurator generates an order that is passed on to Cabletron's back-end order fulfillment systems, which update inventory, accounting, and shipping databases.

Within a year of completing a six-month implementation of Calico's software, Cabletron saw staggering results. Some 60 percent of the businesses using its website now use the configurator. Kirk Estes, Cabletron's director of e-commerce, estimates Calico's software saved $12 million in one year by whittling down the percentage of misconfigured orders—and subsequent returns—to nearly nothing. "We think it's 99.8 percent accurate," Estes says. Order processing costs also dropped 96 percent, and customers can now place online orders in 10 to 20 minutes—a fraction of the two to three days it takes through a sales rep [5].

The role of catalog/content management and workflow management in a Web-based procurement process: the MS Market system used by Microsoft Corporation.

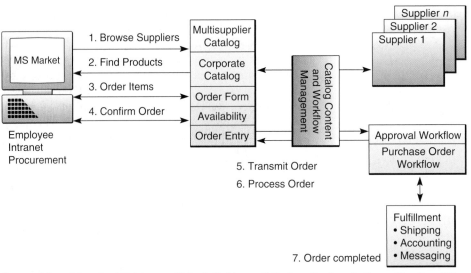

Source: Adapted from Ravi Kalakota and Marcia Robinson, *E-Business: Roadmap for Success* (Reading, MA: Addison-Wesley, 1999), p. 243. © 1999 Addison-Wesley Publishing Company, Inc. Reprinted by permission of Addison-Wesley Longman Inc.

Workflow Management

Many of the business processes in e-commerce applications can be managed and partially automated with the help of workflow management software. E-business workflow systems for enterprise collaboration help employees electronically collaborate to accomplish structured work tasks within knowledge-based business processes. Workflow management in both e-business and e-commerce depends on a *workflow software engine* containing software models of the business processes to be accomplished. The workflow models express the predefined sets of business rules, roles of stakeholders, authorization requirements, routing alternatives, databases used, and sequence of tasks required for each e-commerce process. Thus, workflow systems ensure that the proper transactions, decisions, and work activities are performed, and the correct data and documents are routed to the right employees, customers, suppliers, and other business stakeholders.

For example, Figure 8.7 illustrates the e-commerce procurement processes of the MS Market system of Microsoft Corporation. Microsoft employees use their global intranet and the catalog/content management and workflow management software engines built into MS Market to electronically purchase more than $3 billion annually of business supplies and materials from approved suppliers connected to the MS Market system by their corporate extranets [17].

Microsoft Corporation: e-Commerce Purchasing Processes

MS Market is an internal e-commerce purchasing system that works on Microsoft's intranet. MS Market drastically reduced the personnel required to manage low-cost requisitions and gives employees a quick, easy way to order materials without being burdened with paperwork and bureaucratic processes. These high-volume, low-dollar transactions represent about 70 percent of total volume, but only 3 percent of Microsoft's accounts payable. Employees were wasting time turning requisitions into purchase orders (POs) and trying to follow business rules and processes. Managers wanted to streamline this process, so the decision was made to create a requisitioning tool that would take all the controls and validations used by requisition personnel and push them onto the Web. Employees wanted an easy-to-use online form for ordering supplies that included extranet interfaces to procurement partners, such as Boise Cascade and Marriott.

How does this system work? Let's say a Microsoft employee wants a technical book. He goes to the MS Market site on Microsoft's intranet, and MS Market immediately identifies his preferences and approval code through his log-on ID. The employee selects the Barnes & Noble link, which brings up a catalog, order form, and a list of hundreds of books with titles and prices that have been negotiated between Microsoft buyers and Barnes & Noble. He selects a book, puts it in the order form, and completes the order by verifying his group's cost center number and manager's name.

The order is transmitted immediately to the supplier, cutting down on delivery time as well as accounting for the payment of the supplies. Upon submission of the order, MS Market generates an order tracking number for reference, sends notification via e-mail to the employee's manager, and transmits the order over the Internet to Barnes & Noble for fulfillment. In this case, since the purchase total is only $40, the manager's specific approval is not required. Two days later, the book arrives at the employee's office. Thus, MS Market lets employees easily order low-cost items in a controlled fashion at a low cost, without going through a complicated PO approval process [17].

Event Notification

Most e-commerce applications are *event-driven* systems that respond to a multitude of events—from a new customer's first website access, to payment and delivery processes, and to innumerable customer relationship and supply chain management activities. That is why **event notification** processes play an important role in e-commerce systems, since customers, suppliers, employees, and other stakeholders must be notified of all events that might affect their status in a transaction. Event notification software works with the workflow management software to monitor all e-commerce processes and record all relevant events, including unexpected changes or problem situations. Then it works with user-profiling software to automatically notify all involved stakeholders of important transaction events using appropriate user-preferred methods of electronic messaging, such as e-mail, newsgroup, pager, and fax communications. This includes notifying a company's management so they can monitor their employees' responsiveness to e-commerce events and customer and supplier feedback.

For example, when you purchase a product at a retail e-commerce website like Amazon.com, you automatically receive an e-mail record of your order. Then you may receive e-mail notifications of any change in product availability or shipment status, and finally, an e-mail message notifying you that your order has been shipped and is complete.

Collaboration and Trading

This major category of e-commerce processes are those that support the vital collaboration arrangements and trading services needed by customers, suppliers, and other stakeholders to accomplish e-commerce transactions. Thus, in Chapter 2, we discussed how a customer-focused e-business uses tools such as e-mail, chat systems, and discussion groups to nurture online *communities of interest* among employees and customers to enhance customer service and build customer loyalty in e-commerce. The essential collaboration among business trading partners in e-commerce may also be provided by Internet-based trading services. For example, B2B e-commerce Web portals provided by companies like Ariba and Commerce One support matchmaking, negotiation, and mediation processes among business buyers and sellers. In addition, B2B e-commerce is heavily dependent on Internet-based trading platforms and portals that provide online exchange and auctions for e-business enterprises. Therefore, the online auctions and exchange developed by companies like FreeMarkets are revolutionizing the procurement processes of many major corporations. We will discuss these and other e-commerce applications in Section II.

Electronic Payment Processes

Payment for the products and services purchased is an obvious and vital set of processes in electronic commerce transactions. But payment processes are not simple, because of the near-anonymous electronic nature of transactions taking place between the networked computer systems of buyers and sellers, and the many security issues involved. Electronic commerce payment processes are also complex because of the wide variety of debit and credit alternatives and financial institutions and intermediaries that may be part of the process. Therefore, a variety of **electronic payment systems** have evolved over time. In addition, new payment systems are being developed and tested to meet the security and technical challenges of electronic commerce over the Internet.

Web Payment Processes

Most e-commerce systems on the Web involving businesses and consumers (B2C) depend on credit card payment processes. But many B2B e-commerce systems rely on more complex payment processes based on the use of purchase orders, as was illustrated in Figure 8.7. However, both types of e-commerce typically use an electronic *shopping cart* process, which enables customers to select products from website catalog displays and put them temporarily in a virtual shopping basket for later checkout and processing. Figure 8.8 illustrates and summarizes a B2C electronic payment system with several payment alternatives.

Electronic Funds Transfer

Electronic funds transfer (EFT) systems are a major form of electronic payment systems in banking and retailing industries. EFT systems use a variety of information technologies to capture and process money and credit transfers between banks and businesses and their customers. For example, banking networks support teller terminals at all bank offices and automated teller machines (ATMs) at locations throughout the world. Banks, credit card companies, and other businesses may

---

Figure 8.8

An example of a secure electronic payment system with many payment alternatives.

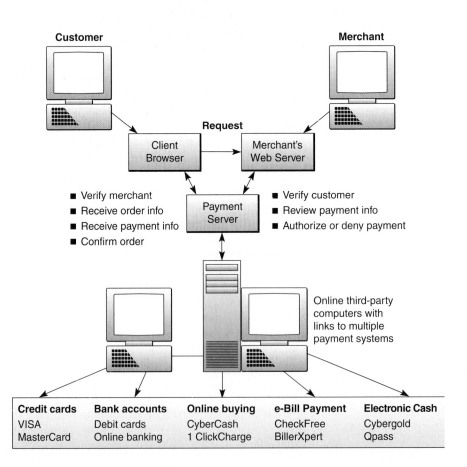

Credit cards	Bank accounts	Online buying	e-Bill Payment	Electronic Cash
VISA	Debit cards	CyberCash	CheckFree	Cybergold
MasterCard	Online banking	1 ClickCharge	BillerXpert	Qpass

support pay-by-phone and Web-based bill payment services, which enable customers to use their telephones or networked PCs to electronically pay bills. In addition, most point-of-sale terminals in retail stores are networked to bank EFT systems. This makes it possible for you to use a credit card or debit card to instantly pay for gas, groceries, or other purchases at participating retail outlets.

Micropayment Systems

Other electronic payment systems include *micropayment* systems like Cybergold and Qpass. Some of these technologies create *electronic scrip* or *digital cash*, sometimes called e-cash, for making payments that are too small for credit card transactions. Encryption and authentication techniques are used to generate strings of data that can be handled like currency for making cash payments. For example, websites like ESPNET SportsZone, Discovery Online, and *The Wall Street Journal Interactive Edition* let you chat with superstars, download video segments, or pay for business reports by using digital cash micropayment systems [1, 27].

Secure Electronic Payments

When you make an online purchase on the Internet, your credit card information is vulnerable to interception by *network sniffers*, software that easily recognizes credit card number formats. Several basic security measures are being used to solve this security problem: (1) encrypt (code and scramble) the data passing between the customer and merchant, (2) encrypt the data passing between the customer and the company authorizing the credit card transaction, or (3) take sensitive information offline. (Note: Because encryption and other security issues are discussed in Chapter 11, we will not explain how they work in this section.)

For example, many companies use the Secure Socket Layer (SSL) security method developed by Netscape Communications that automatically encrypts data passing between your Web browser and a merchant's server. However, sensitive information is still vulnerable to misuse once it's decrypted (decoded and unscrambled) and stored on a merchant's server. So a digital wallet approach such as the CyberCash payment system was developed. In this method, you add security software add-on modules to your Web browser: That enables your browser to encrypt your credit card data in such a way that only the bank that authorizes credit card transactions for the merchant gets to see it. All the merchant is told is whether your credit card transaction is approved or not.

The Secure Electronic Transaction, or SET, standard for electronic payment security extends the CyberCash digital wallet approach. In this method, EC software encrypts a digital envelope of digital certificates specifying the payment details for each transaction. SET has been agreed to by VISA, MasterCard, IBM, Microsoft, Netscape, and most other industry players. Therefore, SET is expected to eventually become the dominant standard for secure electronic payments on the Internet. However, SET has been stalled by the reluctance of companies to incur its increased hardware, software, and cost requirements [28]. See Figure 8.9.

Figure 8.9

CyberCash provides electronic payment services on the World Wide Web including a digital wallet system for secure credit card transactions.

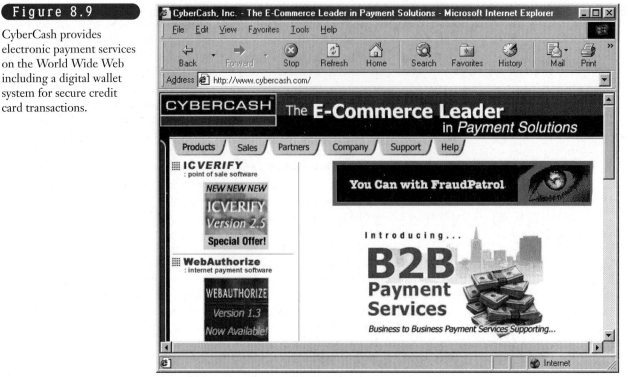

Source: Courtesy of CyberCash, © 2000.

e-Commerce Applications and Issues

e-Commerce Application Trends

E-commerce is here to stay. In the new millennium, the Web and e-commerce are key industry drivers. It's changed how many companies do business. It's created new channels for our customers, making leaders in many different industries sit up and take notice. Managers everywhere are feeling the heat: their companies are at the e-commerce crossroads and there are many ways to go [17].

Thus, e-commerce is changing how companies do business both internally and externally with their customers, suppliers, and other business partners. How companies apply e-commerce to their business is also subject to change as their managers confront a variety of e-commerce alternatives. The applications of e-commerce by many companies have gone through several major stages as e-commerce matures in the world of business. For example, e-commerce between businesses and consumers (B2C) moved from merely offering multimedia company information at corporate websites *(brochureware)*, to offering products and services at Web storefront sites via electronic catalogs and online sales transactions. B2B e-commerce, on the other hand, started with website support to help business customers serve themselves, and then moved toward automating intranet and extranet procurement systems. But before we go any further, let's look at a real world example.

Analyzing the Boeing Company

Read the Real World Case on the Boeing Company on the next page. We can learn a lot about the challenges that companies face as they develop major e-commerce marketplaces. See Figure 8.10.

The Boeing Company is implementing internal and external B2B e-commerce marketplaces aimed at significantly reducing the costs and complexity of procurement processes. For example, Boeing's SSPN online catalog marketplace is being

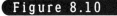

Figure 8.10

Candace Ismael is Director of Supplier Management and Procurement for the Boeing Company and leads the implementation of their online catalog marketplace for nonproduction procurement.

Source: © Brian Smale.

The Boeing Company:
Implementing Internal and External B2B Marketplaces

How hard can it be to manage the purchase of office supplies and professional services? Very hard. Just ask the Boeing Company. As the world's largest airplane manufacturer, Boeing generates millions of purchase orders and spends about $3.5 billion annually on nonproduction goods and services such as office and shop supplies, professional services, machine tools, vehicles, computers, and software.

The huge task is managed by Boeing's Shared Services Group, which was set up to handle, among other things, all nonproduction purchases after the company's acquisitions of Milwaukee-based Rockwell International Corp. and St. Louis–based McDonnell Douglas Corp. When the new organization first took over the task, it found it had to deal with 18 purchase systems across the three companies, all based on technologies from the 1960s and 70s. As a result, much of the purchase information needed to aggregate orders and negotiate volume discounts had to be collected manually and wasn't always accurate. Employees often circumvented Boeing's systems and paid full retail price, even if the vendor had already negotiated a volume discount on that item.

In 1999, the group launched an enterprise-wide Web-based system for ordering, acquiring, and paying for nonproduction items, says Candace Ismael, director of Boeing's supplier management and procurement functions. The system is the first company-wide e-procurement system deployed at Boeing; it lets users worldwide access it in the same manner. "The vision was to take all of those multiple back-end purchasing systems and create a single B2B e-procurement process and supporting system for purchasing indirect parts," says Ismael.

The Shared Service Procurement/Payables Network (SSPN, or Spin in Boeing-speak) is still being rolled out, but it already lets thousands of Boeing employees worldwide purchase and pay for office supplies from a Web page. To buy an item, a Boeing user connects to the SSPN Web page, searches an online catalog of preapproved items for which prices have already been negotiated, adds it to a shopping cart, and submits the order. User profiles determine the employee's buying authority, and orders are routed to managers for approval when necessary.

Suppliers electronically bill Boeing and are paid via electronic funds transfer directly to their banks. The system is built around Oracle's Internet Procurement software and allows for better volume discounts and supplier management, and greater efficiencies in purchasing. But Ismael says a big challenge has been managing changes brought on by the new e-procurement system. "There is a lot of resistance to change in an organization this large," Ismael says. Consequently, one of her roles has been that of change management agent getting support needed across Boeing.

And now Boeing has begun the gritty detail work of building links to its chosen online B2B marketplaces. Boeing is nine months into a two-and-a-half-year integration project with Exostar LLC, the online B2B aerospace industry marketplace being developed by a consortium of companies, including Boeing, Lockheed Martin, and Raytheon. While it undertakes that work, Exostar is building links to other marketplaces such as Enporion, a gas and energy exchange, and the regional markets operated by Deutsche Telekom AG and British Telecom PLC. "That was a major criterion for selection for us," said Kristina Erickson, Boeing's director of venture relations. "It might not be something we can take advantage of immediately, but we fully expect to take advantage of a global network once we've got all our functionality in place."

According to Erickson, Boeing has had to build a method of accessing 18 different procurement systems in order to do business with Exostar. Boeing has a polyglot of legacy procurement systems built by Baan, Oracle, and WDS Technologies, in addition to some homegrown systems. Erickson explained that the data from all 18 systems must be converted to XCBL terminology (a variant of XML created by Commerce One Inc.) and then pumped through the corporate fire wall to Exostar.

In addition, the business units in 54 locations that use the 18 procurement systems are being asked to change their rules and processes to enable a reduction to only four or five systems that will route their procurement efforts through Exostar. "That's what makes this a whole lot harder," Erickson said. "If e-business was just installing technology, it would be a whole lot easier."

But the new system will enable more suppliers to participate in the e-commerce marketplace, since Exostar will be open to any supplier with a browser, Internet connection, and security password. And different units at Boeing will be able to use the same Web interface to connect to suppliers for accounting, inventory, and shipping functions.

Case Study Questions

1. What are Boeing's major implementation challenges and business opportunities in developing its SSPN online catalog marketplace?

2. What are the business benefits and implementation challenges of Boeing's use of the Exostar B2B marketplace?

3. What strategic risks for Boeing do you see in the Exostar marketplace? Are they offset by Exostar's strategic benefits? Explain.

Source: Adapted from Pimm Fox, "Boeing Shows How XML Can Help Business," *Computerworld*, March 12, 2001, pp. 28, 29; Jalkumar Vijayan, "Procurement Network Harnesses Buying Power," *Computerworld*, June 4, 2001, p. 33; and Michael Meehan, "Boeing, UPS Push Marketplace Links to Ease Procurement," *Computerworld*, July 20, 2001, p. 15. Reprinted by permission.

used by employees worldwide to purchase office supplies and other nonproduction items. Boeing is also implementing a major project to reduce the number of company procurement systems and build Web links to Exostar, the aerospace B2B marketplace, as well as other online marketplaces. And Boeing is finding that dealing with the people and organizational issues caused by the major changes required in procurement processes is a major challenge in both e-commerce projects.

e-Commerce Trends

Figure 8.11 illustrates some of the trends taking place in the e-commerce applications that we introduced at the beginning of this section. Notice how B2C e-commerce moves from simple Web storefronts to interactive marketing capabilities that provide a personalized shopping experience for customers, and then toward a totally integrated Web store that supports a variety of customer shopping experiences. B2C e-commerce is also moving toward a self-service model where customers configure and customize the products and services they wish to buy, aided by configuration software and online customer support as needed.

B2B e-commerce participants moved quickly from self-service on the Web to configuration and customization capabilities and extranets connecting trading partners. As B2C e-commerce moves toward full-service and wide-selection retail Web portals, B2B is also trending toward the use of e-commerce portals that provide catalog, exchange, and auction markets for business customers within or across industries. Of course, both of these trends are enabled by e-business capabilities like customer relationship management and supply chain management, which are the hallmarks of the customer-focused and internetworked supply chains of the successful e-business enterprise [30].

Figure 8.11   Trends in B2C and B2B e-commerce, and the business strategies and value driving these trends.

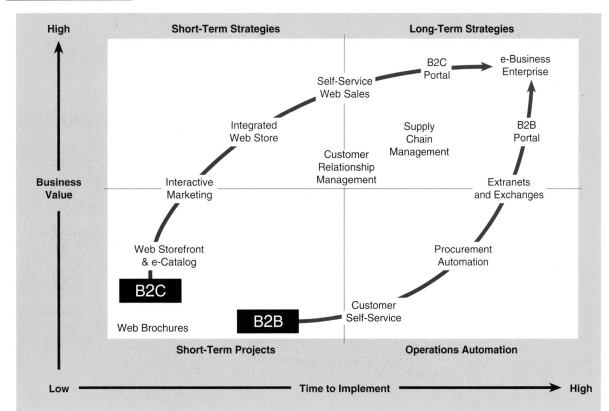

Source: Adapted from Jonathan Rosenoer, Douglas Armstrong, and J. Russell Gates, *The Clickable Corporation: Successful Strategies for Capturing the Internet Advantage* (New York: The Free Press, 1999), p. 24.

Business-to-Consumer e-Commerce

E-commerce applications that focus on the consumer share an important goal: to attract potential buyers, transact goods and services, and build customer loyalty through individual courteous treatment and engaging community features [15].

What does it take to create a successful B2C e-commerce business venture? That's the question that many are asking in the wake of the failures of many pure B2C *dotcom* companies. One obvious answer would be to create a Web business initiative that offers attractive products or services of great customer value, and whose business plan is based on realistic forecasts of profitability within the first year or two of operation—a condition that was lacking in many failed dot-coms. But such failures have not stemmed the tide of millions of businesses, both large and small, that are moving at least part of their business to the Web. So let's take a look at some essential success factors and website capabilities for companies engaged in either B2C or B2B e-commerce. Figure 8.12 provides examples of a few top-rated retail Web companies.

e-Commerce Success Factors

On the Internet, the barriers of time, distance, and form are broken down, and businesses are able to transact the sale of goods and services 24 hours a day, 7 days a week, 365 days a year with consumers all over the world. In certain cases, it is even possible to convert a physical good (CDs, packaged software, a newspaper) to a virtual good (MP3 audio, downloadable software, information in HTML format) [15].

A basic fact of Internet retailing *(e-tailing)* is that all retail websites are created equal as far as the "location, location, location" imperative of success in retailing is concerned. No site is any closer to its Web customers, and competitors offering similar goods and services may be only a mouse click away. This makes it vital that businesses find ways to build customer satisfaction, loyalty, and relationships, so customers keep coming back to their Web stores. Thus the key to e-tail success is to optimize several key factors such as selection and value, performance and service efficiency, the look and feel of the site, advertising and incentives to purchase, personal attention, community relationships, and security and reliability. Let's briefly examine each of these factors that are essential to the success of a B2C Web business. See Figure 8.13.

Top Retail Websites
● **Amazon.com www.amazon.com** Amazon.com is the exception to the rule that consumers prefer to shop "real world" retailers online. The mother of all shopping sites, Amazon features a vast selection of books, videos, DVDs, CDs, toys, kitchen items, electronics, and even home and garden goods sold to millions of loyal customers.
● **eBay www.ebay.com** The fabled auction site operates the world's biggest electronic flea market, with everything from antiques, computers, and coins to Pez dispensers and baseball cards. This site boasts billions of page views per month, and millions of items for sale in thousands of categories supported by thousands of special-interest groups.
● **Eddie Bauer www.eddiebauer.com** Sportswear titan Eddie Bauer has integrated its retail channels-store, website, and catalog. Shoppers can return an item to any Eddie Bauer store, no matter where it was purchased—a policy other merchants should follow.
● **Lands' End www.landsend.com** With several seasons as an online retailer, Lands' End is a pro at meeting shoppers' expectations. One of the best features: Specialty Shoppers. A customer service rep will help you make your selections and answer questions by phone or via a live chat.

Source: Adapted from "Tech Lifestyles: Shopping," *Technology Buyers Guide, Fortune*, Winter 2001, pp. 288–90. © 2001 Time Inc. All rights reserved.

Figure 8.13

Some of the key factors for success in e-commerce.

e-Commerce Success Factors
● **Selection and Value.** Attractive product selections, competitive prices, satisfaction guarantees, and customer support after the sale.
● **Performance and Service.** Fast, easy navigation, shopping, and purchasing, and prompt shipping and delivery.
● **Look and Feel.** Attractive Web storefront, website shopping areas, multimedia product catalog pages, and shopping features.
● **Advertising and Incentives.** Targeted Web page advertising and e-mail promotions, discounts and special offers, including advertising at affiliate sites.
● **Personal Attention.** Personal Web pages, personalized product recommendations, Web advertising and e-mail notices, and interactive support for all customers.
● **Community Relationships.** Virtual communities of customers, suppliers, company representatives, and others via newsgroups, chat rooms, and links to related sites.
● **Security and Reliability.** Security of customer information and website transactions, trustworthy product information, and reliable order fulfillment.

Selection and Value. Obviously, a business must offer Web shoppers a good selection of attractive products and services at competitive prices or they will quickly click away from a Web store. But a company's prices don't have to be the lowest on the Web if they build a reputation for high quality, guaranteed satisfaction, and top customer support while shopping and after the sale. For example, top-rated e-tailer REI.com helps you select quality outdoor gear for hiking and other activities with a "How to Choose" section, and gives a money-back guarantee on your purchases.

Performance and Service. People don't want to be kept waiting when browsing, selecting, or paying in a Web store. A site must be efficiently designed for ease of access, shopping, and buying, with sufficient server power and network capacity to support website traffic. Web shopping and customer service must also be friendly and helpful, as well as quick and easy. In addition, products offered should be available in inventory for prompt shipment to the customer.

Look and Feel. B2C sites can offer customers an attractive Web storefront, shopping areas, and multimedia product catalogs. These could range from an exciting shopping experience with audio, video, and moving graphics, to a more simple and comfortable look and feel. Thus, most retail e-commerce sites let customers browse product sections, select products, drop them into a virtual shopping cart, and go to a virtual checkout station when they are ready to pay for their order.

Advertising and Incentives. Some Web stores may advertise in traditional media, but most advertise on the Web with targeted and personalized banner ads and other Web page and e-mail promotions. Most B2C sites also offer shoppers incentives to buy and return. Typically, this means coupons, discounts, special offers, and vouchers for other Web services, sometimes with other e-tailers at cross-linked websites. Many Web stores also increase their market reach by being part of Web banner advertising exchange programs with thousand of other Web retailers.

Personal Attention. Personalizing your shopping experience encourages you to buy and make return visits. Thus, e-commerce software can automatically record details of your visits and build user profiles of you and other Web shoppers. Many sites also encourage you to register with them and fill out a personal interest profile. Then, whenever you return, you are welcomed by name or with a personal Web page, greeted with special offers, and guided to those parts of the site that you are most interested in. This *one-to-one marketing* and relationship building power is one of the major advantages of personalized Web retailing.

Community Relationships. Giving online customers with special interests a feeling of belonging to a unique group of like-minded individuals helps build customer loyalty and value. Thus, website relationship and affinity marketing programs build and promote virtual communities of customers, suppliers, company representatives, and others via a variety of Web-based collaboration tools. Examples include discussion forums or newsgroups, chat rooms, message board systems, and cross-links to related website communities.

Security and Reliability. As a customer of a successful Web store, you must feel confident that your credit card, personal information, and details of your transactions are secure from unauthorized use. You must also feel that you are dealing with a trustworthy business, whose products and other website information you can trust to be as advertised. Having your orders filled and shipped as you requested, in the time frame promised, and with good customer support are other measures of an e-tailer's reliability.

Amazon.com: Tops in B2C Retailing	Amazon (www.amazon.com) is rated as one of the biggest and best virtual retailers on the Web, though it has lost its luster with investors because it has yet to make a profit. The site is designed to speed you through the process of browsing and ordering merchandise while giving you reassuring, personal service at discount prices. For example, the search engine for finding the products you want is quick and accurate, and the ordering process easy and fast. Confirmation is quick, notifications are accurate and friendly, and delivery is prompt. Buyers are e-mailed both when their order is confirmed, as well as the day their order is shipped. The company also offers customers a complete money-back guarantee.

In creating this potential powerhouse of shopping services and offerings, Amazon.com wants to be not simply a Wal-Mart of the Web but rather a next-generation retail commerce portal. Imagine a customized site where—through a personalized shopping service and communities of other shoppers—you will not only shop easily with a trusted brand for books, videos, gifts, and more, but you will also research the features, price, and availability of millions of products from a single storefront that has Amazon's—and your—name on it.

That's what has gotten Amazon this far in its first years of business: exhaustive focus on convenience, selection, and personalization. It lived up to its billing as "Earth's Biggest Selection" by building an inventory of millions of products. It was also among the first Net stores to facilitate credit card purchases; greet customers by name and offer customized home pages; send purchase recommendations via e-mail; and number and explain each step in the purchasing process. This combination of vast selection, efficiency, discount prices, and personal service is why Amazon is frequently mentioned as the top retailer on the Web [6, 36].

Web Store Requirements

Most business-to-consumer e-commerce ventures take the form of retail business sites on the World Wide Web. Whether a huge retail Web portal like Amazon.com, or a small specialty Web retailer, the primary focus of such e-tailers is to develop, operate, and manage their websites so they become high-priority destinations for consumers who will repeatedly choose to go there to buy products and services. Thus, these websites must be able to demonstrate the key factors

Figure 8.14

These Web store requirements must be implemented by a company or its website hosting service, in order to develop a successful e-commerce business.

Developing a Web Store		
● **Build**	● **Market**	
Website design tools	Web page advertising	
Site design templates	E-mail promotions	
Custom design services	Web advertising exchanges with affiliate sites	
Website hosting	Search engine registrations	

Serving Your Customers		
● **Serve**	● **Transact**	● **Support**
Personalized Web pages	Flexible order process	Website online help
Dynamic multimedia catalog	Credit card processing	Customer service e-mail
Catalog search engine	Shipping and tax calculations	Discussion groups and chat rooms
Integrated shopping cart	E-mail order notifications	Links to related sites

Managing a Web Store		
● **Manage**	● **Operate**	● **Protect**
Website usage statistics	24x7 website hosting	User password protection
Sales and inventory reports	Online tech support	Encrypted order processing
Customer account management	Scalable network capacity	Encrypted website administration
Links to accounting system	Redundant servers and power	Network fire walls and security monitors

for e-commerce success that we have just covered. In this section, let's discuss the essential Web store requirements that you would have to implement to support a successful retail business on the Web, as summarized and illustrated in Figure 8.14.

Developing a Web Store

Before you can launch your own retail store on the Internet, you must build an e-commerce website. Many companies use simple website design software tools and predesigned templates provided by their website hosting service to construct their Web retail store. That includes building your Web storefront and product catalog Web pages, as well as tools to provide shopping cart features, process orders, handle credit card payments, and so forth. Of course, larger companies can use their own software developers or hire an outside website development contractor to build a custom-designed e-commerce site. Also, like most companies, you can contract with your ISP (Internet service provider) or a specialized Web hosting company to operate and maintain your B2C website.

Once you build your website, it must be developed as a retail Web business by marketing it in a variety of ways that attract visitors to your site and transform them into loyal Web customers. So your website should include Web page and e-mail advertising and promotions for Web visitors and customers, and Web advertising exchange programs with other Web stores. Also, you can register your Web business with its own domain name (for example, yourstore.com), as well as registering your website with the major Web search engines and directories to help Web surfers find your site more easily. In addition, you might consider affiliating as a small business partner with large Web portals like Yahoo! and Netscape, large e-tailers and auction sites like Amazon and eBay, and small business Web centers like Microsoft bCentral and Prodigy Biz.

Freemerchant and Prodigy Biz: Getting Started

Freemerchant and Prodigy Biz are examples of the many companies that help small businesses get on the Web. Freemerchant.com enables you to set up a Web store for free by choosing from nearly 60 design templates. That includes Web hosting on secure networks, shopping cart and order processing, and providing common database software for importing your product catalog data. Fee-based services include banner ad exchanges, domain and search engine registrations, and enabling product data to be listed on eBay and sales data to be exported to the Quickbooks accounting system.

Prodigybiz.com is designed to serve small e-tail businesses with a full range of Web store development services. Prodigy Biz features both free and fee-based site design and Web publishing tools, website hosting and site maintenance, full e-commerce order and credit card processing, Internet access and e-mail services, and a variety of management reports and affiliate marketing programs [34]. See Figure 8.15.

Serving Your Customers

Once your retail store is on the Web and receiving visitors, the website must help you welcome and serve them personally and efficiently so that they become loyal customers. So most e-tailers use several website tools to create user profiles, customer files, and personal Web pages and promotions that help them develop a one-to-one relationship with their customers. This includes creating incentives to encourage visitors to register, developing *Web cookie files* to automatically identify returning visitors, or contracting with website tracking companies like DoubleClick and others for software to automatically record and analyze the details of the website behavior and preferences of Web shoppers.

Of course, your website should have the look and feel of an attractive, friendly, and efficient Web store. That means having e-commerce features like a dynamically changing and updated multimedia catalog, a fast catalog search engine, and a

---

Figure 8.15

Prodigy Biz is one of many companies offering retail website development and hosting services.

Source: Courtesy of Prodigy Biz.

convenient shopping cart system that is integrated with Web shopping, promotions, payment, shipping, and customer account information. Your e-commerce order processing software should be fast and able to adjust to personalized promotions and customer options like gift handling, special discounts, credit card or other payments, and shipping and tax alternatives. Also, automatically sending your customers e-mail notices to document when orders are processed and shipped is a top customer service feature of e-tail transaction processing.

Providing customer support for your Web store is an essential website capability. So many e-tail sites offer help menus, tutorials, and lists of FAQs (frequently asked questions) to provide self-help features for Web shoppers. Of course, e-mail correspondence with customer service representatives of your Web store offers more personal assistance to customers. Establishing website discussion groups and chat rooms for your customers and store personnel to interact helps create a more personal community that can provide invaluable support to customers, as well as building customer loyalty. Providing links to related websites from your Web store can help customers find additional information and resources, as well as earning commission income from the affiliate marketing programs of other Web retailers. For example, the Amazon.com Affiliate program pays commissions of up to 15 percent for purchases made by Web shoppers clicking to their Web store from your site.

Managing a Web Store

A Web retail store must be managed as both a business and a website, and most e-commerce hosting companies offer software and services to help you do just that. For example, companies like Freemerchant, Prodigy Biz, and Verio provide their hosting clients with a variety of management reports that record and analyze Web store traffic, inventory, and sales results. Other services build customer lists for e-mail and Web page promotions, or provide customer relationship management features to help retain Web customers. Also, some e-commerce software includes links to download inventory and sales data into accounting packages like Quickbooks for bookkeeping and preparation of financial statements and reports.

Of course, Web hosting companies must enable their Web store clients to be available online twenty-four hours a day and seven days a week all year. This requires them to build or contract for sufficient network capacity to handle peak Web traffic loads, and redundant network servers and power sources to respond to system or power failures. Most hosting companies provide e-commerce software that uses passwords and encryption to protect Web store transactions and customer records, and employ network fire walls and security monitors to repel hacker attacks and other security threats. Many hosting services also offer their clients twenty-four hour tech support to help them with any technical problems that arise. We will discuss these and other e-commerce security management issues in Chapter 11.

NTT/Verio Inc.: Website Management

NTT/Verio Inc. (www.verio.com) is an example of one of the world's leading Web hosting companies. Verio provides complete software, computing, and network resources to Web hosting companies, as well as offering e-commerce development and hosting services to Web retailers. Verio also offers a Web startup and development service for small businesses called SiteMerlin (www.sitemerlin.com). Verio guarantees 99.9 percent website uptime to its e-commerce customers, with 24 × 7 server monitoring and customer support. Verio hosts more than 10,000 small and medium-sized Web businesses; has a network hosting alliance with Sun Microsystems, an Oracle Web database application service; and provides hosting services to Terra Lycos and other Web hosting companies [34].

Business-to-Business e-Commerce

Business-to-business electronic commerce is the wholesale and supply side of the commercial process, where businesses buy, sell, or trade with other businesses. B2B electronic commerce relies on many different information technologies, most of which are implemented at e-commerce websites on the World Wide Web and corporate intranets and extranets. B2B applications include electronic catalog systems, electronic trading systems such as exchange and auction portals, electronic data interchange, electronic funds transfers, and so on. All of the factors for building a successful retail website we discussed earlier also apply to wholesale websites for business-to-business electronic commerce.

In addition, many businesses are integrating their Web-based e-commerce systems with their e-business systems for supply chain management, customer relationship management, and online transaction processing, as well as to their traditional, or legacy, computer-based accounting and business information systems. This ensures that all electronic commerce activities are integrated with e-business processes and supported by up-to-date corporate inventory and other databases, which in turn are automatically updated by Web sales activities. Let's look at a successful example.

Cisco Systems: B2B Marketplace Success

The e-commerce website Cisco Connection Online enables corporate users to purchase routers, switches, and other hardware that enables customers to build high-speed information networks. Over 70 percent of Cisco's sales take place at this site.

So what has made Cisco so successful? Some would argue that its market—networking hardware—is a prime product to sell online because the customer base is composed almost entirely of IT department staffers and consultants. To some degree, this is certainly true. On the other hand, competitors initially scoffed at Cisco's efforts due to the inherent complexity of its product. However, it's difficult to dispute that Cisco has built an online store with functionality and usefulness that is a model of success in the B2B commerce world.

Cisco was able to achieve success largely due to the variety of service offerings made available throughout its purchasing process. In addition to simply providing a catalog and transaction processing facilities, Cisco includes a personalized interface for buyers, an extensive customer support section with contact information, technical documents, software updates, product configuration tools, and even online training and certification courses for Cisco hardware. Also, Cisco provides direct integration with its internal back-end systems for frequent customers, and makes software available that customers can use to design custom links to their own line-of-business software from such players as SAP America, PeopleSoft, and Oracle.

Cisco has also made a concerted effort to ensure that post-sale customer support is available to buyers of every kind. For most large corporations, this means diligent account management and dedicated support representatives to troubleshoot problems and aid in complex network design. For smaller businesses that may be installing their first routers or switches, Cisco includes recommended configurations and simple FAQs to get users up and running.

Like any mature virtual marketplace, Cisco Connection Online integrates directly with Cisco's internal applications and databases to automatically manage inventory and production. Cisco even allows vendors such as HP, PeopleSoft, and IBM to exchange design data to enable easy network configuration troubleshooting online [15].

e-Commerce Marketplaces

The latest e-commerce transaction systems are scaled and customized to allow buyers and sellers to meet in a variety of high-speed trading platforms: auctions, catalogs, and exchanges [23].

Figure 8.16

Types of e-commerce marketplaces.

e-Commerce Marketplaces
● **One to many:** Sell-side marketplaces. Host one major supplier, who dictates product catalog offerings and prices. Examples: Cisco.com and Dell.com.
● **Many to one:** Buy-side marketplaces. Attract many suppliers that flock to these exchanges to bid on the business of a major buyer like GE or AT&T.
● **Some to many:** Distribution marketplaces. Unite major suppliers who combine their product catalogs to attract a larger audience of buyers. Examples: VerticalNet and Works.com
● **Many to some:** Procurement marketplaces. Unite major buyers who combine their purchasing catalogs to attract more suppliers and thus more competition and lower prices. Examples: the auto industry's Covisint and energy industry's Pantellos.
● **Many to many:** Auction marketplaces used by many buyers and sellers that can create a variety of buyers' or sellers' auctions to dynamically optimize prices. Examples are eBay and FreeMarkets.

Source: Adapted from Edward Robinson, "Battle to the Bitter End (-to-End)," *Business2.0*, July 25, 2000, pp. 140–141.

Businesses of any size can now buy everything from chemicals to electronic components, excess electrical energy, construction materials, or paper products at business-to-business **e-commerce marketplaces.** Figure 8.16 outlines five major types of e-commerce marketplaces used by businesses today. However, many B2B **e-commerce portals** provide several types of marketplaces. Thus they may offer an electronic **catalog** shopping and ordering site for products from many suppliers in an industry. Or they may serve as an **exchange** for buying and selling via a bid-ask process, or at negotiated prices. Very popular are electronic **auction** websites for business-to-business auctions of products and services. Figure 8.17 illustrates a B2B trading system that offers exchange, auction, and reverse auction (where sellers bid for the business of a buyer) electronic markets.

Many of these B2B **e-commerce portals** are developed and hosted by third-party *market-maker* companies who serve as **infomediaries** that bring buyers and sellers together in catalog, exchange, and auction markets. Infomediaries are companies that

Figure 8.17

This is an example of a B2B e-commerce Web portal that offers exchange, auction, and reverse auction electronic markets.

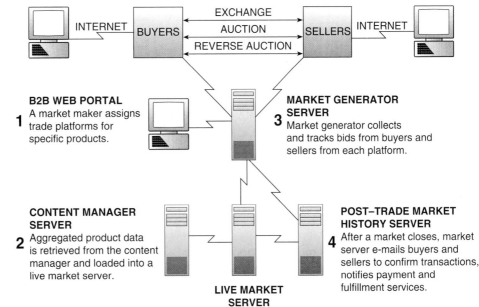

Source: Adapted from Mark Leon, "Trading Spaces," *Business 2.0*, February 2000, p. 129.

serve as intermediaries in e-business and e-commerce transactions. Examples are Ariba, Commerce One, VerticalNet, and FreeMarkets, to name a few. All provide e-commerce marketplace software products and services to power their Web portals for e-commerce transactions.

These B2B e-commerce sites make business purchasing decisions faster, simpler, and more cost effective, since companies can use Web systems to research and transact with many vendors. Business buyers get one-stop shopping and accurate purchasing information. They also get impartial advice from infomediaries that they can't get from the sites hosted by suppliers and distributors. Thus, companies can negotiate or bid for better prices from a larger pool of vendors. And of course, suppliers benefit from easy access to customers from all over the globe [23, 25]. Figure 8.18 illustrates the huge B2B procurement marketplaces formed by consortiums of major corporations in various industries to trade with their thousands of suppliers. Now, let's look at a real world example.

FreeMarkets.com: B2B e-Commerce Auctions	Auction sites like e-Steel, MetalSite, and PlasticsNet.com create lively global spot markets for standard processed materials like steel, chemicals, and plastics. On MetalSite, for example, Weirton or LTV can put sheet or rolled steel on the block anytime the market looks hungry. Buyers then enter their bids over two or three days, and the highest price wins. This is called a sellers' auction: Think of it as the business version of the familiar estate sale for rugs or antiques.

Figure 8.18   Examples of the B2B procurement marketplaces formed by major corporations in various industries.

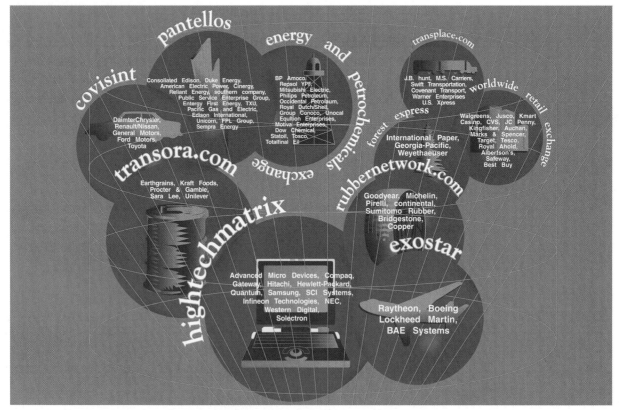

Source: Adapted from Peter Henig, "Revenge of the Bricks," *Red Herring*, August 2000, p. 123.

The FreeMarkets online auction model takes the Internet into a much bigger, far more complex kind of corporate purchase: the individually crafted parts—the motors, gears, circuit boards, and plastic casings that producers forge into their finished automobiles, washing machines, and locomotives—that are purchased on contracts typically running three or four years, and there is nothing standard about them.

However, the FreeMarkets model standardizes absolutely every item in a buyer's RFQ or "request for quotation" that documents the specifications for a part. To participate in a FreeMarkets auction, suppliers must offer not only to deliver the same part but also to do it on the same schedule, with the same payment terms, inventory arrangements, and everything else. That way each package is practically the same; plastic refrigerator shelves and automobile bumpers become almost as much a commodity as bushels of wheat. All that remains is to find the lowest price, and the best way to do that is through an auction.

The auction itself is a tense, 20-to-30-minute sweepstakes. The events are called buyers' or reverse auctions because, unlike the exchange sponsored by e-Steel, the price starts high and moves downward. Linked over the Internet, the sellers don't have to guess at their competitors' bids as they do with RFQs. They see exactly what the opposition is bidding, in real time—and how low they must go to pocket the order.

General Motors, United Technologies, Raytheon, and Quaker Oats have saved more than 15 percent on average buying parts, materials, and even services at FreeMarkets auctions. Says Kent Brittan, vice president of supply management for United Technologies: "This FreeMarkets auction idea is revolutionizing procurement as we know it" [41].

Electronic Data Interchange

Electronic data interchange (EDI) was one of the earliest forms of electronic commerce. EDI involves the electronic exchange of business transaction documents over the Internet and other networks between supply chain trading partners (organizations and their customers and suppliers). Data representing a variety of business transaction documents (such as purchase orders, invoices, requests for quotations, and shipping notices) are automatically exchanged between computers using standard document message formats. Typically, EDI software is used to convert a company's own document formats into standardized EDI formats as specified by various industry and international protocols. Thus, EDI is an example of the almost complete automation of an e-commerce supply chain process. And EDI over the Internet, using secure *virtual private networks*, is a growing B2B e-commerce application.

Formatted transaction data are transmitted over network links directly between computers, without paper documents or human intervention. Besides direct network links between the computers of trading partners, third-party services are widely used. Value-added network companies like GE Global Exchange Services and Computer Associates offer a variety of EDI services. Many EDI service providers now offer secure, lower cost EDI services over the Internet. Figure 8.19 illustrates a typical EDI system [33].

EDI is still a popular data-transmission format among major trading partners, primarily to automate repetitive transactions. It automatically tracks inventory changes; triggers orders, invoices, and other documents related to transactions; and schedules and confirms delivery and payment. By digitally integrating the supply chain, EDI streamlines processes, saves time, and increases accuracy. And by using Internet technologies, lower cost Internet-based EDI services are now available to smaller businesses [37, 39].

Figure 8.19   A typical example of electronic data interchange activities, an important form of business-to-business electronic commerce. EDI over the Internet is a major B2B e-commerce application.

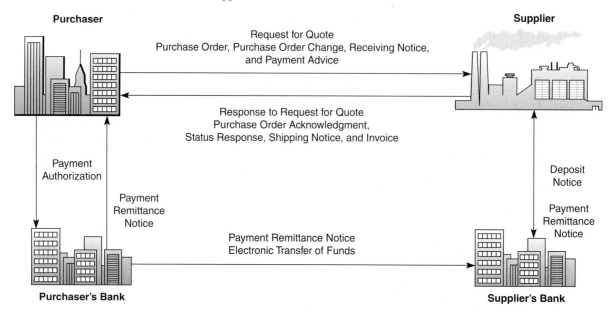

| **Telefónica's TSAI: Internet EDI** | Telefónica is Spain's largest supplier of telecommunications services, serving the Spanish-speaking and Portuguese-speaking world with affiliates in Latin America and the United States. Telefónica Serviciós Avanzados de Información (TSAI) is a subsidiary of Telefónica that handles 60 percent of Spain's electronic data interchange (EDI) traffic. TSAI's customers are supply chain trading partners—merchants, suppliers, and others involved in business supply chains from design to delivery.

To tap into the sizable market of smaller businesses that can't afford standard EDI services, TSAI offers an Internet EDI service, InfoEDI, based on Netscape ECXpert electronic commerce software. InfoEDI allows transactions to be entered and processed on the Internet, so smaller trading partners no longer have to buy and install special connections, dedicated workstations, and proprietary software. Instead, they can access the EDI network through the Internet via TSAI's Web portal.

InfoEDI's forms-based interface lets businesses connect with InfoEDI simply by using modems and Web browsers. They can then interact with the largest suppliers and retailers to send orders, issue invoices based on orders, send invoice summaries, track status of documents, and receive messages. InfoEDI also provides a product database that lists all details of trading partners' products. Once a trading relationship has been established, each partner has encrypted access to details of its own products. Because those details remain accessible on TSAI's Web server, users need enter only minimal information to create links to that data, which is then plugged in as needed [39]. |

Clicks and Bricks in e-Commerce

Companies are recognizing that success in the new economy will go to those who can execute clicks-and-mortar strategies that bridge the physical and virtual worlds. Different companies will need to follow very different paths in deciding how closely—or loosely—to integrate their Internet initiatives with their traditional operations [13].

Figure 8.20 illustrates the spectrum of alternatives and benefit trade-offs that e-business enterprises face when choosing an e-commerce "clicks and bricks" strategy. E-business

Figure 8.20 Companies have a spectrum of alternatives and benefits trade-offs when deciding upon an integrated or separate e-commerce business.

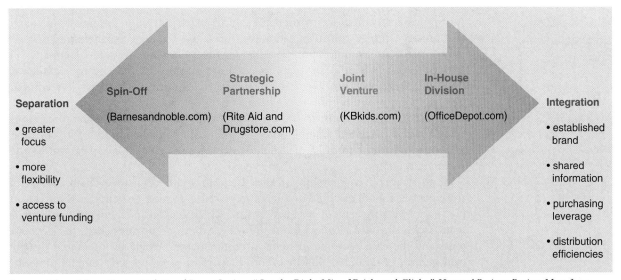

Source: Adapted from Ranjay Gulati and Jason Garino, "Get the Right Mix of Bricks and Clicks," *Harvard Business Review*, May–June 2000, p. 110.

managers must answer this question: Should we integrate our e-commerce virtual business operations with our traditional physical business operations, or keep them separate? As Figure 8.20 shows, companies have been implementing a range of integration/separation strategies and made key benefits trade-offs in answering that question. Let's take a look at several alternatives [13].

e-Commerce Integration

The Internet is just another channel that gets plugged into the business architecture [13].

So says CIO Bill Seltzer of office supply retailer Office Depot, which fully integrates their OfficeDepot.com e-commerce venture into their traditional business operations. Thus, Office Depot is a prime example of why many companies have chosen integrated clicks and bricks strategies, where their e-commerce business is integrated in some major ways into the traditional business operations of a company. The business case for such strategies rests on:

- Capitalizing on any unique strategic capabilities that may exist in a company's traditional business operations that could be used to support an e-commerce business.

- Gaining several strategic benefits of integrating e-commerce into a company's traditional business; such as the sharing of established brands and key business information, and joint buying power and distribution efficiencies.

For example, Office Depot already had a successful catalog sales business with a professional call center and a fleet of over 2,000 delivery trucks. Its 1,825 stores and 30 warehouses were networked by a sophisticated information system that provided complete customer, vendor, order, and product inventory data in real time. These business resources made an invaluable foundation for coordinating Office Depot's e-commerce activities and customer services with its catalog business and physical stores. Thus, customers can shop at OfficeDepot.com at their home or business, or at in-store kiosks. Then they can choose to pick up their purchases at the stores or have them delivered. In addition, the integration of Web-enabled e-commerce applications within Office Depot's traditional store and catalog operations has helped to increase the traffic at their physical stores and improved the catalog operation's productivity and average order size.

Other Clicks and Bricks Strategies

As Figure 8.20 illustrates, other clicks and bricks strategies range from partial e-commerce integration using joint ventures and strategic partnerships, to complete separation via the spin-off of an independent e-commerce company. For example, Kbkids.com is an e-commerce joint venture created by toy retailer KB Toys and BrainPlay.com, formerly an e-tailer of children's products. The company is 80 percent owned by KB Toys, but has independent management teams and separate distribution systems. However, Kbkids.com has successfully capitalized on the shared brand name and buying power of KB Toys, and the ability of its customers to return purchases to over 1,300 KB Toys stores which also heavily promote their e-commerce site.

The strategic partnership of the Rite-Aid retail drugstore chain and Drugstore.com is a good example of a less integrated e-commerce venture. Rite-Aid only owns about 25 percent of Drugstore.com, which has an independent management team and a separate business brand. However, both companies share the decreased costs and increased revenue benefits of joint buying power, an integrated distribution center, co-branded pharmacy products, and joint prescription fulfillment at Rite-Aid stores.

Finally, let's look at an example of the benefits and challenges of a completely separate clicks and bricks strategy. Barnesandnoble.com was created as an independent e-commerce company that was spun off by the Barnes & Noble book retail chain. This enabled it to gain several hundred million dollars in venture capital funding, create an entrepreneurial culture, attract quality management, maintain a high degree of business flexibility, and accelerate decision making. But the book e-retailer has done poorly since its founding, and has failed to gain market share from Amazon.com, its leading competitor. Many e-commerce analysts say that the failure of Barnes & Noble to integrate some of the marketing and operations of Barnesandnoble.com within their thousands of bookstores forfeited a strategic business opportunity in e-commerce.

The previous examples emphasize that there is no universal clicks and bricks e-commerce strategy for every company, industry, or type of business. Both e-commerce integration and separation have major business benefits and shortcomings. Thus, deciding on a clicks and bricks strategy depends heavily on whether or not a company's unique business operations provide strategic capabilities and resources to successfully support integration with an e-commerce venture. As these examples show, most companies are implementing some measure of clicks and bricks integration, because "the benefits of integration are almost always too great to abandon entirely" [13].

Summary

- **Electronic Commerce.** Electronic commerce encompasses the entire online process of developing, marketing, selling, delivering, servicing, and paying for products and services. The Internet and related technologies and e-commerce websites on the World Wide Web and corporate intranets and extranets serve as the business and technology platform for e-commerce marketplaces for consumers and businesses in the basic categories of business-to-consumer (B2C), business-to-business (B2B), and consumer-to-consumer (C2C) e-commerce. The essential processes that should be implemented in all e-commerce applications—access control and security, personalizing and profiling, search management, content management, catalog management, payment systems, workflow management, event notification, and collaboration and trading—are summarized in Figure 8.5.

- **e-Commerce Issues.** Many e-business enterprises are moving toward offering full-service B2C and B2B e-commerce portals supported by integrated customer-focused processes and internetworked supply chains as illustrated in Figure 8.11. In addition, e-business companies must evaluate a variety of e-commerce integration or separation alternatives and benefit trade-offs when choosing a clicks and bricks strategy, as summarized in Figure 8.20.

- **B2C e-Commerce.** Businesses typically sell products and services to consumers at e-commerce websites that provide attractive Web pages, multimedia catalogs, interactive order processing, secure electronic payment systems, and online customer support. However, successful e-tailers build customer satisfaction and loyalty by optimizing factors outlined in Figure 8.13, such as selection and value, performance and service efficiency, the look and feel of the site, advertising and incentives to purchase, personal attention, community relationships, and security and reliability. In addition, a Web store has several key business requirements, including building and marketing a Web business, serving and supporting customers, and managing a Web store, as summarized in Figure 8.14.

- **B2B e-Commerce.** Business-to-business applications of e-commerce involve electronic catalog, exchange, and auction marketplaces that use Internet, intranet, and extranet websites and portals to unite buyers and sellers, as summarized in Figure 8.16 and illustrated in Figure 8.17. Many B2B e-commerce portals are developed and operated for a variety of industries by third-party market-maker companies called infomediaries, which may represent consortiums of major corporations. B2B e-commerce also includes applications like electronic data interchange, which automates the exchange of business documents on the Internet.

Key Terms and Concepts

These are the key terms and concepts of this chapter. The page number of their first explanation is in parentheses.

1. Clicks and bricks alternatives (282)
2. E-commerce marketplaces (277)
   - *a.* Auction (277)
   - *b.* Catalog (277)
   - *c.* Exchange (277)
   - *d.* Portal (277)
3. E-commerce success factors (269)
4. E-commerce technologies (258)
5. Electronic commerce (256)

   - *a.* Business-to-business (257)
   - *b.* Business-to-consumer (256)
   - *c.* Consumer-to-consumer (257)
6. Electronic data interchange (279)
7. Electronic funds transfer (264)
8. Essential e-commerce processes (258)
   - *a.* Access control and security (259)
   - *b.* Catalog management (260)
   - *c.* Collaboration and trading (263)

   - *d.* Content management (260)
   - *e.* Electronic payment systems (264)
   - *f.* Event notification (263)
   - *g.* Profiling and personalizing (259)
   - *h.* Search management (260)
   - *i.* Workflow management (262)
9. Infomediaries (277)
10. Trends in e-commerce (267)
11. Web store requirements (275)

Review Quiz

Match one of the key terms and concepts listed previously with one of the brief examples or definitions that follow. Try to find the best fit for the answers that seem to fit more than one term or concept. Defend your choices.

_____ 1. The online process of developing, marketing, selling, delivering, servicing, and paying for products and services.

_____ 2. Business selling to consumers at retail Web stores is an example.

_____ 3. Using an e-commerce portal for auctions by business customers and their suppliers is an example.

_____ 4. Using an e-commerce website for auctions among consumers is an example.

_____ 5. E-commerce depends on the Internet and the World Wide Web, and on other networks of browser-equipped client/server systems and hypermedia databases.

_____ 6. E-commerce applications must implement several major categories of interrelated processes such as search management and catalog management.

_____ 7. Helps to establish mutual trust between you and an e-tailer at an e-commerce site.

_____ 8. Tracks your website behavior to provide you with an individualized Web store experience.

_____ 9. Develops, generates, delivers, and updates information to you at a website.

_____ 10. Ensures that proper e-commerce transactions, decisions, and activities are performed to better serve you.

_____ 11. Sends you an e-mail when what you ordered at an e-commerce site has been shipped.

_____ 12. Includes matchmaking, negotiation, and mediation processes among buyers and sellers.

_____ 13. Companies that serve as intermediaries in e-commerce transactions.

_____ 14. A website for e-commerce transactions.

_____ 15. An e-commerce marketplace that may provide catalog, exchange, or auction service for businesses or consumers.

_____ 16. Buyers bidding for the business of a seller.

_____ 17. Marketplace for bid (buy) and ask (sell) transactions.

_____ 18. The most widely used type of marketplace in B2C e-commerce.

_____ 19. The exchange of business documents between the networked computers of business partners.

_____ 20. The processing of money and credit transfers between businesses and financial institutions.

_____ 21. Ways to provide efficient, convenient, and secure payments in e-commerce.

_____ 22. E-businesses are increasingly developing full-service B2C and B2B e-commerce portals.

_____ 23. E-businesses can evaluate and choose from several e-commerce integration alternatives.

_____ 24. Successful e-tailers build customer satisfaction and loyalty in several key ways.

_____ 25. Successful e-commerce ventures must build, market, and manage their Web businesses while serving their customers.

Discussion Questions

1. Most businesses should engage in electronic commerce on the Internet. Do you agree or disagree with this statement? Explain your position.

2. Are you interested in owning, managing, or working for a business that is primarily engaged in electronic commerce on the Internet? Explain your position.

3. Refer to the Real World Case on Orvis, Supergo, and ComfortLiving in the chapter. What other website capabilities might help increase customer purchases at a Web store? Explain.

4. Why do you think there have been so many business failures among "dot-com" companies that were devoted only to retail e-commerce?

5. Do the e-commerce success factors listed in Figure 8.13 guarantee success for an e-commerce business venture? Give a few examples of what else could go wrong and how you would confront such challenges.

6. If personalizing a customer's website experience is a key success factor, then electronic profiling processes to track visitor website behavior are necessary. Do you agree or disagree with this statement? Explain your position.

7. All corporate procurement should be accomplished in e-commerce auction marketplaces, instead of using B2B websites that feature fixed-price catalogs or negotiated prices. Explain you position on this proposal.

8. Refer to the Real World Case on the Boeing Company in the chapter. When should a company build its own e-marketplace? Join an industry consortium e-marketplace? Use such e-marketplaces?

9. If you were starting an e-commerce Web store, which of the business requirements summarized in Figure 8.14 would you primarily do yourself, and which would you outsource to a Web development or hosting company? Why?

10. Which of the e-commerce clicks and bricks alternatives illustrated in Figure 8.20 would you recommend to Barnes & Noble? Amazon.com? Wal-Mart? Any business? Explain your position.

Application Exercises

Complete the following exercises as individual or group projects that apply chapter concepts to real world business situations.

1. bCentral.com: Small Business e-Commerce Portals

On the net, small businesses have become big news. And a really big business, Microsoft, wants a piece of the action. The company's bCentral Web portal (www.bcentral.com) is one of many sites offering advice and services for small businesses moving online. Most features, whether free or paid, are what you'd expect: lots of links and information along the lines established by Excite's Work.com, and other competitors like ECongo.com or GoBizGo.com. BCentral, however, stands out for its affordable advertising and marketing services. See Figure 8.21.

One bCentral program allows you to put banner ads on other sites in exchange for commissions from click-throughs and sales. As on other sites, a banner ad exchange program lets you place one ad on a member site in exchange for displaying two ads on your own. For as little as $20 a month, you can buy a marketing package that includes ads on sites such as Yahoo and Excite, and get help with direct e-mail campaigns, as well as track all activities on your personal "my business" page.

a. Check out bCentral and the other e-commerce portals mentioned. Identify several benefits and limitations for a business using their websites.

b. Which is your favorite. Why?

c. Which site would you recommend or use to help a small business wanting to get into e-commerce? Why?

Source: Adapted from Anush Yegazarian, "BCentral.com Puts Your Business on the Web," *PC World*, December 1999, p. 64.

2. Ford, Microsoft, GM, and Others: e-Commerce Websites for Car Buying

Ford and Microsoft—leaders in their respective industries—have forged an alliance that may have a big impact on the future of online car buying. Customers will be able to configure the car of their dreams on Microsoft's CarPoints website. While the giants share the spotlight, other online car sellers have begun to offer similar innovations. See Figure 8.22.

For now, the majority of car buyers are still using the Internet as a place to research rather than buy. Most auto sites simply put consumers in touch with a local dealer, where they test drive a vehicle and negotiate a price. Autobytel.com of Irvine, Calif., for example, has been referring buyers to new and used car dealers since 1995, as well as offering online financing and insurance. General Motors' BuyPower site provides access to a vast inventory of cars, though shoppers still have to go to a dealer to close the sale.

The Microsoft-Ford alliance will make consumers less dependent on what cars a dealer has on the lot. At CarPoint and Ford.com, buyers can customize a car—

Figure 8.21

Microsoft's bCentral is a small business e-commerce portal.

Source: Courtesy of Microsoft Corporation.

Figure 8.22

Some of the top e-commerce websites for car buying and researching.

Top Car Buying Websites
● **Autobytel.com**   www.autobytel.com Enter make and model, and a local dealer will contact you with a price offer. Home delivery is an option.
● **AutoNation**   www.autonation.com Every make and model available, as well as financing and insurance information, home delivery, and test drives.
● **carOrder.com**   www.carorder.com Configure, price, and directly order a car. If no partner dealership has it, the manufacturer will build it.
● **Microsoft CarPoint**   www.carpoint.com Auto reviews, detailed vehicle specifications, safety ratings, and buying services for new and used cars, including customizing your very own Ford.
● **cars.com**   www.cars.com Research tools include automotive reviews, model reports, dealer locators, and financing information.
● **CarsDirect.com**   www.carsdirect.com Research price and design, then order your car. CarsDirect will deliver it to your home—wrapped, if you like, in a bow.
● **Edmunds.com**   www.edmunds.com For an objective opinion, Edmunds.com provides reviews, safety updates, and rebate news for car buyers.
● **GM BuyPower**   www.gmbuypower.com With access to nearly 6,000 GM dealerships, car shoppers can get a price quote, schedule a test drive, and buy.

any car as long as it's a Ford—by selecting trim, paint color, and other options before purchase. Buyers will still pick up and pay for the cars at local dealerships.

   a. Check out several of the websites shown in Figure 8.22. Evaluate them based on ease of use, response times, relevance of information provided, and other criteria you feel are important. Don't forget the classic: "Did they make you want to buy?"

   b. Which sites would you use or recommend if you or a friend actually wanted to buy a car? Why?

Source: Adapted from "E-Commerce Cars," in Technology Review, *Fortune*, Winter 2000, p. 42. © 2000 Time Inc. All rights reserved.

3. Comparing e-Commerce Sites

In this exercise you will experiment with electronic shopping and compare alternative electronic commerce sites. First you will need to select a category of product widely available on the Web, such as books, CDs, toys, etcetera. Next select five specific products to price on the Internet, e.g., five specific CDs you might be interested in buying. Search three prominent electronic commerce sites selling this type of product and record the price charged for each product by each site.

   a. Using a spreadsheet record a set of information similar to that shown below for each product. (Categories describing the product will vary depending upon the type of product you select—CDs might require the title of the CD and the performer[s], while toys or similar products would require the name of the product and its description.)

   b. For each product rank each company based on the price charged. Give a rating of 1 for the lowest price and 3 for the highest and split the ratings for ties—two sites tying for 1st and 2nd lowest price would each receive a 1.5. If a site does not have one of the products available for sale, give that site a rating of 4 for that product. Add the ratings across your products to produce an overall price/availability rating for each site.

Title of Book	Author	Price at: Site A	Site B	Site C	Rating A	B	C
The Return of Little Big Man	Berger, T.	$15.00	$16.95	$14.50	2	3	1
Learning Perl/Tk	Walsh, N. & Mui, L.	$26.36	$25.95	$25.95	3	1.5	1.5
Business at the Speed of Thought	Gates, W.	$21.00	$22.95	$21.00	1.5	3	1.5
Murders for the Holidays	Smith, G.		$8.25	$7.95	4	2	1
Design for Dullards	Jones	$17.95	$18.50	$18.50	1	2.5	3
Sum of ratings (low score represents most favorable rating)					11.5	12	8

c. Based on your experience with these sites rate them on their ease of use, completeness of information, and order-filling and shipping options. As in part B, give a rating of 1 to the site you feel is best in each category, a 2 to the second best and a 3 to the poorest site.

d. Prepare a set of PowerPoint slides or similar presentation materials summarizing the key results and including an overall assessment of the sites you compared.

4. Evaluating the Market for B2C Electronic Commerce

In assessing the potential for business-to-consumer (B2C), electronic commerce, it is important to know how many people are using the Internet for business transactions and what segments of the population are using the Internet in this manner. In August of 2000 the U.S. Census Bureau asked a number of questions about Internet use as a part of its monthly Current Population Survey. This survey is administered to over 100,000 individuals and its results are used to create projected rates of use for the full population. Among the questions was one that asked each respondent whether they used the Internet to shop, to pay bills, or for other commercial purposes. A number of general demographic characteristics, such as age, education level, and household income level are also gathered for each respondent.

The sample table below shows summary results for different education levels. Data showing the distribution of Internet use for shopping across age categories and levels of family income have also been collected from this survey data and are available as a download file for this application exercise in the website for this textbook. The textbook website is www.mhhe.com/business/mis/obrien/obrien11e/index.html. Click on downloads under the student resources section of that page.

a. Download the initial spreadsheet file for this exercise and modify it to include percentage use calculations for each age, education level, and income category.

b. Create appropriate graphs to illustrate how the distribution of use of the Internet for shopping varies across age, income, and education level categories.

c. Write a short memorandum to your instructor summarizing your results and describing their implications for a Web-based retailer that is designing a marketing strategy.

| | Have Used Internet to Shop / Pay Bills | | % Using Internet to |
Education Level	**Yes**	**No**	**Shop / Pay Bills**
Less than High School	598824	32354711	1.8%
High School Grad	5104952	60930000	7.7%
Some College No Degree	6613400	32290000	17.0%
Associate Degree	7840540	38855612	16.8%
Bachelors Degree	9581979	22830000	29.6%
Masters Degree or Higher	5196040	10280934	33.6%

Citigroup and Deere & Co.:
Moving from Failure to Success in e-Commerce

Companies short on patience and shorter on cash are stepping back and trying to figure out what has worked and what hasn't in the e-commerce world. Executives are demanding to see proof of future returns before deciding to keep projects going. Top management wants Web initiatives tied directly to core business goals, such as better relations with customers and more emphasis on brand-building. "People are going back to two things: What is the strategic rationale for getting into this, and what is the return on investment?" says Tim Byrne, a vice president at Mercer Management Consulting.

Two companies have spent considerable time finding this out. Their sagas hold lessons for any business now struggling to untangle its snarl of websites.

Citigroup. Few companies blew more money trying to build independent e-commerce divisions than Citigroup, parent company of Citibank, Salomon Smith Barney, and Travelers Insurance. In 1997, it launched e-Citi with high hopes and a big task. E-Citi's job was to keep all of Citigroup on its toes—partly by competing with the very bank, credit card company, and other businesses that made Citigroup a $230 billion giant. There was to be an e-Citibank called Citi.f/i and a financial portal called Finance.com. The e-Citi unit soon had 1,600 employees and more than 100 U.S. websites. The idea: to cannibalize your business before someone else did.

The only thing e-Citi gobbled was money. Citigroup's e-commerce effort lost over $1 billion between 1998 and 2000. In online banking, for example, Citigroup was so determined to make Citi.f/i an independent operation that customers of the online bank couldn't use Citibank branches. That turned off depositors. The online bank drew 30,000 accounts versus 146 million for the rest of Citigroup's banking operation. By March 2000, word came down from Citigroup Chairman Sandy Weill: E-commerce initiatives must be part of the existing business, not self-appointed upstarts trying to overturn them. "At the beginning of 2000, people were dreaming that you could take e-Citi public," says Deryck C. Maughan, Citigroup's vice-chairman. "I looked very carefully and asked, could it make a profit? Not in our lifetime."

Still, Citigroup wanted to keep e-commerce innovation humming. So last year, the company formed an Internet Operating Group of top execs to help Citigroup units share e-business technology and to ensure that they all have a common look and feel.

A year later, the results are easy to see. The number of online customers are up 80 percent because Citibank and Citi's credit card operations are pushing Web services themselves, instead of leaving that mostly to e-Citi. Citigroup now serves 10 million customers online. E-Citi has scaled back to only 100 people, who implement projects the operating groups propose. The 100 websites have been

trimmed to 38. The reported loss for online efforts in the first half of this year was down 41 percent, to $67 million, from $114 million a year ago. And counting savings from moving procurement, human resources, and other back-office functions online, Citigroup says e-business systems will cut $1 billion off annual costs by next year. "I promise you, we are going to be saving a lot more than we are spending," Maughan pledges.

Deere & Co. When the e-commerce craze hit in the mid-1990s, managers at equipment-maker Deere & Co. jumped into the Internet like everyone else. For example, the 13 major e-commerce initiatives that just one division put up, were narrowly focused with overlapping missions. Three websites focused on used equipment alone: one to list it, one to sell it through an online marketplace, and one to support used equipment dealers. The sites targeted Deere's largely Web-allergic dealers, not customers who bought Deere products and might save time by locating parts or seeking repair know-how online.

Two years ago, with the sites developing little revenue, Deere hired consultants to advise the company on overall e-commerce strategy. By the end of 2000, a plan was in place: The $13 billion company created an e-business group to oversee e-commerce initiatives for its financing arm and its equipment division targeting farmers, consumers, and construction companies. Deere would create one website with areas for each customer group, and it would enable customers to search for parts or information about equipment online. The site offers "a new set of Web tools that enables Deere to provide information to help everyone's day-to-day business," says Kirk Siefkas, Deere's chief information officer.

Thus by centralizing everything at deere.com, Deere not only reasserted control over its business, but also is using the Web to make life a lot easier for its 4,000 independent dealers and their customers.

Case Study Questions

1. What is Citigroup doing differently to change from an e-commerce failure to a success? What else should they be doing in e-commerce? Visit www.citionthenet.com to help you answer.

2. How is Deere moving from failure to success in e-commerce? What else should they do to improve their e-commerce performance? Visit www.deere.com to help you answer.

3. What are several lessons that you learned from this case that can be applied to help any business be more successful in its e-commerce efforts?

Source: Adapted from Faith Keenan and Timothy Mullaney, "Let's Get Back to Basics," *Business Week e.biz*, October 29, 2001, pp. 26–28. © 2001 McGraw Hill Companies. Reprinted by permission.

Covisint, Johnson Controls, and Dana Corp.: Challenges of B2B e-Commerce Marketplaces

In just about every industry—from automobile manufacturing to chemical production—electronic marketplaces have been created to handle the buying and selling of goods and services between manufacturers and suppliers. One common bond that unites these B2B e-commerce markets is the hope that the automation of exchange processes will dramatically cut time, cost, and waste. But while information technology is a key enabler behind the scenes, one of the biggest challenges online e-market creators face is translating paper-based processes to more efficient, electronic approaches that support strategic relationships with their suppliers, customers, and even competitors.

A prime example of that is Covisint LLC, a business-to-business e-marketplace created by Ford Motor, General Motors, and DaimlerChrysler in February 2000. The automotive exchange could potentially handle more than $240 billion in annual procurements of raw materials and vehicle parts by these manufacturers alone.

Detroit-based GM plans to reduce the average cost of processing a purchase order from $100 to $10 by using Covisint. The world's largest automaker spends more than $80 billion in procurements each year, so even a minor improvement in how these activities are handled could save the company billions.

Most of the big automotive suppliers acknowledge that they'll work with Covisint, but that hasn't stopped them from creating e-marketplaces of their own. For example, Johnson Controls, Inc., a manufacturer of car parts and environmental systems in Milwaukee, launched a design and collaboration exchange for its 600 suppliers in March 2001.

Mike Suman, group vice president for e-business and marketing at Johnson Controls, says the company needed to replace its homegrown product development software with a B2B exchange that will address the bidding process with suppliers and the management of design collaboration. E-commerce software from MatrixOne will form the bulk of the technology infrastructure for the e-marketplace.

Johnson Controls generated $6.8 billion in revenue last year—or 40 percent of its $16.14 billion in total sales—from contracts to build car interiors, seats, and batteries for the Big Three. But Suman says the company also works with nonautomotive customers, and other automakers like Volkswagen AG in Germany, that don't plan to join Covisint.

Dana Corporation is another major automotive supplier that's building a private e-marketplace. Officials say Dana is building its own exchange to handle purchasing transactions with its 86,000 suppliers. But the Toledo, Ohio–based driveshaft and piston ring maker, which drummed up one-third of its $13 billion-plus revenue from sales to Ford and DaimlerChrysler, will also work with Covisint.

And Covisint is trying to get its act together by signing a critical deal with webMethods, Inc., to integrate its growing list of technology products and platforms. Covisint is creating a central e-commerce hub that links to its diverse application set and provides a single "on-ramp" to suppliers, said Dan Skrbina, lead integration architect at the Southfield, Michigan–based business-to-business procurement exchange.

Once that has been accomplished, suppliers should be able to access Covisint's internal applications, such as Commerce One's procurement system and Oracle's enterprise resource planning (ERP) system as well as project development tools, product visualization tools, and supply chain execution software from other vendors.

Still, that might be too little, too late. Dan Garretson, an analyst at Forrester Research, said Covisint's ongoing integration woes and limited service offerings spell trouble for the fledgling exchange. "They've been in existence for a year and a half but they have no real product offerings other than auctions," he said. "As a result a lot of projects being conducted by the automakers are going on in parallel, which reduces the critical role that Covisint will play."

For example, DaimlerChrysler is rolling out an Advanced Product Quality Planning (APQP) business system from Powerway, Inc., to 1,000 of its suppliers without waiting for Covisint to develop such a system. The Powerway system is meant to provide the automaker's suppliers with extranet-based access to an analysis of the complex and constantly changing APQP requirements for new parts. However, at DaimlerChrysler's urging, Covisint also struck a deal to partner with Powerway.

Covisint also recently won a key contract with Delphi Automotive Systems Corp. to build a supplier B2B portal for the GM parts maker. Thus, rather than integrate its applications with those of suppliers and other vendors, Covisint must offer a set of mission-critical applications of its own, which is something that is lacking, analysts said. "The question remains whether Covisint will have the time and resources to create compelling applications before its automaker partners get tired of waiting, and do critical e-commerce stuff on their own," said Kevin Prouty, an analyst at AMR Research.

Case Study Questions

1. What do the automakers that founded Covisint hope to gain from this e-marketplace? Are such gains feasible? Why or why not?

2. Why are major suppliers to the auto industry like Johnson Controls and Dana Corporation establishing their own e-marketplaces instead of working through Covisint? Is this the best approach? Explain.

3. What must Covisint do to succeed as an e-marketplace for the auto industry? Visit www.covisint.com to help you answer.

Source: Adapted from Lee Gladwin, "E-Marketplaces," *Computerworld*, February 12, 2001, p. 45; and "Covisint Focuses on Tech Integration," *Computerworld*, July 2, 2001, p. 10. Reprinted by permission.

Management
Challenges

Business
Applications

Module
III

Information
Technologies

Development
Processes

Foundation
Concepts

Chapter 9

Decision Support Systems

Chapter Highlights

Learning Objectives

After reading and studying this chapter, you should be able to:

1. Identify the changes taking place in the form and use of decision support in e-business enterprises.

2. Identify the role and reporting alternatives of management information systems.

3. Describe how online analytical processing can meet key information needs of managers.

4. Explain the decision support system concept and how it differs from traditional management information systems.

5. Explain how the following information systems can support the information needs of executives, managers, and business professionals:

   a. Executive information systems

   b. Enterprise information portals

   c. Enterprise knowledge portals

6. Identify how neural networks, fuzzy logic, genetic algorithms, virtual reality, and intelligent agents can be used in business.

7. Give examples of several ways expert systems can be used in business decision-making situations.

Decision Support in e-Business

e-Business and Decision Support

Conventional wisdom says knowledge is power, but knowledge harvesting without focus can render you powerless. As companies migrate toward responsive e-business models, they are investing in new data-driven decision support application frameworks that help them respond rapidly to changing market conditions and customer needs [32].

So to succeed in e-business and e-commerce, companies need information systems that can support the diverse information and decision-making needs of their managers and business professionals. In this section, we will explore in more detail how this is accomplished by several types of management information, decision support, and executive information systems. We will concentrate our attention on how the Internet, intranets, and other Web-enabled information technologies have significantly strengthened the role information systems play in supporting the decision-making activities of every manager and knowledge worker in the e-business enterprise.

Analyzing International Rectifier, Blair, and Pillsbury

Read the Real World Case on International Rectifier, Blair, and Pillsbury on the next page. We can learn a lot from this case about how a variety of e-business technologies have become key components of successful decision support systems. See Figure 9.1.

Many companies use a variety of data analysis tools to accomplish decision support processes that are sometimes called business analytics. Thus, International Rectifier uses the Essbase online analytical processing software to build and manipulate large multidimensional data cubes to help them analyze their inventory and sales performance. Blair Corp. turned to the IntelliVisor Web-based analytic service from

Figure 9.1

Doug Bourke is manager of financial analytics at International Rectifier Corp., which is using Essbase online analytical processing software to analyze and improve their sales and inventory performance.

Source: David Strick.

International Rectifier, Blair, and Pillsbury:
Business Analytics for Decision Support

Business analytics "makes the difference between an average implementation of an e-business system such as customer relationship management, and an excellent implementation," says Frank Buytendijk, a senior research analyst at Gartner Inc. in the Netherlands. "It's in analytics where you assess and evaluate the effectiveness of what you're doing." So from semiconductors to pharmaceuticals, companies are seeking and using data analysis tools to better understand their businesses, make better decisions, and even to streamline the analytic process itself.

At International Rectifier Corp., an El Segundo, California–based producer of power management semiconductors, manager of financial analytics Doug Burke says Hyperion Solutions' Essbase software has enabled the company to "get a lot more out of our IBM AS/400" midrange system by allowing the company to extract and analyze sales data very inexpensively. Rather than being forced to manipulate and e-mail each other huge spreadsheets, which ties up network bandwidth, users at networked PC workstations can now dynamically retrieve calculated views of just the data they need from the AS/400's databases using the online analytical processing (OLAP) features of Essbase.

Burke says he expects more cost savings in a few weeks when he deploys Essbase Version 6.1, which includes attributes that will allow users to dynamically analyze data across additional dimensions (such as sales areas) without having to store those calculations and thus increase the size of the database. "That's a big payoff," he says, "especially when you want to scale this thing up to hundreds of thousands or even millions of products" to analyze.

When catalog retailer Blair Corp. relaunched its online retail website in December, "we were looking from Day 1 how to be more profitable," says Jeff Parnell, vice president and general manager of e-commerce. The relaunch not only added many more products to the site but was also the first iteration of the site to be promoted in the millions of catalogs the firm mails each year. The Warren, Pennsylvania–based company wanted a Web clickstream analysis tool to tell it which areas within the site attracted the most customers and exactly why those browsing did or didn't buy, says Darren Schott, the company's director of marketing for e-commerce.

For the answers, Blair turned to IntelliVisor, an online analytic service offered by SAS Institute Inc. in Cary, North Carolina, to determine such things as which product categories suffered the most cart abandonment (customers ending their shopping process without completing the order) and which generated the highest conversion rates (turning browsers into buyers). Using SAS as an application service provider was attractive, Schott says, because Blair didn't have to develop the needed know-how in-house. SAS was a natural choice as vendor, because Blair was a longtime SAS customer and the company could easily integrate its clickstream data into the SAS tools it already had, says Parnell.

Parnell declined to specify how IntelliVisor has helped the bottom line, except to say, "We feel very comfortable with the ROI equation." The payoff, he says, lies in "the fact you can make better decisions and make them more quickly."

"Professional statisticians and analysts are a fairly scarce resource," says Fred Hulting, a senior research scientist at the Pillsbury Co. in Minneapolis. To shield them from routine report requests, he's rolling out Web-based statistical applications built on the StatServer decision-support tool from Insightful Corp. in Seattle. By building commonly used reporting capabilities into StatServer, business users can now generate statistical analyses and reports themselves rather than call in an analyst, he says.

Like others, Hulting wouldn't specify the application's benefits but says they have "greatly increased the capacity of my folks to spend more time with the business and focus on the bigger issues." The new applications leverage Pillsbury's existing network infrastructure, require no client software, and run on a portion of a server the company already owns. Pillsbury spent only $40,000 to license StatServer and the underlying S-Plus language used to develop the applications. Hulting and a colleague who was experienced in S-Plus developed the applications without outside assistance, but he warns that others without such experience will need consulting help.

International Rectifier is using Essbase not only to cut the costs and time it takes to collect data but also to standardize how the data is created to improve decision making, says Burke. Using Essbase, the company has built a multidimensional data cube for inventory analysis and will soon roll out another to analyze sales by market sector. Using these common databases, "you don't have costs defined three different ways or revenue defined four different ways by different divisions," Burke says. "Whether people like the numbers or not, everyone agrees on the numbers," and can focus more on analyzing the data than gathering it, he explains.

Case Study Questions

1. What is the business value to International Rectifier of using Essbase for business analytics? Is Essbase a DSS? Why or why not?

2. How might IntelliVisor help Blair Corp.'s e-commerce Web initiative or any Web business venture be more successful?

3. How does StatServer help both business professionals and statisticians at Pillsbury? Is StatServer an MIS or DSS? Explain.

Source: Adapted from Robert Schier, "Finding Pearls in an Ocean of Data," *Computerworld*, July 23, 2001, pp. 48, 49. Reprinted by permission.

SAS Institute to help them continually improve their online catalog sales performance by analyzing the browsing and buying behavior of visitors to their relaunched e-commerce website. And the Pillsbury Co. uses Web-based StatServer decision support applications that enable business users to generate their own statistical analyses and reports.

e-Business Decision Support Trends

The emerging class of applications focuses on personalized decision support, modeling, information retrieval, data warehousing, what-if scenarios, and reporting [32].

As we discussed in Chapter 1, using information systems to support business decision making has been one of the primary thrusts of the business use of information technology. However, the e-commerce revolution spawned by the Internet and the World Wide Web is expanding the information and decision support uses and expectations of a company's employees, managers, customers, suppliers, and other business partners. But this change was noticed even earlier, as both academic researchers and business practitioners began reporting that the traditional managerial focus originating in classic management information systems (1960s), decision support systems (1970s), and executive information systems (1980s) was expanding. The fast pace of new information technologies like PC hardware and software suites, client/server networks, and networked PC versions of DSS/EIS software made decision support available to lower levels of management, as well as to nonmanagerial individuals and self-directed teams of business professionals [25, 46, 50].

This trend has accelerated with the Internet and e-commerce revolutions, and the dramatic growth of intranets and extranets that internetwork e-business enterprises and their stakeholders. Figure 9.2 illustrates that all e-commerce participants expect easy and instant access to information and Web-enabled self-service data analysis. Internetworked e-business enterprises are responding with a variety of personalized and proactive Web-based analytical techniques to support the decision-making requirements of all of their stakeholders.

Thus, the growth of corporate intranets, extranets, as well as the Web, has accelerated the development and use of "executive class" information delivery and decision support software tools by lower levels of management and by individuals and teams of business professionals. In addition, the dramatic expansion of e-commerce has opened the door to the use of such e-business DSS tools by the suppliers, customers, and other business stakeholders of a company for customer relationship management, supply chain management, and other e-business applications.

Figure 9.3 highlights several of the major e-business decision support applications that are being customized, personalized, and Web-enabled for use in e-business and e-commerce [24, 25, 32, 46]. We will emphasize the trend toward such e-business decision support applications in all of the various types of information and decision support systems that are discussed in this chapter.

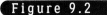

Figure 9.2

An e-business enterprise must meet the information and data analysis requirements of customers and companies in e-commerce with more personalized and proactive Web-based decision support.

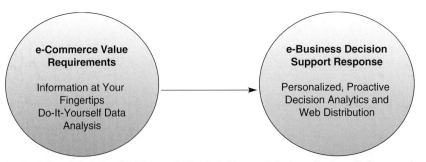

Source: Adapted from Ravi Kalakota and Marcia Robinson, *E-Business: Roadmap for Success* (Reading, MA: Addison-Wesley, 1999), p. 270. © 1999 Addison-Wesley Publishing Company, Inc. Reprinted by permission of Addison-Wesley Longman, Inc.

Figure 9.3

Examples of e-business decision support applications available to employees, managers, customers, suppliers, and other business partners of an e-business enterprise.

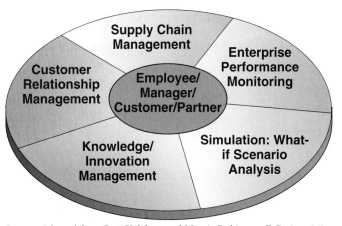

Source: Adapted from Ravi Kalakota and Marcia Robinson, *E-Business 2.0: Roadmap for Success* (Reading, MA: Addison-Wesley, 2001), p. 361. © 2001 Addison-Wesley Publishing Company, Inc. Reprinted by permission of Addison-Wesley Longman, Inc.

Target Corporation: e-Business DSS

Target Corporation's decision support system is composed of several applications known collectively as the Decision Maker's Workbench, which use Decision Suite and WebOLAP software from Information Advantage. The DSS and Target's corporate intranet support more than 1,700 active users creating more than 60,000 adhoc online analytical processing (OLAP) reports each month. During the Christmas season, more than 20,000 analytic OLAP reports are produced each day. By integrating the Web with its corporate data warehouse, Target Stores enable its vendors to access its data warehouse to monitor the sales and performance of their own products via secure extranet links across the Internet.

With the Target Stores system complete, the corporation has standardized it as a model for the entire company. Already the standardized warehouse has enabled Target Corporation to obtain more accurate data on how items are performing across divisions, across the company. This has improved vendor negotiations considerably by enabling the different divisions to consolidate orders and receive a better price. The standardized DSS applications also allow for cross-referencing of fashion trends across divisions, and they have helped validate merchandising hunches through the analysis of cross-company data [14, 43].

Information, Decisions, and Management

Figure 9.4 emphasizes that the type of information required by decision makers in a company is directly related to the **level of management decision making** and the amount of structure in the decision situations they face. You should realize that the framework of the classic *managerial pyramid* shown in Figure 9.4 applies even in today's *downsized* organizations and *flattened* or nonhierarchical organizational structures. Levels of management decision making still exist, but their size, shape, and participants continue to change as today's fluid organizational structures evolve. Thus, the levels of managerial decision making that must be supported by information technology in a successful organization are:

- **Strategic Management.** Typically, a board of directors and an executive committee of the CEO and top executives develop overall organizational goals, strategies, policies, and objectives as part of a strategic planning process. They also monitor the strategic performance of the organization and its overall direction in the political, economic, and competitive business environment.

- **Tactical Management.** Increasingly, business professionals in self-directed teams as well as business unit managers develop short- and medium-range

Figure 9.4

Information requirements of decision makers. The type of information required by directors, executives, managers, and members of self-directed teams is directly related to the level of management decision making involved and the structure of decision situations they face.

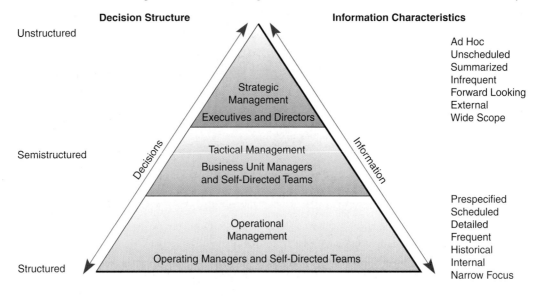

plans, schedules, and budgets and specify the policies, procedures, and business objectives for their subunits of the company. They also allocate resources and monitor the performance of their organizational subunits, including departments, divisions, process teams, project teams, and other workgroups.

● **Operational Management.** The members of self-directed teams or operating managers develop short-range plans such as weekly production schedules. They direct the use of resources and the performance of tasks according to procedures and within budgets and schedules they establish for the teams and other workgroups of the organization.

Decision Structure

Decisions made at the operational management level tend to be more *structured*, those at the tactical level more *semistructured*, and those at the strategic management level more *unstructured*. Structured decisions involve situations where the procedures to follow when a decision is needed can be specified in advance. The inventory reorder decisions faced by most businesses are a typical example. Unstructured decisions involve decision situations where it is not possible to specify in advance most of the decision procedures to follow. At most, many decision situations are semistructured. That is, some decision procedures can be prespecified, but not enough to lead to a definite recommended decision. For example, decisions involved in starting a new line of e-commerce services or making major changes to employee benefits would probably range from unstructured to semistructured. Figure 9.5 provides a variety of examples of business decisions by type of decision structure and level of management [27].

Therefore, information systems must be designed to produce a variety of information products to meet the changing needs of decision makers throughout an organization. For example, decision makers at the strategic management level require more summarized, ad hoc, unscheduled reports, forecasts, and external intelligence to support their more unstructured planning and policy-making responsibilities. Decision makers at the operational management level, on the other hand, may require more prespecified internal reports emphasizing detailed current and historical data comparisons that support their more structured responsibilities in day-to-day operations.

Figure 9.5 Examples of decisions by the type of decision structure and by level of management.

Decision Structure	Operational Management	Tactical Management	Strategic Management
Unstructured	Cash management	Business process reengineering	New e-commerce initiatives
		Work group performance analysis	Company reorganization
Semistructured	Credit management	Employee performance appraisal	Product planning
	Production scheduling	Capital budgeting	Mergers and acquisitions
	Daily work assignment	Program budgeting	Site location
Structured	Inventory control	Program control	

Management Information Systems

Management information systems were the original type of information system developed to support managerial decision making. An MIS produces information products that support many of the day-to-day decision-making needs of managers and business professionals. Reports, displays, and responses produced by management information systems provide information that these decision makers have specified in advance as adequately meeting their information needs. Such predefined information products satisfy the information needs of decision makers at the operational and tactical levels of the organization who are faced with more structured types of decision situations. For example, sales managers rely heavily on sales analysis reports to evaluate differences in performance among salespeople who sell the same types of products to the same types of customers. They have a pretty good idea of the kinds of information about sales results they need to manage sales performance effectively.

Managers and other decision makers use an MIS to request information at their networked workstations that supports their decision-making activities. This information takes the form of periodic, exception, and demand reports and immediate responses to inquiries. Web browsers, application programs, and database management software provide access to information in the intranet and other operational databases of the organization. Remember, operational databases are maintained by transaction processing systems. Data about the business environment are obtained from Internet or extranet databases when necessary.

Management Reporting Alternatives

Management information systems provide a variety of information products to managers. Four major reporting alternatives are provided by such systems.

- **Periodic Scheduled Reports.** This traditional form of providing information to managers uses a prespecified format designed to provide managers with information on a regular basis. Typical examples of such periodic scheduled reports are daily or weekly sales analysis reports and monthly financial statements.

- **Exception Reports.** In some cases, reports are produced only when exceptional conditions occur. In other cases, reports are produced periodically but contain information only about these exceptional conditions. For example, a credit manager can be provided with a report that contains only information on customers who exceed their credit limits. Exception reporting reduces *information overload*, instead of overwhelming decision makers with periodic detailed reports of business activity.

- **Demand Reports and Responses.** Information is available whenever a manager demands it. For example, Web browsers and DBMS query languages and report generators enable managers at PC workstations to get immediate responses or find and obtain customized reports as a result of their requests for the information they need. Thus, managers do not have to wait for periodic reports to arrive as scheduled.

- **Push Reporting.** Information is *pushed* to a manager's networked workstation. Thus, many companies are using webcasting software to selectively broadcast reports and other information to the networked PCs of managers and specialists over their corporate intranets. See Figure 9.6.

Online Analytical Processing

At a recent stockholder meeting, the CEO of PepsiCo, D. Wayne Calloway, said: "Ten years ago I could have told you how Doritos were selling west of the Mississippi. Today, not only can I tell you how well Doritos sell west of the Mississippi, I can also tell you how well they are selling in California, in Orange County, in the town of Irvine, in the local Vons supermarket, in the special promotion, at the end of Aisle 4, on Thursdays" [55].

The competitive and dynamic nature of today's global business environment is driving demands by business managers and analysts for information systems that can provide fast answers to complex business queries. The IS industry has responded to these demands with developments like analytical databases, data marts, data warehouses, data mining techniques, and multidimensional database structures (discussed in Chapter 5), and with specialized servers and Web-enabled software products that support **online analytical processing** (OLAP).

Online analytical processing enables managers and analysts to interactively examine and manipulate large amounts of detailed and consolidated data from many perspectives. OLAP involves analyzing complex relationships among thousands or even millions of data items stored in multidimensional databases to discover patterns, trends, and exception conditions. An OLAP session takes place online in real time, with rapid responses to a manager's or analyst's queries, so that their analytical or decision-making process is undisturbed [21]. See Figure 9.7.

Online analytical processing involves several basic analytical operations, including consolidation, "drill-down," and "slicing and dicing" [20]. See Figure 9.8.

Figure 9.6   An example of the push components in a marketing intelligence system that uses the Internet and a corporate intranet system to provide information to employees.

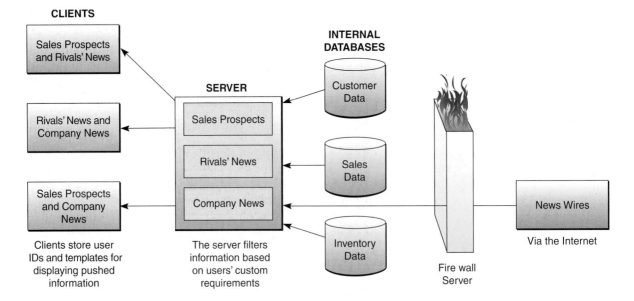

Figure 9.7

Online analytical processing may involve the use of specialized servers and multidimensional databases. OLAP provides fast answers to complex queries posed by managers and analysts using traditional and Web-enabled OLAP software.

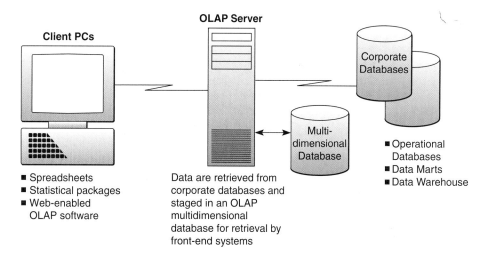

Client PCs

- Spreadsheets
- Statistical packages
- Web-enabled OLAP software

OLAP Server

Data are retrieved from corporate databases and staged in an OLAP multidimensional database for retrieval by front-end systems

Multi-dimensional Database

Corporate Databases

- Operational Databases
- Data Marts
- Data Warehouse

- **Consolidation.** Consolidation involves the aggregation of data. This can involve simple roll-ups or complex groupings involving interrelated data. For example, sales offices can be rolled up to districts and districts rolled up to regions.
- **Drill-Down.** OLAP can go in the reverse direction and automatically display detail data that comprise consolidated data. This is called drill-down. For example, the sales by individual products or sales reps that make up a region's sales totals could be easily accessed.
- **Slicing and Dicing.** Slicing and dicing refers to the ability to look at the database from different viewpoints. One slice of the sales database might show all sales of product type within regions. Another slice might show all sales by sales channel within each product type. Slicing and dicing is often performed along a time axis in order to analyze trends and find patterns.

Figure 9.8

An example of a display produced by a Web-enabled online analytical processing package.

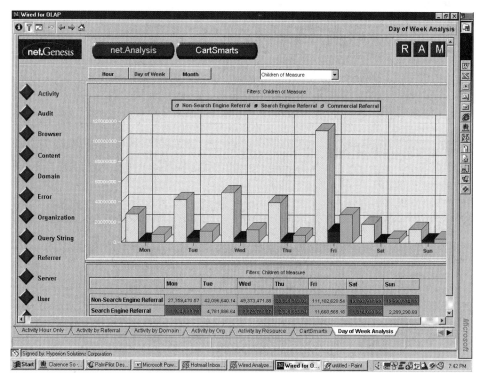

Source: Courtesy of Actuate.

OLAP at MasterCard International

MasterCard International developed OLAP software called Market Advisor, which enables members to query a data warehouse and drill down into information to analyze transactions and trends online. Market Advisor also provides a 13-month historical database, extended report graphing, and triggered marketing alerts based on above- or below-average merchant or cardholder activity.

In a typical application, a marketing analyst can examine a trend in spending at aggregate levels for a particular merchant category, such as hardware store, restaurant, car rental agency, or gas station. By using Market Advisor, analysts can determine which states or provinces accounted for the volume and identify which merchants accounted for the greatest volume. An analyst can even drill into the data to find which cardholder accounts were used at a particular store over a period of time. The analyst can then find common spending patterns among certain categories of cardholders, and tailor marketing promotions appropriately [22].

Decision Support Systems

Decision support systems are computer-based information systems that provide interactive information support to managers and business professionals during the decision-making process. Decision support systems use (1) analytical models, (2) specialized databases, (3) a decision maker's own insights and judgments, and (4) an interactive, computer-based modeling process to support the making of semistructured and unstructured business decisions. See Figure 9.9.

Example

An example might help at this point. Sales managers typically rely on management information systems to produce sales analysis reports. These reports contain sales performance figures by product line, salesperson, sales region, and so on. A decision support system, on the other hand, would also interactively show a sales manager the effects on sales performance of changes in a variety of factors (such as promotion expense and salesperson compensation). The DSS could then use several criteria (such as expected gross margin and market share) to evaluate and rank several alternative combinations of sales performance factors. ●

Therefore, DSS are designed to be ad hoc, quick-response systems that are initiated and controlled by business decision makers. Decision support systems are thus

Figure 9.9

Comparing decision support systems and management information systems. Note the major differences in the information and decision support they provide.

	Management Information Systems	Decision Support Systems
● Decision support provided	Provide information about the performance of the organization	Provide information and decision support techniques to analyze specific problems or opportunities
● Information form and frequency	Periodic, exception, demand, and push reports and responses	Interactive inquiries and responses
● Information format	Prespecified, fixed format	Ad hoc, flexible, and adaptable format
● Information processing methodology	Information produced by extraction and manipulation of business data	Information produced by analytical modeling of business data

Figure 9.10

Components of a Web-enabled marketing decision support system. Note the hardware, software, model, data, and network resources involved.

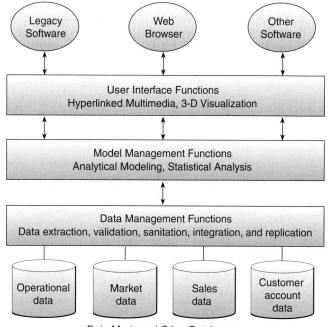

Data Marts and Other Databases

Source: Adapted from Ravi Kalakota and Andrew Whinston, *Electronic Commerce: A Manager's Guide* (Reading, MA: Addison-Wesley, 1997), p. 343. © 1997 by Addison-Wesley Publishing Company, Inc. Reprinted by permission of Addison-Wesley Longman, Inc.

able to directly support the specific types of decisions and the personal decision-making styles and needs of individual executives, managers, and business professionals.

DSS Models and Software

Unlike management information systems, decision support systems rely on **model bases** as well as databases as vital system resources. A DSS model base is a software component that consists of models used in computational and analytical routines that mathematically express relationships among variables. For example, a spreadsheet program might contain models that express simple accounting relationships among variables, such as Revenue − Expenses = Profit. Or a DSS model base could include models and analytical techniques used to express much more complex relationships. For example, it might contain linear programming models, multiple regression forecasting models, and capital budgeting present value models. Such models may be stored in the form of spreadsheet models or templates, or statistical and mathematical programs and program modules. See Figure 9.10.

DSS software packages can combine model components to create integrated models that support specific types of decisions. DSS software typically contains built-in analytical modeling routines and also enables you to build your own models. Many DSS packages are now available in microcomputer and Web-enabled versions. Of course, electronic spreadsheet packages also provide some of the model building (spreadsheet models) and analytical modeling (what-if and goal-seeking analysis) offered by more powerful DSS software. See Figure 9.11.

Web-Enabled DSS at PepsiCo

PepsiCo and Sedgwick James Inc., the world's second largest insurance broker, developed a risk management DSS to help minimize PepsiCo's losses from accidents, theft, and other causes. Every week, Sedgwick loads the latest casualty claims data from the nation's leading insurance carriers into a DSS database resident on IBM RS/6000 servers in the PepsiCo intranet. The database is then accessed by managers and analysts using desktop PCs and remote laptops

Figure 9.11

Examples of special-purpose DSS packages.

DSS Packages
• **Retail:** Information Advantage and Unisys offer the Category Management Solution Suite, an OLAP decision support system and industry-specific data model.
• **Insurance:** Computer Associates offers RiskAdvisor, an insurance risk decision support system whose data model stores information in insurance industry specific tables designed for optimal query performance.
• **Telecom:** NCR and SABRE Decision Technologies have joined forces to create the NCR Customer Retention program for the communications industry including data marts for telephone companies to use for decision support in managing customer loyalty, quality of service, network management, fraud, and marketing.

Source: Adapted from Charles B. Darling, "Ease Implementation Woes with Packaged Data Marts," *Datamation*, March 1997, p. 103. © 1997 by Cahners Publishing Co.

equipped with the INFORM risk management system. Both the RS/6000 servers and local PCs use Information Builders' middleware to provide PepsiCo managers and business analysts with transparent data access from a variety of hardware/software configurations.

The INFORM risk management system combines the analytical power of FOCUS decision support modeling with the graphical analysis capabilities of FOCUS/EIS for Windows. As a result, PepsiCo managers and business analysts at all levels can pinpoint critical trends, drill down for detailed backup information, identify potential problems, and plan ways to minimize risks and maximize profits [41].

Geographic Information and Data Visualization Systems

Geographic information systems (GIS) and *data visualization systems* (DVS) are special categories of DSS that integrate computer graphics with other DSS features. A geographic information system is a DSS that uses *geographic databases* to construct and display maps and other graphics displays that support decisions affecting the geographic distribution of people and other resources. Many companies are using GIS technology along with *global positioning system* (GPS) devices to help them choose new retail store locations, optimize distribution routes, or analyze the demographics of their target audiences. For example, companies like Levi Strauss, Arby's, Consolidated Rail, and Federal Express use GIS packages to integrate maps, graphics, and other geographic data with business data from spreadsheets and statistical packages. GIS software such as MapInfo and Atlas GIS is used for most business GIS applications [36].

Data visualization systems represent complex data using interactive three-dimensional graphical forms such as charts, graphs, and maps. DVS tools help users to interactively sort, subdivide, combine, and organize data while it is in its graphical form. This helps users discover patterns, links, and anomalies in business or scientific data in an interactive knowledge discovery and decision support process. Business applications like data mining typically use interactive graphs that let users drill down in real time and manipulate the underlying data of a business model to help clarify its meaning for business decision making [15, 28]. Figure 9.12 is an example of business data displayed by a data visualization system.

OshKosh B'Gosh Uses Data Visualization

OshKosh B'Gosh, Inc., the Oshkosh, Wisconsin-based maker of children's clothing, uses the data visualization tools built into Cognos PowerPlay DSS software. Visualizing data helps them pinpoint data anomalies and intuitively see what's happening in their business data. The tools have been particularly helpful for analyzing

Figure 9.12

Displays of business data for sales analysis by a data visualization system.

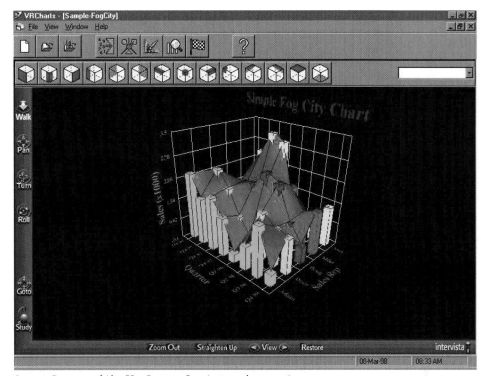

Source: Courtesy of AlterVue Systems, Inc. (www.vrcharts.com).

canceled orders and returns. Business analysts drill into graphs and models to see the underlying cause of their results.

"Say, for example, we're getting lots of items returned from retailers," says CIO Jon Dell'Antonia. "We can drill into the visual model for the data about what plants made the items that are being returned. If they primarily came from one plant, then we may have a manufacturing problem. But if the returns are coming primarily from one retailer, then we know we don't have a product quality issue, but instead might need to talk to that customer. This type of analysis used to take us days and days to do. Now it can take minutes" [15].

Using Decision Support Systems

Using a decision support system involves an interactive **analytical modeling** process. For example, using a DSS software package for decision support may result in a series of displays in response to alternative what-if changes entered by a manager. This differs from the demand responses of management information systems, since decision makers are not demanding prespecified information. Rather, they are exploring possible alternatives. Thus, they do not have to specify their information needs in advance. Instead, they use the DSS to find the information they need to help them make a decision. That is the essence of the decision support system concept.

Using a decision support system involves four basic types of analytical modeling activities: (1) what-if analysis, (2) sensitivity analysis, (3) goal-seeking analysis, and (4) optimization analysis. Let's briefly look at each type of analytical modeling that can be used for decision support. See Figure 9.13.

What-If Analysis

In **what-if analysis,** an end user makes changes to variables, or relationships among variables, and observes the resulting changes in the values of other variables. For example, if you were using a spreadsheet, you might change a revenue

Figure 9.13

Activities and examples of
the major types of analytical
modeling.

Type of Analytical Modeling	Activities and Examples
What-if analysis	Observing how changes to selected variables affect other variables. *Example:* What if we cut advertising by 10 percent? What would happen to sales?
Sensitivity analysis	Observing how repeated changes to a single variable affect other variables. *Example:* Let's cut advertising by $100 repeatedly so we can see its relationship to sales.
Goal-seeking analysis	Making repeated changes to selected variables until a chosen variable reaches a target value. *Example:* Let's try increases in advertising until sales reach $1 million.
Optimization analysis	Finding an optimum value for selected variables, given certain constraints. *Example:* What's the best amount of advertising to have, given our budget and choice of media?

amount (a variable) or a tax rate formula (a relationship among variables) in a simple financial spreadsheet model. Then you could command the spreadsheet program to instantly recalculate all affected variables in the spreadsheet. A managerial user would be very interested in observing and evaluating any changes that occurred to the values in the spreadsheet, especially to a variable such as net profit after taxes. To many managers, net profit after taxes is an example of *the bottom line*, that is, a key factor in making many types of decisions. This type of analysis would be repeated until the manager was satisfied with what the results revealed about the effects of various possible decisions. Figure 9.14 is an example of what-if analysis.

Sensitivity Analysis

Sensitivity analysis is a special case of what-if analysis. Typically, the value of only one variable is changed repeatedly, and the resulting changes on other variables are observed. So sensitivity analysis is really a case of what-if analysis involving repeated

Figure 9.14

What-if analysis involves
the development of
alternative scenarios based
on changing assumptions as
part of the decision-making
process.

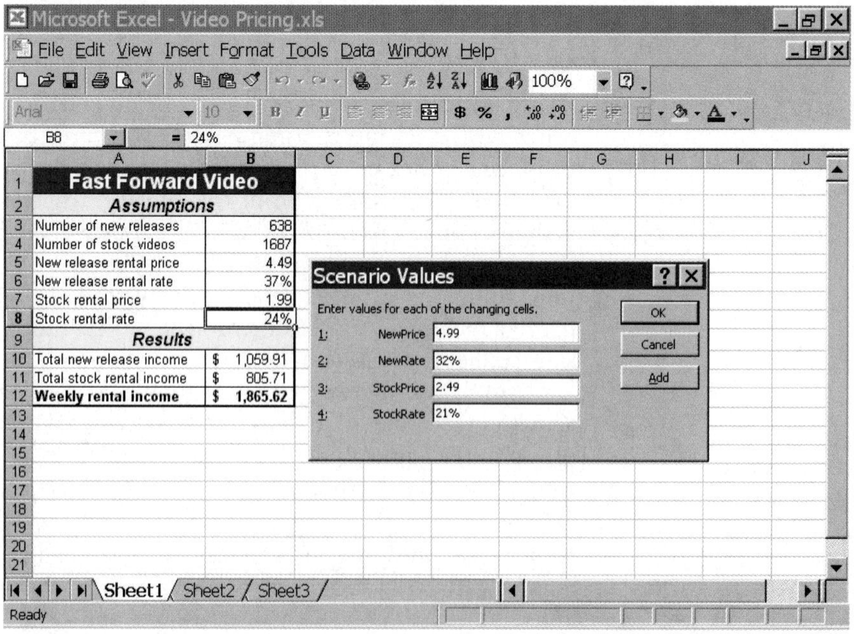

changes to only one variable at a time. Some DSS packages automatically make repeated small changes to a variable when asked to perform sensitivity analysis. Typically, sensitivity analysis is used when decision makers are uncertain about the assumptions made in estimating the value of certain key variables. In our previous spreadsheet example, the value of revenue could be changed repeatedly in small increments, and the effects on other spreadsheet variables observed and evaluated. This would help a manager understand the impact of various revenue levels on other factors involved in decisions being considered.

Goal-Seeking Analysis

Goal-seeking analysis reverses the direction of the analysis done in what-if and sensitivity analysis. Instead of observing how changes in a variable affect other variables, goal-seeking analysis (also called *how can* analysis) sets a target value (a goal) for a variable and then repeatedly changes other variables until the target value is achieved. For example, you could specify a target value (goal) of $2 million for net profit after taxes for a business venture. Then you could repeatedly change the value of revenue or expenses in a spreadsheet model until a result of $2 million is achieved. Thus, you would discover what amount of revenue or level of expenses the business venture needs to achieve in order to reach the goal of $2 million in after-tax profits. Therefore, this form of analytical modeling would help answer the question, "How can we achieve $2 million in net profit after taxes?" instead of the question, "What happens if we change revenue or expenses?" Thus, goal-seeking analysis is another important method of decision support.

Optimization Analysis

Optimization analysis is a more complex extension of goal-seeking analysis. Instead of setting a specific target value for a variable, the goal is to find the optimum value for one or more target variables, given certain constraints. Then one or more other variables are changed repeatedly, subject to the specified constraints, until the best values for the target variables are discovered. For example, you could try to determine the highest possible level of profits that could be achieved by varying the values for selected revenue sources and expense categories. Changes to such variables could be subject to constraints such as the limited capacity of a production process or limits to available financing. Optimization typically is accomplished by special-purpose software packages for optimization techniques such as linear programming, or by advanced DSS generators.

Lexis-Nexis: Web Tools for Decision Support

"Our new subscribers will grow geometrically with Web-based access to our information services," explains Keith Hawk, vice president of sales for the Nexis division of Lexis-Nexis. "And therefore our business model is changing from selling primarily to organizations to selling to individual users." To track their 1.7 million subscribers of legal and news documents, Lexis-Nexis replaced its old decision support system with new DSS tools and an NCR Teradata data warehouse system. The new customer data warehouse lets 475 salespeople and in-house analysts use the corporate intranet and Web browsers to look up daily detailed customer usage data.

The type of data that the company's salespeople sort through and analyze includes subscriber usage patterns—what they look up, what sources they use most often, when they're connecting—along with customer contract details. To get to that data, Lexis-Nexis uses decision support software from MicroStrategy Inc. Field sales representatives who need ad hoc reporting capabilities use MicroStrategy DSS WebPE, a Web-based reporting tool. Power users, such as market research analysis, use DSS Agent, an analytical modeling tool with Web access, to closely analyze and model business processes [16, 24].

Figure 9.15

A display of a data mining
software package.

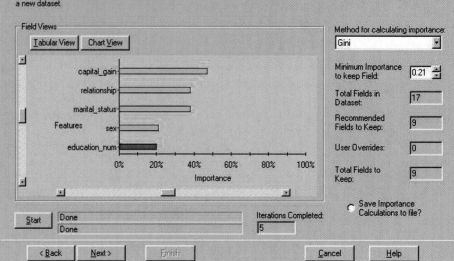

Source: Courtesy of Oracle Corporation.

**Data Mining for
Decision Support**

We discuss data mining and data warehouses in Chapter 5 as applications of data
resource management. However, data mining's main purpose is knowledge discovery
leading to decision support. Data mining software analyzes the vast stores of historical business data that have been prepared for analysis in corporate data warehouses. Data mining attempts to discover patterns, trends, and correlations hidden
in the data that can give a company a strategic business advantage.

Data mining software may perform regression, decision tree, neural network, clus-
ter detection, or market basket analysis for a business. See Figure 9.15. The data mining process can highlight buying patterns, reveal customer tendencies, cut redundant
costs, or uncover unseen profitable relationships and opportunities. For example,
many companies use data mining to find more profitable ways to perform successful
direct mailings, including e-mailings, or to discover better ways to display products
in a store, design a better e-commerce website, reach untapped profitable customers,
or recognize customers or products that are unprofitable or marginal [18].

**KeyCorp and
Peoples Bank: Data
Mining DSS**

Quick payback and support for some surprising, counterintuitive decisions have
been among the benefits early users found with IBM's DecisionEdge for Relationship Marketing decision support software. "We had a full return on our
investment 14 months after installing the data mining component," said Jo Ann
Boylan, an executive vice president in the Key Technology Service division at
KeyCorp, the nation's 13th largest retail bank with 7 million customers. She
added that the data mining and analysis system helped raise the bank's direct-mail
response rate from 1 to as high as 10 percent. It also helped identify unprofitable
product lines.

The DecisionEdge decision support package includes application suites, analytical tools, a mining data tool, industry-specific data models, and consulting
services. Pricing begins at around $150,000.

Peoples Bank & Trust Co. in Indianapolis used the DecisionEdge for Relationship Marketing to delve into some highly profitable bank offerings that turned out to be prohibitively expensive, said Bob Connors, a senior vice president of information services. The DSS pointed out how much it actually costs to bring in each highly profitable home equity loan customer. "Because those loans can be so profitable, it seems like a no-brainer that you'd want to market them," Connors explained. "But we found that the costs to bring them in were far too high, so we've cut way back on that spending. We still offer the loans, but we don't spend so much on advertising or direct mail any more" [17].

Executive Information Systems

Executive information systems (EIS) are information systems that combine many of the features of management information systems and decision support systems. When they were first developed, their focus was on meeting the strategic information needs of top management. Thus, the first goal of executive information systems was to provide top executives with immediate and easy access to information about a firm's *critical success factors* (CSFs), that is, key factors that are critical to accomplishing an organization's strategic objectives. For example, the executives of a retail store chain would probably consider factors such as its e-commerce versus traditional sales results, or its product line mix to be critical to its survival and success.

However, executive information systems are becoming so widely used by managers, analysts, and other knowledge workers that they are sometimes humorously called "everyone's information systems." More popular alternative names are enterprise information systems (EIS) and executive support systems (ESS). These names also reflect the fact that more features, such as Web browsing, electronic mail, groupware tools, and DSS and expert system capabilities, are being added to many systems to make them more useful to managers and business professionals [23, 25, 50].

In an EIS, information is presented in forms tailored to the preferences of the executives using the system. For example, most executive information systems stress the use of a graphical user interface and graphics displays that can be customized to the information preferences of executives using the EIS. Other information presentation methods used by an EIS include exception reporting and trend analysis. The ability to *drill down*, which allows executives to quickly retrieve displays of related information at lower levels of detail, is another important capability. And of course, the growth of Internet and intranet technologies has added Web browsing to the list of EIS capabilities.

Figure 9.16 shows an actual display provided by the Hyperion executive information system. Notice how simple and brief this display is. Also note how it provides users of the system with the ability to drill down quickly to lower levels of detail in areas of particular interest to them. Beside the drill-down capability, the Hyperion EIS also stresses trend analysis and exception reporting. Thus, a business user can quickly discover the direction key factors are heading and the extent to which critical factors are deviating from expected results [53].

EIS have spread into the ranks of middle management and business professionals as they recognized their feasibility and benefits, and as less-expensive systems for client/server networks and corporate intranets became available. For example, one popular EIS software package reports that only 3 percent of its users are top executives. Another example is the EIS of Conoco, one of the world's largest oil companies. Conoco's EIS is used by most senior managers, and by over 4,000 employees located at corporate headquarters in Houston and throughout the world [4, 51, 54].

Displays provided by an executive information system. Note the simplicity and clarity in which key information is provided, and the ability to drill down to lower levels of detail.

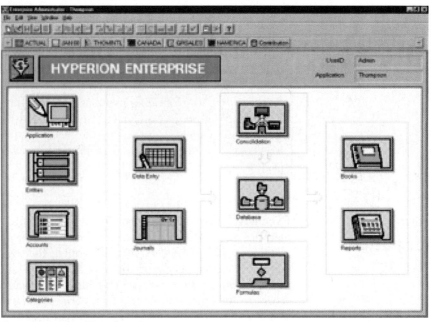

Source: Courtesy of Comshare, Inc.

EIS at Conoco and KeyCorp

As we just mentioned, Conoco, Inc., has a widely used EIS. Conoco's EIS is a large system with 75 different applications and hundreds of screen displays. Senior executives and over 4,000 managers and analysts worldwide use EIS applications ranging from analyzing internal operations and financial results to viewing external events that affect the petroleum industry. Conoco's EIS is popular with its users and has resulted in improved employee productivity and decision making, and significant cost savings compared to alternative methods of generating information for managers and analysts [4].

KeyCorp is a large banking and financial services holding company. It developed Keynet, a corporate intranet that transformed their mainframe-based EIS into a new EIS—a Web-enabled system they call "everyone's information system." Now more than 1,000 managers and analysts have Web access to 40 major business information areas within Keynet, ranging from sales and financial statistics to human resource management.

Enterprise Portals and Decision Support

Don't confuse portals with the executive information systems that have been used in some industries for many years. Portals are for everyone in the company, and not just for executives. You want people on the front lines making decisions using browsers and portals rather than just executives using specialized executive information system software [45].

We began this chapter by observing that major changes and expansion are taking place in traditional MIS, DSS, and EIS tools for providing the information and modeling managers need to support their decision making. Decision support in business is changing, driven by rapid developments in end user computing and networking; Internet, Web browser, and related technologies, and the explosion of e-commerce activity.

Enterprise Information Portals

A user checks his e-mail, looks up the current company stock price, checks his available vacation days, and receives an order from a customer—all from the browser on his desktop. That is the next-generation intranet, also known as a corporate or enterprise information portal. With it, the browser becomes the dashboard to daily business tasks [44].

Figure 9.17

This enterprise information portal was developed by British Petroleum for its North Sea customers using Plumtree portal software.

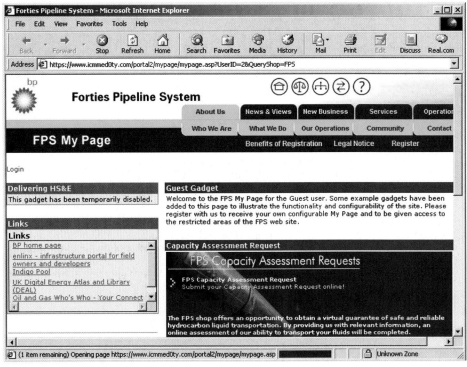

Source: Courtesy of British Petroleum.

An **enterprise information portal** (EIP) is a Web-based interface and integration of intranet and other technologies that gives all intranet users and selected extranet users access to a variety of internal and external business applications and services. For example, internal applications might include access to e-mail, project websites, and discussion groups; human resources Web self-services; customer, inventory, and other corporate databases; decision support systems, and knowledge management systems. External applications might include industry, financial, and other Internet news services; links to industry discussion groups; and links to customer and supplier Internet and extranet websites. Enterprise information portals are typically tailored or personalized to the needs of individual business users or groups of users. See Figure 9.17.

The business benefits of enterprise information portals include providing more specific and selective information to business users, providing easy access to key corporate intranet website resources, delivering industry and business news, and providing better access to company data for selected customers, suppliers, or business partners. Enterprise information portals can also help avoid excessive surfing by employees across company and Internet websites by making it easier for them to receive or find the information and services they need, thus improving the productivity of a company's workforce [45].

Figure 9.18 illustrates how companies are developing enterprise information portals as a way to provide Web-enabled information, knowledge, and decision support to their executives, managers, employees, suppliers, customers, and other business partners. The enterprise information portal (EIP) is a customized and personalized Web-based interface for corporate intranets, which gives users easy access to a variety of internal and external business applications, databases, and services. For example, the EIP in Figure 9.18 might give a qualified user secure access to DSS, data mining, and OLAP tools, the Internet and the Web, the corporate intranet, supplier or customer extranets, operational and analytical databases, a data warehouse, and a variety of business applications [43, 44, 45].

Figure 9.18

The components of this enterprise information portal identify it as an e-business decision support system that can be personalized for executives, managers, employees, suppliers, customers, and other business partners.

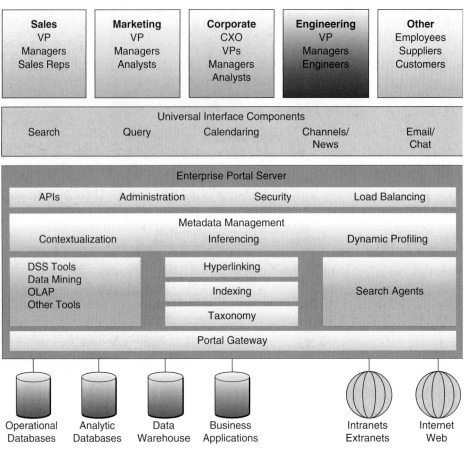

Sales	Marketing	Corporate	Engineering	Other
VP	VP	CXO	VP	Employees
Managers	Managers	VPs	Managers	Suppliers
Sales Reps	Analysts	Managers	Engineers	Customers
		Analysts		

Universal Interface Components

Search	Query	Calendaring	Channels/ News	Email/ Chat

Enterprise Portal Server

APIs	Administration	Security	Load Balancing

Metadata Management

Contextualization	Inferencing	Dynamic Profiling

DSS Tools Data Mining OLAP Other Tools	Hyperlinking Indexing Taxonomy	Search Agents

Portal Gateway

Operational Databases	Analytic Databases	Data Warehouse	Business Applications	Intranets Extranets	Internet Web

Source: Adapted from Gerry Murray, "Making Connections with Enterprise Knowledge Portals," White Paper, *Computerworld*, September 6, 1999, p. 6. Copyright 1999 by Computerworld, Inc., Framingham, MA 01701. Reprinted from *Computerworld*.

Procter & Gamble: How an EIP Provides Decision Support

Back in 1996, when a portal was just a fancy name for a door, Procter & Gamble Co.'s IT division began developing a rudimentary system for sharing documents and information over the company's intranet. As the demands of users and the number of Web pages supported by the system grew, the IT team expanded the scope of this Global Knowledge Catalog. The larger system is a storehouse of information that lets all 97,000 Procter & Gamble employees worldwide find information specific to their needs.

But although the system helped make sense of volumes of data, it still led to information overload. What Procter & Gamble really needed was a way to personalize the information of each employee, based on his or her job, says Dan Gerbus, project manager for the portal project in the Cincinnati company's IT division. "Users wanted one tool on their browser that would consolidate and deliver all the information they needed to do their work without having to navigate through 14 websites," he says.

So in January 2000, Procter & Gamble awarded a contract to Plumtree Software for 100,000 seats of the Plumtree Corporate Portal. Procter & Gamble, which became an investor in Plumtree, uses the portal to deliver marketing, product, and strategic information, as well as industry-news documents in thousands of Lotus Notes databases to its employees. The portal's document directory pulls data from more than 1 million Web pages.

By early 2001, Procter & Gamble's enterprise-wide portal included Web links to the company's SAP R/3 enterprise resource planning system and a wide range of Oracle data warehousing and decision support products. Customer data analyzed by E.piphany's customer relationship management application is also incorporated. The idea, Gerbus says, is to give employees one place to get the information and applications they need. "They used to have to scan multiple intranet sites to find ways to get that. The portal is one-stop shopping," he says.

Gerbus says that Procter & Gamble employees will be able to glance at their "dashboard," which will deliver a preset view into various information sources and find all the up-to-date information they need to make decisions about new products, advertising compaigns, or other initiatives. "If a business manager always needs to track some key pieces of information, we'll be able to build a dashboard for that," Gerbus says. "But we'll also provide the tools for them to get to the application or data source for a more-in-depth analysis" [49].

Enterprise Knowledge Portals

It should also be emphasized that an enterprise information portal is the entry to corporate intranets that serve as the primary **knowledge management systems** for many companies. That's why they are called **enterprise knowledge portals** by some vendors. We introduced knowledge management systems in Chapter 2 as the use of information technology to help gather, organize, and share business knowledge within an organization. In many organizations, hypermedia databases at corporate intranet websites have become the *knowledge bases* for storage and dissemination of business knowledge. This frequently takes the form of best practices, policies, and business solutions at the project, team, business unit, and enterprise levels of the company. Thus, the enterprise knowledge portal can play a major role in helping a company use its intranets as knowledge management systems to share and disseminate knowledge in support of its business decision making [29, 43]. See Figure 9.19.

Shiva Corporation: Web Knowledge Management

Shiva Corporation is in the business of connecting employees, customers, and partners to business networks via remote access technology. Using Verity's Information Server and CD-Web Publisher software, Shiva built a knowledge management application for their corporate intranet and company site on the Web. The solution provides customers and employees with Web-based answers to their technical support questions, access to online peer groups, CD-ROM-based product documentation, and a quarterly CD-ROM containing time-saving information.

The Knowledge Management solution took three months to develop. Within 45 days of use, it surpassed its financial break-even point. Shiva experienced a 22 percent drop in customer support calls in the first three months. Shiva's knowledgebase area is now the second-most-accessed section of the company's website, with 110,000 people hitting the site every month, including Shiva's 500-plus employees worldwide, most of whom access the site through the corporate intranet.

Shiva's knowledgebase is updated primarily by the company's technical support and engineering departments, although anyone in the company can enter a knowledgebase article into the system via the corporate intranet. It then becomes accessible to everyone else on the company's intranet before being placed on the Web. Within the Knowledge Management application, the Lotus Notes knowledgebase is converted to HTML and uploaded to a server. Then, the Verity software indexes all of the available documents and ties all the information together, where it's available to customers via the Web.

The Knowledge Management application has helped foster a corporate culture in which technical information is shared fully via the company intranet and site on the Web, rather than kept under lock and key. In-house staff can track common technical problems and determine what areas need improvement. And customers can obtain instant answers to their questions [29].

Figure 9.19   An example of the capabilities and components of an enterprise knowledge portal.

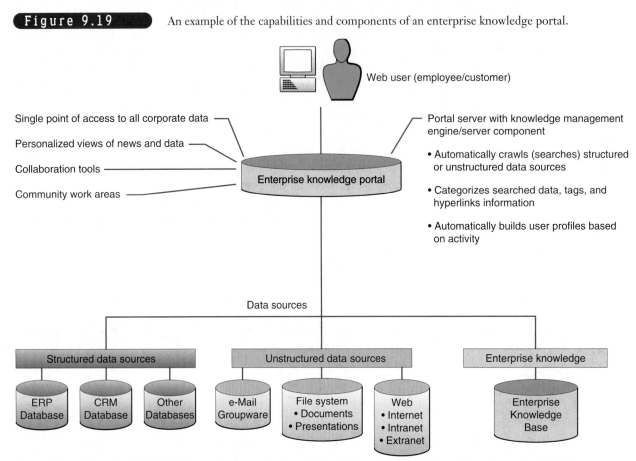

Source: Adapted from Lori Mitchell, "Enterprise Knowledge Portals Wise Up Your Business," *Infoworld.com*, December 1, 2000.

Artificial Intelligence Technologies in Business

Artificial intelligence is making its way back to the mainstream of corporate technology. Designed to leverage the capabilities of humans rather than replace them, today's AI technology enables an extraordinary array of applications that forge new connections among people, computers, knowledge, and the physical world. AI-enabled applications are at work in information distribution and retrieval, database mining, product design, manufacturing, inspection, training, user support, surgical planning, resource scheduling, and complex resource management.

Indeed, for anyone who schedules, plans, allocates resources, designs new products, uses the Internet, develops software, is responsible for product quality, is an investment professional, heads up IT, uses IT, or operates in any of a score of other capacities and arenas, new AI technologies already may be in place and providing competitive advantage [56].

Analyzing Grove Madsen and Cutler-Hammer

Read the Real World Case on Grove Madsen and Cutler-Hammer on the next page. We can learn a lot about the business value of using the Internet and artificial intelligence technologies from this example. See Figure 9.20.

Figure 9.20

Vicky Combs of Grove Madsen Industries uses the Bid Manager expert system to help her design and transmit specifications for equipment via an extranet to a Cutler-Hammer automated factory.

Source: Jason Fulford.

Grove Madsen and Cutler-Hammer:
Using an Expert System for e-Manufacturing

Fifteen minutes after Vicky Combs, in her Las Vegas office transmits her design for a custom $30,000 motor control center intended to run fountains at the Mandalay Bay casino, a big angular machine in Fayetteville, North Carolina, springs into action. Amid a clutter of drills and presses on the factory floor, a spiderlike Finn Power robot lifts steel sheets the size of tabletops and places them one after another on a conveyor. Rollers move the sheets to drill heads nearby. Other machines shape the steel into housings, and workers along the assembly line combine these to build the control center, which consists of adjoining bins crammed with motors, switches, circuit breakers, and other devices.

This is electronic manufacturing at its most advanced. Combs, whose firm, Grove Madsen Industries, supplies equipment to Las Vegas casinos, feeds her design directly to the Cutler-Hammer assembly line 2,050 miles away. Cutler-Hammer's customers, field reps, and distributors now electronically design and place 95 percent of their orders remotely via extranet links, bypassing C-H plant engineers.

E-manufacturing—the e-business marriage of the intelligent factory with the Internet—is finally catching on in a growing number of U.S. companies like Cutler-Hammer, Timken, Ford Motor, and Caterpillar. For a firsthand look at the big payoffs that can be produced, consider Cutler-Hammer, an acknowledged leader in e-manufacturing.

A $1.4 billion-a-year subsidiary of Eaton Corp., located outside of Pittsburgh, Pennsylvania, Cutler-Hammer has boosted its competitiveness as well as sales and profits since launching its e-factory effort. Its products are complex assemblies ranging from panel boards, the industrial counterpart to the boxes of circuit breakers and fuses in your home basement, to motor control centers, which run motors in factories; heating and air conditioning systems in hospitals, schools, and office buildings; pumps and valves in pipelines; and turbines and generators at electric utilities.

Cutler-Hammer's IT people were pioneers when they began work in 1995 on an expert system software program called Bid Manager. Its original purpose was to let customers' engineers deal more directly with the factory. Today Bid Manager has grown into a giant software package with six million lines of code, a far-reaching all-embracing e-manufacturing weapon with a sharp competitive edge. Not surprisingly, Cutler-Hammer has kept it largely under wraps.

To start with, the program allows a customer, a distributor, or one of the company's sales engineers in the field to easily configure the sometimes devilishly complex innards of Cutler-Hammer equipment with its convoluted wiring patterns and precise placement of dozens of electronic and electrical components. The software automatically checks that the engineer does everything right. If he places a switch or a wire in the wrong spot, he gets a gentle electronic slap on the wrist—an onscreen message pointing out the mistake. Bid Manager contains literally thousands of rules to ensure that designs are done correctly; at the same time, it allows for idiosyncrasies—a user may want the equipment to turn on electric motors in a certain way, for instance.

"No outsider could possibly know an industry such as ours well enough to cover it the way Bid Manager does," says Barbara J. Riesmeyer, manager of IT at Cutler-Hammer's power and control systems division and a developer of Bid Manager. To create the software, the company enlisted not only 15 software writers but also experts at the plants, sales engineers, and many others. Director of e-business Ray L. Huber led the team and, with Riesmeyer, created what they call the design-to-delivery (D2D) vision.

Bid Manager is used on the more complex assembled products that make up half the company's sales. Cutler-Hammer makes most of its panel boards at a spacious plant in Sumter, South Carolina, and most of its motor control centers at the almost identical facility in Fayetteville. Sumter runs 11 satellite assembly operations, and Fayetteville has eight. An additional 14 assembly plants in the United States and Mexico also employ Bid Manager.

With more than 61,000 orders processed electronically last year at Cutler-Hammer, the e-factory unquestionably has proved itself. Plant managers Frank C. Campbell at Sumter and Steven R. Kavanaugh at Fayetteville overflow with praise for the software. It's easy to see why. Where in the past paperwork stifled production flow, now Bid Manager takes care of even small but significant details. What's more, says Huber, "Bid Manager has helped us think differently about products." For example, Cutler-Hammer has standardized its products and models, slimming down the number of steel enclosure sizes from more than 400 to only 100.

There's no question that the software has decisively helped Cutler-Hammer's business. CEO Randy Carson reports that Bid Manager has increased Cutler-Hammer's market share for configured products—motor control centers, control panels, and the like—by 15 percent. He adds that Bid Manager has boosted sales of the larger assemblies by 20 percent, doubling profits, increasing productivity by 35 percent, and reducing quality costs by 26 percent. He concludes, "Bid Manager has transformed Cutler-Hammer into a customer-driven company."

Case Study Questions

1. What is e-manufacturing? How are AI technologies involved in Cutler-Hammer's e-manufacturing systems?

2. What is the business value of e-manufacturing and the Bid Manager expert system to Grove Madsen? To Cutler-Hammer?

3. How do e-manufacturing and expert systems like Bid Manager change the relationships and responsibilities between a business and its suppliers and customers? What is the business impact of such changes?

Companies like Cutler-Hammer, Timken, Ford Motor, and Caterpillar are capitalizing on e-manufacturing—the e-business application of automated manufacturing and Internet technologies. For example, Grove Madsen, an equipment supplier to Las Vegas casinos, uses Cutler-Hammer's Bid Manager expert system to help them design and transmit electronic specifications for large equipment assemblies via extranet links to Cutler-Hammer's automated factory in Fayetteville, North Carolina. There Bid Manager directs the fabrication of products by robots and other automated production machinery according to customer-transmitted specifications. Bid Manager automates and enables the online collaboration of customers in the production process in 35 Cutler-Hammer manufacturing facilities in the United States and Mexico. Cutler-Hammer management credits Bid Manager and e-manufacturing with significantly increasing their market share, sales, productivity, product quality, and profitability.

An Overview of Artificial Intelligence

What is artificial intelligence? **Artificial intelligence** (AI) is a field of science and technology based on disciplines such as computer science, biology, psychology, linguistics, mathematics, and engineering. The goal of AI is to develop computers that can think, as well as see, hear, walk, talk, and feel. A major thrust of artificial intelligence is the development of computer functions normally associated with human intelligence, such as reasoning, learning, and problem solving, as summarized in Figure 9.21.

Debate has raged around artificial intelligence since serious work in the field began in the 1950s. Not only technological, but moral and philosophical questions abound about the possibility of intelligent, thinking machines. For example, British AI pioneer Alan Turing in 1950 proposed a test for determining if machines could think. According to the Turing test, a computer could demonstrate intelligence if a human interviewer, conversing with an unseen human and an unseen computer, could not tell which was which [37, 50].

Though much work has been done in many of the subgroups that fall under the AI umbrella, critics believe that no computer can truly pass the Turing test. They claim that developing intelligence to impart true humanlike capabilities to computers is simply not possible. But progress continues, and only time will tell if the ambitious goals of artificial intelligence will be achieved and equal the popular images found in science fiction.

The Domains of Artificial Intelligence

Figure 9.22 illustrates the major domains of AI research and development. Note that AI applications can be grouped under three major areas: cognitive science, robotics, and natural interfaces, though these classifications do overlap each other, and other classifications can be used. Also note that expert systems are just one of many important AI applications. Let's briefly review each of these major areas of AI and some

---

Figure 9.21

Some of the attributes of intelligent behavior. AI is attempting to duplicate these capabilities in computer-based systems.

Attributes of Intelligent Behavior
● Think and reason.
● Use reason to solve problems.
● Learn or understand from experience.
● Acquire and apply knowledge.
● Exhibit creativity and imagination.
● Deal with complex or perplexing situations.
● Respond quickly and successfully to new situations.
● Recognize the relative importance of elements in a situation.
● Handle ambiguous, incomplete, or erroneous information.

Figure 9.22

The major application areas of artificial intelligence. Note that the many applications of AI can be grouped into the three major areas of cognitive science, robotics, and natural interfaces.

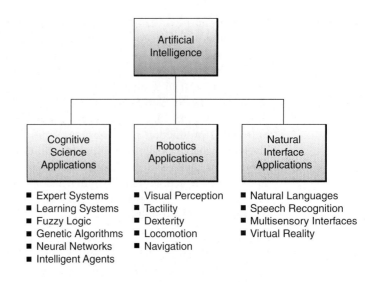

of their current technologies. Figure 9.23 outlines some of the latest developments in commercial applications of artificial intelligence.

Cognitive Science. This area of artificial intelligence is based on research in biology, neurology, psychology, mathematics, and many allied disciplines. It focuses on researching how the human brain works and how humans think and learn. The results of such research in *human information processing* are the basis for the development of a variety of computer-based applications in artificial intelligence.

Applications in the cognitive science area of AI include the development of *expert systems* and other *knowledge-based systems* that add a knowledge base and some reasoning capability to information systems. Also included are *adaptive learning systems* that can modify their behaviors based on information they acquire as they operate. Chess-playing systems are primitive examples of such applications, though many more applications are being implemented. *Fuzzy logic* systems can process data that are incomplete or ambiguous, that is, *fuzzy data*. Thus, they can solve unstructured problems with incomplete knowledge by developing approximate inferences and answers, as humans do. *Neural network* software can learn by processing sample problems and their solutions. As neural nets start to recognize patterns, they can begin to program themselves to solve such problems on their own. *Genetic algorithm* software uses Darwinian (survival of the fittest), randomizing, and other mathematics functions to simulate evolutionary processes that can generate increasingly better solutions to problems. And *intelligent agents* use expert system and other AI technologies to serve as software surrogates for a variety of end user applications.

Robotics. AI, engineering, and physiology are the basic disciplines of robotics. This technology produces robot machines with computer intelligence and computer-controlled, humanlike physical capabilities. This area thus includes applications designed to give robots the powers of sight, or visual perception; touch, or tactile capabilities; dexterity, or skill in handling and manipulation; locomotion, or the physical ability to move over any terrain; and navigation, or the intelligence to properly find one's way to a destination [37]. The use of robotics in computer-aided manufacturing was discussed in Chapter 7.

Natural Interfaces. The development of natural interfaces is considered a major area of AI applications and is essential to the natural use of computers by humans.

Figure 9.23

Examples of some of the latest commercial applications of AI.

Commercial Applications of AI
Decision Support
● Intelligent work environment that will help you capture the *why* as well as the *what* of engineered design and decision making
● Intelligent human-computer interface (HCI) systems that can understand spoken language and gestures, and facilitate problem solving by supporting organizationwide collaborations to solve particular problems
● Situation assessment and resource allocation software for uses that range from airlines and airports to logistics centers
Information Retrieval
● AI-based intra- and Internet systems that distill tidal waves of information into simple presentations
● Natural language technology to retrieve any sort of online information, from text to pictures, videos, maps, and audio clips, in response to English questions
● Database mining for marketing trend analysis, financial forecasting, maintenance cost reduction, and more
Virtual Reality
● X-raylike vision enabled by enhanced-reality visualization that allows brain surgeons to "see through" intervening tissue to operate, monitor, and evaluate disease progression
● Automated animation and haptic interfaces that allow users to interact with virtual objects via touch (i.e., medical students can "feel" what it's like to suture severed aortas)
Robotics
● Machine vision inspections systems for gauging, guiding, identifying, and inspecting products and providing competitive advantage in manufacturing
● Cutting-edge robotics systems from micro robots and hands and legs to cognitive robotic and trainable modular vision systems

Source: Adapted from Patrick Winston, "Rethinking Artificial Intelligence," Program Announcement: Massachusetts Institute of Technology, September 1997, p. 3.

For example, the development of *natural languages* and speech recognition are major thrusts of this area of AI. Being able to talk to computers and robots in conversational human languages and have them "understand" us as easily as we understand each other is a goal of AI research. This involves research and development in linguistics, psychology, computer science, and other disciplines. This area of AI drives developments in the voice recognition and response technology discussed in Chapter 3 and the natural programming languages discussed in Chapter 4. Other natural interface research applications include the development of multisensory devices that use a variety of body movements to operate computers. This is related to the emerging application area of *virtual reality*. Virtual reality involves using multisensory human-computer interfaces that enable human users to experience computer-simulated objects, spaces, activities, and "worlds" as if they actually exist.

Neural Networks

Neural networks are computing systems modeled after the brain's meshlike network of interconnected processing elements, called *neurons*. Of course, neural networks are a lot simpler in architecture (the human brain is estimated to have over

Figure 9.24

A display of a data mining software package that uses neural network technology.

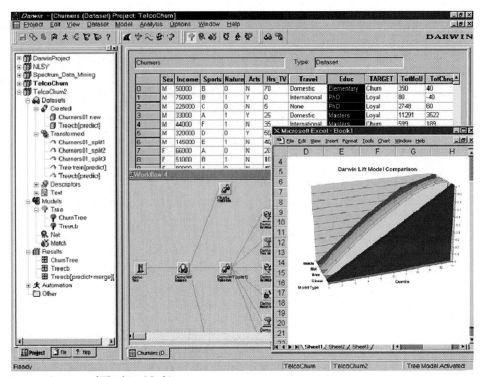

Source: Courtesy of Thinking Machines.

100 billion neuron brain cells!). However, like the brain, the interconnected processors in a neural network operate in parallel and interact dynamically with each other. This enables the network to "learn" from data it processes. That is, it learns to recognize patterns and relationships in the data it processes. The more data examples it receives as input, the better it can learn to duplicate the results of the examples it processes. Thus, the neural network will change the strengths of the interconnections between the processing elements in response to changing patterns in the data it receives and the results that occur [8, 50]. See Figure 9.24.

For example, a neural network can be trained to learn which credit characteristics result in good or bad loans. Developers of a credit evaluation neural network could provide it with data from many examples of credit applications and loan results to process, and opportunities to adjust the signal strengths between its neurons. The neural network would continue to be trained until it demonstrated a high degree of accuracy in correctly duplicating the results of recent cases. At that point it would be trained enough to begin making credit evaluations of its own.

Neural networks can be implemented on microcomputers and other traditional computer systems by using software packages that simulate the activity of a neural network. Specialized neural network coprocessor circuit boards for PCs are also available that provide significantly greater processing power. In addition, special-purpose neural net microprocessor chips are being used in specific application areas such as military weapons systems, image processing, and voice recognition. However, most business applications depend primarily on neural net software packages to accomplish applications ranging from credit risk assessment to check signature verification, investment forecasting, data mining, and manufacturing quality control [8, 55].

<table>
<tr><td>

Neural Nets at Go.com

</td><td>

Go.com has a targeted marketing service that more closely targets advertising on its Internet search engine to users' interests by keeping track of every search that a user makes. The service uses neural network technology from Aptex Software to observe all the searches users run every time they use the Go.com search engine. The neural net software then calculates a numeric value, or "vector," that describes users' interests. Go.com uses that information to match users to the online ads it sells to advertisers on its Web search pages.

Other commercial World Wide Web sites use this technology to build up the usefulness of their websites or encourage repeat business. Many electronic commerce websites use customizing software to track user behavior and predict what a user will be interested in seeing in the future. For example, Aptex has a version of its neural net software designed for sites that sell products and services online. Select-Cast for Commerce Servers analyzes customer buying patterns, and predicts products and services the customer will be likely to buy, based on past behavior [52].

</td></tr>
</table>

Fuzzy Logic Systems

In spite of the funny name, **fuzzy logic** systems represent a small, but serious and growing, application of AI in business. Fuzzy logic is a method of reasoning that resembles human reasoning since it allows for approximate values and inferences (fuzzy logic) and incomplete or ambiguous data (fuzzy data) instead of relying only on *crisp data*, such as binary (yes/no) choices. For example, Figure 9.25 illustrates a partial set of rules (fuzzy rules) and a fuzzy SQL query for analyzing and extracting credit risk information on businesses that are being evaluated for selection as investments.

Notice how fuzzy logic uses terminology that is deliberately imprecise, such as *very high, increasing, somewhat decreased, reasonable,* and *very low.* This enables fuzzy systems to process incomplete data and quickly provide approximate, but acceptable, solutions to problems that are difficult for other methods to solve. Fuzzy logic queries of a database, such as the SQL query shown in Figure 9.25, promise to improve the extraction of data from business databases. Queries can be stated more naturally in words that are closer to the way business specialists think about the topic for which they want information [11, 31].

Fuzzy Logic in Business

Examples of applications of fuzzy logic are numerous in Japan, but rare in the United States. The United States has tended to prefer using AI solutions like expert systems or neural networks. But Japan has implemented many fuzzy logic

Figure 9.25   An example of fuzzy logic rules and a fuzzy logic SQL query in a credit risk analysis application.

Fuzzy Logic Rules

Risk should be acceptable
If debt-equity is very high
  then risk is positively increased
If income is increasing
  then risk is somewhat decreased
If cash reserves are low to very low
  then risk is very increased
If PE ratio is good
  then risk is generally decreased

Fuzzy Logic SQL Query

Select companies
  from financials
    where revenues are very large
    and pe_ratio is acceptable
    and profits are high to very high
    and (income/employee_tot) is reasonable

Figure 9.26

Using genetic algorithm
software for business
problem solving.

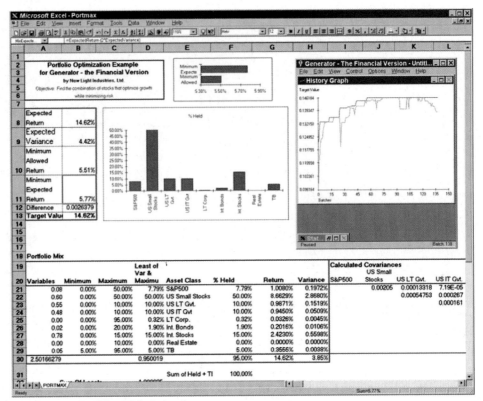

Source: Courtesy of New Light Industries.

applications, especially the use of special-purpose fuzzy logic microprocessor chips, called fuzzy process controllers. Thus, the Japanese ride on subway trains, use elevators, and drive cars that are guided or supported by fuzzy process controllers made by Hitachi and Toshiba. They can even trade shares on the Tokyo Stock Exchange using a stock-trading program based on fuzzy logic rules. Many new models of Japanese-made products also feature fuzzy logic microprocessors. The list is growing, but includes autofocus cameras, autostabilizing camcorders, energy-efficient air conditioners, self-adjusting washing machines, and automatic transmissions [42].

Genetic Algorithms

The use of **genetic algorithms** is a growing application of artificial intelligence. Genetic algorithm software uses Darwinian (survival of the fittest), randomizing, and other mathematical functions to simulate an evolutionary process that can yield increasingly better solutions to a problem. Genetic algorithms were first used to simulate millions of years in biological, geological, and ecosystem evolution in just a few minutes on a computer. Now genetic algorithm software is being used to model a variety of scientific, technical, and business processes [3, 26].

Genetic algorithms are especially useful for situations in which thousands of solutions are possible and must be evaluated to produce an optimal solution. Genetic algorithm software uses sets of mathematical process rules (*algorithms*) that specify how combinations of process components or steps are to be formed. This may involve trying random process combinations (*mutation*), combining parts of several good processes (*crossover*), and selecting good sets of processes and discarding poor ones (*selection*) in order to generate increasingly better solutions. Figure 9.26 illustrates a business use of genetic algorithm software.

GE's Engeneous	General Electric's design of a more efficient jet engine for the Boeing 777 is a classic example of a genetic algorithm application in business. A major engineering challenge was to develop more efficient fan blades for the engine. GE's engineers estimated that it would take billions of years, even with a supercomputer, to mathematically evaluate the astronomical number of performance and cost factors and combinations involved. Instead, GE used a hybrid genetic algorithm/expert system, called Engeneous, that produced an optimal solution in less than a week [3].

Virtual Reality

Virtual reality (VR) is a computer-simulated reality. Virtual reality is a fast-growing area of artificial intelligence that had its origins in efforts to build more natural, realistic, multisensory human–computer interfaces. So virtual reality relies on multisensory input/output devices such as a tracking headset with video goggles and stereo earphones, a *data glove* or jumpsuit with fiber-optic sensors that track your body movements, and a *walker* that monitors the movement of your feet. Then you can experience computer-simulated "virtual worlds" three-dimensionally through sight, sound, and touch. Thus, virtual reality is also called *telepresence*. For example, you can enter a computer-generated virtual world, look around and observe its contents, pick up and move objects, and move around in it at will. Thus, virtual reality allows you to interact with computer-simulated objects, entities, and environments as if they actually exist [2, 48]. See Figure 9.27.

VR Applications

Current applications of virtual reality are wide ranging and include computer-aided design (CAD), medical diagnostics and treatment, scientific experimentation in many physical and biological sciences, flight simulation for training pilots and astronauts, product demonstrations, employee training, and entertainment, especially 3-D video arcade games. CAD is the most widely used industrial VR application. It enables architects and other designers to design and test electronic 3-D models of products and structures by entering the models themselves and examining, touching, and manipulating sections and parts from all angles. This scientific-visualization

Figure 9.27

This environmental designer uses a virtual reality system to design the interiors of an office building.

Source: Image Bank.

capability is also used by pharmaceutical and biotechnology firms to develop and observe the behavior of computerized models of new drugs and materials, and by medical researchers to develop ways for physicians to enter and examine a virtual reality of a patient's body.

VR designers are creating everything from virtual weather patterns and virtual wind tunnels to virtual cities and virtual securities markets. For example, by converting stock market and other financial data into three-dimensional graphic form, securities analysts can use VR systems to more rapidly observe and identify trends and exceptions in financial performance. Also promising are applications in information technology itself. This includes the development of 3-D models of telecommunications networks and databases. These virtual graphical representations of networks and databases make it easier for IS specialists to visualize the structure and relationships of an organization's telecommunications networks and corporate databases, thus improving their design and maintenance.

VR becomes *telepresence* when users who can be anywhere in the world use VR systems to work alone or together at a remote site. Typically, this involves using a VR system to enhance the sight and touch of a human who is remotely manipulating equipment to accomplish a task. Examples range from virtual surgery, where surgeon and patient may be on either side of the globe, to the remote use of equipment in hazardous environments such as chemical plants or nuclear reactors.

VR Limitations. The use of virtual reality seems limited only by the performance and cost of its technology. For example, some VR users develop *cybersickness*, such as eyestrain and motion sickness, from performance problems in the realism of VR systems. The cost of a virtual reality system is another limitation. A VR system consisting of a headset with goggles and headphones, a fiber-optic data glove, motion-sensing devices, and a powerful engineering workstation with top-quality 3-D modeling software can exceed $50,000. If you want less cumbersome devices, more realistic displays, and a more natural sense of motion in your VR world, costs can escalate into several hundred thousand dollars. CAVEs *(cave automatic virtual environments)*, virtual reality rooms that immerse you in a virtual reality experience, cost several million dollars to set up [10, 48].

However, the cost of highly realistic multisensory VR systems is dropping each year. In the meantime some VR developers are using the VRML *(virtual reality modeling language)* to develop 3-D hypermedia graphics and animation products that provide a primitive VR experience for PC users on the World Wide Web and corporate intranets. Further advances in these and other VR technologies are expected to make virtual reality useful for a wide array of business and end user applications [2, 5, 48].

VR at Morgan Stanley	The Market Risks Department of Morgan Stanley & Co. uses Discovery virtual reality software by Visible Decisions to model risks of financial investments in varying market conditions. Discovery displays three-dimensional results using powerful Silicon Graphics workstations.
	Morgan Stanley also uses VRML (virtual reality modeling language) as a way to display the results of risk analyses in three dimensions on PCs in their corporate intranet. (VRML allows developers to create hyperlinks between 3-D objects in files and databases on the World Wide Web and corporate intranets.) 3-D results are displayed on ordinary PCs in a virtual reality experience over an intranet connection to a Sun Microsystems SPARCstation server running a Sun VRML browser. Seeing data in three dimensions and experiencing relationships among data in a virtual reality process make it easier for analysts to make intuitive connections than it would be with a 2-D chart or table of numbers [53].

Intelligent Agents

Intelligent agents are growing in popularity as a way to use artificial intelligence routines in software to help users accomplish many kinds of tasks in e-business and e-commerce. An intelligent agent is a *software surrogate* for an end user or a process that fulfills a stated need or activity. An intelligent agent uses its built-in and learned knowledge base about a person or process to make decisions and accomplish tasks in a way that fulfills the intentions of a user. Sometimes an intelligent agent is given a graphic representation or persona, such as Einstein for a science advisor, Sherlock Holmes for an information search agent, and so on. Thus, intelligent agents (also called *software robots* or "bots") are special-purpose knowledge-based information systems that accomplish specific tasks for users. Figure 9.28 summarizes major types of intelligent agents [30, 40].

One of the most well-known uses of intelligent agents is the wizards found in Microsoft Office and other software suites. These wizards are built-in capabilities that can analyze how an end user is using a software package and offer suggestions on how to complete various tasks. Thus, wizards might help you change document margins, format spreadsheet cells, query a database, or construct a graph. Wizards and other software agents are also designed to adjust to your way of using a software package so that they can anticipate when you will need their assistance. See Figure 9.29.

The use of intelligent agents is growing rapidly as a way to simplify software use, search websites on the Internet and corporate intranets, and help customers do comparison shopping among the many e-commerce sites on the Web. Intelligent agents are becoming necessary as software packages become more sophisticated and powerful, as the Internet and the World Wide Web become more vast and complex, and as information sources and e-commerce alternatives proliferate exponentially. In fact, some commentators forecast that much of the future of computing will consist of intelligent agents performing their work for users. So instead of using agents to help us accomplish computing tasks, we will be managing the performance of intelligent agents as they perform computing tasks for us [34].

Figure 9.28

Examples of different types of intelligent agents.

Types of Intelligent Agents
User Interface Agents
● **Interface Tutors.** Observe user computer operations, correct user mistakes, and provide hints and advice on efficient software use.
● **Presentation Agents.** Show information in a variety of reporting and presentation forms and media based on user preferences.
● **Network Navigation Agents.** Discover paths to information and provide ways to view information that are preferred by a user.
● **Role-Playing Agents.** Play what-if games and other roles to help users understand information and make better decisions.
Information Management Agents
● **Search Agents.** Help users find files and databases, search for desired information, and suggest and find new types of information products, media, and resources.
● **Information Brokers.** Provide commercial services to discover and develop information resources that fit the business or personal needs of a user.
● **Information Filters.** Receive, find, filter, discard, save, forward, and notify users about products received or desired, including e-mail, voice mail, and all other information media.

Intelligent agents like those in Ask Jeeves help you find information in a variety of categories from many online sources.

Source: Courtesy of Ask Jeeves, Inc., © 2000.

Dow Jones & Co.: Intelligent Web Agents

Websites such as Amazon.com's Shop the Web, Excite's Jango.com, and MySimon's MySimon.com use intelligent agent technology to help users compare prices for fragrances, book titles, or other items on multiple sites. Other types of agents can answer e-mail, conduct intelligent searches, or help users find news reports and useful sites based on stated preferences.

For example, dozens of sites can show you the news, but Dow Jones & Co.'s Dow Jones Interactive (www.djinteractive.com) is different. Nearly 600,000 customers pay to search through stories from its 6,000 licensed and internal publications. That's a huge amount of data to filter and the company has applied intelligent agent and other artificial intelligence (AI) technologies to manage the task.

One of the site's most important features is Custom Clips, which allows users to create folders based on predefined topics—such as agribusiness or IBM—or to build their own using custom key words. When the site IS agent retrieves relevant articles, it can post them to a database-generated Web page or send the stories to the user's e-mail address [39, 40].

Expert Systems

One of the most practical and widely implemented applications of artificial intelligence in business is the development of expert systems and other knowledge-based information systems. A *knowledge-based information system* (KBIS) adds a knowledge base to the major components found in other types of computer-based information systems. An **expert system** (ES) is a knowledge-based information system that uses its knowledge about a specific, complex application area to act as an expert consultant to end users. Expert systems provide answers to questions in a very specific problem area by making humanlike inferences about knowledge contained in a specialized knowledge base. They must also be able to explain their reasoning process and conclusions to a user. So expert systems can provide decision support to end users in the form of advice from an expert consultant in a specific problem area [19, 37].

Components of an Expert System

The components of an expert system include a knowledge base and software modules that perform inferences on the knowledge and communicate answers to a user's questions. Figure 9.30 illustrates the interrelated components of an expert system. Note the following components:

- **Knowledge Base.** The knowledge base of an expert system contains (1) facts about a specific subject area (for example, *John is an analyst*) and (2) heuristics (rules of thumb) that express the reasoning procedures of an expert on the subject (for example: IF John is an analyst, THEN he needs a workstation). There are many ways that such knowledge is represented in expert systems. Examples are *rule-based*, *frame-based*, *object-based*, and *case-based* methods of knowledge representation. See Figure 9.31.

Figure 9.30

Components of an expert system. The software modules perform inferences on a knowledge base built by an expert and/or knowledge engineer. This provides expert answers to an end user's questions in an interactive process.

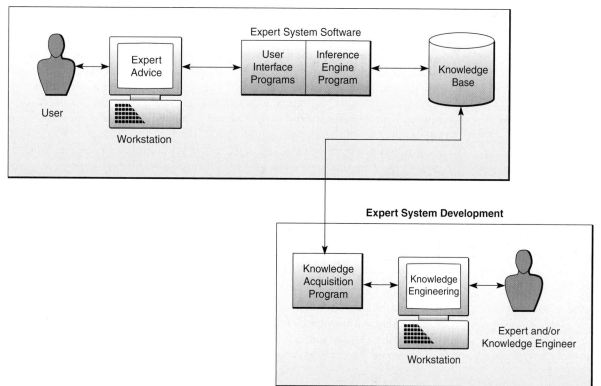

Figure 9.31

A summary of four ways that knowledge can be represented in an expert system's knowledge base.

Methods of Knowledge Representation
● **Case-Based Reasoning.** Representing knowledge in an expert system's knowledge base in the form of cases, that is, examples of past performance, occurrences, and experiences.
● **Frame-Based Knowledge.** Knowledge represented in the form of a hierarchy or network of *frames*. A frame is a collection of knowledge about an entity consisting of a complex package of data values describing its attributes.
● **Object-Based Knowledge.** Knowledge represented as a network of objects. An object is a data element that includes both data and the methods or processes that act on those data.
● **Rule-Based Knowledge.** Knowledge represented in the form of rules and statements of fact. Rules are statements that typically take the form of a premise and a conclusion such as: If (condition), Then (conclusion).

● **Software Resources.** An expert system software package contains an inference engine and other programs for refining knowledge and communicating with users. The **inference engine** program processes the knowledge (such as rules and facts) related to a specific problem. It then makes associations and inferences resulting in recommended courses of action for a user. User interface programs for communicating with end users are also needed, including an explanation program to explain the reasoning process to a user if requested. Knowledge acquisition programs are not part of an expert system but are software tools for knowledge base development, as are *expert system shells*, which are used for developing expert systems.

Expert System Applications

Using an expert system involves an interactive computer-based session in which the solution to a problem is explored, with the expert system acting as a consultant to an end user. The expert system asks questions of the user, searches its knowledge base for facts and rules or other knowledge, explains its reasoning process when asked, and gives expert advice to the user in the subject area being explored. For example, Figure 9.32 illustrates one of the displays of an expert system.

Expert systems are being used for many different types of applications, and the variety of applications is expected to continue to increase. However, you should realize that expert systems typically accomplish one or more generic uses. Figure 9.33 outlines six generic categories of expert system activities, with specific examples of actual expert system applications. As you can see, expert systems are being used in many different fields, including medicine, engineering, the physical sciences, and business. Expert systems now help diagnose illnesses, search for minerals, analyze compounds, recommend repairs, and do financial planning. So from a strategic business standpoint, expert systems can and are being used to improve every step of the product cycle of a business, from finding customers to shipping products to providing customer service.

ES for Advertising Strategy

ADCAD (ADvertising Communications Approach Designer) is an expert system that assists advertising agencies in setting marketing and communications objectives, selecting creative strategies, and identifying effective communications approaches. In particular, it is designed to help advertisers of consumer products with the development of advertising objectives and ad copy strategy, and the selection of communications techniques. ADCAD's knowledge base consists of rules derived from various sources, including consultations with the creative staff of the Young & Rubicam advertising agency. Figure 9.34 gives examples of two of the hundreds of rules in ADCAD's knowledge base [6].

Figure 9.32

This expert system helps a bank analyze and score customers based on various profiles, thus helping it manage the composition and attrition of its customer base.

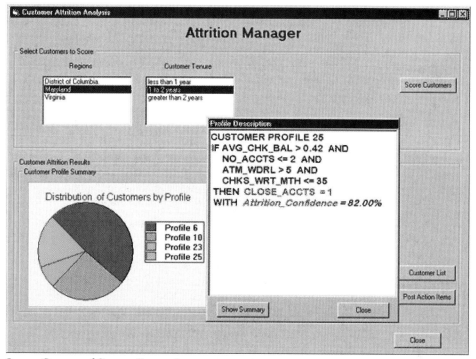

Source: Courtesy of Gensym Corporation.

ADCAD uses a question-and-answer format, asking the user a series of questions about the advertising problem. It then searches through its knowledge base, matching user answers against its rules to draw inferences. Then ADCAD presents its recommendations, along with a rationale for each recommendation if asked. For example, Figure 9.34 shows how ADCAD responded when asked to explain its recommendation to use a celebrity to present an ad on television for a shampoo product.

ADCAD has been popular with advertising and brand managers since it provides them with a rationale for their current advertising, as well as ideas for new communications approaches. Another benefit of ADCAD is its support of what-if analysis of advertising options. ADCAD allows users to easily change their responses to questions and investigate the impact of alternative product or market assumptions. This feature has also made ADCAD a valuable training tool for students and novice advertising managers [6].

Developing Expert Systems

The easiest way to develop an expert system is to use an **expert system shell** as a developmental tool. An expert system shell is a software package consisting of an expert system without its kernel, that is, its knowledge base. This leaves a *shell* of software (the inference engine and user interface programs) with generic inferencing and user interface capabilities. Other development tools (such as rule editors and user interface generators) are added in making the shell a powerful expert system development tool.

Expert system shells are now available as relatively low-cost software packages that help users develop their own expert systems on microcomputers. They allow trained users to develop the knowledge base for a specific expert system application. For example, one shell uses a spreadsheet format to help end users develop IF-THEN rules, automatically generating rules based on examples furnished by a user. Once a knowledge base is constructed, it is used with the shell's inference engine

Application Categories of Expert Systems

- **Decision management**—Systems that appraise situations or consider alternatives and make recommendations based on criteria supplied during the discovery process:
    - Loan portfolio analysis
    - Employee performance evaluation
    - Insurance underwriting
    - Demographic forecasts

- **Diagnostic/troubleshooting**—Systems that infer underlying causes from reported symptoms and history:
    - Equipment calibration
    - Help desk operations
    - Software debugging
    - Medical diagnosis

- **Design/configuration**—Systems that help configure equipment components, given existing constraints:
    - Computer option installation
    - Manufacturability studies
    - Communications networks
    - Optimum assembly plan

- **Selection/classification**—Systems that help users choose products or processes, often from among large or complex sets of alternatives:
    - Material selection
    - Delinquent account identification
    - Information classification
    - Suspect identification

- **Process monitoring/control**—Systems that monitor and control procedures or processes:
    - Machine control (including robotics)
    - Inventory control
    - Production monitoring
    - Chemical testing

and user interface modules as a complete expert system on a specific subject area. Other software tools may require an IT specialist to develop expert systems. See Figure 9.35.

Knowledge Engineering

A **knowledge engineer** is a professional who works with experts to capture the knowledge (facts and rules of thumb) they possess. The knowledge engineer then builds the knowledge base (and the rest of the expert system if necessary), using an iterative, prototyping process until the expert system is acceptable. Thus, knowledge engineers perform a role similar to that of systems analysts in conventional information systems development.

Once the decision is made to develop an expert system, a team of one or more domain experts and a knowledge engineer may be formed. Or experts skilled in the use of expert system shells could develop their own expert systems. If a shell is used, facts and rules of thumb about a specific domain can be defined and entered into a knowledge base with the help of a rule editor or other knowledge acquisition tool. A limited working prototype of the knowledge base is then constructed, tested, and evaluated using the inference engine and user interface programs of the shell. The knowledge engineer and domain experts can modify the knowledge base, then retest the system and evaluate the results. This process is repeated until the knowledge base and the shell result in an acceptable expert system.

Figure 9.34

Examples of the rules and explanations of the ADCAD expert system for developing advertising strategies.

Examples of ADCAD's Rules

- **IF** ad objective = convey brand image or reinforce brand image
  AND brand purchase motivation = sensory stimulation
  AND message processing motivation = high
  THEN emotional tone = elation.

- **IF** ad objective = change brand beliefs
  AND message processing motivation = low
  AND purchase anxiety = low
  AND brand use avoids fearful consequences = yes
  THEN emotional tone = high fear.

Example of an ADCAD explanation of its recommendation to use a celebrity.

- Just a moment please . . .
  The advertising objective is to communicate or reinforce your brand's image, mood, or an associated lifestyle to consumers who are not highly motivated to process your ad message. A celebrity presenter can attract the consumer's attention, enhance your brand's image, and become a memorable cue for brand evaluation.

ES Development at MacMillan Bloedel

MacMillan Bloedel Corp. is a forest products conglomerate in British Columbia, Canada, that produces particleboard used in building items such as bookshelves, furniture, and kitchen cupboards. Due to high staff turnover and a reorganization of divisional personnel at the particleboard plant, only two senior employees had the comprehensive, operational know-how and training needed to operate the facility. After they retired, MacMillan had to call back a former manager, named Herb, as a very expensive consultant to keep the mill running. So MacMillan decided to develop an expert system to capture his knowledge of plant operations. The expert system that resulted documents the

Figure 9.35

Using the Visual Rule Studio and Visual Basic to develop rules for a credit management expert system.

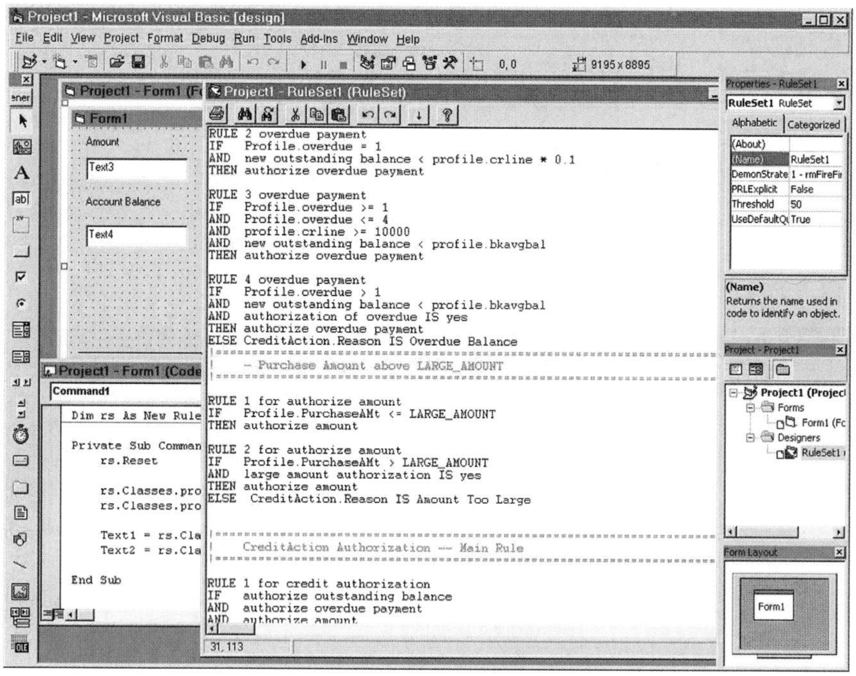

Source: Courtesy of MultiLogic, Inc.

procedures needed to efficiently run the facility, and is also used for training and upgrading employees.

Knowledge engineers used the ACQUIRE expert system shell from Acquired Intelligence to develop the system. The ACQUIRE knowledge-based acquisition system was used to pick Herb's brain for his knowledge of how to start up, clean up, and set up the particleboard coating line. The line consisted of machines whose operations parameters changed according to the coating to be applied. Herb was able to provide expert information, in the form of facts and rules, that was captured in the expert system's knowledge base. The resulting expert system consistently provides quality maintenance and operations advice to the mill operators [19].

The Value of Expert Systems

Obviously, expert systems are not the answer to every problem facing an organization. People using other types of information systems do quite well in many problem situations. So what types of problems are most suitable to expert system solutions? One way to answer this is to look at examples of the applications of current expert systems, including the generic tasks they can accomplish, as were summarized in Figure 9.33. Another way is to identify criteria that make a problem situation suitable for an expert system. Figure 9.36 outlines some important criteria.

Figure 9.36 should emphasize that many real world situations do not fit the suitability criteria for expert system solutions. Hundreds of rules may be required to capture the assumptions, facts, and reasoning that are involved in even simple problem situations. For example, a task that might take an expert a few minutes to accomplish might require an expert system with hundreds of rules and take several months to develop. A task that may take a human expert several hours to do may require an expert system with thousands of rules and take several years to build [1, 9].

Benefits of Expert Systems

An expert system captures the expertise of an expert or group of experts in a computer-based information system. Thus, it can outperform a single human expert in many problem situations. That's because an expert system is faster and more consistent, can have the knowledge of several experts, and does not get tired or distracted by overwork or stress.

Expert systems also help preserve and reproduce the knowledge of experts. They allow a company to preserve the expertise of an expert before she leaves the organization. This expertise can then be shared by reproducing the software and knowledge base of the expert system. This allows novices to be trained and supported by copies of an expert system distributed throughout an organization. Finally, expert

---

Figure 9.36

Criteria for applications that are suitable for expert systems development.

Suitability Criteria for Expert Systems
• **Domain:** The domain, or subject area, of the problem is relatively small and limited to a well-defined problem area.
• **Expertise:** Solutions to the problem require the efforts of an expert. That is, a body of knowledge, techniques, and intuition is needed that only a few people possess.
• **Complexity:** Solution of the problem is a complex task that requires logical inference processing, which would not be handled as well by conventional information processing.
• **Structure:** The solution process must be able to cope with ill-structured, uncertain, missing, and conflicting data, and a problem situation that changes with the passage of time.
• **Availability:** An expert exists who is articulate and cooperative, and who has the support of the management and end users involved in the development of the proposed system.

systems can have the same competitive advantages as other types of information technology. That is, the effective use of expert systems can allow a firm to significantly improve the efficiency of its business processes, or produce new knowledge-based products and services.

Limitations of Expert Systems

The major limitations of expert systems arise from their limited focus, inability to learn, maintenance problems, and developmental cost. Expert systems excel only in solving specific types of problems in a limited domain of knowledge. They fail miserably in solving problems requiring a broad knowledge base and subjective problem solving. They do well with specific types of operational or analytical tasks, but falter at subjective managerial decision making. For example, an expert system might help a financial consultant develop alternative investment recommendations for a client. But it could not adequately evaluate the nuances of current political, economic, and societal developments, or the personal dynamics of a session with a client. These important factors would still have to be handled by the human consultant before a final investment decision could be reached.

Expert systems may also be difficult and costly to develop and maintain properly. The costs of knowledge engineers, lost expert time, and hardware and software resources may be too high to offset the benefits expected from some applications. Also, expert systems can't maintain themselves. That is, they can't learn from experience but must be taught new knowledge and modified as new expertise is needed to match developments in their subject areas. However, some of these limitations can be overcome by combining expert systems with AI technologies such as fuzzy logic and neural networks or by the use of expert system developmental tools that make the job of development and maintenance easier.

Summary

- **e-Business Decision Support Trends.** Major changes are taking place in traditional MIS, DSS, and EIS tools for providing the information and modeling managers need to support their decision making. Decision support in business is changing, driven by rapid developments in end user computing and networking; Internet, Web browser, and related technologies; and the explosion of e-commerce activity. The growth of corporate intranets, extranets, as well as the Web, has accelerated the development of "executive class" interfaces like enterprise information portals, enterprise knowledge portals, and Web-enabled decision support software tools, and their use by lower levels of management and by individuals and teams of business professionals. In addition, the dramatic expansion of e-commerce has opened the door to the use of enterprise portals and DSS tools by the suppliers, customers, and other business stakeholders of a company for customer relationship and supply chain management and other e-business applications.

- **Information, Decisions, and Management.** Information systems can support a variety of management decision-making levels and decisions. These include the three levels of management activity (strategic, tactical, and operational decision making) and three types of decision structures (structured, semistructured, and unstructured). Information systems provide a wide range of information products to support these types of decisions at all levels of the organization.

- **Management Information Systems.** Management information systems provide prespecified reports and responses to managers on a periodic, exception, demand, or push reporting basis, to meet their need for information to support decision making.

- **OLAP and Data Mining.** Online analytical processing interactively analyzes complex relationships among large amounts of data stored in multidimensional databases. Data mining analyzes the vast amounts of historical data that have been prepared for analysis in data warehouses. Both technologies discover patterns, trends, and exception conditions in a company's data that support their business analysis and decision making.

- **Decision Support Systems.** Decision support systems are interactive, computer-based information systems that use DSS software and a model base and database to provide information tailored to support semistructured and unstructured decisions faced by individual managers. They are designed to use a decision maker's own insights and judgments in an ad hoc, interactive, analytical modeling process leading to a specific decision.

- **Executive Information Systems.** Executive information systems are information systems originally designed to support the strategic information needs of top management. However, their use is spreading to lower levels of management and business professionals.

EIS are easy to use and enable executives to retrieve information tailored to their needs and preferences. Thus, EIS can provide information about a company's critical success factors to executives to support their planning and control responsibilities.

- **Enterprise Information and Knowledge Portals.** Enterprise information portals provide a customized and personalized Web-based interface for corporate intranets to give their users easy access to a variety of internal and external business applications, databases, and information services that are tailored to their individual preferences and information needs. Thus, an EIP can supply personalized Web-enabled information, knowledge, and decision support to executives, managers, and business professionals, as well as customers, suppliers, and other business partners. An enterprise knowledge portal is a corporate intranet portal that extends the use of an EIP to include knowledge management functions and knowledge base resources so that it becomes a major form of knowledge management system for a company.

- **Artificial Intelligence.** The major application domains of artificial intelligence (AI) include a variety of applications in cognitive science, robotics, and natural interfaces. The goal of AI is the development of computer functions normally associated with human physical and mental capabilities, such as robots that see, hear, talk, feel, and move, and software capable of reasoning, learning, and problem solving. Thus, AI is being applied to many applications in business operations and managerial decision making, as well as in many other fields.

- **AI Technologies.** The many application areas of AI are summarized in Figure 9.22, including neural networks, fuzzy logic, genetic algorithms, virtual reality, and intelligent agents. Neural nets are hardware or software systems based on simple models of the brain's neuron structure that can learn to recognize patterns in data. Fuzzy logic systems use rules of approximate reasoning to solve problems where data are incomplete or ambiguous. Genetic algorithms use selection, randomizing, and other mathematics functions to simulate an evolutionary process that can yield increasingly better solutions to problems. Virtual reality systems are multisensory systems that enable human users to experience computer-simulated environments as if they actually existed. Intelligent agents are knowledge-based software surrogates for a user or process in the accomplishment of selected tasks.

- **Expert Systems.** Expert systems are knowledge-based information systems that use software and a knowledge base about a specific, complex application area to act as expert consultants to users in many business and technical applications. Software includes an inference engine program that makes inferences based on the facts and rules stored in the knowledge base. A knowledge base consists of facts about a specific subject area and heuristics (rules of thumb) that express the reasoning procedures of an expert. The benefits of expert systems (such as preservation and replication of expertise) must be balanced with their limited applicability in many problem situations.

Key Terms and Concepts

These are the key terms and concepts of this chapter. The page number of their first explanation is in parentheses.

1. Analytical modeling (303)
   a. Goal-seeking analysis (305)
   b. Optimization analysis (305)
   c. Sensitivity analysis (304)
   d. What-if analysis (303)
2. Artificial intelligence (315)
   a. Application areas (316)
   b. Domains (315)
3. Data mining (306)
4. Data visualization system (302)
5. Decision structure (296)
6. Decision support versus management reporting (300)
7. Decision support system (300)
8. DSS software (301)
9. E-business decision support (294)
   a. Applications (294)
   b. Trends (294)

10. Enterprise information portal (309)
11. Enterprise knowledge portal (311)
12. Executive information system (307)
13. Expert system (325)
    a. Applications (326)
    b. Benefits and limitations (330)
    c. Components (325)
    d. System development (327)
14. Expert system shell (327)
15. Fuzzy logic (319)
16. Genetic algorithms (320)
17. Geographic information system (302)
18. Inference engine (326)
19. Intelligent agent (323)
20. Knowledge base (325)
21. Knowledge engineer (328)

22. Knowledge management system (311)
23. Level of management decision making (295)
24. Management information system (297)
25. Model base (307)
26. Neural network (317)
27. Online analytical processing (298)
28. Reporting alternatives (297)
29. Robotics (316)
30. Virtual reality (321)

Review Quiz

Match one of the key terms and concepts listed previously with one of the brief examples or definitions that follow. Try to find the best fit for answers that seem to fit more than one term or concept. Defend your choices.

_____ 1. Internet technologies and e-commerce developments have expanded the form and use of decision support in business.

_____ 2. Web-enabled systems that provide decision support for e-business managers, employees, and business partners.

_____ 3. A CEO and a production team may have different needs for decision making.

_____ 4. Decision-making procedures cannot be specified in advance for some complex decision situations.

_____ 5. Information systems for the strategic information needs of top and middle managers.

_____ 6. Systems that produce predefined reports for management.

_____ 7. Managers can receive reports periodically, on an exception basis, or on demand.

_____ 8. Provide an interactive modeling capability tailored to the specific information needs of managers.

_____ 9. Interactive responses to ad hoc inquiries versus prespecified information.

_____ 10. A collection of mathematical models and analytical techniques.

_____ 11. Analyzing the effect of changing variables and relationships and manipulating a mathematical model.

_____ 12. Changing revenues and tax rates to see the effect on net profit after taxes.

_____ 13. Changing revenues in many small increments to see revenue's effect on net profit after taxes.

_____ 14. Changing revenues and expenses to find how you could achieve a specific amount of net profit after taxes.

_____ 15. Changing revenues and expenses subject to certain constraints in order to achieve the highest profit after taxes.

_____ 16. Realtime analysis of complex business data.

_____ 17. Attempts to find patterns hidden in business data in a data warehouse.

_____ 18. Represents complex data using three-dimensional graphical forms.

_____ 19. A customized and personalized Web interface to internal and external information resources available through a corporate intranet.

_____ 20. Using intranets to gather, store, and share a company's best practices among employees.

_____ 21. An enterprise information portal that can access knowledge management functions and company knowledge bases.

_____ 22. Information technology that focuses on the development of computer functions normally associated with human physical and mental capabilities.

_____ 23. Applications in cognitive science, robotics, and natural interfaces.

_____ 24. Development of computer-based machines that possess capabilities such as sight, hearing, dexterity, and movement.

_____ 25. Computers can provide you with computer-simulated experiences.

_____ 26. An information system that integrates computer graphics, geographic databases, and DSS capabilities.

_____ 27. A knowledge-based information system that acts as an expert consultant to users in a specific application area.

_____ 28. Applications such as diagnosis, design, prediction, interpretation, and repair.

_____ 29. These systems can preserve and reproduce the knowledge of experts but have a limited application focus.

_____ 30. A collection of facts and reasoning procedures in a specific subject area.

_____ 31. A software package that manipulates a knowledge base and makes associations and inferences leading to a recommended course of action.

_____ 32. A software package consisting of an inference engine and user interface programs used as an expert system development tool.

_____ 33. One can either buy a completely developed expert system package, develop one with an expert system shell, or develop one from scratch by custom programming.

_____ 34. An analyst who interviews experts to develop a knowledge base about a specific application area.

_____ 35. AI systems that use neuron structures to recognize patterns in data.

_____ 36. AI systems that use approximate reasoning to process ambiguous data.

_____ 37. Knowledge-based software surrogates that do things for you.

_____ 38. Software that uses mathematical functions to simulate an evolutionary process.

Discussion Questions

1. Is the form and use of information and decision support in e-business changing and expanding? Why or why not?

2. Has the growth of self-directed teams to manage work in organizations changed the need for strategic, tactical, and operational decision making in business?

3. What is the difference between the ability of a manager to retrieve information instantly on demand using an MIS and the capabilities provided by a DSS?

4. Refer to the Real World Case on International Rectifier, Blair, and Pillsbury in the chapter. Are e-business decision support products evolving into hybrid systems that combine MIS, OLAP, DSS, AI, and other related capabilities? Give examples to illustrate your answer.

5. In what ways does using an electronic spreadsheet package provide you with the capabilities of a decision support system?

6. Are enterprise information portals making executive information systems unneccessary? Explain your reasoning.

7. Refer to the Real World Case on Grove Madsen and Cutler-Hammer in the chapter. Could e-manufacturing principles and technologies be used to profitably produce products for individual consumers? Why or why not?

8. Can computers think? Will they ever be able to? Explain why or why not.

9. What are some of the most important applications of AI in business? Defend your choices.

10. What are some of the limitations or dangers you see in the use of AI technologies such as expert systems, virtual reality, and intelligent agents? What could be done to minimize such effects?

Application Exercises

Complete the following exercises as individual or group projects that apply chapter concepts to real world business situations.

1. BizRate: e-Commerce Website Reviews

Visit *www.bizrate.com* and you instantly have information about hundreds of online stores and what thousands of previous shoppers at those stores think about them. See Figure 9.37.

Looking to buy a Miles Davis music CD, I entered *CDnow.com* at BizRate.com's Rapid Reports section. What I got back was an overall customer satisfaction rating of four and a half stars out of a possible five. I scrolled down farther to find individual ratings of the online music store's product selection, pricing, customer support, and on-time delivery record. The rating was based on reports from 22,034 shoppers who had already been to the CDnow site.

BizRate.com users who don't know the name of an online music retailer can go to the site's categories section. Here, I typed in *music* and was given the choice of shopping by product, store, or personal preferences. I wanted to pay by check and receive my CD the next day. Two sites—Cdconnection.com and Playback.com—met my criteria. The first had been reviewed by more than 1,200 shoppers. The other had received 911 reviews.

   a. Check out the reviews of online stores for a product you want to buy at the bizrate.com site. How thorough, valid, and valuable were they to you? Explain.

   b. How could similar Web-enabled reporting systems be used in other business situations? Give an example.

Source: Adapted from Julia King, "Infomediary," *Computerworld*, November 1, 1999, p. 58. Copyright 1999 by Computerworld, Inc., Framingham, MA 01701. Reprinted from *Computerworld*.

2. Jango and mySimon: Intelligent Web Price Comparison Agents

Jango/Excite Product Finder

The Jango award-winning intelligent agent software is used in the Excite shopping area. This agent can use presupplied templates to search categories or adapt new templates from past experiences. The Excite shopping area at www.excite.com covers a range of product categories, although the merchant list in the standard categories is a bit shorter than some others. One nice touch is that some of Jango's price comparisons also list shipping costs along with the product price, so you can compare the total price. You also can search for product reviews in addition to finding merchants that sell a given product.

mySimon

The mySimon site (http://www.mysimon.com) starts from a category listing that covers many different kinds of merchandise. After you find the subcategory that interests you, you can search by manufacturer and

Figure 9.37

The BizRate website offers customer reviews of online stores.

Source: Courtesy of BizRate.com, © 2000.

product keywords. mySimon also offers shopping guides for areas such as Winter Sports or product guides such as Coffeemaker/Espresso. You can register with the site to receive its newsletter, use the talk forums, and save your searches.

a. Visit the Jango and mySimon sites. Which price comparison agent do you prefer? Why?

b. Are these sites examples of Web-enabled decision support systems? Why or why not?

c. How could this technology be used in business situations? Give an example.

Source: Adapted from Jennifer Powell, "Streamline Your Shopping," *Smart Computing*, February 2000, pp. 88–90.

3. Retail Electronic Commerce System for Pinnacle Products

Pinnacle Products is considering developing a strategic system to allow it to sell products through its website. None of Pinnacle's direct competitors currently utilize electronic retailing, but the president of Pinnacle feels that business to consumer electronic commerce is appropriate for Pinnacle's industry and wants to be in a leadership position. You have been asked to assist in preparing a preliminary feasibility study for the system. Your analysis is to be restricted to the first five years of operation.

The Information Systems and Marketing departments have developed estimates for your use. The marketing department estimates that sales will be $1,000,000 in year 2 (the system is expected to take one full year for initial development) and that sales will grow 50 percent per year thereafter. The department also estimates that each dollar of electronic sales will contribute 25 cents to profit. The IS department has estimated the cost of developing and maintaining this system across it first five years of operation, as shown below.

	Year 1	Year 2	Year 3	Year 4	Year 5
System Cost:	$900,000	$400,000	$400,000	$500,000	$600,000
Projected Sales $:	$2,000,000 (50 percent growth per year)				
Sales Contribution Rate:	(25 percent contribution to profits in all years 1–5)				

a. Based upon these figures construct a spreadsheet to analyze the costs and benefits of the proposed system. Projected sales for year 3 will be 1.5 times year 2 sales, year 4's sales will be 1.5 times year 3's and so on. The benefits of the system are equal to new sales times the 25 percent contribution to profits. Your spreadsheet should include a column showing the net contribution (benefits minus system cost) for each year.

b. Assume that ABC Company requires a return of 25 percent on this type of investment. Add an internal rate of return estimate to your spreadsheet and determine whether the return exceeds the 25 percent requirement.

c. This type of investment is risky largely because sales growth is very hard to predict. To assess risk,

marketing has been asked to provide worst-case and best-case estimates for the rate of growth in sales. Their worst-case estimate is a growth of only 10 percent per year while their best-case estimate is 100 percent growth per year. Calculate the returns under best case and worst case assumptions and add these estimates to your spreadsheet.

d. Prepare a set of PowerPoint slides or similar presentation materials summarizing your key results and including a recommendation as to whether this project should be pursued.

4. Palm City Police Department

The Palm City Police Department has eight defined precincts. The police station in each precinct has primary responsibility for all activities in its precinct area. The current population of each precinct, the number of violent crimes committed in each precinct, and the number of officers assigned to each precinct are shown below. The department has established a goal of equalizing access to police services. Ratios of population per police officer and violent crimes per police officer should be calculated for each precinct. These ratios for the city as a whole are shown below.

a. Build a spreadsheet to perform the analysis described above and print it out.

Currently, no funds are available to hire additional officers. Based on the citywide ratios the department has decided to develop a plan to shift resources as needed in order to ensure that no precinct has more than 1,100 residents per police officer and no precinct has more than seven violent crimes per police officer. The department will transfer officers from precincts, that easily meet these goals to precincts that violate one or both of these ratios.

b. Use goal seeking on your spreadsheet to move police officers between precincts until the goals are met. (You can use the goal seek function to see how many officers would be required to bring each precinct into compliance and then judgmentally reduce officers in precincts that are substantially within the criteria.) Print out a set of results that allow the department to comply with these ratios and a memorandum to your instructor summarizing your results and the process you used to develop them.

Precinct	Population	Violent Crimes	Police Officers
Shea Blvd.	96,552	318	85
Lakeland Heights	99,223	582	108
Sunnydale	68,432	206	77
Old Town	47,732	496	55
Mountainview	101,233	359	82
Financial District	58,102	511	70
Riverdale	78,903	537	70
Cole Memorial	75,801	306	82
Total	625,978	3,315	629
Per officer	995.196	5.270	

Ames Department Stores and IBM:
The Business Case for Enterprise Information Portals

We all know that the information is out there, but who knows how to find it? Consider, for example, Ames Department Stores, headquartered in Rock Hill, Connecticut, a discount retail chain with 452 outlets. Until recently sales managers there had to spend as much as a day combing through numerous databases, file servers, and Web documents just to pull together a basic sales report.

Sadly, Ames is not alone it its info-maze dilemma. According to a recent KPMG survey of 423 large companies, 67 percent of respondents claimed they had too much information to manage, and 56 percent complained of having to "reinvent the wheel" every time they started a new project.

So how do you deliver the information your employees need in a way that's easy? Increasingly, big companies are investing in souped-up intranets that consultants call enterprise portals. Think of an enterprise information portal (EIP), not in the sense of Yahoo's consumer service, but rather as a single, well-organized gateway to all the information services and resources within a company.

At their most basic, enterprise portals provide access to human-resources staples like employee benefit forms and employee directories; more advanced versions add critical applications like sales force tools, collaborative features such as whiteboards, and company and industry news. It all gets delivered through a single Web page that each employee can personalize to match his or her job and information needs.

San Francisco–based Plumtree Software built a $1 million portal for Ames that provides easy access to all of the company's databases on one page, letting sales associates monitor data as it comes in, spotting trends and responding instantaneously to match supply and demand. The result: a nimbler and more efficient effort to stock the shelves in a timely manner. Ames CFO Rolando de Aguiar expects a return on investment—in inventory reduction and other cost savings—of at least 20 percent this year.

Stories like de Aguiar's have made portals a hot subject for corporations. The Delphi Group, a Boston-based market research company, estimates that 60 percent of the world's 2,000 largest companies either currently have a portal or will be building one in the next six months. According to Delphi, sales of portal applications are expected to reach $730 million in 2001, five times more than in 1999. "Providing a portal is becoming part of the way you do business," says Hadley Reynolds, Delphi's director of research.

The spur for this growth has been twofold. First, enterprise portal software is finally capable of supporting hundreds of thousands of users, something the earliest versions couldn't do. Second, Web technology provides a shortcut for tying together legacy applications and information systems. Instead of trying to get old applications to exchange data with one another (an extremely costly and difficult undertaking known to IT folks as application integration), a portal takes the data you want from each existing application and displays it on a Web page.

IBM's homegrown portal—nicknamed W_3 for its private Web address, w3.ibm.com—may be one of the most sophisticated in existence. From W_3's home page, IBM's roughly 325,000 employees worldwide can view a host of IBM-related information, all tailored to their individual interests and responsibilities. The portal provides company and industry news, transcripts and videos of recent presentations, and a library of online training courses.

But that's just the tip of the iceberg. W_3 is the front door to dozens of business applications, from procurements to contract requisitions, as well as discussion boards and collaborative workspaces. It also links to a searchable database, called BluePages that helps employees find subject-matter experts within IBM. Currently, W_3 gets 450,000 to 500,000 page views a day, and more than 120,000 employees have created personal profiles for the directory, according to IBM's intranet director, Mike Wing.

The payoff? IBM estimates that W_3 helps the company save more than $500 million a year across many departments. For example, by simply delivering health care benefits information online instead of on paper, IBM saved $1 million last year. Even more impressive, by buying 94 percent of its goods and services through W_3, IBM trimmed $377 million from its budgets.

Do you need a portal? "Portals will become part of the cost of doing business for most corporations over the next four to five years," says Andy Warzecha, a VP at Meta Group. Even for smaller businesses, less expensive outsourced options are available from such companies as SAP (mysap.com), Yahoo! (corporate.yahoo.com), and Intranets.com.

Building and supporting an enterprise portal for a large company is a big—and expensive—undertaking. But in most cases, the payoff for that hard work comes quickly. According to Meta Group senior VP David Yockelson, the average portal project pays for itself in about eight months. "We're seeing enterprise portals have a huge impact on productivity and cost savings," says Delphi's Reynolds. "If your competitors are doing it, in our view, it's risky *not* to deploy something." Yes, that's a hard sell you've heard before, but portals are a simple, proven technology that really does make sense.

Case Study Questions

1. How does an enterprise information portal differ from an intranet in terms of technologies used and applications provided to business users?

2. What are the business benefits of an EIP to Ames and IBM and their employees?

3. How might an EIP help you as a business professional in your work activities? Give several examples to illustrate your answer.

Source: Adapted from Dylan Tweeney, "Whip, Beat, and Stomp Your Data Into Submission," *eCompany Now*, May 2001, pp. 110–112. © 2001 Time Inc. All rights reserved.

Eli Lilly and Anadarko Petroleum:
Data Visualization Systems for Decision Support

Businesses are drowning, just drowning in data. And they asked for it. Computers today make it relatively easy for industries ranging from pharmaceuticals to oil exploration to amass vast archives of information. The data can be of the utmost importance in figuring out where to drill an oil well, or which of a zillion chemical compounds to bet on as the next blockbuster drug. But the payoffs go only to those who can somehow drag a net through tidal waves of raw information and capture the little fishes of opportunity swimming within them.

A new idea in software is beginning to help these companies reduce the time and money they spend searching for patterns and meaning in their data oceans. It's an approach that started as a doctoral thesis by Christopher Ahlberg, the 32-year-old Swedish-born founder of software company Spotfire, in Somerville, Massachusetts. Part of his inspiration was to make examining the contents of different databases as easy as surfing different websites with a Web browser. His other goal was to use visually compelling displays to present the results in ways that mere mortals can quickly and intuitively grasp. "Databases were the last area where graphic design was waiting to happen," Ahlberg says.

Spotfire's software is the first to combine both "data visualization" and a powerful database querying flexibility. Known as DecisionSite, the data visualization system (DVS) software isn't cheap—installations start at $100,000. That hasn't stopped customers in a wide range of industries from buying more than 16,000 licenses. Recently IBM's life-sciences division puts its marketing muscle behind the product. Big Blue is combining its data-management software with Spotfire's tools in a package aimed at drug companies that hope to speed up their R&D.

The magic in Spotfire's software is that it lets users easily do what-if queries and comparisons of data from different sources by moving sliders on a computer screen with a mouse. The results appear as brightly colored bar graphs, pie charts, scatter plots, and even maps.

When Spotfire rolled out its software four years ago, it aimed first at the drug industry, where the data explosion has been immense. An early adopter was Sheldon Ort, Eli Lilly's information officer for manufacturing and supply services. Ort now has some 1,500 company scientists around the world hooked up to Spotfire's software. "We primarily use it to facilitate decision making," Ort says. "With its ability to represent multiple sources of information and interactively change your view, it's helpful for homing in on specific molecules and deciding whether we should be doing further testing on them."

Using Spotfire, researchers avoid having to construct multiple queries in perfect syntax. Dragging the sliders to and fro, the user is actually launching a sequence of queries in rapid succession and seeing the outcomes expressed graphically onscreen. Lilly uses the software to conduct meetings among researchers at multiple sites who are linked on a computer network. As the person making a presentation moves the sliders on his or her screen, everyone can see the families, clusters, outliers, gaps, anomalies, and other statistical nuggets that database users fish for. Ideas can be tried out collaboratively in real time. Ort is now experimenting with using Spotfire to streamline Lilly's supply chain.

Ahlberg says he had never thought about applying his software to the energy business until Anadarko Petroleum called. "I didn't see any analogy between drug discovery and the oil and gas industry. Then I realized that the oil and gas equivalent of the chemical-structure libraries that drugmakers want was maps—geographical maps." Spotfire formed an alliance with ESRI in Redlands, California, a prominent supplier of geographical information systems. The final touches are now being put on a version of DecisionSite incorporating a map visualizer feature for Anadarko's people to use in planning oil-field operations.

Says Ron Bain, manager of international exploration at Anadarko: "A lot of the databases our geoscientists and engineers query read out as Excel spreadsheets, and comparing 1,000 data points from a few of them is mentally difficult. Spotfire is like Excel on steroids. It does all the cross-plotting instantaneously, looking for trends."

With oil prices up, Anadarko is starting a new well somewhere in the world every five hours. To decide where the wells should be, the company's geophysicists consult databases of magnetic data, gravity data, information from sensors in existing wells, and the results of seismic surveys of subsurface rock structures. Disk drives fill quickly in this business. A survey of a nine-square-mile block of Gulf of Mexico sea floor, for example, comprises five or six gigabytes of data; Anadarko has thousands of such survey blocks in its gigantic 20-terabyte archives.

The promise Spotfire holds is "streamlining the decision process," Bain says. "I can have a lot of information without it making me very smart or very successful. The idea here is to find oil economically and produce it. We like to say that we drill where oil *should* be, not here it *could* be. DecisionSite guides us to a quicker answer."

Case Study Questions

1. How does the DecisionSite data visualization system provide decision support to companies like Eli Lilly and Anadarko Petroleum?

2. What are the business benefits of using DecisionSite for Eli Lilly and Anadarko?

3. How could DVS products like DecisionSite help business professionals in other industries? Give several examples to illustrate your answer.

Management
Challenges

Business
Applications

Module
IV

Information
Technologies

Development
Processes

Foundation
Concepts

Module IV

Development Processes

How can business professionals help to develop and implement information system solutions to meet the challenges and opportunities faced by today's e-business enterprises? Answering that question is the goal of the chapter of this module, which focuses on the processes for developing and implementing e-business applications.

- Chapter 10, **Developing e-Business Solutions,** introduces the traditional, prototyping, and end user approaches to the development of e-business systems, and discusses the processes and managerial issues involved in the implementation of new e-business applications.

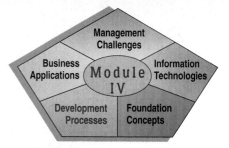

Chapter 10

Developing e-Business

Solutions

Chapter Highlights

Learning Objectives

After reading and studying this chapter, you should be able to:

1. Use the systems development process outlined in this chapter, and the model of IS components from Chapter 1 as problem-solving frameworks to help you propose information systems solutions to simple business problems.

2. Describe and give examples to illustrate how you might use each of the steps of the information systems development cycle to develop and implement an e-business system.

3. Explain how prototyping improves the process of systems development for end users and IS specialists.

4. Identify the activities involved in the implementation of new information systems.

5. Describe several evaluation factors that should be considered in evaluating the acquisition of hardware, software, and IS services.

6. Identify several change management solutions for end user resistance to the implementation of new e-business applications.

Developing e-Business Systems

IS Development

Suppose the chief executive of the company where you work asks you to find a Web-enabled way to get information to and from the salespeople in your company. How would you start? What would you do? Would you just plunge ahead and hope you could come up with a reasonable solution? How would you know whether your solution was a good one for your company? Do you think there might be a systematic way to help you develop a good solution to the CEO's request? There is. It's a problem-solving process called *the systems approach.*

When the systems approach to problem solving is applied to the development of information system solutions to business problems, it is called *information systems development* or *application development.* This section will show you how the systems approach can be used to develop e-business systems and applications that meet the business needs of a company and its employees and stakeholders.

Analyzing AvantGo, Sparklist, BuyerZone, and OfficeMax

Read the Real World Case on AvantGo, Sparklist, BuyerZone, and OfficeMax on the next page. We can learn a lot about the challenges of good Web systems design for B2B e-commerce. See Figure 10.1.

This case dramatizes some of the common failures in good business system design found in many B2B e-commerce websites. The case author is a principal in a Web design and usability evaluation consultancy who emphasizes that the

Figure 10.1

Jakob Nielsen, a principal of Nielsen Norman Group, finds that the design of many B2B e-commerce websites fails to provide adequate support for business users.

Source: Jakob Nielsen

AvantGo, Sparklist, BuyerZone, and OfficeMax:
Failures in B2B Website Design

I t is almost impossible to do business with most B2B sites. How often do the sites provide the answers to the simplest questions a business must ask before deciding on a vendor: Exactly what does the product or service do? What are the terms and conditions? What is the price?

Bottom line: B2B sites often lose customers because it is impossible to discover the answers to essential questions early in the process, while the user is still evaluating potential vendors. For example, let's evaluate two B2B sites. One does a poor job of providing basic purchasing information. The other offers enough information to encourage and facilitate a transaction.

Bad: The developer Web page of AvantGo.com is a particularly clueless example of B2B usability. A prospective customer cannot see the customer agreement without having to complete a long inquisitive form. AvantGo has it wrong. At this stage in the online process, I don't want to "apply" to become a customer. I want to see what the company has to offer and at what terms. In particular, I don't want to disclose sensitive information about my own business. The site asks for information such as the number of visitors to my website and my audience demographics. I am not going to reveal confidential company information to some website just because it asks for it. Most users, when faced with such a screen, will either go away or enter fake data.

Better: Sparklist.com clearly discloses its prices for hosting e-mail newsletters on an e-mail newsletter-hosting Web page, which is one click from the home page. Of course, no site is perfect. Some items on the Web page are unclear. Are all customers subject to a three-month minimum or is it a three-month contract? The "have a salesperson call" area uses a U.S. format for phone numbers and time zones, a disadvantage if trying to attract global customers.

Another Study. Customers of business-to-business sites are also faced with much more difficult decisions than the customers of business-to-consumer sites. We recently studied the reactions of users who were trying to decide whether to lease or buy office equipment.

BuyerZone.com and OfficeMax both failed because they didn't support users going through a process. In order to support a customer's process, businesses need to understand it from the user's perspective. If users feel pushed through a process or can't figure out what to do next, you're skipping steps that matter to them. Don't just design Web pages. Design support for users' tasks. Here's how:

Support Processes before Pushing Transactions. Customers need compelling reasons to complete complex tasks on the Web. It's usually easier to pick up the phone and deal with a salesperson than to go it alone on the Web. Users often tell us that the Web is OK for preliminary research, but useless for closing deals. Most B2B sites overlook their users' perspectives in their eagerness to move them to the checkout line. For example, users don't want to click Buy Now until they select their payment options on BuyerZone.com. Unfortunately, clicking Buy Now is the only way to see both leasing and purchase prices.

Provide the Right Tools at the Right Time. Complex processes require different tools for different stages of the process. Early in a process, customers need ways to quickly look at their purchasing options in many ways, without commitment. Let users easily manipulate data they care about, and carry that forward to their transaction when they're ready. For example, while it's good that BuyerZone.com offers a calculator to explore leasing prices, users struggle to understand the leasing terminology and want more guidance and recommendations from the tool.

Integrate Related Tasks. From a customer's prospective, leasing is just a payment option and is a part of a larger acquisition process, not a separate task. Yet OfficeMax separates leasing from purchasing, as if a user would get leases in an independent project. A user who has selected office equipment on OfficeMax's website can't explore how to lease that equipment. Instead, she must abandon her selection, find leasing services from the site's Business Services section, and then suffer through an awkward registration process.

Don't Push the Cart. The only purpose of a shopping cart is to hold items until users are ready for checkouts. Yet many B2B sites inappropriately use shopping carts as mandatory gateways to vital sales information, such as shipping costs or availability. If your shopping cart plays a larger role than a holding tank on your site, you're probably forcing users to do things out of their preferred sequence. For example, in order to compare leasing and purchase payments on BuyerZone.com, users must add an item to their cart by clicking a Buy Now button. Imagine how quickly you would spurn a human salesperson who forced you to "buy now" every time you wanted a question answered.

Case Study Questions

1. What failures in B2B website design are being made by AvantGo.com and Sparklist.com? How would you fix these problems?

2. What failures in B2B website design are being made by BuyerZone.com and OfficeMax.com? How would you fix these problems?

3. Visit each of the above websites. Have they fixed their design problems? Do you see any other design shortcomings? Discuss your findings.

Source: Adapted from Jakob Nielsen, "Better Data Brings Better Sales," *Business 2.0*, May 15, 2001, p. 34; and "Design for Process, Not for Products," *Business 2.0*, July 10, 2001, p. 28. © 2001 Time Inc. All rights reserved.

customers of business-to-business websites must make more difficult purchasing and financing decisions during their online experience than users of business-to-consumer sites. Thus, online business customers need much better information, tools, and other support than they are getting from the B2B sites of many companies. This finding is detailed in the examples of the system design failures found at the websites of the four companies discussed in the case.

The Systems Approach

The systems approach to problem solving uses a systems orientation to define problems and opportunities and develop solutions. Studying a problem and formulating a solution involves the following interrelated activities:

1. Recognize and define a problem or opportunity using *systems thinking*.
2. Develop and evaluate alternative system solutions.
3. Select the system solution that best meets your requirements.
4. Design the selected system solution.
5. Implement and evaluate the success of the designed system.

Systems Thinking

Using **systems thinking** to understand a problem or opportunity is one of the most important aspects of the systems approach. Management consultant and author Peter Senge calls systems thinking *the fifth discipline*. Senge argues that mastering systems thinking (along with the disciplines of personal mastery, mental models, shared vision, and team learning) is vital to personal fulfillment and business success in a world of constant change. The essence of the discipline of systems thinking is "seeing the forest *and* the trees" in any situation by:

- Seeing *interrelationships* among *systems* rather than linear cause-and-effect chains whenever events occur.
- Seeing *processes* of change among *systems* rather than discrete "snapshots" of change, whenever changes occur [32].

One way of practicing systems thinking is to try to find systems, subsystems, and components of systems in any situation you are studying. This is also known as using a *systems context*, or having a *systemic view* of a situation. For example, the business organization or business process in which a problem or opportunity arises could be viewed as a system of input, processing, output, feedback, and control components. Then to understand a problem and solve it, you would determine if these basic systems functions are being properly performed. See Figure 10.2.

Example

The sales process of a business can be viewed as a system. You could then ask: Is poor sales performance (output) caused by inadequate selling effort (input), out-of-date sales procedures (processing), incorrect sales information (feedback), or inadequate sales management (control)? Figure 10.2 illustrates this concept. ●

Figure 10.2

An example of systems thinking. You can better understand a sales problem or opportunity by identifying and evaluating the components of a sales system.

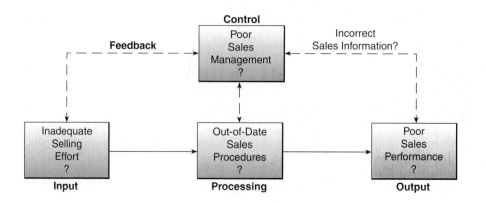

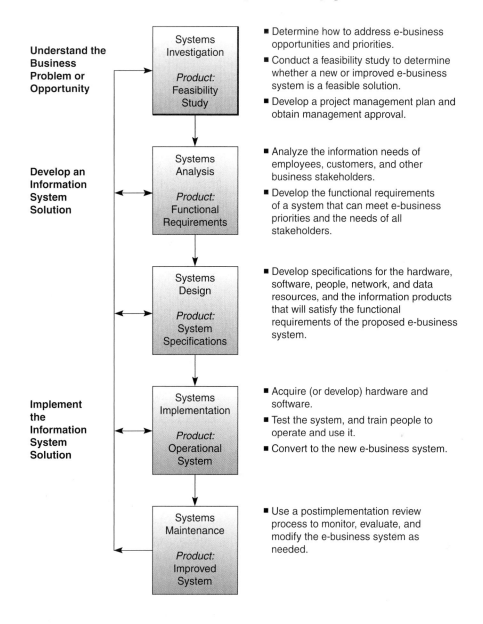

The traditional information systems development cycle. Note how the five steps of the cycle are based on the stages of the systems approach. Also note the products that result from each step in the cycle, and that you can recycle back to any previous step if more work is needed.

Understand the Business Problem or Opportunity

Systems Investigation

Product: Feasibility Study

- Determine how to address e-business opportunities and priorities.
- Conduct a feasibility study to determine whether a new or improved e-business system is a feasible solution.
- Develop a project management plan and obtain management approval.

Develop an Information System Solution

Systems Analysis

Product: Functional Requirements

- Analyze the information needs of employees, customers, and other business stakeholders.
- Develop the functional requirements of a system that can meet e-business priorities and the needs of all stakeholders.

Systems Design

Product: System Specifications

- Develop specifications for the hardware, software, people, network, and data resources, and the information products that will satisfy the functional requirements of the proposed e-business system.

Implement the Information System Solution

Systems Implementation

Product: Operational System

- Acquire (or develop) hardware and software.
- Test the system, and train people to operate and use it.
- Convert to the new e-business system.

Systems Maintenance

Product: Improved System

- Use a postimplementation review process to monitor, evaluate, and modify the e-business system as needed.

The Systems Development Cycle

Using the systems approach to develop information system solutions can be viewed as a multistep process called the **information systems development cycle,** also known as the *systems development life cycle* (SDLC). Figure 10.3 illustrates what goes on in each stage of this process, which includes the steps of (1) investigation, (2) analysis, (3) design, (4) implementation, and (5) maintenance.

You should realize, however, that all of the activities involved are highly related and interdependent. Therefore, in actual practice, several developmental activities can occur at the same time, so different parts of a development project can be at different stages of the development cycle. In addition, you and IS specialists may recycle back at any time to repeat previous activities in order to modify and improve a system you are developing.

Prototyping

The systems development process frequently takes the form of, or includes, a *prototyping* approach. **Prototyping** is the rapid development and testing of working models, or **prototypes,** of new applications in an interactive, iterative process that can be used by both IS specialists and business professionals. Prototyping makes the development process faster and easier, especially for projects where end user requirements are hard to define. Thus, prototyping is sometimes called *rapid application design* (RAD). Prototyping has also opened up the application development process

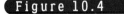

Figure 10.4

Application development using prototyping. Note how prototyping combines the steps of the systems development cycle and changes the traditional roles of IS specialists and end users.

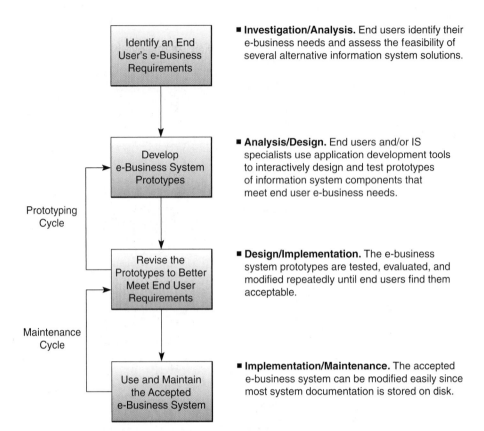

to end users because it simplifies and accelerates systems design. Thus prototyping has enlarged the role of end users and changed the methods of IS specialists in systems development. See Figure 10.4.

The Prototyping Process

Prototyping can be used for both large and small applications. Typically, large e-business systems still require using a traditional systems development approach, but parts of such systems can frequently be prototyped. A prototype of a business application needed by an end user is developed quickly using a variety of application development software tools. The prototype system is then repeatedly refined until it is acceptable.

As Figure 10.4 illustrates, prototyping is an iterative, interactive process that combines steps of the traditional systems development cycle. End users with sufficient experience with application development tools can do prototyping themselves. Alternatively, you could work with an IS specialist to develop a prototype system in a series of interactive sessions. For example, you could develop, test, and refine prototypes of management reports, data entry screens, or output displays.

Usually, a prototype is modified several times before end users find it acceptable. Any program modules that are not generated by application development software can then be coded by programmers using conventional programming languages. The final version of the application system is then turned over to its end users for operational use. Figure 10.5 outlines a typical prototyping-based systems development process for an e-business application.

Amway, Inc.: Doing Prototyping

To keep development times to a minimum, Amway, Inc. sought to build an enterprise information portal that would essentially perform as an intelligent assistant, able to retrieve and format relevant information for employees in research and

Figure 10.5

An example of a typical prototyping-based systems development process for an e-business application.

Example of Prototyping Development
● **Team.** A few end users and IS developers form a team to develop an e-business application.
● **Schematic.** The initial prototype schematic design is developed.
● **Prototype.** The schematic is converted into a simple point-and-click prototype using prototyping tools.
● **Presentation.** A few screens and routine linkages are presented to users.
● **Feedback.** After the team gets feedback from users, the prototype is reiterated.
● **Reiteration.** Further presentations and reiterations are made.
● **Consultation.** Consultations are held with IT consultants to identify potential improvements and conformance to existing standards.
● **Completion.** The prototype is converted into a finished application.
● **Acceptance.** Users review and sign off on their acceptance of the new e-business system.
● **Installation.** The new e-business software is installed on network servers.

development. Craig Abbott, IT group leader, developed a Web-based application using Lotus Notes and Domino groupware systems.

After a series of prototypes and a pilot project, the portal (code-named Artemis) was rolled out to a cross-section of approximately 100 users in the product development and process development areas of the division. It retrieved information for costing, forecasting, and project management activities, and was slated to integrate with Amway's document management system.

To understand its business drivers, Amway set up a user development group that identified the information needed and how difficult it was to retrieve it. The initial prototype EIP was then tailored to help the project team meet its top three objectives: speed, accuracy, and ease of use. "The rapid development of prototypes (in a series of prototyping sessions with users) was important to help refine the system, because users sometimes have a hard time communicating the results they're looking for," says Steve Klemm, director of engineering R&D.

Artemis is still being phased in, but it's already having an impact. "The biggest benefit has been to provide a source of consistent information to the research and development staff," Klemm says. "There's less confusion during project discussions because everyone is looking at the same set of information" [36].

Starting the Systems Development Process

Do we have e-business opportunities? What are our e-business priorities? How can information technologies provide information system solutions that address our e-business priorities? These are the questions that have to be answered in the **systems investigation stage**—the first step in the systems development process. This stage may involve consideration of proposals generated by an e-business planning process, which we will discuss in Chapter 12. The investigation stage also includes the preliminary study of proposed information system solutions to meet a company's e-business priorities and opportunities. See Figure 10.6.

Feasibility Studies

Because the process of development can be costly, the systems investigation stage may require a preliminary study called a **feasibility study.** A feasibility study is a preliminary study where the information needs of prospective users and the resource requirements, costs, benefits, and feasibility of a proposed project are determined. Then you might formalize the findings of this study in a written report that includes preliminary specifications and a developmental plan for a proposed e-business

Figure 10.6

An e-business application planning process includes consideration of IT proposals for addressing the strategic e-business priorities of a company and planning for e-business application development and implementation.

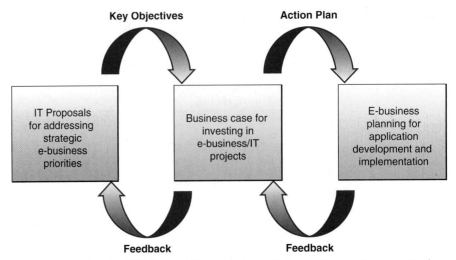

Source: Adapted from Ravi Kalakota and Marcia Robinson, *E-Business: Roadmap for Success* (Reading, MA: Addison-Wesley, 1999), p. 341. © 1999 Addison-Wesley Publishing Company, Inc. Reprinted by permission of Addison-Wesley Longman Inc.

application. If management approves the recommendations of the feasibility study, the development process can continue.

The goal of feasibility studies is to evaluate alternative system solutions and to propose the most feasible and desirable e-business application for development. The feasibility of a proposed e-business system can be evaluated in terms of four major categories, as illustrated in Figure 10.7.

The focus of **organizational feasibility** is on how well a proposed system supports the strategic e-business priorities of the organization. **Economic feasibility** is concerned with whether expected cost savings, increased revenue, increased profits, reductions in required investment, and other types of benefits will exceed the costs of developing and operating a proposed system. For example, if an e-business project can't cover its development costs, it won't be approved, unless mandated by government regulations or strategic business considerations.

Technical feasibility can be demonstrated if reliable hardware and software capable of meeting the needs of a proposed system can be acquired or developed by the business in the required time. Finally, **operational feasibility** is the willingness and ability of the management, employees, customers, suppliers, and others to operate, use, and support a proposed system. For example, if the software for a new e-commerce system is too difficult to use, customers or employees may make too many errors and avoid using it. Thus, it would fail to show operational feasibility. See Figure 10.8.

Cost/Benefit Analysis. Feasibility studies typically involve **cost/benefit analysis.** If costs and benefits can be quantified, they are called tangible; if not, they are called

Figure 10.7

Organizational, economic, technical, and operational feasibility factors. Note that there is more to feasibility than cost savings or the availability of hardware and software.

Organizational Feasibility	Economic Feasibility
• How well the proposed system supports the e-business priorities of the organization	• Cost savings • Increased revenue • Decreased investment requirements • Increased profits

Technical Feasibility	Operational Feasibility
• Hardware, software, and network capability, reliability and availability	• Employee, customer, supplier acceptance • Management support • Government or other requirements

Figure 10.8

Examples of how a feasibility study might measure the feasibility of a proposed e-commerce system.

Organizational Feasibility	Economic Feasibility
• How well a proposed e-commerce system fits the company's plans for integrating sales, marketing, and financial e-business systems	• Savings in labor costs • Increased sales revenue • Decreased investment in inventory • Increased profits
Technical Feasibility	**Operational Feasibility**
• Capability, reliability and availability of e-commerce hardware, software, and website management services	• Acceptance of employees • Management support • Customer and supplier acceptance

intangible. Examples of tangible costs are the costs of hardware and software, employee salaries, and other quantifiable costs needed to develop and implement an IS solution. **Intangible costs** are difficult to quantify; they include the loss of customer goodwill or employee morale caused by errors and disruptions arising from the installation of a new system.

Tangible benefits are favorable results, such as the decrease in payroll costs caused by a reduction in personnel or a decrease in inventory carrying costs caused by reduction in inventory. **Intangible benefits** are harder to estimate. Such benefits as better customer service or faster and more accurate information for management fall into this category. Figure 10.9 lists typical tangible and intangible benefits with examples. Possible tangible and intangible costs would be the opposite of each benefit shown.

Systems Analysis

What is **systems analysis?** Whether you want to develop a new application quickly or are involved in a long-term project, you will need to perform several basic activities of systems analysis. Many of these activities are an extension of those used in conducting a feasibility study. However, systems analysis is not a preliminary study. It is an in-depth study of end user information needs that produces *functional*

Figure 10.9

Possible benefits of e-commerce systems, with examples. Note that an opposite result for each of these benefits would be a cost or disadvantage of e-commerce systems.

Tangible Benefits	Example
• Increase in sales or profits	• Development of e-commerce-based products
• Decrease in information processing costs	• Elimination of unnecessary documents
• Decrease in operating costs	• Reduction in inventory carrying costs
• Decrease in required investment	• Decrease in inventory investment required
• Increased operational efficiency	• Less spoilage, waste, and idle time
Intangible Benefits	**Example**
• Improved information availability	• More timely and accurate information
• Improved abilities in analysis	• OLAP and data mining
• Improved customer service	• More timely service response
• Improved employee morale	• Elimination of burdensome job tasks
• Improved management decision making	• Better information and decision analysis
• Improved competitive position	• Systems that lock in customers
• Improved business image	• Progressive image as perceived by customers, suppliers, and investors

requirements that are used as the basis for the design of a new information system. Systems analysis traditionally involves a detailed study of:

- The information needs of a company and end users like yourself.
- The activities, resources, and products of one or more of the present information systems being used.
- The information system capabilities required to meet your information needs, and those of other e-business stakeholders that may use the system.

Organizational Analysis

An **organizational analysis** is an important first step in systems analysis. How can anyone improve an information system if they know very little about the organizational environment in which that system is located? They can't. That's why the members of a development team have to know something about the organization, its management structure, its people, its business activities, the environmental systems it must deal with, and its current information systems. Someone on the team must know this information in more detail for the specific business units or end user workgroups that will be affected by the new or improved information system being proposed. For example, a new inventory control system for a chain of department stores cannot be designed unless someone on a development team knows a lot about the company and the types of business activities that affect its inventory. That's why business end users are frequently added to systems development teams.

Analysis of the Present System

Before you design a new system, it is important to study the system that will be improved or replaced (if there is one). You need to analyze how this system uses hardware, software, network, and people resources to convert data resources, such as transactions data, into information products, such as reports and displays. Then, you should document how the information system activities of input, processing, output, storage, and control are accomplished.

For example, you might evaluate the format, timing, volume, and quality of input and output activities. Such *user interface* activities are vital to effective interaction between end users and a computer-based system. Then, in the systems design stage, you can specify what the resources, products, and activities should be to support the user interface in the system you are designing. Figure 10.10 presents a Web page from the analysis of an e-commerce website.

Panasonic.com: Evaluating an e-Commerce Website

Buying electronics direct from the manufacturer should be a cinch. But if you're looking for a VCR, don't go to Panasonic's online store, which sells a random selection of products (manicure sets and camcorder batteries were featured when I visited), but no VCRs. In addition to being very slow, the graphics-heavy pages don't provide the answers a customer needs to make a purchase.

The product catalog on Panasonic's home page is relegated to a pop-up menu that requires extensive scrolling. The menu has no entry for "VCR," although selecting "video" does lead to a page that lists VCRs as one of the choices. With two more clicks, you finally arrive at a product list that includes the PV–8400 (4-Head VHS Mono Video Cassette Recorder) and the PV–9400 (4-Head VHS Mono VCR). The latter is $40 cheaper. What's the difference? The site doesn't say—unless using acronyms saves money.

The page for the PV–S7680, the most expensive model, also fails to justify the price difference in terms that make sense to normal people. Are there any links to independent reviews that would be more credible than the manufacturer's own claim of "excellent picture quality"? No. Even though I'm in the market for a high-end VCR, I didn't buy this machine.

Most companies would do more business on the Internet if they fired their entire Web marketing department and replaced it with people who could produce interactive content that actually makes it easier for users to buy [26].

Figure 10.10

A Web page from Panasonic's e-commerce site at www.panasonic.com.

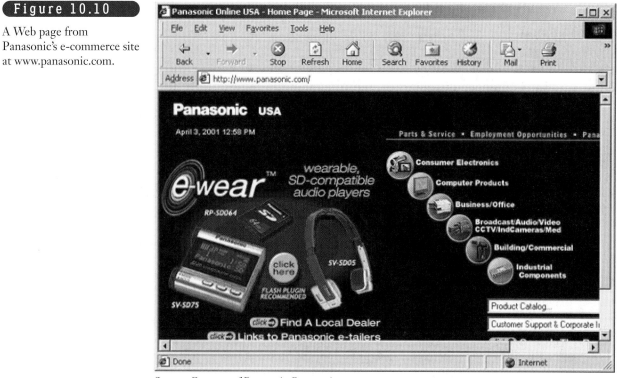

Source: Courtesy of Panasonic Corporation.

Functional Requirements Analysis

This step of systems analysis is one of the most difficult. You may need to work as a team with IS analysts and other end users to determine your specific business information needs. For example, first you need to determine what type of information each business activity requires; what its format, volume, and frequency should be; and what response times are necessary. Second, you must try to determine the information processing capabilities required for each system activity (input, processing, output, storage, control) to meet these information needs. *Your main goal is to identify what should be done, not how to do it.*

Finally, you should try to develop **functional requirements.** Functional requirements are end user information requirements that are not tied to the hardware, software, network, data, and people resources that end users presently use or might use in the new system. That is left to the design stage to determine. For example, Figure 10.11 shows examples of functional requirements for a proposed e-commerce application.

Systems Design

Systems analysis describes *what* a system should do to meet the information needs of users. **Systems design** specifies *how* the system will accomplish this

Figure 10.11

Examples of functional requirements for a proposed e-commerce system.

Examples of Functional Requirements
● **User Interface Requirements** Automatic entry of product data and easy-to-use data entry screens for Web customers.
● **Processing Requirements** Fast, automatic calculation of sales totals and shipping costs.
● **Storage Requirements** Fast retrieval and update of data from product, pricing, and customer databases.
● **Control Requirements** Signals for data entry errors and quick e-mail confirmation for customers.

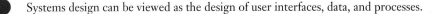

Figure 10.12 Systems design can be viewed as the design of user interfaces, data, and processes.

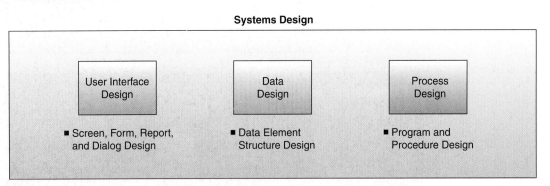

objective. Systems design consists of design activities that produce system specifications satisfying the functional requirements that were developed in the systems analysis process.

A useful way to look at systems design is illustrated in Figure 10.12. This concept focuses on three major products, or *deliverables* that should result from the design stage. In this framework, systems design consists of three activities: user interface, data, and process design. This results in specifications for user interface methods and products, database structures, and processing and control procedures. Let's take a closer look at userinterface design, since it is the system component closest to business end users, and the one they will most likely help design.

User Interface Design

The user interface design activity focuses on supporting the interactions between end users and their computer-based applications. Designers concentrate on the design of attractive and efficient forms of user input and output, such as easy-to-use Internet or intranet Web pages.

As we mentioned earlier, user interface design is frequently a *prototyping* process, where working models or prototypes of user interface methods are designed and modified several times with feedback from end users. The user interface design process produces detailed design specifications for information products such as display screens, interactive user/computer dialogues (including the sequence or flow of dialogue), audio responses, forms, documents, and reports. Figure 10.13 gives examples of user interface design elements and guidelines suggested for the multimedia

Figure 10.13 Useful guidelines for the user interface design of business websites.

Checklist for Corporate Websites

- **Remember the Customer:** Successful websites are built solely for the customer, not to make company vice presidents happy.
- **Aesthetics:** Successful designs combine fast-loading graphics and simple color palettes for pages that are easy to read.
- **Broadband Content:** The Web's coolest stuff can't be accessed by most Web surfers. Including a little streaming video isn't bad, but don't make it the focus of your site.
- **Easy to Navigate:** Make sure it's easy to get from one part of your site to another. Providing a site map, accessible from every page, helps.

- **Searchability:** Many sites have their own search engines; very few are actually useful. Make sure yours is.
- **Incompatibilities:** A site that looks great on a PC using Internet Explorer can often look miserable on an iBook running Netscape.
- **Registration Forms:** Registration forms are a useful way to gather customer data. But make your customers fill out a three-page form, and watch them flee.
- **Dead Links:** Dead links are the bane of all Web surfers—be sure to keep your links updated. Many Web-design software tools can now do this for you.

Figure 10.14 An example of the user interface design process. State Farm developers changed this work scheduling and assignment application's interface after usability testing showed that end users working with the old interface (at left) didn't realize that they had to follow a six-step process. If users jumped to a new page out of order, they would lose their work. The new interface (at right) made it clearer that a process had to be followed.

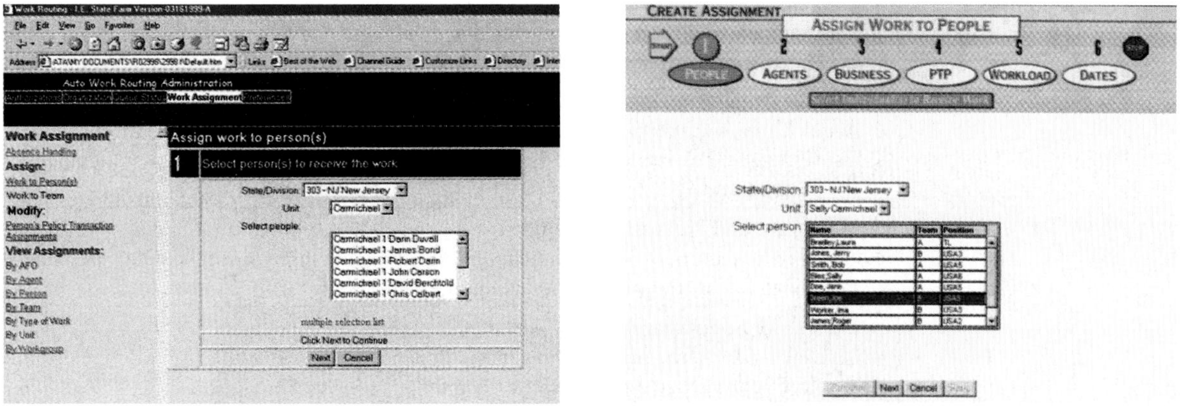

Source: Courtesy of the Usability Lab of State Farm and ComputerWorld.

Web pages of e-commerce websites. Figure 10.14 presents actual before and after screen displays of the user interface design process for a work scheduling application of State Farm Insurance Company [27].

| Quicken Loans: Web Page Design | One yellow box. A measly 150 by 72 pixels on the QuickenLoans.com home page. Fifteen minutes of coding on a Tuesday afternoon. Yet it boosted Quicken Loans Inc.'s user return rates from 2 percent to 11 percent. Talk about an inexpensive way to recapture customer loyalty. That's the power of proper Web design. The problem isn't so much the coding but knowing what to code. And that's where Web redesign plans like those of QuickenLoans.com come in.

Creating a good design is a challenge all e-commerce sites face because a poor design can frustrate customers and have a bad financial impact. As studies from Zona Research have shown, more than one-third of online shoppers who have trouble finding a product just give up altogether. And really dissatisfied customers don't just stay away; they discourage their friends from visiting, too.

QuickenLoans.com, a leader in the booming online mortgage business, has been through the website redesign trenches and has deduced three key lessons: keep testing to see what works and what's wrong, keep tweaking (modifying features) to fix what's wrong and, when necessary, tell customers what they should buy instead of giving them too many choices [31]. |
|---|---|

System Specifications

System specifications formalize the design of an application's user interface methods and products, database structures, and processing and control procedures. Therefore, systems designers will frequently develop hardware, software, network, data, and personnel specifications for a proposed system. Figure 10.15 shows examples of system specifications that could be developed for an e-commerce system.

End User Development

In a traditional systems development cycle, your role as a business end user is similar to that of a customer or a client. Typically, you make a request for a new or improved system, answer questions about your specific information needs and

Examples of System Specifications
● **User Interface Specifications** Use personalized screens that welcome repeat Web customers and make product recommendations.
● **Database Specifications** Develop databases that use object/relational database management software to organize access to all customer and inventory data, and multimedia product information.
● **Software Specifications** Acquire an e-commerce software engine to process all e-commerce transactions with fast responses, i.e., retrieve necessary product data, and compute all sales amounts in less than one second.
● **Hardware and Network Specifications** Install redundant networked Web servers and sufficient high-bandwidth telecommunications lines to host the company e-commerce website.
● **Personnel Specifications** Hire an e-commerce manager and specialists and a webmaster and Web designer to plan, develop, and manage e-commerce strategies.

information processing problems, and provide background information on your existing e-business systems. IS professionals work with you to analyze your problem and suggest alternative solutions. When you approve the best alternative, it is designed and implemented. Here again, you may be involved in a prototyping design process or be on an implementation team with IS specialists.

However, in **end user development,** IS professionals play a consulting role, while you do your own application development. Sometimes a staff of user consultants may be available to help you and other end users with your application development efforts. This may include training in the use of application packages; selection of hardware and software; assistance in gaining access to organization databases; and, of course, assistance in analysis, design, and implementing your e-business application.

Focus on IS Activities

It is important to remember that end user development should focus on the fundamental activities of any information system: input, processing, output, storage, and control. Figure 10.16 illustrates these system components and the questions they address.

In analyzing a potential application, you should focus first on the **output** to be produced by the application. What information is needed and in what form should it be presented? Next, look at the **input** data to be supplied to the application. What data are available? From what sources? In what form? Then you should examine the **processing** requirements. What operations or transformation processes will be required to convert the available inputs into the desired output? Among software packages the developer is able to use, which package can best perform the operations required?

You may find that the desired output cannot be produced from the inputs that are available. If this is the case, you must either make adjustments to the output expected, or find additional sources of input data, including data stored in files and databases from external sources. The **storage** component will vary in importance in end user applications. For example, some applications require extensive use of stored data or the creation of data that must be stored for future use. These are better suited for database management development projects than for spreadsheet applications.

Necessary **control** measures for end user applications vary greatly depending upon the scope and duration of the application, the number and nature of the users of the application, and the nature of the data involved. For example, control measures are needed to protect against accidental loss or damage to end user files.

Figure 10.16   End user development should focus on the basic information processing activity components of an information system.

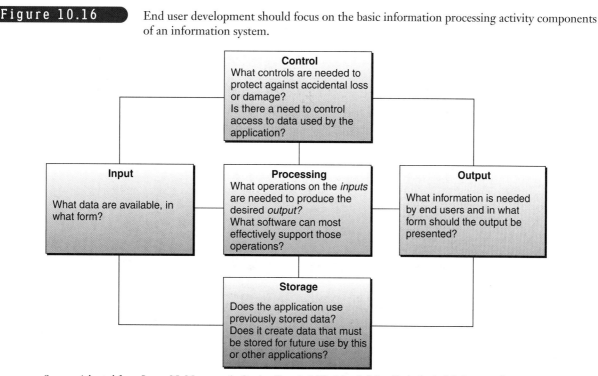

Control
What controls are needed to protect against accidental loss or damage?
Is there a need to control access to data used by the application?

Input
What data are available, in what form?

Processing
What operations on the *inputs* are needed to produce the desired *output*?
What software can most effectively support those operations?

Output
What information is needed by end users and in what form should the output be presented?

Storage
Does the application use previously stored data?
Does it create data that must be stored for future use by this or other applications?

Source: Adapted from James N. Morgan, *Application Cases in MIS*, 4th ed. (New York: Irwin/McGraw-Hill, 2001), p. 4.

The most basic protection against this type of loss is simply to make backup copies of application files on a frequent and systematic basis. Another example is the cell protection feature of spreadsheets that protects key cells from accidental erasure by users.

Doing End User Development

In end user development, you and other business professionals can develop new or improved ways to perform your jobs without the direct involvement of IS specialists. The application development capabilities built into a variety of end user software packages have made it easier for many users to develop their own computer-based solutions. For example, you can use a website development tool to help you develop, update, and manage an intranet website for your business unit. Or you might use an electronic spreadsheet package as a tool to develop a way to easily analyze weekly sales results for the sales managers in a company. Or you could use a website development package to design Web pages for a small business e-commerce Web store or a departmental intranet website. Let's take a look at a real world example of how many companies are encouraging business end users to do their own website development. See Figures 10.17 and 10.18.

Providence Health Systems: End User Web Development

Business groups at Providence Health systems in Portland, Oregon, complained to information technology staff about the sometimes outdated and incorrect content of the company's intranet websites. That was especially frustrating to IT workers, because the content originated from and belonged to the business groups, says Erik Sargent, lead Internet developer at the health care provider. So Providence Health's IT and Web development group did what many companies are considering. They gave up some of their central power to let business personnel in different departments contribute directly to corporate Internet and intranet sites with the help of Web content development tools.

More IT groups can do this because the tools have made it easier for users to create, manage, and update websites without knowing the intricacies of the Internet programming language HTML. Sargent and his team at Providence Health used

Figure 10.17

Microsoft FrontPage is an example of an easy-to-use end user website development tool.

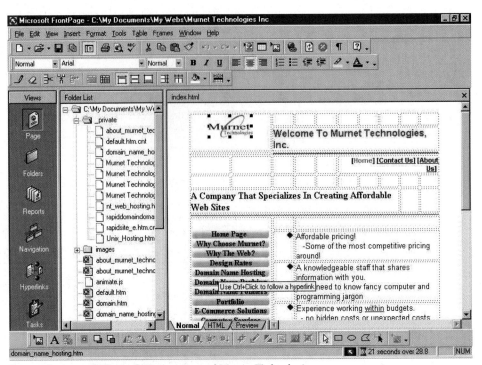

Source: Courtesy of Microsoft Corporation and Murnet Technologies.

Microsoft FrontPage on their development efforts. And because the company standardized on Microsoft Office productivity tools, it made sense to stay with FrontPage when allowing employees to do the intranet publishing duties.

One reason was that FrontPage maintained the same look and feel as Office, so there was a gentler learning curve. The other reason: FrontPage was cheaper to roll out to the 108 non-IT people now contributing to the intranet, rather than buying high-end tools with big price tags [28].

Figure 10.18

How companies are encouraging and managing intranet website development by business end users.

Encouraging End User Web Development
● Look for Tools That Make Sense. Some Web development tools may be too powerful and more costly than what your business end users really need.
● Spur Creativity. Consider a competition among business departments for the best website, to help spur users to more creative uses of their intranet sites.
● Set Some Limits. Yes, you have to keep some control. Consider putting limits on exactly what parts of a Web page users can change and who can change what pages. You still want some consistency across the organization.
● Give Managers Responsibility. Make business unit managers sign off on who will be Web publishing from their groups, and make the managers personally responsible for the content that goes on their websites. That will help prevent the publishing of inappropriate content by some users.
● Make Users Comfortable. Training users well on the tools will help users become confident in their ability to properly manage and update their sites—and save IT the trouble of fixing problems later on or providing continuous support for minor problems.

Source: Adapted from Tim Ouellette, "Giving Users the Key to Their Web Content," *Computerworld*, July 26, 1999, p. 67. Copyright 1999 by Computerworld, Inc., Framingham, MA 01701. Reprinted from *Computerworld*.

Section II ▸ Implementing e-Business Systems

Implementation

Once a new e-business system has been designed, it must be implemented and maintained. The implementation process we will cover in this section follows the investigation, analysis, and design stages of the systems development cycle we discussed in Section I. Implementation is a vital step in the deployment of information technology to support the e-business systems developed by a company for employees, customers, and other business stakeholders.

Analyzing Amazon, Verizon, and Boise Cascade

Read the Real World Case on Amazon, Verizon, and Boise Cascade on the next page. We can learn a lot from this case about the challenges of implementing customer-centric e-business systems. See Figure 10.19.

This case discusses the challenges faced by companies trying to implement a customer-centric business strategy. The experiences of both Amazon and Verizon emphasize that customer-centric solutions require cultural and structural changes in an organization, as well as the implementation of customer-support technologies. This is highlighted in the example of Boise Cascade Office Products, which installed a new customer relationship management system that required integrating the access to dozens of different databases. In addition, the new system required that the job responsibilities of service representatives be broadened, that sales reps share more data about their clients, and that formerly autonomous brands be consolidated. The result is a successful customer-centric strategic initiative that integrates customer databases, call centers, and customer Web access in a quick-response customer information and support system.

Figure 10.19

Verizon executive Stephen Butler believes that a change in culture, organization, and technology is needed to move his company toward a customer-centric business model.

Source: Craig Cameron Olsen

Amazon, Verizon, and Boise Cascade: Implementing Customer-Centric e-Business Systems

At most companies, the world revolves around products or functions or geography. Customers endure the all-to-familiar experience of contacting different parts of an organization and finding that each part knows nothing about that customer's experience with other parts of the company. Have you ever called your local phone company and tried to order a new service like, say, a DSL connection? Depending on where you live, you may be treated like a total stranger, even if you've been a customer for decades.

For that to change, someone must "own" the customer—and that means each customer segment must be a business unit run by a manager with profit-and-loss accountability. This is a radical change at most companies, but it works. Dell is organized this way, a key element in its knockout performance during the past 15 years. Why don't more companies follow suit? Corporate politics are a major factor. A customer-centric reorganization would take power from today's product-, function-, and territory-based barons, all of whom command formidable resources with which to kill the new system.

More fundamentally, the problem is one of mind-set—what the company perceives itself to be all about. No company uses customer data better than Amazon. Ask former CFO Joy Covey why, and she replies immediately, "It's the mind-set." From day one, founder Jeff Bezos made clear that Amazon would use the vast amount of information about customers it gathers on its website to build relationships with them and make them happy. There simply was no other way of operating.

Not many companies inherit a customer-centric mind-set from their founders. But those that weren't born with one will need to get one—and organize on that basis—before hoping to turn customer data into shareholder value. "We're building toward that customer-centric model," says Stephen Butler, a Verizon executive who's among those trying to shake things up at a company with roots going back more than a century to life as a regulated utility. It's a long slog, but Butler is starting with the right insight. "It's more than just implementing customer support technology," he says. "It's a change in culture and organization."

A few companies—Amazon, for one—were born to turn customer data to competitive advantage. For most established firms, however, it often takes fundamental tear-up-the-org-chart reorientation. One company of the latter type is Boise Cascade Office Products (BCOP), a $4 billion subsidiary of paper giant Boise Cascade, and a purveyor to large and midsize businesses of everything from paper to paper clips to office furniture.

About two years ago, the company had its "eureka" moment. "Here we had tons of data on our customers and were doing nothing with it," says senior VP for marketing Dave Goudge, the leader of BCOP's customer data initiative. "We could distinguish ourselves in an increasingly competitive industry by collecting that data in one place, organizing it, and then using it to create great customer service."

Easier said than done. For starters, BCOP's customer information was buried in dozens of separate databases that couldn't speak to one another. Liberating that data and installing a new customer relationship management (CRM) system without disrupting BCOP's ongoing business would be challenge enough—a bit like changing the tires on a race car in motion. But the organizational hurdles were higher still. For BCOP to make full use of its data, service representatives would have to learn to sell, territorial sales reps would have to share data on the their clients, and once-autonomous brands within BCOP would have to be consolidated.

Still, phase one of the initiative dubbed One Boise went into effect on April 1, 2001, on time and within 1 percent of the $20 million the firm had budgeted—and life began to get dramatically easier for BCOP clients. Now when you call to place an order (or log on—about 18 percent of sales come via the Web), you key in an identifying number and are soon greeted by name by a rep whose screen shows all of your most recent BCOP interactions. Based on your past dealings with the company, your call might get special routing—to a specialist in a particular kind of merchandise, say, or to a Spanish-speaking rep—all before the rep even picks up the phone.

Lost on the website? Click "Need Assistance?" and a pop-up screen asks whether you would like help by instant message or by phone. Choose the former and a rep will be on your screen immediately. Choose the latter and the phone will ring within 30 seconds. "BCOP has taken much of the aggravation out of ordering supplies," says Bob Powell, purchasing manager at Citizens Banking Corp., an $8 billion Midwestern bank. "That lets us spend more time doing what we're supposed to do, which is banking."

Goudge and his team have to live up to present return-on-investment goals. In this case ROI is admittedly fuzzy, estimated from measures such as customer retention and share of total office-product spending. But Goudge has his own yardstick. "When customers finish placing an order with us," he says, "I want them to say, 'God, that was slick.'"

Case Study Questions

1. Why is a customer-centric business model missing from so many companies? What should a company do to implement a customer-centric focus?

2. What are several ways that information technology and e-business systems can support a company's customer-centric strategy? What challenges are involved?

3. Has Boise Cascade Office Products successfully implemented a customer-centric e-business system? Why or why not?

Figure 10.20

An overview of the implementation process. Implementation activities are needed to transform a newly developed information system into an operational system for end users.

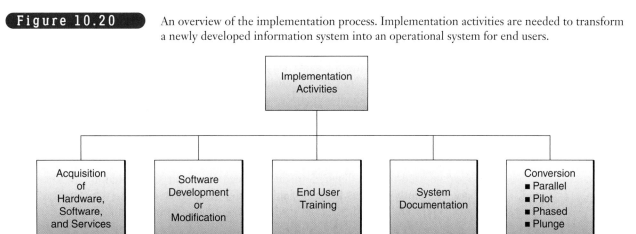

Implementing New Systems

Figure 10.20 illustrates that the **systems implementation** stage involves hardware and software acquisition, software development, testing of programs and procedures, development of documentation, and a variety of conversion alternatives. It also involves the education and training of end users and specialists who will operate a new system.

Implementation can be a difficult and time-consuming process. However, it is vital in ensuring the success of any newly developed system, for even a well-designed system will fail if it is not properly implemented. Figure 10.21 illustrates the activities and time lines that might be required to implement an intranet for a new employee benefits system in the human resources department of a company.

Evaluating Hardware, Software, and Services

How do companies evaluate and select hardware and software? Large companies may require suppliers to present bids and proposals based on system specifications developed during the design stage of systems development. Minimum acceptable physical and performance characteristics for all hardware and software requirements are established. Most large business firms and all government agencies formalize these requirements by listing them in a document called an RFP (request for proposal) or RFQ (request for quotation). Then they send the RFP or RFQ to appropriate vendors, who use it as the basis for preparing a proposed purchase agreement.

Figure 10.21

An example of the implementation process activities and time lines for a company installing an intranet-based employee benefits system in its human resource management department.

Intranet Implementation Activities	Month 1	Month 2	Month 3	Month 4
Acquire and install server hardware and software	■			
Train administrators	■			
Acquire and install browser software	■	■		
Acquire and install publishing software	■			
Train benefits employees on publishing software	■			
Convert benefits manuals and add revisions	■			
Create Web-based tutorials for the intranet		■		
Hold rollout meetings				■

Source: Adapted from Mclanie Hills, *Intranet Business Strategy* (New York: John Wiley & Sons, 1997), p. 193. Reprinted by permission of John Wiley & Sons, Inc. Copyright © 1997 by John Wiley & Sons, Inc.

Companies may use a *scoring* system of evaluation when there are several competing proposals for a hardware or software acquisition. They give each **evaluation factor** a certain number of maximum possible points. Then they assign each competing proposal points for each factor, depending on how well it meets the specifications of the computer user. Scoring each evaluation factor for several proposals helps organize and document the evaluation process. It also spotlights the strengths and weaknesses of each proposal.

Whatever the claims of hardware manufacturers and software suppliers, the performance of hardware and software must be demonstrated and evaluated. Independent hardware and software information services (such as Datapro and Auerbach) may be used to gain detailed specification information and evaluations. Other users are frequently the best source of information needed to evaluate the claims of manufacturers and suppliers. That's why Internet newsgroups established to exchange

Figure 10.22

Example of e-commerce hardware, software, and services offered by IBM and IPlanet, a joint venture of Sun Microsystems and Netscape. These are the kinds of hardware, software, and IS services that many e-business companies are evaluating and acquiring to support their moves into e-commerce.

IPlanet	IBM
Hardware	**Hardware**
Full range of Sun offerings, including low-end desktop and workgroup servers, midrange E3500, E4500, E5500, and E6500 servers and mainframe-class E10,000 server. Also has storage systems.	Full range of offerings, including Netfinity servers, AS/400 midrange for small and midsize businesses, RS6000 servers for UNIX customers and System 390 mainframes for large enterprises. Also has full range of storage options
Software	**Software**
Web server: IPlanet Web Server (formerly Netscape Enterprise Server).	**Web server:** Lotus DominoGo Web server.
Storefront: IPlanet MerchantXpert (formerly Netscape MerchantXpert).	**Storefront:** WebSphere Commerce Suite (formerly known as Net.Commerce) for storefront and catalog creation, relationship marketing, and order management. Can add Commerce Integrator to integrate with back-end systems and Catalog Architect for content management.
Middleware/transaction services: IPlanet Application Server (also NetDynamics Application Server, Netscape Application Server).	**Middleware/transaction services:** WebSphere application server manages transactions. MQ Series queues messages and manages connections. CICS processes transactions.
Database: None.	**Database:** DB2 Universal Database.
Tools: Recently acquired Forte tools and NetBeans for building Java components.	**Tools:** WebSphere Studio includes set of predefined templates and common business logic.
Other applications include: IPlanet Certificate Management Solution, IPlanet BillerXpert for Internet bill presentment and payment, IPlanet PublishingXpert for digital goods delivery and selling and IPlanet Portal Server to help companies set up personalized websites.	**Other applications include:** IBM Payment Suite for handling credit cards and managing digital certificates.
Services	**Services**
IPlanet Professional Services, Sun Professional Services. Also, Sun has "dotcom" practice to strategize and build e-commerce sites.	IBM Global Services, which includes groups organized by each major industry, including retail and financial. Can design, build and host e-commerce applications.

Source: Adapted from Carol Sliwa, "E-Commerce Solutions: How Real?" *Computerworld*, February 28, 2000, pp. 68–69. Copyright 2000 by Computerworld, Inc., Framingham, MA 01701. Reprinted from *Computerworld*.

information about specific software or hardware vendors and their products have become one of the best sources for obtaining up-to-date information about the experiences of users of the products. See Figure 10.22.

Large e-business companies frequently evaluate proposed hardware and software by requiring the processing of special *benchmark* test programs and test data. Benchmarking simulates the processing of typical jobs on several computers and evaluates their performances. Users can then evaluate test results to determine which hardware device or software package displayed the best performance characteristics.

Hardware Evaluation Factors

When you evaluate hardware for an e-business system, you should investigate specific physical and performance characteristics for each hardware component to be acquired. This is true whether you are evaluating microcomputers, mainframes, or peripheral devices. Specific questions must be answered concerning many important factors. Ten of these **hardware evaluation factors** and questions are summarized in Figure 10.23.

Notice that there is much more to evaluating hardware than determining the fastest and cheapest computing device. For example, the question of obsolescence must be addressed by making a technology evaluation. The factor of ergonomics is also very important. Ergonomic factors ensure that computer hardware and software are user-friendly, that is, safe, comfortable, and easy to use. Connectivity is another important evaluation factor, since so many network technologies and bandwidth alternatives are available to connect computer systems to the Internet, intranet, and extranet networks.

Figure 10.23

A summary of ten major hardware evaluation factors. Notice how you can use this to evaluate a computer system or a peripheral device.

Hardware Evaluation Factors	Rating
Performance What are its speed, capacity, and throughput?	
Cost What is its lease or purchase price? What will be its cost of operations and maintenance?	
Reliability What are the risk of malfunction and its maintenance requirements? What are its error control and diagnostic features?	
Compatibility Is it compatible with existing hardware and software? Is it compatible with hardware and software provided by competing suppliers?	
Technology In what year of its product life cycle is it? Does it use a new untested technology or does it run the risk of obsolescence?	
Ergonomics Has it been "human factors engineered" with the user in mind? Is it user-friendly, designed to be safe, comfortable, and easy to use?	
Connectivity Can it be easily connected to wide area and local area networks that use different types of network technologies and bandwidth alternatives?	
Scalability Can it handle the processing demands of a wide range of end users, transactions, queries, and other information processing requirements?	
Software Is system and application software available that can best use this hardware?	
Support Are the services required to support and maintain it available?	
Overall Rating	

Figure 10.24

A summary of selected software evaluation factors. Note that most of the hardware evaluation factors in Figure 10.23 can also be used to evaluate software packages.

Software Evaluation Factors	Rating
Quality Is it bug free, or does it have many errors in its program code?	
Efficiency Is the software a well-developed system of program code that does not use much CPU time, memory capacity, or disk space?	
Flexibility Can it handle our e-business processes easily, without major modification?	
Security Does it provide control procedures for errors, malfunctions, and improper use?	
Connectivity Is it *Web-enabled* so it can easily access the Internet, intranets, and extranets, on its own, or by working with Web browsers or other network software?	
Language Is it written in a programming language that is familiar to our own software developers?	
Documentation Is the software well documented? Does it include help screens and helpful software agents?	
Hardware Does existing hardware have the features required to best use this software?	
Other Factors What are its performance, cost, reliability, availability, compatibility, modularity, technology, ergonomics, scalability, and support characteristics? (Use the hardware evaluation factor questions in Figure 10.23)	
Overall Rating	

Software Evaluation Factors

You should evaluate software according to many factors that are similar to those used for hardware evaluation. Thus, the factors of performance, cost, reliability, availability, compatibility, modularity, technology, ergonomics, and support should be used to evaluate proposed software acquisitions. In addition, however, **the software evaluation factors** summarized in Figure 10.24 must also be considered. You should answer the questions they generate in order to properly evaluate software purchases. For example, some software packages are notoriously slow, hard to use, bug-filled, or poorly documented. They are not a good choice, even if offered at attractive prices.

Evaluating IS Services

Most suppliers of hardware and software products and many other firms offer a variety of **IS services** to end users and organizations. Examples include assistance during e-commerce website development, installation or conversion of new hardware and software, employee training, and hardware maintenance. Some of these services are provided without cost by hardware manufacturers and software suppliers.

Other types of IS services needed by a business can be outsourced to an outside company for a negotiated price. For example, *systems integrators* take over complete responsibility for an organization's computer facilities when an organization outsources its computer operations. They may also assume responsibility for developing and implementing large systems development projects that involve many vendors and subcontractors. Value-added resellers (VARs) specialize in providing industry-specific hardware, software, and services from selected manufacturers. Many other services are available to end users, including systems design, contract programming, and consulting services. Evaluation factors and questions for IS services are summarized in Figure 10.25.

Figure 10.25

Evaluation factors for IS services. These factors focus on the quality of support services e-business users may need.

Evaluation Factors for IS Services	Rating
Performance What has been their past performance in view of their past promises?	
Systems Development Are website and other e-business developers available? What are their quality and cost?	
Maintenance Is equipment maintenance provided? What are its quality and cost?	
Conversion What systems development and installation services will they provide during the conversion period?	
Training Is the necessary training of personnel provided? What are its quality and cost?	
Backup Are similar computer facilities available nearby for emergency backup purposes?	
Accessibility Does the vendor provide local or regional sites that offer sales, systems development, and hardware maintenance services? Is a customer support center at the vendor's website available? Is a customer hot line provided?	
Business Position Is the vendor financially strong, with good industry market prospects?	
Hardware Do they provide a wide selection of compatible hardware devices and accessories?	
Software Do they offer a variety of useful e-business software and application packages?	
Overall Rating	

Microsoft and IBM: Customer Service Satisfaction

Microsoft

The effectiveness of Microsoft's support depends on who you are, or whom you know, according to a recent *Computerworld* survey. The company is highly selective in determining who receives its Premier Support plan, the very attentive service it's using to get deeper into the corridors of Fortune 500 corporations. Very large—2,500 users or more—companies fortunate enough to be included in Premier Support receive Microsoft's undivided and very effective attention. But the mediocre grades Microsoft received from *Computerworld*'s survey come largely from the rank-and-file companies that don't quality for Premier class. These users, the vast majority of Microsoft business customers, are bounced to one of the company's many support partners.

One bright spot for Microsoft: Users really like its website support and gave it the highest grade of any in the survey. Respondents said that between its website and its TechNet informational CD-ROM service, Microsoft is the best at letting its users help themselves.

IBM

IBM's whatever-the-customer-wants approach to service has made it the benchmark by which other vendors are measured, according to several *Computerworld* survey respondents. Big Blue scored highest in six of eight rating categories and achieved the highest customer-satisfaction grade in the entire survey for its emergency and mission-critical service. IT managers gave the highest grades to the responsiveness and knowledge demonstrated by IBM's phone staff. IBM, they said, best follows the priorities users set when calling in problems. Priority 1 means a system is down. When that happens, IBM's goal is to connect the user to the person best qualified to fix the system within the hour.

IBM lost ground in *Computerworld*'s survey over website support, however. Surveyed managers said IBM's site is OK for logging minor problems into a queue but not among the best when users need to quickly locate specific solutions. IBM wasn't alone in the area of weak Web-based support, but it's certainly one place that IBM needs to work on [2].

Other Implementation Activities

Testing, documentation, and training are keys to successful implementation of a new e-business system.

Testing

System testing may involve testing website performance, testing and debugging software, and testing new hardware. An important part of testing is the review of prototypes of displays, reports, and other output. Prototypes should be reviewed by end users of the proposed systems for possible errors. Of course, testing should not occur only during the system's implementation stage, but throughout the system's development process. For example, you might examine and critique prototypes of input documents, screen displays, and processing procedures during the systems design stage. Immediate end user testing is one of the benefits of a prototyping process.

Documentation

Developing good user **documentation** is an important part of the implementation process. Sample data entry display screens, forms, and reports are good examples of documentation. When *computer-aided systems engineering* methods are used, documentation can be created and changed easily since it is stored and accessible on disk in a *system repository*. Documentation serves as a method of communication among the people responsible for developing, implementing, and maintaining a computer-based system. Installing and operating a newly designed system or modifying an established application requires a detailed record of that system's design. Documentation is extremely important in diagnosing errors and making changes, especially if the end users or systems analysts who developed a system are no longer with the organization.

Training

Training is a vital implementation activity. IS personnel, such as user consultants, must be sure that end users are trained to operate a new e-business system or its implementation will fail. Training may involve only activities like data entry, or it may also involve all aspects of the proper use of a new system. In addition, managers and end users must be educated in how the new technology impacts the company's business operations and management. This knowledge should be supplemented by training programs for any new hardware devices, software packages, and their use for specific work activities. Figure 10.26 illustrates how one business coordinated its e-business training program with each stage of its implementation process for developing intranet and e-commerce access within the company.

Clarke American Checks: Web-Based ERP Training

If it's 10 A.M., workers at Clarke American Checks Inc. are firing up their Web browsers for a collaborative training lesson on how to perform purchasing with their new SAP AG enterprise resource planning (ERP) software. During the daily sessions, end users in more than 20 locations either watch their colleagues perform simulated transactions with the software, or do it themselves.

Self-paced ERP training delivered via the Web is becoming a popular concept. Users say training eats up 10 to 20 percent of an ERP project's budget and is one of the more vexing parts of an ERP development project. Many ERP systems have tricky user interfaces and are highly customized, making generic, computer-based training courses ineffective. Clarke American, a San Antonio–based check printer, is in a growing group of companies using Web-based training to get workers up to speed on enterprise resource planning applications. Doing so can trim up to 75 percent off the cost of traditional training methods, such as instructor-led sessions, users said [4].

Conversion Methods

The initial operation of a new e-business system can be a difficult task. This typically requires a **conversion** process from the use of a present system to the operation of a new or improved application. Conversion methods can soften the impact of introducing new information technologies into an organization. Four major forms of system conversion are illustrated in Figure 10.27. They include:

- Parallel conversion.
- Phased conversion.
- Pilot conversion.
- Plunge or direct cutover.

Figure 10.26 How one company developed e-business training programs for the implementation of Internet e-commerce and intranet access for its employees.

Figure 10.27

The four major forms of conversion to a new system.

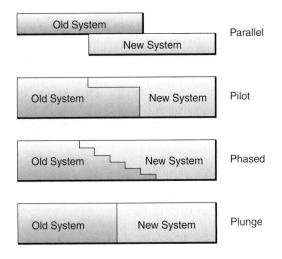

Conversions can be done on a *parallel* basis, whereby both the old and the new systems are operating until the project development team and end user management agree to switch completely over to the new system. It is during this time that the operations and results of both systems are compared and evaluated. Errors can be identified and corrected, and the operating problems can be solved before the old system is abandoned. Installation can also be accomplished by a direct cutover or *plunge* to a newly developed system.

Conversion can also be done on a *phased basis*, where only parts of a new application or only a few departments, branch offices, or plant locations at a time are converted. A phased conversion allows a gradual implementation process to take place within an organization. Similar benefits accrue from using a *pilot conversion*, where one department or other work site serves as a test site. A new system can be tried out at this site until developers feel it can be implemented throughout the organization.

IS Maintenance

Once a system is fully implemented and is being used in business operations, the maintenance function begins. **Systems maintenance** is the monitoring, evaluating, and modifying of operational e-business systems to make desirable or necessary improvements. For example, the implementation of a new system usually results in the phenomenon known as the *learning curve*. Personnel who operate and use the system will make mistakes simply because they are not familiar with it. Though such errors usually diminish as experience is gained with a new system, they do point out areas where a system may be improved.

Maintenance is also necessary for other failures and problems that arise during the operation of a system. End users and information systems personnel then perform a *troubleshooting* function to determine the causes of and solutions to such problems.

The maintenance activity includes a **postimplementation review** process to ensure that newly implemented systems meet the e-business objectives established for them. Errors in the development or use of a system must be corrected by the maintenance process. This includes a periodic review or audit of a system to ensure that it is operating properly and meeting its objectives. This audit is in addition to continually monitoring a new system for potential problems or necessary changes.

Maintenance also includes making modifications to an e-business system due to changes in the business organization or the business environment. For example, new tax legislation, company reorganizations, and new e-business and e-commerce ventures may require major changes to current e-business systems.

Farmland Industries and Lockheed Martin: Implementing ERP Systems	Farmland Industries, a $10.7 billion farmer-owned cooperative in Kansas City, Missouri, installed a version of the SAP R/3 enterprise resource planning (ERP) software tailored for oil and gas users two years ago. Farmland has had only minor problems with the software, said Dick Weaver, technology manager at its petroleum and crop production units. But changing the way the company does business to take full advantage of R/3 has been a sticky proposition. Because Farmland didn't do much of that work up front, its finance and order-entry operations didn't see the kind of savings they were looking for. Now the cooperative is going back and making the business-process changes that were put off earlier in the project. "If you just put in SAP, you haven't gained a whole lot," Weaver said. "Two years into it, we're getting a lot of value. The first year, we didn't." At Lockheed Martin Aeronautics, 900 business users from its three aircraft manufacturing companies have been working to design common ways to enter orders and process other transactions in using R/3. When that's done, several hundred users will test the system for another six months. Lockheed Martin first rolled out R/3 at an aircraft maintenance operation, and installed SAP's human resources module a few months later, to get its feet wet before bigger installations at the manufacturing units. Its project team also sought advice from Pratt & Whitney Canada, an aircraft engine supplier that had previously done an R/3 rollout [34].

Managing Organizational Change

Implementing new e-business systems requires managing the effects of major changes in key organizational dimensions such as business processes, organizational structures, managerial roles, employee work assignments, and stakeholder relationships that arise from the deployment of new e-business systems. For example, Figure 10.28 emphasizes the variety and extent of the challenges reported by 100 companies that developed and implemented new enterprise information portals and ERP systems.

End Users and Change

Any new way of doing things generates some resistance by the people affected. Thus, the implementation of new e-business work support technologies can generate fear

Figure 10.28

The ten greatest challenges of developing and implementing intranet enterprise portals and enterprise resource planning systems reported by 100 e-business companies.

Intranet Enterprise Portal Challenges	Enterprise Resource Planning Challenges
● Security, security, security	● Getting end-user buy-in
● Defining the scope and purpose of the portal	● Scheduling/planning
● Finding the time and the money	● Integrating legacy systems/data
● Ensuring consistent data quality	● Getting management buy-in
● Getting employees to use it	● Dealing with multiple/international sites and partners
● Organizing the data	● Changing culture/mind-sets
● Finding technical expertise	● IT training
● Integrating the pieces	● Getting, keeping IT staff
● Making it easy to use	● Moving to a new platform
● Providing all users with access	● Performance/system upgrades

Source: Adapted from Kathleen Melymuka, "An Expanding Universe," *Computerworld*, September 14, 1998, p. 57; and Tim Ouellette, "Opening Your Own Portal," *Computerworld*, August 9, 1999. p. 79. Copyright 1998 and 1999 by Computerworld, Inc., Framingham, MA 01701, Reprinted from *Computerworld*.

and resistance to change by employees. One of the keys to solving problems of **end user resistance** to new information technologies is proper education and training. Even more important is **end user involvement** in organizational changes, and in the development of new information systems. Organizations have a variety of strategies to help manage business change, and one basic requirement is the involvement and commitment of top management and all business stakeholders affected by a new e-business application.

Direct end user participation in e-business planning and application development projects before a new system is implemented is especially important in reducing the potential for end user resistance. That is why end users frequently are members of e-business systems development teams or do their own development work. Such involvement helps ensure that end users assume ownership of a system, and that its design meets their needs. Systems that tend to inconvenience or frustrate users cannot be effective systems, no matter how technically elegant they are and how efficiently they process data. For example, Figure 10.29 illustrates some of the major obstacles to knowledge management systems in business. Notice that end user resistance to sharing knowledge is the biggest obstacle to the implementation of knowledge management applications.

Change Management

People are the major focus of organizational **change management.** This includes activities such as developing innovative ways to measure, motivate, and reward performance. So is designing programs to recruit and train employees in the core competencies required in a changing workplace. Change management also involves analyzing and defining all changes facing the organization, and developing programs to reduce the risks and costs and to maximize the benefits of change. For example, implementing a new e-business process such as customer relationship management might involve developing a *change action plan*, assigning selected managers as *change sponsors*, developing employee *change teams*, and encouraging open communications and feedback about organizational changes. Some key tactics change experts recommend include:

- Involve as many people as possible in e-business planning and application development.

- Make constant change an expected part of the culture.

- Tell everyone as much as possible about everything as often as possible, preferably in person.

- Make liberal use of financial incentives and recognition.

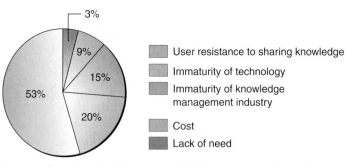

Figure 10.29

Obstacles to knowledge management systems. Note that end user resistance to knowledge sharing is the biggest obstacle.

- 3%
- 9%
- 15%
- 53%
- 20%

- User resistance to sharing knowledge
- Immaturity of technology
- Immaturity of knowledge management industry
- Cost
- Lack of need

Source: Adapted from Barb Cole-Gomolski, "Users Loathe to Share Their Know-How," *Computerworld*, November 17, 1997, p. 6. Copyright 1997 by Computerworld, Inc. Framingham, MA 01701. Reprinted from *Computerworld*.

Context Integration: User Resistance to Knowledge Management

In a Web consulting firm, the whole business is pretty much locked away in the minds of employees. And Chairman Bruce Strong didn't feel that the consultants were sharing the ideas they had stored there. So he decided to design a knowledge-management system to help them unlock their thoughts and be more productive. After all, using technology to solve problems was what the company he had co-founded, Context Integration, was all about. Six months and half a million dollars later, he unveiled a new tool with a friendly acronym, IAN (Intellectual Assets Network). Just one snag: Few of his people actually wanted to use it.

The truth is that getting people to participate is the hardest part of knowledge management. Carla O'Dell, president of the American Productivity & Quality Center, says that of the companies trying knowledge management, less than 10 percent have succeeded in making it part of their culture.

Some reluctance surfaced at Context simply because IAN was a bother. Depositing notes or project records into the database was one more task in a consultant's busy day—and worse yet, it was a task that didn't have any obvious urgency. Even more important, IAN forced consultants to reveal their ignorance. Asking a trusted colleague a question is one thing; posting it for the whole company to see can be downright intimidating. Abdou Touray, who's been at Context even longer than IAN, says that consultants don't like admitting that they can't solve a problem. Moreover, they resented management's trying to impose what seemed like a rigid structure on their work.

But Strong made IAN usage part of everyone's job description. He even started paying them to use it. Each IAN task has now been assigned points, and the score accounts for 10 percent of a consultant's quarterly bonus. Before these metrics were introduced, only a third of Context employees were rated as good or better for IAN usage. Two months later, that IAN usage had almost doubled. "You don't want to be the person that doesn't use IAN at all," says Strong. "It's your performance—it's how we view you as a person in the company" [19].

Summary

- **The Systems Development Cycle.** Business end users and IS specialists may use a systems approach to help them develop information system solutions to meet e-business opportunities. This frequently involves a systems development cycle where IS specialists and end users conceive, design, and implement e-business systems. The stages, activities, and products of the information systems development cycle are summarized in Figure 10.3.

- **Prototyping.** Prototyping is a major alternative methodology to the traditional information systems development cycle. It includes the use of prototyping tools and methodologies, which promote an iterative, interactive process that develops prototypes of user interfaces and other information system components. See Figure 10.4.

- **End User Development.** The application development capabilities built into many end user software packages have made it easier for end users to develop their own e-business applications. End users should focus their development efforts on the system components of business processes that can benefit from the use of information technology, as summarized in Figure 10.16.

- **Implementing IS.** The implementation process for information system projects is summarized in Figure 10.30. Implementation involves acquisition, testing,

documentation, training, installation, and conversion activities that transform a newly designed e-business system into an operational system for end users.

- **Evaluating Hardware, Software, and Services.** Business professionals should know how to evaluate the acquisition of information system resources. IT vendors' proposals should be based on specifications developed during the design stage of systems development. A formal evaluation process reduces the possibility of incorrect or unnecessary purchases of hardware or software. Several major evaluation factors, summarized in Figures 10.23, 10.24, and 10.25, can be used to evaluate hardware, software, and IS services.

- **Implementing e-Business Change.** Implementation activities include managing the introduction and implementation of changes in business processes, organizational structures, job assignments, and work relationships resulting from e-business strategies and applications such as e-commerce initiatives, reengineering projects, supply chain alliances, and the introduction of new technologies. Companies use change management tactics such as user involvement in e-business planning and development to reduce end user resistance and maximize acceptance of e-business changes by all stakeholders.

Figure 10.30

An overview of the implementation process. Implementation activities are needed to transform a newly developed information system into an operational system for end users.

Implementing New Systems
● **Acquisition**   Evaluate and acquire necessary hardware and software resources and information system services. Screen vendor proposals.
● **Software Development**   Develop any software that will not be acquired externally as software packages. Make any necessary modifications to software packages that are acquired.
● **Training**   Educate and train management, end users, customers and other business stakeholders. Use consultants or training programs to develop user competencies.
● **Testing**   Test and make necessary corrections to the programs, procedures, and hardware used by a new system.
● **Documentation**   Record and communicate detailed system specifications, including procedures for end users and IS personnel and examples of input screens and output displays and reports.
● **Conversion**   Convert from the use of a present system to the operation of a new or improved system. This may involve operating both new and old systems in *parallel* for a trial period, operation of a *pilot* system on a trial basis at one location, *phasing* in the new system one location at a time, or an immediate *plunge* or *cutover* to the new system.

Key Terms and Concepts

These are the key terms and concepts of this chapter. The page number of their first explanation is in parentheses.

1. Change management (368)
2. Conversion methods (365)
3. Cost/benefit analysis (348)
4. Documentation (364)
5. Economic feasibility (348)
6. End user development (354)
7. End user involvement (368)
8. End user resistance (368)
9. Evaluation factors (360)
   a. Hardware (361)
   b. IS services (362)
   c. Software (362)
10. Feasibility study (347)
11. Functional requirements (351)
12. Implementation process (359)
13. Intangible (349)
    a. Benefits (349)
    b. Costs (349)
14. Operational feasibility (348)
15. Organizational analysis (350)
16. Organizational feasibility (348)
17. Postimplementation review (366)
18. Prototype (345)
19. Prototyping (345)
20. Systems analysis (349)
21. Systems approach (344)
22. Systems design (351)
23. Systems development life cycle (345)
24. Systems implementation (359)
25. Systems investigation (347)
26. Systems maintenance (366)
27. Systems specifications (353)
28. System testing (364)
29. Systems thinking (344)
30. Tangible (349)
    a. Benefits (349)
    b. Costs (349)
31. Technical feasibility (348)
32. User interface design (352)

Review Quiz

Match one of the key terms and concepts listed previously with one of the brief examples or definitions that follow. Try to find the best fit for answers that seem to fit more than one term or concept. Defend your choices.

_____ 1. Using an organized sequence of activities to study a problem or opportunity using systems thinking.

_____ 2. Trying to recognize systems and the new interrelationships and components of systems in any situation.

_____ 3. Evaluating the success of a solution after it has been implemented.

_____ 4. Your evaluation shows that benefits outweigh costs for a proposed system.

_____ 5. The costs of acquiring computer hardware, software, and specialists.

_____ 6. Loss of customer goodwill caused by errors in a new system.

_____ 7. Increases in profits caused by a new system.

_____ 8. Improved employee morale caused by efficiency and effectiveness of a new system.

_____ 9. A multistep process to conceive, design, and implement an information system.

_____ 10. The first stage of the systems development cycle.

_____ 11. Determines the organizational, economic, technical, and operational feasibility of a proposed information system.

_____ 12. Cost savings and additional profits will exceed the investment required.

_____ 13. Reliable hardware and software are available to implement a proposed system.

_____ 14. Customers will not have trouble using a proposed system.

_____ 15. The proposed system supports the strategic plan of the business.

_____ 16. Studying in detail the information needs of users and any information systems presently used.

_____ 17. A detailed description of user information needs and the input, processing, output, storage, and control capabilities required to meet those needs.

_____ 18. The process that results in specifications for the hardware, software, people, network, and data resources and information products needed by a proposed system.

_____ 19. Systems design should focus on developing user-friendly input and output methods for a system.

_____ 20. A detailed description of the hardware, software, people, network, and data resources and information products required by a proposed system.

_____ 21. Acquiring hardware and software, testing and documenting a proposed system, and training people to use it.

_____ 22. Making improvements to an operational system.

_____ 23. A working model of an information system.

_____ 24. An interactive and iterative process of developing and refining information system prototypes.

_____ 25. Managers and business specialists can develop their own e-business applications.

_____ 26. Includes acquisition, testing, training, and conversion to a new system.

_____ 27. Performance, cost, reliability, technology, and ergonomics are examples.

_____ 28. Performance, cost, efficiency, language, and documentation are examples.

_____ 29. Maintenance, conversion, training, and business position are examples.

_____ 30. Operate in parallel with the old system, use a test site, switch in stages, or cut over immediately to a new system.

_____ 31. Checking whether hardware and software work properly for end users.

_____ 32. A user manual communicates the design and operating procedures of a system.

_____ 33. Modifying an operational system by adding e-commerce website access would be an example.

_____ 34. End users frequently resist the introduction of new technology.

_____ 35. End users should be part of planning for organizational change and e-business project teams.

_____ 36. Companies should try to minimize the resistance and maximize the acceptance of major changes in e-business and information technology.

Discussion Questions

1. Why do you think prototyping has become a popular way to develop e-business applications?

2. Refer to the Real World Case on AvantGo, Sparklist, BuyerZone, and OfficeMax in the chapter. What are your choices for the top five design failures at business websites? Defend your selections.

3. Review the Panasonic and Quicken Loans real world examples in the text. What design changes should Panasonic make to correct the design flaws at their site and bring their website design up to Quicken's standard? Explain your reasoning.

4. What are the three most important factors you would use in evaluating computer hardware? Computer software? Explain why.

5. Assume that in your first week on a new job you are asked to use a type of business software that you have never used before. What kind of user training should your company provide to you before you start?

6. Refer to the Real World Case on Amazon, Verizon, and Boise Cascade in the chapter. What are your choices for the top five ways in which you would use e-business applications and technologies to implement a customer-centric business strategy at Verizon or other telephone companies? Defend your selections.

7. What is the difference between the parallel, plunge, phased, and pilot forms of IS conversion? Which conversion strategy is best? Explain why.

8. What are several key factors in designing a successful e-commerce or intranet website? Refer to Figure 10.13 as a starting point. Explain why the design factors you chose are important to Web success.

9. How can a company use change management to minimize the resistance and maximize the acceptance of changes in business and technology? Give several examples.

10. Pick a business task you would like to computerize. How could you use the steps of the information systems development cycle as illustrated in Figure 10.3 to help you? Use examples to illustrate your answer.

Application Exercises

Complete the following exercises as individual or group projects that apply chapter concepts to real world business situations.

1. The Sports Authority and Others: e-Commerce Website Design Requirements

Depending on which survey you choose, customers abandon online shopping carts at a rate of between 25 percent and 77 percent. Shoppers abandon their online carts for many reasons. Turn-offs include poor site navigation, hard-to-find shopping carts, and time-consuming checkouts. Let's look at how several companies are confronting this e-commerce problem.

Web Site Navigation

Consistent design throughout your site makes it easier for your customers to find their way: Users can always click on product images for most information. Buttons use a consistent color. Links are always underlined. If your site is simple for users to understand, they will happily keep moving toward the checkout. Walmart.com's recent redesign came under fire by industry critics for being too boring. However, the changes made the site cleaner, simpler, and easier for shoppers to master.

Shopping Cart Design

Whatever you do, make sure your site's shopping cart is a clearly identified link placed on the top right corner of the page, traditionally a high-click area. Moreover, make it available on every page in the same place.

Also try bringing your site's shopping cart area to life. Sports retailer The Sports Authority (*www.thesportsauthority.com*) does that with its dynamic shopping cart. The cart displays the latest item added, allowing the customer to keep a running tab more easily. The company also made sure customers could click on the cart icon to start shopping.

Don't expect people to instantly notice items added to a dynamic cart. When shoppers add items, route them to a cart summary page each time—even if it seems redundant. This page indicates confirmation and invites the shopper to check out.

Checkout Process

Shopping online is all about convenience, and nothing is a bigger pain than lengthy forms that extend the checkout process. No wonder people click away in disgust. While there may be no way around forms for the time being, keep information that you request to a minimum. Demographics are nice to know, but they can also kill sales.

A winning checkout system needs to be fast and easy. Any good checkout process makes a distinction between a repeat shopper and a first-time buyer. Greet returning customers by getting them as close as possible to single-click shopping process. Amazon.com leads in this area with the fastest possible checkout. The Gap (www.gap.com) also offers shoppers two clear shopping tracks, as well as an easy way to retrieve an account password.

Trust and Security

Shoppers demand more than security online. Getting customers to trust you must happen throughout the site, not just when they use their credit card. Establishing trust with your customers means making service a priority by giving them multiple ways to contact you and providing them with a timely reply.

The human touch, especially in a faceless online world, is important to customers. Land's End (www.landsend.com) has 250 sales reps ready to answer questions live online—and it pays: Their Internet orders end up averaging $10 more than catalog orders.

Ensure the privacy of your customer data in a clearly worded and easy-to-find policy. Also, make sure you spell out your encryption standard by using recognizable signs such as the VeriSign logo, and explain how credit card information is transmitted to your site's servers.

Website Speed

As long as shoppers use dial-up modems to access the Web, overall site speed will be a fundamental measurement to live and die by. Browse the top ten Media Metrix sites with stopwatch in hand and you can almost feel the wind in your hair. You won't get a gratuitous 20-second splash screen on Yahoo or wait for graphic after graphic to download. The fastest sites help you get in and get out by making each subsequent clock and page view as fast-loading as possible. How fast is fast enough? There is no set rule, but for a fast and free look at how your site's speed stacks up, visit Web Site Garage, a website maintenance service, at websitegarage.netscape.com.

a. Visit the Walmart.com and SportsAuthority.com websites. Which one has the better website navigation and shopping cart design? Why?

b. Compare the Amazon.com website with one of the websites mentioned in this case. Which one has the fastest website and checkout processes? Defend your choices.

c. Evaluate the LandsEnd.com privacy and security policies at their website. Does this information help build trust in the security of their e-commerce transactions? Explain.

Source: Adapted from Alice Hill, "Top 5 Reasons Your Customers Abandon Their Shopping Carts," *Smart Business*, March 2001, pp. 80–84.

2. Amazon and eBay: Evaluating e-Commerce Website Behavior

Stanford University communications professors and NetSage officers Byron Reeves and Clifford Nass evaluate e-commerce websites for their human interfaces and social behavior. Their position is that people dislike some websites not because they are badly designed, but because the sites behave badly during people's visits. Here's their evaluation of Amazon and eBay.

Amazon.com Inc.: Overall Grade = **A−**
Bottom Line: *Successfully applies social rules to create a bookstore rather than a warehouse or a library.*

Befitting its reputation as the premier e-commerce player, Amazon's book-buying site follows many social rules to great effect. The consistent style and tone throughout the site communicates a reliable personality that builds comfort and trust in the business relationship. Appropriate for its products, the tone of the site is casual.

For example, Amazon tells users, "For now, you just need to . . ." Visitors have a sense that the same person is communicating with them consistently throughout their visit at the site. This promotes a feeling that customers have a single personal assistant rather than a confusing group of merchants—all with different methods and personalities—to help with purchases. Amazon maximizes personalization with minimal information by offering suggestions based on previous purchases, discussing what people in geographic areas are buying and offering one-click shopping that uses information previously stored on the site.

It continually tells users where they are in the ordering and registration process, particularly when they're about to purchase something. A confirmation to customers that they're "doing the right things" to accomplish a transaction—commonplace in real-life transactions—is used effectively at Amazon.

Amazon also effectively uses physical places on its site to let people know what to expect of the information presented in those places. For example, the largest column of information (the middle two-thirds of each page from the top to the bottom) is devoted to product information. And regardless of whether a shopper is looking for books, music, or electronic gear, the function of the space is unchanged. Even the details of price, shipping, and discounts are identical among products.

Amazon-generated book reviews and postings from customers are mixed with book reviews (from, for example, *The New York Times*) to produce commentary relevant to many items. Through careful use of language for related groups of customers (for example, *Purchase Circles* rather than, say, folksier *Neighbors*) and the avoidance of visual clutter around the buttons that execute the purchase, they remind the customer that this isn't a library.

eBay Inc.: Overall Grade = **D**
Bottom Line: *An expert auctioneer that doesn't behave like one.*

People labeled as experts, whether by others or themselves, are perceived as more competent, more trusting, and more likely to provide unique knowledge and expertise. But eBay's reputation as an expert suffers because it doesn't correct sellers' mistakes and is considered to be complicit in these errors. For example, typographical errors in product descriptions reduce credibility, yet eBay doesn't edit that text. There are trade-offs among image size, picture quality, and details of the background in product presentations, but eBay doesn't make suggestions or offer ways to improve them.

A lesson here is that people hopelessly confuse the errors of the "message" with the competence of the "messenger"; poor presentation undermines eBay as well as the sale items. eBay is also impolite. For example, signing up for an account can take as long as 24 hours for confirmation. eBay users also aren't alerted when they omit a field during registration. Instead of dismissing people during that period, eBay should invite customers to browse. A good social partner tries to own the problems and makes an attempt at resolution.

eBay also fails to carry through on the notion of a "personal" shopper. It's unclear how to submit the initial form that activates the personal shopper, and the shopper doesn't save a list of items on which the customer might want to bid. Having someone remember things for you is essential in personalization. Finally, eBay users must traverse many pages to find the personal shopper—the exact opposite of what a "personal" shopper should be. The idea of an automatic bidder, someone working on your behalf, is a social plus. However, eBay should place more attention and emphasis on making the bidding process personal rather than simply automatic.

a. Visit the Amazon.com and eBay.com websites. Do you agree with the evaluations of Professors Reeves and Nass? Why or why not?

b. How could Amazon improve the experience it offers its e-commerce shoppers? Give several examples.

c. What should eBay do to improve the experience it provides to customers at its auction site? Give several examples.

Source: Adapted from Kevin Fogarty, "Net Manners Matter: How Top Sites Rank in Social Behavior," *Computerworld*, October 18, 1999, pp. 40–41. Copyright 1999 by Computerworld, Inc., Framingham, MA 01701. Reprinted from *Computerworld*.

3. e-Business System Report
Study an e-business system described in a case study in this text or one used by an organization to which you have access. Write up the results in an e-business system report. Make a presentation to the class based on the results of your study of an e-business system. Use the outline in Figure 10.31 as a table of contents for your report and the outline of your presentation. Use presentation software and/or overhead transparencies to display key points of your analysis.

4. Creating a Personal Web Page
Create a personal Web page for yourself using appropriate software recommended by your instructor. If you use Microsoft Word to create your Web page, a brief description of special features of Word that are particularly useful in developing Web pages is available on the website for my textbooks at www.mhhe.com/business/mis/obrien.

Or you may want to try the free website building and hosting services offered by sites like Homestead.com and Webprovider.com and many others, including those provided to members of online Web communities and services like AOL, GeoCities, Tripod, and EarthLink.

Your website should begin with an attractive home page that contains links to the other, more detailed pages. You may also want to include bookmarks within a page linking to other sections of the same page and/or links to the websites of others.

Figure 10.31   Outline of an e-business system report.

● **Introduction to the organization and e-business system.** Briefly describe the organization you selected and the type of e-business system you have studied.

● **Analysis of an e-business system.** Identify the following system components of a business use of the Internet, intranets, extranets, or electronic commerce.

  ● Input, processing, output, storage, and control methods currently used.

  ● Hardware, software, networks, and people involved.

  ● Data captured and information products produced.

  ● Files and databases accessed and maintained

● **Evaluation of the e-business system.**

  ● **Efficiency:** Does it do the job right? Is the e-business system well organized? Inexpensive? Fast? Does it require minimum resources? Process large volumes of data, produce a variety of information products?

  ● **Effectiveness:** Does it do the right job? The way the employees, customers, suppliers, or other end users want it done? Does it give them the information they need, the way they want it? Does it support the e-business objectives of the organization? Provide significant customer and business value?

● **Design and implementation of an e-business system proposal.**

  ● Do end users need a new system or just improvements? Why?

  ● What exactly are you recommending they do?

  ● Is it feasible? What are its benefits and costs?

  ● What will it take to implement your recommendations?

Frito-Lay Inc.:
Failure and Success in Knowledge Portal Development

Some big blunders bring great opportunities; others just waste time and energy. At Plano, Texas–based Frito-Lay Inc., one error led to the creation of an impressive knowledge management system; a second mistake undermined users' acceptance of it. The story begins in the late 1990s, when one of Frito-Lay's biggest customers adopted a more centralized decision-making structure. Frito-Lay's regional sales teams, designed to deal with regional offices of customers, found themselves struggling to work effectively with this huge account.

Moreover, the customer—a sophisticated, multibillion-dollar supermarket chain—began demanding more from the Frito-Lay sales teams. When a Frito-Lay salesperson suggested a new way to merchandise a product, the supermarket wanted the facts and figures to back it up. "They were pushing us to support our plans with quantitative and qualitative research," recalls Mike Marino, Frito-Lay's vice president for category and customer development.

Sensing a trend, Frito-Lay created a handful of national sales teams to focus on top customers such as the supermarket chain. But the teams, used to working regionally, found nationwide collaboration difficult. Although Frito-Lay had rich stores of market research and other pertinent customer information housed in databases at its headquarters, there was no easy way for team members to find what they needed. Frustration rose, performance suffered, and sales team turnover reached 25 percent.

Then, in early 1999, Marino engaged Dallas-based Navigator Systems Inc. to help. Navigator consultants envisioned a Web-based enterprise knowledge portal that would combine tools for knowledge management and collaboration, enabling the team to better serve the customer while helping reduce frustration and turnover.

A portal development project team was formed to work with the national supermarket team because it had the most centralized and demanding customers. "We knew if we could deliver there, we could satisfy any customer," Marino says.

The supermarket sales team told the project team what kind of knowledge they needed. The request ranged from simple information, such as why Frito-Lay merchandises Lays and Ruffles products in one part of a store and Doritos in another, to more complex research on what motivates shoppers as they move through a store.

Then the project team had to find the knowledge. The team went prospecting in Frito-Lay's databases in departments such as marketing, sales, and operations. They scoured the Web for external sources such as trade publications and industry organizations. They identified in-house subject matter experts and noted their areas of expertise in an online database.

In October 1999, the project team presented a working prototype they had developed to a group of beta users from the supermarket sales team only to find that in the quest for speed, a classic and crippling error had been made. Because the project team had not involved the sales team in the design of the prototype, the portal they had built could be marginally useful to a sales team, but it wasn't specific enough for the supermarket team.

"Conceptually, it was a great idea," says Frito-Lay sales team leader Joe Ackerman. "But when folks are not on the front line, their view of what is valuable is different from those running 100 miles an hour in the field." The project team needed to backtrack and plug in the missing features, but it also had to win back the sales force, who now suspected that even a revised tool would be a waste of time.

The project team then spent the next four months working with salespeople to evolve the prototype into a system they would embrace. For example, a call-reporting feature was added. "So many people want to know what happened on a sales call, the account manager involved can be on the phone for days," Ackerman explains. "Now, we're able to post that to a website. It frees up the account manager to document the call once and move on."

Other changes included enabling users to analyze and manipulate data rather than just viewing it, and developing reports tailored to customers' needs. "The original reports were very general," Ackerman says, so users would have had to spend lots of time reformatting them for customer presentations. Ackerman was also enlisted for the official rollout of the portal. "If it comes from the field, it's really better received than if it's from headquarters," he says. "So we made sure it was embraced by the team leader—me."

Now Ackerman says that better collaboration with the portal has helped to significantly reduce turnover, while improved access to knowledge-base data has enabled account managers to present themselves to customers as consultants with important data to share.

Marino claims that the portal has been a big success. The supermarket team, whose first year as a customer-based team in 1999 was a bad one from a financial standpoint, exceeded its sales plan for 2000 and grew its business at a rate almost twice that of Frito-Lay's other customer teams. There was no turnover except for promotions. The concept is now being tailored to three other Frito-Lay sales teams and departments, and studied by other divisions of PepsiCo, Frito-Lay's parent company.

Case Study Questions

1. What mistakes in systems development were made by the Frito-Lay portal development project team? By Frito-Lay management?

2. What else could you recommend to the project team for the redesign and implementation of the revised portal system? Explain your answer.

3. What is the business value of the redesigned enterprise knowledge portal to Frito-Lay?

Source: Adapted from Kathleen Melymuka, "Profiting from Mistakes," *Computerworld*, April 30, 2001, pp. 42, 43. Reprinted by permission

Ryder System and Others:
Strategies for Successful User Involvement in Systems Development

In the mid-1980s, Shirley Wong was part of a team developing software for an automated 411 system at a large West Coast telephone company. After a great deal of work, the team unveiled the system to telephone operators and were greeted with universal hisses and boos. "The operators didn't want it," recalls Wong, who is now the Webmaster at Optodyne, Inc. The company had wasted at least $1 million on the effort, and as a result of the fiasco, the project director and three managers were fired.

The problem: The operators who would be using the system were never consulted about their needs.

Times change and many IT project managers realize how crucial users are to a project's success. But how do you get users to take system requirements seriously? "This is probably the biggest problem at most companies," says Bill Berghel, a project manager at FedEx Corp. in Memphis.

To get users engaged, start by educating their bosses, says Naomi Karten, president of Karten Associates, a customer service consulting firm. Demonstrate how important user input is to the success of systems. Use real examples to show the benefits of doing things right and the consequences of doing things wrong. Once they get it, make sure they buy in on every project, she says. "Senior managers have to make sure that people below them make the time," says Peter Goundry, MIS manager at Aircast Inc., a medical device maker in Summit, New Jersey.

Don't ask what users want; find out what they need. "Focus on what ails the user, not what the user wants in a system," says Rob Norris, CIO at Pinocol Assurance in Denver. "Users don't always know what they want," says Sue McKay, CIO at Aircast. "Sometimes, you have to help them understand that what they think they want won't give them what they need." For example, end users may have heard about some cool system to produce management reports and may not realize the same information is already easily available through existing databases.

And don't make the mistake Wong's group made. Talk with enough people to really understand the business process you're trying to facilitate. "If you are creating a new sales system and you're only dealing with the VP of sales, you're doomed," Aircast's McKay says. Don't forget the sales representatives, sales assistants, and customers.

One of the best ways to get users interested and keep them engaged is to make them partners through rapid application development. "We show a series of prototypes to the users and work toward what they do want," says Berghel of FedEx. And each iteration should take only a few days, to keep up the momentum, he says.

Ryder System, Inc. At least one Ryder executive, John Wormwood, the company's director of e-commerce solutions, credits user involvement with alerting Ryder to its Web problems. It was Web-surfing customers who pointed out what a mess the site was. "We got feedback from users saying 'the website is unusable, difficult to navigate,'" he says.

About 10 sites had sprung up, some without a link to Ryder.com, the corporate site that explains the company's business. Although Ryder sells used tractor-trailers, for instance, buying them online required a visit to usedtrucks.ryder.com. "It was really a patchwork quilt of navigation, colors, and styles," says Wormwood. Separate divisions put up 10 websites for everything from selling used tractor-trailers to emergency roadside service. But many didn't link to the corporate site, Ryder.com. And its shipment-tracking service was buried 10 clicks deep into the Ryder.com site.

Ryder needed to unravel the threads. In late 1999, it created an e-commerce group, including business users from all its major divisions. They agreed that Ryder needed a common look and produce a style guide to lay out where logos, photos, and text should go on all Ryder Web pages. So now all the company's websites are linked to Ryder.com. A redesign helps customers locate their shipments within two clicks. Now Ryder uses the Web to coordinate its picking, packing, and shipping for customers.

A renewed focus on customers, and on making it a snap for them to use the Web, has driven the $5.3 billion company's e-strategy ever since, and upped its IT spending 15 percent, to $100 million. Of that, $500,000 went toward a website makeover this year. Before the redesign, it took 10 clicks to track a shipment. Since the new site was launched in July, the function is just one click from Ryder's home page. Before, there was no search mechanism. There is today.

These and other improvements have helped Ryder attract new customers, including Northrop Grumman. The defense contractor hopes to cut its transportation costs by taking advantage of better rates Ryder gets through bulk buys of cargo space. Northrop is pleased that it can electronically track the shipments every step of the way. "We're able to pull out a lot of manual processes that sometimes introduce errors," says T.W. Scott, director of supply-chain management systems.

Case Study Questions

1. Do you agree with all of the strategies to "get users to take system requirements gathering seriously" outlined in this case? Why or why not?

2. How else could Ryder System have involved users in their Web systems redesign projects? What benefits would result from such involvement?

3. What else should user managers and IT development managers and specialists do to successfully involve users in business systems development projects?

Source: Adapted from Kathleen Meylmuka, "Engaging Users," *Computerworld*, September 24, 2001, p. 32; and Faith Keenan and Timothy Mullaney, "Let's Get Back to Basics, Folks!" *Business Week e.biz*, October 29, 2001, pp. 27, 28. Reprinted by permission.

Management
Challenges

Business
Applications   Module   Information
                   V   Technologies

Development   Foundation
Processes   Concepts

Module V

Management Challenges

What managerial challenges do information systems pose for
e-business enterprises? The two chapters of this module emphasize how managers and business professionals can manage the
successful use of e-business technologies in a global information society.

- Chapter 11, **Security and Ethical Challenges of e-Business,** discusses
  the threats against, and defenses needed for e-business performance and
  security, as well as the ethical implications and societal impacts of information technologies.

- Chapter 12, **Enterprise and Global Management of e-Business Technology,** emphasizes the impact of e-business technologies on management and organizations, the components of information systems management, and the managerial implications of the use of information
  technology in global e-business.

Management
Challenges

Business
Applications   Module
V   Information
Technologies

Development
Processes   Foundation
Concepts

Chapter 11

Security and Ethical

Challenges of e-Business

Chapter Highlights

Learning Objectives

After reading and studying this chapter, you should be able to:

1. Identify several ethical issues in how the use of information technologies in e-business affects employment, individuality, working conditions, privacy, crime, health, and solutions to societal problems.

2. Identify several types of security management strategies and defenses, and explain how they can be used to ensure the security of e-business applications.

3. Propose several ways that business managers and professionals can help to lessen the harmful effects and increase the beneficial effects of the use of information technology.

Security, Ethical, and Societal Challenges of e-Business

Introduction

There is no question that the use of information technology in e-business operations presents major security challenges, poses serious ethical questions, and affects society in significant ways. Therefore, in this section we will explore the threats to e-business security posed by many types of computer crime and unethical behavior. In Section II, we will examine a variety of methods that companies use to manage the security and integrity of today's e-business enterprise. Now let's look at a realworld example.

Analyzing Exodus Communications

Read the Real World Case on Exodus Communications on the next page. We can learn a lot from this case about the ethical and security issues and challenges that surround the business use of Internet technologies. See Figure 11.1.

This case reveals some of the dimensions and trends of the threat of cybercrime to business. The distributed denial of service attacks on major e-commerce websites by Mafiaboy showed that cybercrime weapons are becoming increasingly automated and easy to use by even the most inexperienced hackers. The attacks also showed that the vulnerability and number of potential cybercrime victims are expanding as more people and organizations are networked by the Internet. The case also reveals the security measures being employed by Exodus, a major Internet facilities and services provider. One of these services is CATT, the Cyber Attack Tiger Team, which offers companies a range of managed security services by a team of expert and experienced security specialists. Many companies have thus outsourced some of their security management to Exodus. The case concludes with examples of two companies that demonstrates how they used the security expertise of the CATT group to solve several cybercrimes.

Figure 11.1

Preventing and solving cybercrimes is the goal of the Cyber Attack Tiger Team (CATT) of Exodus Communications, which is led by former FBI computer intrusion team leader Charles Neal (second from right).

Source: Eean Wei.

Exodus Communications:
Protecting Companies against Cybercrime

For Charles Neal, a 20-year veteran of the FBI, Mafiaboy was the watershed case for cybercrime. On Monday, February 7, 2000, a 15-year old from suburban Montreal with the online moniker Mafiaboy launched a week-long Internet attack on Yahoo, CNN.com, Amazon.com, eBay, Dell, Buy.com, and several others causing losses estimated in the millions. The hacker hit the companies with what is now commonly known as a distributed denial-of-service attack, which flooded the victims' Internet servers with messages until they collapsed.

Mafiaboy was a newbie hacker, a "script kiddie." He begged the software—now widely available on several Internet hacker sites—from other hackers and then used it to break into and gain root access to more than 50 servers, most of them located at American universities. He then used those servers to launch his assault.

That morning, calls began coming into Neal's office at the FBI's Los Angeles computer intrusion squad. Neal sent an agent to the Irvine, California, data center of Exodus Communications, one of the world's largest providers of Internet services and network facilities, whose corporate customers included many of Mafiaboy's victims. Neal's team soon began poring over Exodus's network logs, ultimately tracing the attacks to Mafiaboy's home computer. Jill Knesek, the case agent, then flew to Montreal where the Royal Canadian Mounted Police were placing a phone tap on Mafiaboy's house.

What made Mafiaboy so important? It proved to Neal that anybody, even someone with very limited talent, could launch a massive cyberattack. And while Mafiaboy primarily targeted dot-coms, almost every company, and maybe your home, is now online and networked to some extent. The case exposed two major trends in cybercrime weapons and vulnerability. The weapons are becoming increasingly automated and easy to use, and the pool of vulnerable potential victims is expanding. Automation, Neal argues, opens up cybercrime to all sorts of groups, from hacktivists to career criminals and terrorists.

The Exodus data center in El Segundo, California, one of 43 worldwide, sits utterly undistinguished amid the sprawl fanning out from Los Angeles International Airport. The company's name doesn't even appear on the building, but the unassuming façade, which is wrapped in bulletproof Kevlar, belies its extremely high security, almost to the point of paranoia.

Inside, a biometric hand scanner, another layer of bulletproof glass, two Pinkerton security guards, and a 500-pound door block access to 66,000 climate-controlled square feet of Internet servers, the online backbones of Exodus clients like Best Buy, eBay, KPMG Consulting, British Airways, Virgin, Merrill Lynch, Yahoo, and some 4,500 other customers. It's estimated that as many as one-third of all Internet clicks pass through Exodus servers.

If Exodus is the switchboard of the Internet, then its Cyber Attack Tiger Team, or CATT, aspires to be the Internet's detectives. Neal formed the group after retiring from the FBI and joining Exodus to sell managed security services to Exodus's clients. So far it's signed up more than 250 of the most security-conscious among them.

CATT's thesis is relatively simple: Internet security is complex. If you have poor security, you will be hacked. If you have the latest security hardware but don't use it properly, you will be hacked. Furthermore, if you are hacked, and you do nothing about it, you will be sued.

For roughly $5,000 a month—the price varies widely depending on a company's needs and size—a CATT infrastructure team installs a "content integrity monitoring system" on the client's servers. The CIMS can tell if key data is ever altered (like select passwords). An unexpected change probably means a hacker has breached the system, which pages one of CATT's incident responders, who then immediately sets to work ejecting the intruder. At the same time, the team starts investigating where the hack originated, what systems the hacker used, and exactly who it is. Meanwhile, an intelligence group monitors hacker sites, interviews insiders, and lurks undercover in hacker chat rooms.

Neal sits in his spartan office above the El Segundo data center. He wants to talk about the cases they're investigating to shed light on the problem—and his group, which now includes some of his ex-FBI colleagues—so he gives a few examples without mentioning clients' names.

Neal's first case at Exodus centered on a European client in a lawsuit with a competitor. In court one day the competitors showed up with a thick stack of e-mail messages from Exodus's client that they claimed had been mailed to them anonymously. In truth the competitor had hired a hacker to break into the Exodus's client's network and steal its e-mail database. The hacker-for-hire, whom Neal interviewed later, ultimately confessed because he felt underpaid for his services.

This past spring, a high-tech client in California was in the running for a large contract that promised to make or break its business. Company executives detected something suspicious on their networks and contacted Exodus. Neal's group ran forensic tests on the client's servers to find that its primary competitor for the contract had broken into the network to steal trade secrets. Neal called in the FBI.

Case Study Questions

1. What major trends in cybercrime weapons and vulnerability were exposed by the attacks on large e-commerce websites by Mafiaboy?

2. Do you think that a security initiative like the Exodus CATT team provides adequate security measures against cybercrime for a company? Why or why not?

3. What are several security measures besides those mentioned in the case that a company might employ to protect itself from cybercrime? Explain their benefits and limitations.

Source: Bill Breen, "Bankers Hours," **Fast Company**, November 2001, pp. 196–203. Copyright 2001 by Bus Innovator Group Resources, Inc. Reproduced with permission of Bus Innovator Group Resources, Inc. via Copyright Clearance Center.

Figure 11.2

Important aspects of the security, ethical, and societal dimensions of e-business. Remember that information technologies can support both beneficial or detrimental effects on society in each of the areas shown.

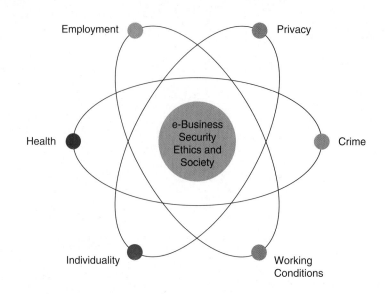

e-Business Security, Ethics, and Society

The use of information technologies in e-business systems has had major impacts on society, and thus raises ethical issues in the areas of crime, privacy, individuality, employment, health, and working conditions. See Figure 11.2.

However, you should also realize that information technology has had beneficial results as well as detrimental effects on society and people in each of these areas. For example, computerizing a manufacturing process may have the adverse effect of eliminating people's jobs, but also have the beneficial result of improving working conditions and producing products of higher quality at less cost. So your job as a manager or business professional should involve managing your work activities and those of others to minimize the detrimental effects of e-business systems and optimize their beneficial effects. That would represent an ethically responsible use of information technology.

Computer Crime in e-Business

Cyber crime is becoming one of the Net's growth businesses. Today, criminals are doing everything from stealing intellectual property and committing fraud to unleashing viruses and committing acts of cyber terrorism [36].

Computer crime is a growing threat to society caused by the criminal or irresponsible actions of individuals who are taking advantage of the widespread use and vulnerability of computers and the Internet and other networks. It thus presents a major challenge to the ethical use of information technologies. Computer crime poses serious threats to the integrity, safety, and survival of most e-business systems, and thus makes the development of effective security methods a top priority. See Figure 11.3.

Computer crime is defined by the Association of Information Technology Professionals (AITP) as including (1) the unauthorized use, access, modification, and destruction of hardware, software, data, or network resources; (2) the unauthorized release of information; (3) the unauthorized copying of software; (4) denying an end user access to his or her own hardware, software, data, or network resources; and (5) using or conspiring to use computer or network resources to illegally obtain information or tangible property. This definition was promoted by the AITP in a Model Computer Crime Act, and is reflected in many computer crime laws.

Yahoo! and Others: Cybercrime on the Internet

First it was Yahoo! Inc. The portal giant was shut down for three hours. Then retailer Buy.com Inc. was hit the next day, hours after going public. By that evening, eBay, Amazon.com, and CNN had gone dark. And in the morning, the

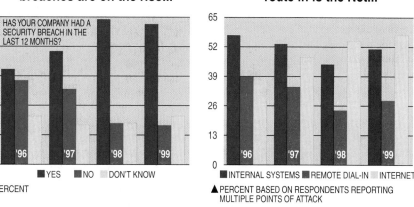

Figure 11.3

The growth in electronic assaults and break-ins on business and government organizations via internal systems, the Internet, and other networks.

DATA: FBI/COMPUTER SECURITY INSTITUTE.
SURVEY BASED ON APPROXIMATELY 500 RESPONSES FROM PRIVATE CORPORATIONS AND LARGE GOVERNMENT AGENCIES.

Source: Adapted from Ira Sager, Steve Hamm, Neil Gross, John Carey, and Robert Hoff, "Cyber Crime," *Business Week*, February 21, 2000, p. 39. Reprinted with special permission, copyright © 2000 by The McGraw-Hill Companies, Inc.

mayhem continued with online broker E*TRADE and others having traffic to their sites virtually choked off.

Gridlock. For all the sophisticated work on fire walls, intrusion-detection systems, encryption and computer security, e-businesses are at risk from *denial of service* (DOS) attacks, a relatively simple technique that's akin to dialing a telephone number repeatedly so that everyone else trying to get through will hear a busy signal.

Cybercrime on the Internet is on the rise. Consider just a quick smattering of recent events: In December, 1999, 300,000 credit card numbers were snatched from online music retailer CD Universe. In March, the Melissa virus caused an estimated $80 million in damage when it swept around the world, paralyzing e-mail systems. That same month, hackers-for-hire pleaded guilty to breaking into phone giants AT&T, GTE, and Sprint, among others, for calling card numbers that eventually made their way to organized crime gangs in Italy. According to the FBI, the phone companies were hit for an estimated $2 million.

But one good thing: Such events are delivering a wake-up call to businesses that they need to spend as much time protecting their websites and networks as they do linking them with customers, suppliers, contractors—and you [36].

Hacking

Cyber thieves have at their fingertips a dozen dangerous tools, from "scans" that ferret out weaknesses in website software programs to "sniffers" that snatch passwords. All told, the FBI estimates U.S. computer losses at up to $10 billion a year [36].

Hacking, in computerese, is the obsessive use of computers, or the unauthorized access and use of networked computer systems. Illegal hackers (also called *crackers*) frequently assault the Internet and other networks to steal or damage data and programs. One of the issues in hacking is what to do about a hacker who commits only *electronic breaking and entering*; that is, gets access to a computer system, reads some files, but neither steals nor damages anything. This situation is common in computer crime cases that are prosecuted. In several states, courts have found that the typical computer crime statute language prohibiting malicious access to a computer system did apply to anyone gaining unauthorized access to another's computer networks. See Figure 11.4.

Figure 11.4

Examples of common hacking tactics to assault e-business enterprises and other organizations through the Internet and other networks.

Common Hacking Tactics

Denial of Service This is becoming a common networking prank. By hammering a website's equipment with too many requests for information, an attacker can effectively clog the system, slowing performance or even crashing the site. This method of overloading computers is sometimes used to cover up an attack.

Scans Widespread probes of the Internet to determine types of computers, services, and connections. That way the bad guys can take advantage of weaknesses in a particular make of computer or software program.

Sniffer Programs that covertly search individual packets of data as they pass through the Internet, capturing passwords or the entire contents.

Spoofing Faking an e-mail address or Web page to trick users into passing along critical information like passwords or credit card numbers.

Trojan Horse A program that, unknown to the user, contains instructions that exploit a known vulnerability in some software.

Back Doors In case the original entry point has been detected, having a few hidden ways back makes reentry easy—and difficult to detect.

Malicious Applets Tiny programs, sometimes written in the popular Java computer language, that misuse your computer's resources, modify files on the hard disk, send fake e-mail, or steal passwords.

War Dialing Programs that automatically dial thousands of telephone numbers in search of a way in through a modem connection.

Logic Bombs An instruction in a computer program that triggers a malicious act.

Buffer Overflow A technique for crashing or gaining control of a computer by sending too much data to the buffer in a computer's memory.

Password Crackers Software that can guess passwords.

Social Engineering A tactic used to gain access to computer systems by talking unsuspecting company employees out of valuable information such as passwords.

Dumpster Diving Sifting through a company's garbage to find information to help break into their computers. Sometimes the information is used to make a stab at social engineering more credible.

Source: Adapted from Ira Sager, Steve Hamm, Neil Gross, John Carey, and Robert Hoff, "Cyber Crime," *Business Week*, February 21, 2000, p. 40. Reprinted with special permission, copyright © 2000 by The McGraw-Hill Companies. Inc.

Hackers can monitor e-mail, Web server access, or file transfers to extract passwords or steal network files, or to plant data that will cause a system to welcome intruders. A hacker may also use remote services that allow one computer on a network to execute programs on another computer to gain privileged access within a network. Telnet, an Internet tool for interactive use of remote computers, can help hackers discover information to plan other attacks. Hackers have used Telnet to access a computer's e-mail port, for example, to monitor e-mail messages for passwords and other information about privileged user accounts and network resources. These are just some of the typical types of computer crimes that hackers commit on the Internet on a regular basis. That's why Internet security measures like encryption and fire walls, as discussed in the next section, are so vital to the success of electronic commerce and other e-business applications.

Cyber Theft

Many computer crimes involve the theft of money. In the majority of cases, they are "inside jobs" that involve unauthorized network entry and fraudulent alteration of computer databases to cover the tracks of the employees involved. Of course, more recent examples involve the use of the Internet, such as the widely publicized theft of $11 million from Citibank in late 1994. Russian hacker Vladimir Levin and his accomplices in St. Petersburg used the Internet to electronically break into Citibank's mainframe systems in New York. They then succeeded in transferring the funds from several Citibank accounts to their own accounts at banks in Finland, Israel, and California [34].

In most cases, the scope of such financial losses is much larger than the incidents reported. Most companies don't reveal that they have been targets or victims of computer crime. They fear scaring off customers and provoking complaints by shareholders. In fact, several British banks, including the Bank of London, paid hackers more than a half million dollars not to reveal information about electronic break-ins [34].

BuyDirect Inc.: Internet Credit Card Fraud	Fraud nearly vanquished San Francisco-based BuyDirect Inc. when it opened for business, said William Headapohl, president of the online software store. "Our fraud rate was unacceptably high and banks wanted to drop us. If we hadn't had strong financial backing and worked hard to reduce our fraud rates, we would have been put out of business pretty quickly." Using antifraud software and elaborate screening systems, the company reduced its fraud rate to under 1 percent. "The more it costs, the more someone will try to steal it," said Headapohl. "One of our first defenses was not to sell the really expensive products online."

Selling internationally is one of the key reasons for starting an electronic-commerce site, yet foreign sales are the riskiest of all. "Our international fraud rates were so bad in the beginning, we thought we were going to have to exclude overseas sales altogether," Headapohl said. "Companies like ours were routinely seeing fraud rates in excess of 20 percent."

Most successful Web merchants avoid fraud by outsourcing credit card verification to third parties with sophisticated (and expensive) neural-net antifraud software. Or they develop their own antifraud systems. Another approach is to take verification procedures off-line and check cards manually [28].

Unauthorized Use at Work

The unauthorized use of computer systems and networks can be called *time and resource theft*. A common example is unauthorized use of company-owned computer networks by employees. This may range from doing private consulting or personal finances, or playing video games, to unauthorized use of the Internet on company networks. Network monitoring software, called *sniffers*, is frequently used to monitor network traffic to evaluate network capacity, as well as reveal evidence of improper use. See Figures 11.5 and 11.6.

According to one survey, 90 percent of U.S. workers admit to surfing recreational sites during office hours, and 84 percent say they send personal e-mail from work. So this kind of activity alone may not get you fired from your job. However, other Internet activities at work can bring instant dismissal. For example, *The New York Times* fired 23 workers in November of 1999 because they were distributing racist and sexually offensive jokes on the company's e-mail system [44].

Xerox Corporation fired more than 40 workers in 1999 for spending up to eight hours a day on pornography sites on the Web. Several employees even downloaded pornographic videos which took so much network bandwidth that it choked the company network and prevented co-workers from sending or receiving e-mail. Xerox instituted an eight-member SWAT team on computer abuse that uses software to review every website its 40,000 computer users view each day. Other companies clamp down even harder, by installing software like SurfWatch, which enables them to block, as well as monitor access to off-limit websites [29].

American Fast Freight: Stealing Time and Resources	Pornography, check. Online auctions, check. Sports sites, check. MIS director Jeff LePage thought his company's network was insulated from the Internet sites that typically lure employees away from their work. Those activities are policed and in some cases blocked with monitoring software because the company policy at

Figure 11.5

Online non-work-related employee activity and corporate policies.

Use of Non-Work-Related Websites

Most frequent recreational surfing by employees:

1. Sports
2. Stock trading
3. Job hunting
4. Pornography

Base: Survey of 102 network administrators at companies with 500 or more employees

Online activities specifically discouraged by corporate policies:

CATEGORY	RESPONDENTS
Pornography	79
Gambling	51
Chat	37
Shopping	27
Sports	25
Stock trading	24
Job hunting	23

Base: 98 network administrators; multiple responses allowed

Source: Adapted from Stacy Collett, "Net Managers Battle Online Trading Boom," *Computerworld*, July 5, 1999, p. 24. Copyright 1999 by Computerworld, Inc., Framingham, MA 01701. Reprinted from *Computerworld*.

American Fast Freight Inc., in Seattle, clearly states that any online activity "not specifically and exclusively work related" is prohibited.

So imagine LePage's surprise when a new culprit emerged: He recently discovered that one employee had visited a stock-monitoring website 186 times during a 12-day period. "We've been bitten by the online investing bug," LePage said. He isn't alone.

The stock market boom and the day-trading frenzy at websites such as E*TRADE.com and Schwab.com created a form of recreational surfing that hit employers especially hard. The best time to trade is during business hours, and that means greater demands on a company's network bandwidth and resources, as well as a substantial productivity hit.

Experts said it's time for companies to drag out their Internet policy and specifically include a limit on personal investment activity. "If there's not a policy, there's going to be an argument," said Peter Kershaw, president of Content Technologies. Since the online trading incident at American Fast Freight, the company has amended its Internet usage policy to specifically prohibit use of online investing sites during work hours—except for lunchtime [6].

Software Piracy

Computer programs are valuable property and thus are the subject of theft from computer systems. However, unauthorized copying of software, or **software piracy,** is also a major form of software theft. Several major cases involving the unauthorized copying of software have been widely reported. These include lawsuits by the Software Publishers Association, an industry association of software developers, against major corporations that allowed unauthorized copying of their programs.

Unauthorized copying is illegal because software is intellectual property that is protected by copyright law and user licensing agreements. For example, in the United States, commercial software packages are protected by the Computer Software Piracy and Counterfeiting Amendment to the Federal Copyright Act. In most cases, the

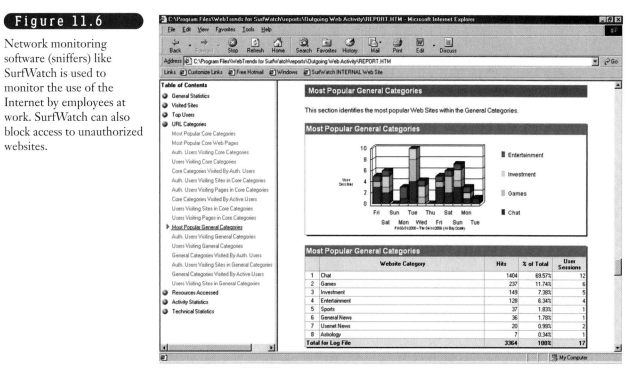

Figure 11.6

Network monitoring software (sniffers) like SurfWatch is used to monitor the use of the Internet by employees at work. SurfWatch can also block access to unauthorized websites.

Source: Courtesy of SurfWatch.com.

purchase of a commercial software package is really a payment to license its fair use by an individual end user. Therefore, many companies sign *site licenses* that allow them to legally make a certain number of copies for use by their employees at a particular location. Other alternatives are *shareware*, which allows you to make copies of software for others, and *public domain software*, which is not copyrighted.

Piracy of Intellectual Property

Software is not the only intellectual property subject to computer-based piracy. Other forms of copyrighted material, such as music, videos, images, articles, books and other written works are especially vulnerable to copyright infringement, which most courts have deemed illegal. Digitized versions can easily be captured by computer systems and made available for people to access or download at Internet websites, or can be readily disseminated by e-mail as file attachments. The development of peer-to-peer (P2P) networking technologies like the Napster and Gnutella models (discussed in Chapter 6) have made digital versions of copyrighted material even more vulnerable to unauthorized use. For example, Napster and other similar software enable direct MP3 audio file transfers of specified tracks of music between your PC and those of other users on the Internet. Thus, such software creates a *peer-to-peer network* of millions of Internet users who electronically trade digital versions of copyrighted or public domain music stored on their PC's hard drives. Let's look at the ongoing debate in this controversial area of intellectual property rights more closely with a real world example.

Napster: Intellectual Property Battleground

The Recording Industry Association of America (RIAA) won its suit in U.S. courts against Napster, a San Mateo, California, dot-com, charging that Napster's primary function is to enable and encourage copyright violations.

Napster invented Web software which is free to anyone who wants to download it, that allows you to zap a song from your computer via the Internet to another user's hard drive in under a minute. But RIAA execs had sued, charging that Napster "has created and is operating a haven for music piracy on an unprecedented scale."

Though that seems to be exactly what Napster was doing, two intellectual-property lawyers had argued that the law favored Napster. For one thing, Napster doesn't actually control any of the music—it never even passes through the website. "Napster is saying, 'We just put software out there,'" said John Lynch of Howrey Simon Arnold & White. "So the plaintiff has to prove Napster is inducing illegal activity. And inducing is not what they're really doing."

What's more, the RIAA had to prove that Napster is used almost exclusively for illegal activity, argued Mark Lemley, a law professor at University of California at Berkeley. That would be difficult because Napster provides access to new, uncopyrighted artists as well.

Napster argued that it is essentially powerless to prevent users from trading copyrighted music and that it shouldn't be held responsible for their misconduct. RIAA general counsel Cary Sherman had emphatically dismissed that argument. "If you have knowledge that what you are doing is causing infringement," he says, "you're liable." And the courts agreed [22].

Computer Viruses

One of the most destructive examples of computer crime involves the creation of **computer viruses** or *worms*. *Virus* is the more popular term but, technically, a virus is a program code that cannot work without being inserted into another program. A worm is a distinct program that can run unaided. In either case, these programs copy annoying or destructive routines into the networked computer systems of anyone who accesses computers infected with the virus or who uses copies of magnetic disks taken from infected computers. Thus, a computer virus or worm can spread destruction among many users. Though they sometimes display only humorous messages, they more often destroy the contents of memory, hard disks, and other storage devices. Copy routines in the virus or worm spread the virus and destroy the data and software of many computer users. See Figure 11.7.

Computer viruses typically enter a computer system through e-mail and file attachments via the Internet and online services, or through illegal or borrowed copies of software. Copies of *shareware* software downloaded from the Internet can be another source of viruses. A virus usually copies itself into the files of a computer's

Figure 11.7

Examples of computer viruses.

Computer Virus Facts
● **Melissa Virus** **Type:** Computer virus designed to attack files on a single PC. **Replication method:** Prompts Microsoft Outlook to send infected document to first 50 addresses in address book. **Damage:** Overwhelms corporate e-mail servers.
● **CIH, or Chernobyl Virus** **Type:** Data-triggered computer virus designed to attack files on a single PC. **Replication method:** Executes infected files sent via e-mail or on the Web. **Damage:** Erases entire hard drive and attempts to overwrite BIOS.
● **W32/Explorerzip.worm** **Type:** Internet worm designed to infect PCs on a network. **Replication method:** Sends infected e-mail attachment as response to incoming mail. **Damage:** Will delete .c, .cpp, .asm, .doc, .xls, and .ppt files from local hard drive.

Source: Adapted from Ann Harrison, "Internet Worm Destroys Data," *Computerworld*, June 14, 1999. Copyright 1999 by Computerworld, Inc., Framingham, MA 01701. Reprinted from *Computerworld*.

operating system. Then the virus spreads to the main memory and copies itself onto the computer's hard disk and any inserted floppy disks. The virus spreads to other computers through e-mail, file transfers, other telecommunications activities, or floppy disks from infected computers. Thus, as a good practice, you should avoid using software from questionable sources without checking for viruses. You should also regularly *use antivirus programs* that can help diagnose and remove computer viruses from infected files on your hard disk.

Anatomy of a Virus: Melissa	If you receive an e-mail with the subject line "Important message from . . . ," be suspicious. If that message comes with a Word document attached called "List.Doc," you've likely been sent the Word/Melissa macro virus or worm. And if you open the document, it will send copies of itself to 50 e-mail addresses it gleans from your personal e-mail file. That gives it the ability to propagate very quickly—much quicker than the Happy99.exe worm, according to virus experts, which is why Melissa swept around the globe in a few days.

The document itself contains a list of 73 pornographic websites, along with user names and passwords for those sites. The virus can allow documents to be e-mailed to other people without warning, a potential security breach that should worry businesses and governments. About 60,000 users were infected at the company that made the first complaint, said Srivhes Sampath, general manager of McAfee Online. "It pretty much brings mail systems to a halt. . . . We've never seen anything spread like this" [41]. |

Privacy Issues

Information technology makes it technically and economically feasible to collect, store, integrate, interchange, and retrieve data and information quickly and easily. This characteristic has an important beneficial effect on the efficiency and effectiveness of computer-based information systems. However, the power of information technology to store and retrieve information can have a negative effect on the **right to privacy** of every individual. For example, confidential e-mail messages by employees are monitored by many companies. Personal information is being collected about individuals every time they visit a site on the World Wide Web. Confidential information on individuals contained in centralized computer databases by credit bureaus, government agencies, and private business firms has been stolen or misused, resulting in the invasion of privacy, fraud, and other injustices. The unauthorized use of such information has seriously damaged the privacy of individuals. Errors in such databases could seriously hurt the credit standing or reputation of an individual.

Important privacy issues are being debated in business and government, as Internet technologies accelerate the ubiquity of global telecommunications connections in business and society. For example:

- Accessing individuals' private e-mail conversations and computer records, and collecting and sharing information about individuals gained from their visits to Internet websites and newsgroups (violation of privacy).

- Always knowing where a person is, especially as mobile and paging services become more closely associated with people rather than places (computer monitoring).

- Using customer information gained from many sources to market additional business services (computer matching).

- Collecting telephone numbers, e-mail addresses, credit card numbers, and other personal information to build individual customer profiles (unauthorized personal files).

Privacy on the Internet

If you don't take the proper precautions, any time you send an e-mail, access a website, post a message to a newsgroup, or use the Internet for banking and shopping . . . whether you're online for business or pleasure, you're vulnerable to anyone bent on collecting data about you without your knowledge. Fortunately, by using tools like encryption and anonymous remailers—and by being selective about the sites you visit and the information you provide—you can minimize, if not completely eliminate, the risk of your privacy being violated [35].

The Internet is notorious for giving its users a feeling of anonymity, when in actuality, they are highly visible and open to violations of their privacy. Most of the Internet and its World Wide Web, e-mail, chat, and newsgroups are still a wide open, unsecured electronic frontier, with no tough rules on what information is personal and private. Information about Internet users is captured legitimately and automatically each time you visit a website or newsgroup and recorded as a "cookie file" on your hard disk. Then the website owners, or online auditing services like WebTrack and DoubleClick, may sell the information from cookie files and other records of your Internet use to third parties. To make matters worse, much of the net and Web are easy targets for the interception or theft by hackers of private information furnished to websites by Internet users [29].

Of course, you can protect your privacy in several ways. For example, sensitive e-mail can be protected by encryption, if both e-mail parties use compatible encryption software built into their e-mail programs. Newsgroup postings can be made privately by sending them through *anonymous remailers* that protect your identity when you add your comments to a discussion. You can ask your Internet service provider not to sell your name and personal information to mailing list providers and other marketers. Finally, you can decline to reveal personal data and interests on online service and website user profiles to limit your exposure to electronic snooping [29].

Acxiom Inc.: Challenges to Consumer Privacy

What detail of you private life would you least like to see splashed across the Internet? Or added to a database, linked to your name and sold in a mailing list?

The privacy problem is simple. Companies need to glean information that will help target sales. Consumers want the convenience of secure e-commerce without worrying about having their identities stolen, being spammed, or having the aggregators of personal data knowing—and profiting from—every detail of their lives. As retailers and consumers force this issue, e-commerce could get squeezed in the process—particularly among companies that minimize the privacy concerns of their customers. Take Acxiom.

You may not know Acxiom. But the Conway, Arkansas, company probably knows you, having spent 30 years amassing a monster database of consumer information. It has dossiers on 160 million Americans—90 percent of U.S. households.

Acxiom has 20 million unlisted telephone numbers—gleaned mostly from those warranty cards you filled out when you bought that new coffeemaker—that it sells to law enforcement agencies, lawyers, private investigators, debt collectors, and just about anybody else willing to pay its fee. Acxiom is often better at tracking down deadbeat dads than the police. That's because Acxiom combines the most extensive public records database ever gathered by a nongovernmental entity with consumer information it purchases from the private sector.

The company's biggest clients are data-hungry telemarketers, retailers, e-commerce companies, and direct mail marketers. For example, Acxiom advises Wal-Mart on how to stock its shelves, while helping Citicorp decide the creditworthiness of potential customers.

Computer Matching

Computer profiling and mistakes in the **computer matching** of personal data are other controversial threats to privacy. Individuals have been mistakenly arrested and jailed, and people have been denied credit because their physical profiles or personal data have been used by profiling software to match them incorrectly or improperly with the wrong individuals. Another threat is the unauthorized matching of computerized information about you extracted from the databases of sales transaction processing systems, and sold to information brokers or other companies. A more recent threat is the unauthorized matching and sale of information about you collected from Internet websites and newsgroups you visit, as we discussed earlier. You are then subjected to a barrage of unsolicited promotional material and sales contacts as well as having your privacy violated [7, 35].

Privacy Laws

Many countries strictly regulate the collection and use of personal data by business corporations and government agencies. Many government **privacy laws** attempt to enforce the privacy of computer-based files and communications. For example, in the United States, the Electronic Communications Privacy Act and the Computer Fraud and Abuse Act prohibit intercepting data communications messages, stealing or destroying data, or trespassing in federal-related computer systems. Since the Internet includes federal-related computer systems, privacy attorneys argue that the laws also require notifying employees if a company intends to monitor Internet usage. Another example is the U.S. Computer Matching and Privacy Act, which regulates the matching of data held in federal agency files to verify eligibility for federal programs.

Computer Libel and Censorship

The opposite side of the privacy debate is the right of people to know about matters others may want to keep private (freedom of information), the right of people to express their opinions about such matters (freedom of speech), and the right of people to publish those opinions (freedom of the press). Some of the biggest battlegrounds in the debate are the bulletin boards, e-mail boxes, and online files of the Internet and public information networks such as America Online and the Microsoft Network. The weapons being used in this battle include *spamming*, *flame mail*, libel laws, and censorship.

Spamming is the indiscriminate sending of unsolicited e-mail messages *(spam)* to many Internet users. Spamming is the favorite tactic of mass-mailers of unsolicited advertisements, or *junk e-mail*. Spamming has also been used by cyber criminals to spread computer viruses or infiltrate many computer systems.

Flaming is the practice of sending extremely critical, derogatory, and often vulgar e-mail messages *(flame mail)*, or newsgroup postings to other users on the Internet or online services. Flaming is especially prevalent on some of the Internet's special-interest newsgroups.

There have been many incidents of racist or defamatory messages on the Web that have led to calls for censorship and lawsuits for libel. In addition, the presence of sexually explicit material at many World Wide Web locations has triggered lawsuits and censorship actions by various groups and governments.

Other Challenges

Let's now explore some other important challenges that arise from the use of information technologies in e-business systems that were illustrated in Figure 11.2. These challenges include ethical and societal impacts of e-business in the areas of employment, individuality, working conditions, and health.

Employment Challenges

The impact of information technologies on **employment** is a major ethical concern and is directly related to the use of computers to achieve automation of work activities. There can be no doubt that the use of e-business technologies has created new jobs and increased productivity, while also causing a significant reduction in some types of job opportunities. For example, when computers are used for accounting systems or for the automated control of machine tools, they are accomplishing tasks formerly performed by many clerks and machinists. Also, jobs created by some e-business systems may require different types of skills and education than do the jobs that are eliminated. Therefore, individuals may become unemployed unless they can be retrained for new positions or new responsibilities.

However, there can be no doubt that e-business and e-commerce have created a host of new job opportunities. Many new jobs, including Internet webmasters, e-commerce directors, systems analysts, and user consultants, have been created in e-business organizations. New jobs have also been created in service industries that provide services to e-business firms. Additional jobs have been created because information technologies make possible the production of complex industrial and technical goods and services that would otherwise be impossible to produce. Thus, jobs have been created by activities that are heavily dependent on information technology, in such areas as space exploration, microelectronic technology, and telecommunications.

Computer Monitoring

One of the most explosive ethical issues concerning workplace privacy and the quality of working conditions in e-business is **computer monitoring.** That is, computers are being used to monitor the productivity and behavior of millions of employees while they work. Supposedly, computer monitoring is done so employers can collect productivity data about their employees to increase the efficiency and quality of service. However, computer monitoring has been criticized as unethical because it monitors individuals, not just work, and is done continually, thus violating workers' privacy and personal freedom. For example, when you call to make a reservation, an airline reservation agent may be timed on the exact number of seconds he or she took per caller, the time between calls, and the number and length of breaks taken. In addition, your conversation may also be monitored. See Figure 11.8.

Computer monitoring has been criticized as an invasion of the privacy of employees because, in many cases, they do not know that they are being monitored or don't know how the information is being used. Critics also say that an employee's right

Figure 11.8

Computer monitoring can be used to record the productivity and behavior of people while they work.

Source: Index Stock Imagery/Picture Quest.

of due process may be harmed by the improper use of collected data to make personnel decisions. Since computer monitoring increases the stress on employees who must work under constant electronic surveillance, it has also been blamed for causing health problems among monitored workers. Finally, computer monitoring has been blamed for robbing workers of the dignity of their work. In effect, computer monitoring creates an "electronic sweatshop," where workers are forced to work at a hectic pace under poor working conditions.

Political pressure is building to outlaw or regulate computer monitoring in the workplace. For example, public advocacy groups, labor unions, and many legislators are pushing for action at the state and federal level in the United States. The proposed laws would regulate computer monitoring and protect the worker's right to know and right to privacy. In the meantime, lawsuits by monitored workers against employers are increasing. So computer monitoring of workers is one ethical issue in e-business that won't go away.

Challenges in Working Conditions

Information technology has eliminated monotonous or obnoxious tasks in the office and the factory that formerly had to be performed by people. For example, word processing and desktop publishing make producing office documents a lot easier to do, while robots have taken over repetitive welding and spray painting jobs in the automotive industry. In many instances, this allows people to concentrate on more challenging and interesting assignments, upgrades the skill level of the work to be performed, and creates challenging jobs requiring highly developed skills in the computer industry and within computer-using organizations. Thus, information technology can be said to upgrade the quality of work because it can upgrade the *quality of working conditions* and the content of work activities.

Of course, it must be remembered that some jobs in e-business systems—data entry, for example—are quite repetitive and routine. Also, to the extent that computers are utilized in some types of automation, IT must take some responsibility for the criticism of assembly-line operations that require the continual repetition of elementary tasks, thus forcing a worker to work like a machine instead of like a skilled craftsperson. Many automated operations are also criticized for relegating people to a "do-nothing" standby role, where workers spend most of their time waiting for infrequent opportunities to push some buttons. Such effects do have a detrimental effect on the quality of work, but they must be compared to the less burdensome and more creative jobs created by information technology.

Challenges to Individuality

A frequent criticism of e-business systems concerns their negative effect on the **individuality** of people. Computer-based systems are criticized as impersonal systems that dehumanize and depersonalize activities that have been computerized, since they eliminate the human relationships present in noncomputer systems.

Another aspect of the loss of individuality is the regimentation of the individual that seems to be required by some computer-based systems. These systems do not seem to possess any flexibility. They demand strict adherence to detailed procedures if the system is to work. The negative impact of IT on individuality is reinforced by horror stories that describe how inflexible and uncaring some organizations with computer-based processes are when it comes to rectifying their own mistakes. Many of us are familiar with stories of how computerized customer billing and accounting systems continued to demand payment and send warning notices to a customer whose account has already been paid, despite repeated attempts by the customer to have the error corrected.

However, many e-business systems have been designed to minimize depersonalization and regimentation. And many e-commerce systems are designed to stress personalization and community features to encourage repeated visits to e-commerce websites. Thus, the widespread use of personal computers and the Internet has dramatically improved the development of people-oriented and personalized information systems.

Health Issues

The use of information technology in the workplace raises a variety of **health issues.** Heavy use of computers is reportedly causing health problems like job stress, damaged arm and neck muscles, eye strain, radiation exposure, and even death by computer-caused accidents. For example, computer monitoring is blamed as a major cause of computer-related job stress. Workers, unions, and government officials criticize computer monitoring as putting so much stress on employees that it leads to health problems [9, 11].

People who sit at PC workstations or visual display terminals (VDTs) in fast-paced, repetitive keystroke jobs can suffer a variety of health problems known collectively as *cumulative trauma disorders* (CTDs). Their fingers, wrists, arms, necks, and backs may become so weak and painful that they cannot work. Many times strained muscles, back pain, and nerve damage may result. In particular, some computer workers may suffer from *carpal tunnel syndrome,* a painful, crippling ailment of the hand and wrist that typically requires surgery to cure.

Prolonged viewing of video displays causes eyestrain and other health problems in employees who must do this all day. Radiation caused by the cathode ray tubes (CRTs) that produce most video displays is another health concern. CRTs produce an electromagnetic field that may cause harmful radiation of employees who work too close for too long in front of video monitors. Some pregnant workers have reported miscarriages and fetal deformities due to prolonged exposure to CRTs at work. However, several studies have failed to find conclusive evidence concerning this problem. Still, several organizations recommend that female workers minimize their use of CRTs during pregnancy [9, 11].

Ergonomics

Solutions to some of these health problems are based on the science of **ergonomics,** sometimes called *human factors engineering.* See Figure 11.9. The goal of ergonomics is to design healthy work environments that are safe, comfortable, and pleasant for people to work in, thus increasing employee morale and productivity. Ergonomics stresses the healthy design of the workplace, workstations, computers and other machines, and even software packages. Other health issues may require ergonomic solutions emphasizing job design, rather than workplace design. For example, this may require policies providing for work breaks from heavy VDT use every few hours, while limiting the CRT exposure of pregnant workers. Ergonomic

Figure 11.9

Ergonomic factors in the workplace. Note that good ergonomic design considers tools, tasks, the workstation, and environment.

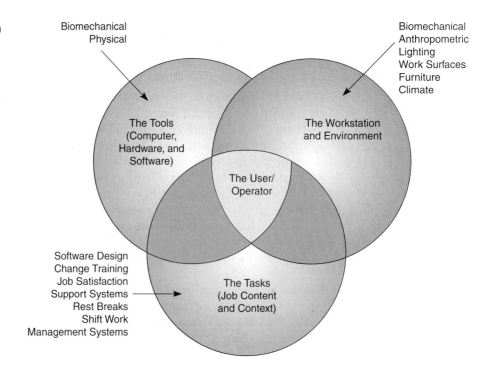

job design can also provide more variety in job tasks for those workers who spend most of their workday at computer workstations.

Societal Solutions

Computers and networks like the Internet and other information technologies can have many beneficial effects on society. We can use information technologies to solve human and social problems through **societal solutions** such as medical diagnosis, computer-assisted instruction, governmental program planning, environmental quality control, and law enforcement. For example, computers can help diagnose an illness, prescribe necessary treatment, and monitor the progress of hospital patients. Computer-assisted instruction (CAI) and computer-based training (CBT) enable interactive instruction tailored to the needs of students. Distance learning is supported by telecommunications networks, video conferencing, e-mail, and other technologies.

Information technologies can be used for crime control through various law enforcement applications. For example, computerized alarm systems allow police to identify and respond quickly to evidences of criminal activity. Computers have been used to monitor the level of pollution in the air and in bodies of water, to detect the sources of pollution, and to issue early warnings when dangerous levels are reached. Computers are also used for the program planning of many government agencies in such areas as urban planning, population density and land use studies, highway planning, and urban transit studies. Computers are being used in job placement systems to help match unemployed persons with available jobs. These and other applications illustrate that information technology can be used to help solve the problems of society.

You and Ethical Responsibility

As a business end user, you have a responsibility to promote ethical uses of information technology in the workplace. Whether you are a manager, business professional, or IS professional, you should accept the ethical responsibilities that come with your work activities. That includes properly performing your role as a vital human resource in the e-business systems you help develop and use in your organization. As a manager or business professional, it will be your responsibility to make decisions about business activities and the use of information technologies, which may have an ethical dimension that must be considered.

For example, should you electronically monitor your employees' work activities and electronic mail? Should you let employees use their work computers for private business or take home copies of software for their personal use? Should you electronically access your employees' personnel records or workstation files? Should you sell customer information extracted from transaction processing systems to other companies? These are a few examples of the types of decisions you will have to make that have a controversial ethical dimension. So let's take a closer look at several ethical foundations in business and information technology.

Ethical Foundations

People may use **ethical philosophies** or hold *ethical values* that guide them in ethical decision making. For example, four basic ethical philosophies are: egoism, natural law, utilitarianism, and respect for persons [9]. Briefly, these alternative ethical philosophies are:

- **Egoism.** What is best for a given individual is right.
- **Natural law.** Humans should promote their own health and life, propagate, pursue knowledge of the world and God, pursue close relationships with other people, and submit to legitimate authority.
- **Utilitarianism.** Those actions are right that produce the greatest good for the greatest number of people.
- **Respect for persons.** People should be treated as an end and not as a means to an end; and actions are right if everyone adopts the moral rule presupposed by the action.

Source: Adapted and reprinted by permission of *Harvard Business Review* from Thomas Donaldson, "Values in Tension: Ethics Away from Home," September–October 1996, p. 7. Copyright © 1996 by the President and Fellows of Harvard College; all rights reserved.

Figure 11.10

Western and non-Western values and how they converge to support three common ethical values.

Non-Western	Western	Common Values
● *Kyosei* (Japanese): Living and working together for the common good. ● *Dharma* (Hindu): The fulfillment of inherited duty. ● *Santutthi* (Buddhist): The importance of limited desires. ● *Zakat* (Muslim): The duty to give alms to the Muslim poor.	● Individual liberty ● Egalitarianism ● Political participation ● Human rights	● Respect for human dignity ● Respect for basic rights ● Good citizenship

Ethical values are more specific ethical concepts that people hold, and are heavily influenced by one's cultural background. For example, Figure 11.10 lists several Western and non-Western values. Notice that these values converge to support three basic ethical values that are common across many cultures today [10].

There are many **ethical models** of how humans apply their chosen ethical philosophies to the decisions and choices they have to make daily in work and other areas of their lives. For example, some theories focus on people's decision-making processes and stress how various factors or our perceptions of them affect our ethical decision-making processes. Thus, our personal, professional, and work environments and governmental/legal and social environments may affect our decision processes and lead to ethical or unethical behavior.

Another example is a *behavioral stage theory*, which says that people go through several stages of moral evolution before they settle on one level of ethical reasoning. In this model, if you reach the final stage of moral evolution, your actions are guided by self-chosen ethical principles, not by fear, guilt, social pressure, and so on.

A final dimension includes *ethical principles* that deal specifically with the ethics of the use of any form of technology. For example, Figure 11.11 lists four ethical principles that can serve as guidelines for the implementation of e-business systems and their technologies.

Business Ethics

Business ethics is concerned with the numerous ethical questions that managers must confront as part of their daily business decision making. For example, Figure 11.12

Figure 11.11

Ethical principles to help evaluate the potential harms or risks of the use of e-business technologies.

Principles of Technology Ethics
● **Proportionality.** The good achieved by the technology must outweigh the harm or risk. Moreover, there must be no alternative that achieves the same or comparable benefits with less harm or risk.
● **Informed Consent.** Those affected by the technology should understand and accept the risks.
● **Justice.** The benefits and burdens of the technology should be distributed fairly. Those who benefit should bear their fair share of the risks, and those who do not benefit should not suffer a significant increase in risk.
● **Minimized Risk.** Even if judged acceptable by the other three guidelines, the technology must be implemented so as to avoid all unnecessary risk.

Figure 11.12	Basic categories of ethical business issues. Information technology has caused ethical controversy in the areas of intellectual property rights, customer and employee privacy, security of company information, and worplace safety.

Equity	Rights	Honesty	Exercise of Corporate Power
Executive Salaries	Corporate Due Process	Employee Conflicts	Product Safety
Comparable Worth	Employee Health	of Interest	Environmental Issues
Product Pricing	Screening	**Security of Company**	Disinvestment
Intellectual	**Customer Privacy**	**Information**	Corporate Contributions
Property Rights	**Employee Privacy**	Inappropriate Gifts	Social Issues Raised by
Noncompetitive	Sexual Harassment	Advertising Content	Religious Organizations
Agreements	Affirmative Action	Government Contract	Plant/Facility Closures and
	Equal Employment	Issues	Downsizing
	Opportunity	Financial and Cash	Political Action Committees
	Shareholder Interests	Management Procedures	**Workplace Safety**
	Employment at Will	Questionable Business	
	Whistle-Blowing	Practices in Foreign	
		Countries	

Source: Adapted from The Conference Board, "Defending Corporate Ethics," in Peter Madsen and Jay Shafritz, *Essentials of Business Ethics* (New York: Meridian, 1990), p. 18.

outlines some of the basic categories of ethical issues and specific business practices that have serious ethical consequences. Notice that the issues of employee privacy, security of company records, and workplace safety are highlighted because they have been major areas of ethical controversy in information technology.

How can managers make ethical decisions when confronted with business issues such as those listed in Figure 11.12? Several important alternatives based on theories of corporate social responsibility can be used [38, 39].

- **The stockholder theory** holds that managers are agents of the stockholders, and their only ethical responsibility is to increase the profits of the business without violating the law or engaging in fraudulent practices.

- **The social contract theory** states that companies have ethical responsibilities to all members of society, which allow corporations to exist based on a social contract. The first condition of the contract requires companies to enhance the economic satisfaction of consumers and employees. They must do that without polluting the environment or depleting natural resources, misusing political power, or subjecting their employees to dehumanizing working conditions. The second condition requires companies to avoid fraudulent practices, show respect for their employees as human beings, and avoid practices that systematically worsen the position of any group in society.

- **The stakeholder theory** maintains that managers have an ethical responsibility to manage a firm for the benefit of all its stakeholders, which are all individuals and groups that have a stake in or claim on a company. This usually includes the corporation's stockholders, employees, customers, suppliers, and the local community. Sometimes the term is broadened to include all groups who can affect or be affected by the corporation, such as competitors, government agencies, special interest groups, and the media. Balancing the claims of conflicting stakeholders is obviously not an easy task for managers.

Ethical Guidelines

We have now outlined several ethical principles that can serve as the basis for ethical conduct by managers, end users, and IS professionals. But what more specific guidelines might help your ethical use of information technology?

Figure 11.13

Part of the AITP standards of professional conduct. This code can serve as a model for ethical conduct by business end users as well as IS professionals.

AITP Standards of Professional Conduct
In recognition of my obligation to my employer I shall:
● Avoid conflicts of interest and ensure that my employer is aware of any potential conflicts.
● Protect the privacy and confidentiality of all information entrusted to me.
● Not misrepresent or withhold information that is germane to the situation.
● Not attempt to use the resources of my employer for personal gain or for any purpose without proper approval.
● Not exploit the weakness of a computer system for personal gain or personal satisfaction.
In recognition of my obligation to society I shall:
● Use my skill and knowledge to inform the public in all areas of my expertise.
● To the best of my ability, ensure that the products of my work are used in a socially responsible way.
● Support, respect, and abide by the appropriate local, state, provincial, and federal laws.
● Never misrepresent or withhold information that is germane to a problem or a situation of public concern, nor will I allow any such known information to remain unchallenged.
● Not use knowledge of a confidential or personal nature in any unauthorized manner to achieve personal gain.

One way to answer this question is to examine statements of responsibilities contained in codes of professional conduct for IS professionals. A good example is the code of professional conduct of the Association of Information Technology Professionals (AITP), an organization of professionals in the computing field. Its code of conduct outlines the ethical considerations inherent in the major responsibilities of an IS professional. Figure 11.13 is a portion of the AITP code of conduct.

Business end users and IS professionals would live up to their ethical responsibilities by voluntarily following such guidelines. For example, you can be a **responsible end user** by (1) acting with integrity, (2) increasing your professional competence, (3) setting high standards of personal performance, (4) accepting responsibility for your work, and (5) advancing the health, privacy, and general welfare of the public. Then you would be demonstrating ethical conduct, avoiding computer crime, and increasing the security of any information system you develop or use.

As a business manager or professional, you should insist that the ethical and societal dimensions of information technology be considered when e-business and e-commerce systems are being developed and used. For example, a major design objective should be to develop systems that can be easily and effectively used by people. The objectives of the system must also include protection of the privacy of the individuals and the defense of the system against computer crime. The potential for misuse and malfunction of a proposed system must be analyzed and controlled to minimize such effects on its users. In that way, the security of people, hardware, software, networks, and data resources will be included in the systems design.

It should be obvious to you that many of the detrimental effects of information technology are caused by individuals or organizations that are not accepting the ethical responsibility for their actions. Like other powerful technologies, information technology possesses the potential for great harm or great good for all humankind. If managers, business professionals, and IS specialists accept their ethical responsibilities, then information technology can help make this world a better place for all of us.

Security Management of e-Business

e-Business Security

With Internet access proliferating rapidly, one might think that the biggest obstacle to electronic commerce would be bandwidth. But it's not; the number one problem is security. And part of the problem is that the Internet was developed for interoperability, not impenetrability [42].

As we saw in Section I, there are many significant threats to the security of e-business and e-commerce. That's why this section is dedicated to exploring the methods that e-business enterprises can use to manage their security. Business managers and professionals alike are responsible for the security, quality, and performance of the e-business systems in their business units. Like any other vital business assets, their information systems hardware, software, networks, and data resources need to be protected by a variety of security measures to ensure their quality and beneficial use. That's the business value of e-business security.

Analyzing Visa International Inc.

Read the Real World Case on Visa International Inc. on the next page. We can learn a lot from this case about the security challenges and security measures needed to protect corporate and financial websites. See Figure 11.14.

This case demonstrates a wide range of security measures used by Visa International to ensure a flawless level of payment card processing and financial settlements generated by over one billion outstanding cards, 23 million merchants, and 21,000

Figure 11.14

Richard Knight, senior vice president of Visa International's Inovant data center subsidiary, is responsible for ensuring a flawless level of payment processing through a range of security management measures.

Source: Douglas Woods.

Visa International Inc.:
Strategies for Global Security Management

One of the largest financial systems in the world is hidden in a nondescript building near Washington, D.C. The owner, Visa International Inc., hasn't put its name on the building, nor will it allow a reporter to say exactly where it is. The secret data center is a fireproof, earthquakeproof concrete fortress with 5,000-pound doors and a basement full of backup gear, but it has fake windows to make it look like any of hundreds of ordinary office buildings in the area. Paranoia? Not when you consider the stakes. Five minutes of downtime in Visa's worldwide processing system, called VisaNet, would block $55 million in payment transactions, estimates the Foster City, California–based firm.

"There is no such thing as 99.9 percent reliability; it has to be 100 percent," says Richard L. Knight, senior vice president for operations at Inovant Inc., the Visa subsidiary that runs its data centers. "Anything less than 100 percent, and I'm looking for a job." The company has had 98 minutes of downtime in 12 years. Visa fights the battle against outages and defects on two broad fronts: Its physical processing plant is protected by multiple layers of redundancy and backups, and the company's IT shop has raised software testing to a fine art.

There are more than 1 billion Visa payment cards outstanding around the world, spawning $2 trillion in transactions per year for 23 million merchants and automated teller machines and Visa's 21,000 member financial institutions. "We run the biggest payments engine in the world," says Sara Garrison, senior vice president for systems development at Visa U.S.A. Inc. in Foster City, California. "If you took all the traffic on all the stock markets in the world in 24 hours, we do that on a coffee break. And our capacity grows at 20 to 30 percent year to year, so every three years, our capacity doubles."

Visa has four major processing centers to handle that load, but the Washington facility is the largest, with half of all global payment transactions flowing through the building. It shares U.S. traffic with a center in San Mateo, California, but it can instantly pick up the full United States if San Mateo goes down.

Indeed, everything in Visa's processing infrastructure—from entire data centers to computers, individual processors, and communications switches—has a backup. Even the backups have backups. For example, the Washington center has four rotating uninterruptible power supply (UPS) units (only three are needed) driven by the local utility and backed up by an array of batteries and four 1-megawatt diesel-powered generators. The 24,000 gallons of diesel fuel stored on-site is enough to power the center for a week. The UPS units protect the center from possible power fluctuations. The facility has enough redundant cooling capacity to air-condition 300 homes.

The eight IBM mainframes at the Washington data center are rated collectively at 3,000 MIPS. Altogether, worldwide, 7,000 MIPS of processing power can conduct 10,000 payment-authorization transactions per second. Visa's network, one of the largest private networks in the world, consists of 9 million miles of copper and optical fiber, and every Visa customer has two paths into Visa via commercial carriers.

Visa's Washington-area processing center houses 50 million lines of code for some 300 applications. Major functions include the following:

- **Authorization system.** This online IBM-mainframe–based system propels a payment card request from a cardholder to a merchant, to the merchant bank, then on to the card issuer and back to the merchant.

- **Clearing and settlement system.** This mainframe batch system runs nightly and settles accounts among merchants, merchants' banks, and card issuers.

- **Fraud-detection system.** This online system runs on Sun Microsystems servers and uses neural networks and pattern-recognition algorithms to look for fraud in each payment transaction.

- **Data warehouse.** This mammoth storage facility consists of 18 Storage Technology Corp. silos and a 250,000-volume tape library holding up to seven years' worth of transaction histories. It grows by 250TB each month.

While all these backups and safeguards contribute to Visa's ultrareliable operations, they're only part of the story. Every summer, well in advance of its year-end peak processing season, Visa runs a full-scale stress test at IBM's $1 billion Performance & Scalability Center in Gaithersburg, Maryland, where IBM has 14,000 MIPS of processing power. The tests cap months of requirements analysis, modeling, and testing at Visa's own facilities.

"We introduce failures at that point as well," says Mike Wolfson, senior vice president of engineering at Inovant. "So while we are processing 5,000 messages a second, we'll knock off a storage controller and make sure the system doesn't skip a beat." This kind of full-volume testing—which Visa doesn't have the capacity to do in-house—has proved itself many times. For example, several applications that ran flawlessly in production at peak loads failed when the test load was increased to reflect volumes projected for the coming holiday season, Wolfson says.

Case Study Questions

1. What examples of security measures can you identify being used by Visa International? Refer to Figure 11.15 in the chapter to help organize your answer.

2. What proactive (versus defensive) security management tactics do you recognize in this case? Evaluate their effectiveness for Visa International.

3. What is the strategic business value of Visa's security management excellence and processing efficiency in the payment card industry?

Source: Adapted from Gary Anthers, "When Five 9s Aren't Enough," *Computerworld*, October 8, 2001, pp. 48, 49. Reprinted by permission.

Figure 11.15

Examples of important security measures that are part of the security management of e-business systems.

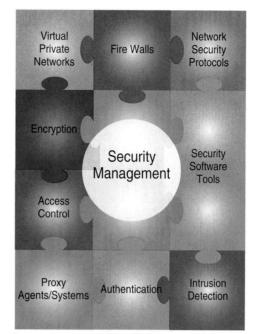

Source: Courtesy of Wang Global.

financial institutions. The top quality security management required to support 100 percent availability of this worldwide electronic payment system is demonstrated in both traditional and high-tech defensive and proactive measures like biometric identification, neural net fraud detection, and offsite high volume–high performance stress testing of Visa's global payment processing systems.

Security Management

The goal of **security management** is the accuracy, integrity, and safety of all e-business processes and resources. Thus, effective security management can minimize errors, fraud, and losses in the internetworked computer-based systems that interconnect today's e-business enterprises. As Figure 11.15 illustrates, security management is a complex task. As you can see, security managers must acquire and integrate a variety of security tools and methods to protect a company's e-business and e-commerce systems. We will discuss many of these security measures in this section.

Intel Corporation: Security Management Issues

"Protection of our information assets is paramount," explains Rich Cower, information security analyst at Intel Corp.'s Online Services Division. "But the difficulty is that this is a web of businesses. Intel has business connections all over the world to suppliers, contractors and others. Protecting your assets in an environment like this is especially tricky."

That's why access controls are keys to security. Developers should access information related only to their products. Ditto for vendors, he says. Thus, Cower advises all high-tech companies to separate Internet, intranet, and extranet servers if necessary, especially those in research and development and other laboratories where free-sharing of information takes place. And, he says, install fire walls in all servers with connections to the outside and close off unused ports on corporate intranet and extranet servers. But with Intel's e-commerce activity growing, the company puts a lot of emphasis on employee awareness and collaboration with its vendor partners. So Intel, through employee orientation, newsletters, and spot checks, teaches its employees that "security is everyone's job," Cower adds [32].

Internetworked e-Business Defenses

Few professionals today face greater challenges than those IT managers who are developing Internet security policies for rapidly changing network infrastructures. How can they balance the need for Internet security and Internet access? Are the budgets for Internet security adequate? What impact will intranet, extranet and Web application development have on security architectures? How can they come up with best practices for developing Internet security policy? [42]

Thus, the security of today's internetworked e-business enterprises is a major management challenge. Many companies are still rushing to get fully connected to the Web and the Internet for e-commerce, and to reengineer their internal business processes with intranets, enterprise software, and extranet links to customers, suppliers, and other business partners. Vital network links and business flows need to be protected from external attack by cyber criminals or subversion by the criminals or irresponsible acts of insiders. This requires a variety of security tools and defensive measures, and a coordinated security management program. Let's take a look at some of these important security defenses.

Encryption

Encryption of data has become an important way to protect data and other computer network resources especially on the Internet, intranets, and extranets. Passwords, messages, files, and other data can be transmitted in scrambled form and unscrambled by computer systems for authorized users only. Encryption involves using special mathematical algorithms, or keys, to transform digital data into a scrambled code before they are transmitted, and to decode the data when they are received. The most widely used encryption method uses a pair of public and private keys unique to each individual. For example, e-mail could be scrambled and encoded

Figure 11.16 How public key/private key encryption works.

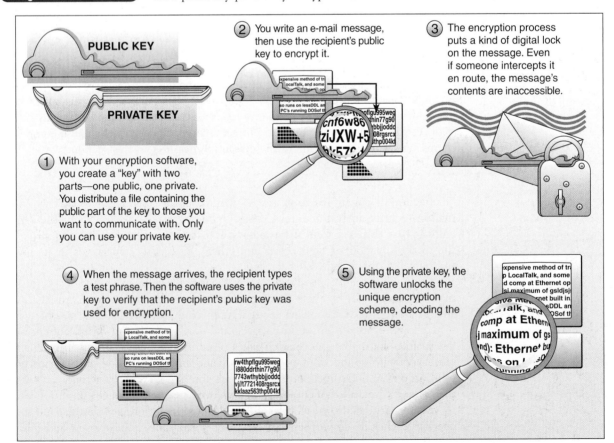

using a unique *public key* for the recipient that is known to the sender. After the e-mail is transmitted, only the recipient's secret *private key* could unscramble the message [35]. See Figure 11.16.

Encryption programs are sold as separate products or built into other software used for the encryption process. There are several competing software encryption standards, but the top two are RSA (by RSA Data Security) and PGP (pretty good privacy), a popular encryption program available on the Internet. Software products including Microsoft Windows NT, Novell Netware, Lotus Notes, and Netscape Communicator offer encryption features using RSA software.

Fire Walls

Another important method for control and security on the Internet and other networks is the use of **fire wall** computers and software. A network fire wall can be a communications processor, typically a *router*, or a dedicated server, along with fire wall software. A fire wall serves as a "gatekeeper" system that protects a company's intranets and other computer networks from intrusion by providing a filter and safe transfer point for access to and from the Internet and other networks. It screens all network traffic for proper passwords or other security codes, and only allows authorized transmissions in and out of the network. Fire walls have become an essential component of organizations connecting to the Internet, because of its vulnerability and lack of security. Figure 11.17 illustrates an Internet/intranet fire wall system for a company [23].

Fire walls can deter, but not completely prevent, unauthorized access (hacking) into computer networks. In some cases, a fire wall may allow access only from trusted locations on the Internet to particular computers inside the fire wall. Or it may allow only "safe" information to pass. For example, a fire wall may permit users to read e-mail from remote locations but not to run certain programs. In other cases, it is impossible to distinguish safe use of a particular network service from unsafe use and so all requests must be blocked. The fire

Figure 11.17   An example of the Internet and intranet fire walls in a company's networks.

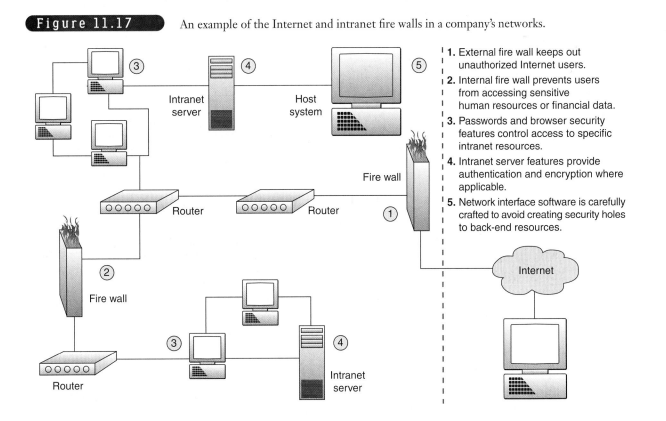

1. External fire wall keeps out unauthorized Internet users.
2. Internal fire wall prevents users from accessing sensitive human resources or financial data.
3. Passwords and browser security features control access to specific intranet resources.
4. Intranet server features provide authentication and encryption where applicable.
5. Network interface software is carefully crafted to avoid creating security holes to back-end resources.

Defending Against Denial of Service
● **At the zombie machines:** Set and enforce security policies. Scan regularly for Trojan Horse programs and vulnerabilities. Close unused ports. Remind users not to open .exe mail attachments.
● **At the ISP:** Monitor and block traffic spikes. Filter spoofed IP addresses. Coordinate security with network providers.
● **At the victim's website:** Create backup servers and network connections. Limit connections to each server. Install multiple intrusion-detection systems and multiple routers for incoming traffic to reduce choke points.

Source: Adapted from Deborah Radcliff, "Fighting the Flood," *Computerworld*, March 6, 2000, p. 66. Copyright 2000 by Computerworld, Inc., Framingham, MA 01701. Reprinted from *Computerworld*.

wall may then provide substitutes for some network services (such as e-mail or file transfer) that perform most of the same functions but are not as vulnerable to penetration.

Denial of Service Defenses

As attacks against major e-commerce players (described in Section I) have demonstrated, the Internet is extremely vulnerable to a variety of assaults by criminal hackers, especially **denial of service** (DOS) attacks. Figure 11.18 outlines the steps organizations can take to protect themselves from DOS attacks.

Denial of service assaults via the Internet depend on three layers of networked computer systems: (1) the victim's website, (2) the victim's Internet service provider (ISP), and (3) the sites of "zombie" or slave computers that were commandeered by the cyber criminals. For example, in the DOS attacks described in Section I, the hackers broke into hundreds of servers, mostly poorly protected servers at universities, and planted Trojan Horse .exe programs, which were then used to launch a barrage of service requests in a concerted attack at e-commerce websites like Yahoo! and eBay [31].

As Figure 11.18 shows, defensive measures and security precautions need to be taken at all three levels of the computer networks involved. These are the basic steps e-business companies and other organizations can take to protect their websites from denial of service and other hacking attacks.

e-Mail Monitoring

Spot checks just aren't good enough anymore. The tide is turning toward systematic monitoring of corporate e-mail traffic using content-monitoring software that scans for troublesome words that might compromise corporate security. The reason: Users of monitoring software said they're concerned about protecting their intellectual property and guarding themselves against litigation [8].

As we mentioned in Section I, Internet and other online e-mail systems are one of the favorite avenues of attack by hackers for spreading computer viruses or breaking into networked computers. E-mail is also the battleground for attempts by companies to enforce policies against illegal, personal, or damaging messages by employees, and the demands of some employees and others, who see such policies as violations of privacy rights. Figure 11.19 highlights reasons why 75 surveyed companies are monitoring employees' e-mail, and outlines what statements should be in a company's e-mail monitoring policy [8].

American Fast Freight: Corporate e-Mail Monitoring

"I didn't really realize how much of a problem I had until I started using monitoring software," said Jeff LePage, director of MIS at American Fast Freight (AFF) in Kent, Washington. LePage is using MIME-sweeper software from Content Technologies to scan the content of e-mail on the company network.

Figure 11.19	Reasons for e-Mail Monitoring	e-Mail Monitoring Policy
Why companies monitor e-mail, and what a company's e-mail monitoring policy should contain.	**57%** Potential legal liability from information contained in e-mail **51%** Potential leaking of corporate secrets **47%** Use of e-mail for racial or sexual harassment **19%** Complying with official regulations **9%** Personal (nonbusiness) use of e-mail	● A statement that computer systems are the company's property and are to be used for business purposes only. ● A clear definition of what is and isn't appropriate use of e-mail. ● A statement to employees that they can't expect e-mail to be private and that all e-mail may be monitored. ● An explanation that violations can lead to disciplinary action, up to and including termination.

Source: Adapted from Dominique Deckmyn, "More Managers Monitor e-Mail," *Computerworld*, October 18, 1999, pp. 1, 97. Copyright 1999 by Computerworld, Inc., Framingham, MA 01701. Reprinted from *Computerworld*.

"Probably 30 percent of the e-mails going through our servers were not work-related," said LePage—an infraction of the company's e-mail usage policy.

At AFF, most of the problem was with joke mail, but there were also some inappropriate e-mail attachments. A year after putting monitoring software in place, the software is now capturing only two or three inappropriate e-mails per week from the company's 330 employees—requiring only a quick once-per-week check, LePage said. Although the monitoring software is fairly processor-intensive and can take several months to fine-tune, LePage said, "I'm very happy with the solution we've come up with" [8].

Virus Defenses

Is your PC protected from the latest viruses, worms, Trojan horses, and other malicious programs like Back Orifice that can wreak havoc on your PC? Chances are it is, if it's periodically linked to the corporate network. These days, corporate antivirus protection is a centralized function of information technology. Someone installs it for you on your PC and notebook or, increasingly, distributes it over the network. The antivirus software runs in the background, popping up every so often to reassure you. The trend right now is to automate the process entirely [13].

Thus many companies are building defenses against the spread of viruses by centralizing the distribution and updating of antivirus software as a responsibility of their IS departments. Other companies are outsourcing the virus protection responsibility to their Internet service providers or to telecommunications or security management companies.

One reason for this trend is that the major antivirus software companies like Trend Micro (eDoctor and PC-cillin), McAfee (VirusScan), and Symantec (Norton Antivirus) have developed network versions of their programs which they are marketing to ISPs and others as a service they should offer to all their customers. The antivirus companies are also beginning to market *security suites* of software that integrate virus protection with fire walls, Web security, and content blocking features [18]. See Figure 11.20.

Sprint and US West: Antivirus Software Services

Trend Micro's eDoctor Global Network Internet antivirus software service builds malicious-code protection into service providers' networks, allowing customers to get virus scanning as a service from their Internet providers and managed service providers. This strategy delivers updated virus protection, around-the-clock support and faster virus response.

Figure 11.20

An example of the display from an antivirus program to eliminate computer viruses.

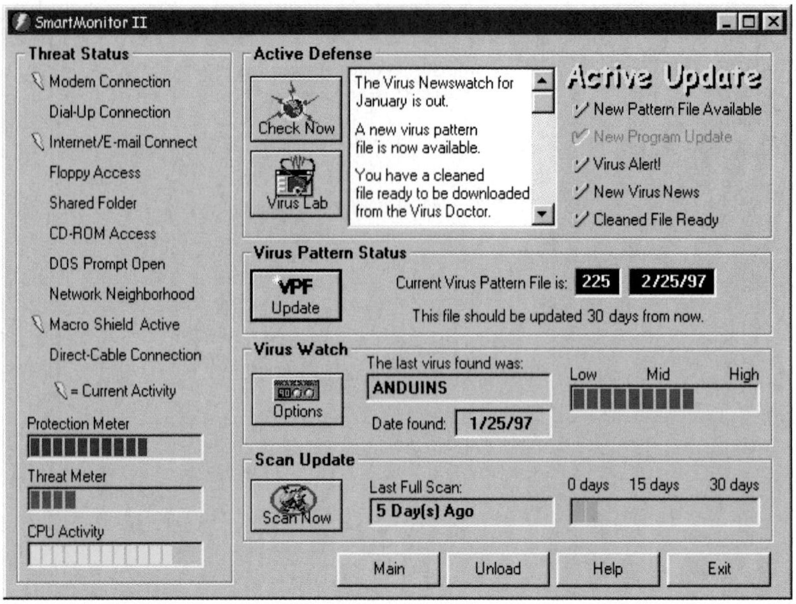

Source: Courtesy of Touchstone Software.

Sprint Corp. in Kansas City, is licensing Trend Micro technology to provide corporate Internet gateway virus scanning as part of a suite of managed security applications for corporate customers. And US West Inc., the telecommunications company based in Denver, is using eDoctor to provide e-mail virus protection to its consumer and business Internet access subscribers. Breakwater Security Associates, a Seattle-based managed information security services provider, will also use the eDoctor technology, along with specialized training, to remotely manage network antivirus strategies for their customers [18].

Other Security Measures

Let's now briefly examine a variety of security measures that are commonly used to protect e-business systems and networks. These include both hardware and software tools like faulttolerant computers and security monitors, and security policies and procedures like passwords and backup files. All of them are part of an integrated security management effort at many e-business enterprises today.

Security Codes

Typically, a multilevel **password** system is used for security management. First, an end user logs on to the computer system by entering his or her unique identification code, or user ID. The end user is then asked to enter a password in order to gain access into the system. (Passwords should be changed frequently and consist of unusual combinations of upper- and lowercase letters and numbers.) Next, to access an individual file, a unique file name must be entered. In some systems, the password to read the contents of a file is different from that required to write to a file (change its contents). This feature adds another level of protection to stored data resources. However, for even stricter security, passwords can be scrambled, or *encrypted*, to avoid their theft or improper use, as we will discuss shortly. In addition, *smart cards*, which contain microprocessors that generate random numbers to add to an end user's password, are used in some secure systems.

Backup Files

Backup files, which are duplicate files of data or programs, are another important security measure. Files can also be protected by *file retention* measures that involve storing copies of files from previous periods. If current files are destroyed, the files

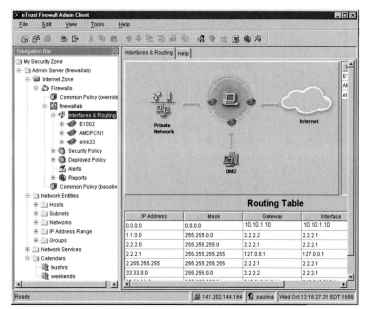

Figure 11.21

The eTrust security monitor manages a variety of security functions for major corporate networks, including monitoring the status of fire walls throughout a network.

Source: Computer Associates International, Inc.

from previous periods can be used to reconstruct new current files. Sometimes, several generations of files are kept for control purposes. Thus, master files from several recent periods of processing (known as *child, parent, grandparent* files, etc.) may be kept for backup purposes. Such files may be stored off-premises, that is, in a location away from a company's data center, sometimes in special storage vaults in remote locations.

Security Monitors

Security of a network may be provided by specialized system software packages known as **system security monitors.** See Figure 11.21. System security monitors are programs that monitor the use of computer systems and networks and protect them from unauthorized use, fraud, and destruction. Such programs provide the security measures needed to allow only authorized users to access the networks. For example, identification codes and passwords are frequently used for this purpose. Security monitors also control the use of the hardware, software, and data resources of a computer system. For example, even authorized users may be restricted to the use of certain devices, programs, and data files. Additionally, security programs monitor the use of computer networks and collect statistics on any attempts at improper use. They then produce reports to assist in maintaining the security of the network.

Biometric Security

Biometric security is a fast-growing area of computer security. These are security measures provided by computer devices that measure physical traits that make each individual unique. This includes voice verification, fingerprints, hand geometry, signature dynamics, keystroke analysis, retina scanning, face recognition, and genetic pattern analysis. Biometric control devices use special-purpose sensors to measure and digitize a biometric profile of an individual's fingerprints, voice, or other physical trait. The digitized signal is processed and compared to a previously processed profile of the individual stored on magnetic disk. If the profiles match, the individual is allowed entry into a computer network and given access to secure system resources. See Figure 11.22.

Computer Failure Controls

Sorry, our computer systems are down is a well-known phrase to many end users. A variety of controls can prevent such computer failure or minimize its effects. Computer systems fail for several reasons—power failure, electronic circuitry malfunctions, telecommunications network problems, hidden programming errors, computer viruses, computer operator errors, and electronic vandalism. For example, computers

Figure 11.22

An evaluation of common biometric security techniques based on user requirements, accuracy, and cost.

Evaluation of Biometric Techniques	USER CRITERIA		SYSTEM CRITERIA	
	INTRUSIVENESS	EFFORT	ACCURACY	COST
Dynamic signature verification	Excellent	Fair	Fair	Excellent
Face geometry	Good	Good	Fair	Good
Finger scan	Fair	Good	Good	Good
Hand geometry	Fair	Good	Fair	Fair
Passive iris scan	Poor	Excellent	Excellent	Poor
Retina scan	Poor	Poor	Very good	Fair
Voice print	Very good	Poor	Fair	Very good

Source: Adapted from Gary Anthes, "Biometrics," *Computerworld*, October 12, 1998, p. 30. Copyright 1998 by Computerworld, Inc., Framingham, MA 01701. Reprinted from *Computerworld*.

are available with automatic and remote maintenance capabilities. Programs of preventive maintenance of hardware and management of software updates are commonplace. A backup computer system capability can be arranged with *disaster recovery* organizations. Major hardware or software changes are usually carefully scheduled and implemented to avoid problems. Finally, highly trained data center personnel and the use of performance and security management software help keep a company's computer system and networks working properly.

Fault Tolerant Systems

Many firms also use **fault tolerant** computer systems that have redundant processors, peripherals, and software that provide a *fail-over* capability to back up components in the event of system failure. This may provide a *fail-safe* capability where the computer system continues to operate at the same level even if there is a major hardware or software failure. However, many fault tolerant computer systems offer a *fail-soft* capability where the computer system can continue to operate at a reduced

Figure 11.23

Methods of fault tolerance in computer-based information systems.

Layer	Threats	Fault Tolerant Methods
Applications	Environment, hardware, and software faults	Application-specific redundancy and rollback to previous checkpoint
Systems	Outages	System isolation, data security, system integrity
Databases	Data errors	Separation of transactions and safe updates, complete transaction histories, backup files
Networks	Transmission errors	Reliable controllers; safe asynchrony and handshaking; alternative routing; error-detecting and error-correcting codes
Processes	Hardware and software faults	Alternative computations, rollback to checkpoints
Files	Media errors	Replication of critical data on different media and sites; archiving, backup, retrieval
Processors	Hardware faults	Instruction retry; error-correcting codes in memory and processing; replication; multiple processors and memories

Source: Adapted from Peter Neumann, *Computer-Related Risks* (New York: ACM Press, 1995), p. 231. Copyright © 1995, Association for Computing Machinery, Inc. By permission.

but acceptable level in the event of a major system failure. Figure 11.23 outlines some of the fault tolerant capabilities used in many computer systems and networks.

Disaster Recovery

Natural and man-made disasters do happen. Hurricanes, earthquakes, fires, floods, criminal and terrorist acts, and human error can all severely damage an organization's computing resources, and thus the health of the organization itself. Many companies, especially online e-commerce retailers and wholesalers, airlines, banks, and Internet service providers, for example, are crippled by losing even a few hours of computing power. Many firms could survive only a few days without computing facilities. That's why organizations develop **disaster recovery** procedures and formalize them in a *disaster recovery plan*. It specifies which employees will participate in disaster recovery and what their duties will be; what hardware, software, and facilities will be used; and the priority of applications that will be processed. Arrangements with other companies for use of alternative facilities as a disaster recovery site and offsite storage of an organization's databases are also part of an effective disaster recovery effort.

e-Business System Controls and Audits

Information System Controls

Two final security management requirements that need to be mentioned are the development of information system controls and the accomplishment of e-business system audits. Let's take a brief look at these two security measures.

Information system controls are methods and devices that attempt to ensure the accuracy, validity, and propriety of information system activities. Information system (IS) controls must be developed to ensure proper data entry, processing techniques, storage methods, and information output. Thus, IS controls are designed to monitor and maintain the quality and security of the input, processing, output, and storage activities of any information system. See Figure 11.24.

For example, IS controls are needed to ensure the proper entry of data into an e-business system and thus avoid the garbage in, garbage out (GIGO) syndrome.

Figure 11.24

Examples of information system controls. Note that they are designed to monitor and maintain the quality and security of the input, processing, output, and storage activities of an information system.

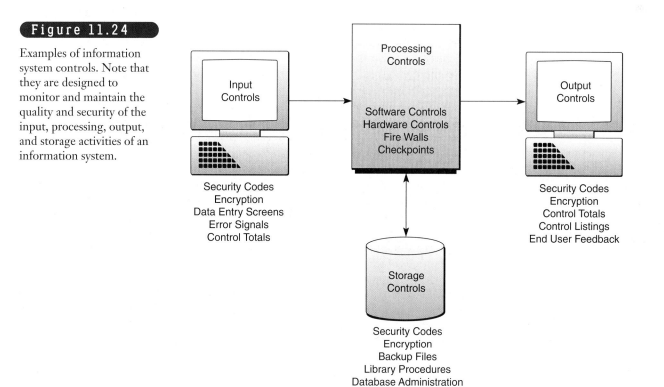

Examples include passwords and other security codes, formatted data entry screens, and audible error signals. Computer software can include instructions to identify incorrect, invalid, or improper input data as it enters the computer system. For example, a data entry program can check for invalid codes, data fields, and transactions, and conduct "reasonableness checks" to determine if input data exceed specified limits or are out of sequence.

Auditing e-Business Systems

E-business systems should be periodically examined, or audited, by a company's internal auditing staff or external auditors from professional accounting firms. Such audits review and evaluate whether proper and adequate security measures and management policies have been developed and implemented. This typically involves verifying the accuracy and integrity of the e-business software used, as well as the input of data and output produced. Some firms employ special EDP auditors for this assignment. They may use special test data to test processing accuracy and the control procedures built into the software. The auditors may develop special test programs or use audit software packages.

Another important objective of e-business system audits is testing the integrity of an application's *audit trail*. An **audit trail** can be defined as the presence of documentation that allows a transaction to be traced through all stages of its information processing. This journey may begin with a transaction's appearance on a source document and may end with its transformation into information on a final output document or report. The audit trail of manual information systems is quite visible and easy to trace. However, e-business systems have changed the form of the audit trail. Now auditors must know how to search electronically through disk and tape files of past activity to follow the audit trail of e-business systems.

Many times, this *electronic audit trail* takes the form of *control logs* that automatically record all computer network activity on magnetic disk or tape devices. This audit feature can be found on many online transaction processing systems, performance and security monitors, operating systems, and network control programs. Software that records all network activity is also widely used on the Internet, especially the World Wide Web, as well as corporate intranets and extranets. Such an audit trail helps auditors check for errors or fraud, but also helps IS security specialists trace and evaluate the trail of hacker attacks on computer networks.

Figure 11.25 summarizes 10 security management steps you can take to protect your computer system resources from hacking and other forms of cybercrime.

Figure 11.25

How to protect yourself from cybercrime and other computer security threats.

Security Management for Internet Users

1. Use antivirus software and update it often to keep destructive programs off your computer.

2. Don't allow online merchants to store your credit card information for future purchases.

3. Use a hard-to-guess password that contains a mix of numbers and letters, and change it frequently.

4. Use different passwords for different websites and applications to keep hackers guessing.

5. Use the most up-to-date version of your Web browser, e-mail software and other programs.

6. Send credit card numbers only to secure sites; look for a padlock or key icon at the bottom of the browser.

7. Confirm the site you're doing business with. Watch your typing; it's amazon.com, not amazon.com.

8. Use a security program that gives you control over "cookies" that send information back to websites.

9. Install fire wall software to screen traffic if you use DSL or a cable modem to connect to the Net.

10. Don't open e-mail attachments unless you know the source of the incoming message.

Source: Adapted from Bill Joy, "Report from the Cyberfront," *Newsweek*, February 21, 2000, p. 44.

Summary

- **Ethical and Societal Dimensions of e-Business.** The vital role of e-business and e-commerce systems in society raises serious ethical and societal issues in terms of their impact on employment, individuality, working conditions, privacy, health, and computer crime. Managers, business professionals, and IS specialists can help solve the problems of improper use of IT by assuming their ethical responsibilities for the ergonomic design, beneficial use, and enlightened management of e-business technologies in our society. See Figure 11.2.

- **The Ethical Foundations of e-Business.** Business and IT activities involve many ethical considerations. Various ethical philosophies and models of ethical behavior may be used by people in forming ethical judgments. These serve as a foundation for ethical principles that can serve as guidelines for dealing with ethical business issues that may arise in e-business and e-commerce.

- **e-Business Security Management.** One of the most important responsibilities of the management of a company is to assure the security and quality of its e-business activities. Security management tools and policies can ensure the accuracy, integrity, and safety of the e-business systems and resources of a company, and thus minimize errors, fraud, and security losses in their e-commerce activities. See Figure 11.15.

Key Terms and Concepts

These are the key terms and concepts of this chapter. The page number of their first explanation is in parentheses.

1. Antivirus software (405)
2. Audit trail (410)
3. Auditing e-business systems (410)
4. Backup files (406)
5. Biometric security (407)
6. Business ethics (396)
7. Computer crime (382)
8. Computer matching (391)
9. Computer monitoring (392)
10. Computer virus (388)
11. Denial of service (404)
12. Disaster recovery (409)
13. Encryption (402)
14. Ergonomics (394)
15. Ethical and societal impacts of e-business (382)
    a. Employment (391)
    b. Health (394)
    c. Individuality (393)
    d. Societal solutions (395)
    e. Working conditions (393)
16. Ethical foundations (395)
17. Fault tolerant (408)
18. Fire wall (403)
19. Flaming (391)
20. Hacking (383)
21. Information system controls (409)
22. Intellectual property piracy (387)
23. Passwords (406)
24. Privacy issues (389)
25. Responsible end user (398)
26. Security management (401)
27. Software piracy (386)
28. Spamming (391)
29. System security monitor (407)
30. Unauthorized use (385)

Review Quiz

Match one of the key terms and concepts listed previously with one of the brief examples or definitions that follow. Try to find the best fit for the answers that seem to fit more than one term or concept. Defend your choices.

_____ 1. Ensuring the accuracy, integrity, and safety of e-business activities and resources.

_____ 2. Control totals, error signals, backup files, and security codes are examples.

_____ 3. Software that can control access and use of a computer system.

_____ 4. A computer system can continue to operate even after a major system failure if it has this capability.

_____ 5. A computer system that serves as a filter for access to and from other networks by a company's networked computers.

_____ 6. Periodically examine the accuracy and integrity of computer processing.

_____ 7. The presence of documentation that allows a transaction to be traced through all stages of information processing.

_____ 8. Using your voice or fingerprints to identify you electronically.

_____ 9. A plan to continue IS operations during an emergency.

_____ 10. Scrambling data during its transmission.

_____ 11. Ethical choices may result from decision-making processes, cultural values, or behavioral stages.

_____ 12. Managers must confront numerous ethical questions in their businesses.

_____ 13. Sending unsolicited e-mail indiscriminately.

_____ 14. Employees may have to retrain or transfer.

_____ 15. Computer-based systems may depersonalize human activities.

_____ 16. Constant long-term use of computers at work may cause health problems.

_____ 17. Computer-based monitoring of environmental quality is an example.

_____ 18. Tedious jobs are decreased and jobs are made more challenging.

_____ 19. Using computers to identify individuals that fit a certain profile.

_____ 20. Collecting information about you without your consent.

_____ 21. Using computers to monitor the activities of workers.

_____ 22. Overwhelming a website with requests for service from captive computers.

_____ 23. Using computers and networks to steal money, services, software, or data.

_____ 24. Using company computers to access the Internet during work hours for personal business.

_____ 25. Unauthorized copying of software.

_____ 26. Unauthorized copying of copyrighted material.

_____ 27. Electronic breaking and entering into a computer system.

_____ 28. A program makes copies of itself and destroys data and programs.

_____ 29. Finds and eliminates computer viruses.

_____ 30. Sending extremely critical, derogatory, and vulgar e-mail messages.

_____ 31. Designing computer hardware, software, and workstations that are safe, comfortable, and easy to use.

_____ 32. End users should act with integrity and competence in their use of information technology.

Discussion Questions

1. What can be done to improve e-commerce security on the Internet? Give several examples of security measures, and technologies you would use.

2. What potential security problems do you see in the increasing use of intranets and extranets in business? What might be done to solve such problems? Give several examples.

3. What artificial intelligence techniques can a business use to improve computer security and fight computer crime?

4. What are your major concerns about computer crime and privacy on the Internet? What can you do about it? Explain.

5. What is disaster recovery? How could it be implemented at your school or work?

6. Refer to the Real World Case on Exodus Communications in the chapter. How vulnerable to cybercrime by hackers, criminals, or terrorists are the networked computer systems at your home, school, and place of business? Discuss the reasons for your conclusions.

7. Is there an ethical crisis in e-business today? What role does information technology play in unethical business practices?

8. What are several business decisions that you will have to make as a manager that have both an ethical and IT dimension? Give examples to illustrate your answer.

9. Refer to the Real World Case on Visa International in the chapter. What are several security measures being taken to protect your home, school, and business from cybercrime, natural disasters, and system malfunctions? What are some other security measures that should be taken? Why?

10. What would be examples of one positive and one negative effect of the use of e-business technologies in each of the ethical and societal dimensions illustrated in Figure 11.2? Explain several of your choices.

Application Exercises

Complete the following exercises as individual or group projects that apply chapter concepts to real world business situations.

1. **Internet Privacy and Anonymity:
   An Ethical Dilemma**
   I recently came across some software that lets you cloak your identity on the Internet. It got me

thinking about the whole issue of anonymity on the Net. Suppose a political activist in a country with limited civil rights sends an e-mail to an American human-rights group describing dreadful working conditions in a U.S.-owned factory. The plant's owners have to make changes—but not before local authorities, who monitor Internet traffic, throw the activist in jail. There, anonymity would have helped illuminate a problem.

Now suppose a child pornographer delivers his wares by e-mail. Authorities intercept the transmissions, but because the pornographer has successfully hidden his identity on the Net, they are unable to identify or find him. In that case, anonymity has protected a felon.

Whether you find these scenarios troubling will probably determine how you react to new software designed to allow people to send and receive e-mail, post messages to discussion groups, and participate in online chats in perfect anonymity. If, like me, you find both scenarios troubling, then what we have is an ethical dilemma.

I believe fervently in the right to free speech. I'm pleased that the Internet means that freedom of the press no longer is restricted, as A. J. Liebling once said, to the person who owns one. But I've also seen enough damage done by anonymous rumor and innuendo to recognize the danger that lurks in freedom without responsibility. I'm glad that such software for Internet anonymity will be available. But in the end, I hope that not many people will feel a need to use it.

a. Do you share the ethical misgivings of the author on this issue? Why or why not?

b. Should there be unrestricted use of software that provides anonymity on the Internet? Why or why not?

c. If you were able to decide this issue now, how would you decide for yourself? Your company? For society? Explain the reasons for your decisions.

Source: Adapted from Stephen Wildstrom, "A Big Boost for Net Privacy," *Business Week*, April 5, 1999, p. 23. Reprinted with special permission, copyright © 1999 by The McGraw-Hill Companies, Inc.

2. **Your Internet Job Rights:**
Three Ethical Scenarios
Whether you're an employer or an employee, you should know what your rights are when it comes to Internet use in the workplace. Mark Grossman, a Florida attorney who specializes in computer and Internet law, gives answers to some basic questions.

Scenario 1
Nobody told you that your Internet use in the office was being monitored. Now you've been warned you'll be fired if you use the Internet for recreational surfing again. What are your rights?

Bottom line. When you're using your office computer, you have virtually no rights. You'd have a tough time convincing a court that the boss invaded your privacy by monitoring your use of the company PC on company time. You should probably be grateful you got a warning.

Scenario 2
Your employees are abusing their Internet privileges, but you don't have an Internet usage policy. What do you do?

Bottom line. Although the law isn't fully developed in this area, courts are taking a straightforward approach:

If it's a company computer, the company can control the way it's used. You don't need an Internet usage policy to prevent inappropriate use of your company computers. To protect yourself in the future, distribute an Internet policy to your employees as soon as possible.

Scenario 3
Employee John Doe downloads adult material to his PC at work, and employee Jane Smith sees it. Smith then proceeds to sue the company for sexual harassment. As the employer, are you liable?

Bottom line. Whether it comes from the Internet or from a magazine, adult material simply has no place in the office. So Smith could certainly sue the company for making her work in a sexually hostile environment. The best defense is for the company to have an Internet usage policy that prohibits visits to adult sites. (Of course, you have to follow through. If someone is looking at adult material in the office, you must at least send the offending employee a written reprimand.) If the company lacks a strict Internet policy, though, Smith could prevail in court.

Ethical Questions
a. Do you agree with the advice of attorney Mark Grossman in each of the scenarios? Why or why not?

b. What would your advice be? Explain your positions.

c. Identify any ethical philosophies, values, or models you may be using in explaining your position in each of the scenarios.

Source: Adapted from James Martin. "You Are Being Watched," *PC World*, November 1997, p. 258. Reprinted with the permission of *PC World* Communications Inc.

3. **A Gantt Chart for an Intranet Development Project**
Gantt charts are used primarily as a scheduling tool to determine the length of time required to complete a project and the steps in the project that are most critical to its timely completion. A Gantt chart identifies the shortest time in which a project can be completed. It begins each step as soon as all of its predecessor steps (those which must be compete in order to perform the current step) have been completed. By plotting the timing of elements in a project in a manner similar to that shown in Figure 3.29, a Gantt chart shows interdependencies among steps in a project and makes clear which steps are most critical to completing a project on time.

The data below list a hypothetical set of steps needed to complete an intranet project. Step A is to begin at week 1 of the project. Since steps B, C, and E have A as a predecessor step, they can only begin at week 4 after step A has been completed. Step D requires that steps B and C both be completed, so it can only begin at week 8, and so on.

If you do not have access to project management software, a Gantt chart can be presented on a standard spreadsheet by laying out a set of columns of equal width to represent elapsed weeks of project time. You can use cell outlining and filling to illustrate the timing of each step. A portion of this type of layout is illustrated on the next page.

a. Using project planning software or a spreadsheet create an appropriate Gantt chart for this project. How will the completion of this project be affected if the time to complete step B runs 2 weeks longer than planned? If step C runs 2 weeks longer?

b. Prepare a brief presentation of your results using PowerPoint or similar presentation software. Be sure that your presentation highlights the steps that are most critical to rapid completion of the project.

Steps Required for an Intranet Development Project

Project Step	Description of Step	Weeks Required	Predecessor Steps	Elapsed Weeks			
				1	2	3	4
A	Gather Site Requirements	3	None	▓	▓	▓	
B	Design Navigation Structure	2	A				▓
C	Develop Prototype Content	4	A				▓
D	Create/Test/Revise Prototype Site	3	B and C				
E	Design Supporting Database	2	A				▓
F	Create/Test Supporting Database	3	E				
G	Link Site Pages to Database	2	F and D				
H	Test/Revise/Implement Completed Site	3	G				

4. Tracking Project Work at AAA Systems 2

Database systems typically involve multiple tables that are related to each other and can be combined on the basis of their logical relationship. In this exercise, we will take the database file created in **Application Exercise 5.2,** modify it, and add a second related table containing information about Employees.

The data for the Employee Table shown below is quite simple and consist only of the Employee ID, the Employee Name, and the Billing rate used when charging the employee's work against a project task. The Employee ID is used to identify the employee and to link this data to the project hours data in the existing table.

Employee_Id	Employee_Name	Billing_Rate
123	C. Davis	$70.00
234	J. Jones	$90.00
345	B. Bates	$110.00
456	B. Smith	$80.00

a. If you have not completed **Application Exercise 5.2** complete part A of that exercise now. Open up the database file you created for **Application Exercise 5.2.** Next create an employee table with the structure and data shown in the example below. Make sure that the Employee Id column in this new table has exactly the same data type and length that you used for the Employee Id column on the previous table. Create and print a listing of a query that joins the two tables based on the common Employee ID column and displays all columns of both tables.

b. Create a report grouped by employee that lists their Id and Name and then shows the production week, hours worked that week and amount billed (hours worked times billing rate) for that week.

c. Create a report grouped project name that shows the total amount billed for each task within each project.

AGM Container Controls and Sonalysts, Inc.: The Business Case for Workplace Monitoring

John Conlin is browsing around some company's network again. *Click-click*—now he's searching employees' e-mail by key words. Not only can he sniff out which websites workers have visited, but he can see how long they were there and at what time. All this snooping leaves no tracks. What Conlin does is not illegal. In fact, it's probably already happening at your company. If not, just wait. Conlin's company, eSniff, sells an electronic monitoring device that allows businesses to spy on their workers. It may sound like a scene from a movie, but as either an employee or a manager, you'd better get used to it. Last year some 82 percent of businesses monitored their employees in some way, according to the American Management Association.

It's not hard to see why the Net provides all kinds of productivity-frittering distractions—from instant messaging socializing, to eBay, pornography, and sports scores. Worse, company secrets may be floating across your fire wall. And what you dismiss as simple time wasting could be setting you up for harassment, discrimination, copyright infringement, and other lawsuits. Lawsuits are not the only risk employers face. Intellectual property can make its way out of the office more easily than ever with the help of electronic communications.

eSniff logs all Internet traffic, recording and reporting anything that's been labeled as suspicious. The administrator can then view the log summaries and quickly drill down to the actual content of any questionable e-mail to make sure it hasn't fallen into the wrong in-box. "It's rare for eSniff to be installed on a network and not find a lot of inappropriate activity," Conlin says, adding that close to 100 percent of workers register some kind of improper use.

Despite the threat of lawsuits, a study from the Society for Human Resource Management found that among companies that monitor employees electronically, less than one-quarter do so to mitigate legal risk. Some 45 percent do it because they suspect employees are slacking. "The problem is, people think it's their God-given right to be on the Internet," says Conlin. "People who wouldn't dream of removing a paper clip from the office think nothing of taking 20 minutes to check yesterday's baseball scores. It's not any different from stealing pencils or paper or anything else from the office."

There are two ways to remedy cyber-slacking: monitoring Internet use (and making sure employees know you're doing it), and simply blocking sites deemed unrelated to work. Neither is an easy—or bulletproof—fix. If nothing else, a monitoring system with the right amount of follow-up can help employees realize how much company time they waste on the Internet—and help get them back on track.

Howard Stewart, president of AGM Container Controls in Tucson, Arizona, had a feeling that one of his employees was using her PC for personal use a little too much. "When I talked to the employee, she denied she was using e-mail or the Internet for personal use," he says, explaining that the company has a written policy against using the Internet for anything other than work. "However, I knew that this policy was ineffective because a few of my employees had come to the realization that I couldn't monitor their usage."

Stewart chose a simple program from Strategic Business Solutions called Resource Monitor. "Boy, oh boy! Was that employee ever surprised when I was able to negate point-by-point each of her denials that she was using the computer for personal business," Stewart says. "She was shocked to discover that I could give her the exact dates and times she was on and how long she had been at inappropriate sites. Up to that point, she had claimed that she didn't have enough time to take on additional projects at work."

When Randy Dickson, a systems analyst for the Connecticut-based multimedia production firm Sonalysts, Inc., revealed at the company's 2001 annual meeting that employee Internet use had been monitored using eSniff, the reaction was surprisingly positive. "There was some shock value, but most of the folks were happy to see it because we're an employee-owned business. If something is going to distress the company financially, they want to see it dealt with in a logical manner," he says. Dickson was pleased to find there was less abuse going on than he thought.

For instance, Dickson had been concerned about time wasted using instant messaging, but found that most of the IM activity was for legitimate business use and was actually saving the company money on phone bills. He also found system abuse that was caused by simple ignorance and easily corrected. "One guy was playing Internet radio all the time. He assumed the service was free, but it was eating up bandwidth and we pay for our T1 line based on use," Dickson explains. Once informed, the employee stopped using the service.

"That's one of the virtues of eSniff," says Dickson. "When we first started the monitoring, people hadn't quite gotten the message about acceptable use. Since telling them about eSniff, though, it's gotten much easier."

Case Study Questions

1. Is employer monitoring of employee online computer activity a good business practice? An ethical business practice? Why or why not?

2. Is unauthorized use by employees of an employer's computer networks and online services for nonbusiness use during work hours an ethical business practice? Why or why not?

3. How lenient would you be as a manager or employer towards personal use of company network resources during work hours by your employees? Explain the rationale for your position.

Source: Adapted from Kayte VanScoy, "What Your Workers Are Really Up To," *Ziff Davis Smart Business*, September 2001, pp. 50–54. Reprinted by permission.

Microsoft, DoubleClick, and Others: Evaluating Privacy Challenges and Solutions

Say one thing, do another. Since the birth of the Web, there's been a chasm separating consumers' stated feelings about online privacy and how they act with a mouse in their hand. Eighty-six percent of Internet users worry about online privacy, according to the Pew Internet and American Life Project. However, nearly 50 percent say they'll give out personal information in exchange for the chance to win a sweepstakes, reports Jupiter Media Metrix.

Or will they? While there is a disparity between what many online users say and do when their privacy is at stake, another subset of consumers is more steeled. Of those who are connected but do not transact online—which is over half of all Internet users—58 percent say it's because they fear their information will be stolen or misused, according to Jupiter. Thus billions of dollars in e-commerce revenue is being left on the table because businesses have not done enough to quell consumers' fears about privacy. Bandwidth, the wireless Web, and convergence aside: Build the Net with more privacy options and the dollars will come.

The first incarnation of the Internet was built with virtually no thought to privacy. Websites weren't crafted with confidentiality in mind, and corporations had little concern for the issue when setting up their internal databases. Only after high-profile privacy flameouts involving Microsoft, RealNetworks, and DoubleClick in 1999 and 2000 did companies realize that they had to retrofit their operations to reach privacy-conscious customers.

Starting in 1998 with the GeoCities case in which the company was charged with violating its own privacy policy by sharing customer data, companies have been caught surreptitiously collecting personal information and re-selling it to third-party marketers. Credit card files stolen from merchant databases have revealed companies' faulty security. Two years ago, Willingford, Connecticut–based CD Universe learned this lesson the hard way, when thousands of its customers' credit card numbers were stolen and posted on the Web, nearly putting the company out of business.

DoubleClick Inc., an online profiler in New York, initiated a merger two years ago with an information aggregator, Abacas Direct Corp., and announced its intent to share their respective databases. After an investigation, the FTC decided not to file charges. Nevertheless, the incident prompted DoubleClick to hire New York's former consumer affairs commissioner, Jules Polonetsky, as its chief privacy officer in March 2000. He quickly brought other privacy experts onboard to establish and carry out best practices. And 50 clients who had violated their privacy agreements with DoubleClick have since been dropped.

Still, the fact remains that only about half of online Americans "trust valuable personal information to Web companies that require it," according to the Pew Internet and American Life Project. And Statistical Research found that 67 percent of active Internet users tend to abandon sites that request personal information. These are the statistics that vex Internet companies, and have them looking at various privacy rights management technologies.

For companies like Microsoft, which have much more comprehensive plans involving the Web and personal information, such negative Web surfer sentiments loom like storm clouds. So Microsoft built a feature called P3P (Platform for Privacy Preferences) into Internet Explorer 6.0, allowing consumers to check out and leave websites without privacy policies that match their privacy preferences.

However, Microsoft has more ambitious plans. Through a service code-named HailStorm within its .Net initiative, Microsoft hopes to become the trusted repository of a laundry list of personal information about millions of Internet users, which could conceivably include bank account and credit card numbers, cell phone numbers, and, via calendar software, a person's physical whereabouts. The service should roll out sometime in the Spring of 2002, according to Ruthann Lorentzen, general manager of Microsoft .Net services marketing and business development.

The idea is to streamline everyday transactions by linking together information about consumers. For example, Lorentzen says, the service could make receiving goods bought online or via mail order much more convenient. If shippers like UPS and FedEx HailStorm-enable their sites, customers could keep much closer tabs on deliveries—and even decide when and where to receive packages.

For some privacy advocates, the idea of trusting Microsoft with such information is suspect. "This is not a company that anybody in their right mind would trust with their home telephone number," says Jason Catlett, president of Junkbusters, an online-privacy advocacy firm. And when Jupiter Media Metrix asked Internet users how they would feel about having a site on the Web keep their personal information in one place, to send to companies at their request, a mere 4 percent said they'd be in favor of such an arrangement.

Case Study Questions

1. Does the Internet privacy issue affect the success of e-commerce? Explain your position.

2. Do you support Microsoft's HailStorm initiative to be a repository of personal information for Internet users? Why or why not?

3. What alternatives can you propose to help solve the Internet privacy problems revealed in this case? Defend your proposals.

Source: Adapted from Deborah Radcliff, "Privacy: The Liability Link," *Computerworld*, August 27, 2001, pp. 36–37; and Bob Tedeschi, "Privacy vs. Profits," *Ziff Davis Smart Business*, October 2001, pp. 56–60. Reprinted with permission.

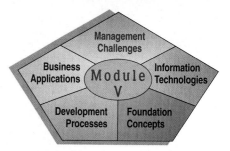

Management
Challenges

Business
Applications

Module
V

Information
Technologies

Development
Processes

Foundation
Concepts

Chapter 12

Enterprise and Global Management

of e-Business Technology

Chapter Highlights

Learning Objectives

After reading and studying this chapter, you should be able to:

1. Identify several ways that information technologies have affected the job of managers in e-business companies.

2. Explain how problems of information system performance can be reduced by the involvement of business managers in IS planning and management.

3. Identify the seven major dimensions of the e-business organization and explain how they affect the success of e-business companies.

4. Identify each of the three components of e-business technology management and use examples to illustrate how they might be implemented in an e-business enterprise.

5. Identify several cultural, political, and geoeconomic challenges that confront managers in the management of global e-business technologies.

6. Explain the effect on global e-business strategy of the trend toward a transnational business strategy by international business organizations.

7. Identify several considerations that affect the choice of IT applications, IT platforms, data access policies, and systems development methods by a global e-business enterprise.

Managing e-Business Technologies

e-Business and IT

Information technology is the bloodstream that feeds the business process [25].

The strategic and operational importance of information technology in e-business enterprises is no longer questioned.

As the 21st century unfolds, many companies throughout the world are intent on transforming themselves into global e-business enterprises and major players in global e-commerce. Thus, there is a real need for business managers and professionals to understand how to manage this vital organizational function. In this section, we will explore how IT affects managers and e-business organizations, and stress the importance of a customer and business value focus for the management of e-business technologies. So whether you plan to be an entrepreneur and run your own business, a manager in a corporation, or a business professional, managing e-business systems and technologies will be one of your major responsibilities.

Analyzing Mellon Financial Corp.

Read the Real World Case on Mellon Financial Corp. on the next page. We can learn a lot about the challenges of developing e-commerce strategies in today's economic environment. See Figure 12.1.

Figure 12.1

Janey Place is manager of e-commerce strategy for Mellon Financial and leads the development of their e-commerce initiatives.

Source: Eric Ogden.

Mellon Financial Corp.:
The Business Case for Hybrid e-Commerce Strategies

Janey Place heads up e-commerce strategy for Mellon Financial Corp., the Pittsburgh-based parent of subsidiaries such as Dreyfus Corp. and Newton Investment Management Ltd. When Place signed on with Mellon in 1999, the financial-service powerhouse essentially had no e-commerce strategy, and was way behind other big banks and brokerage firms. Place had already led many major-league online initiatives. Within the banking industry, she was widely regarded as an e-commerce and business-technology futurist with extensive experience in developing technology-enabled business strategies at Bank of America and Wells Fargo Bank in California.

Place's plan for Mellon's e-commerce strategy was decidedly simple: Instead of spinning off a separate, headline-grabbing Web channel, she would integrate the Web into all of Mellon's existing lines of business. "We felt we could add more value to the market by bringing such capabilities as our asset management, asset serving, and employee-benefits consulting to the Web," says Place.

It's not a radical plan—and that's exactly the point. But Place and her team are moving aggressively to leverage the Web: They have deployed 12 major applications; they are launching a new online application or enhancement every six weeks; and currently, they have 42 applications in development. In an interview with *Fast Company*, Place highlighted five rules for Webifying financial institutions and services.

Rule 1: The Internet changes everything—but it doesn't change everything overnight. The Internet changes everything: how we get information, how we learn, how we conduct business. But back in 1999, when I joined Mellon, quite a few people hoped that I would come in with great ideas for building e-marketplaces and communities of interest and self-service on the Web. But other processes need to come into play.

For example, there's a lot of excitement over EBPP (electronic bill presentment and payment). But we still haven't worked out the basic business model for EBPP. Who should pay for it? And who should be the beneficiary? Will it be banks, online payment services, merchants, or their customers?

Rule 2: There is no such thing as first-mover advantage. When I joined Mellon, my colleagues and I set about creating a company-wide e-commerce framework that assists all lines of business without constricting them. This was at a time when the major events in the banking world were Bank One launching WingspanBank.com and Citigroup Inc. launching Citi f/i as pure dot-com subsidiaries. Bank One and Citigroup bet that the Internet would lower costs, raise customer retention, and make it easier to cross-sell additional products.

Wingspan and Citi f/i were aimed solely at attaining first-mover advantage. But where was the advantage? Being first doesn't mean that you claim an unlimited amount of cyberspace—not when your competition is just one click away. As Wingspan and Citi f/i fell back to earth, losing hundreds of millions of dollars, we realized that second place is a good place to be. We could learn from others' mistakes.

Rule 3: Some of the old rules still rule. Technology, in and of itself, isn't enough of a reason to invest in the Internet. There has to be a reasonable, logical business model. Either you're saving money or you're making money.

For example, we're seeing this reality come into play with digital signatures. Right now, there are many technological solutions for securing digital signatures for online transactions. The technology exists to make you feel secure when you transfer $100,000. And the electronic-signature legislation that has been passed by most countries lays the necessary legal foundation. But that's just a start. The legal infrastructure that keeps commerce running in the real world still needs to be developed for the virtual world. So if your $100,000 disappears into a black hole, someone is legally liable for it.

Rule 4: Your choice: dot-com, dotcorp, or both? A dot-com strategy is one where you take an existing expertise, put it on the Internet, and try to build a new line of business around it. Forrester Research coined the term "dotcorp." In a dotcorp, you drive the benefits of e-commerce through your existing products for the benefit of your existing customers.

For example, we could have dot-commed the investment methodology that we use with Mellon Private Asset Management, our high-net-worth application that we launched in August 2000. We could have standardized and commoditized it, and sold it to third-party investment advisers. Instead, we followed a dotcorp strategy: We focused on adding Web services for our large institutional clients and our very wealthy individual clients at the retail level.

Rule 5: First we overestimated the Internet; don't underestimate it now. Looking ahead, I am convinced that the business impact of the Internet will exceed our expectations. The dot-com explosion proved that technology matters—big time. But the fallout proves that old-economy rules haven't been completely repealed. This isn't the new economy. This is a combination of the two. This is the hybrid economy. And the challenge for every e-commerce strategist is to meld hybrid strategies from both economies that will thrive in this new era.

Case Study Questions

1. Has Janey Place chosen the right e-commerce strategies for Mellon Financial? Why or why not?

2. Do you agree with Janey Place's rules for e-commerce strategies for financial institutions and services? Why or why not?

3. Do these rules also apply to other industries and companies, both large and small? Use several examples from the business world to support your answer.

Source: Adapted from Bill Breen, "Bankers' Hours," *Fast Company*, November 2001, pp. 196–203. Reprinted by permission.

Janey Place came to Mellon Financial in 1999 from Bank of America and Wells Fargo Bank, when Mellon had no e-commerce strategy and was way behind other large banks and brokerage firms in its Web services. As manager of e-commerce strategy, Place decided against developing a separate Mellon dot-com subsidiary, like Citigroup's Citi f/i or Bank One's Wingspan Bank. Instead Place has championed a "dotcorp" e-commerce strategy of integrating the Web into all of Mellon's existing lines of business. Time has proven the wisdom of Place's choice, as Wingspan and f/i have lost their banks hundreds of millions of dollars. Under Place's leadership, Mellon has deployed 12 major e-commerce applications, and has 42 others under development. Place is convinced that the business impact of the Internet will exceed expectations. Thus, she says companies should devise hybrid new economy/old economy e-commerce strategies that will thrive in this new e-business era.

Managers and e-Business Technologies

Really difficult business problems always have many aspects. Often a major decision depends on an impromptu search for one or two key pieces of auxiliary information and a quick ad hoc analysis of several possible scenarios. You need software tools that easily combine and recombine data from many sources. You need Internet access for all kinds of research. Widely scattered people need to be able to collaborate and work the data in different ways [11].

So says Bill Gates, chairman of Microsoft Corporation, of his own and his management team's experience with the managerial effects of e-business technologies. Thus, as Figure 12.2 illustrates, the competitive pressures of today's e-business and technology environment are encouraging managers to rethink their use and management of information technology. Many business executives now see information technology as an enabling platform for electronic commerce, and for managing the cross-functional and interorganizational e-business processes of their business units. In addition, the Internet, intranets, extranets, and the Web are interconnecting individuals, teams, business units, and business partners in close business relationships that promote the communication, collaboration, and decision making needed in today's competitive global marketplace.

| **Figure 12.2** | Information technology must be managed to meet the challenges of today's internetworked e-business and technology environment, and the customer value and business value imperatives for success in a dynamic global economy. |

E-Business Developments

Suppliers → Customers

Information Technology Developments

Customer Value Business Value

- E-business and e-commerce transformation of business strategies and processes
- Agility, flexibility, and time compression of development, manufacturing, and delivery supply chain cycles
- Reengineering and cross-functional integration of business processes using Internet technologies
- Competitive advantage, total quality, and customer value focus

- Use of the Internet, intranets, extranets, and the Web as the primary IT infrastructure
- Diffusion of technology to internetwork employees, customers and suppliers
- Global and enterprise computing, collaboration and decision support systems
- Integrated cross-functional enterprise software replaces legacy systems

- Give customers what they want, when and how they want it, at the lowest cost
- Interenterprise coordination of manufacturing and business processes
- Effective distribution and channel partnerships
- Responsiveness and accountability to customers

Source: Adapted in part from Ravi Kalakota and Marcia Robinson, *e-Business 2.0: Roadmap for Success* (Reading, MA: Addison-Wesley, 2001), pp. 273, 279. © 2001 Addison-Wesley Publishing Company, Inc. Reprinted by permission of Addison-Wesley Longman Inc.

Thus, information technology has become a major force for precipitating or enabling organizational and managerial change. Thanks to Internet technologies and other dynamic hardware, software, data, and network developments, computing power and information resources are now more readily available to more managers than ever before. In fact, these and other information technologies have already enabled innovative changes in managerial decision making, organizational structures, and managerial work activities [8, 16, 29].

For example, the decision support capabilities provided by Web-enabled decision support system technologies are changing the focus of managerial decision making. Managers freed from number-crunching chores must now face tougher strategic policy questions in order to develop realistic alternatives for today's dynamic e-business and e-commerce environment. In addition, many companies now use the Internet, intranets, and enterprise collaboration systems to coordinate their work activities and business processes. Middle managers no longer need to serve as conduits for the transmission of operations feedback or control directives between operational managers and teams, and top management. Thus, many companies have reduced the layers and numbers of middle management, and encouraged the growth of workgroups of task-focused teams. Let's take a look at a real world example given by Bill Gates of Microsoft.

Microsoft: The Impact of IT on District Sales Managers	At Microsoft, our information systems have changed the role of our district sales managers. When MS Sales (our intranet-based revenue measurement and decision support system) first came online, our Minneapolis general manager ran a variety of numbers for her district at a level of detail never possible before. She discovered that excellent sales among other customer segments were obscuring a poor showing among large customers in her district. In fact, the district was dead last among U.S. districts in that category. Finding that out was a shock but also a big motivator for the large-customer teams in the district. By the end of the year Minneapolis was the top-growing district for sales to large customers. If you're a district manager at Microsoft today, you must be more than a good sales leader helping your team close the big deals, which has been the traditional district sales manager role. Now you can be a business thinker. You have numbers to help you run your business. Before, even if you were concerned about the retail store revenue in your area, you had no view whatsoever of those results. Now you can look at sales figures and evaluate where your business is strong, where your business is weak, and where your business has its greatest potential, product by product, relative to other districts. You can try out new programs and see their impact. You can talk to other managers about what they're doing to get strong results. Being a district sales manager in our organization is a much broader role than what it was five years ago because of the digital tools we've developed and their ease of use [11].

Poor IS Performance

The future arrived a little early for Hershey Foods. In July, to be exact, when a botched big-software project meant the chocolate maker literally couldn't deliver the goods. The failure jacked up product delivery times from five days to 12, increased inventory costs by 29 percent and kicked the props from under Hershey's third-quarter sales (a $150 million drop, or 12 percent) and profits (down almost $20 million, or 19 percent). After a catastrophe like that, could anybody still believe IT can't have a big impact on business? [14]

So, managing information technology is not an easy task. The information systems function has performance problems in many organizations. The promised benefits of information technology have not occurred in many documented cases. Studies by management consulting firms and university researchers have shown that many businesses have not been successful in managing their use of information

Figure 12.3

The perils of poor IS performance. Hershey suffered severe business losses after the failure of a major ERP implementation to reengineer its business processes.

The Results of Hershey's Big IT Failure
• A 19% drop in third-quarter profits and a 12% sales decline • A 29% increase in year-to-year inventory costs • An inability to ship complete orders to some retail customers • Strained customer relations and major market-share losses • An increase in typical delivery times from 5 days to 12

Source: Adapted from Craig Steadman, "Failed ERP Gamble Haunts Hershey," *Computerworld*, November 1, 1999, p. 1. Copyright 1999 by Computerworld, Inc., Framingham, MA 01701. Reprinted from *Computerworld*.

technology. Figure 12.3 dramatizes the results of the failure of a large corporation to manage the development and implementation of a major ERP project to reengineer its business processes. Thus, it is evident that in many organizations, information technology is not being used effectively and efficiently. For example:

- Information technology is not being used *effectively* by companies that use IT primarily to computerize traditional business processes instead of using it for electronic commerce, Web-enabled decision support, and innovative e-business processes and products.

- Information technology is not being used *efficiently* by information systems that provide poor response times and frequent downtimes, or IS professionals and consultants who do not properly manage application development projects.

Let's look closer at Hershey Foods as a real world example.

Hershey Foods: Anatomy of a Disaster

A $112 million ERP project blew up in the face of Hershey Foods Corp. Now it is struggling to fix order-processing problems that are hampering its ability to ship candy and other products to retailers. Analysts and sources in the industry said the Hershey, Pennsylvania, manufacturer appears to have lost a gamble when it installed a wide swath of SAP AG's R/3 enterprise resource planning applications, plus companion packages from two other vendors, simultaneously during one of its busiest shipping seasons. The sources said Hershey squeezed what was originally envisioned as a four-year project into just 30 months before going live with the full ERP system in July of 1999. That's when retailers begin ordering large amounts of candy for back-to-school and Halloween sales.

Hershey wouldn't specify whether the problems stem from its configuration of the system or the software itself, which also includes planning and scheduling applications developed by Manugistics Group, and a pricing promotions package from Siebel Systems. Manugistics said it's working with Hershey and the other vendors on "business process improvements." A spokesman for IBM, the lead consultant on the project, said the new system required "enormous" changes in the way Hershey's workers do their jobs. Siebel officials weren't available for comment.

Hershey turned on some of SAP's finance applications, plus its purchasing, materials management, and warehousing modules, in January. The order-processing and billing portions of R/3 were added along with the Manugistics and Siebel packages in July. Jim Shepherd, an analyst at AMR Research, said most companies install ERP systems in a more staged manner, especially when applications from multiple vendors are involved. "These systems tie together in very intricate ways, and things that work fine in testing can turn out to be a disaster when you go live," Shepherd said. He added that the software Hershey turned on all at once in July was "a huge bite to take, given that processing orders is the lifeblood of their business" [31].

Management Involvement and Governance

What is the solution to problems of poor performance in the information systems function? There are no quick and easy answers. However, the experiences of successful organizations reveal that extensive and meaningful **managerial and end user involvement** is the key ingredient of high-quality information systems performance. Involving business managers in the governance of the IS function and business professionals in the development of IS applications should thus shape the response of management to the challenge of improving the business value of information technology [8, 16].

Involving managers in the management of IT (from the CEO to the managers of business units) requires the development of *governance structures* (such as executive councils and steering committees) that encourage their active participation in planning and controlling the business uses of IT. Thus, many organizations have policies that require managers to be involved in IT decisions that affect their business units. This helps managers avoid IS performance problems in their business units and development projects. Without this high degree of involvement, managers cannot hope to improve the strategic business value of information technology. Also, as we said in Chapter 10, the problems of employee resistance and poor user interface design can only be solved by direct end user participation in systems development projects.

The e-Business Organization

Just as the value chain has been disintermediated, so too has the traditional organization. The Digital Age organization is no longer a single corporate entity, but rather an extended network consisting of a streamlined global core, market-focused business units and shared support services [29].

E-business companies are reengineering (or *e-engineering*) their organizational structures and roles, as well as their business processes, as they strive to become agile, customer-focused, value-driven enterprises. One way to express this phenomenon is illustrated in Figure 12.4, which outlines several key dimensions of the new e-business organization, compared to the same dimensions of a pre-e-business organization model used by many companies. The seven dimensions of the *e-organization*

Figure 12.4 Comparing the e-organization model of internetworked e-business enterprises to the pre-e-organization model used by many companies.

	Pre-e-Organization	e-Organization
Organization Structure	• Hierarchical • Command-and-control	• Centerless, networked • Flexible structure that is easily modified
Leadership	• Selected "stars" step above • Leaders set the agenda • Leaders force change	• Everyone is a leader • Leaders create environment for success • Leaders create capacity for change
People and Culture	• Long-term rewards • Vertical decision making • Individuals and small teams are rewarded	• "Own your own career" mentality • Delegated authority • Collaboration expected and rewarded
Coherence	• Hard-wired into processes • Internal relevance	• Embedded vision in individuals • Impact projected externally
Knowledge	• Focused on internal processes • Individualistic	• Focused on customers • Institutional
Alliances	• Complement current gaps • Ally with distant partners	• Create new value and outsource uncompetitive services • Ally with competitors, customers, and suppliers
Governance	• Internally focused • Top-down	• Internal and external focus • Distributed

Source: Adapted from Gary Neilson, Bruce Pasternack, and Albert Visco, "Up the E-Organization! A Seven-Dimensional Model of the Centerless Enterprise," *Strategy & Business*, First Quarter 2000, p. 53.

model demonstrate that e-business and e-commerce appear to provide a major impetus for companies to make major changes to their organizational structures and roles. Let's look at a real world example that exemplifies and illustrates all seven dimensions of this new e-business organization model [29].

Cisco Systems: The Ultimate e-Organization

Cisco Systems Inc. may well be the best example of what we mean by an e.org. At present, Cisco does more business online than any other company, with electronic sales averaging more than $20 million a day. The clear market leader in the business-to-business networking hardware industry, it is the ultimate networked enterprise.

Organization Structure: Cisco maintains a strong web of strategic partnerships and systems integration with suppliers, contractors, and assemblers. This network of alliances provides a flexible structure that enables the "e-stended" Cisco enterprise to shift toward new market opportunities, and away from old ones. Although it outsources functions, including a large part of its manufacturing, it also leverages its innovative human resources and IT departments as shared services to the benefit of all its business units.

Leadership: John Chambers has proven to be a strong, visionary leader, but Cisco is led by more than just a single person. The company has made more than 40 acquisitions in its short history, and many acquired companies live on as autonomous Cisco business units. But Cisco does not install new leadership for those business units; managers of the acquired companies usually have the independence to run their business units. Even more telling, Cisco's senior management is filled with executives from acquired companies. These entrepreneurial managers are not pushed out of the company; their skills as leaders are valued at all levels of Cisco.

People and Culture: Cisco's culture is straight out of the e.org textbook, and extends all the way to the company's endless search for talent. Cisco has proven to be very effective at recruiting those whom the company calls "passive" job seekers—people who aren't actively looking for a new job. The company is a recruitment innovator in the competitive Silicon Valley marketplace. The company has a Web page, for example, to connect a potential hire with a Cisco employee who works in the same sort of position. The volunteer employee "friend," and not a trained recruiter, will then call the prospect to talk about life at Cisco. This inside view of the company is an important selling tool for recruitment; it also gives employees a voice in the continued growth of the company. And Cisco's human resources ability extends to the culture of the organization and its ability to retain talent. The result? Turnover is low, at 6.7 percent annually, compared to an industry average of 18 percent. And turnover of acquired-company staff at Cisco is even lower—just 2.1 percent, compared to an industry average of more than 20 percent. (Of course, a relentlessly increasing stock price doesn't hurt.)

Coherence: Cisco is almost religious when it comes to customer focus, and the customer focus goes right to the top. CEO John Chambers was reportedly late for his very first board meeting in 1994 because he was on the phone with an unhappy customer. The board excused him. Under Chambers, Cisco senior executives have their bonuses tied to customer satisfaction ratings, and the company has spared no expense developing its online service and support model to provide its customers with the industry's broadest range of hardware products, as well as related software and services. The customer focus permeates the entire organization—even to the engineering department, a group not traditionally thought of as customer oriented.

Knowledge: Cisco has leveraged the Internet to optimize every step in the value chain from sales to order-processing to customer service to manufacturing. The extent to which Cisco has tied its business partners together with shared knowledge is staggering. Web-based systems allow suppliers to tap directly into Cisco's manufacturing and order systems with realtime access to product logistics information, and order flow. Cisco also shares demand forecasts, intellectual capital, electronic communication tools, and volume targets. The result? Suppliers' production processes are "pulled" by Cisco's customer demand. The company's knowledge-sharing goes even further, providing online service and support to end customers; 70 percent of technical support requests are now filed electronically, generating an average customer service rating of 4+ on a 5-point scale. Cisco has saved considerable money from this online migration—an estimated $500 million a year from improved supply chain management, online technical support, software distribution via downloads and other Internet-enabled processes.

Alliances: It's not just knowledge that Cisco distributes electronically with its network of partners. Cisco's alliance partners are an integral component of the company's ability to serve customers, and Cisco treats them as part of the company. Indeed, half of customer orders that come in over its website are routed electronically to a supplier who ships directly to the customer.

Governance: Cisco's ability to grow while managing its autonomous business units and bringing together its alliance partners is indicative of its internal and external governance policies. Perhaps this is best illustrated by Cisco's acquisitions ability. The company is well known for its rapid acquisitions process, and for its ability to integrate its acquisitions quickly into the Cisco family. The Cisco integration team has the acquisitions process down to a science.

Cisco has upped the ante and established the table stakes in the industry, not only for its competitors, but also for its suppliers, by utilizing the Internet to maximum advantage. Yet its primary product, networking hardware, is not even a product that lends itself to Internet distribution. These components are not only difficult to subdivide and describe for an e-commerce website, they are highly specialized. Still Cisco has been able to make the sales and buying experience very Web accessible and very lucrative [29].

Figure 12.5 provides an example of the e-organization structure of an e-business company. Notice that there is a global executive core, four market-focused business units, and two shared support services business units. However, all six business units

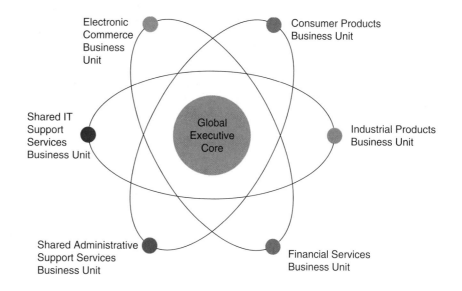

Figure 12.5

An example of the organizational structure of an e-business enterprise.

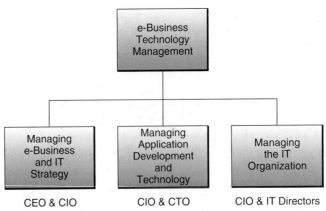

Figure 12.6

The major components of e-business technology management. Note the executives with primary responsibilities in each area.

Source: Derived in part from Omar El Sawy, Arvind Malhotra, Sanjay Go-sain, and Kerry Young, "IT-Intensive Value Innovation in the Electronic Economy: Insights from Marshall Industries," *MIS Quarterly*, September 1999, pp. 323–27. Reprinted with permission from the *MIS Quarterly*.

are customer and market focused. Even the shared support services units must provide competitive services to the global core, other business units, and external customers, since uncompetitive services may be outsourced to external vendors [29].

e-Business Technology Management

Figure 12.6 illustrates a popular approach to managing information technology in an e-business enterprise. This managerial approach has three major components:

- Managing the joint development and implementation of e-business and IT strategies.
- Managing the development of e-business applications and the research and implementation of new information technologies.
- Managing the IT processes, professionals, and subunits within a company's IT organization and IS function.

Let's look at a real world example.

Avnet Marshall: Managing IT

Figure 12.7 contrasts how Avnet Marshall's information technology management differs from conventional IT management. Notice that they use the model of e-business technology management illustrated in Figure 12.6. For example, in technology management, Avnet Marshall uses a best-of-breed approach that supports business needs, instead of enforcing a standardized and homogeneous choice of hardware, software, database, and networking technologies. In managing its IT organization, Avnet Marshall hires IS professionals who can integrate IT with business. These IS professionals are organized in workgroups around e-business initiatives that focus on building e-commerce services for customers [8].

e-Business Planning

Figure 12.8 illustrates the **e-business planning** process, which focuses on discovering innovative approaches to satisfying a company's customer value and business value goals. This planning process leads to development of strategies and business models for new e-business and e-commerce platforms, processes, products, and services. Then a company can develop IT strategies and an IT architecture that supports building and implementing their newly planned e-business applications.

Both the CEO and the chief information officer (CIO) of a company must manage the development of complementary e-business and IT strategies to meet its customer

Figure 12.7

Comparing conventional and e-business IT management approaches.

IT Management	Conventional Practices	Avnet Marshall's e-Business Practices
Technology Management	• Approach to IT infrastructure may sacrifice match with business needs for vendor homogeneity and technology platform choices	• Best-of-breed approach to IT infrastructure in which effective match with business needs takes precedence over commitment to technology platform choices and vender homogeneity
Managing the IT Organization	• Hire "best by position" who can bring specific IT expertise • Departments organized around IT expertise with business liaisons and explicit delegation of tasks • IT projects have separable cost/value considerations. Funding typically allocated within constraints of yearly budget for IT function	• Hire "best athletes" IS professionals who can flexibly integrate new IT and business competencies • Evolving workgroups organized around emerging IT-intensive business initiatives with little explicit delegation of tasks • IT funding typically based on value proposition around business opportunity related to building services for customers. IT project inseparable part of business initiative

Source: Adapted from Omar El Sawy, Arvind Malhotra, Sanjay Gosain, and Kerry Young, "IT-Intensive Value Innovation in the Electronic Economy: Insights from Marshall Industries," *MIS Quarterly*, September 1999, p. 324. Reprinted with permission from the *MIS Quarterly*.

value and business value vision. This *co-adaptation* process is necessary because as we have seen so often in this text, information technologies are a fast changing, but vital component in all e-business and e-commerce initiatives. The e-business planning process has three major components:

- **Strategy development.** Developing e-business and e-commerce strategies that support a company's e-business vision, and use information technology to create innovative e-business systems that focus on customer and business value.

Figure 12.8

The e-business planning process emphasizes a customer and business value focus for developing e-business strategies and models, and an IT architecture for e-business applications.

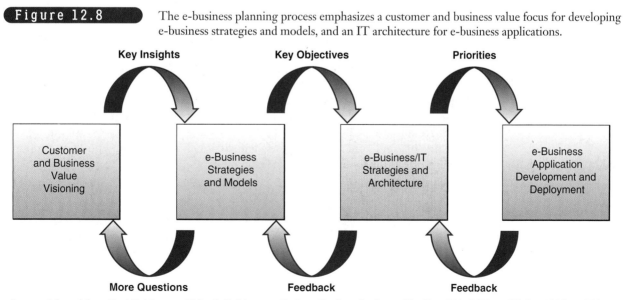

Source: Adapted from Ravi Kalakota and Marcia Robinson, *e-Business: Roadmap for Success* (Reading, MA: Addison-Wesley, 1999), p. 305. © 1999 Addison-Wesley Publishing Company, Inc. Reprinted by permission of Addison-Wesley Longman Inc.

- **Resource management.** Developing strategic plans for managing or outsourcing a company's IT resources, including IS personnel, hardware, software, data, and network resources.

- **Technology architecture.** Making strategic IT choices that reflect an information technology architecture designed to support a company's e-business and e-commerce initiatives.

Information Technology Architecture

The **IT architecture** that is created by the strategic e-business planning process is a conceptual design, or blueprint, that includes the following major components:

- **Technology platform.** The Internet, intranets, extranets and other networks, computer systems, system software, and integrated enterprise application software provide a computing and communications infrastructure, or platform, that supports the strategic use of information technology for e-business and e-commerce.

- **Data resources.** Many types of operational and specialized databases, including data warehouses and Internet/intranet databases (as reviewed in Chapter 5) store and provide data and information for business processes and decision support.

- **Applications architecture.** Business applications of information technology are designed as an integrated architecture of enterprise systems that support strategic e-business initiatives, as well as cross-functional business processes. For example, an applications architecture should include support for developing and maintaining interenterprise supply chain applications, and integrated enterprise resource planning and customer relationship management applications we discussed in Chapter 7.

- **IT organization.** The organizational structure of the IS function within a company and the distribution of IS specialists are designed to meet the changing strategies of a business. The form of the IT organization depends on the managerial philosophy and business/IT strategies formulated during the strategic planning process.

Avnet Marshall: e-Business Planning

Avnet Marshall weaves both e-business and IT strategic planning together *co-adaptively* under the guidance of the CEO and the CIO, instead of developing IT strategy by just tracking and supporting business strategies. Avnet Marshall also locates IT application development projects within the business units that are involved in an e-business initiative to form centers of e-business/IT expertise throughout the company. Finally, Avnet Marshall uses an application development process with rapid deployment of e-business applications, instead of a traditional systems development approach. This application development strategy trades the risk of implementing incomplete applications with the benefits of gaining competitive advantages from early deployment of e-business services to employees, customers, and other stakeholders, and of involving them in the "fine-tuning" phase of e-business application development [9].

Managing the IS Function

A radical shift is occurring in corporate computing—think of it as the recentralization of management. It's a step back toward the 1970s, when a data-processing manager could sit at a console and track all the technology assets of the corporation. Then came the 1980s and early 1990s. Departments got their own PCs and software; client/server networks sprang up all across companies.

Three things have happened in the past couple of years: The Internet boom inspired businesses to connect all those networks; companies put on their intranets essential applications without which their businesses could not function; and it became

Figure 12.9

The organizational structure of the IT function at Avnet Marshall.

Global Alliances Group

Electronic Commerce and Supply Chain Management Group

CIO
CEO

Computer/Communication Operations Group

Marketing and Visibility Initiatives Group

Enterprise Integration Group

Source: Adapted from Omar El Sawy, Arvind Malhotra, Sanjay Gosain, and Kerry Young, "IT-Intensive Value Innovation in the Electronic Economy: Insights from Marshall Industries," *MIS Quarterly*, September 1999, p. 325. Reprinted with permission from the *MIS Quarterly*.

apparent that maintaining PCs on a network is very, very expensive. Such changes create an urgent need for centralization [21].

Organizing IT

In the early years of computing, the development of large mainframe computers and telecommunications networks and terminals caused a **centralization** of computer hardware and software, databases, and information specialists at the corporate level of organizations. Next, the development of minicomputers and microcomputers accelerated a **downsizing** trend, which prompted a move back toward **decentralization** by many business firms. Distributed client/server networks at the corporate, department, workgroup, and team levels came into being. This promoted a shift of databases and information specialists to some departments, and the creation of *information centers* to support end user and workgroup computing.

Lately, the trend is to establish more centralized control over the management of the IS resources of a company, while still serving the strategic needs of its business units, especially their e-business and e-commerce initiatives. This has resulted in the development of hybrid structures with both centralized and decentralized e-business-focused components. See Figure 12.9.

Some companies spin off their information systems function into IS *subsidiaries* that offer IS services to external organizations as well as to their parent company. Recently, large companies have created or spun off their e-commerce and Internet-related business units or IT groups into separate ".com" companies or business units. Other corporations **outsource**, that is, turn over all or parts of their IS operations to outside contractors known as *systems integrators*. In addition, many companies are outsourcing software procurement and support to *application service providers* (ASPs), who provide and support business application and other software via the Internet and intranets to all of a company's employee workstations. Let's look at some real world examples.

Premiere, Monsanto, and Fleetwood: Using ASPs

Premiere Technologies, Inc.
IT leader: Douglas B. Hadaway, vice president of finance
Goal: Rescue a failing PeopleSoft ERP project without compromising core business efforts.
ASP: TransChannel LLC, Atlanta
Solution: Premiere turned the whole project over to the ASP to manage.

Result: "We're saving about $3 million over five years by giving the work to TransChannel," Hadaway says.

Monsanto Co.
IT leader: Kathryn Kissam, director of corporate branding and identity
Goal: Centralize Monsanto's vast, very distributed library of logos, images, and branding specifications into a single library that employees can access worldwide —and do it quickly.
ASP: Imation Corp., Oakdale, Minn.
Solution: Imation created and maintains the Monsanto Image Gallery, an application that lets any company intranet user search, sort, and use Monsanto's logos and images.
Result: "We save money because we don't have to commission new images with every new project or distribute new logo updates to every office in the world," Kissam says.

Fleetwood Retail Corp.
IT leader: Don Palmour, vice president of technology.
Goal: Deploy and manage an entire suite of Lotus Domino applications in Fleetwood's more than 200 mostly rural sales centers.
ASP: Interliant Inc., Purchase, N.Y.
Solution: Fleetwood bought the Domino licenses but turned everything else over to Interliant, which centrally manages the entire suite. Everything—including tape backup—is done in the ASP's central offices.
Result: "This was the only way we could ramp up that quickly. There's no question we get better service than we could provide ourselves," Palmour says [27].

Managing Application Development

Application development management involves managing activities such as systems analysis and design, prototyping, applications programming, project management, quality assurance, and system maintenance for all major e-business/IT development projects. Managing application development requires managing the activities of teams of systems analysts, software developers, and other IS professionals working on a variety of information systems development projects. In addition, some systems development groups have established *development centers* staffed with IS professionals. Their role is to evaluate new application development tools and to help information systems specialists use them to improve their application development efforts.

Managing IS Operations

IS operations management is concerned with the use of hardware, software, network, and personnel resources in the corporate or business unit **data centers** (computer centers) of an organization. Operational activities that must be managed include computer system operations, network management, production control, and production support.

Most operations management activities are being automated by the use of software packages for computer system performance management. These **system performance monitors** monitor the processing of computer jobs, help develop a planned schedule of computer operations that can optimize computer system performance, and produce detailed statistics that are invaluable for effective planning and control of computing capacity. Such information evaluates computer system utilization, costs, and performance. This evaluation provides information for capacity planning, production planning and control, and hardware/software acquisition planning. It is also used in quality assurance programs, which stress quality of services to business end users. See Figure 12.10.

System performance monitors also supply information needed by **chargeback systems** that allocate costs to users based on the information services rendered. All

Figure 12.10

A computer system performance monitor in action. The CA-Unicenter TNG package includes an Enterprise Management Portal module that helps IT specialists monitor and manage a variety of networked computer systems and operating systems.

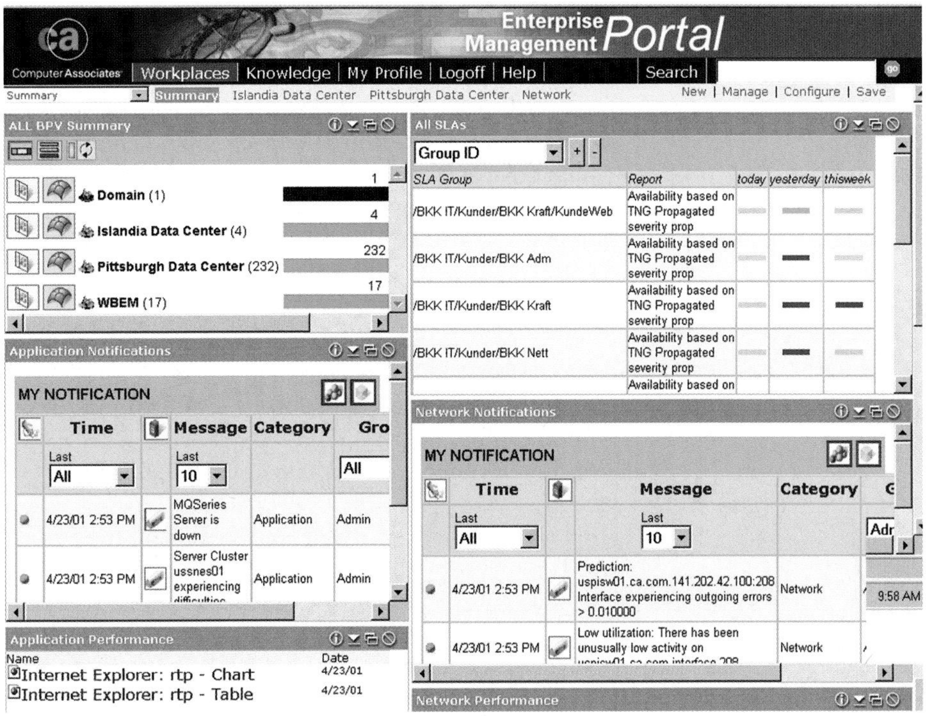

Source: Courtesy of Computer Associates International, Inc.

costs incurred are recorded, reported, allocated, and charged back to specific end user business units, depending on their use of system resources. When companies use this arrangement, the information services department becomes a service center whose costs are charged directly to business units, rather than being lumped with other administrative service costs and treated as an overhead cost.

Many performance monitors also feature **process control** capabilities. Such packages not only monitor but automatically control computer operations at large data centers. Some use built-in expert system modules based on knowledge gleaned from experts in the operations of specific computer systems and operating systems. These performance monitors provide more efficient computer operations than human-operated systems. They also enable "lights out" data centers at some companies, where computer systems are operated unattended, especially after normal business hours.

Human Resource Management of IT

The success or failure of an information services organization rests primarily on the quality of its people. Many computer-using firms consider recruiting, training, and retaining qualified IS personnel as one of their greatest challenges. Managing information services functions involves the management of managerial, technical, and clerical personnel. One of the most important jobs of information services managers is to recruit qualified personnel and to develop, organize, and direct the capabilities of existing personnel. Employees must be continually trained to keep up with the latest developments in a fast-moving and highly technical field. Employee job performances must be continually evaluated and outstanding performances rewarded with salary increases or promotions. Salary and wage levels must be set, and career paths must be designed so individuals can move to new jobs through promotion and transfer as they gain in seniority and expertise.

The CIO and Other IT Executives

The **chief information officer** (CIO) oversees all use of information technology in many companies, and brings them into alignment with strategic business goals. Thus, all traditional computer services, Internet technology, telecommunications network services, and other IS technology support services are the responsibility of this executive. Also, the CIO does not direct day-to-day information services activities. Instead, CIOs concentrate on business/IT planning and strategy. They also work with the CEO and other top executives to develop strategic uses of information technology in electronic business and commerce that help make the firm more competitive in the marketplace. Many companies have also filled the CIO position with executives from the business functions or units outside the IS field. Such CIOs emphasize that the chief role of information technology is to help a company meet its strategic business objectives.

Top IT Jobs: Requirements and Compensation

- **Chief technology officer**

Base salary range: $100,000 to $250,000-plus; varies by location
Bonus range: Up to 30% of salary

If you're second-in-command to the CIO or chief technology officer and you have years of applications development experience, your next move should be into the chief technology officer's spot. To land this job, you'll need to be a passionate problem-solver with a demonstrated record of reducing cycle time. "You have to talk in terms of 'Damn the torpedoes, let's get this straight into production,'" says Phil Schneidermeyer, an executive recruiter at Korn/Ferry International in Los Angeles.

- **E-commerce architect**

Base salary range: $120,000 to $200,000-plus; varies by location
Bonus range: Up to 20% of salary

If you know Java, Perl, C++, and CORBA and have experience in systems architecture, deep-pocketed companies are dying to have you work on their e-commerce sites. "Architects who can design the Internet solution from concept through implementation are probably the hottest thing going," says Heinz Bartesch, a recruiter at Professional Consulting Network Inc. (PCN) in San Francisco.

- **Technical team leader**

Base salary range: $100,000 to $200,000-plus; varies by location
Bonus range: Up to 20% of salary

Senior technical team leaders with good communication, project management, and leadership skills, as well as knowledge of Web languages and databases, are now worth their weight in gold.

- **Practice manager**

Base salary range: $80,000 to $200,000-plus; varies by location
Bonus range: Up to 20% of salary

If you've got a background in IT assessment and a pedigree in business development (MBA preferred), you can land a job as a point person for big projects. You'll need skills in IT operations and software assessment, as well as in marketing, staffing, budgeting, and building customer relationships [10].

Technology Management

The management of rapidly changing technology is important to any organization. Changes in information technology, like the rise of the PC, client/server networks, and the Internet and intranets, have come swiftly and dramatically and are expected to continue into the future. Developments in information systems technology have had, and will continue to have, a major impact on the operations, costs, management work environment, and competitive position of many organizations.

Thus, all information technologies must be managed as a technology platform for integrated e-business and e-commerce systems. Such technologies include the

Internet, intranets, and a variety of electronic commerce and collaboration technologies, as well as integrated enterprise software for customer relationship management, enterprise resource planning, and supply chain management. In many companies, technology management is the primary responsibility of a *chief technology officer* (CTO) who is in charge of all information technology planning and deployment.

Managing User Services

Teams and workgroups of business professionals commonly use PC workstations, software packages, and the Internet, intranets, and other networks to develop and apply information technology to their work activities. Thus many companies have responded by creating **user services,** or *client services,* functions to support and manage end user and workgroup computing.

End user services provide both opportunities and problems for business unit managers. For example, some firms create an *information center* group staffed with user liaison specialists, or Web-enabled intranet help desks. IS specialists with titles such as user consultant, account executive, or business analyst may also be assigned to end user work groups. These specialists perform a vital role by troubleshooting problems, gathering and communicating information, coordinating educational efforts, and helping business professionals with application development.

In addition to these measures, most organizations still establish and enforce policies for the acquisition of hardware and software by end users and business units. This ensures their compatibility with company standards for hardware, software, and network connectivity. See Figure 12.11. Also important is the development of applications with proper security and quality controls to promote correct performance and safeguard the integrity of corporate and departmental networks and databases.

Figure 12.11 The benefits derived from company IT standards.

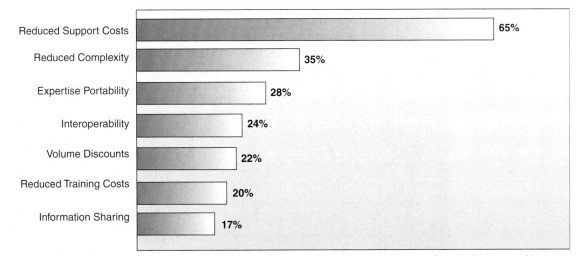

Source: Adapted in part from Jan Rowell, "Getting Control of TCO." Special Advertising Supplement, *Computerworld,* November 17, 1997.

Global e-Business Technology Management

The International Dimension

Whether they are in Berlin or Bombay, Kuala Lumpur or Kansas, San Francisco or Seoul, companies around the globe are developing new models to operate competitively in a digital economy. These models are structured, yet agile; global, yet local; and they concentrate on maximizing the risk-adjusted return from both knowledge and technology assets [16].

Thus, international dimensions have become a vital part of managing an e-business enterprise in the internetworked global economies and markets of today. Whether you become a manager in a large corporation or the owner of a small business, you will be affected by international business developments, and deal in some way with people, products, or services whose origin is not from your home country.

Analyzing DHL and ApplianceWare

Read the Real World Case on DHL and ApplianceWare on the next page. We can learn a lot about the challenges and opportunities facing companies involved in global e-business. See Figure 12.12.

Companies like DHL Worldwide Express and ApplianceWare are implementing global systems development strategies by establishing development centers around the world that perform development work on e-business projects with U.S. counterparts in a shared team environment. Doing systems development in multiple time zones enables companies to accelerate the development work on e-business projects where time to market is critical to success. The lower turnover rates and salaries in many foreign countries are also driving this trend, as well as the high level of development skills available, and the necessity to tailor e-business applications to country-specific requirements. Both companies emphasize that global systems development strategies require significant investments in communications, training, and developing international managers who understand both the global business and its IT infrastructure requirements.

Figure 12.12

Colum Joyce is a global e-business strategy manager at DHL Worldwide Express in Brussels. DHL is committed to a global systems development strategy.

Source: Jock Fistick.

DHL Worldwide Express and ApplianceWare:
Challenges of Global Systems Development

For global companies developing business-critical applications, time to market is of the essence, particularly as they launch e-business initiatives. Because global companies have offices in multiple time zones, they have learned that they can expand the number of development hours available each day by establishing development centers around the world and staffing them with people who work in shared environments with U.S. and other global teams.

DHL Worldwide

One company that's doing so is San Francisco–based DHL Worldwide Express Inc., which has opened centers in the U.K. and in Malaysia, India, and other parts of Asia. The international delivery giant is able to take advantage of time differences between these locations and California to create an extended workday. More important, it's able to put more bodies on problems at a time when IT hiring in the United States isn't easy.

"For us, large-scale development is not a hothouse environment, it's an everyday reality," says Colum Joyce, a global e-business strategy manager based in DHL's offices in Brussels. That means establishing development facilities around the world, as well as working with outsourcers where necessary, he says. These realities, combined with the lower turnover rates and salaries in many foreign countries—the average salary for a skilled programmer in India, for example, is about $30,000, according to Niven—are driving global companies to open offshore facilities.

DHL's offshore developers tailor e-business applications to country-specific requirements and even take lead roles in some development efforts, such as a wireless service applications project that's underway in Europe and Asia.

Joyce says the company looks at several factors when hiring in these locations, including the technical and linguistic skills of local workers, long-term business viability, and knowledge transfer. "A mastery of English is a key skill set, as it is the operating language of all cross-group communication for all development, whether it be verbal, hard copy, or electronic communication," Joyce says.

Though hiring isn't easy in these global locations, Joyce says there are now advantages to hiring outside the United States for development work. "PC skills are universal now, and I would say that it is actually easier to find cost-efficient development skill sets that provide a good fit to our business needs outside the United States, than in it," Joyce says. "We find less of a tendency toward flavor-of-the-month technologism outside the United States.

"It is not so much the knowledge but the willingness and flexibility to learn that is important in hiring global IT workers," Joyce explains. "In an incredibly dynamic environment, it is the attitude, rather than gross development capability, that counts the most in recruitment." Nonetheless, Joyce acknowledges that success in such endeavors depends heavily on adopting market standards in technology infrastructures and on ensuring that there's continual communication among development teams in disparate locations. To that end, DHL puts a great deal of effort into developing what Joyce calls "hybrid managers" who are heavily immersed in both IT and business.

"This has been a process we have engaged in for over 15 years," Joyce says. "The boundaries are really transparent now, and managers and personnel are cross-comfortable with the global business and its supporting infrastructure."

ApplianceWare

Like other global companies, Fremont, California–based ApplianceWare Inc. looked outside the United States when it couldn't find the development talent it needed here. "Our location in Silicon Valley places us in the most competitive software environment on the planet. The lack of available talent and the exorbitant prices mean we can't afford to expand development operations here," says ApplianceWare President Stacy Kenworthy.

Initially, ApplianceWare decided to open its own facilities in Minsk, Belarus, to take advantage of a sizable pool of talented developers and a 10-hour time difference that, when complemented by the West Coast time zone, would increase the number of hours the company could work on projects. However, says Kenworthy, the company found that Belarus government restrictions on private enterprise would make doing so prohibitive. ApplianceWare's solution was to partner with SamSolutions, a development firm in Minsk.

ApplianceWare now considers SamSolutions to be part of its business. Therefore, it worked with the developer to appoint a manager to oversee work and handle translation issues between Fremont and Belarus. The company also frequently sends an IT manager who works in Denmark to Minsk to ensure that processes and delivery are on track.

There are cost advantages to doing development in offshore locations, but they shouldn't be a primary driver, says Kenworthy. And those savings can be offset by additional travel and communication costs, he says. "You need to make substantial investments in communications," he says. "And there's no getting away from face-to-face contact, so there's airfare, investments in process creation, investments in the learning curve, and other front-end work. You're basically changing your organizational structure."

Case Study Questions

1. Is global systems development a good business strategy? Why or why not?

2. Do you approve of the global systems development strategy of DHL? Why or why not?

3. What are the benefits and limitations of ApplianceWare's international systems development initiative?

Source: Adapted from Kym Gilhooly, "The Staff That Never Sleeps," *Computerworld*, June 25, 2001, p. 66. Reprinted by permission.

Figure 12.13

The major dimensions of global e-business technology management.

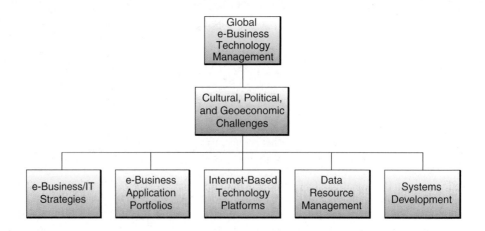

Global e-Business Technology Management

Figure 12.13 illustrates the major dimensions of the job of managing global information technology that we will cover in this section. Notice that all global IT activities must be adjusted to take into account the cultural, political, and geoeconomic challenges that exist in the international business community. Developing appropriate e-business and IT strategies for the global marketplace should be the first step in **global e-business technology management.** Once that is done, end user and IS managers can move on to developing the portfolio of applications needed to support e-business/IT strategies; the hardware, software, and Internet-based technology platforms to support those applications; the data resource management methods to provide necessary databases; and finally the systems development projects that will produce the global information systems required.

Cultural, Political, and Geoeconomic Challenges

"Business as usual" is not good enough in global business operations. The same holds true for global e-business technology management. There are too many cultural, political, and geoeconomic (geographic and economic) realities that must be confronted in order for a business to succeed in global markets. As we have just said, global e-business technology management must focus on developing global e-business IT strategies and managing global e-business application portfolios, Internet technologies, platforms, databases, and systems development projects. But managers must also accomplish that from a perspective and through methods that take into account the cultural, political, and geoeconomic differences that exist when doing business internationally.

For example, a major **political challenge** is that many countries have rules regulating or prohibiting transfer of data across their national boundaries (transborder data flows), especially personal information such as personnel records. Others severely restrict, tax, or prohibit imports of hardware and software. Still others have local content laws that specify the portion of the value of a product that must be added in that country if it is to be sold there. Other countries have reciprocal trade agreements that require a business to spend part of the revenue they earn in a country in that nation's economy [28].

Geoeconomic challenges in global business and IT refer to the effects of geography on the economic realities of international business activities. The sheer physical distances involved are still a major problem, even in this day of Internet telecommunications and jet travel. For example, it may still take too long to fly in specialists when IT problems occur in a remote site. It is still difficult to communicate in real time across the world's 24 time zones. It is still difficult to get good-quality telephone and telecommunications service in many countries. There are still problems finding the job skills required in some countries, or enticing specialists from other countries to live and work there. Finally, there are still problems (and opportunities) in the great differences in the cost of living and labor costs in various countries. All of these geoeconomic challenges must be addressed when developing a company's global business and IT strategies.

Cultural challenges facing global business and IT managers include differences in languages, cultural interests, religions, customs, social attitudes, and political philosophies. Obviously, global IT managers must be trained and sensitized to such cultural differences before they are sent abroad or brought into a corporation's home country. Other cultural challenges include differences in work styles and business relationships. For example, should one take one's time to avoid mistakes, or hurry to get something done early? Should one go it alone or work cooperatively? Should the most experienced person lead, or should leadership be shared? The answers to such questions depend on the culture you are in and highlight the cultural differences that might exist in the global workplace. Let's take a look at a real world example involving the Internet and electronic commerce.

Challenges in the European Union

The non-European student might imagine that the European Union (EU)—a highly sophisticated "single market" embracing 370 million citizens in 15 countries—is ideal ground for a fertile and orderly multinational marketplace in e-commerce. But most Europeans would greet that assumption with a cynical shrug.

The EU's worst-kept secret is that it is a continent of thinly disguised (and sometimes wholly undisguised) national protectionism; of no common language; of widely differing legal and consumer cultures and attitudes toward privacy; and of elaborate trade legislation arrived at by grindingly slow negotiation and imposed with varying degrees of vigor in different member states.

But it would be wrong to imply that there is no hope for a coordinated European e-commerce regime. In fact there is everything to play for, and the game has barely begun [34].

From Paris, Texas, to Paris, France, information technology experts believe that the European e-commerce market is set to blossom over the next five years. But is business ready for Europe's imminent e-revolution? European Internet use is growing at an annual rate of 99 percent, and companies will have to act quickly to satisfy the demand that will result from improved technologies and increased Internet access. European e-commerce will be further boosted over the next few years by the use of the Euro currency.

However, Americans who want to lure European buyers to their websites will have to jump many hurdles they don't see in the United States. One hindrance is the tangle of cross-border regulations governing commerce. E-commerce legal specialist Holly Towle, a partner at Washington law firm Preston Gates & Ellis LLP, points out that many companies wrongly assume that EU directives are the equivalent of U.S. federal legislation. Towle cites the EU Distance Contract Directive as a case in point. "Under the EU rule, a company could deliver an absolutely perfect product after making full disclosure of all elements required by the rule, and still the EU customer could return it for any or no reason," she says. "That concept simply does not exist in the U.S. and should cause many sellers to refuse to incur the costs, delays, and risks of shipping products into the EU" [24].

Global e-Business Strategies

Figure 12.14 illustrates that many firms are moving toward **transnational strategies** in which they integrate their global e-business activities through close cooperation and interdependence among their international subsidiaries and their corporate headquarters. Businesses are moving away from (1) multinational strategies where foreign subsidiaries operate autonomously; (2) international strategies in

Figure 12.14 Companies operating internationally are moving toward transnational e-business strategies. Note some of the chief differences between international, global, and transnational business and IT strategies.

Comparing Global e-Business Strategies		
International	**Global**	**Transnational**
• Autonomous operations.	• Global sourcing.	• Virtual e-business operations via global alliances.
• Region specific.	• Multiregional.	
• Vertical integration.	• Horizontal integration.	• World markets and mass customization.
• Specific customers.	• Some transparency of customers and production.	
• Captive manufacturing.		• Global e-commerce and customer service.
• Customer segmentation and dedication by region and plant.	• Some cross regionalization.	• Transparent manufacturing.
		• Global supply chain and logistics.
		• Dynamic resource management.
Information Technology Characteristics		
• Stand-alone systems.	• Regional decentralization.	• Logically consolidated, physically distributed, Internet connected.
• Decentralized/no standards.	• Interface dependent.	
• Heavy reliance on interfaces.	• Some consolidation of applications and use of common systems.	• Common global data resources.
• Multiple systems, high redundancy and duplication of services and operations.	• Reduced duplication of operations.	• Integrated global enterprise systems.
	• Some worldwide IT standards.	• Internet, intranet, extranet Web-based applications.
• Lack of common systems and data.		• Transnational IT policies and standards.

Source: Adapted and reprinted from Michael Mische, "Transnational Architecture: A Reengineering Approach," *Information Systems Management* (New York: Auerbach Publications), Winter 1995, p. 18. © 1995 Research Institute of America. Used with permission; and Nicholas Vitalari and James Wetherbe, "Emerging Best Practices in Global Systems Development," in *Global Information Technology and Systems Management*, Prashant Palvia et al., editors (Marietta, GA: Ivy League Publishing, 1996), p. 336.

which foreign subsidiaries are autonomous but are dependent on headquarters for new processes, products, and ideas; or (3) global strategies, where a company's worldwide operations are closely managed by corporate headquarters [26].

In the transnational approach, a business depends heavily on its information systems and Internet technologies to help it integrate its global business activities. Instead of having independent IS units at its subsidiaries, or even a centralized IS operation directed from its headquarters, a transnational business tries to develop an integrated and cooperative worldwide hardware, software, and Internet-based architecture for its IT platform. Figure 12.15 illustrates how transnational business and IT strategies were implemented by global companies [35].

Global e-Business Applications

The applications of information technology developed by global companies depend on their e-business and IT strategies and their expertise and experience in IT. However, their IT applications also depend on a variety of **global business drivers,** that is, business requirements caused by the nature of the industry and its competitive or environmental forces. One example would be companies like airlines or hotel chains that have global customers, that is, customers who travel widely or have global operations. Such companies will need global e-business capabilities for online transaction processing so they can provide fast, convenient service to their customers or face losing them to their competitors. The economies of scale provided by global e-business operations are other business drivers that require the support of global IT applications. Figure 12.16 summarizes some of the business requirements that make global e-business a competitive necessity [15].

Of course, many global IT applications, particularly finance, accounting, and office applications, have been in operation for many years. For example, most

Source: Adapted from Nicholas Vitalari and James Wetherbe, "Emerging Best Practices in Global System Development," in *Global Information Technology and Systems Management*, Prashant Palvia et al., editors (Marietta, GA: Ivy League Publishing, 1996), pp. 338–42.

Figure 12.15	Examples of how transnational business and IT strategies were implemented by global companies.

Tactic	Global Alliances	Global Sourcing and Logistics	Global Customer Service
Examples	British Airways / US Air KLM / Northwest Qantas / American	Benetton	American Express
IT Environment	Global network (online reservation system)	Global network, EPOS terminals in 4,000 stores, CAD/CAM in central manufacturing, robots and laser scanner in their automated warehouse	Global network linked from local branches and local merchants to the customer database and medical or legal referrals database
Results	• Coordination of schedules • Code sharing • Coordination of flights • Co-ownership	• Produce 2,000 sweaters per hour using CAD/CAM • Quick response (in stores in 10 days) • Reduced inventories (just-in-time)	• Worldwide access to funds • "Global Assist" hotline • Emergency credit card replacement • 24-hour customer service

multinational companies have global financial budgeting and cash management systems, and office automation applications such as fax and e-mail systems. However, as global operations expand and global competition heats up, there is increasing pressure for companies to install global e-commerce and e-business applications for their customers and suppliers. Examples include global e-commerce websites and customer service systems for customers and global supply chain management systems for suppliers. In the past, such systems relied almost exclusively on privately constructed or government-owned telecommunications networks. But the explosive business use of the Internet, intranets, and extranets for electronic commerce has made such applications much more feasible for global companies.

Figure 12.16	**Business Drivers for Global e-Business**
These are some of the business reasons driving global e-business applications.	• **Global customers.** Customers are people who may travel anywhere or companies with global operations. Global IT can help provide fast, convenient service. • **Global products.** Products are the same throughout the world or are assembled by subsidiaries throughout the world. Global IT can help manage worldwide marketing and quality control. • **Global operations.** Parts of a production or assembly process are assigned to subsidiaries based on changing economic or other conditions. Only global IT can support such geographic flexibility. • **Global resources.** The use and cost of common equipment, facilities, and people are shared by subsidiaries of a global company. Global IT can keep track of such shared resources. • **Global collaboration.** The knowledge and expertise of colleagues in a global company can be quickly accessed, shared, and organized to support individual or group efforts. Only global IT can support such enterprise collaboration.

Gillette and Nypro: Global ERP Issues

For a company like the Gillette Co. in Boston, consistency of product—and therefore consistency of operations—is of paramount importance. Gillette installed ERP applications from SAP AG and PeopleSoft Inc. because they automatically create reports in different languages. "We select vendors who can satisfy global needs," explains CIO Pat Zilvitis. Although development work is done in Boston, deployment and screen labeling is handled locally to overcome language barriers.

Other companies approach globalization strategies differently, allowing for more decentralized control where factories produce products for local customers. Nypro Inc., a plastics molding company based in Clinton, Massachusetts, operates in 12 countries and uses its global presence as a selling point. To meet the needs of global customers, Nypro runs an ERP system from Chicago-based System Software Associates called eBPCS.

Building plants in China and providing them with networked ERP systems is the latest project for Jay Leader, Nypro's director of application development. He points out that it's no more feasible for him to modify code written in Chinese than it is to have Chinese employees operate systems in English. He says he believes that Internet-based applications, with their capacity to personalize what each user sees, represent the best hope for localization of content, because one system can personalize content and data sources for each user. For ERP, localization is more difficult because the systems aren't meant to be flexible. Nypro, however, puts control over ERP data extraction and manipulation in local hands [30].

Global IT Platforms

The management of technology platforms (also called the technology infrastructure) is another major dimension of global IT management—that is, managing the hardware, software, data resources, Internet, intranet, extranet sites, and computing facilities that support global e-business operations. The management of a global IT platform is not only technically complex but also has major political and cultural implications.

For example, hardware choices are difficult in some countries because of high prices, high tariffs, import restrictions, long lead times for government approvals, lack of local service or spare parts, and lack of documentation tailored to local conditions. Software choices can also present unique problems. Software packages developed in Europe may be incompatible with American or Asian versions, even when purchased from the same hardware vendor. Well-known U.S. software packages may be unavailable because there is no local distributor, or because the software publisher refuses to supply markets that disregard software licensing and copyright agreements [15].

Establishing computing facilities internationally is another global challenge. Companies with global business operations usually establish or contract with systems integrators for additional data centers in their subsidiaries in other countries. These data centers meet local and regional computing needs, and even help balance global computing workloads through communications satellite links. However, offshore data centers can pose major problems in headquarter's support, hardware and software acquisition, maintenance, and security. That's why many global companies turn to application service providers or systems integrators like EDS or IBM to manage their overseas operations.

The Internet as a Global IT Platform

What makes the Internet and the World Wide Web so important for international business? This interconnected matrix of computers, information, and networks that reaches tens of millions of users in over one hundred countries is a business environment free of traditional boundaries and limits. Linking to an online global infrastructure offers companies unprecedented potential for expanding markets, reducing costs, and improving profit margins at a price that is typically a small percentage of the corporate communications budget. The Internet provides an interactive channel for direct communication and data exchange with customers, suppliers, distributors, manufacturers, product developers, financial backers, information providers—in fact, with all parties involved in a given business venture [6].

So the Internet and the World Wide Web have now become vital components in international business and commerce. Within a few years, the Internet, with its interconnected network of thousands of networks of computers and databases, has established itself as a technology platform free of many traditional international boundaries and limits. By connecting their businesses to this online global infrastructure, companies can expand their markets, reduce communications and distribution costs, and improve their profit margins without massive cost outlays for new telecommunications facilities. Figure 12.17 outlines key considerations for global e-commerce websites.

The Internet, along with its related intranet and extranet technologies, provides a low-cost interactive channel for communications and data exchange with employees, customers, suppliers, distributors, manufacturers, product developers, financial backers, information providers, and so on. In fact, all parties involved can use the Internet and other related networks to communicate and collaborate to bring a business venture to its successful completion [6]. However, as Figure 12.18 illustrates, much work needs to be done to bring secure Internet access and electronic commerce to more people in more countries. But the trend is clearly on continued expansion of the Internet as it becomes a pervasive IT platform for global business.

Global Data Access Issues

The British and European legislative framework for e-commerce is still in its infancy, and there are large areas yet to be tackled. These include the full gamut of data protection and privacy issues. Under the European Convention on Human Rights, for example, employees are entitled to e-mail privacy; yet employers are regarded in law as the publishers of their employees' e-mails, and—as test cases against companies such as Norwich Union P.L.C. and British Gas have established—can be held legally responsible for their content [34].

Global data access issues have been a subject of political controversy and technology barriers in global business operations for many years, but have become more visible with the growth of the Internet and the pressures of e-commerce. A major example is the issue of **transborder data flows** (TDF), in which business data flow across international borders over the telecommunications networks of global information

Figure 12.17

Key questions for companies establishing global Internet websites.

Key Questions for Global Websites
● Will you have to develop a new navigational logic to accommodate cultural preferences?
● What content will you translate, and what content will you create from scratch to address regional competitors or products that differ from those in the United States?
● Should your multilingual effort be an adjunct to your main site, or will you make it a separate site, perhaps with a country-specific domain name?
● What kinds of traditional and new media advertising will you have to do in each country to draw traffic to your site?
● Will your site get so many hits that you'll need to set up a server in a local country?
● What are the legal ramifications of having your website targeted at a particular country, such as laws on competitive behavior, treatment of children, or privacy?

Source: Adapted from Alice Laplante, "Global Boundaries.com," Global Innovators Series, *Computerworld*, October 6, 1997, p. 17. Copyright 1997 by Computerworld, Inc., Framingham, MA 01701. Reprinted from *Computerworld*.

Figure 12.18

Current and projected numbers of Internet users by world region.

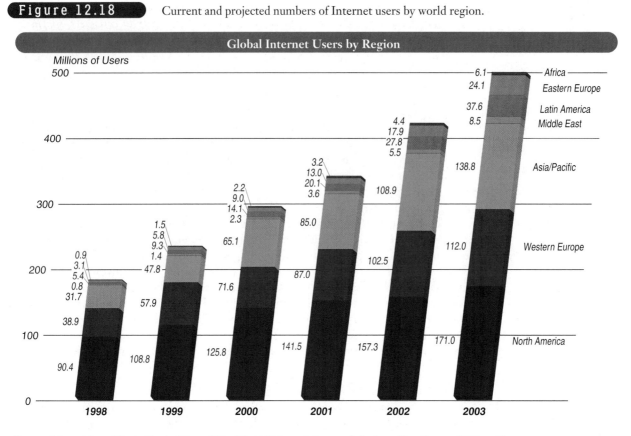

Global Internet Users by Region

Source: Adapted from Martin VanderWeyer, "The World Debates," *Strategy & Business*, First Quarter 2000, p. 69.

systems. Many countries view TDF as violating their national sovereignty because transborder data flows avoid customs duties and regulations for the import or export of goods and services. Others view transborder data flows as violating their laws to protect the local IT industry from competition, or their labor regulations for protecting local jobs. In many cases, the data flow business issues that seem especially politically sensitive are those that affect the movement out of a country of personal data in e-commerce and human resource applications.

Many countries, especially those in the European Union, may view transborder data flows as a violation of their privacy legislation since, in many cases, data about individuals are being moved out of the country without stringent privacy safeguards. For example, Figure 12.19 outlines the key provisions of a data privacy agreement between the United States and the European Union. The agreement exempts U.S. companies engaging in international e-commerce from EU data privacy sanctions if

Figure 12.19

Key data privacy provisions of the agreement to protect the privacy of consumers in e-commerce transactions between the U.S. and the European Union.

U.S. – EU Data Privacy Requirements
● Notice of purpose and use of data collected
● Ability to opt out of third-party distribution of data
● Access for consumers to their information
● Adequate security, data integrity, and enforcement provisions

Source: Adapted from Patrick Thibodeau, "Europe and U.S. Agree on Data Rules," *Computerworld*, March 20, 2000, p. 6. Copyright 2000 by Computerworld, Inc., Framingham, MA 01701. Reprinted from *Computerworld*.

they join a self-regulatory program that provides EU consumers with basic information about and control over how their personal data are used. Thus, the agreement is said to provide a "safe harbor" for such companies from the requirements of the EU's Data Privacy Directive, which bans the transfer of personal information on EU citizens to countries that do not have adequate data privacy protection [32].

iXL Enterprises: Global e-Commerce Data Issues	E-commerce applications are, by default, accessible to almost anyone in the world who has Internet access. Their extensive reach doesn't, however, automatically translate into global business. Victoria Bracewell-Short, who leads the globalization practice at e-commerce consultancy iXL Enterprises Inc. in Atlanta, says clients often ask her, "Isn't this just a translation or content management issue?" But companies that treat it as such can run into problems. Asking for information as basic as a name, a mailing address, or an e-mail address during initial registration can raise hackles in countries where citizens are nervous about giving out personal data.

"Americans take it for granted that when they log on a site, it recognizes and displays their preferences," says Bracewell-Short. But in Germany, she points out, there are much more stringent regulations governing how e-commerce sites gather customer data. For example, using cookies to collect customer preference data without telling the user is illegal there, so companies that hope to build online relationships with customers must adapt their technology plans accordingly [30].

Internet Access Issues

The Paris-based organization Reporters Without Borders (RSF) reports that there are 45 countries that "restrict their citizens' access to the Internet." At its most fundamental, the struggle between Internet censorship and openness at the national level revolves around three main means: controlling the conduits, filtering the flows, and punishing the purveyors. In countries such as Burma, Libya, North Korea, Syria, and the countries of Central Asia and the Caucasus, Internet access is either banned or subject to tight limitations through government-controlled ISPs, says the RSF [33].

Figure 12.20 outlines the restrictions to public Internet access by the governments of 20 countries deemed most restrictive by the Paris-based Reporters Without Borders (RSF). See their website at www.rsf.fr.

So the Internet has become a global battleground over public access to data and information at business and private sites on the World Wide Web. Of course this becomes a business issue because restrictive access policies severely inhibit the growth of e-commerce with such countries. Most of the rest of the world has decided

Figure 12.20

Countries that restrict or forbid Internet access by their citizens.

Global Government Restrictions on Internet Access

- **High Government Access Fees**
  Kazakhstan, Kyrgyzstan
- **Government Monitored Access**
  China, Iran, Saudi Arabia, Azerbaijan, Uzbekistan
- **Government Filtered Access**
  Belarus, Cuba, Iraq, Tunisia, Sierra Leone, Tajikistan, Turkmenistan, Vietnam
- **No Public Access Allowed**
  Burma, Libya, North Korea, Sudan

Source: Data from Reporters Without Borders in Stewart Taggart, "Censor Census," *Business 2.0*, March 2000, pp. 358–59.

that restricting Internet access is not a viable policy, and in fact, would hurt their countries' opportunities for economic growth and prosperity. Instead, national and international efforts are being made to rate and filter Internet content deemed inappropriate or criminal, such as websites for child pornography or terrorism. In any event, countries that significantly restrict Internet access are also choosing to restrict their participation in the growth of electronic commerce [33].

> *To RSF and others, these countries' rulers face a lose-lose struggle against the Information Age. By denying or limiting Internet access, they stymie a major engine of economic growth. But by easing access, they expose their citizenry to ideas potentially destabilizing to the status quo. Either way, many people will get access to the electronic information they want. "In Syria, for example, people go to Lebanon for the weekend to retrieve their e-mail," says Virginie Locussol, RSF's desk officer for the Middle East and North Africa [33].*

Global Systems Development

Just imagine the challenges of developing efficient, effective, and responsive applications for business end users domestically. Then multiply that by the number of countries and cultures that may use a global e-business system. That's the challenge of managing global systems development. Naturally, there are conflicts over local versus global system requirements, and difficulties in agreeing on common system features such as multilingual user interfaces and flexible design standards. And all of this effort must take place in an environment that promotes involvement and "ownership" of a system by local end users. Thus, one IT manager estimates:

> *It takes 5 to 10 times more time to reach an understanding and agreement on system requirements and deliverables when the users and developers are in different countries. This is partially explained by travel requirements and language and cultural differences, but technical limitations also contribute to the problem [15].*

Other systems development issues arise from disturbances caused by systems implementation and maintenance activities. For example: "An interruption during a third shift in New York City will present midday service interruptions in Tokyo." Another major development issue relates to the trade-offs between developing one system that can run on multiple computer and operating system platforms, or letting each local site customize the software for its own platform [15]. See Figure 12.21.

Figure 12.21

The global use of information technology depends on international systems development efforts.

Source: Michael Yamishita/Corbis.

Other important global systems development issues are concerned with global standardization of data definitions. Common data definitions are necessary for sharing data among the parts of an international business. Differences in language, culture, and technology platforms can make global data standardization quite difficult. For example, a sale may be called "an 'order booked' in the United Kingdom, an 'order scheduled' in Germany, and an 'order produced' in France" [28]. However, businesses are moving ahead to standardize data definitions and structures. By moving their subsidiaries into data modeling and database design, they hope to develop a global data architecture that supports their global business objectives.

Systems Development Strategies

Several strategies can be used to solve some of the systems development problems that arise in global IT. First is transforming an application used by the home office into a global application. However, often the system used by a subsidiary that has the best version of an application will be chosen for global use. Another approach is setting up a *multinational development team* with key people from several subsidiaries to ensure that the system design meets the needs of local sites as well as corporate headquarters.

A third approach is called *parallel development*. That's because parts of the system are assigned to different subsidiaries and the home office to develop at the same time, based on the expertise and experience at each site. Another approach is the concept of *centers of excellence*. In this approach, an entire system may be assigned for development to a particular subsidiary based on their expertise in the business or technical dimensions needed for successful development. Obviously, all of these approaches require development team collaboration and managerial oversight to meet the global needs of a business. So, global systems development teams are making heavy use of the Internet, intranets, groupware, and other electronic collaboration technologies [15].

Guy Carpenter & Co.: Global Systems Development

Guy Carpenter & Co., a $450 million New York reinsurance company, outsourced development of a Web-based insurance brokerage system to PRT Group Ltd., which operates out of Bridgetown, Barbados. "We have half the systems development team on-site in New York, and half the people in Barbados," said John Gropper, CIO at Guy Carpenter. The two groups are connected via a high-speed communications link, and Barbados is a four-hour flight from New York. With this kind of project management and communication in place, "there's very little difference in executing a project on the other side of the world versus executing it on the other side of the street," says outsourcing consultant Chris Kizzier.

PRT Group is just a short stroll from a sun-drenched, white-sand Caribbean beach, housed in a 55,000-square-foot software development center, staffed by about 200 English-speaking IT workers from India, Jamaica, Malaysia, the United Kingdom, and elsewhere around the globe. They work on software development and maintenance projects for U.S. clients, including J.P. Morgan & Co. and Prudential Insurance Company of America, which have both invested in the company, and Travelers Corp. and Pfizer Inc.

Big factors contributing to the growth of global systems development team projects include the ever-increasing speed and reliability of communications technology and better project-management discipline. "With advancements in communications and the Internet, the world has shrunk down to the size of a pea, and the fact that you might be 9,000 miles away is irrelevant once you put the right project management disciplines in place," says Kizzier [18, 19].

Summary

- **Managers and IT.** E-business technologies are changing the distribution, relationships, resources, and responsibilities of managers. That is, IT is helping to eliminate layers of management, enabling more collaborative forms of management, providing managers with significant information technology resources, and confronting managers with major e-business and e-commerce challenges.

- **IS Performance.** Information systems are not being used effectively or efficiently by many organizations. The experiences of successful organizations reveal that the basic ingredient of high-quality information system performance is extensive and meaningful management and user involvement in the governance and development of IT applications. Thus, managers may serve on executive IT groups and create IS management functions within their business units.

- **The e-Business Organization.** The organizational structure and roles of e-business companies are undergoing major changes as they strive to become agile, customer focused, value-driven enterprises. Figure 12.4 summarizes the major characteristics of the e-business organization compared to the structure and roles of a previous organization model.

- **e-Business Technology Management.** Managing IT in an e-business company can be viewed as having three major components: (1) managing the joint development and implementation of e-business and IT strategies, (2) managing the development of e-business applications and the research and implementation of new information technologies, and (3) managing IT processes, professionals, and subunits within a company's IT orga-

nization and IS function. Refer to Figures 12.6 and 12.7, which illustrate components and examples of e-business technology management and strategic planning.

- **Managing Global IT.** The international dimensions of managing global e-business technologies include dealing with cultural, political, and geoeconomic challenges posed by various countries; developing appropriate business and IT strategies for the global marketplace; and developing a portfolio of global e-business and e-commerce applications and an Internet-based technology platform to support them. In addition, data access methods have to be developed and systems development projects managed to produce the global e-business applications that are required to compete successfully in the global marketplace. See Figure 12.13.

- **Global e-Business and IT Strategies and Issues.** Many businesses are becoming global companies and moving toward transnational e-business strategies in which they integrate the global business activities of their subsidiaries and headquarters. This requires that they develop a global IT platform, that is, an integrated worldwide hardware, software, and Internet-based network architecture. Global companies are increasingly using the Internet and related technologies as a major component of this IT platform to develop and deliver global IT applications that meet their unique global business requirements. Global IT and end user managers must deal with limitations on the availability of hardware and software, restrictions on transborder data flows, Internet access, and movement of personal data, and difficulties with developing common data definitions and system requirements.

Key Terms and Concepts

These are the key terms and concepts of this chapter. The page number of their first explanation is in parentheses.

1. Application development management (430)
2. Centralization or decentralization of IT (429)
3. Chargeback systems (430)
4. Chief information officer (431)
5. Chief technology officer (433)
6. Cultural, political, and geoeconomic challenges (436)
7. Data center (430)
8. Downsizing (429)
9. E-business organization (423)
10. E-business planning (426)
11. Global business drivers (438)
12. Global e-business technology management (436)
    a. E-business applications (438)
    b. E-business/IT strategies (437)
    c. Data access issues (441)
    d. IT platforms (440)
    e. Systems development issues (445)
13. Human resource management of IT (431)
14. Information systems performance (430)
15. Information technology architecture (428)
16. Internet access issues (443)
17. Internet as a global IT platform (440)
18. Management impact of e-business technologies (423)
19. Management involvement in IT (428)
20. Managing e-business technologies (432)

21. Managing the IS function (428)

22. Operations management (420)

23. Outsourcing IS operations (429)

24. Spinning off IT business units (429)

25. System performance
monitor (430)

26. Technology management (426)

27. Transborder data flows (441)

28. Transnational strategy (437)

29. User services (433)

Review Quiz

Match one of the key terms and concepts listed previously with one of the brief examples or definitions that follow. Try to find the best fit for the answers that seem to fit more than one term or concept. Defend your choices.

____ 1. Managers now have a lot of information processing power and responsibility for the use of e-business technologies.

____ 2. Information systems have not been used efficiently or effectively.

____ 3. An executive IT council is an example.

____ 4. E-business and e-commerce processes affect organizational roles and structures.

____ 5. Managing e-business/IT planning and the IS function within a company.

____ 6. Managing application development, data center operations, and user services are examples.

____ 7. Many IT organizations have centralized and decentralized units.

____ 8. Managing the creation and implementation of new e-business applications.

____ 9. End users need liaison, consulting, and training services.

____ 10. Planning and controlling data center operations.

____ 11. Corporate locations for computer system operations.

____ 12. Rapidly changing technological developments must be anticipated, identified, and implemented.

____ 13. Recruiting and developing IT professionals.

____ 14. The executive responsible for strategic e-business/IT planning and management.

____ 15. The executive in charge of researching and implementing new information technologies.

____ 16. Software that helps monitor and control computer systems in a data center.

____ 17. The cost of IS services may be allocated back to end users.

____ 18. Many business firms are replacing their mainframe systems with networked PCs and servers.

____ 19. Using outside contractors to provide and manage IS operations.

____ 20. Companies may create independent IT or e-commerce business units.

____ 21. Managing IT to support a company's international e-business operations.

____ 22. Integrating global e-business activities through cooperation among international subsidiaries and corporate headquarters.

____ 23. Differences in customs, governmental regulations, and the cost of living are examples.

____ 24. Global customers, products, operations, resources, and collaboration.

____ 25. Applying IT to global e-commerce systems is an example.

____ 26. The goal of some organizations is to develop integrated Internet-based networks for global electronic commerce.

____ 27. Transborder data flows and security of personal databases are top concerns.

____ 28. Standardizing global use of computer systems, software packages, telecommunications networks, and computing facilities is an example.

____ 29. The Internet is a natural global networking choice.

____ 30. Global telecommunications networks like the Internet move data across national boundaries.

____ 31. Some countries deny or limit Internet access.

____ 32. Agreement is needed on common user interfaces and website design features in global IT.

____ 33. Outlines an e-business vision, e-business/IT strategies, and technical architecture for a company.

____ 34. A blueprint for information technology in a company that specifies a technology platform, applications architecture, data resources, and IT organization structure.

Discussion Questions

1. What has been the impact of e-business technologies on the work relationships, activities, and resources of managers?

2. What can business unit managers do about performance problems in the use of information technology and the development and operation of information systems in their business units?

3. Refer to the Real World Case on Mellon Financial Corp. in the chapter. What should determine whether a company uses a dot-com or dotcorp strategy for its e-commerce initiatives? Use an example of companies you know from the real world to support your answer.

4. How are Internet technologies affecting the structure and work roles of modern organizations? For example, will middle management wither away? Will companies consist primarily of self-directed project teams of knowledge workers? Explain your answers.

5. Should the IS function in a business be centralized or decentralized? What recent developments support your answer?

6. Refer to the Real World Case on DHL Worldwide Express and ApplianceWare in the chapter. DHL finds a better fit to their business needs in developers outside of the United States because they have less of a "flavor-of-the-month technologism." What does this mean? Do you agree with DHL's conclusion? Why or why not?

7. How will the Internet, intranets, and extranets affect each of the components of global e-business technology management, as illustrated in Figure 12.13? Give several examples.

8. How might cultural, political, or geoeconomic challenges affect a global company's use of the Internet? Give several examples.

9. Will the increasing use of the Internet by firms with global e-business operations change their move toward a transnational business strategy? Explain.

10. How might the Internet, intranets, and extranets affect the business drivers or requirements responsible for a company's use of global IT, as shown in Figure 12.16? Give several examples to illustrate your answer.

Application Exercises

Complete the following exercises as individual or group projects that apply chapter concepts to real world business situations.

1. CEO Express: Top-Rated Website for Executives
Check out this top-rated site (www.ceoexpress.com) for busy executives. See Figure 12.22. Membership is free and open to students and professors, too. Great news from hundreds of links to top U.S. and international newspapers, business and technology magazines, and news services. Hundreds of links to business and technology research sources and references are provided, as well as to travel services, online shopping, and recreational websites.
   a. Evaluate the CEO Express website as a source of useful links to business and technology news, analysis, and research sources for business executives and professionals.
   b. Report on one item of business or IT news, analysis, or research that might have value for your present or future career in business.

2. The Worldly Investor: Global Business Issues
Check out worldlyinvestor.com (www.worldlyinvestor. com). See Figure 12.23. This easy-to-use website features concise commentary on global business, finance, and technology issues and emerging markets, as well as Q&As. For example, a commentator recently noted that Indian stocks were down and likely to take another hit from international index reshuffling. Other stories featured international auto industry analysis and commentary on several global e-commerce deals.
   a. Evaluate the worldlyinvestor.com website as a source of useful global business and IT news and analysis for the business professional or investor.
   b. Report on one item of global business or IT news or analysis that might have value for your present or future career in business.

Source: Adapted from "Net Finance," Technology Buyers Guide, *Fortune*, Winter 2000, p. 246. © 2000 Time Inc. All rights reserved.

(Continued on page 450.)

Figure 12.22

The CEO Express website.

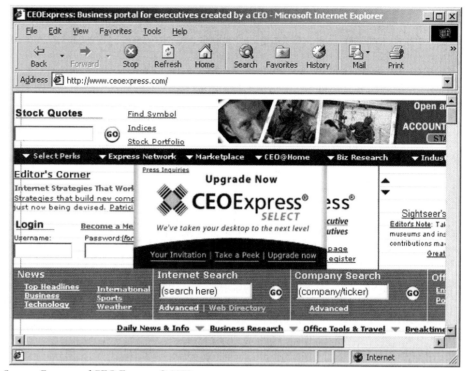

Source: Courtesy of CEO Express, © 2000.

Figure 12.23

The worldlyinvestor.com website.

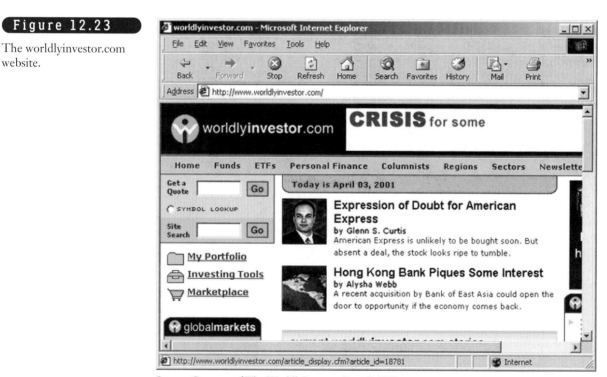

Source: Courtesy of The WorldlyInvestor, Inc., © 2000.

3. **Tracking Shopping-Related Internet Use across the United States**

The U.S. Census Bureau has surveyed households concerning their use of the Internet in December of 1998 and in August of 2000. The sample records shown below illustrate the structure of a database table based on data from these surveys that has been extracted and is available on the website for this textbook. The Use98 column indicates the estimated number of individuals in each state who regularly used the Internet to shop, pay bills, or for some other commercial purpose in December of 1998. The No_Use98 column provides an estimate of the number not using the Internet for those purposes in December of 1998. The Use00 and No_Use00 columns provide the same type of data for August of 2000. These figures are based on survey data and may be subject to significant error, especially for less populous states, but they do allow you to assess the degree of state-to-state variation in e-commerce related Internet use. Download the database file for this exercise from the website for this textbook. The textbook website is *www.mhhe.com/business/mis/obrien/obrien11e/index.html*. Click on downloads under the student resources section of that page.

a. Create and print a query that shows the proportion of the population in each state who used the Internet for shopping and related activities in August of 2000: Use00/(Use00/No_Use00) and sort the states in descending order by this usage proportion.

State	Use98	No_Use98	Use00	No_Use00
AL	183641	4107068	447023	4132225
AK	61261	533460	102968	481889
AZ	258602	4500880	528993	4417750
AR	53658	2448054	183010	2323339
CA	2036246	30804742	4475743	29460000

b. Calculate the usage proportion described in part A for the country as a whole for both December of 1998 and August of 2000 and determine the change in the commercial usage proportion between the two periods. Produce similar proportions for your home state and at least two adjacent states. (You may use database queries to find these proportions or you may copy the data to a spreadsheet and perform the calculations there.)

c. Prepare a set of PowerPoint slides or similar presentation materials summarizing the results in parts A and B and describing their implications for Web-based marketing.

4. **Worldwide Internet Users**

Figure 12.18 provides a set of estimates and projections of the numbers of Internet users in various regions of the world. Record the data from that table into a spreadsheet for further analysis or copy it from the download file for this exercise in the website for this textbook at *www.mhhe.com/business/mis/obrien/obrien11e/index.html*. To download the file click on downloads under the student resources section of that page and find the file for this exercise.

a. Add a section to the spreadsheet showing the percentage growth from year to year for each region. Then create an appropriate chart of this data.

b. Add a section showing the absolute change in users each year for each region. For instance, the absolute change figures for North America would be 108.8 − 90.4 or 18.4 for 1999, 125.8 − 108.8 or 17 for 2000 and so on. Create pie charts to show the distribution of projected Internet growth for the years 2002 and 2003.

c. Create a memorandum to your instructor summarizing your results and their implications. Include an assessment of how accurate you feel these projections are likely to be.

Nike and Connecticut General:
Failures in e-Business System Implementation

Early in 2001, Beaverton, Oregon–based footwear maker Nike, Inc., faced serious inventory reduction and misplacement as it rolled out a highly customized retail supply chain system that included applications from Dallas-based i2 Technologies Inc. At the time, i2 said the difficulties stemmed from tying the customized applications to Nike's enterprise resource planning (ERP) and back-end systems.

And this case isn't unique, say those who advise against tinkering with ERP applications. While customizing may give you industry-specific capabilities, it can be expensive and difficult, and the custom software may require special maintenance, say critics. It may also make the core application unstable and prone to glitches.

The trouble, of course, is that botched customization jobs can lead to disaster—as in Nike's case. The wide range of footwear products Nike sells also led to further difficulties in mapping the supply chain software to internal business processes. Nike Chairman and CEO Philip Knight, facing a drop in stock price and revenue, told shareholders, "I guess my immediate reaction is, 'This is what we get for $400 million?'"

Such crises discourage users from venturing out onto the thin ice of customization. "It's a risky strategy," says Walter Taylor, ERP program director at Atlanta-based Delta Air Lines Inc. Taylor is overseeing an SAP R/3 implementation for Delta. He says he opposes customizing because SAP already has solid applications with best practices built in. When you start tinkering with the code, you make the application unstable and start losing benefits. "It's better too for a company to reengineer its business processes than to rewrite code," Taylor says.

Connecticut General Life Insurance Co. is suing PeopleSoft, Inc., over the aborted installation of a new financial system. The 13-count suit, filed in August 2001 in U.S. District Court in San Francisco, claims that Connecticut General was forced to develop a homegrown application after the vendor failed to deliver customized software that was promised as part of a 1999 contract.

Connecticut General charges that PeopleSoft breached an agreement for support and consulting services and falsely claimed that it could customize and install an accounts receivable billing system for the insurer. After investing more than $5 million, Connecticut General said it didn't get the promised software and had to develop its own application. The suit also claims that Pleasanton, California–based PeopleSoft ballooned its tab for the project from the original figure of $5.15 million to $11.7 million and indicated that the final cost could go even higher.

Connecticut General, a subsidiary of CIGNA Corp. in Philadelphia, wants PeopleSoft to refund the $5.16 million that was paid up front and was supposed to include five years of technical support. The insurer wants PeopleSoft to pay the unspecified cost of the internal application development and is seeking punitive damages plus interest and legal fees.

PeopleSoft declined to comment on the specifics of the suit, saying it hadn't seen the complaint yet. "But PeopleSoft provided CIGNA with software that it licensed and performed services that CIGNA contracted for," a PeopleSoft spokesman said. "It is unfortunate that for internal reasons, CIGNA was unable to successfully adopt our software, but this was not related to the quality of the software or services provided by PeopleSoft."

However, Connecticut General's complaint alleges that it isn't the only company to be mistreated by PeopleSoft. "The 200-page suit includes supplementary legal documents from lawsuits filed in recent years by several other PeopleSoft customers, including Home Products International Inc. in Chicago, McNaughton-McKay Electric Co. in Madison Heights, Michigan, and the now-defunct retailer Bradlees Inc.

According to the legal filing, Connecticut General decided four years ago that its accounts receivable billing system, which handles $5 billion in transactions annually, was outdated and needed to be replaced with a new e-business system. In mid-1999, the suit states, the company signed a $5 million-plus deal with PeopleSoft covering software licenses, technical support, and implementation and customization services.

The project started in October 1999 and was supposed to be based on PeopleSoft 7.5 or a subsequent release, according to the suit. But by the following month, Connecticut General personnel "began to suspect that the PeopleSoft team was having difficulty performing the customization and implementation services." PeopleSoft replaced the workers assigned to the project and sent in a "crisis management team," the suit states.

But early in 2000, Connecticut General charged, PeopleSoft said the original project bid was flawed and raised the price to $11.76 million, with the possibility of another 20 percent increase on top of that amount. Connecticut General further claimed that PeopleSoft "failed to properly customize and implement" the promised software, leaving it "inoperable . . . and entirely useless."

Case Study Questions

1. What are the benefits and risks of customizing software packages for vital business processes? Use the experiences of Nike and Connecticut General to illustrate your answer.

2. How could Nike and Connecticut General have avoided the failures of their e-business development projects? Defend your proposals.

3. Why do you think failures in business/IT development projects continue to occur to large companies with so much IT expertise and financial resources?

Source: Adapted from Marc Songini, "To Customize or Not," *Computerworld*, September 3, 2001, pp. 42,43; and "PeopleSoft Project Ends in Court," *Computerworld*, September 10, 2001, pp. 1, 61. Reprinted by permission.

IBM and the Timken Company:
Evaluating Global e-Business Management Strategies

Bob Moffat, General Manager of IBM's PC division, is sitting at a small conference table in his office in Raleigh, North Carolina. A dozen sheets of paper lay before him that detail the performance of his worldwide group during the past month. His laptop—cordless but fully connected through IBM's wireless network—is at his elbow, so he can send and receive instant messages during a two-hour global conference call with his senior managers in cities as diverse as Lima, Paris, and Tokyo.

If he didn't have a visitor, Moffat would be alone with his data and his speakerphone. His remote location does nothing to dilute his commanding personality. This "weekly operations meeting" among international managers is a global conference call that has been an institution in the PC division.

Moffat opens the meeting by saying, "I wouldn't call it a terrible July, but a mixed one. The question is, How do we get it done in August? Because if we don't, we'll never make it up in September." Characteristically, he asks for an explanation not only of weak desktop sales, but also of unexpectedly strong ThinkPad sales. "Let's talk about why that's happening. How do we capitalize on it?"

Moffat doesn't talk much, but he also doesn't let someone else's bluster pass without a challenge. In fact, one of Moffat's signature phrases is, "Let's not perfume the pig." He is known as a consummate straight talker: He tells people what he thinks, he wants the truth back in return, and he prefers to receive bad news early.

At this meeting, after listening to his European sales chief's report, Moffat is so disappointed that he rises to pace and shouts, "You guys are rallying around the lower sales number, the must-make number. That's a failure number. You need to shoot higher, damn it! You need to change that."

What distinguishes Moffat's leadership, of course, isn't his ability to raise his voice. What's notable about Moffat is that he does a remarkable job of keeping opposing forces in balance. He knows that strategy is critical, but he also knows that it takes more than that. "The people who win are the people who execute," he says. "They have milestones for what they are going to do and metrics to measure if they are reaching those milestones. Many managers stop after developing a strategy. They expect people to just get it." At the same time, Moffat strongly believes in thinking beyond the horizon to what might happen next. And he also believes that kind of thinking is everyone's job, not just his.

Moffat's group designs and sells personal computers—just like Dell, the market leader, does. But Moffat says that it is critical to his success to understand the differences there too. "Michael Dell and I look at the business differently," he says. "Dell is in the PC business. IBM is not in the PC business. We must fit the PC business into the global strategy of the larger IBM." PCs are something that IBM must offer business customers who are buying a full suite of services and who don't want to have to shop elsewhere for hardware. And in developing international markets like China and India,

says Moffat, quality IBM PC products are a way of establishing credibility until global markets mature in the direction of IBM's more profitable services.

The Timken Company

To outsiders, says president James W. Griffith, Timken may seem old-economy, but to people inside, it is a high-tech operation. Just walk through its huge R&D center and see the sophisticated instruments that some 450 scientists and engineers are applying to product design. The Timken Company, based in Canton, Ohio, is a global manufacturer of precision bearings and specialty alloys with operations in 24 countries. Timken has embarked on major e-business initiatives in electronic commerce, engineering design collaboration, and global e-manufacturing.

A year ago Timken hired a GE executive, Curt J. Andersson, and named him to a new post, senior vice president for e-business. Andersson and his team have concentrated on establishing "electronic visibility" through Timken's global supply chain. Within eight weeks the team created a system that lets a Timken dealer see exactly where a part is available in any of a dozen warehouses spread around the world. Such searches previously took lots of faxing, telephoning, and paperwork. The improvement will save Timken millions of dollars annually.

Connecting design to the factory floor comes next in the Andersson team's plans. Engineers in the company's main R&D center already initiate, modify, and complete product designs jointly with customers in real time via the Internet. Soon newly developed e-manufacturing software will allow the designs to flow immediately to Timken's sophisticated production plants all over the world.

Such instant access to information anywhere, anytime, and its meaningful manipulation, are what all e-manufacturers strive for. "We're combining the Internet benefits of speed and worldwide access with the real world capabilities of automated manufacturing plants, warehouses, freight, and global logistics management," says Timken's Andersson. "This bricks-and-clicks e-business combination is what the real Internet is all about."

Case Study Questions

1. Is the global PC strategy of Bob Moffat the best one for IBM? Why or why not?

2. Do you agree with the global "bricks and clicks" e-business strategy of the Timken Company? Why or why not?

3. What are several strategic e-business moves you could recommend to IBM and the Timken Company? Defend the global business value of your proposals.

Source: Charles Fishman, "Leader: Bob Moffat," **Fast Company,** November 2001, pp. 96–104. Copyright 2001 by Bus Innovator Group Resources, Inc. Reproduced with permission of Bus Innovator Group Resources, Inc. via Copyright Clearance Center.

Chapter 1

Foundations of Information Systems in Business

1. 21	7. 26c	13. 11	19. 4	25. 27a	31. 17d	37. 29
2. 22	8. 16	14. 28	20. 18	26. 27b	32. 17e	38. 20
3. 19	9. 1	15. 13	21. 14	27. 25	33. 30	39. 12
4. 26	10. 10	16. 2	22. 14a	28. 17a	34. 30c	40. 23a
5. 26a	11. 7	17. 3	23. 14b	29. 17b	35. 30b	41. 23
6. 26b	12. 9	18. 15	24. 27	30. 17c	36. 30a	42. 8

Chapter 2

Competing with Information Technology

1. 3	4. 11	7. 6	10. 14	13. 1	15. 15	17. 9
2. 4	5. 5	8. 17	11. 2	14. 18	16. 8	18. 7
3. 12	6. 13	9. 10	12. 16			

Chapter 3

Computer Hardware

1. 45	9. 30	17. 31	25. 40e	33. 26	41. 36b	49. 27
2. 7	10. 25	18. 20	26. 32	34. 12	42. 36a	50. 27d
3. 3	11. 24	19. 21	27. 29	35. 38	43. 47	
4. 2	12. 1	20. 23	28. 32a	36. 4	44. 6	
5. 9	13. 17	21. 22	29. 44	37. 5	45. 37	
6. 8	14. 16	22. 42	30. 34	38. 10	46. 36	
7. 33	15. 18	23. 13	31. 39	39. 48	47. 11	
8. 35	16. 15	24. 43c	32. 28	40. 41	48. 14	

Chapter 4

Computer Software

1. 33	7. 36	13. 18	18. 7	23. 16	28. 14	33. 29
2. 2	8. 12	14. 37	19. 8	24. 31	29. 10	34. 15
3. 26	9. 38	15. 11	20. 40	25. 13	30. 25	35. 17
4. 34	10. 22	16. 3	21. 6	26. 19	31. 24	36. 1
5. 30	11. 23	17. 39	22. 27	27. 4	32. 21	37. 35
6. 9	12. 5					

Chapter 5

Data Resource Management

1. 9	5. 1	9. 11d	13. 2	17. 14c	21. 11a	25. 8a
2. 12	6. 17	10. 18d	14. 4	18. 14d	22. 11e	26. 18e
3. 7	7. 10	11. 5	15. 3	19. 14e	23. 11b	27. 18a
4. 16	8. 18b	12. 6	16. 14b	20. 13	24. 8b	28. 18c

Chapter 6

Telecommunications and Networks

1. 36	7. 10	13. 11	19. 26	24. 29	29. 13	34. 17
2. 4	8. 33	14. 5	20. 40	25. 21a	30. 6	35. 1
3. 2	9. 38	15. 34	21. 25	26. 21b	31. 22	36. 30
4. 3	10. 18	16. 35	22. 37	27. 27	32. 28	37. 39
5. 12	11. 31	17. 19	23. 24	28. 14	33. 9	38. 23
6. 16	12. 32	18. 20				

Chapter 7

Electronic Business Systems

1. 9	7. 22	13. 5	18. 16	23. 18	28. 13	33. 4
2. 7	8. 17	14. 11	19. 24	24. 3	29. 25	34. 30
3. 14	9. 32	15. 29	20. 1	25. 2	30. 20	35. 26
4. 9a	10. 8	16. 19	21. 23	26. 28	31. 35	36. 33
5. 10	11. 21	17. 31	22. 27	27. 15	32. 36	37. 34
6. 12	12. 6					

Chapter 8

Electronic Commerce Systems

1. 5	5. 4	9. 8d	13. 9	17. 2c	20. 7	23. 1
2. 5b	6. 8	10. 8i	14. 2	18. 2b	21. 8e	24. 3
3. 5a	7. 8a	11. 8f	15. 2d	19. 6	22. 10	25. 11
4. 5c	8. 8g	12. 8c	16. 2a			

Chapter 9

Decision Support Systems

1. 9*b*	7. 28	13. 1*c*	19. 10	24. 29	29. 13*b*	34. 21
2. 9*a*	8. 7	14. 1*a*	20. 22	25. 30	30. 20	35. 26
3. 23	9. 6	15. 1*b*	21. 11	26. 17	31. 18	36. 15
4. 5	10. 25	16. 27	22. 2	27. 13	32. 14	37. 19
5. 12	11. 1	17. 3	23. 2*a*	28. 13*a*	33. 13*d*	38. 16
6. 24	12. 1*d*	18. 4				

Chapter 10

Developing e-Business Solutions

1. 21	7. 30*a*	12. 5	17. 11	22. 26	27. 9*a*	32. 4
2. 29	8. 13*a*	13. 31	18. 22	23. 18	28. 9*c*	33. 26
3. 17	9. 23	14. 14	19. 32	24. 19	29. 9*b*	34. 8
4. 3	10. 25	15. 16	20. 27	25. 6	30. 2	35. 7
5. 30*b*	11. 10	16. 20	21. 24	26. 12	31. 28	36. 1
6. 13*b*						

Chapter 11

Security and Ethical Challenges of e-Business

1. 26	6. 3	11. 16	16. 15*b*	21. 9	25. 27	29. 1
2. 21	7. 2	12. 6	17. 15*d*	22. 11	26. 22	30. 19
3. 29	8. 5	13. 28	18. 15*e*	23. 7	27. 20	31. 14
4. 17	9. 12	14. 15*a*	19. 8	24. 30	28. 10	32. 25
5. 18	10. 13	15. 15*c*	20. 24			

Chapter 12

Enterprise and Global Management of e-Business Technology

1. 18	6. 21	11. 7	16. 25	21. 12	26. 12*b*	31. 16
2. 14	7. 2	12. 26	17. 3	22. 28	27. 12*c*	32. 12*e*
3. 19	8. 1	13. 11	18. 8	23. 6	28. 12*d*	33. 10
4. 9	9. 29	14. 4	19. 23	24. 11	29. 17	34. 15
5. 20	10. 22	15. 5	20. 24	25. 12*a*	30. 27	

Selected References

Chapter 1—Foundations of Information Systems in Business

1. Emigh, Jacquiline. "E-Commerce Strategies." *Computerworld*, August 16, 1999.

2. Ewusi-Mensah, Kewku. "Critical Issues in Abandoned Information Systems Development Projects." *Communications of the ACM*, September 1997.

3. Fingar, Peter; Harsha Kumar; and Tarun Sharma. *Enterprise E-Commerce*. Tampa, FL: Meghan-Kiffer Press, 2000.

4. Haylock, Christina Ford, and Len Muscarella. *Net Success*. Holbrook, MA: Adams Media Corporation, 1999.

5. Hills, Mellanie. *Intranet Business Strategies*. New York: John Wiley & Sons, 1997.

6. Iansiti, Marco, and Alan MacCormick. "Developing Products on Internet Time." *Harvard Business Review*, September–October 1997.

7. Kalakota, Ravi, and Marcia Robinson. *E-Business: Roadmap for Success*. Reading, MA: Addison-Wesley, 1999.

8. Kalakota, Ravi, and Andrew Whinston. *Electronic Commerce: A Manager's Guide*. Reading, MA: Addison-Wesley, 1997.

9. Lee, Allen. "Inaugural Editor's Comments." *MIS Quarterly*, March 1999.

10. Leinfuss, Emily. "Making the Cut." *Computerworld*, September 20, 1999.

11. Marion, Larry. "Snap, Crackle, Pop, and Crash—Go the Income Statements." *Datamation* (www.datamation.com), February 1999.

12. Norris, Grant; James Hurley; Kenneth Hartley; John Dunleavy; and John Balls. *E-Business and ERP: Transforming the Enterprise*. New York: John Wiley & Sons, 2000.

13. Radcliff, Deborah. "Aligning Marriott." *Computerworld*, April 20, 2000.

14. Seybold, Patricia. *Customers.com: How to Create a Profitable Business Strategy for the Internet and Beyond*. New York: Times Business, 1998.

15. Shapiro, Carl, and Hal Varian. *Information Rules: A Strategic Guide to the New Economy*. Boston, MA: Harvard Business School Press, 1999.

16. Silver, Mark; M. Lynn Markus; and Cynthia Mathis Beath. "The Information Technology Interaction Model: A Foundation for the MBA Core Course." *MIS Quarterly*, September 1995.

17. Steadman, Craig. "ERP Pioneers." *Computerworld*, January 18, 1999.

18. Stewart, Thomas. "How Alcoa and Cisco Make Real-time Work," *Fortune*, May 29, 2000.

19. Wagner, Mitch. "Firms Spell Out Appropriate Internet Use for Employees." *Computerworld*, February 5, 1996.

Chapter 2—Competing with Information Technology

1. Applegate, Lynda; F. Warren McFarlan; and James McKenney. *Corporate Information Systems Management: Text and Cases*. Burr Ridge, IL: Irwin/McGraw-Hill, 1999.

2. Bowles, Jerry. "Best Practices for Global Competitiveness." Special Advertising Section. *Fortune*, November 24, 1997.

3. Caron, J. Raymond; Sirkka Jarvenpaa; and Donna Stoddard. "Business Reengineering at CIGNA Corporation: Experiences and Lessons from the First Five Years." *MIS Quarterly*, September 1994.

4. Cash, James I., Jr.; Robert G. Eccles; Nitin Nohria; and Richard L. Nolan. *Building the Information-Age Organization: Structure, Control, and Information Technologies*. Burr Ridge, IL: Richard D. Irwin, 1994.

5. Christensen, Clayton. *The Innovators Dilemma: When New Technologies Cause Great Firms to Fail*. Boston: Harvard Business School Press, 1997.

6. Clemons, Eric, and Michael Row. "Sustaining IT Advantage: The Role of Structural Differences." *MIS Quarterly*, September 1991.

7. Collett, Stacy. "Spun-off Sabre to Sell Software to AMR Rivals." *Computerworld*, December 20, 1999.

8. Cronin, Mary. *Doing More Business on the Internet*. 2nd ed. New York: Van Nostrand Reinhold, 1995.

9. Cronin, Mary. *The Internet Strategy Handbook*. Boston: Harvard Business School Press, 1996.

10. Davenport, Thomas H. *Process Innovation: Reengineering Work through Information Technology*. Boston: Harvard Business School Press, 1993.

11. Deckmyn, Dominique. "Product Data Management Moves Toward Mainstream." *Computerworld*, November 8, 1999.

12. El Sawy, Omar, and Gene Bowles. "Redesigning the Customer Support Process for the Electronic Economy: Insights from Storage Dimensions." *MIS Quarterly*, December 1997.

13. El Sawy, Omar; Arvind Malhotra; Sanjay Gosain; and Kerry Young. "IT-Intensive Value Innovation in the Electronic Economy: Insights from Marshall Industries." *MIS Quarterly*, September 1999.

14. Emigh, Jacquiline. "E-Commerce Strategies." *Computerworld*, August 16, 1999.

15. Ewing, Jack. "Sharing the Wealth," *Business Week e-biz*, March 19, 2001.

16. Frye, Colleen. "Imaging Proves Catalyst for Reengineering." *Client/Server Computing*, November 1994.

17. Garner, Rochelle. "Please Don't Call IT Knowledge Management!" *Computerworld*, August 9, 1999.

18. Garvin, David. "Building a Learning Organization." *Harvard Business Review*, July–August 1995.

19. Goldman, Steven; Roger Nagel; and Kenneth Preis. *Agile Competitors and Virtual Organizations: Strategies for Enriching the Customer*. New York: Van Nostrand Reinhold, 1995.

20. Grover, Varun, and Pradipkumar Ramanlal. "Six Myths of Information and Markets: Information Technology Networks, Electronic Commerce, and the Battle for Consumer Surplus." *MIS Quarterly*, December 1999.

21. Hamm, Steve, and Marcia Stepaneck. "From Reengineering to E-Engineering." *Business Week e.biz*, March 22, 1999.

22. Hibbard, Justin. "Spreading Knowledge." *Computerworld*, April 7, 1997.

23. Kalakota, Ravi, and Marcia Robinson. *E-Business: Roadmap For Success*. Reading, MA: Addison-Wesley, 1999.

24. Kerwin, Kathleen; Marcia Stepanek; and David Welch. "At Ford, E-Commerce is Job 1." *Business Week*, February 28, 2000.

25. Kettinger, William; Varun Grover; Subashish Guha; and Albert Segars. "Strategic Information Systems Revisited: A Study in Sustainability and Performance." *MIS Quarterly*, March 1994.

26. Kettinger, William; Varun Grover; and Albert Segars. "Do Strategic Systems Really Pay Off? An Analysis of Classic Strategic IT Cases." *Information Systems Management*, Winter 1995.

27. Kettinger, William; James Teng; and Subashish Guha. "Business Process Change: A Study of Methodologies, Techniques, and Tools." *MIS Quarterly*, March 1997.

28. Kover, Amy. "Schwab Makes a Grand Play for the Rich." *Fortune*, February 7, 2000.

29. Melymuka, Kathleen. "GE's Quality Gamble," *Computerworld*, June 8, 1998, p. 64.

30. Mooney, John; Vijay Gurbaxani; and Kenneth Kramer. "A Process Oriented Framework for Assessing the Business Value of Information Technology." *The Data Base for Advances in Information Systems*, Spring 1996.

31. Neumann, Seev. *Strategic Information Systems: Competition through Information Technologies*. New York: Macmillan College Publishing Co., 1994.

32. Nonaka, Ikujiro. "The Knowledge Creating Company." *Harvard Business Review*, November–December 1991.

33. Pegels, C. Carl. *Total Quality Management: A Survey of Its Important Aspects*. Danvers, MA: Boyd & Fraser Publishing Co., 1995.

34. Porter, Michael, and Victor Millar. "How Information Gives You Competitive Advantage." *Harvard Business Review*, July–August 1985.

35. Prokesch, Steven. "Unleashing the Power of Learning: An Interview with British Petroleum's John Browne." *Harvard Business Review*, September–October 1997.

36. Resnick, Rosalind. "The Virtual Corporation." *PC Today*, February 1995.

37. Seybold, Patricia. *Customers.com: How to Create a Profitable Business Strategy for the Internet and Beyond*. New York: Times Books, 1998.

38. Shapiro, Carl, and Hal Varian. *Information Rules: A Strategic Guide to the Network Economy*. Boston: Harvard Business School Press, 1999.

39. Siekman, Philip. "Why Infotech Loves Its Giant Job Shops." *Fortune*, May 12, 1997.

40. Weill, Peter, and Michael Vitale. *Place to Space: Migrating to E-Business Models*. Boston: Harvard Business School Press, 2001.

Chapter 3—Computer Hardware

1. *Computerworld*, *PC Week*, *PC Magazine*, and *PC World* are just a few examples of many good magazines for current information on computer systems hardware and its use in end user and enterprise applications.

2. The World Wide Web sites of computer manufacturers such as Apple Computer, Dell Computer, Gateway, IBM, Hewlett-Packard, Compaq, and Sun Microsystems are good sources of information on computer hardware developments.

3. Alexander, Steve. "Speech Recognition." *Computerworld*, November 8, 1999.

4. Collette, Stacy. "Thin Client Devices Shipments Soar." *Computerworld*, September 20, 1999.

5. "Computing in the New Millenium." *Technology Buyers Guide*, *Fortune*, Winter 2000.

6. Crothers, Brooke. "IBM Wins Big on Supercomputer Deal." CNETNews.com, April 28, 1999.

7. Deckmyn, Dominique. "Dell Joins the Legacy-Free PC Movement." *Computerworld*, December 6, 1999.

8. "Desktop Power." In Technology Buyer's Guide. *Fortune*, Winter 1999.

9. Guyon, Janet. "Smart Plastic." *Fortune*, October 13, 1997.

10. "Hardware." In Technology Buyer's Guide. *Fortune*, Winter 1999.

11. Judge, Paul. "High Tech Star." *Business Week*, March 15, 1999.

12. Kennedy, Ken, and others. "A Nationwide Parallel Computing Environment." *Communications of the ACM*, November 1997.

13. Messerschmitt, David. *Networked Applications: A Guide to the New Computing Infrastructure*. San Francisco: Morgan Kaufmann Publishers, 1999.

14. Morgan, Cynthia. "Speech Recognition." *Computerworld*, September 27, 1998.

15. Ouellette, Tim. "Goodbye to the Glass House." *Computerworld*, May 26, 1997.

16. Ouellette, Tim. "Tape Storage Put to New Enterprise Uses." *Computerworld*, November 10, 1997.

17. Simpson, David. "The Datamation 100." *Datamation*, July 1997.

18. San Diego Supercomputer Center (SDSC), Resources, "Blue Horizon: NPACI Teraflops IBM SP," www.sdsc.edu, October 17, 2001.

Chapter 4—Computer Software

1. Examples of many good magazines for current information and reviews of computer software for business applications can be found at ZD Net, the website for ZD Publications (www.zdnet.com), including *PC Magazine*, *PC Week*, *PC Computing*, *Macworld*, *Inter@ctive Week*, and *Computer Shopper*.

2. The World Wide Web sites of computer manufacturers and software companies like Microsoft, Sun Microsystems, Lotus, IBM, Apple Computer, Oracle, and Netscape Communications are good sources of information on computer software developments.

3. Hamm, Steve; Peter Burrows; and Andy Reinhardt. "Is Windows Ready to Run E-Business?" *Business Week*, January 24, 2000.

4. Jacobsen, Ivar; Maria Ericcson; and Ageneta Jacobsen. *The Object Advantage: Business Process Reengineering with Object Technology*. New York: ACM Press, 1995.

5. Johnson, Amy Helen. "XML Xtends Its Reach." *Computerworld*, October 18, 1999.

6. Kalish, David. "Computer Language Consensus Sought." Associated Press Online, www.marketwatch.com, February 1, 2000.

7. Nance, Barry. "Linux in a 3-Piece Suit?" *Computerworld*, September 6, 1999.

8. Satran, Dick. "Sun's Shooting Star." *Business 2.0*, February 2000.

9. Schlender, Brent. "Steve Jobs' Apple Gets Way Cooler." *Fortune*, January 24, 2000.

10. "Suite Deals," Technology Buyer's Guide, *Fortune*, Winter 2000.

11. Udell, John. "Java: The Actions on the Server." *Computerworld*, July 5, 1999.

Chapter 5—Data Resource Management

1. Ahrens, Judith, and Chetan Sankar. "Tailoring Database Training for End Users." *MIS Quarterly*, December 1993.

2. Anthes, Gary. "Minding the Storage." *Computerworld*. March 22, 1999.

3. Atwood, Thomas. "Object Databases Come of Age," *OBJECT Magazine*, July 1996.

4. Baer, Tony. "Object Databases." *Computerworld*, January 18, 1999.

5. "Borders Knows No Bounds in E-Business." From www.software.ibm/eb/borders, March 1999.

6. Bose, Ranjit, and Vijayan Sugumaran. "Application of Intelligent Agent Technology for Managerial Data Analysis and Mining." *The Data Base for Advances in Information Systems*, Winter 1999.

7. Finkelstein, Richard. *Understanding the Need for On-Line Analytical Servers*. Ann Arbor, MI: Arbor Software Corporation, 1994.

8. Jacobsen, Ivar; Maria Ericsson; and Ageneta Jacobsen. *The Object Advantage: Business Process Reengineering with Object Technology.* New York: ACM Press, 1995.

9. Judge, Paul. "High-Tech Star." *Business Week*, March 15, 1999.

10. Kalakota, Ravi, and Marcia Robinson. *E-Business: Roadmap for Success.* Reading, MA: Addison-Wesley, 1999.

11. Morgan, Cynthia. "Data Is King." *Computerworld*, March 27, 2000.

12. Lorents, Alden, and James Morgan. *Database Systems: Concepts, Management and Applications.* Fort Worth: The Dryden Press, 1998.

13. Mannino, Michael. *Database Application Development and Design.* Burr Ridge, IL: McGraw-Hill Irwin, 2001.

14. "Shedding Light on Data Warehousing for More Informed Business Solutions." Special Advertising Supplement. *Computerworld*, February 13, 1995.

15. Smith, Heather A., and James D. McKeen. "Object-Oriented Technology: Getting Beyond the Hype." *The Data Base for Advances in Information Systems*, Spring 1996.

16. Spiegler, Israel. "Toward a Unified View of Data: Bridging Data Structure and Content." *Information Systems Management*, Spring 1995.

17. Stedman, Craig. "Databases Grab Hold of Objects, Multimedia on the Web." *Computerworld*, October 21, 1996.

18. Storey, Veda, and Robert Goldstein. "Knowledge-Based Approaches to Database Design." *MIS Quarterly*, March 1993.

19. Ta Check, James. "IBM: Not by Databases Alone." *ZD Net*, February 3, 2000.

20. White, Colin, "Data Warehousing: Choosing the Right Tools." *Computerworld*, Special Advertising Supplement, March 2, 1998.

Chapter 6—Telecommunications and Networks

1. Anderson, Heidi. "The Rise of the Extranet." *PC Today*, February 1997.

2. Barksdale, Jim. "The Next Step: Extranets." *Netscape Columns: The Main Thing*, December 3, 1996.

3. Blum, Jonathan. "Peering into the Future." *Red Herring*, November 13, 2000.

4. Campbell, Ian. "The Intranet: Slashing the Cost of Doing Business." Research Report, International Data Corporation, 1996.

5. Cronin, Mary. *Doing More Business on the Internet.* New York: Van Nostrand Reinhold, 1995.

6. Cronin, Mary. *Global Advantage on the Internet.* New York: Van Nostrand Reinhold, 1996.

7. "Dialing for Data." In Technology Buyer's Guide, *Fortune*, Winter 2000.

8. Fernandez, Tony. "Beyond the Browser." *NetWorker*, March/April 1997.

9. Harler, Curt, and Donell Short. "Building Broadband Networks." Special advertising section, *Business Week*, July 12, 1999.

10. Housel, Thomas, and Eric Skopec. *Global Telecommunications Revolution: The Business Perspective.* Burr Ridge, IL: McGraw-Hill Irwin, 2001.

11. Kalakota, Ravi, and Marcia Robinson. *E-Business: Roadmap for Success.* Reading, MA: Addison-Wesley, 1999.

12. Kover, Amy. "Napster: Hot Idea of the Year." *Fortune*, June 26, 2000.

13. "Life on the Web." In Technology Buyer's Guide, *Fortune*, Winter 1999.

14. Martin, Chuck. *The Digital Estate: Strategies for Competing, Surviving, and Thriving in an Internetworked World.* New York: McGraw-Hill, 1997.

15. Messerschmitt, David. *Network Applications: A Guide to the New Computing Infrastructure.* San Francisco: Morgan Kaufmann Publishers, 1999.

16. Murphy, Kate. "Cruising the Net in Hyperdrive." *Business Week*, January 24, 2000.

17. Nee, Eric. "The Upstarts are Rocking Telecom." *Fortune*, January 24, 2000.

18. O'Brien, Atiye. "Friday Intranet Focus." *Upside.com: Hot Private Companies*, Upside Publishing Company, 1996.

19. Papows, Jeff. "Endquotes." *NetReady Adviser*, Winter 1997.

20. "Phones to Go." In Technology Buyer's Guide. *Fortune*, Winter 1999.

21. Reingold, Jennifer; Marcia Stepanek; and Diane Brady. "Why the Productivity Revolution Will Spread." *Business Week*, February 14, 2000.

22. Rosenbush, Steve. "Charge of the Light Brigade," *Business Week*, January 31, 2000.

23. Stuart, Anne. "Cutting the Cord." *Inc. Tech*, 2001, No. 1.

24. Wallace, Bob. "Hotels See Service From Virtual Net." *Computerworld*, February 9, 1998.

Chapter 7—Electronic Business Systems

1. Armor, Daniel. *The E-Business (R)Evolution: Living and Working in an Interconnected World*. Upper Saddle River, NJ: Prentice Hall, 2000.

2. Ashbrand, Deborah. "Squeeze Out Excess Costs with Supply Chain Solutions." *Datamation*, March 1997.

3. Caulfield, Brian. "Systems That Talk Together, Kick Butt Together." *eCompany*, January/February 2001.

4. "Communications Leader Becomes Customer-Focused E-Business." *Siebel.com*, March 12, 2001.

5. "Davenport, Thomas. *Process Innovation: Reengineering Work Through Information Technology*. Boston: Harvard Business School Press, 1993.

6. Diese, Martin; Conrad Nowikow; Patrick King; and Amy Wright. *Executives Guide to E-Business: From Tactics to Strategy*. New York: John Wiley & Sons, 2000.

7. Donahue, Sean. "Supply Traffic Control." *Business 2.0*. February 2000.

8. El Sawy, Omar; Arvind Malhotra; Sanjay Gosain; and Kerry Young. "IT-Intensive Value Innovation in the Electronic Economy: Insights from Marshal Industries." *MIS Quarterly*, September 1999.

9. El Sawy, Omar. *Redesigning Enterprise Processes for E-Business*. New York: McGraw-Hill Irwin, 2001.

10. Essex, David. "Enterprise Application Integration." *Computerworld*, October 4, 1999.

11. Essex, David. "Get into Web Portals." *Computerworld*, March 15, 1999.

12. Fellenstein, Craig, and Ron Wood. *Exploring E-Commerce, Global E-Business, and E-Societies*. Upper Saddle River, NJ: Prentice Hall, 2000.

13. Gates, Bill. *Business @ the Speed of Thought*. New York: Warner Books, 1999.

14. Geoff, Leslie. "CRM: The Cutting Edge of Serving Customers." *Computerworld*, February 28, 2000.

15. Hamel, Gary, and Jeff Sandler. "The E-Corporation." *Fortune*, December 7, 1998.

16. Hamm, Steve, and Robert Hoff. "An Eagle Eye on Customers." *Business Week*, February 21, 2000.

17. Hodges, Judy. "The Rise of the Self Service Employee." *Computerworld HR Online*, September 8, 1997.

18. Johnson, Amy. "CRM Rises to the Top." *Computerworld*, August 16, 1999.

19. Kalakota, Ravi, and Marcia Robinson. *E-Business: Roadmap for Success*. Reading, MA: Addison-Wesley, 1999.

20. Keen, Peter, and Craigg Balance. *Online Profits: A Manager's Guide to Electronic Commerce*. Boston: Harvard Business School Press, 1997.

21. McCann, Stefanie. "Career Opportunities in Enterprise Resource Planning." *Computerworld*, February 7, 2000.

22. McCarthy, Vance. "ERP Gets Down to E-Business." *HP World*, January 2000.

23. Norris, Grant; James Hurley; Kenneth Hartley; John Dunleavy; and John Balls. *E-Business and ERP: Transforming the Enterprise*. New York: John Wiley & Sons, 2000.

24. Orenstein, David. "Enterprise Application Integration." *Computerworld*, October 4, 1999.

25. Papows, Jeff. *Enterprise.com: Market Leadership in the Information Age*. Reading, MA: Perseus Books, 1998.

26. Ranadive, Vivek. *The Power of Now*. New York: McGraw-Hill, 1999.

27. Steadman, Craig. "ERP Guide: Vendor Strategies, Future Plans." *Computerworld*, July 19, 1999.

28. Stewart, Thomas. "How Cisco and Alcoa Make Real-time Work." *Fortune*, May 29, 2000.

29. Tapscott, Don; David Ticoll; and Alex Lowy. *Digital Capital: Harnessing the Power of Business Webs*. Boston: Harvard Business School Press, 2000.

30. Tucker, Jay. "The New Money: Transactions Pour Across the Web." *Datamation*, April 1997.

31. "Your Body, Your Job." Technology Buyer's Guide. *Fortune*, Winter 2000.

Chapter 8—Electronic Commerce Systems

1. Anthes, Gary. "Cha Aims Big with Micropayment Service." *Computerworld*, July 26, 1999.

2. Armor, Daniel. *The E-Business (R)Evolution: Living and Working in an Interconnected World*. Upper Saddle River, NJ: Prentice Hall, 2000.

3. "Click Here to Shop." Technology Buyers Guide. *Fortune*, Winter 2000.

4. Collett, Stacy. "Sun, Newscape Develop Bill Payment Software." *Computerworld*, December 13, 1999.

5. Cross, Kim. "Need Options? Go Configure." *Business 2.0*, February 2000.

6. Davis, Jeffrey. "How IT Works." *Business 2.0*, February 2000.

7. Davis, Jeffrey. "Mall Rats." *Business 2.0*, January 1999.

8. Diese, Martin; Conrad Nowikow; Patrick King; and Amy Wright. *Executives Guide to E-Business: From Tactics to Strategy*. New York: John Wiley & Sons, 2000.

9. El Sawy, Omar; Arvind Malhotra; Sanjay Gosain; and Kerry Young. "IT-Intensive Value Innovation in the Electronic Economy: Insights from Marshal Industries." *MIS Quarterly*, September 1999.

10. Fellenstein, Craig, and Ron Wood. *Exploring E-Commerce, Global E-Business, and E-Societies*. Upper Saddle River, NJ: Prentice Hall, 2000.

11. Fingar, Peter; Harsha Kumar; and Tarun Sharma. *Enterprise E-Commerce*. Meghan-Kiffer Press: Tampa, FL, 2000.

12. Gates, Bill. *Business @ the Speed of Thought*. New York: Warner Books, 1999.

13. Gulati, Ranjay, and Jason Garino. "Get the Right Mix of Clicks and Bricks." *Harvard Business Review,* May–June 2000.

14. Haylock, Christina, and Len Muscarella. *Net Success.* Holbrook, MA: Adams Media Corporation, 1999.

15. Hoque, Faisal. *E-Enterprise: Business Models, Architecture and Components*. Cambridge, UK: Cambridge University Press, 2000.

16. Kalakota, Ravi, and Marcia Robinson. *E-Business: Roadmap for Success*. Reading, MA: Addison-Wesley, 1999.

17. Kalakota, Ravi, and Andrew Whinston. *Electronic Commerce: A Manager's Guide*. Reading, MA: Addison-Wesley, 1997.

18. Kalakota, Ravi, and Andrew Whinston. *Frontiers of Electronic Commerce*. Reading, MA: Addison-Wesley, 1996.

19. Kastner, Peter, and Christopher Stevens. "Electronic Commerce: A True Challenge for IT Managers." In "Enterprise Solutions: Electronic Commerce." Special Advertising Supplement to *Computerworld*, January 13, 1997.

20. Keen, Peter, and Craigg Balance. *Online Profits: A Manager's Guide to Electronic Commerce*. Boston: Harvard Business School Press, 1997.

21. "Keep the 0010001 Happy." Technology Buyers Guide. *Fortune*, Summer 2000.

22. Korper, Steffano, and Juanita Ellis. *The E-Commerce Book: Building the E-Empire*. San Diego: Academic Press, 2000.

23. Leon, Mark. "Trading Spaces." *Business 2.0*, February 2000.

24. Loshin, Peter. "The Electronic Marketplace." *PC Today*, July 1996.

25. Machlis, Sharon. "Portals Link Buyers, Sellers." *Computerworld*, January 25, 1999.

26. Machlis, Sharon. "Web Retailers Try to Keep Their Hits Up." *Computerworld*, February 8, 1999.

27. Martin, Chuck. *The Digital Estate: Strategies for Competing, Surviving, and Thriving in an Internetworked World*. New York: McGraw-Hill, 1997.

28. Morgan, Cynthia. "Dead Set Against SET?" *Computerworld*, March 29, 1999.

29. Robinson, Edward. "Battle to the Bitter End(-to-End)." *Business 2.0*, July 25, 2000.

30. Rosenoer, Jonathan; Douglas Armstrong; and J. Russell Gates. *The Clickable Corporation: Successful Strategies for Capturing the Internet Advantage*. New York: The Free Press, 1999.

31. Schwartz, Evan. *Digital Darwinism*. New York: Broadway Books, 1999.

32. Schwartz, Evan. *Webonomics*. New York: Broadway Books, 1997.

33. Senn, James. "Electronic Data Interchange: Elements of Implementation." *Information Systems Management*, Winter 1992.

34. "Servers with a Smile." Technology Buyers Guide. *Fortune*, Summer 2000.

35. Seybold, Patricia, with Ronnie Marshak. *Customers Com: How to Create a Profitable Business Strategy for the Internet and Beyond*. New York: Times Business, 1998.

36. Shapiro, Carl, and Hal Varian. *Information Rules: A Strategic Guide to the Network Economy*. Boston: Harvard Business School Press, 1999.

37. Sliwa, Carol. "Users Cling to EDI for Critical Transactions." *Computerworld*, March 15, 1999.

38. Tapscott, Don; David Ticoll; and Alex Lowy. *Digital Capital: Harnessing the Power of Business Webs*. Boston: Harvard Business School Press, 2000.

39. "Telefónica Servicios Avanzados De Informació Leads Spain's Retail Industry into Global Electronic Commerce." At www.netscape.com/solutions/business/profiles, March 1999.

40. Trombly, Marcia. "Electronic Billing Merger Should Benefit Billers, Banks." *Computerworld*, February 21, 2000.

41. Tully, Shawn. "The B2B Tool That Is Really Changing the World." *Fortune*, March 20, 2000.

Chapter 9—Decision Support Systems

1. Allen, Bradley. "Case-Based Reasoning: Business Applications." *Communications of the ACM*, March 1994.

2. Ashline, Peter, and Vincent Lai. "Virtual Reality: An Emerging User-Interface Technology." *Information Systems Management*, Winter 1995.

3. Begley, Sharon. "Software au Naturel." *Newsweek*, May 8, 1995.

4. Belcher, Lloyd, and Hugh Watson. "Assessing the Value of Conoco's EIS." *MIS Quarterly*, September 1993.

5. Blackburn, David; Rik Henderson; and Gary Welz. "VRML Evolution: State of the Art Advances." *Internet World*, December 1996.

6. Blattberg, Robert C.; Rashi Glazer; and John D. C. Little. *The Marketing Information Revolution*. Boston: The Harvard Business School Press, 1994.

7. Bose, Ranjit, and Vijayan Sugumaran. "Application of Intelligent Agent Technology for Managerial Data Analysis and Mining." *The Data Base for Advances in Information Systems*, Winter 1999.

8. Botchner, Ed. "Data Mining: Plumbing the Depths of Corporate Databases." Special Advertising Supplement. *Computerworld*, April 21, 1997.

9. Buta, Paul. "Mining for Financial Knowledge with CBR." *AI Expert*, February 1994.

10. Bylinsky, Gene. "To Create Products, Go into a CAVE." *Fortune*, February 5, 1996.

11. Cox, Earl. "Relational Database Queries Using Fuzzy Logic." *AI Expert*, January 1995.

12. Cronin, Mary. "Using the Web to Push Key Data to Decision Makers." *Fortune*, September 29, 1997.

13. Darling, Charles. "Ease Implementation Woes with Packaged Datamarts." *Datamation*, March 1997.

14. "Dayton Hudson Knows What's in Store for Their Customers." Advertising Section. *Intelligent Enterprise*, January 5, 1999.

15. Deck, Stewart. "Data Visualization." *Computerworld*, October 11, 1999.

16. Deck, Stewart. "Data Warehouse Project Starts Simply." *Computerworld*, February 15, 1999.

17. Deck, Stewart. "Early Users Give Nod to Analysis Package." *Computerworld*, February 22, 1999.

18. Deck, Stewart. "Mining Your Business." *Computerworld*, May 17, 1999.

19. Egan, Richard. "The Expert Within." *PC Today*, January 1995.

20. Finkelstein, Richard. *Understanding the Need for Online Analytical Servers.* Ann Arbor, MI: Comshare, 1994.

21. Finkelstein, Richard. "When OLAP Does Not Relate." *Computerworld*, December 12, 1994.

22. Freeman, Eva. "Birth of a Terabyte Data Warehouse." *Datamation*, April 1997.

23. Freeman, Eva. "Desktop Reporting Tools." *Datamation*, June 1997.

24. Gantz, John. "The New World of Enterprise Reporting Is Here." *Computerworld*, February 1, 1999.

25. Gates, Bill. *Business @ the Speed of Thought.* New York: Warner Books, 1999.

26. Goldberg, David. "Genetic and Evolutionary Algorithms Come of Age." *Communications of the ACM*, March 1994.

27. Gorry, G. Anthony, and Michael Scott Morton. "A Framework for Management Information Systems." *Sloan Management Review*, Fall 1971; republished Spring 1989.

28. Hall, Mark. "Supercomputing: From R&D to P&L." *Computerworld*, December 13, 1999.

29. "Helping Customers Help Themselves." Advertising Section. *Intelligent Enterprise*, January 5, 1999.

30. Higgins, Kelly. "Your Agent Is Calling." *Communications Week*, August 5, 1996.

31. Jablonowski, Mark. "Fuzzy Risk Analysis: Using AI Systems." *AI Expert*, December 1994.

32. Kalakota, Ravi, and Marcia Robinson. *E-Business: Roadmap for Success.* Reading, MA: Addison-Wesley, 1999.

33. Kalakota, Ravi, and Andrew Whinston. *Electronic Commerce: A Manager's Guide.* Reading, MA: Addison-Wesley, 1997.

34. King, James. "Intelligent Agents: Bringing Good Things to Life." *AI Expert*, February 1995.

35. King, Julia. "Infomediaries." *Computerworld*, November 1, 1999.

36. King, Julia. "Sharing GIS Talent with the World." *Computerworld*, October 6, 1997.

37. Kurszweil, Raymond. *The Age of Intelligent Machines.* Cambridge, MA: The MIT Press, 1992.

38. Lais, Sami. "CA Advances Neural Network System." *Computerworld*, December 13, 1999.

39. Lundquist, Christopher. "Personalization in E-Commerce." *Computerworld*, March 22, 1999.

40. Machlis, Sharon. "Agent Technology." *Computerworld*, March 22, 1999.

41. Mailoux, Jacquiline. "New Menu at PepsiCo." *Computerworld*, May 6, 1996.

42. McNeill, F. Martin, and Ellen Thro. *Fuzzy Logic: A Practical Approach.* Boston: AP Professional, 1994.

43. Murray, Gerry. "Making Connections with Enterprise Knowledge Portals." White Paper. *Computerworld*, September 6, 1999.

44. Orenstein, David. "Corporate Portals." *Computerworld*, June 28, 1999.

45. Ouellette, Tim. "Opening Your Own Portal." *Computerworld*, August 9, 1999.

46. Papows, Jeff. *Enterprise.com: Market Leadership in the Information Age.* Reading, MA: Perseus Books, 1998.

47. Phelps, Alan. "Knowledge Is Power." *Smart Computing*, February 2000.

48. Pimentel, Ken, and Kevin Teixeira. *Virtual Reality Through the New Looking Glass.* 2nd ed. New York: Intel/McGraw-Hill, 1995.

49. Plumtree Corporation. "Customer: Proctor and Gamble," *Plumtree.com*, March 16, 2001.

50. Turban, Efraim, and Jay Aronson. *Decision Support Systems and Intelligent Systems.* Upper Saddle River, NJ: Prentice Hall, 1998.

51. Vandenbosch, Betty, and Sid Huff. "Searching and Scanning: How Executives Obtain Information from Executive Information Systems." *MIS Quarterly*, March 1997.

52. Wagner, Mitch. "Engine Links Ads to Searches." *Computerworld*, June 2, 1997.

53. Wagner, Mitch. "Reality Check." *Computerworld,* February 26, 1997.

54. Watson, Hugh, and John Satzinger. "Guidelines for Designing EIS Interfaces." *Information Systems Management,* Fall 1994.

55. Watterson, Karen. "Parallel Tracks." *Datamation,* May 1997.

56. Winston, Patrick. "Rethinking Artificial Intelligence." Program Announcement, Massachusetts Institute of Technology, September 1997.

57. Wreden, Nick. "Enterprise Portals: Integrating Information to Drive Productivity." *Beyond Computing,* March 2000.

Chapter 10—Developing e-Business Solutions

1. Anthes, Gary. "The Quest for E-Quality." *Computerworld,* December 13, 1999.

2. Burden, Kevin. "IBM Waxes, Others Wane." *Computerworld,* March 15, 1999.

3. Clark, Charles; Nancy Cavanaugh; Carol Brown; and V. Sambamurthy. "Building Change-Readiness Capabilities in the IS Organization: Insights from the Bell Atlantic Experience." *MIS Quarterly,* December 1997.

4. Cole-Gomolski, Barbara. "Companies Turn to Web for ERP Training." *Computerworld,* February 8, 1999.

5. Cole-Gomolski, Barbara. "Users Loath to Share Their Know-How." *Computerworld,* November 17, 1997.

6. Cronin, Mary. *The Internet Strategy Handbook.* Boston: Harvard Business School Press, 1996.

7. Cross, John; Michael Earl; and Jeffrey Sampler. "Transformation of the IT Function at British Petroleum." *MIS Quarterly,* December 1997.

8. El Sawy, Omar, and Gene Bowles. "Redesigning the Customer Support Process for the Electronic Economy: Insights from Storage Dimensions." *MIS Quarterly,* December 1997.

9. El Sawy, Omar; Arvind Malhotra; Sanjay Gosain; and Kerry Young. "IT Intensive Value Innovation in the Electronic Economy: Insights from Marshall Industries." *MIS Quarterly,* September 1999.

10. Fogarty, Kevin. "Net Manners Matter: How Top Sites Rank in Social Behavior." *Computerworld,* October 18, 1999.

11. Grover, Varun; James Teng; and Kirk Fiedler. "IS Investment Priorities in Contemporary Organizations." *Communications of the ACM,* February 1998.

12. Haskin, David. "If I Had a Cyberhammer." *Business Week Enterprise,* March 29, 1999.

13. Hawson, James, and Jesse Beeler. "Effects of User Participation in Systems Development: A Longitudinal Field Experiment." *MIS Quarterly,* December 1997.

14. Hills, Melanie. *Intranet Business Strategies.* New York: John Wiley & Sons, 1997.

15. Holtz, Shel. *PCWeek: The Intranet Advantage.* Emeryville, CA: Ziff-Davis Press, 1996.

16. Iansiti, Marco, and Alan MacCormack. "Developing Products on Internet Time." *Harvard Business Review,* September–October 1997.

17. Kalakota, Ravi, and Marcia Robinson. *E-Business: Roadmap for Success.* Reading, MA: Addison-Wesley, 1999.

18. Kettinger, William; James Teng; and Subashish Guha. "Business Process Change: A Study of Methodologies, Techniques, and Tools." *MIS Quarterly,* March 1997.

19. Koudsi, Suzanne. "Actually, It Is Like Brain Surgery." *Fortune,* March 20, 2000.

20. LaPlante, Alice. "Eyes on the Customer." *Computerworld,* March 15, 1999.

21. Machlis, Sharon. "Web Retailers Retool for Mainstream Users." *Computerworld,* March 22, 1999.

22. Maglitta, Joseph. "Rocks in the Gears: Reengineering the Workplace." *Computerworld,* October 3, 1994.

23. Martin, Chuck. *The Digital Estate: Strategies for Competing, Surviving, and Thriving in an Internet-Worked World.* New York: McGraw-Hill, 1997.

24. Millard, Elizabeth, "Big Company Weakened." *Business 2.0,* January 2000.

25. Morgan, James N. *Application Cases in MIS.* 3rd ed. New York: Irwin/McGraw-Hill, 1999.

26. Nielsen, Jakob. "Jakob Nielsen on www.panasonic.com." *Red Herring,* February 2000.

27. Orenstein, David. "Software Is Too Hard to Use." *Computerworld,* August 23, 1999.

28. Ouellette, Tim. "Giving Users the Key to Their Web Content." *Computerworld,* July 26, 1999.

29. Ouellette, Tim. "Opening Your Own Portal." *Computerworld,* August 9, 1999.

30. Pereira, Rex Eugene. "Resource View of SAP as a Source of Competitive Advantage for Firms." *The Database for Advances in Information Systems,* Winter 1999.

31. Schwartz, Matthew. "Tweak This!" *Computerworld,* January 31, 2000.

32. Senge, Peter. *The Fifth Discipline: The Art and Practice of the Learning Organization.* New York: Currency Doubleday, 1994.

33. Sliwa, Carol. "E-Commerce Solutions: How Real?" *Computerworld,* February 28, 2000.

34. Steadman, Craig. "ERP Flops Point to Users' Plans." *Computerworld,* November 15, 1999.

35. Whitten Jeffrey, and Lonnie Bentley. *Systems Analysis and Design Methods*. 4th ed. New York: Irwin/McGraw-Hill, 1998.

36. Wreden, Nick. "Enterprise Portals: Integrating Information to Drive Productivity." *Beyond Computing*, March 2000.

Chapter 11—Security and Ethical Challenges of e-Business

1. Anthes, Gary. "Biometrics." *Computerworld*, October 12, 1998.

2. Anthes, Gary. "Lotsa Talk, Little Walk." In "Managing." *Computerworld*, September 21, 1998.

3. Bahar, Richard. "Who's Reading Your E-Mail?" *Fortune*, February 3, 1997.

4. Bloom, Paul; Robert Adler; and George Milne. "Identifying the Legal and Ethical Risks and Costs of Using New Information Technologies to Support Marketing Programs." In *The Marketing Information Revolution*, ed. Robert C. Blattberg, Rashi Glazer, and John D. C. Little. Boston: Harvard Business School Press, 1994.

5. Cole-Gomolski, Barb. "Quick Fixes Are of Limited Use in Deterring Force Diet of Spam." *Computerworld*, October 20, 1997.

6. Collett, Stacy. "Net Managers Battle Online Trading Boom." *Computerworld*, July 5, 1999.

7. Culnane, Mary. "How Did They Get My Name? An Exploratory Investigation of Consumer Attitudes Toward Secondary Information Use." *MIS Quarterly*, September 1993.

8. Deckmyn, Dominique. "More Managers Monitor E-Mail." *Computerworld*, October 18, 1999.

9. Dejoie, Roy; George Fowler; and David Paradice, eds. *Ethical Issues in Information Systems*. Boston: Boyd & Fraser, 1991.

10. Donaldson, Thomas. "Values in Tension: Ethics Away from Home." *Harvard Business Review*, September–October 1996.

11. Dunlop, Charles, and Rob Kling, eds. *Computerization and Controversy: Value Conflicts and Social Choices*. San Diego: Academic Press, 1991.

12. Duvall, Mel. "Protecting Against Viruses." *Inter@ctive Week*, February 28, 2000.

13. Essex, David. "Stop Desktop Virus Gremlins." *Computerworld*, December 6, 1999.

14. Ganesan, Ravi, and Ravi Sandhu, guest editors. "Security in Cyberspace." Special Section, *Communications of the ACM*, November 1994.

15. Harrison, Ann. "FBI Issues Software to Help Detect Web Attacks." *Computerworld*, February 14, 2000.

16. Harrison, Ann. "Internet Worm Destroys Data." *Computerworld*, June 14, 1999.

17. Harrison, Ann. "RealNetworks Slapped With Privacy Lawsuits." *Computerworld*, November 15, 1999.

18. Harrison, Ann. "Virus Scanning Moving to ISPs." *Computerworld*, September 20, 1999.

19. Joy, Bill. "Report From the Cyberfront." *Newsweek*, February 21, 2000.

20. Johnson, Deborah. "Ethics Online." *Communications of the ACM*, January 1997.

21. Kallman, Earnest, and John Grillo. *Ethical Decision Making and Information Technology: An Introduction with Cases*. New York: Mitchel McGraw-Hill, 1993.

22. Kover, Amy. "Who's Afraid of This Kid?" *Fortune*, March 20, 2000.

23. Liebman, Lenny. "Are Intranets Safe?" *Communications Week*, August 5, 1996.

24. Levy, Stephen, and Brad Stone. "Hunting the Hackers." *Newsweek*, February 21, 2000.

25. Martin, James. "You Are Being Watched." *PC World*, November 1997.

26. McCarthy, Michael. "Keystroke Cops." *The Wall Street Journal*, March 7, 2000.

27. McFarland, Michael. "Ethics and the Safety of Computer Systems." *Computer*, February 1991.

28. Morgan, Cynthia. "Web Merchants Stung by Fraud." *Computerworld*, March 8, 1999.

29. Naughton, Keith. "CyberSlacking," *Newsweek*, November 29, 1999.

30. Neumann, Peter. *Computer-Related Risks*. New York: ACM Press, 1995.

31. Radcliff, Deborah. "Fighting the Flood." *Computerworld*, March 6, 2000.

32. Radcliff, Deborah. "Three Industries: Three Security Needs." *Computerworld*, November 29, 1999.

33. Robinson, Lori. "How It Works: Viruses." *Smart Computing*, March 2000.

34. Rothfeder, Jeffrey. "Hacked! Are Your Company Files Safe?" *PC World*, November 1996.

35. Rothfeder, Jeffrey. "No Privacy on the Net." *PC World*, February 1997.

36. Sager, Ira; Steve Hamm; Neil Gross; John Carey; and Robert Hoff. "Cyber Crime." *Business Week*, February 21, 2000.

37. Sandberg, Jared. "Holes in the Net." *Newsweek*, February 21, 2000.

38. Smith, H. Jefferson, and John Hasnas. "Debating the Stakeholder Theory." *Beyond Computing*, March–April 1994.

39. Smith, H. Jefferson, and John Hasnas. "Establishing an Ethical Framework," *Beyond Computing*, January–February 1994.

40. Stark, Andrew. "What's the Matter with Business Ethics?" *Harvard Business Review*, May–June 1993.

41. Sullivan, Bob. "Melissa Macro Worms Around Web." MSNBC.com, March 27, 1999.

42. Tate, Priscilla. "Internet Security: Can Best Practices Overcome Worst Perils?" White Paper. *Computerworld*, May 4, 1998.

43. Willard, Nancy. *The Cyberethics Reader.* Burr Ridge, IL: Irwin/McGraw-Hill, 1997.

44. York, Thomas. "Invasion of Privacy? E-Mail Monitoring Is on the Rise." *Information Week Online*, February 21, 2000.

Chapter 12—Enterprise and Global Management of e-Business Technology

1. Alter, Allan. "Harmonic Convergence." In "The Premier 100." *Computerworld*, November 16, 1998.

2. Brandel, Mary. "Think Global, Act Local." *Computerworld Global Innovators*, Special Section, March 10, 1997.

3. Bryan, Lowell; Jane Fraser; Jeremy Oppenheim; and Wilhelm Rall. *Race for the World: Strategies to Build a Great Global Firm.* Boston: Harvard Business School Press, 1999.

4. Christensen, Clayton. *The Innovators Dilemma: When New Technologies Cause Great Firms to Fail.* Boston: Harvard Business School Press, 1997.

5. Corbett, Michael. "Outsourcing: Creating Competitive Advantage Through Specialization, Alliances, and Innovation." *Fortune*, Special Advertising Section, October 14, 1996.

6. Cronin, Mary. *Global Advantage on the Internet.* New York: Van Nostrand Reinhold, 1996.

7. DeGeus, Arie. "The Living Company." *Harvard Business Review*, March–April, 1997.

8. El Sawy, Omar; Arvind Malhotra; Sanjay Gosain; and Kerry Young. "IT Intensive Value Innovation in the Electronic Economy: Insights from Marshall Industries." *MIS Quarterly*, September 1999.

9. El Sawy, Omar, and Gene Bowles. "Redesigning the Customer Support Process for the Electronic Economy: Insights from Storage Dimensions." *MIS Quarterly*, December 1997.

10. Fryer, Bronwyn. "Payroll Busters." *Computerworld*, March 6, 2000.

11. Gates, Bill. *Business @ the Speed of Thought.* New York: Warner Books, 1999.

12. Grover, Varun; James Teng; and Kirk Fiedler. "IS Investment Opportunities in Contemporary Organizations." *Communications of the ACM*, February 1998.

13. Hall, Mark. "Service Providers Give Users More IT Options." *Computerworld*, February 7, 2000.

14. Hayes, Frank. "The Main Event." *Computerworld*, November 8, 1999.

15. Ives, Blake, and Sirkka Jarvenpaa. "Applications of Global Information Technology: Key Issues for Management." *MIS Quarterly*, March 1991.

16. Kalakota, Ravi, and Marcia Robinson. *E-Business: Roadmap for Success.* Reading, MA: Addison-Wesley, 1999.

17. Kalin, Sari. "The Importance of Being Multiculturally Correct." Global Innovators Series, *Computerworld*, October 6, 1997.

18. King, Julia. "Exporting Jobs Saves IT Money." *Computerworld*, March 15, 1999.

19. King, Julia. "Sun and Pay Lures Coders to Barbados Outsourcer." *Computerworld*, March 15, 1999.

20. King, Julia. "The Lure of Internet Spin-Offs." *Computerworld*, October 18, 1999.

21. Kirkpatrick, David. "Back to the Future with Centralized Computing." *Fortune*, November 10, 1997.

22. LaPlante, Alice. "Global Boundaries.com." Global Innovators Series, *Computerworld*, October 6, 1997.

23. Luftman, Jerry. "Align in the Sand." Leadership Series. *Computerworld*, February 17, 1997.

24. McGrath, Dermot. "When 'E' Stands for Europe." *Computerworld*, September 6, 1999.

25. Melymuka, Kathleen. "Ford's Driving Force." *Computerworld*, August 30, 1999.

26. Mische, Michael. "Transnational Architecture: A Reengineering Approach." *Information Systems Management*, Winter 1995.

27. Morgan, Cynthia. "ASPs Speak the Corporate Language." *Computerworld*, October 25, 1999.

28. Palvia, Prashant; Shailendra Palvia; and Edward Roche, eds. *Global Information Technology and Systems Management.* Marietta, GA: Ivy League Publishing, 1996.

29. Neilson, Gary; Bruce Pasternack; and Albert Visco. "Up the E-Organization! A Seven-Dimensional Model of the Centerless Enterprise." *Strategy & Business*, First Quarter 2000.

30. Shand, Dawne. "All Information Is Local." *Computerworld*, April 10, 2000.

31. Steadman, Craig. "Failed ERP Gamble Haunts Hershey." *Computerworld*, November 1, 1999.

32. Thibodeau, Patrick. "Europe and U.S. Agree on Data Rules." *Computerworld*, March 20, 2000.

33. Taggart, Stewart. "Censor Census." *Business 2.0*, March 2000.

34. Vander Weyer, Martin. "The World Debates." *Strategy & Business*, First Quarter 2000.

35. Vitalari, Nicholas, and James Wetherbe. "Emerging Best Practices in Global Systems Development." In *Global Information Technology and Systems Management*, ed. Prashant Palvia et al. Marietta, GA: Ivy League Publishing, 1996.

Accounting Information Systems
Information systems that record and report business transactions, the flow of funds through an organization, and produce financial statements. These provide information for the planning and control of business operations, as well as for legal and historical record-keeping.

Ad Hoc Inquiries
Unique, unscheduled, situation-specific information requests.

Ada
A programming language named after Augusta Ada Byron, considered the world's first computer programmer. Developed for the U.S. Department of Defense as a standard high-order language.

Agile Competition
The ability of a company to profitably operate in a competitive environment of continual and unpredictable changes in customer preferences, market conditions, and business opportunities.

Algorithm
A set of well-defined rules or processes for the solution of a problem in a finite number of steps.

Analog Computer
A computer that operates on data by measuring changes in continuous physical variables such as voltage, resistance, and rotation. Contrast with Digital Computer.

Analytical Database
A database of data extracted from operational and external databases to provide data tailored to online analytical processing, decision support, and executive information systems.

Analytical Modeling
Interactive use of computer-based mathematical models to explore decision alternatives using what-if analysis, sensitivity analysis, goal-seeking analysis, and optimization analysis.

Applet
A small limited-purpose application program, or small independent module of a larger application program.

Application Development
See Systems Development.

Application Generator
A software package that supports the development of an application through an interactive terminal dialogue, where the programmer/analyst defines screens, reports, computations, and data structures.

Application Portfolio
A planning tool used to evaluate present and proposed information systems applications in terms of the amount of revenue or assets invested in information systems that support major business functions and processes.

Application Server
System software that provides a middleware interface between an operating system and the application programs of users.

Application Software
Programs that specify the information processing activities required for the completion of specific tasks of computer users. Examples are electronic spreadsheet and word processing programs or inventory or payroll programs.

Applications Architecture
A conceptual planning framework in which business applications of information technology are designed as an integrated architecture of enterprise systems that support strategic business initiatives and cross-functional business processes.

Application-Specific Programs
Application software packages that support specific applications of end users in business, science and engineering, and other areas.

Arithmetic-Logic Unit (ALU)
The unit of a computing system containing the circuits that perform arithmetic and logical operations.

Artificial Intelligence (AI)
A science and technology whose goal is to develop computers that can think, as well as see, hear, walk, talk, and feel. A major thrust is the development of computer functions normally associated with human intelligence, for example, reasoning, inference, learning, and problem solving.

ASCII: American Standard Code for Information Interchange
A standard code used for information interchange among data processing systems, communication systems, and associated equipment.

Assembler
A computer program that translates an assembler language into machine language.

Assembler Language
A programming language that utilizes symbols to represent operation codes and storage locations.

Asynchronous
Involving a sequence of operations without a regular or predictable time relationship. Thus operations do not happen at regular timed intervals, but an operation will begin only after a previous operation is completed. In data transmission, involves the use of start and stop bits with each character to indicate the beginning and end of the character being transmitted. Contrast with Synchronous.

Audit Trail
The presence of media and procedures that allow a transaction to be traced through all stages of information processing, beginning with its appearance on a source document and ending with its transformation into information on a final output document.

Automated Teller Machine (ATM)
A special-purpose transaction terminal used to provide remote banking services.

Back-End Processor
Typically, a smaller general-purpose computer that is dedicated to database processing using a database management system (DBMS). Also called a database machine or server.

Background Processing
The automatic execution of lower-priority computer programs when higher-priority programs are not using the resources of the computer system. Contrast with Foreground Processing.

Backward-Chaining
An inference process that justifies a proposed conclusion by determining if it will result when rules are applied to the facts in a given situation.

Bandwidth
The frequency range of a telecommunications channel, which determines its maximum transmission rate. The speed and capacity of transmission rates are typically measured in bits per second (BPS). Bandwidth is a function of the telecommunications hardware, software, and media used by the telecommunications channel.

Bar Codes
Vertical marks or bars placed on merchandise tags or packaging that can be sensed and read by optical character-reading devices. The width and combination of vertical lines are used to represent data.

Barriers to Entry
Technological, financial, or legal requirements that deter firms from entering an industry.

BASIC: Beginner's All-Purpose Symbolic Instruction Code
A programming language developed at Dartmouth College designed for programming by end users.

Batch Processing
A category of data processing in which data are accumulated into batches and processed periodically. Contrast with Realtime Processing.

Baud
A unit of measurement used to specify data transmission speeds. It is a unit of signaling speed equal to the number of discrete conditions or signal events per second. In many data communications applications it represents one bit per second.

Binary
Pertaining to a characteristic or property involving a selection, choice, or condition in which there are two possibilities, or pertaining to the number system that utilizes a base of 2.

Biometric Controls
Computer-based security methods that measure physical traits and characteristics such as fingerprints, voice prints, retina scans, and so on.

Bit
A contraction of "binary digit." It can have the value of either 0 or 1.

Block
A grouping of contiguous data records or other data elements that are handled as a unit.

Branch
A transfer of control from one instruction to another in a computer program that is not part of the normal sequential execution of the instructions of the program.

Browser
See Web Browser.

Buffer
Temporary storage used when transmitting data from one device to another to compensate for a difference in rate of flow of data or time of occurrence of events.

Bug
A mistake or malfunction.

Bulletin Board System (BBS)
A service of online computer networks in which electronic messages, data files, or programs can be stored for other subscribers to read or copy.

Bundling
The inclusion of software, maintenance, training, and other products or services in the price of a computer system.

Bus
A set of conducting paths for movement of data and instructions that interconnects the various components of the CPU.

Business Ethics
An area of philosophy concerned with developing ethical principles and promoting ethical behavior and practices in the accomplishment of business tasks and decision making.

Business Process Reengineering (BPR)
Restructuring and transforming a business process by a fundamental rethinking and redesign to achieve dramatic improvements in cost, quality, speed, and so on.

Byte
A sequence of adjacent binary digits operated on as a unit and usually shorter than a computer word. In many computer systems, a byte is a grouping of eight bits that can represent one alphabetic or special character or can be packed with two decimal digits.

C
A low-level structured programming language that resembles a machine-independent assembler language.

C++
An object-oriented version of C that is widely used for software package development.

Cache Memory
A high-speed temporary storage area in the CPU for storing parts of a program or data during processing.

Capacity Management
The use of planning and control methods to forecast and control information processing job loads, hardware and software usage, and other computer system resource requirements.

Case-Based Reasoning
Representing knowledge in an expert system's knowledge base in the form of cases, that is, examples of past performance, occurrences, and experiences.

Cathode Ray Tube (CRT)
An electronic vacuum tube (television picture tube) that displays the output of a computer system.

CD-ROM
An optical disk technology for microcomputers featuring compact disks with a storage capacity of over 500 megabytes.

Cellular Phone Systems
A radio communications technology that divides a metropolitan area into a honeycomb of cells to greatly increase the number of frequencies and thus the users that can take advantage of mobile phone service.

Central Processing Unit (CPU)
The unit of a computer system that includes the circuits that control the interpretation and execution of instructions. In many computer systems, the CPU includes the arithmetic-logic unit, the control unit, and the primary storage unit.

Change Management
Managing the process of implementing major changes in information technology, business processes,

organizational structures, and job assignments to reduce the risks and costs of change, and optimize its benefits.

Channel
(1) A path along which signals can be sent. (2) A small special-purpose processor that controls the movement of data between the CPU and input/output devices.

Chargeback Systems
Methods of allocating costs to end user departments based on the information services rendered and information system resources utilized.

Chat Systems
Software that enables two or more users at networked PCs to carry on online, realtime text conversations.

Check Bit
A binary check digit; for example, a parity bit.

Check Digit
A digit in a data field that is utilized to check for errors or loss of characters in the data field as a result of data transfer operations.

Checkpoint
A place in a program where a check or a recording of data for restart purposes is performed.

Chief Information Officer
A senior management position that oversees all information technology for a firm concentrating on long-range information system planning and strategy.

Client
(1) An end user. (2) The end user's networked microcomputer in client/server networks. (3) The version of a software package designed to run on an end user's networked microcomputer, such as a Web browser client, a groupware client, and so on.

Client/Server Network
A computer network where end user workstations (clients) are connected via telecommunications links to network servers and possibly to mainframe superservers.

Clock
A device that generates periodic signals utilized to control the timing of a computer. Also, a register whose contents change at regular intervals in such a way as to measure time.

Coaxial Cable
A sturdy copper or aluminum wire wrapped with spacers to insulate and protect it. Groups of coaxial cables may also be bundled together in a bigger cable for ease of installation.

COBOL: COmmon Business Oriented Language
A widely used business data processing programming language.

Code
Computer instructions.

Cognitive Science
An area of artificial intelligence that focuses on researching how the human brain works and how humans think and learn, in order to apply such findings to the design of computer-based systems.

Cognitive Styles
Basic patterns in how people handle information and confront problems.

Cognitive Theory
Theories about how the human brain works and how humans think and learn.

Collaborative Work Management Tools
Software that helps people accomplish or manage joint work activities.

Communications Satellite
Earth satellites placed in stationary orbits above the equator that serve as relay stations for communications signals transmitted from earth stations.

Competitive Advantage
Developing products, services, processes, or capabilities that give a company a superior business position relative to its competitors and other competitive forces.

Competitive Forces
A firm must confront (1) rivalry of competitors within its industry, (2) threats of new entrants, (3) threats of substitutes, (4) the bargaining power of customers, and (5) the bargaining power of suppliers.

Competitive Strategies
A firm can develop cost leadership, product differentiation, and business innovation strategies to confront its competitive forces.

Compiler
A program that translates a high-level programming language into a machine-language program.

Computer
A device that has the ability to accept data; internally store and execute a program of instructions; perform mathematical, logical, and manipulative operations on data; and report the results.

Computer-Aided Design (CAD)
The use of computers and advanced graphics hardware and software to provide interactive design assistance for engineering and architectural design.

Computer-Aided Engineering (CAE)
The use of computers to simulate, analyze, and evaluate models of product designs and production processes developed using computer-aided design methods.

Computer-Aided Manufacturing (CAM)
The use of computers to automate the production process and operations of a manufacturing plant. Also called factory automation.

Computer-Aided Planning (CAP)
The use of software packages as tools to support the planning process.

Computer-Aided Software Engineering (CASE)
Same as Computer-Aided Systems Engineering, but emphasizing the importance of software development.

Computer-Aided Systems Engineering (CASE)
Using software packages to accomplish and automate many of the activities of information systems development, including software development or programming.

Computer Application
The use of a computer to solve a specific problem or to accomplish a particular job for an end user. For example, common business computer applications include sales order processing, inventory control, and payroll.

Computer-Assisted Instruction (CAI)
The use of computers to provide drills, practice exercises, and tutorial sequences to students.

Computer-Based Information System
An information system that uses computer hardware and software to perform its information processing activities.

Computer Crime
Criminal actions accomplished through the use of computer systems, especially with intent to defraud, destroy, or make unauthorized use of computer system resources.

Computer Ethics
A system of principles governing the legal, professional, social, and moral responsibilities of computer specialists and end users.

Computer Generations
Major stages in the historical development of computing.

Computer Graphics
Using computer-generated images to analyze and interpret data, present

information, and do computer-aided design and art.

Computer Industry
The industry composed of firms that supply computer hardware, software, and services.

Computer-Integrated Manufacturing (CIM)
An overall concept that stresses that the goals of computer use in factory automation should be to simplify, automate, and integrate production processes and other aspects of manufacturing.

Computer Matching
Using computers to screen and match data about individual characteristics provided by a variety of computer-based information systems and databases in order to identify individuals for business, government, or other purposes.

Computer Monitoring
Using computers to monitor the behavior and productivity of workers on the job and in the workplace.

Computer Program
A series of instructions or statements in a form acceptable to a computer, prepared in order to achieve a certain result.

Computer System
Computer hardware as a system of input, processing, output, storage, and control components. Thus a computer system consists of input and output devices, primary and secondary storage devices, the central processing unit, the control unit within the CPU, and other peripheral devices.

Computer Terminal
Any input/output device connected by telecommunications links to a computer.

Computer Virus or Worm
Program code that copies its destructive program routines into the computer systems of anyone who accesses computer systems that have used the program, or anyone who uses copies of data or programs taken from such computers. This spreads the destruction of data and programs among many computer users. Technically, a virus will not run unaided, but must be inserted into another program, while a worm is a distinct program that can run unaided.

Concurrent Processing
The generic term for the capability of computers to work on several tasks at the same time, that is, concurrently. This may involve specific capabilities such as

overlapped processing, multiprocessing, multiprogramming, multitasking, parallel processing, and so on.

Connectivity
The degree to which hardware, software, and databases can be easily linked together in a telecommunications network.

Control
(1) The systems component that evaluates feedback to determine whether the system is moving toward the achievement of its goal and then makes any necessary adjustments to the input and processing components of the system to ensure that proper output is produced. (2) A management function that involves observing and measuring organizational performance and environmental activities and modifying the plans and activities of the organization when necessary.

Control Listing
A detailed report that describes each transaction occurring during a period.

Control Totals
Accumulating totals of data at multiple points in an information system to ensure correct information processing.

Control Unit
A subunit of the central processing unit that controls and directs the operations of the computer system. The control unit retrieves computer instructions in proper sequence, interprets each instruction, and then directs the other parts of the computer system in their implementation.

Conversion
The process in which the hardware, software, people, network, and data resources of an old information system must be converted to the requirements of a new information system. This usually involves a parallel, phased, pilot, or plunge conversion process from the old to the new system.

Cooperative Processing
Information processing that allows the computers in a distributed processing network to share the processing of parts of an end user's application.

Cost/Benefit Analysis
Identifying the advantages or benefits and the disadvantages or costs of a proposed solution.

Critical Success Factors
A small number of key factors that executives consider critical to the success of the enterprise. These are key areas where successful performance will assure the success of the organization and attainment of its goals.

Cross-Functional Information Systems
Information systems that are integrated combinations of business information systems, thus sharing information resources across the functional units of an organization.

Cursor
A movable point of light displayed on most video display screens to assist the user in the input of data.

Customer Relationship Management (CRM)
A cross-functional e-business application that integrates and automates many customer serving processes in sales, direct marketing, account and order management, and customer service and support.

Cybernetic System
A system that uses feedback and control components to achieve a self-regulating capability.

Cylinder
An imaginary vertical cylinder consisting of the vertical alignment of tracks on each surface of magnetic disks that are accessed simultaneously by the read/write heads of a disk drive.

Data
Facts or observations about physical phenomena or business transactions. More specifically, data are objective measurements of the attributes (characteristics) of entities such as people, places, things, and events.

Data Administration
A data resource management function that involves the establishment and enforcement of policies and procedures for managing data as a strategic corporate resource.

Database
An integrated collection of logically re-lated data elements. A database consol-idates many records previously stored in separate files so that a common pool of data serves many applications.

Database Administration
A data resource management function that includes responsibility for developing and maintaining the organization's data dictionary, designing and monitoring the performance of databases, and enforcing standards for database use and security.

Database Administrator
A specialist responsible for maintaining standards for the development, maintenance, and security of an organization's databases.

Database Maintenance
The activity of keeping a database up-to-date by adding, changing, or deleting data.

Database Management Approach
An approach to the storage and processing of data in which independent files are consolidated into a common pool, or database, of records available to different application programs and end users for processing and data retrieval.

Database Management System (DBMS)
A set of computer programs that controls the creation, maintenance, and utilization of the databases of an organization.

Database Processing
Utilizing a database for data processing activities such as maintenance, information retrieval, or report generation.

Data Center
An organizational unit that uses centralized computing resources to perform information processing activities for an organization. Also known as a computer center.

Data Conferencing
Users at networked PCs can view, mark up, revise, and save changes to a shared whiteboard of drawings, documents, and other material.

Data Design
The design of the logical structure of databases and files to be used by a proposed information system. This produces detailed descriptions of the entities, relationships, data elements, and integrity rules for system files and databases.

Data Dictionary
A software module and database containing descriptions and definitions concerning the structure, data elements, interrelationships, and other characteristics of a database.

Data Entry
The process of converting data into a form suitable for entry into a computer system. Also called data capture or input preparation.

Data Flow Diagram
A graphic diagramming tool that uses a few simple symbols to illustrate the flow of data among external entities, processing activities, and data storage elements.

Data Management
Control program functions that provide access to data sets, enforce data storage conventions, and regulate the use of input/output devices.

Data Mining
Using special-purpose software to analyze data from a data warehouse to find hidden patterns and trends.

Data Model
A conceptual framework that defines the logical relationships among the data elements needed to support a basic business or other process.

Data Modeling
A process where the relationships between data elements are identified and defined to develop data models.

Data Planning
A corporate planning and analysis function that focuses on data resource management. It includes the responsibility for developing an overall information policy and data architecture for the firm's data resources.

Data Processing
The execution of a systematic sequence of operations performed upon data to transform it into information.

Data Resource Management
A managerial activity that applies information systems technology and management tools to the task of managing an organization's data resources. Its three major components are database administration, data administration, and data planning.

Data Warehouse
An integrated collection of data extracted from operational, historical, and external databases, and cleaned, transformed, and cataloged for retrieval and analysis (*data mining*), to provide business intelligence for business decision making.

Debug
To detect, locate, and remove errors from a program or malfunctions from a computer.

Decision Support System (DSS)
An information system that utilizes decision models, a database, and a decision maker's own insights in an ad hoc, interactive analytical modeling process to reach a specific decision by a specific decision maker.

Demand Reports and Responses
Information provided whenever a manager or end user demands it.

Desktop Publishing
The use of microcomputers, laser printers, and page-makeup software to produce a variety of printed materials that were formerly produced only by professional printers.

Desktop Videoconferencing
The use of end user computer workstations to conduct two-way interactive video conferences.

Development Centers
Systems development consultant groups formed to serve as consultants to the professional programmers and systems analysts of an organization to improve their application development efforts.

Digital Computer
A computer that operates on digital data by performing arithmetic and logical operations on the data. Contrast with Analog Computer.

Digitizer
A device that is used to convert drawings and other graphic images on paper or other materials into digital data that are entered into a computer system.

Direct Access
A method of storage where each storage position has a unique address and can be individually accessed in approximately the same period of time without having to search through other storage positions. Same as Random Access. Contrast with Sequential Access.

Direct Access Storage Device (DASD)
A storage device that can directly access data to be stored or retrieved, for example, a magnetic disk unit.

Direct Data Organization
A method of data organization in which logical data elements are distributed randomly on or within the physical data medium. For example, logical data records distributed randomly on the surfaces of a magnetic disk file. Also called direct organization.

Direct Input/Output
Methods such as keyboard entry, voice input/output, and video displays that allow data to be input into or output from a computer system without the use of machine-readable media.

Disaster Recovery
Methods for ensuring that an organization recovers from natural and human-caused disasters that have affected its computer-based operations.

Discussion Forum
An online network discussion platform to encourage and manage online text discussions over a period of time among members of special interest groups or project teams.

Distributed Databases
The concept of distributing databases or portions of a database at remote sites where the data are most frequently referenced. Sharing of data is made possible through a network that interconnects the distributed databases.

Distributed Processing
A form of decentralization of information processing made possible by a network of computers dispersed throughout an organization. Processing of user applications is accomplished by several computers interconnected by a telecommunications network, rather than relying on one large centralized computer facility or on the decentralized operation of several independent computers.

Document
(1) A medium on which data have been recorded for human use, such as a report or invoice. (2) In word processing, a generic term for text material such as letters, memos, reports, and so on.

Documentation
A collection of documents or information that describes a computer program, information system, or required data processing operations.

Downsizing
Moving to smaller computing platforms, such as from mainframe systems to networks of personal computers and servers.

Downtime
The time interval during which a device is malfunctioning or inoperative.

DSS Generator
A software package for a decision support system that contains modules for database, model, and dialogue management.

Duplex
In communications, pertains to a simultaneous two-way independent transmission in both directions.

EBCDIC: Extended Binary Coded Decimal Interchange Code
An eight-bit code that is widely used by mainframe computers.

e-Business Decision Support
The use of Web-enabled DSS software tools by managers, employees, customers, suppliers, and other business partners of an internetworked e-business enterprise for customer relationship management, supply chain management, and other e-business applications.

e-Business Enterprise
A business that uses the Internet, intranets, extranets, and other computer networks to support electronic commerce and other electronic business processes, decision making, and team and workgroup collaboration within the enterprise and among its customers, suppliers, and other business partners.

e-Business Organization
An e-business enterprise whose organizational structure and roles have been reengineered to help it become a flexible, agile, customer-focused, value-driven leader in e-commerce.

e-Business Planning
The process of developing a company's e-business vision, strategies, goals, and how they will be supported by the company's information technology architecture and implemented by its e-business application development process.

e-Business Technology Management
Managing information technologies in an e-business enterprise by (1) the joint development and implementation of e-business and IT strategies by business and IT executives, (2) managing the research and implementation of new information technologies and the development of e-business applications, and (3) managing IT processes, professionals, and subunits within a company's IT organization and IS function.

Echo Check
A method of checking the accuracy of transmission of data in which the received data are returned to the sending device for comparison with the original data.

e-Commerce Marketplaces
Internet, intranet, and extranet websites and portals hosted by individual companies, consortiums of organizations, or third-party intermediaries providing electronic catalog, exchange, and auction markets to unite buyers and sellers to accomplish e-commerce transactions.

Economic Feasibility
Whether expected cost savings, increased revenue, increased profits, and reductions in required investment exceed the costs of developing and operating a proposed system.

EDI: Electronic Data Interchange
The automatic electronic exchange of business documents between the computers of different organizations.

Edit
To modify the form or format of data. For example: to insert or delete characters such as page numbers or decimal points.

Edit Report
A report that describes errors detected during processing.

EFT: Electronic Funds Transfer
The development of banking and payment systems that transfer funds electronically instead of using cash or paper documents such as checks.

Electronic Business (e-Business)
The use of Internet technologies to internetwork and empower business processes, electronic commerce, and enterprise communication and collaboration within a company and with its customers, suppliers, and other business stakeholders.

Electronic Commerce (e-Commerce)
The buying and selling, marketing and servicing, and delivery and payment of products, services, and information over the Internet, intranets, extranets, and other networks, between an internetworked enterprise and its prospects, customers, suppliers, and other business partners. Includes business-to-consumer (B2C), business-to-business (B2B), and consumer-to-consumer (C2C) e-commerce.

Electronic Communications Tools
Software that helps you communicate and collaborate with others by electronically sending messages, documents, and files in data, text, voice, or multimedia over the Internet, intranets, extranets, and other computer networks.

Electronic Conferencing Tools
Software that helps networked computer users share information and collaborate while working together on joint assignments, no matter where they are located.

Electronic Data Processing (EDP)
The use of electronic computers to process data automatically.

Electronic Document Management
An image processing technology in which an electronic document may consist of digitized voice notes and electronic graphics images, as well as digitized images of traditional documents.

Electronic Mail
Sending and receiving text messages between networked PCs over telecommunications networks. E-mail can also include data files, software, and multimedia messages and documents as attachments.

Electronic Meeting Systems (EMS)
Using a meeting room with networked PCs, a large-screen projector, and EMS software to facilitate communication, collaboration, and group decision making in business meetings.

Electronic Payment Systems
Alternative cash or credit payment methods using various electronic technologies to pay for products and services in electronic commerce.

Electronic Spreadsheet Package
An application program used as a

computerized tool for analysis, planning, and modeling that allows users to enter and manipulate data into an electronic worksheet of rows and columns.

Emulation
To imitate one system with another so that the imitating system accepts the same data, executes the same programs, and achieves the same results as the imitated system.

Encryption
To scramble data or convert it, prior to transmission, to a secret code that masks the meaning of the data to unauthorized recipients. Similar to enciphering.

End User
Anyone who uses an information system or the information it produces.

End User Computing Systems
Computer-based information systems that directly support both the operational and managerial applications of end users.

Enterprise Application Integration (EAI)
A cross-functional e-business application that integrates front-office applications like customer relationship management with back-office applications like enterprise resource management.

Enterprise Collaboration Systems
The use of groupware tools and the Internet, intranets, extranets, and other computer networks to support and enhance communication, coordination, collaboration, and resource sharing among teams and workgroups in an internetworked enterprise.

Enterprise Information Portal
A customized and personalized Web-based interface for corporate intranets and extranets that gives qualified users access to a variety of internal and external e-business and e-commerce applications, databases, software tools, and information services.

Enterprise Knowledge Portal
An enterprise information portal that serves as a knowledge management system by providing users with access to enterprise knowledge bases.

Enterprise Model
A conceptual framework that defines the structures and relationships of business processes and data elements, as well as other planning structures, such as critical success factors, and organizational units.

Enterprise Resource Planning (ERP)
Integrated cross-functional software

that reengineers manufacturing, distribution, finance, human resources and other basic business processes of a company to improve its efficiency, agility, and profitability.

Entity Relationship Diagram (ERD)
A data planning and systems development diagramming tool that models the relationships among the entities in a business process.

Entropy
The tendency of a system to lose a relatively stable state of equilibrium.

Ergonomics
The science and technology emphasizing the safety, comfort, and ease of use of human-operated machines such as computers. The goal of ergonomics is to produce systems that are user-friendly: safe, comfortable, and easy to use. Ergonomics is also called human factors engineering.

Exception Reports
Reports produced only when exceptional conditions occur, or reports produced periodically that contain information only about exceptional conditions.

Executive Information Systems (EIS)
An information system that provides strategic information tailored to the needs of executives and other decision makers.

Executive Support System (ESS)
An executive information system with additional capabilities, including data analysis, decision support, electronic mail, and personal productivity tools.

Expert System (ES)
A computer-based information system that uses its knowledge about a specific complex application area to act as an expert consultant to users. The system consists of a knowledge base and software modules that perform inferences on the knowledge and communicate answers to a user's questions.

Extranet
A network that links selected resources of a company with its customers, suppliers, and other business partners, using the Internet or private networks to link the organizations' intranets.

Facilities Management
The use of an external service organization to operate and manage the information processing facilities of an organization.

Fault Tolerant Systems
Computers that have multiple central processors, peripherals, and system

software and that are able to continue operations even if there is a major hardware or software failure.

Faxing (Facsimile)
Transmitting and receiving images of documents over the telephone or computer networks using PCs or fax machines.

Feasibility Study
A preliminary study that investigates the information needs of end users and the objectives, constraints, basic resource requirements, cost/benefits, and feasibility of proposed projects.

Feedback
(1) Data or information concerning the components and operations of a system. (2) The use of part of the output of a system as input to the system.

Fiber Optics
The technology that uses cables consisting of very thin filaments of glass fibers that can conduct the light generated by lasers for high-speed telecommunications.

Field
A data element that consists of a grouping of characters that describe a particular attribute of an entity. For example: the name field or salary field of an employee.

Fifth Generation
The next generation of computers. Major advances in parallel processing, user interfaces, and artificial intelligence may provide computers that will be able to see, hear, talk, and think.

File
A collection of related data records treated as a unit. Sometimes called a data set.

File Management
Controlling the creation, deletion, access, and use of files of data and programs.

Financial Management Systems
Information systems that support financial managers in the financing of a business and the allocation and control of financial resources. These include cash and securities management, capital budgeting, financial forecasting, and financial planning.

Fire Wall Computer
Computers, communications processors, and software that protect computer networks from intrusion by screening all network traffic and serving as a safe transfer point for access to and from other networks.

Firmware
The use of microprogrammed read only memory circuits in place of

hard-wired logic circuitry. See also Microprogramming.

Floating Point
Pertaining to a number representation system in which each number is represented by two sets of digits. One set represents the significant digits or fixed-point "base" of the number, while the other set of digits represents the "exponent," which indicates the precision of the number.

Floppy Disk
A small plastic disk coated with iron oxide that resembles a small phonograph record enclosed in a protective envelope. It is a widely used form of magnetic disk media that provides a direct access storage capability for microcomputer systems.

Flowchart
A graphical representation in which symbols are used to represent operations, data, flow, logic, equipment, and so on. A program flowchart illustrates the structure and sequence of operations of a program, while a system flowchart illustrates the components and flows of information systems.

Foreground Processing
The automatic execution of the computer programs that have been designed to preempt the use of computing facilities. Contrast with Background Processing.

Format
The arrangement of data on a medium.

FORTRAN: FORmula TRANslation
A high-level programming language widely utilized to develop computer programs that perform mathematical computations for scientific, engineering, and selected business applications.

Forward Chaining
An inference strategy that reaches a conclusion by applying rules to facts to determine if any facts satisfy a rule's conditions in a particular situation.

Fourth-Generation Languages (4GL)
Programming languages that are easier to use than high-level languages like BASIC, COBOL, or FORTRAN. They are also known as nonprocedural, natural, or very-high-level languages.

Frame
A collection of knowledge about an entity or other concept consisting of a complex package of slots, that is, data values describing the characteristics or attributes of an entity.

Frame-Based Knowledge
Knowledge represented in the form of a hierarchy or network of frames.

Front-End Processor
Typically a smaller, general-purpose computer that is dedicated to handling data communications control functions in a communications network, thus relieving the host computer of these functions.

Functional Business Systems
Information systems within a business organization that support one of the traditional functions of business such as marketing, finance, or production. Functional business systems can be either operations or management information systems.

Functional Requirements
The information system capabilities required to meet the information needs of end users. Also called system requirements.

Fuzzy Logic Systems
Computer-based systems that can process data that are incomplete or only partially correct, that is, fuzzy data. Such systems can solve unstructured problems with incomplete knowledge, as humans do.

General-Purpose Application Programs
Programs that can perform information processing jobs for users from all application areas. For example, word processing programs, electronic spreadsheet programs, and graphics programs can be used by individuals for home, education, business, scientific, and many other purposes.

General-Purpose Computer
A computer that is designed to handle a wide variety of problems. Contrast with Special-Purpose Computer.

Generate
To produce a machine-language program for performing a specific data processing task based on parameters supplied by a programmer or user.

Genetic Algorithm
An application of artificial intelligence software that uses Darwinian (survival of the fittest) randomizing and other functions to simulate an evolutionary process that can yield increasingly better solutions to a problem.

Gigabyte
One billion bytes. More accurately, 2 to the 30th power, or 1,073,741,824 in decimal notation.

GIGO
A contraction of "Garbage In, Garbage Out," which emphasizes that information systems will produce erroneous and invalid output when provided with erroneous and invalid input data or instructions.

Global Company
A business that is driven by a global strategy so that all of its activities are planned and implemented in the context of a whole-world system.

Global e-Business Technology Management
Managing information technologies in a global e-business enterprise, amid the cultural, political, and geoeconomic challenges involved in developing e-business/IT strategies, global e-business and e-commerce applications portfolios, Internet-based technology platforms, and global data resource management policies.

Global Information Technology
The use of computer-based information systems and telecommunications networks using a variety of information technologies to support global business operations and management.

Globalization
Becoming a global enterprise by expanding into global markets, using global production facilities, forming alliances with global partners, and so on.

Goal-Seeking Analysis
Making repeated changes to selected variables until a chosen variable reaches a target value.

Graphical User Interface
A software interface that relies on icons, bars, buttons, boxes, and other images to initiate computer-based tasks for users.

Graphics
Pertaining to symbolic input or output from a computer system, such as lines, curves, and geometric shapes, using video display units or graphics plotters and printers.

Graphics Pen and Tablet
A device that allows an end user to draw or write on a pressure-sensitive tablet and have the handwriting or graphics digitized by the computer and accepted as input.

Graphics Software
A program that helps users generate graphics displays.

Group Decision Making
Decisions made by groups of people coming to an agreement on a particular issue.

Group Decision Support System (GDSS)
A decision support system that provides support for decision making by groups of people.

Group Support Systems (GSS)
An information system that enhances communication, coordination, collaboration, decision making, and group work activities of teams and workgroups.

Groupware
Software to support and enhance the communication, coordination, and collaboration among networked teams and workgroups, including software tools for electronic communications, electronic conferencing, and cooperative work management.

Hacking
(1) Obsessive use of a computer.
(2) The unauthorized access and use of computer systems.

Handshaking
Exchange of predetermined signals when a connection is established between two communications terminals.

Hard Copy
A data medium or data record that has a degree of permanence and that can be read by people or machines.

Hardware
(1) Machines and media. (2) Physical equipment, as opposed to computer programs or methods of use.
(3) Mechanical, magnetic, electrical, electronic, or optical devices. Contrast with Software.

Hash Total
The sum of numbers in a data field that are not normally added, such as account numbers or other identification numbers. It is utilized as a control total, especially during input/output operations of batch processing systems.

Header Label
A machine-readable record at the beginning of a file containing data for file identification and control.

Heuristic
Pertaining to exploratory methods of problem solving in which solutions are discovered by evaluation of the progress made toward the final result. It is an exploratory trial-and-error approach guided by rules of thumb. Opposite of algorithmic.

Hierarchical Data Structure
A logical data structure in which the relationships between records form a hierarchy or tree structure. The relationships among records are one to many, since each data element is related only to one element above it.

High-Level Language
A programming language that utilizes macro instructions and statements that closely resemble human language or mathematical notation to describe the problem to be solved or the procedure to be used. Also called a compiler language.

Homeostasis
A relatively stable state of equilibrium of a system.

Host Computer
Typically a larger central computer that performs the major data processing tasks in a computer network.

Human Factors
Hardware and software capabilities that can affect the comfort, safety, ease of use, and user customization of computer-based information systems.

Human Information Processing
A conceptual framework about the human cognitive process that uses an information processing context to explain how humans capture, process, and use information.

Human Resource Information Systems (HRIS)
Information systems that support human resource management activities such as recruitment, selection and hiring, job placement and performance appraisals, and training and development.

Hybrid AI Systems
Systems that integrate several AI technologies, such as expert systems and neural networks.

Hypermedia
Documents containing multiple forms of media, including text, graphics, video, and sound, that can be interactively searched, like Hypertext.

Hypertext
Text in electronic form that has been indexed and linked (hyperlinks) by software in a variety of ways so that it can be randomly and interactively searched by a user.

Hypertext Markup Language (HTML)
A popular page description language for creating hypertext and hypermedia documents for World Wide Web and intranet websites.

Icon
A small figure on a video display that looks like a familiar office or other device such as a file folder (for storing a file) or a wastebasket (for deleting a file).

Image Processing
A computer-based technology that allows end users to electronically capture, store, process, and retrieve images that may include numeric data, text, handwriting, graphics, documents, and photographs. Image processing makes heavy use of optical scanning and optical disk technologies.

Impact Printers
Printers that form images on paper through the pressing of a printing element and an inked ribbon or roller against the face of a sheet of paper.

Index
An ordered reference list of the contents of a file or document together with keys or reference notations for identification or location of those contents.

Index Sequential
A method of data organization in which records are organized in sequential order and also referenced by an index. When utilized with direct access file devices, it is known as index sequential access method, or ISAM.

Inference Engine
The software component of an expert system, which processes the rules and facts related to a specific problem and makes associations and inferences resulting in recommended courses of action.

Infomediaries
Third-party market-maker companies who serve as intermediaries to bring buyers and sellers together by developing and hosting electronic catalog, exchange, and auction markets to accomplish e-commerce transactions.

Information
Information is data placed in a meaningful and useful context for an end user.

Information Appliance
Small Web-enabled microcomputer devices with specialized functions, such as hand-held PDAs, TV set-top boxes, game consoles, cellular and PCS phones, wired telephone appliances, and other Web-enabled home appliances.

Information Architecture
A conceptual framework that defines the basic structure, content, and relationships of the organizational databases that provide the data needed to support the basic business processes of an organization.

Information Center
A support facility for the end users of an organization. It allows users to learn to develop their own application programs and to accomplish their own information processing tasks. End users

are provided with hardware support, software support, and people support (trained user consultants).

Information Float
The time when a document is in transit between the sender and receiver, and thus unavailable for any action or response.

Information Processing
A concept that covers both the traditional concept of processing numeric and alphabetic data, and the processing of text, images, and voices. It emphasizes that the production of information products for users should be the focus of processing activities.

Information Quality
The degree to which information has content, form, and time characteristics that give it value to specific end users.

Information Resource Management (IRM)
A management concept that views data, information, and computer resources (computer hardware, software, networks, and personnel) as valuable organizational resources that should be efficiently, economically, and effectively managed for the benefit of the entire organization.

Information Retrieval
The methods and procedures for recovering specific information from stored data.

Information Superhighway
An advanced high-speed Internet-like network that connects individuals, households, businesses, government agencies, libraries, schools, universities, and other institutions with interactive voice, video, data, and multimedia communications.

Information System
(1) A set of people, procedures, and resources that collects, transforms, and disseminates information in an organization. (2) A system that accepts data resources as input and processes them into information products as output.

Information System Model
A conceptual framework that views an information system as a system that uses the resources of hardware (machines and media), software (programs and procedures), people (users and specialists), and networks (communications media and network support) to perform input, processing, output, storage, and control activities that transform data resources (databases and knowledge bases) into information products.

Information System Specialist
A person whose occupation is related to the providing of information system services. For example: a systems analyst, programmer, or computer operator.

Information Systems Development
See Systems Development.

Information Technology (IT)
Hardware, software, telecommunications, database management, and other information processing technologies used in computer-based information systems.

Information Technology Architecture
A conceptual blueprint that specifies the components and interrelationships of a company's technology infrastructure, data resources, applications architecture, and IT organization.

Information Theory
The branch of learning concerned with the likelihood of accurate transmission or communication of messages subject to transmission failure, distortion, and noise.

Input
Pertaining to a device, process, or channel involved in the insertion of data into a data processing system. Opposite of Output.

Input/Output (I/O)
Pertaining to either input or output, or both.

Input/Output Interface Hardware
Devices such as I/O ports, I/O buses, buffers, channels, and input/output control units, which assist the CPU in its input/output assignments. These devices make it possible for modern computer systems to perform input, output, and processing functions simultaneously.

Inquiry Processing
Computer processing that supports the realtime interrogation of online files and databases by end users.

Instruction
A grouping of characters that specifies the computer operation to be performed.

Intangible Benefits and Costs
The nonquantifiable benefits and costs of a proposed solution or system.

Integrated Circuit
A complex microelectronic circuit consisting of interconnected circuit elements that cannot be disassembled because they are placed on or within a "continuous substrate" such as a silicon chip.

Integrated Packages
Software that combines the ability to do several general-purpose applications (such as word processing, electronic spreadsheet, and graphics) into one program.

Intelligent Agent
A special-purpose knowledge-based system that serves as a software surrogate to accomplish specific tasks for end users.

Intelligent Terminal
A terminal with the capabilities of a microcomputer that can thus perform many data processing and other functions without accessing a larger computer.

Interactive Marketing
A dynamic collaborative process of creating, purchasing, and improving products and services that builds close relationships between a business and its customers, using a variety of services on the Internet, intranets, and extranets.

Interactive Processing
A type of realtime processing in which users can interact with a computer on a realtime basis.

Interactive Video
Computer-based systems that integrate image processing with text, audio, and video processing technologies, which makes interactive multimedia presentations possible.

Interface
A shared boundary, such as the boundary between two systems. For example, the boundary between a computer and its peripheral devices.

Internet
The Internet is a rapidly growing computer network of millions of business, educational, and governmental networks connecting hundreds of millions of computers and their users in over 200 countries.

Internetwork Processor
Communications processors used by local area networks to interconnect them with other local area and wide area networks. Examples include switches, routers, hubs, and gateways.

Internetworks
Interconnected local area and wide area networks.

Interoperability
Being able to accomplish end user applications using different types of computer systems, operating systems, and application software, interconnected by different types of local and wide area networks.

Interorganizational Information Systems
Information systems that interconnect an organization with other organizations, such as a business and its customers and suppliers.

Interpreter
A computer program that translates and executes each source language statement before translating and executing the next one.

Interrupt
A condition that causes an interruption in a processing operation during which another task is performed. At the conclusion of this new assignment, control may be transferred back to the point where the original processing operation was interrupted or to other tasks with a higher priority.

Intranet
An Internet-like network within an organization. Web browser software provides easy access to internal websites established by business units, teams, and individuals, and other network resources and applications.

Inverted File
A file that references entities by their attributes.

IT Architecture
A conceptual design for the implementation of information technology in an organization, including its hardware, software, and network technology platforms, data resources, application portfolio, and IS organization.

Iterative
Pertaining to the repeated execution of a series of steps.

Java
An object-oriented programming language designed for programming realtime, interactive Web-based applications in the form of applets for use on clients and servers on the Internet, intranets, and extranets.

Job
A specified group of tasks prescribed as a unit of work for a computer.

Job Control Language (JCL)
A language for communicating with the operating system of a computer to identify a job and describe its requirements.

Joystick
A small lever set in a box used to move the cursor on the computer's display screen.

K
An abbreviation for the prefix kilo-, which is 1,000 in decimal notation. When referring to storage capacity it is equivalent to 2 to the 10th power, or 1,024 in decimal notation.

Key
One or more fields within a data record that are used to identify it or control its use.

Keyboarding
Using the keyboard of a microcomputer or computer terminal.

Knowledge Base
A computer-accessible collection of knowledge about a subject in a variety of forms, such as facts and rules of inference, frames, and objects.

Knowledge-Based Information System
An information system that adds a knowledge base to the database and other components found in other types of computer-based information systems.

Knowledge Engineer
A specialist who works with experts to capture the knowledge they possess in order to develop a knowledge base for expert systems and other knowledge-based systems.

Knowledge Management
Organizing and sharing the diverse forms of business information created within an organization. Includes managing project and enterprise document libraries, discussion databases, intranet website databases, and other types of knowledge bases.

Knowledge Workers
People whose primary work activities include creating, using, and distributing information.

Language Translator Program
A program that converts the programming language instructions in a computer program into machine language code. Major types include assemblers, compilers, and interpreters.

Large-Scale Integration (LSI)
A method of constructing electronic circuits in which thousands of circuits can be placed on a single semiconductor chip.

Legacy Systems
The older, traditional mainframe-based business information systems of an organization.

Light Pen
A photoelectronic device that allows data to be entered or altered on the face of a video display terminal.

Liquid Crystal Displays (LCDs)
Electronic visual displays that form characters by applying an electrical charge to selected silicon crystals.

List Organization
A method of data organization that uses indexes and pointers to allow for nonsequential retrieval.

List Processing
A method of processing data in the form of lists.

Local Area Network (LAN)
A communications network that typically connects computers, terminals, and other computerized devices within a limited physical area such as an office, building, manufacturing plant, or other work site.

Locking in Customers and Suppliers
Building valuable relationships with customers and suppliers that deter them from abandoning a firm for its competitors or intimidating it into accepting less-profitable relationships.

Logical Data Elements
Data elements that are independent of the physical data media on which they are recorded.

Logical System Design
Developing general specifications for how basic information systems activities can meet end user requirements.

Loop
A sequence of instructions in a computer program that is executed repeatedly until a terminal condition prevails.

Machine Cycle
The timing of a basic CPU operation as determined by a fixed number of electrical pulses emitted by the CPU's timing circuitry or internal clock.

Machine Language
A programming language where instructions are expressed in the binary code of the computer.

Macro Instruction
An instruction in a source language that is equivalent to a specified sequence of machine instructions.

Mag Stripe Card
A plastic wallet-size card with a strip of magnetic tape on one surface; widely used for credit/debit cards.

Magnetic Disk
A flat circular plate with a magnetic surface on which data can be stored by selective magnetization of portions of the curved surface.

Magnetic Ink
An ink that contains particles of iron

oxide that can be magnetized and detected by magnetic sensors.

Magnetic Ink Character Recognition (MICR)
The machine recognition of characters printed with magnetic ink. Primarily used for check processing by the banking industry.

Magnetic Tape
A plastic tape with a magnetic surface on which data can be stored by selective magnetization of portions of the surface.

Mainframe
A larger-size computer system, typically with a separate central processing unit, as distinguished from microcomputer and minicomputer systems.

Management Information System (MIS)
A management support system that produces prespecified reports, displays, and responses on a periodic, exception, demand, or push reporting basis.

Management Support System (MSS)
An information system that provides information to support managerial decision making. More specifically, an information-reporting system, executive information system, or decision support system.

Managerial End User
A manager, entrepreneur, or managerial-level professional who personally uses information systems. Also, the manager of the department or other organizational unit that relies on information systems.

Managerial Roles
Management as the performance of a variety of interpersonal, information, and decision roles.

Manual Data Processing
Data processing that requires continual human operation and intervention and that utilizes simple data processing tools such as paper forms, pencils, and filing cabinets.

Manufacturing Information Systems
Information systems that support the planning, control, and accomplishment of manufacturing processes. This includes concepts such as computer-integrated manufacturing (CIM) and technologies such as computer-aided manufacturing (CAM) or computer-aided design (CAD).

Marketing Information Systems
Information systems that support the planning, control, and transaction processing required for the accomplishment of marketing activities,

such as sales management, advertising, and promotion.

Mass Storage
Secondary storage devices with extra-large storage capacities such as magnetic or optical disks.

Master File
A data file containing relatively permanent information that is utilized as an authoritative reference and is usually updated periodically. Contrast with Transaction File.

Mathematical Model
A mathematical representation of a process, device, or concept.

Media
All tangible objects on which data are recorded.

Megabyte
One million bytes. More accurately, 2 to the 20th power, or 1,048,576 in decimal notation.

Memory
Same as Primary Storage.

Menu
A displayed list of items (usually the names of alternative applications, files, or activities) from which an end user makes a selection.

Menu Driven
A characteristic of interactive computing systems that provides menu displays and operator prompting to assist an end user in performing a particular job.

Metadata
Data about data; data describing the structure, data elements, interrelationships, and other characteristics of a database.

Microcomputer
A very small computer, ranging in size from a "computer on a chip" to hand-held, laptop, and desktop units, and servers.

Micrographics
The use of microfilm, microfiche, and other microforms to record data in greatly reduced form.

Microprocessor
A microcomputer central processing unit (CPU) on a chip. Without input/output or primary storage capabilities in most types.

Microprogram
A small set of elementary control instructions called microinstructions or microcode.

Microprogramming
The use of special software (microprograms) to perform the

functions of special hardware (electronic control circuitry). Microprograms stored in a read-only storage module of the control unit interpret the machine language instructions of a computer program and decode them into elementary microinstructions, which are then executed.

Microsecond
A millionth of a second.

Middleware
Software that helps diverse networked computer systems work together, thus promoting their interoperability.

Midrange Computer
A computer category between microcomputers and mainframes. Examples include minicomputers, network servers, and technical workstations.

Millisecond
A thousandth of a second.

Minicomputer
A type of midrange computer.

Model Base
An organized software collection of conceptual, mathematical, and logical models that express business relationships, computational routines, or analytical techniques.

Modem
(MOdulator-DEModulator) A device that converts the digital signals from input/output devices into appropriate frequencies at a transmission terminal and converts them back into digital signals at a receiving terminal.

Monitor
Software or hardware that observes, supervises, controls, or verifies the operations of a system.

Mouse
A small device that is electronically connected to a computer and is moved by hand on a flat surface in order to move the cursor on a video screen in the same direction. Buttons on the mouse allow users to issue commands and make responses or selections.

Multidimensional Structure
A database model that uses multidimensional structures (such as cubes or cubes within cubes) to store data and relationships between data.

Multimedia Presentations
Providing information using a variety of media, including text and graphics displays, voice and other audio, photographs, and video segments.

Multiplex
To interleave or simultaneously

transmit two or more messages on a single channel.

Multiplexer
An electronic device that allows a single communications channel to carry simultaneous data transmissions from many terminals.

Multiprocessing
Pertaining to the simultaneous execution of two or more instructions by a computer or computer network.

Multiprocessor Computer Systems
Computer systems that use a multiprocessor architecture in the design of their central processing units. This includes the use of support microprocessors and multiple instruction processors, including parallel processor designs.

Multiprogramming
Pertaining to the concurrent execution of two or more programs by a computer by interleaving their execution.

Multitasking
The concurrent use of the same computer to accomplish several different information processing tasks. Each task may require the use of a different program, or the concurrent use of the same copy of a program by several users.

Nanosecond
One billionth of a second.

Natural Language
A programming language that is very close to human language. Also called very-high-level language.

Network
An interconnected system of computers, terminals, and communications channels and devices.

Network Architecture
A master plan designed to promote an open, simple, flexible, and efficient telecommunications environment through the use of standard protocols, standard communications hardware and software interfaces, and the design of a standard multilevel telecommunications interface between end users and computer systems.

Network Computer
A low-cost networked microcomputer with no or minimal disk storage, which depends on Internet or intranet servers for its operating system and Web browser, Java-enabled application software, and data access and storage.

Network Computing
A network-centric view of computing in which "the network is the

computer," that is, the view that computer networks are the central computing resource of any computing environment.

Network Data Structure
A logical data structure that allows many-to-many relationships among data records. It allows entry into a database at multiple points, because any data element or record can be related to many other data elements.

Neural Networks
Computer processors or software whose architecture is based on the human brain's meshlike neuron structure. Neural networks can process many pieces of information simultaneously and can learn to recognize patterns and programs themselves to solve related problems on their own.

Node
A terminal point in a communications network.

Nonprocedural Languages
Programming languages that allow users and professional programmers to specify the results they want without specifying how to solve the problem.

Numerical Control
Automatic control of a machine process by a computer that makes use of numerical data, generally introduced as the operation is in process. Also called machine control.

Object
A data element that includes both data and the methods or processes that act on those data.

Object-Based Knowledge
Knowledge represented as a network of objects.

Object-Oriented Language
An object-oriented programming (OOP) language used to develop programs that create and use objects to perform information processing tasks.

Object Program
A compiled or assembled program composed of executable machine instructions. Contrast with Source Program.

OEM: Original Equipment Manufacturer
A firm that manufactures and sells computers by assembling components produced by other hardware manufacturers.

Office Automation (OA)
The use of computer-based information systems that collect, process, store, and transmit electronic messages,

documents, and other forms of office communications among individuals, workgroups, and organizations.

Offline
Pertaining to equipment or devices not under control of the central processing unit.

Online
Pertaining to equipment or devices under control of the central processing unit.

Online Analytical Processing (OLAP)
A capability of some management, decision support, and executive information systems that supports interactive examination and manipulation of large amounts of data from many perspectives.

Online Transaction Processing (OLTP)
A realtime transaction processing system.

Open Systems
Information systems that use common standards for hardware, software, applications, and networking to create a computing environment that allows easy access by end users and their networked computer systems.

Operand
That which is operated upon. That part of a computer instruction that is identified by the address part of the instruction.

Operating Environment
Software packages or modules that add a graphics-based interface between end users, the operating system, and their application programs, and that may also provide a multitasking capability.

Operating System
The main control program of a computer system. It is a system of programs that controls the execution of computer programs and may provide scheduling, debugging, input/output control, system accounting, compilation, storage assignment, data management, and related services.

Operation Code
A code that represents specific operations to be performed upon the operands in a computer instruction.

Operational Feasibility
The willingness and ability of management, employees, customers, and suppliers to operate, use, and support a proposed system.

Operations Support System (OSS)
An information system that collects, processes, and stores data generated by

the operations systems of an organization and produces data and information for input into a management information system or for the control of an operations system.

Operations System
A basic subsystem of the business firm that constitutes its input, processing, and output components. Also called a physical system.

Optical Character Recognition (OCR)
The machine identification of printed characters through the use of light-sensitive devices.

Optical Disks
A secondary storage medium using CD (compact disk) and DVD (digital versatile disk) technologies to read tiny spots on plastic disks. The disks are currently capable of storing billions of characters of information.

Optical Scanner
A device that optically scans characters or images and generates their digital representations.

Optimization Analysis
Finding an optimum value for selected variables in a mathematical model, given certain constraints.

Organizational Feasibility
How well a proposed information system supports the objectives of an organization's strategic plan for information systems.

Output
Pertaining to a device, process, or channel involved with the transfer of data or information out of an information processing system. Opposite of Input.

Outsourcing
Turning over all or part of an organization's information systems operation to outside contractors, known as systems integrators or service providers.

Packet
A group of data and control information in a specified format that is transmitted as an entity.

Packet Switching
A data transmission process that transmits addressed packets such that a channel is occupied only for the duration of transmission of the packet.

Page
A segment of a program or data, usually of fixed length.

Paging
A process that automatically and continually transfers pages of programs and data between primary storage and direct access storage devices. It provides computers with multiprogramming and virtual memory capabilities.

Parallel Processing
Executing many instructions at the same time, that is, in parallel. Performed by advanced computers using many instruction processors organized in clusters or networks.

Parity Bit
A check bit appended to an array of binary digits to make the sum of all the binary digits, including the check bit, always odd or always even.

Pascal
A high-level, general-purpose, structured programming language named after Blaise Pascal. It was developed by Niklaus Wirth of Zurich in 1968.

Pattern Recognition
The identification of shapes, forms, or configurations by automatic means.

PCM: Plug-Compatible Manufacturer
A firm that manufactures computer equipment that can be plugged into existing computer systems without requiring additional hardware or software interfaces.

Peer-to-Peer Network (P2P)
A computing environment where end user computers connect, communicate, and collaborate directly with each other via the Internet or other telecommunications network links.

Pen-Based Computers
Tablet-style microcomputers that recognize handwriting and hand drawing done by a pen-shaped device on their pressure-sensitive display screens.

Performance Monitor
A software package that monitors the processing of computer system jobs, helps develop a planned schedule of computer operations that can optimize computer system performance, and produces detailed statistics that are used for computer system capacity planning and control.

Periodic Reports
Providing information to managers using a prespecified format designed to provide information on a regularly scheduled basis.

Peripheral Devices
In a computer system, any unit of equipment, distinct from the central processing unit, that provides the system with input, output, or storage capabilities.

Personal Digital Assistant (PDA)
Hand-held microcomputer devices that enable you to manage information such as appointments, to-do lists, and sales contacts, send and receive e-mail, access the Web, and exchange such information with your desktop PC or network server.

Personal Information Manager (PIM)
A software package that helps end users store, organize, and retrieve text and numerical data in the form of notes, lists, memos, and a variety of other forms.

Physical System Design
Design of the user interface methods and products, database structures, and processing and control procedures for a proposed information system, including hardware, software, and personnel specifications.

Picosecond
One trillionth of a second.

Plasma Display
Output devices that generate a visual display with electrically charged particles of gas trapped between glass plates.

Plotter
A hard-copy output device that produces drawings and graphical displays on paper or other materials.

Pointer
A data element associated with an index, a record, or other set of data that contains the address of a related record.

Pointing Devices
Devices that allow end users to issue commands or make choices by moving a cursor on the display screen.

Pointing Stick
A small buttonlike device on a keyboard that moves the cursor on the screen in the direction of the pressure placed upon it.

Point-of-Sale (POS) Terminal
A computer terminal used in retail stores that serves the function of a cash register as well as collecting sales data and performing other data processing functions.

Port
(1) Electronic circuitry that provides a connection point between the CPU and input/output devices. (2) A connection point for a communications line on a CPU or other front-end device.

Postimplementation Review
Monitoring and evaluating the results of an implemented solution or system.

Presentation Graphics
Using computer-generated graphics to

enhance the information presented in reports and other types of presentations.

Prespecified Reports
Reports whose format is specified in advance to provide managers with information periodically, on an exception basis, or on demand.

Private Branch Exchange (PBX)
A switching device that serves as an interface between the many telephone lines within a work area and the local telephone company's main telephone lines or trunks. Computerized PBXs can handle the switching of both voice and data.

Procedure-Oriented Language
A programming language designed for the convenient expression of procedures used in the solution of a wide class of problems.

Procedures
Sets of instructions used by people to complete a task.

Process Control
The use of a computer to control an ongoing physical process, such as petrochemical production.

Process Design
The design of the programs and procedures needed by a proposed information system, including detailed program specifications and procedures.

Processor
A hardware device or software system capable of performing operations upon data.

Program
A set of instructions that cause a computer to perform a particular task.

Programmed Decision
A decision that can be automated by basing it on a decision rule that outlines the steps to take when confronted with the need for a specific decision.

Programmer
A person mainly involved in designing, writing, and testing computer programs.

Programming
The design, writing, and testing of a program.

Programming Language
A language used to develop the instructions in computer programs.

Programming Tools
Software packages or modules that provide editing and diagnostic capabilities and other support facilities to assist the programming process.

Project Management
Managing the accomplishment of an information system development project according to a specific project plan, in order that a project is completed on time, and within its budget, and meets its design objectives.

Prompt
Messages that assist a user in performing a particular job. This would include error messages, correction suggestions, questions, and other messages that guide an end user.

Protocol
A set of rules and procedures for the control of communications in a communications network.

Prototype
A working model. In particular, a working model of an information system that includes tentative versions of user input and output, databases and files, control methods, and processing routines.

Prototyping
The rapid development and testing of working models, or prototypes, of new information system applications in an interactive, iterative process involving both systems analysts and end users.

Pseudocode
An informal design language of structured programming that expresses the processing logic of a program module in ordinary human language phrases.

Pull Marketing
Marketing methods that rely on the use of Web browsers by end users to access marketing materials and resources at Internet, intranet, and extranet websites.

Push Marketing
Marketing methods that rely on Web broadcasting software to push marketing information and other marketing materials to end users' computers.

Quality Assurance
Methods for ensuring that information systems are free from errors and fraud and provide information products of high quality.

Query Language
A high-level, humanlike language provided by a database management system that enables users to easily extract data and information from a database.

Queue
(1) A waiting line formed by items in a system waiting for service. (2) To arrange in or form a queue.

RAID
Redundant array of independent disks. Magnetic disk units that house many interconnected microcomputer hard disk drives, thus providing large, fault-tolerant storage capacities.

Random Access
Same as Direct Access. Contrast with Sequential Access.

Random Access Memory (RAM)
One of the basic types of semiconductor memory used for temporary storage of data or programs during processing. Each memory position can be directly sensed (read) or changed (write) in the same length of time, irrespective of its location on the storage medium.

Reach and Range Analysis
A planning framework that contrasts a firm's ability to use its IT platform to reach its stakeholders, with the range of information products and services that can be provided or shared through IT.

Read Only Memory (ROM)
A basic type of semiconductor memory used for permanent storage. Can only be read, not "written," that is, changed. Variations are Programmable Read Only Memory (PROM) and Erasable Programmable Read Only Memory (EPROM).

Real Time
Pertaining to the performance of data processing during the actual time a business or physical process transpires, in order that results of the data processing can be used to support the completion of the process.

Realtime Processing
Data processing in which data are processed immediately rather than periodically. Also called online processing. Contrast with Batch Processing.

Record
A collection of related data fields treated as a unit.

Reduced Instruction Set Computer (RISC)
A CPU architecture that optimizes processing speed by the use of a smaller number of basic machine instructions than traditional CPU designs.

Redundancy
In information processing, the repetition of part or all of a message to increase the chance that the correct information will be understood by the recipient.

Register
A device capable of storing a specified amount of data such as one word.

Relational Data Structure
A logical data structure in which all data elements within the database are viewed as being stored in the form of simple tables. DBMS packages based on the relational model can link data elements from various tables as long as the tables share common data elements.

Remote Access
Pertaining to communication with the data processing facility by one or more stations that are distant from that facility.

Remote Job Entry (RJE)
Entering jobs into a batch processing system from a remote facility.

Report Generator
A feature of database management system packages that allows an end user to quickly specify a report format for the display of information retrieved from a database.

Reprographics
Copying and duplicating technology and methods.

Resource Management
An operating system function that controls the use of computer system resources such as primary storage, secondary storage, CPU processing time, and input/output devices by other system software and application software packages.

Robotics
The technology of building machines (robots) with computer intelligence and humanlike physical capabilities.

Routine
An ordered set of instructions that may have some general or frequent use.

RPG: Report Program Generator
A problem-oriented language that utilizes a generator to construct programs that produce reports and perform other data processing tasks.

Rule
Statements that typically take the form of a premise and a conclusion such as If-Then rules: If (condition), Then (conclusion).

Rule-Based Knowledge
Knowledge represented in the form of rules and statements of fact.

Scalability
The ability of hardware or software to handle the processing demands of a wide range of end users, transactions, queries, and other information processing requirements.

Scenario Approach
A planning approach where managers, employees, and planners create scenarios of what an organization will be like three to five years or more into the future, and identify the role IT can play in those scenarios.

Schema
An overall conceptual or logical view of the relationships between the data in a database.

Scientific Method
An analytical methodology that involves (1) recognizing phenomena, (2) formulating a hypothesis about the causes or effects of the phenomena, (3) testing the hypothesis through experimentation, (4) evaluating the results of such experiments, and (5) drawing conclusions about the hypothesis.

Secondary Storage
Storage that supplements the primary storage of a computer. Synonymous with Auxiliary Storage.

Sector
A subdivision of a track on a magnetic disk surface.

Security Codes
Passwords, identification codes, account codes, and other codes that limit the access and use of computer-based system resources to authorized users.

Security Management
Protecting the accuracy, integrity, and safety of the processes and resources of an internetworked e-business enterprise against computer crime, accidental or malicious destruction, and natural disasters, using security measures such as encryption, fire walls, antivirus software, faulttolerant computers, and security monitors.

Security Monitor
A software package that monitors the use of a computer system and protects its resources from unauthorized use, fraud, and vandalism.

Semiconductor Memory
Microelectronic storage circuitry etched on tiny chips of silicon or other semiconducting material. The primary storage of most modern computers consists of microelectronic semiconductor storage chips for random access memory (RAM) and read only memory (ROM).

Semistructured Decisions
Decisions involving procedures that can be partially prespecified, but not enough to lead to a definite recommended decision.

Sensitivity Analysis
Observing how repeated changes to a single variable affect other variables in a mathematical model.

Sequential Access
A sequential method of storing and retrieving data from a file. Contrast with Random Access and Direct Access.

Sequential Data Organization
Organizing logical data elements according to a prescribed sequence.

Serial
Pertaining to the sequential or consecutive occurrence of two or more related activities in a single device or channel.

Server
(1) A computer that supports applications and telecommunications in a network, as well as the sharing of peripheral devices, software, and databases among the workstations in the network. (2) Versions of software for installation on network servers designed to control and support applications on client microcomputers in client/server networks. Examples include multiuser network operating systems and specialized software for running Internet, intranet, and extranet Web applications, such as electronic commerce and enterprise collaboration.

Service Bureau
A firm offering computer and data processing services. Also called a computer service center.

Smart Products
Industrial and consumer products, with "intelligence" provided by built-in microcomputers or microprocessors that significantly improve the performance and capabilities of such products.

Software
Computer programs and procedures concerned with the operation of an information system. Contrast with Hardware.

Software Package
A computer program supplied by computer manufacturers, independent software companies, or other computer users. Also known as canned programs, proprietary software, or packaged programs.

Software Piracy
Unauthorized copying of software.

Software Suites
A combination of individual software packages that share a common graphical user interface and are designed for easy transfer of data between applications.

Solid State
Pertaining to devices such as transistors and diodes whose operation depends on the control of electric or magnetic phenomena in solid materials.

Source Data Automation
The use of automated methods of data entry that attempt to reduce or eliminate many of the activities, people, and data media required by traditional data entry methods.

Source Document
A document that is the original formal record of a transaction, such as a purchase order or sales invoice.

Source Program
A computer program written in a language that is subject to a translation process. Contrast with Object Program.

Special-Purpose Computer
A computer designed to handle a restricted class of problems. Contrast with General-Purpose Computer.

Speech Recognition
Direct conversion of spoken data into electronic form suitable for entry into a computer system. Also called voice data entry.

Spooling
Simultaneous peripheral operation online. Storing input data from low-speed devices temporarily on high-speed secondary storage units, which can be quickly accessed by the CPU. Also, writing output data at high speeds onto magnetic tape or disk units from which it can be transferred to slow-speed devices such as a printer.

Stage Analysis
A planning process in which the information system needs of an organization are based on an analysis of its current stage in the growth cycle of the organization and its use of information systems technology.

Standards
Measures of performance developed to evaluate the progress of a system toward its objectives.

Storage
Pertaining to a device into which data can be entered, in which they can be held, and from which they can be retrieved at a later time. Same as Memory.

Strategic Information Systems
Information systems that provide a firm with competitive products and services that give it a strategic advantage over its competitors in the marketplace. Also, information systems that promote business innovation, improve business processes, and build strategic information resources for a firm.

Strategic Opportunities Matrix
A planning framework that uses a matrix to help identify opportunities with strategic business potential, as well

as a firm's ability to exploit such opportunities with IT.

Structure Chart
A design and documentation technique to show the purpose and relationships of the various modules in a program.

Structured Decisions
Decisions that are structured by the decision procedures or decision rules developed for them. They involve situations where the procedures to follow when a decision is needed can be specified in advance.

Structured Programming
A programming methodology that uses a top-down program design and a limited number of control structures in a program to create highly structured modules of program code.

Structured Query Language (SQL)
A query language that is becoming a standard for advanced database management system packages. A query's basic form is SELECT . . . FROM . . . WHERE.

Subroutine
A routine that can be part of another program routine.

Subschema
A subset or transformation of the logical view of the database schema that is required by a particular user application program.

Subsystem
A system that is a component of a larger system.

Supercomputer
A special category of large computer systems that are the most powerful available. They are designed to solve massive computational problems.

Superconductor
Materials that can conduct electricity with almost no resistance. This allows the development of extremely fast and small electronic circuits. Formerly only possible at supercold temperatures near absolute zero. Recent developments promise superconducting materials near room temperature.

Supply Chain
The network of business processes and interrelationships among businesses that are needed to build, sell, and deliver a product to its final customer.

Supply Chain Management
Integrating management practices and information technology to optimize information and product flows among the processes and business partners within a supply chain.

Switch
(1) A device or programming technique for making a selection. (2) A computer that controls message switching among the computers and terminals in a telecommunications network.

Switching Costs
The costs in time, money, effort, and inconvenience that it would take a customer or supplier to switch its business to a firm's competitors.

Synchronous
A characteristic in which each event, or the performance of any basic operation, is constrained to start on, and usually to keep in step with, signals from a timing clock. Contrast with Asynchronous.

System
(1) A group of interrelated or interacting elements forming a unified whole. (2) A group of interrelated components working together toward a common goal by accepting inputs and producing outputs in an organized transformation process. (3) An assembly of methods, procedures, or techniques unified by regulated interaction to form an organized whole. (4) An organized collection of people, machines, and methods required to accomplish a set of specific functions.

System Flowchart
A graphic diagramming tool used to show the flow of information processing activities as data are processed by people and devices.

System Software
Programs that control and support operations of a computer system. System software includes a variety of programs, such as operating systems, database management systems, communications control programs, service and utility programs, and programming language translators.

System Specifications
The product of the systems design stage. It consists of specifications for the hardware, software, facilities, personnel, databases, and the user interface of a proposed information system.

System Support Programs
Programs that support the operations, management, and users of a computer system by providing a variety of support services. Examples are system utilities and performance monitors.

Systems Analysis
(1) Analyzing in detail the components and requirements of a system.
(2) Analyzing in detail the information needs of an organization, the

characteristics and components of presently utilized information systems, and the functional requirements of proposed information systems.

Systems Approach
A systematic process of problem solving that defines problems and opportunities in a systems context. Data are gathered describing the problem or opportunity, and alternative solutions are identified and evaluated. Then the best solution is selected and implemented, and its success evaluated.

Systems Design
Deciding how a proposed information system will meet the information needs of end users. Includes logical and physical design activities, and user interface, data, and process design activities that produce system specifications that satisfy the system requirements developed in the systems analysis stage.

Systems Development
(1) Conceiving, designing, and implementing a system. (2) Developing information systems by a process of investigation, analysis, design, implementation, and maintenance. Also called the systems development life cycle (SDLC), information systems development, or application development.

Systems Development Tools
Graphical, textual, and computer-aided tools and techniques used to help analyze, design, and document the development of an information system. Typically used to represent (1) the components and flows of a system, (2) the user interface, (3) data attributes and relationships, and (4) detailed system processes.

Systems Implementation
The stage of systems development in which hardware and software are acquired, developed, and installed; the system is tested and documented; people are trained to operate and use the system; and an organization converts to the use of a newly developed system.

Systems Investigation
The screening, selection, and preliminary study of a proposed information system solution to a business problem.

Systems Maintenance
The monitoring, evaluating, and modifying of a system to make desirable or necessary improvements.

Systems Thinking
Recognizing systems, subsystems, components of systems, and system interrelationships in a situation. Also known as a systems context or a systemic view of a situation.

Tangible Benefits and Costs
The quantifiable benefits and costs of a proposed solution or system.

Task and Project Management
Managing team and workgroup projects by scheduling, tracking, and charting the completion status of tasks within a project.

Task Management
A basic operating system function that manages the accomplishment of the computing tasks of users by a computer system.

TCP/IP
Transmission control protocol/Internet protocol. A suite of telecommunications network protocols used by the Internet, intranets, and extranets that has become a de facto network architecture standard for many companies.

Technical Feasibility
Whether reliable hardware and software capable of meeting the needs of a proposed system can be acquired or developed by an organization in the required time.

Technology Management
The organizational responsibility to identify, introduce, and monitor the assimilation of new information system technologies into organizations.

Telecommunications
Pertaining to the transmission of signals over long distances, including not only data communications but also the transmission of images and voices using radio, television, and other communications technologies.

Telecommunications Channel
The part of a telecommunications network that connects the message source with the message receiver. It includes the hardware, software, and media used to connect one network location to another for the purpose of transmitting and receiving information.

Telecommunications Control Program
A computer program that controls and supports the communications between the computers and terminals in a telecommunications network.

Telecommunications Controller
A data communications interface device (frequently a special-purpose mini- or microcomputer) that can control a telecommunications network containing many terminals.

Telecommunications Monitors
Computer programs that control and support the communications between the computers and terminals in a telecommunications network.

Telecommunications Processors
Internetwork processors such as switches and routers, and other devices such as multiplexers and communications controllers that allow a communications channel to carry simultaneous data transmissions from many terminals. They may also perform error monitoring, diagnostics and correction, modulation-demodulation, data compression, data coding and decoding, message switching, port contention, and buffer storage.

Telecommuting
The use of telecommunications to replace commuting to work from one's home.

Teleconferencing
The use of video communications to allow business conferences to be held with participants who are scattered across a country, continent, or the world.

Telephone Tag
The process that occurs when two people who wish to contact each other by telephone repeatedly miss each other's phone calls.

Teleprocessing
Using telecommunications for computer-based information processing.

Terabyte
One trillion bytes. More accurately, 2 to the 40th power, or 1,009,511,627,776 in decimal notation.

Text Data
Words, phrases, sentences, and paragraphs used in documents and other forms of communication.

Throughput
The total amount of useful work performed by a data processing system during a given period of time.

Time Sharing
Providing computer services to many users simultaneously while providing rapid responses to each.

Total Quality Management
Planning and implementing programs of continuous quality improvement, where quality is defined as meeting or exceeding the requirements and expectations of customers for a product or service.

Touch-Sensitive Screen
An input device that accepts data input by the placement of a finger on or close to the CRT screen.

Track
The portion of a moving storage medium, such as a drum, tape, or disk, that is accessible to a given reading head position.

Trackball
A rollerball device set in a case used to move the cursor on a computer's display screen.

Transaction
An event that occurs as part of doing business, such as a sale, purchase, deposit, withdrawal, refund, transfer, payment, and so on.

Transaction Document
A document produced as part of a business transaction. For instance: a purchase order, paycheck, sales receipt, or customer invoice.

Transaction File
A data file containing relatively transient data to be processed in combination with a master file. Contrast with Master File.

Transaction Processing Cycle
A cycle of basic transaction processing activities including data entry, transaction processing, database maintenance, document and report generation, and inquiry processing.

Transaction Processing System (TPS)
An information system that processes data arising from the occurrence of business transactions.

Transaction Terminals
Terminals used in banks, retail stores, factories, and other work sites that are used to capture transaction data at their point of origin. Examples are point-of-sale (POS) terminals and automated teller machines (ATMs).

Transborder Data Flows (TDF)
The flow of business data over telecommunications networks across international borders.

Transform Algorithm
Performing an arithmetic computation on a record key and using the result of the calculation as an address for that record. Also known as key transformation or hashing.

Transnational Strategy
A management approach in which an organization integrates its global business activities through close cooperation and interdependence among its headquarters, operations, and international subsidiaries, and its use of appropriate global information technologies.

Turnaround Document
Output of a computer system (such as customer invoices and statements) that is designed to be returned to the organization as machine-readable input.

Turnaround Time
The elapsed time between submission of a job to a computing center and the return of the results.

Turnkey Systems
Computer systems where all of the hardware, software, and systems development needed by a user are provided.

Unbundling
The separate pricing of hardware, software, and other related services.

Uniform Resource Locator (URL)
An access code (such as http://www.sun.com) for identifying and locating hypermedia document files, databases, and other resources at websites and other locations on the Internet, intranets, and extranets.

Universal Product Code (UPC)
A standard identification code using bar coding, printed on products that can be read by the optical supermarket scanners of the grocery industry.

Unstructured Decisions
Decisions that must be made in situations where it is not possible to specify in advance most of the decision procedures to follow.

User Friendly
A characteristic of human-operated equipment and systems that makes them safe, comfortable, and easy to use.

User Interface
That part of an operating system or other program that allows users to communicate with it to load programs, access files, and accomplish other computing tasks.

User Interface Design
Designing the interactions between end users and computer systems, including input/output methods and the conversion of data between human-readable and machine-readable forms.

Utility Program
A standard set of routines that assists in the operation of a computer system by performing some frequently required process such as copying, sorting, or merging.

Value-Added Carriers
Third-party vendors who lease telecommunications lines from common carriers and offer a variety of telecommunications services to customers.

Value-Added Resellers (VARs)
Companies that provide industry-specific software for use with the computer systems of selected manufacturers.

Value Chain
Viewing a firm as a series, chain, or network of basic activities that adds value to its products and services and thus adds a margin of value to the firm.

Videoconferencing
Realtime video and audio conferencing (1) among users at networked PCs (desktop videoconferencing), or (2) among participants in conference rooms or auditoriums in different locations (teleconferencing). Videoconferencing can also include whiteboarding and document sharing.

Virtual Communities
Groups of people with similar interests who meet and share ideas on the Internet and online services and develop a feeling of belonging to a community.

Virtual Company
A form of organization that uses telecommunications networks and other information technologies to link the people, assets, and ideas of a variety of business partners, no matter where they may be located, in order to exploit a business opportunity.

Virtual Machine
Pertaining to the simulation of one type of computer system by another computer system.

Virtual Mall
An online multimedia simulation of a shopping mall with many different interlinked retail websites.

Virtual Memory
The use of secondary storage devices as an extension of the primary storage of the computer, thus giving the appearance of a larger main memory than actually exists.

Virtual Private Network
A secure network that uses the Internet as its main backbone network to connect the intranets of a company's different locations, or to establish extranet links between a company and its customers, suppliers, or other business partners.

Virtual Reality
The use of multisensory human/computer interfaces that enable human users to experience computer-simulated objects, entities, spaces, and "worlds" as if they actually existed.

Virtual Storefront
An online multimedia simulation of a retail store shopping experience on the Web.

Virtual Team
A team whose members use the Internet, intranets, extranets, and other networks to communicate, coordinate, and collaborate with each other on tasks and projects, even though they may work in different geographic locations and for different organizations.

VLSI: Very-Large-Scale Integration
Semiconductor chips containing hundreds of thousands of circuits.

Voice Conferencing
Telephone conversations shared among several participants via speaker phones or networked PCs with Internet telephone software.

Voice Mail
Unanswered telephone messages are digitized, stored, and played back to the recipient by a voice messaging computer.

Volatile Memory
Memory (such as electronic semiconductor memory) that loses its contents when electrical power is interrupted.

Wand
A hand-held optical character recognition device used for data entry by many transaction terminals.

Web Browser
A software package that provides the user interface for accessing Internet, intranet, and extranet websites. Browsers are becoming multifunction universal clients for sending and receiving e-mail, downloading files, accessing Java applets, participating in discussion groups, developing Web pages, and other Internet, intranet, and extranet applications.

Web Publishing
Creating, converting, and storing hyperlinked documents and other material on Internet or intranet Web servers so they can easily be shared via Web browsers with teams, workgroups, or the enterprise.

What-If Analysis
Observing how changes to selected variables affect other variables in a mathematical model.

Whiteboarding
See Data Conferencing.

Wide Area Network (WAN)
A data communications network covering a large geographic area.

Window
One section of a computer's multiple-section display screen, each of which can have a different display.

Wireless LANs
Using radio or infrared transmissions to link devices in a local area network.

Wireless Technologies
Using radio wave, microwave, infrared, and laser technologies to transport digital communications without wires between communications devices. Examples include terrestrial microwave, communications satellites, cellular and PCS phone and pager systems, mobile data radio, and various wireless Internet technologies.

Word
(1) A string of characters considered as a unit. (2) An ordered set of bits (usually larger than a byte) handled as a unit by the central processing unit.

Word Processing
The automation of the transformation of ideas and information into a readable form of communication. It involves the use of computers to manipulate text data in order to produce office communications in the form of documents.

Workgroup Computing
Members of a networked workgroup may use groupware tools to communicate, coordinate, and collaborate, and to share hardware, software, and databases to accomplish group assignments.

Workstation
(1) A computer system designed to support the work of one person. (2) A high-powered computer to support the work of professionals in engineering, science, and other areas that require extensive computing power and graphics capabilities.

World Wide Web (WWW)
A global network of multimedia Internet sites for information, education, entertainment, e-business, and e-commerce.

XML (Extensible Markup Language)
A Web document content description language that describes the content of Web pages by applying hidden identifying tags or contextual labels to the data in Web documents. By categorizing and classifying Web data this way, XML makes Web content easier to identify, search, analyze, and selectively exchange between computers.

Company Index

Subject Index